Securities & Investment Institute Diploma

STUDY BOOK
Global Operations Management

2008

In this 2008 edition

- A **user-friendly format** for easy navigation

- **Updated** on recent developments

- A **chapter roundup** and **test your knowledge** quiz at the end of each chapter

- A full **index**

APPROVED WORKBOOK

Published February 2008

ISBN 9780 7517 5442 1

British Library Cataloguing-in-Publication Data
A catalogue record for this book
is available from the British Library

Published by

BPP Learning Media Ltd
BPP House, Aldine Place
London W12 8AA

www.bpp.com/learningmedia

Printed in Great Britain

Your learning materials, published by BPP Learning Media Ltd,
are printed on paper sourced from sustainable, managed
forests.

CONTENTS

BPP LEARNING MEDIA

1

Global Operations Management

INTRODUCTION

We start by defining the scope of operations management and what, more specifically, is meant by 'global operations management'.

What is the operations manager's role in measuring and controlling risk, and what sorts of 'risk' do we mean here?

We also ask: in what types of financial institution or business is the operations manager found?

BPP LEARNING MEDIA

1

1 WHAT IS GLOBAL OPERATIONS MANAGEMENT?

1.1 Introduction

Operations management is concerned with managing the **Operations Department** of a financial institution.

Fundamentally, the Operations Department is responsible for:

- Processing and settling trades
- Monitoring and controlling risk
- Complying with the regulatory and legal framework

An **Operations Manager** needs to have both a detailed working knowledge of trade processing and settlement and to possess a high level overview of the role and responsibilities of other departments within a financial institution.

An Operations Manager must be able to identify practical solutions to a range of risks and problems. The solutions need to address both the high-level business requirement for management and yet be detailed enough for operations staff to implement. It is this area in particular that the Diploma examination seeks to test.

In the context of Global Operations Management, this extends to a full understanding of both the domestic and international markets and settlement conventions. It also encompasses the important issues of international business, such as:

- Time zones
- Different settlement conventions
- Different regulatory regimes
- Customs and working practices
- Communication
- Currency and funding issues
- Cross-border settlement

It will be important to recognise **local issues** as well as the bigger picture.

Global Operations Management thus reflects the fact that markets are global, exchanges are global, investment is global and products are global. The modern firm needs to be able to manage its domestic and cross-border business across international marketplaces providing professional services to customers from all parts of the world. This is a major challenge for the men and women in these roles and, as one can imagine, things never stand still!

1.2 Processing and settling trades

The core role of an Operations Department is to ensure that trades are processed efficiently and effectively and settle on the intended settlement date.

The roles in a securities trading operation include, *inter alia:*

- Input of the transactions dealt by the front office

- Processing of transactions through the financial institution's accounting and settlement systems

- Ensuring that the trade matches with the counterparty and resolving any problems

- Ensuring that the relationships and operational procedures with external exchanges, central counterparty clearing houses and central securities depositories are properly controlled and operate efficiently

- Ensuring that the trade settles on the intended settlement date and resolving any problems

- Holding the securities either in the safe, at the custodian, at a settlement agency or at another financial institution

- Identifying and processing corporate actions

1.3 Monitoring and controlling risk

Risk can be defined as the measurable possibility of losing or not gaining value. Risk can be major or minor. Major risks facing a financial institution are those which impact on its future business viability, e.g. a major financial loss, a major reputational or regulatory scandal. Minor risks are those which affect the profitability and efficiency of the financial institution. Minor risks that are not dealt with can grow into major risks. A number of minor risks can also create a major risk. An Operations Manager is responsible for measuring **operational risks** such as ensuring that all trades settle on time, resolving problems and reconciling items on a timely basis.

Having a good **control environment** controls risk. This entails:

- The appropriate risk culture with clearly defined responsibilities and organisational structure
- Competent and timely reviews
- Up-to-date Procedures Manual
- Adequate and trained staff resources
- Timely reconciliation
- Efficient and reliable IT systems

We look at operational risks in more detail in Chapter 14 of this Study Book.

1.4 Complying with the regulatory and legal framework

The financial services industry is one of the most regulated sectors of the economy. A financial institution must comply with legislation, rules and regulations in the UK and with regulatory institutions, including the following.

- Financial Services Authority
- Companies Acts 1985 and 2006
- Markets in Financial Instruments Directive (MiFID)
- Data Protection Act 1998
- The rules of the exchange(s) upon which it trades, e.g. London Stock Exchange rules
- Money Laundering Regulations and Proceeds of Crime Act 2002
- Criminal Justice Act 1993
- Trustee Act 2000
- Panel on Takeovers and Mergers
- Various pieces of employment legislation

An Operations Manager must be aware of the interaction of these laws, rules and regulations on the Operations Department.

The same awareness is needed for **international regulation** where appropriate, covering such bodies as:

- Ministry of Finance and Financial Services Agency (Japan)
- Securities and Exchange Commission (SEC) and the Commodities and Futures Trading Commission (CFTC) in the United States
- Irish Financial Services Regulatory Authority (IFSRA)
- Financial regulators in France and Germany – AMF and BaFin respectively
- Central banks (Bank of England, European Central Bank, Federal Reserve)

Particular attention is needed in respect of the European regulatory environment which impacts on the business of UK-based organisations.

2 THE FINANCIAL INSTITUTION

2.1 Types of financial institution

The role of an Operations Manager will depend on the size of an organisation and the breadth of services offered. The range of financial institutions varies.

- **Niche players** are small financial institutions offering specialised services, e.g. spread betting, soft commission, links to an overseas stock exchange, private clients. Frequently the settlement department is outsourced.
- **Medium size players** with a strong customer base and efficient operations department.
- **Internet execution-only brokers** who process large volumes of trades as cheaply as possible.
- **'Bulge Bracket'**, **'super firms'** or **'powerhouses'**, like Merrill Lynch and Morgan Stanley which offer a full range of financial services.

The so-called 'Bulge Bracket' firms are global players providing their services into the major markets and do so for a global client base.

The requirements of investment and corporate clients extend to international securities markets, foreign exchange, derivatives and corporate finance activities.

2.2 Organisational structures

Every bank and securities firm has its own unique **organisational structure**, reflecting that institution's:

- Key lines of business
- Products
- Customers
- Size
- Personnel
- Geography

These organisational structures are constantly changing to reflect new strategies, new opportunities and changing management. However, most organisational structures are a combination of two or three of the following generic types of organisations.

- **Product-based organisations.** In a product-based organisational structure, the institution is organised into individual product business units. At the highest level, the institution is organised along its major product lines. Very often these are referred to as 'silos'. In turn, each business unit is organised along individual (or closely related) products and services. Each of these requires separate sets of systems (including IT) to support its activities.

  These individual business units focus on product profitability and innovation. Distribution channels are developed and supported by the individual business units, so they tend to be focused on specific products. This organisation model also creates internal product knowledge that is concentrated into each business unit.

- **Customer-focused organisations.** In this structure, the institution is organised into business units by customer group. At the highest level, the institution is organised along its major customer groups. Individual business units are then organised along sub-segments of the institution's customer base.

  These individual business units focus on customer profitability with an emphasis on multi-product relationships. Distribution channels tend to be focused on specific groups, with branches and sales offices as the primary channels.

- **Geographically-based organisations.** Global securities firms are often organised geographically because of the unique regulatory environments found in different countries or regions. Some institutions may create separate entities for their foreign business.

3 INTERACTION WITH OTHER DEPARTMENTS

An Operations Manager must interact with other departments within the financial institution. The Operations Manager will have to present the operational impact of ideas and issues to the Board. Issues might include, for example, extending the current product line into international securities, or ISAs, or expanding the existing customer base by using the internet or advertising overseas, or changing the IT supplier or preparing for a major industry change to a new standard procedure, e.g. Y2K (year 2000 changeover), the euro currency, ISO 15022 SWIFT standards or MiFID.

The departments within a financial institution could include:

- Front Office or Dealing Desks
- Finance, Credit and Accounting
- IT
- Compliance
- Legal
- Customer Services
- Corporate Finance
- Research
- Marketing
- Internal Audit
- Human Resources

CHAPTER ROUNDUP

- Operations management involves managing the operations department of a financial institution.

- The Operations Department is responsible for: processing and setting trades; monitoring and controlling risk; complying with regulations and the law.

- Financial institutions include specialised niche players, internet brokers and larger firms offering a full range of services.

- An organisation's structure reflects product lines, customers, size, personnel and geography.

- The Operations Manager will interact with and present operational issues to other departments.

TEST YOUR KNOWLEDGE

Check your knowledge of the Chapter here, without referring back to the text.

1   What are the three fundamental areas of responsibility of the Operations Department?

2   Among the roles in securities trading are the following. *[Fill in the blanks, using one of the following words or phrases: Settlement; Custodian; Counterparty; Front office; One word or phrase is to be used twice.]*

Input of transactions is dealt with by the ....

Trades must be matched with the .... and any problems resolved.

Trades should be settled on the agreed .... date.

Securities may be held by a .... or by a .... agency.

3   Give a brief definition of 'risk'.

4   Match each piece of legislation with the relevant year: 1985; 1993; 1998; 2002; 2006.

(a)   Criminal Justice Act
(b)   Data Protection Act
(c)   Proceeds of Crime Act
(d)   Companies Acts

TEST YOUR KNOWLEDGE: ANSWERS

1   Processing and settling trades; monitoring and controlling risk; compliance with law and regulation. (See 1.1.)

2   Input of transactions is dealt with by the *front office*.

    Trades must be matched with the *counterparty* and any problems resolved.

    Trades should be settled on the agreed *settlement* date.

    Securities may be held by a *custodian* or by a *settlement* agency. (See 1.2.)

3   Risk may be defined as 'the measurable possibility of losing or not gaining value'. (See 1.3.)

4   The relevant years are as follows. (See 1.4.)

    (a)   Data Protection Act 1998
    (b)   Criminal Justice Act 1993
    (c)   Proceeds of Crime Act 2002
    (d)   Companies Acts 1985 and 2006

BPP)))
LEARNING MEDIA

2

Instruments and Characteristics – Equities

INTRODUCTION

For the examination, you need to understand the features of equities and the different forms equity investment can take.

The limited company with share capital is a fundamental form of business organisation. Companies work within a legal framework and within various types of regulation, depending on the particular types of company and its sector.

We need to set out the rules governing different types of shares.

There are certain special instruments giving rights over shares, including warrants and convertibles. There are special instruments also to enable a share to be traded in a different country from the country in which it is listed.

This is a chapter with quite a large amount of detail.

CHAPTER CONTENTS

1 INTRODUCTION

1.1 What are equities?

For the examination, you need to understand the features of equities and the different forms they can take. **Equities** is the generic name for company **shares**.

A share represents ownership in a corporation. A corporation is owned by its shareholders and managed on a daily basis by its directors. A shareholder will be able to vote in major policy decisions and question the Board of Directors at the **Annual General Meeting (AGM)**.

Investors generally buy equities to make money in two ways. Firstly, to receive **dividend income** when they own the stock. Secondly, to make a **capital gain** if they sell the shares for more than they bought it.

1.2 Incorporation

1.2.1 Legal separation of the business from its owners

If a business is carried on as a sole trade or as a partnership there is no legal distinction between the business and its owners; the actions of the business are those of its owners and in most cases the owners themselves run the risk, if the business fails, of having to pay creditors out of their personal assets.

If however the business is **incorporated**, for example as a limited company, the law regards the company as a 'person' in its own right, separate from the shareholders who are its owners. The separate legal personality of the company enables it to enter into binding contracts in its own name, to sue and to be sued.

What is the essential difference between a 'plc' and a 'Limited' company? A **public limited company** ('plc') is allowed to offer its shares to the general public, while a **private company** ('Ltd') is not.

1.2.2 Limited liability

Being an owner of a business incorporated as a company with **limited liability** means that, in the event of business failure, the shareholder is not liable to make contributions from his personal assets to pay creditors who are owed money by the company other than the amount of share capital itself. The concept of limited liability clearly reduces risk for owners and represents one of the major benefits of incorporation.

1.2.3 Nominal value

A share represents part ownership of the company, each of which is ascribed a fixed **nominal value**, sometimes known as **par value**.

The nominal value is of little relevance other than as follows.

- Shares issued in future cannot be issued at a price below nominal value, and

- When shares are subsequently issued at a price in excess of nominal value (at a premium), the nominal value is recorded in the balance sheet as 'share capital' and the premium (excess of issue price over nominal value) is recorded in a special reserve in the balance sheet '**share premium account**'.

1.2.4 Shareholders' rights

A shareholder acquires various rights and entitlements. Companies may issue different classes of share capital offering different rights. These rights are established when issuing the shares and are set out in the company's Articles of Association.

Money having been subscribed to the company by the shareholder when the shares were issued, the shareholder's principal rights will be as follows.

- **Dividends** – Cash distributions out of profits earned by the company.

- **Capital repayment** – If and when the business is legally wound up although as an Ordinary shareholder they are the last category to be repaid.

- **Votes** – The extent to which the shareholder can influence the conduct of the business, e.g. appointment and removal of directors, the level of dividend payments and approval of a takeover bid.

- **To receive advance notices of all meetings** of the company and to attend, speak and vote at such meetings.

- To be given the opportunity to subscribe for a rights issue on a *pro rata* basis (**pre-emption rights**) If this right did not apply, new shares might be issued to certain shareholders only, as a way of giving that group effective control of the company.

- To sell their shares or transfer them without restriction. The Stock Exchange insists on **free transferability**, although the Articles of Association of some private companies may restrict the transfer of shares.

2 UK EQUITIES

2.1 Types of ordinary share capital

The principal distinctions between classes of ordinary share capital relate to voting rights.

Historically, companies may have wished to raise money by issuing shares to the public but were reluctant to dilute the control exercised by existing shareholders. One means of achieving this might have been to have issued a class of ordinary share capital which entitled the holder to participate fully in profits and capital repayment but which did not carry voting rights. These non-voting shares are frequently described as 'A' Ordinary shares.

Preference shares	Ordinary shares
Dividend is a fixed amount per share. Cumulative means that if a dividend is not paid one year, it will be paid the following year. Non-cumulative means that if it is not paid one year, the dividend has been lost forever.	Dividend is at the discretion of the company. Preference dividends are always paid before Ordinary shareholders.
No or limited voting rights	Voting rights
Upon liquidation, preference shareholders are repaid before Ordinary shareholders but after all other creditors.	Upon liquidation, Ordinary shareholders are paid after all other creditors and preference shareholders.

Investors are nowadays opposed to the issuing of equity without votes or with restricted voting rights in the belief that all shareholders who bear the same risk should have an equal voice in the management of the business.

2.2 Distribution on winding up

In the liquidation or winding up of a company, the order in which various persons owed money by the company are repaid is subject to company law.

Order of distribution of assets on a winding up

1   Costs of the liquidator

2   Loans and bonds secured on assets of the company by a fixed charge – a charge over a specific asset or assets of the company

3   Preferential creditors: unpaid wages, up to a limit per employee; unpaid contributions to an occupational pension scheme (Since the **Enterprise Act 2002**, there is no longer a Crown preference for unpaid taxes.)

4   Fund pool for ordinary creditors (persons owed money by the company), comprising 50% of the first £10,000 of the company's assets and 20% of net property over £10,000 and up to £600,000

5   Loans and bonds secured on assets of the company by a floating charge – charges over the assets of the company generally, excluding any assets covered by a fixed charge

6   Other ordinary (unsecured) creditors

7   Subordinated loan stocks

8   Preference shares

9   Ordinary shares

2.3 Ordinary shares

2.3.1 General ordinary shares

As for preference shares, a number of sub-categories of **ordinary shares** exist, conferring slightly different rights on the shareholder. We start with a general consideration of these rights and then look at some specific sub-categories.

Ordinary shares usually form the bulk of the share capital of the company. The Ordinary shareholders are normally entitled to all profits remaining after tax and preference dividends have been deducted. These profits will either be paid out to them as a dividend or retained within the company, increasing its value and hence generating capital growth in the value of their shares.

Some general characteristics of ordinary shares are as follows.

- **Annual returns.** Ordinary shareholders are entitled to a declared dividend, which (if any) will be proposed by the directors at each AGM.

- **Dividends** can only be paid out of profits available for distribution, basically accumulated realised profits as disclosed in the company's income statement.

- **Capital repayment.** Ordinary shareholders are not usually entitled to any capital repayment from the company. If they wish to realise their investment, they must sell their shares to another investor.

- **Security.** Ordinary shareholders are the first people to lose, should a company become insolvent, i.e. they are the last people to be paid out if there are any financial resources left in the business in such a circumstance.

- **Influence.** Ordinary shareholders are generally entitled to vote at general meetings, giving them control over the directors of the company and hence, the operations of the business. It is usual for each Ordinary share to carry one vote, so the level of influence a particular investor has will be determined by the number of shares he holds.

  These are generalisations however, and it would be necessary to look to the Articles of Association to find out the specific rules for each Ordinary share.

- **Negotiability.** The general rules outlined above apply to ordinary shares.

2.3.2 Non-voting ordinary shares

When companies wish to raise finance from people other than the existing shareholders without diluting the control of the existing shareholders, they may issue non-voting shares.

These shares are identical in all respects to the Ordinary shares, except that they carry no voting rights (called 'N/V' or 'A' shares) or restricted voting rights ('R/V' shares).

Such shares offer no greater return (they receive the same Ordinary dividend), though the shareholder faces a much higher risk, since he cannot influence the operations of the company. As a result, it is becoming increasingly difficult for companies to raise new capital by issuing non-voting shares.

There are, however, a small number of companies that still have non-voting shares in issue, such as Young's Brewers.

Example: Voting rights

We illustrate below the financing provided by and voting rights of Young's Brewers.

Share category	Shares issued		Voting influence	
	'000	%	m	%
A Ordinary shares	3,141	24.3	3,141	43.2
B Ordinary shares	4,125	31.8	4,125	56.7
Non-voting shares	5,684	43.9	–	–
	12,950	100.0	7,266	100.0

2.3.3 Redeemable ordinary shares

Since the Companies Act 1985 (CA 1985), companies have been allowed to issue **redeemable ordinary shares**, providing they also have shares in issue that are not redeemable (s159 CA 1985).

A company may now also purchase its own shares, subject to satisfying a number of conditions as we will see later.

2.3.4 Deferred shares

Deferred shares are shares that do not rank for a dividend until a particular circumstance is satisfied, typically either:

- Until the Ordinary dividends have reached a predetermined level, or

- Until a specified period after they are issued. For example, Croda issued shares in 1978 that did not rank for a dividend until 1988

2.4 Preference shares

2.4.1 General preference shares

In practice, a number of sub-categories of preference shares are frequently encountered, each giving different rights to the relevant shareholders. We will start with a general consideration of the rights that preference shares confer, then look at the sub-categories.

- **Annual returns.** Preference shares carry a fixed rate of dividend, normally payable half-yearly. This rate is fixed, regardless of the levels of profit of the company.

- As the name suggests, these shares receive preferential treatment by the company with regard to **dividend distribution and capital repayment** on a winding up. In particular, no dividend may be paid on any other class of shares until the preference dividend has been paid for the year. This does not, however, mean that a preference dividend must be declared. Preference shareholders are in an inferior position to lenders from this viewpoint, since any loan interest must always be paid.

- **Capital repayment.** In general, there is no entitlement to any capital repayment from the company, though certain sub-categories do confer this right. On a winding up, preference shareholders are generally only entitled to the repayment of the nominal value of their shares: they do not participate in any remaining profits.

- **Security.** There is no specific security attached to preference shares.

- **Influence.** When a preference dividend is not declared, preference shareholders usually become entitled to vote at shareholders' general meetings, along with Ordinary shareholders. Normally, provided preference dividends are paid, preference shares do not carry any voting rights.

- **Negotiability.** The general rules outlined above apply to preference shares.

2.4.2 Cumulative preference shares

If the dividend on a **cumulative preference share** is not paid in any one year, then it must be accumulated and paid later. That is, it should be accrued in the accounts even if the company cannot afford to pay it this year. This accumulated liability must be paid off in full in later years before any Ordinary dividend can be paid.

2.4.3 Redeemable preference shares

These are shares that are repayable:

- At a predetermined price – normally quoted at a premium above their nominal value
- At a predetermined date or dates

As such, they represent a temporary source of financing for the company that will rank for dividends for a short period of time and then be repaid.

2.4.4 Participating preference shares

As noted above, preference shares usually carry a fixed dividend, representing their full annual return entitlement. Participating preference shares will receive this fixed dividend and an additional dividend, which is usually a proportion of any Ordinary dividend declared. As such, they participate more in the risks and rewards of ownership of the company.

2.4.5 Convertible preference shares

Up to the date of conversion, a convertible preference share offers the shareholder all the normal risks and returns associated with preference shares, i.e. fixed dividend returns and preferential rights to any capital repayment. On reaching the date of conversion, the shareholders will have the option of converting the preference shares into Ordinary shares or taking a predetermined cash alternative.

2.5 Warrants

2.5.1 What are warrants and why are they issued?

Warrants in a company give the holder the right to subscribe for ordinary shares in that company on the terms set out in the Articles of Association. Holders of warrants are not entitled to any dividend or voting rights, and if the subscription has not been exercised by the expiry date, the warrant becomes valueless.

Warrants are traded on the Stock Exchange in exactly the same way as any other quoted security. The holder will receive a certificate which usually sets out the number of warrants held, and the terms on which ordinary shares can be purchased.

Companies have often issued warrants as part of a 'package deal' whereby the warrants and a loan stock were issued together to make the loan stock more attractive. On completion of the issue formalities the warrants and loan stock were then quoted and dealt in as separate entities.

Benefits to the company from issue of warrants

- **Reducing the financial burden.** No dividends or interest are paid on the warrants themselves. The company has the benefit of the proceeds of the issue of warrants (which are shown as a capital reserve in the balance sheet) at no cost to itself until and unless conversion takes place. Warrants are not normally converted early in their life, so the company has the benefit of the capital reserve at no cost to itself for many years.

- **Taking advantage of an overvalued share price.** If a company believes its share price to be overvalued, it can sell warrants to outsiders. If the company's share price does indeed fall far enough to make conversion unattractive, then the conversion will never take place, and the capital reserve will have been acquired at no cost. However, to prevent abuses, the Stock Exchange insists that a new issue of warrants can only be offered to outsiders with the consent of the existing shareholders.

- **Enhancing the attraction of other issues.** In cases where the warrants are issued as part of a 'package', the accompanying loan stock may be issued at a lower coupon because of the added attraction of the warrant.

Example: Warrant

The warrants of the XYZ Investment Trust are priced at 29p while its ordinary shares stand at 160p. The conversion terms give warrant holders the right to subscribe for one ordinary share for each warrant held at a subscription price of 177p any time until say January 2009.

If we ignore dealing costs, we can see that the price of obtaining the shares via the warrants is at a premium of 28.75%. The cost of a warrant is 29p which when added to the subscription price of 177p makes a total cost of 206p. This means that the shares cost 46p more when obtained via the warrants, and there is a premium of $46/160 \times 100 = 28.75\%$.

2.5.2 Premiums and discounts

Generally speaking, the **premium** on a warrant will be higher the longer the period for subscription, although much must depend on the prospects of the underlying shares. There have been instances, however, where the warrant price has not moved as quickly as the underlying share price, and in these instances a **discount** can arise. These circumstances can also cause discounts on convertible loans.

As the warrant nears the end of its life, the premium will tend to disappear as the warrants will either be exercised or will be allowed to lapse.

2.5.3 Time value and intrinsic value

A warrant is essentially a long dated call option with an **intrinsic value** and a **time value**. The principles of options apply: the 'intrinsic value' of a warrant is the amount, if any, by which the current share price exceeds the subscription price.

If we look back at the XYZ Investment Trust warrant in the Example above, we can see that its intrinsic value is nil since the current share price is below the subscription price. The 29p warrant price consists entirely of 'time value' which can be described as the price paid now for the opportunity to acquire the shares at a later date at a pre-determined price.

2.5.4 Evaluating a warrant

Takeovers. If there is a likelihood of a takeover, the warrant holder could suffer very badly if the warrant is 'out of the money'.

Under the terms of the issue of almost all warrants there is a clause stating that in the event of a successful takeover of the company, the subscription expiry date will be brought forward to coincide with the bid. The successful bidder must then offer the intrinsic value of the warrants calculated on his offer price to the ordinary shareholders. However, there is no obligation to compensate the warrant holders for lost 'time value'.

Therefore when a warrant's price consists mainly of time value, the warrant holder might choose to sell his warrant on the first news of a takeover bid, unless the offer price is vastly above the current share price.

Having no votes, warrant holders cannot exercise any influence on the outcome of the takeover.

Bonus issues and rights issues. The warrant holder can view such issues with equanimity, since the Stock Exchange requires the company to protect warrant holders from suffering any loss due from a fall in the ex-capitalisation or ex-rights price.

Liquidation. The rights of a warrant holder in liquidation will depend on the terms of the issue. In any event a warrant is classed as capital, and the warrant holder will rank behind all external creditors.

Expiry date. The longer the expiry date the better, as there is a greater chance of a favourable movement in the price of the underlying shares. The current market price of the warrant could well contain a large 'time value' in recognition of the value of a long time scale.

The warrant, when exercised, involves the company in an issue of shares and therefore a dilution of share capital. As the warrant represents a long dated call option – a deferred purchase – the investor should only invest in companies which should be successful.

2.6 Covered warrants

A **covered warrant** is a contract that confers upon the buyer the right, but not the obligation, to buy or sell an asset at a given price on or before a given date. You may have noticed that this definition is identical to that of a traded option, which is effectively what a covered warrant is. Covered warrants are available on the London Stock Exchange, covering a range of blue chip and mid-cap shares and indices.

The main **differences between** the **covered warrants** traded on the London Stock Exchange and the **traded options** traded on Euronext.liffe are as follows.

- A covered warrant is issued by a financial institution who must play an active role as an equity market maker. The word 'covered' denotes the fact that the institution will cover (hedge) their exposure by an offsetting position in the underlying asset market.

- Covered warrants normally have a life of six to twelve months at issue, though this may be up to five years.

- Covered warrants on any assets may be either physically settled or cash settled (contract for differences), though cash settlement is most common as a result of the avoidance of stamp duty. Settlement is specified contract by contract for traded options.

The fact that covered warrants must be issued by a financial institution means that investors cannot short-sell covered warrants.

Other than these points, the uses, terminology and pricing principles of both covered warrants and traded options are the same, for example:

- There are two basic forms, namely calls and puts
- They can have either American or European style exercise

The cost of each type is called the **premium** (which represents the maximum potential loss to the holder). They are both exercised at the exercise price, and expire at the expiry date. Covered warrants can be referred to as **securitised options**.

2.7 Dividends

Dividends are cash payments to shareholders out of the profits of a company. Usually there are two dividends on UK shares: an interim dividend and a final dividend.

- **Interim dividends** may be declared by the directors and are usually paid at the start of the second half of a company's accounting year.

- **Final dividends** are proposed by the directors and are usually paid the day after the company's annual general meeting. Shareholders at the AGM have the power to reduce or prevent payment of any final dividend, but they may not vote to increase the dividend which has been proposed.

Dividends can only be paid from available profits. Thus, the maximum dividend which the directors could propose is limited by the profits available. However, retained profits from previous years can be used to maintain a dividend, for example if the current year has seen relatively low profits.

2.8 Scrip issues

A **scrip issue**, also known as a **bonus issue** or **capitalisation issue**, represents an issue without charge of further shares at nominal value to existing shareholders in proportion to their holdings.

The issue represents a 'capitalisation' of reserves in the sense that the effect on the balance sheet is to convert reserves into issued share capital. Any category of reserves can be used for scrip issues.

Example: Scrip issue

Arnold plc has in issue 4 million ordinary shares of nominal value 50p each. The company makes a scrip issue of 1 share for every 4 held.

The balance sheets before and after the issue will be as follows.

	Before (£'000)	Scrip issue (£'000)	After (£'000)
Net assets	5,000	–	5,000
Called up share capital			
Ordinary shares of 50p	2,000	+500	2,500
Income statement	3,000	–500	2,500
Shareholders' funds	5,000	–	5,000

The issue of a further one million ordinary shares is recorded at nominal value 50p and is 'financed' by reducing reserves by the same amount. It is clear that no cash has been raised and that shareholders' funds in total are unchanged; £500,000 of the reserve 'income statement' has been converted into share capital.

Theoretical impact on share price. A scrip issue does not affect the ability of the company to make profits. Theoretically the total value of the company (market capitalisation) should therefore not change and similarly the total value of an individual's holding should not change. However, the value per share should fall in proportion to the weight of the scrip issue. Assume that the market price was 200p per share prior to the scrip issue. This capitalises the company at £8m (4 million × 200p) and an individual holding of 1,000 shares is worth £2,000.

When a scrip issue is made, these total values ought not to change; if the scrip is a 1 for 4 the holder of 1,000 shares receives an additional 250 shares (a 25% increase in his holding) but the 1,250 shares are still worth £2,000 in total. The price of each share should fall to 160p (£2,000/1,250), which is 20% less than before. The price per share is now 80% of its pre-scrip level. If the scrip had been a 1 for 1 the price per share would be expected to halve to 100p given the 100% increase in the number of shares to 2,000 shares and no change in the total value of the holding (£2,000).

Despite the fact that there should be no change in the share price, historical evidence supports the view that investor expectations are such that the share price increases whether through increased marketability or through the expectation of higher dividends.

2.9 Share splits

A **share split** or subdivision should be distinguished from a scrip issue. The effect on the market price per share is similar but the impact on the balance sheet is different. Splits are sometimes used to reduce the price per share to increase marketability of the shares.

A split involves dividing the existing issued share capital into a greater number of shares of a reduced nominal value per share. There is no capitalisation of reserves; the only effect on the balance sheet is that the note on share capital shows the increased number of shares and the reduced nominal value per share.

Example: Share split

Elizabethan plc has in issue 4 million ordinary shares of nominal value 50p each. The company splits each ordinary share of 50p each into five ordinary shares of 10p each.

The balance sheet before and after the split will be as follows.

	Before (£'000)	Split (£'000)	After (£'000)
Net assets	5,000	–	5,000
Called up share capital			
Ordinary shares			
4 million of 50p	2,000	–	
20 million of 10p			2,000
Income statement	3,000	–	3,000
Shareholders' funds	5,000	–	5,000

Theoretical impact on share price. Suppose that the market price per share was 200p before the split and that an individual held 1,000 shares. As with a scrip issue, the total value of the holding should remain £2,000. On a per-share basis, however, the market price 200p should fall to 40p per share since the individual now holds 5,000 shares.

2.10 Share consolidations

A **share consolidation** is the opposite of a share split. The shares are consolidated so that, for example, four shares with a nominal value of 25p each become one share with £1 nominal value.

2.11 Rights issues

Exam tip

> In the Summer 2006 exam, a four-mark compulsory question asked about investors' choices when a rights issue is made, and their consequences.

The Companies Act 1985 provides that when UK companies issue equity shares for cash they must firstly offer shareholders the right to subscribe for the new shares in proportion to their existing holdings. These provisions conferring **pre-emption rights** account for the fact that UK companies have in the past used rights issues as the standard method of issuing equity for cash.

Traditionally, rights issues have been made at a price below the existing market price in order to persuade existing shareholders to subscribe for additional shares. It has also been normal practice for the issue to be '**underwritten**' by institutional investors. In exchange for agreeing to subscribe for shares if existing shareholders do not take up their rights, the underwriters receive a commission which represents a kind of insurance premium from the issuing company's point of view since it guarantees that the company will receive its money. From time to time companies have priced the issue at a 'deep discount' to the existing market price and have avoided the necessity (and cost) of underwriting.

A rights issue may be either **renounceable** or **non-renounceable**. Non-renounceable rights cannot be bought or sold. With a renounceable issue, the investor may sell the rights.

The **allotment letter** is the document detailing the amount or number of securities allotted to an applicant for a rights issue (or a new issue).

What if the investor chooses not to subscribe for the rights issue? The allotment letters for renounceable rights issues are negotiable instruments and the rights can be sold and bought on a '**nil paid**' basis.

The investor may allow the rights to lapse. The new shares will not be received, and there will be a dilution in the investor's shareholding.

Example: Rights issue

Godzilla plc has in issue 4,000,000 ordinary shares of 50p each. The market price of each share is 200p. The company wishes to raise £1,500,000 to finance a new project by means of a rights issue. If it does so by issuing one new share for every four held, at a price of 150p, the balance sheets before and after the issue will be as follows.

	Before (£'000)	Rights issue (£'000)	After (£'000)
Net assets	5,000	+1,500	6,500
Called up share capital			
Ordinary shares of 50p	2,000	+500	2,500
Share premium account		+1,000	1,000
Income statement	3,000	–	3,000
Shareholders' funds	5,000	+1,500	6,500

Theoretical impact on share price. If a holder of 1,000 ordinary shares takes up the entitlement to subscribe for 250 additional shares at 150p, theoretically the value of the existing holding (£2,000) should be increased by the new money subscribed £375 (250 × 150p)

	Shares		£
Pre-rights issue	1,000	× 200p	2,000
Rights issue (1 for 4)	250	– 150p	375
Ex-rights (after the rights issue)	1,250		2,375

On a per share basis, the shares should be worth 190p ex-rights. In practice, what happens to the share price depends on market sentiment regarding factors such as the purpose to which the new money is to be applied and the trading background against which the issue is made.

2.12 Placings

S95 Companies Act 1985 requires that if shares are to be issued for cash other than on a pre-emption basis, shareholders must vote by means of a special resolution to empower the directors to issue the shares in this way. This power can last for up to five years.

The London Stock Exchange requires that a special resolution is passed at each Annual General Meeting permitting **placings** of new equity for cash. There are no monetary limits on the amounts which can be raised in this way and authority need not be acquired for each individual placing. However, the Stock Exchange requires that, in the notes to its annual report and accounts, the company must give details of all issues of shares for cash other than *pro rata*.

2.12.1 Comparing rights issues and placings

The merits of placings are held to be as follows.

- The company saves underwriting commission which normally has to be paid in rights issues (unless they are issued at a deep discount).

- The company can issue the new shares in a placing at a narrower discount to the existing market price than would be the case with a rights issue.

- The company gets its money more quickly because the formalities are fewer and the time scale is compressed.

Note that the principles of accounting for an issue by means of a placing are identical to those applied to rights issues.

2.13 Companies buying back their own shares

The Companies Acts 1985 and 2006 gives companies the right to **purchase their own shares**.

In theory, if a company buys back its own shares when their market price is below net asset value, the supply of ordinary shares is reduced with the remaining shares having a greater earning capacity and net asset backing per share. Net asset value in this context is the theoretical surplus available to ordinary shareholders in a possible liquidation, divided by the number of shares. The resultant figure is the theoretical amount per share which a shareholder would receive in liquidation.

The theory of finance generally welcomes buy-backs of share capital as an acceptable way of returning companies' funds to shareholders. If a company has surplus cash, the directors could feel obliged to find projects to use the surplus cash, for example to diversify or carry out ambitious acquisitions, which in the long term could result in losses for the company.

2.14 Individual and institutional investors

Investors include **individuals** and **institutional investors**.

Institutional investors are organisations whose purpose is to invest its own assets or those managed on behalf of others. Examples are pension funds, insurance companies and banks. The institutions manage investments either directly, or indirectly through investment companies.

3 INTERNATIONAL ASPECTS

3.1 Depository receipts

3.1.1 American Depository Receipts (ADRs)

American Depository Receipts (ADRs) enable trading in a foreign stock or share. An American Depository Receipt is a certificate issued by a depository bank stating that a specific number of a company's shares have been deposited with that bank. The underlying securities are deposited with the bank (or its custodian bank abroad). The US bank then issues an ADR against them. ADRs can be traded on major exchanges or on the over-the-counter market.

American Depository Shares (ADSs) are the shares which are embodied within an American Depository Receipt. ADSs are shares issued under a deposit agreement that represent an underlying security in the issuer's home country. Technically, an ADS is the actual share trading, while an ADR represents a bundle of ADSs.

The American Depository Shares are a US dollar-denominated form of equity ownership in a non-US company. It represents the foreign shares of the company held on deposit by a custodian bank in the company's home country and carries the corporate and economic rights of the foreign shares, subject to the terms specified on the ADR certificate.

3.1.2 Global Depository Receipts (GDRs)

Global Depository Receipts (GDRs) were developed to help international trading of stocks and shares. The underlying securities are deposited with a bank or with the bank's custodian in the country of origin. The bank then issues a GDR against them. GDRs are bought and sold outside the USA; inside the USA, ADRs are used.

Different types available are called by their initials, for example Global Depository Receipts are GDRs (used primarily for shares listed in Japan or Hong Kong) and European Depository Receipts EDRs. In each case, the shares concerned are issued in a country, or in the case of EDRs a continent, other than the one issuing the depository receipts.

Since 1994, various depository receipts of overseas companies have been traded on the London Stock Exchange.

3.1.3 Euroclear Depository Interests (CDIs)

Euroclear Depository Interests (CDIs) are instruments based on an underlying international security. They may be traded and settled in exactly the same manner as a UK stock but are fully **fungible** with their international parent. The attraction of this 'class' of security is the **lower cost of settlement** that use of the Euroclear settlement system provides.

Exam tip

> In the Summer 2006 exam, 2 marks were available for explaining fungibility. Do not confuse fungibility with convertibility, as many candidates did.
>
> CDIs appeared in the Winter 2007 exam.

Definition: **Fungible assets** are interchangeable assets which are identical in terms of quality. For example, an investor's holding of shares in BP plc left in custody at a brokerage firm are interchangeable with other customers' BP shares. Investors may buy futures contracts for the purchase of wheat, but the wheat stored in a grain silo is not specifically identified with regard to ownership.

The London Stock Exchange's IRS (**International Retail Service**) – aimed specifically at the UK retail client – offers the possibility of competing quotes in many foreign-denominated securities settled in sterling via Euroclear (CDIs). All dealings on the IRS are in CDIs.

3.1.4 Use of ADRs

Use of ADRs has grown, largely as a result of American fund managers emerging as major purchasers of overseas securities. Many British companies have used the American markets to raise funds through primary issues of ADRs.

ADRs represent a means by which shares of foreign companies listed on foreign stock exchanges can be traded in dollar denominations and in bearer form in the United States stock market. 'Foreign' in relation to ADRs means companies that are **not** US companies.

The holder of the ADR certificate has all dividend rights belonging to the shares, and he has the right to have votes cast on his behalf at company meetings. This is done by the depository bank in the United States acting as his proxy.

From the point of view of the company, which could have anything up to 20% of its equity in ADR form, problems can arise because of an inability to trace the beneficial owners of their share capital. This is because the ADRs effectively turn registered shares into bearer shares. It can be vital to a company to know who owns its share capital in the event of a takeover bid, and it is not impossible that a prospective purchaser of the company could acquire a sizeable holding via ADRs without the knowledge of the directors of the company.

Whilst ADRs are an American creation, some UK institutional investors have purchased shares of UK companies through ADRs in New York rather than on the UK Stock Exchange. The reason for this operation is that the securities are in bearer form, thus there was no stamp duty payable on their purchase, and at ½% of the total consideration this could have added greatly to the institutional investors' dealing costs. However, a special rate of stamp duty of $1\frac{1}{2}$% applies to the conversion of UK shares into depository receipts. This is often referred to as the 'season ticket'.

For more information, see www.global-investor.com.

3.2 Overseas government bonds

Apart from investing in company securities, it is possible to purchase securities issued by **foreign governments and public bodies**. The standing of these securities depends greatly on the standing of the issuing authority. This is covered in greater depth in the section on bonds – see Chapter 3 on Fixed Income Instruments.

Some foreign government securities have virtually 'gilt-edged' status, such as USA Treasury Bonds and Japanese Government Bonds, while some others are virtually worthless except as collectors' items.

Some foreign governments have defaulted or deferred on interest payments. In such cases the Council of Foreign Bondholders will exert pressure on the defaulting government to make it pay. Its main weapon is that eventually defaulting governments will need to raise fresh capital, and when this happens the Council has enough power to insist upon agreement being reached with existing creditors before the new loan can be agreed.

The majority of foreign government securities issued in London are issued in sterling and these have been nicknamed 'bulldog bonds'. Interest is payable in sterling on these bonds.

Overseas issues in other currencies are affected by the exchange risk, and the fluctuations of the currency must be taken into account when investing.

Many foreign government bonds have had much higher yields than UK gilts in the recent past. This reflects the greater risk, with some countries' bonds now being designated as junk bonds (i.e. sub-investment grade). This means that the credit rating of the issuing government indicates a significant chance of default on the debt.

Chapter 3 describes bonds and fixed income products in greater detail.

3.3 Bearer securities

Bearer securities are stocks and shares issued by companies, public bodies and governments where the issuing authority does not maintain a register of ownership. Ownership of these securities passes by mere delivery. This type of instrument is relatively rare in the UK, with eurobonds and ADRs (American Depository Receipts) being the main examples.

A few UK-registered companies also have part of their share capital in bearer form, two examples here being RTZ and Shell Transport.

Ownership of a bearer security vests in the holder of the certificate, and ownership passes by mere delivery. A problem here arises if the share certificate is stolen, and a *bona-fide* transferee for value purchases the certificate from the thief. If this occurred the original owner would lose all his rights to the shares. To safeguard against this occurrence, a bearer certificate should be kept in a safe place, such as with a stockbroker or at a custody bank.

Keeping a bearer certificate with a custodian has other advantages. Because there is no register of holders, the issuing authority does not know where to send notice of meetings, circulars and dividends. Such items are always preceded by advertisements in the financial press or on the Bondholders Register. In the case of dividend payments the advertisement will inform holders which coupon to submit in order to claim the dividend.

Coupons are attached to the certificate and are numbered. Each time a dividend is claimed the relevantly numbered coupon is detached and sent to the issuing authority. At some time the coupons will run out and the next set of coupons in numerical order will be claimed by submission of the 'talon', which is the last coupon and is larger than the other coupons. Obviously for the private investor it can be easy to miss the dividend notice, and failure to claim the dividend might lead to forfeiting that dividend. If the certificate is lodged with a custodian then there is no likelihood of this happening because the custodian is geared up to check such items. Another advantage here is that the custodian will lump together all the coupons and make one claim. If the cheque received is in foreign currency, it must be converted into sterling.

In order for a bearer certificate to be sold there must be 'good delivery'. This means that the certificate must be in good condition and all coupons that should be attached are attached.

The final area that can be a problem with bearer securities is the danger of forged documents. Obviously as ownership can pass by mere delivery, it is quite feasible that a forged document could escape careful scrutiny resulting in a purchaser holding a worthless piece of paper. Here again the bank would be in a position to verify the authenticity of the certificate purchased.

3.4 Marking certificates

These are share certificates issued primarily by American companies. They are registered shares; the name of the registered holder appears on the front of the certificate and the company maintains a register of holders in exactly the same way as for any registered share.

The difference between marking certificates and ordinary registered share certificates is that the transfer form on the reverse of the share certificate is blank endorsed. This means that the registered holder signs the form in front of a witness, who also must sign it, but then leaves the rest of the form blank. This has the effect of making title pass by mere delivery, i.e. the certificate acquires most of the characteristics of a bearer security.

The registered holder is called the '**marking name**' or '**street name**' and appears as the holder of the certificate in the issuing company's books. The marking name receives all correspondence, rights and bonus issue details, and dividends. The marking name must then account to the true owner for all of these. It is usual for the marking name to be a stockbroker, bank or a financial institution recognised as being of impeccable standing by the London Stock Exchange.

A marking name is classified as a 'good marking name' or 'recognised marking name', and shares registered in a 'good or recognised marking name' command a higher price than ones in a 'bad marking name', i.e. in the name of someone or somebody not recognised by the Stock Exchange for this purpose. The 'good marking name' will give the Stock Exchange an undertaking to pay interest and dividends to the true owner when he claims them. Interest and dividends are paid in the currency of the issuing company's country and the 'good marking name' also undertakes to the Stock Exchange to convert the currency cheques at the approved rate of exchange.

There is no reason why the true owner of a marking certificate should not have the shares registered in his own name. To do so he will complete the Stock Power form on the back of the certificate which is left blank, showing himself as assignee. He will then send the certificate and the required fee to the issuing authority who will delete the 'good marking name' from their books as holder and insert the true owner's name. They will then issue a new share certificate showing him as registered owner on the front of the certificate.

It is inadvisable for the true owner to carry out this operation, for the following reasons.

- The shares will command a lower price in a 'bad marking name', i.e. his own name, than in a 'good marking name'.

- There is a fee to be paid to carry out this operation.

- The true owner will receive a currency cheque and will have to pay the full cost of converting this into sterling. If his holding is not very large, or the dividend is small, he may find that the charges virtually take the whole of the value of the cheque. The issuing authority itself also deducts a charge for paying a dividend to an individual.

- It takes a long time for ownership to be transferred, one reason being that you are dealing with a company abroad, and postal times can cause delays.

In conclusion, it can be seen that it is better to retain the shares in a good marking name. As the shares are bank-endorsed they are effectively bearer shares, and for safety should be kept in the bank. The bank will claim the dividends due, and in the same way as with true bearer shares, the costs of changing the dividend cheque into sterling is divided between all the holders, thus the true owner will effectively receive a higher dividend than he would if he transferred the shares into his own name.

These certificates have the name 'marking certificates' because, theoretically at least, each time the dividend is claimed the certificate is marked. However, not all banks now mark the certificate every time the dividend is claimed.

3.5 Comparison of bearer securities and marking certificates

There is often confusion as to where bearer shares end and marking certificates begin. Because they are both bearer in nature does not mean they are totally identical. Marking certificates only acquire **some** of the attributes of bearer shares, and the differences and similarities are seen in the following table of comparison.

Marking certificates	Bearer securities
1 Shares endorsed on the back by a UK institution (e.g. a bank or insurance company) in blank. They then acquire most of the attributes of a bearer security.	1 Stocks and shares of a company which are not registered shares. Mainly issued by overseas companies or bodies, but some are issued by UK companies, e.g. Shell Transport.
2 Dividends are claimed from the marking name by the beneficial owner.	2 Dividends are claimed by submitting coupons attached to the certificate to the issuing company.
3 A marking certificate can be transferred out of the marking name into the name of the beneficial owner by completion of the registration form on the back of the certificate by the beneficial owner. He will send it to the company. In return he will receive a share certificate showing him as the registered owner. This is expensive and results in a lower share price.	3 Bearer securities can never be made registered securities.
4 Good delivery does not apply.	4 Bearer securities must always be 'good delivery', i.e. all coupons and talons that should be attached must be attached and the certificate itself must not be defaced.

The following points apply in common to bearer securities and marking certificates.

- All bearer or marking certificates should be kept with an approved custodian in safe custody for the following reasons.

    - Title passes by delivery and a thief could pass on a good title to a *bona fide* transferee for value.

    - Custodians are geared up to claiming dividends from the company/issuing authority. If a dividend is missed it may be lost forever.

    - Because the custodian aggregates all the claims together it only receives one currency cheque, thus the costs involved in collecting the cheque are much lower and are divided *pro-rata* amongst all the customers.

- When either security is bought it is cheaper than buying a registered security because there is no stamp duty payable on the purchase.

- Secrecy – no one knows that you own the certificates (apart from the custodian).

4 CONVERTIBLES

4.1 What is a convertible?

A **convertible loan stock** is a fixed interest loan stock or a preference share which carries the right to **convert into ordinary shares** on the terms and conditions set out in the Articles of Association. The stockholder has the right, but not the obligation, to convert within stipulated time limits. If conversion rights are not exercised by the expiry date, the stock will revert to a conventional dated loan stock.

The holder of a convertible loan stock has a legal right to receive his fixed interest in the same way as any other creditor is entitled to money owing. In addition the loan stock is of course an external liability which must be met in full in any liquidation before the shareholders receive a penny. However, should the company prosper, the loan stockholder can obtain an equity stake by converting.

The classic example of 'having your cake and eating it' occurs when the trustee of a trust buys convertible loans to help maintain the income of the life tenant, whilst retaining the possibility of capital growth through exercise of the conversion rights on behalf of the reversionary interest after the life tenant's death.

Usually a convertible loan stock will be priced above a comparable 'straight' loan stock because of the attraction of the conversion option. However, if the prospects for the shares seem to be poor, the convertible loan stock price should be supported at the level of a comparable fixed interest stock. This support level is sometimes known as the 'bond support price'.

To sum up, income from a fixed interest stock will generally exceed the dividend income from shares in the short term, but in the longer term there is scope for growth in the dividend income and market price of shares. A convertible loan stock enables the investor to take advantage of the higher fixed income in the short term, whilst retaining the option to benefit from growth of capital and income from the shares in the long term. If the shares do not perform very well then he will simply retain the convertible as a straight fixed interest stock.

4.2 Weighing up the merits of convertibles

4.2.1 Choice of company

The golden rule for an investor is only to choose a convertible loan in a company which is likely to be successful. If the company is unsuccessful, then the share price will fall and the conversion rights will become worthless. If matters become even more desperate, the value of the convertible loan stock could even fall below the bond support price because of fears of default.

4.2.2 Length of option period

If you like the company, then the next consideration is the length of the conversion option. The longer the conversion period the more chance there is for the investor to benefit, since there is a greater time during which the share price could 'take off'.

4.2.3 Conversion premium or discount

The conversion premium is the premium effectively paid by the investor by purchasing shares via a convertible rather than purchasing them directly.

Example: Convertible loan stock

Consider a hypothetical company JKL plc, with 6% Convertible Unsecured Loan Stock 2002 (CULS).

The conversion terms are that each £100 nominal value can be converted into 30 ordinary shares between February 2002 and February 2008. Any stock unconverted will be redeemed at par in February 2008.

Market prices

CULS	£85	Flat yield	7.1%
Ordinary	260p	Dividend yield	4.0%

If a person purchases £100 of CULS now and later converts into ordinary shares, he will have effectively paid

$$\frac{85}{30} = 283 \text{ pence per share}$$

This represents a premium of $\frac{283-260}{260} \times 100\% = 8.8\%$ over the current market price.

This is quite a low premium and combined with the healthy flat yield would make this an attractive stock.

Sometimes the market price of the shares can rise very quickly, and there can be a time lag before the convertible follows suit. In such cases purchase of the convertible can be a cheap way of obtaining the shares because there is a conversion discount.

4.2.4 Taxation

Tax considerations also apply, since a high flat yield on a convertible may deter a higher rate taxpayer, but he may still feel the investment to be worthwhile if he sees the possibility of a good capital gain on conversion.

5 VALUES OF SHARES

5.1 Influences on share prices

The value of a share at any time is on what another person will pay for it.

Factors affecting share prices

- The **demand** for the stock – if many investors want to buy the share price will increase
- **Supply** factors also apply
- Optimism about the future of the economy as a whole
- Expectation about the future profitability or operations of the firm
- News or rumour of a takeover/merger
- The strength of the Board
- The activities and profits of competitors
- General consensus and sentiment among investors
- Expectations about the dividend

The equity market goes through cycles. A persistent rising period is known as a **bull market** while a persistently falling market is known as a **bear market**. The term 'bear' is derived from bear skin traders who had a reputation for selling skins before the bears were caught. Therefore the term was applied to traders who sold the stock before they owned it because they were confident that the price would fall. Due to the popularity of bull and bear baiting, the term bull was used to signify the opposite of bear and thus those believing the price would increase.

5.2 Share price indices

Share price indices measure the rises and falls of share prices. An **index** is a number that shows the value of something relative to a base value.

The following diagram shows the main indices for the UK market. The constituents of the indices are reviewed every three months and appropriate promotions and demotions are made.

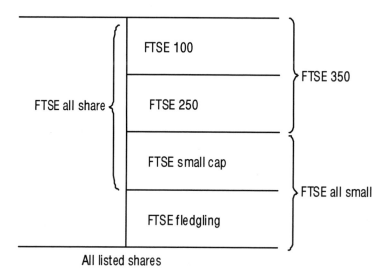

The FTSE Eurotop 300, FTSE Eurobloc 100 and FTSE Eurotop 100 are designed to reflect the trends on the European stock markets.

International indices

- Dow Jones Industrial Average (USA)
- Standard and Poor's (S&P) 500 (USA)
- Nikkei 250 (Japan)
- Hang Seng (Hong Kong)
- CAC 40 (France)
- DAX (Germany)
- STI (Straits Times Index, Singapore)
- SMI (Swiss Market Index)
- MIB (Italy)
- IBEX 35 (Spain)
- Euros Stoxx 50

5.3 Short selling and stock lending

The mechanism of **stock** lending enables someone to take a short position in a stock and it is frequently the means by which short selling – sale of a security that the seller does not own – takes place. The seller may have already borrowed the necessary securities on a temporary basis in order to deliver the stock to the buyer, or may not yet hold them at all – the latter situation often being referred to as a 'naked short'.

The practice of **short selling** has long been a subject of considerable debate and differing views.

- Critics of short selling argue that it increases share price volatility, exaggerates share price declines and forces the price of individual stocks down to levels which might not otherwise be reached. It is argued that, in extreme cases, short selling may depress the price of a security so much that it could create problems for the company in question, either by undermining commercial confidence or making fundraising more difficult.

- Defenders of the practice of short selling see it as a necessary and desirable feature of the market that plays an important role both in providing liquidity and accelerating price corrections. Some believe that short sellers tend to stabilise prices in a declining market by covering their short sale positions often opened at the start of a downturn.

The FSA considered short selling in **Discussion Paper 17** (2003). The FSA's assessment was that short selling is a legitimate investment activity which plays an important role in supporting efficient markets. Short selling can accelerate price corrections in overvalued securities, and it supports derivatives trading and hedging activities, facilitating liquidity and trading opportunities. The practice acts as a necessary brake on overly bullish markets.

It has been estimated that around 5% of UK-listed stock is on loan at any one time. On investigation, it was found that most stock lending was undertaken for the purpose of equity financing: lending assets to secure cash finance via a stock loan is seen as efficient and often the cheapest way to borrow funds. Stock lending can create revenue from long-term docile assets held by institutional investors such as pension funds and insurance companies.

In some markets, the potential for market abuse through short selling is recognised, for example with the 'uptick' rule in the US, whereby market participants may only short sell if the last share price movement has been an increase. However, the case for such measures is largely unproven.

It has been suggested that activist fund managers are willing to borrow significant positions in order to secure associated voting rights and so bolster their influence. While this practice is not unlawful, it is highly visible in the share register. Furthermore, the lender can recall the stock if they wish to exercise their votes on a contentious issue.

Exam tip

> The Summer 2007 exam included a question on stock lending, involving the above arguments for and against.

CHAPTER ROUNDUP

- An incorporated business (company) is a legal person, owned by the holders of shares (equity).

- Shareholders have rights to dividends, capital repayments, voting and notice of meetings. They also have pre-emption rights if there is a rights issue.

- Ordinary shareholders may receive dividends, at the company's discretion. They rank lower than all other creditors in a liquidation.

- Preference shareholders are entitled to a fixed dividend, which (if paid) must be paid before ordinary dividends. Preference shareholders have limited or no voting rights, and rank above ordinary shareholders but after other creditors in a liquidation.

- If preference shares are 'cumulative', any unpaid dividends accrue and must be paid in later periods when the company's financial situation permits payment.

- A warrant is a security giving the right to subscribe for a company's shares at a specified price during a specified time period.

- A covered warrant is a type of warrant issued by a financial institution which acts as a market maker in the warrants and covers its position in the underlying market.

- A special resolution is required for a placing of shares for cash, as opposed to a rights issue.

- Companies may use surplus cash to buy back the company's own shares.

- ADRs, ADSs, GDRs and CDIs provide ways in which a company's shares can be traded internationally.

- Foreign government securities issued in sterling in London are nicknamed 'bulldog bonds'.

- With bearer securities, no register of ownership is held and the holder must claim dividends. For US companies, marking certificates enable shares to be held in a 'street name' – usually, a financial institution.

- Share prices are determined by various factors – some related to the company, some to the wider market and the economy.

TEST YOUR KNOWLEDGE

Check your knowledge of the Chapter here, without referring back to the text.

1   The essential difference between a public limited company and a private company is that the former:

    A   Is a legal person with limited liability

    B   Is permitted to offer shares to the public

    C   Is listed on the Stock Exchange

    D   Is owned by its equity stockholders

    [Choose one option.]

2   Put the following into the order of priority on a winding up, starting with the highest priority.

    (a) Ordinary shares   (b) Unpaid taxes   (c) A loan secured by a fixed charge   (d) Preference shares

3   If the dividend on preference shares in GreatWheel plc is not paid in any year, the amount unpaid must be paid in a later year when the company is in a position to do so. This means that the shares are:

    A   Cumulative preference shares

    B   Participating preference shares

    C   Redeemable preference shares

    D   Convertible preference shares

4   Which one of the following is *not* a feature of covered warrants?

    A   Issued by a financial institution which acts as market maker

    B   Have no expiry date

    C   May take the form of calls or puts

    D   Confers on the buyer the right but not the obligation to buy or sell an asset on specified terms

5   Each of the following terms means the same, except which *one*?

    A Rights issue   B Capitalisation issue   C Scrip issue   D Bonus issue

6   What do the initials 'ADR and 'CDI' stand for?

7   If the regulatory system is functioning successfully, which one of the following should *not* be a determinant of the price of a share?

    A   Expectations of future dividend growth

    B   The market's view of the quality of Board members

    C   The activities of competitors

    D   Key investors' special knowledge of the company's affairs, such as takeover approaches not yet made public

8   Which share price indices have constituents that are combinations of the following indices?

    (a)   FTSE 100, FTSE 250 and FTSE Small Cap

    (b)   FTSE 100 and FTSE 250

    (c)   FTSE Small Cap and FTSE Fledgling

TEST YOUR KNOWLEDGE: ANSWERS

1   The correct answer is B. A and D apply to both plcs and private companies. A plc may, or may not, be listed. (See 1.2.1.)

2   The correct order is (c), (b), (d), (a). Note that equity shareholders come last in the queue. (See 2.2.)

3   The correct answer is A, as the word 'cumulative' indicates. (See 2.4.)

4   The correct answer is B. Covered warrants typically have a life of six to twelve months from issue, but the life may be up to five years. (See 2.6.)

5   With a rights issue, those taking up the rights make a further subscription, and so the correct answer is A. (See 2.8, 2.11.)

6   American Depository Receipts; Euroclear Depository Interests. (See 3.1.)

7   Key investors' special knowledge of the company's affairs, such as takeover approaches not yet made public, is 'insider knowledge', and it is against the law to trade on it. So, D is the correct answer. (See 5.1.)

8   The relevant indices are:

   (a)   FTSE All-Share
   (b)   FTSE 350
   (c)   FTSE All Small (See 5.2.)

3

Instruments and Characteristics
– Fixed Income

INTRODUCTION

Having looked at equities in the previous Chapter, in this Chapter we consider the characteristics of another major asset class: 'bonds' or 'fixed income' securities.

We will consider: what is a bond, who are the issuers and what are their features?

What are the different ways of evaluating the return earned on bonds? How do different sectors of the market – for example, Government bonds and corporate bonds – compare? What are Eurobonds?

We also look at bond markets around the world, and at how bonds are rated by credit agencies.

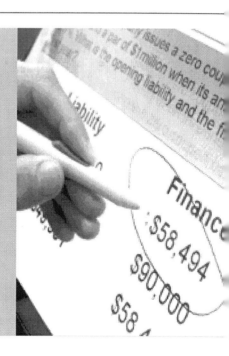

CHAPTER CONTENTS

1 GENERAL FEATURES OF BONDS

1.1 Definition and development of bonds

> A **bond** may be defined as a negotiable debt instrument for a fixed principal amount issued by a borrower for a specific period of time, making a regular payment of interest/coupon to the holder until it is redeemed at maturity, when the principal amount is repaid.

Historically, **bonds** began as very simple negotiable debt instruments, paying a fixed coupon (rate of interest) for a specified period, then being redeemed at face value – a 'straight bond'. In the 1960s and 1970s, bond markets were seen as being investment vehicles for 'widows and orphans'. They were thought to be dull markets with predictable returns and very little in the way of gains to be made from trading.

The bond markets emerged from this shadow during the mid-1970s when both interest rates and currencies became substantially more volatile. Bonds have emerged over the past 20 years to be much more complex investments, and there are now a significant number of variations on the basic theme.

Whilst it is perhaps easy to be confused by the variety of 'bells and whistles' that have been introduced into the market in recent years, one should always bear in mind that the vast majority of issues are still straight bonds. The reason for this is that investors are wary of buying investments that they do not fully understand. If an issue is too complex, it will be difficult to market.

Bonds are often referred to as '**fixed interest**' investments.

1.2 Who issues bonds and why

Bonds are used by a number of issuers as a means of raising finance.

Major bond issuers

- **Sovereign governments** which need to raise finance to cover any national debt or budget shortfall
- **Local authorities** needing to raise finance to help them cover any local budget shortfall
- **Companies** wanting to raise cash to help them finance business requirements

Regardless of who the issuer is, there are a number of general characteristics that any bond is likely to have, which we will examine next.

1.3 General characteristics

Examining the above definition in a little more detail reveals the general characteristics that a bond may have.

1.3.1 Negotiable instrument

Negotiability means that it is a piece of paper that can be bought and sold. For certain types of bonds, this is easier than for others. Government bonds tend to be highly liquid, i.e. very easy to buy or sell, whereas certain corporate bonds are almost illiquid and are usually held to maturity by the initial buyer.

1.3.2 Nominal value

As we noted above, all bonds are issued for a fixed principal amount or nominal value, which historically represented the amount invested. On UK bonds, it is normal to have a bond nominal or **par value** of £100, and bond prices are quoted on this basis.

This **nominal value** determines:

- The scale of the coupon (interest) payments
- The value of the redemption proceeds

We will discuss both of these below.

1.3.3 Maturity

Initially, all bonds were redeemable after a specific maturity date, which determines when the principal is due for repayment. However, there are now a number of variations we will need to consider.

We can sub-categorise bonds as:

- Redeemable bonds, or
- Irredeemable/perpetual bonds

1.3.4 Redeemable bonds

The majority of bonds are redeemable, although there are some subsets we will need to consider, as follows.

- **Single-dated bonds** – bonds which mature at a pre-set date only.

- **Double-dated bonds** – bonds that can be redeemed by the issuer between the specified dates. On a double-dated bond, the earlier date specifies when the issuer may redeem, the later date specifies when the bond must be redeemed.

- **Callable bonds** – where the issuer of the bond is able to redeem the bond at an earlier date, should they wish to do so. Double-dated bonds may be considered as a subset of callable bonds, are though callable bonds may have many other features (e.g. call premiums) and may be callable throughout their lives.

- **Putable bonds** – a more recent innovation, which gives the holder the ability to sell the bond back to the issuer at a premium over the face value.

1.3.5 Irredeemable bonds

On irredeemable or perpetual or undated bonds, there is no maturity date and the issuer is under no obligation to redeem the principal sum, though he may have the right to do so if he wishes. On these bonds, the coupon will be paid into perpetuity.

1.3.6 Coupon

The basis for the determination of the **coupon** on a bond is set before issue, though this does not mean that the value is known at that date. Whilst the vast majority of bonds issued are straights (i.e. with a fixed coupon), there are a number of variants on this theme. There are also bonds whose coupons vary with economic factors.

Bond coupons may be:

- Predetermined, or
- Variable

However the amount is calculated, the full coupon for the period will be paid to the holder of the bond on the **ex-div date**.

Predetermined coupons would include, as we have already stated, the vast majority of bonds. On these bonds, the gross annual coupon (i.e. the amount due to be paid in a one-year period, irrespective of the frequency of payment) is specified as a percentage of the nominal value of the bond.

Sub-classes here would include the following.

- **Straight/fixed coupon bonds** – where the coupon is at a set level for the entire life of the bond.

- **Stepped coupon bonds** – where the coupon increases in steps to pre-specified amounts as the bond moves through its life, for example as follows.

Year 1	4%
Year 2	6%
Year 3	8%
Years 4 to 10	10%

  The advantage to the issuer is that it will not be burdened by the full interest cost in the early years of the debt. However, overall the issuer will be paying a higher coupon rate. It is also possible to issue a reversed stepped coupon with the coupon rate declining progressively over the life of the bond.

- **Zero-coupon bonds** – bonds that carry no coupon and simply redeem at face value at maturity. On such bonds, the investors realise a return by paying only a fraction of the face value.

Variable coupons would include:

- **Floating rate bonds**, where the coupon varies as interest rates vary, and

- **Index-linked bonds**, where the coupon and redemption proceeds figures get scaled for the effects of inflation

1.3.7 Coupon frequency

The **frequency of payment** of the coupons is predetermined before issue, usually following the local market conventions. As a result, all investors will be (or should be) aware of those dates.

Conventions regarding the frequency of payment differ between the various bond markets. Some markets have a convention of paying semi-annual coupons, as is the case in the UK and the US, whereas other markets, in particular the Eurobond market, France and Germany, pay coupons on an annual basis.

1.3.8 Recipient

The norm is that the holder of the bond receives all of the asset flows from that bond throughout its life to the maturity date. There are, however, some markets where it is possible to strip the coupons and the bond apart so that the holder of the underlying bond may receive the redemption proceeds, while the coupons (the 'tint') are paid to another party.

1.3.9 Redemption at maturity

As we noted above, it is possible for bonds to be issued that will not redeem at maturity, namely irredeemables. Most bonds are however redeemed though, once again, there are a few variations.

The primary consideration here is the form that the redemption proceeds takes, which may be either

- Cash, or
- Other assets

1.3.10 Cash redemption proceeds

Once more, the vast majority of bonds fall into this category, whereby the bonds are redeemed in cash at maturity.

This redemption may be:

- **At par value** – redeemed at the nominal value of the bond at the redemption date
- **At a premium** – redeemed at a specified premium above the nominal value of the bond at the redemption date

1.3.11 Other assets

Instead of obliging the issuer to repay cash at maturity, the bond may offer the holder the choice between normal cash redemption proceeds and some other asset, such as:

- An alternative bond of a later maturity
- Shares issued by a corporation

1.4 Clean prices and dirty prices

1.4.1 Introduction

A further pricing aspect is clean and dirty pricing, the distinction being made for tax purposes as income and capital gains may be taxed differently on bonds.

The value of a bond has **two elements**, the underlying capital value of the bond itself (the **clean price** which is quoted) and the coupon that it is accruing over time (**accrued interest**). Periodically, this coupon is distributed as income to the holders or, more specifically, the individual who was the registered holder on the ex-div date (normally, **seven business days** prior to payment date).

The **dirty price** is the price that is paid for a bond, which combines these two elements. Consequently, ignoring all other factors that might affect the price, a dirty price will rise gradually as the coupon builds up and then fall back as the stock is marked either ex-div or pays the dividend (see the diagram below).

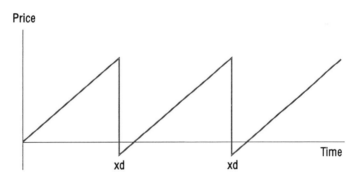

The advantage that this offered investors in the past was that rather than claiming the dividend, they could sell the bond at the high price just prior to the payment of the dividend, and this gain would be free of tax. This process was known as **bond washing**. In 1986, the UK moved to a system of clean pricing that separates the two elements.

Under clean pricing, whenever an investor purchases a bond, they pay the quoted price (the **clean price**), which represents the capital value of the underlying bond with an allowance made for the interest element, allowing the **two elements** (**income** and **gain**) to be taxed separately.

1.4.2 Cum-dividend bargains

A purchase made before the ex-dividend date is referred to as a **cum-div bargain**. In this situation, the buyer of the bond will be the holder on the next ex-div date and will, therefore, receive the full coupon for the period. The seller, however, has held the bond for part of this period and is therefore entitled to a part of that coupon. To account for this, the purchaser of the bond must compensate the seller for the dividend which he has earned.

As a result, the purchaser will pay the clean price plus the interest from the last payment date up to the purchase. On the next payment date, the holder will receive the whole of the interest for the six months. However, on a net basis, they will only have received the interest for the period of ownership.

The formula used by the Debt Management Office in the gilts market is as follows.

Formula to learn

$$\text{Dirty price} = \text{Clean price} + \text{Periods coupon} \times \frac{\text{Days}}{\text{Days in period}}$$

where:

Days = number of days from the last coupon payment date up to and including the calendar day before the settlement day (next business day following the trade)

Days in period = number of days from the last coupon payment date up to and including the calendar day before the next coupon

Thus, the periods coupon is spread over the number of days in the period, giving a coupon per day, then allocated to the relevant holder on a daily basis.

Example: Clean prices and dirty prices

Coupons are paid on 1 April and 1 October. On 10 July, an investor buys £10,000 nominal of Treasury 8% @ 101.50 for settlement on 11 July.

How much is paid?

Solution

		£
Clean Price	£10,000 @ 101.50	10,150.00
Accrued Interest	$(£10,000 \times 4\% = £400) \times \dfrac{101}{183}$	220.77
Dirty Price		10,370.77

The number of days having been calculated as follows.

Month		Days	Days in period
April	From last coupon (inclusive)	30	30
May		31	31
June		30	30
July	To day before settlement	10	31
August			31
September			30
		101	183

1.4.3 Ex-dividend bargains

An **ex-div bargain** is one occurring after the ex-dividend date, but before the coupon is paid. Gilt-edged stocks, for example, are usually marked 'ex-div' seven business days prior to the payment day in order to allow the DMO to ensure that the dividend is paid to the appropriate party. Any person buying the stock after it has been marked 'ex-div' will not, therefore, be entitled to the interest. Consequently, the pricing must reflect this.

In this situation, the buyer of the bond will be entitled to the coupon for the last few days of the period, but will receive nothing, as this will all go to the seller who held at the ex-div date. He will, therefore, require this to be adjusted in the price.

Accordingly, he pays the clean price as determined by the market less the number of days worth of interest that he is not receiving.

The formula used in this situation by the Debt Management Office in the gilts market is as follows.

Formula to learn

$$\text{Dirty price} = \text{Clean price} - \text{Periods coupon} \times \frac{\text{Days}}{\text{Days in period}}$$

where:

Days = number of days from the settlement day (next business day) to the calendar day before the next coupon payment date (inclusive)

Days in period = number of days from the last coupon payment date up to and including the calendar day before the next coupon

1.5 Interest rates and the price of bonds

1.5.1 The general relationship

The relationship between the price and the level of interest rates (yield) for a straight bond can be illustrated as follows.

Price/Yield Curve for a Straight Bond

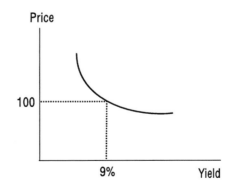

In other words, as interest rates fall, the price of the bond becomes higher.

1.5.2 Callable bonds

Bonds with a call provision enable the issuer to repurchase the bond at a set price prior to its stated maturity. For example, a bond with a 105 call could be bought back by the issuer at a price of £105.

Exam tip

> A call option should not be confused with a redemption clause. It is often the case that a bond may be redeemed under predetermined circumstances, so long as the redemption is not being refinanced by a new bond issue. For example, a company may have excess cash balances (possibly due to the sale of assets) available to retire the bond.

The price of a **callable bond** will change at a different rate to the price of an equivalent straight bond as interest rates change.

For a callable bond (assuming that it is callable immediately), the price will not rise as much – for a given fall in interest rates – as a straight bond. For example, take a bond that can be called at 105. As interest rates fall, bond prices rise. The price of a straight bond will continue to rise as interest rates fall and may go above 105. However, the price of the callable bond can never rise above the call price of 105, since the company can buy it back at that price.

Consequently, as interest rates fall, the rate at which the price of the callable bond increases will be slower than the rate at which the straight bond price increases. Once the callable bond price is close to 105, it will hardly change at all, even if interest rates continue to fall.

Price-Yield Curve for a Straight Versus a Callable Bond

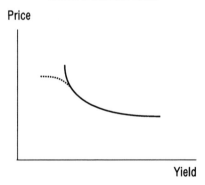

The curve to the right gives the price/yield relationship for both bonds. However, at lower interest rates, the relationships diverge, with the straight bond's price continuing to rise while the price of the callable bond first increases at a declining rate, then stays static.

A callable bond could be viewed as a straight bond with an embedded option. The company has sold a straight bond to investors but at the same time has bought a call option from the investors, enabling the company to buy back the straight bond at the agreed call price.

As a result, the proceeds on the issue of a callable bond are less than that for an equivalent straight bond. The company effectively receives the proceeds from the straight bond, but then uses part of those proceeds to buy a call option from the bond investors. The net proceeds received are therefore lower.

The bond investor's position is as follows.

> Long callable bond = Long straight bond and short call option

The value is given by:

> Callable bond value = Straight bond value – Issuers call option value

If the value of the call option increases, then the value of the callable bond will decrease. For example, an increase in the price of the straight bond (caused by a decrease in interest rates) will also result in an increase in the intrinsic value of the call option. Although the straight bond will increase in value, the call option also increases in value, meaning that the callable bond value hardly changes at all.

1.5.3 Basis Point Value (BPV)

Sometimes referred to as the **price value of a basis point or the dollar value of a basis point**. This is the change in price if the yield changes by one basis point. The more sensitive stocks will have a high BPV.

1.6 Taxation

Interest on government stocks (**gilts**) is paid gross, unless:

- The investor elects to have 20% tax deducted at source, or

- Tax has been deducted at source for a gilt purchased before 6 April 1998 and the investor has not elected for gross payments

Interest on corporate bonds may be received gross, but some UK bond issues pay interest net of 20% tax.

Eurobonds are international bonds and are not issued under the auspices of any domestic economy. Coupons are paid **gross of tax**. In each domestic tax regime, the Eurobond interest is taxed in accordance with normal rules.

Gilts, and **qualifying corporate bonds**, are exempt from **capital gains tax**.

Qualifying corporate bonds comprise:

- All **company loan stock and debentures** (except loan stock convertible into shares) that are issued in sterling and bought by the investor after 13 March 1984

- Building societies' **Permanent Interest Bearing Shares (PIBS)**

1.7 Forward rates

1.7.1 Spot interest rates and forward interest rates

A **spot rate** is a rate of interest that can be agreed today for a deposit or borrowing from today for a fixed period. A **forward rate** is a rate of interest that can be agreed today for a deposit or borrowing from one future date to another.

Forward rates allow people to lock rates today for any future deposit or borrowing in order to avoid the risk of adverse interest rate movements before actually undertaking the deposit or borrowing.

Clearly, no one ever knows future interest rates with certainty. Hence the borrower or depositor may typically find that the normal market rate ultimately proves to be better or worse than the forward rate that he has locked into. However, by locking in today with forward rates as, say, a borrower, we are avoiding the difficulty that we would suffer if interest rates rose, but giving up the opportunity of a benefit if interest rates fall.

The motivation here is to fix a rate, and hence cash flow levels, at something that represents a definitely affordable cost or reasonable income, e.g. locking into a fixed rate mortgage that you know you can afford rather than risking the variable rate. In the fullness of time, the variable rate may turn out to be lower, but that lost opportunity is the price paid to avoid risk of rates moving up dramatically, which they have been known to do.

1.7.2 Derivation of forward rates

How then does a bank determine today the rate that it is prepared to offer in, say, one year's time for a one-year borrowing? Does it take a guess as to what interest rates will be at that time and take the risk of being wrong? This idea does seem to pose an intriguing problem as if the borrower is avoiding risk, then the bank must be taking it on.

Banks could adopt this approach, i.e. guessing what interest rates will be next year, although this could hardly be considered prudent and could result in disaster. There must be some other factors at work here.

The answer lies in the idea of **arbitrage**. That is, if the bank is happy to lend to someone today for two years at the two-year spot rate, then they should be happy to agree today to lend to two people over the same period (one for the first year and one for the second) so long as the total returns are the same. The first-year borrower would be charged the one-year spot rate, as this is the rate appropriate for his borrowing term. The second-year borrower would be charged the forward rate for a one-year borrowing starting in one year's time.

Similarly, there should be no difference between investing the money for two years and investing it for one year and agreeing now to roll this over in a year's time into another one-year deposit.

Either arrangement could be pictured as follows.

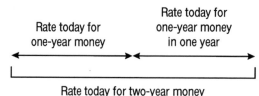

Mathematically, the relationship that we have here is as follows.

Formula to learn

$$(1 + r_1) \times (1 + {}_1f_2) = (1 + r_2)^2$$

where:

r_1 and r_2 are the one and two-year spot rates respectively

${}_1f_2$ is the forward rate from Time 1 to Time 2

Note that the forward rate is **not** necessarily the rate that will eventually be available in the market in a year's time. As we have already noted, this cannot be predicted with certainty.

1.8 Characteristics of sources of finance

The main characteristics that distinguish the various **sources of finance** are as follows.

- **Annual returns** – the dividends or interest that must be paid by the company on an ongoing basis

- **Capital repayment** – any provisions relating to the return of capital for the particular instrument

- **Security** – any rights that the provider of finance has over various assets of the business

- **Influence** – the voting rights or other influence that the provider of finance has and hence, his ability to impact on the operations of the business

- **Negotiability** – the ability of the holder of the financial instrument to trade the instrument and realise its value

Each of these factors will be specified in a loan agreement in the same way that they are specified for share finance in the Memorandum and Articles of Association.

1.9 Comparison of ordinary shares and loan stocks

Ordinary shares	Company loan stocks
1 Ordinary shareholders are members of the company. They own the company and can vote at meetings. However, a private individual will often own insufficient shares to exert a decisive vote. Day-to-day control is in the hands of the directors.	1 Holders of loan stocks are creditors who cannot normally vote at meetings. However, the terms of the issue will sometimes allow loan stockholders a vote if the payment of interest or capital is in arrears. Loan stocks are normally held by institutions not private investors.
2 Ordinary shares are never secured.	2 Loans can be secured (debentures usually are) or unsecured depending on the terms of issue.
3 Ordinary shares are not normally redeemed except by special court order.	3 Loan stocks normally carry a redemption date.
4 Dividends are paid only from distributable profits, but may not be paid out even when profits are available. It is for the directors to recommend whether to pay out profits as dividends or to retain profits in the company to finance expansion or reduce borrowing. Shareholders can vote to reduce the recommended dividend but cannot vote to increase it.	4 Interest is a debt and is payable irrespective of whether profits are available.
5 In inflationary times, companies can sometimes increase prices, and hence turnover and profits. Thus the share price may increase with inflation and dividends may also grow. Much depends on the choice of the company and timing of purchase of shares but the possibility of growth exists.	5 (a) The interest remains the same irrespective of inflation. It therefore declines in purchasing power. (b) The loans are normally redeemed at par at maturity. Thus there is no scope for capital gains unless the stocks are purchased below par.
6 Capital gains are subject to Capital Gains Tax (CGT).	6 Capital gains on fixed interest stocks are free of CGT, unless the stock is convertible.

2 BOND STRUCTURES

2.1 Vanilla (or 'straight') bonds

This is the classic form for a bond, with no complicating attributes. It has a fixed nominal value, a fixed coupon, and a fixed maturity date.

2.2 Zero-coupon bonds

Zero coupon bonds are straight bonds with a coupon of 0%, so the only payment by the issuer is of the principal at maturity. Clearly, these will have to be issued (and will trade subsequently) at a discount. (If yields are high this may well be a large, or **deep discount**.)

They are likely to be more attractive to tax-exempt investors since taxable investors will have to pay tax on the **imputed** interest income (a percentage of the ultimate capital gain) each period, despite receiving no actual income.

A company receives corporation tax relief over the bond's life, based on an interest accrual calculation. An investor pays income tax on the final redemption of the bond, based on the difference between the issue price and par.

2.3 Irredeemables (or 'perpetual') bonds

These are like straight bonds except that they do not have a specified maturity. It may be that redemption will never take place, but it is more likely (as with UK Government perpetuals, for instance) that the issuer has the **right, but not the obligation** to redeem. In the latter case we have a **callable bond** with no fixed maturity.

2.4 Index-linked bonds

With **index-linked bonds**, the redemption value (and possibly the coupon as well) is adjusted in line with some specified index (probably an index of consumer prices) or with a commodity price level. In high-inflation economies, this might be the only way of inducing investors to purchase bonds (whose value would otherwise fall with the real value of the coupons and principal).

2.5 Floating (or variable) rate notes (FRNs/VRNs)

Whereas with vanilla bonds the annual interest is a fixed percentage of the principal, with **FRNs** the payment is calculated by reference to a key interest rate (commonly LIBOR or London Inter Bank Offered Rates; or LIMEAN, the average of the offered and bid rates).

The coupon on these bonds is comprised of two elements. Firstly, the reference or **index rate**, for example LIBOR and secondly, a **quoted margin**, the rate above LIBOR which must be paid. An example might be a five-year bond with a coupon of LIBOR (the index rate) plus 25bp (the quoted margin, 25bp or 0.25%).

Initially, in this market, the quoted margins used to be measured in half and a quarter per cent, but with competitive pricing, these have come down now to a matter of mere basis points. The quoted margin is established at the outset of the deal and reflects the borrower's credit rating and the size of the issue, along with the market conditions at the time.

Other conditions may be included. A bond may be a **drop lock** where the coupon is allowed to float but, once it reaches its set minimum, the bond locks into being a fixed coupon bond at that minimum interest rate.

These are obviously fairly rigid structures and have been replaced frequently by floors where the bond's coupon level cannot fall below a certain point. For example, the floor of a bond might be 5%. If the index rate and the quoted margin gradually floated down to this level, then at the point of 5%, the coupon would be locked. However, as the index rate begins to pick up, then the coupon will increase beyond 5%, unlike with a drop lock.

The minimum rate or floor is obviously a protection for the investor purchasing the floating rate note. It is possible for the issuer also to take up protection in the form of a ceiling or a cap whereby, as interest rates rise, the coupon on the FRN also rises, but not beyond this preset ceiling.

It has been common for issuers to offset the costs of establishing a ceiling by including a floor value (**minimax bonds**) which, in effect, collars the interest rate available on the floating rate note. It cannot exceed a preset ceiling nor can it fall beneath a preset floor. Within these basic market conventions, a number of variants have been introduced.

A further issue to consider is the frequency of refixing the coupon. Most Eurobonds pay annual coupons. However, with floating rate notes, the convention is normally to refix the coupon rate on a six-monthly basis. Depending on the nature of the market, it may even be that the refixing frequency is greater, perhaps refixing on a six-weekly basis.

By refixing more rapidly than the coupon is paid, the bond closely tracks markets rates. FRNs, which refix more frequently than they pay coupons, are referred to as mismatched floating rate notes or mismatched floaters.

2.6 Cap/collar bonds

Cap/collar bonds are FRNs, but with limits on the extent to which the rate can float. A bond with a cap has an upper limit on the interest rate (which should prove attractive to issuers), while a floor places a lower limit (appealing to investors).

2.7 Structured products

Various more exotic and innovative bond structures can be created. Frequently, these are created by taking a basic fixed-income product and embedding within it a series of options. As we have seen, these can link to the underlying equity, currency, interest rates, and commodities.

Clearly, the more exotic the product, the more difficult it becomes to sell the bond to underlying investors. In many cases, the more exotic bond issues are created in order to satisfy a demand from investors and are effectively pre-sold.

2.8 Loan stock and debenture stock

Loan stock and **debenture stock** represent a borrowing by a company in evidence of which the company issues marketable certificates.

Listed **loan stocks and debentures** usually carry a fixed coupon and have a redemption date. Technically speaking, there is no difference between the two stocks, as a debenture is strictly a 'written acknowledgement of debt'. However, debentures are commonly so called because there is some security available to the stockholders to enforce their rights against the company. Loan stock is sometimes called 'ULS' because it is unsecured. In practice, this generalisation is too sweeping, and the precise position can be determined only by examining the terms of each individual issue. In particular, subordinated loans may rank after other loans, trade creditors or may even rank with equity in the event of the company being liquidated.

The three main degrees of security

- **Secured loans – Debentures**. Secured by fixed or floating charges, fixed charges being the more secure (discussed further below).

- **Unsecured loans – Loan stock.** A variation of such loan stock is convertible loan stock.

- **Subordinated loan stock.** Ranks after unsecured creditors/loans in a winding up.

Many companies have issued unsecured loan stock in the UK markets, but they tend to be only those companies with a high credit rating or good name recognition. The consequence of not giving security will be that the coupon will be higher.

Most debentures and ULS carry a fixed annual **coupon** (interest) rate, which is payable half yearly. The coupon rate shows the **gross** interest that the company will have to pay, which will be treated as an allowable expense for tax purposes.

Repayment dates are normally determined at the outset, typically as:

- A fixed repayment date on which the company must repay the debt, or

- A repayment period during which the company must repay the debt. The exact timing will be at the choice of the company within that period.

As written acknowledgements of debt, debentures and loan stock are frequently **negotiable**, although not always.

Most public companies which issue debentures or loans appoint a **trustee** to look after the interests of the loan stockholders. The trustee is usually a bank or insurance company and must be independent of the company. A trust deed governing the terms of the issue will be drawn up. The trustee will ensure that the terms of the trust deed are complied with.

2.8.1 Matters covered by the trust deed

- Rate of interest and dates of payment

- Redemption date

- Details of any sinking fund arrangement – discussed below

- Details of security for the loan

  The security may be a **fixed charge** over a specific asset. In this case the company cannot deal with it in any way without the trustees' consent. Alternatively, it may be a **floating charge** covering all assets. With a floating charge the company may deal with the assets without restriction in the ordinary course of business. A combination of a fixed charge over the land, buildings and book debts with a floating charge over other assets could be taken.

- Details of the rights of the trustee if the company is in default of the terms of the issue

- The realisation of the security can only be undertaken by the trustees on behalf the loan stockholders. An individual loan stockholder cannot do this.

2.8.2 Advantages of appointing a trustee

- It would be difficult for the company to make arrangements with each individual loan stockholder regarding the creation of security.

- A trustee with professional expertise is better placed to act in the interests of the loan shareholders.

- When decisive action is called for, the various loan stockholders probably would not be able to agree amongst themselves.

2.8.3 Security

Debentures will be secured by one or both of:

- A fixed charge
- A floating charge

As indicated above, a **fixed charge** is a charge over an identifiable asset of the company and the debenture deed will note the specific asset in question. Typically, a specific fixed asset, such as land or a freehold building, will be used for this purpose as it can be readily identified and should not deteriorate substantially in value over the term of the debenture.

The commercial impact of having a fixed charge is that the company cannot sell the asset in question, unless the debenture holder releases the charge. The debenture holder is unlikely to do this, unless he is offered some equally good asset over which he can have an alternative charge.

If the company falls into arrears with its interest payments or defaults on its capital repayment, then the debenture holder can either:

- Appoint a receiver and obtain income from the assets held under charge, or

- Take possession of the asset and sell it, using the proceeds to repay the debentures in full. Any excess proceeds will be returned to the company, any shortfall will become an unsecured liability of the company.

A **floating charge** is a general charge over the assets of the company, which allows them to be freely traded (unlike a fixed charge) until such time as the charge **crystallizes**, i.e. there are arrears in interest payment or a default of capital repayment. When a charge crystallizes, it becomes attached to the assets in the company at the time of the crystallization.

2.8.4 Influence

Debenture or loan stockholders do not automatically have any influence over the day-to-day operations of the company. However, they exercise influence in the following ways.

- Certain clauses in any loan agreements may restrict the levels of gearing at which the company can operate, thus restricting its ability to raise further debt finance.

- If there is a default, then any charged assets can be seized.

2.9 Building Society Permanent Interest Bearing Shares (PIBS)

PIBS are a fixed interest, **irredeemable** listed security issued by a building society on which interest is paid semi-annually. **Permanent Interest Bearing Shares (PIBS)** were first issued in 1991. Around fifteen building societies have issued these shares as a means of raising capital.

The minimum investment could be as low as £1,000, although some societies place a minimum of £50,000. PIBS would typically be used by institutional investors, although private investors have also been attracted by the high yields available. Private investors can buy PIBS via a broker or via one of the main market makers.

PIBS are issued as subordinated loan stock and hence rank for repayment on a winding up behind other creditors. As they are a form of loan stock, PIBS are exempt from capital gains tax as **qualifying corporate bonds**.

Interest on PIBS is now paid gross, but is taxable. The society is not under an obligation to pay the interest, although it would have to be in a very poor financial position not to do so.

There is no protection for holders of PIBS in the case of default, as they are not covered by the Financial Services Compensation Scheme.

PIBS are like an unsecured, irredeemable loan stock and must be analysed and viewed as such. However, no society has yet failed to meet an interest payment, resulting in PIBS starting to seem less risky than when the market began. As a result, yields have become lower in recent years.

Some PIBS issuers have converted to plc status. Examples include the Halifax (now HBOS) and Northern Rock. Where this has happened, the PIBS have become **perpetual subordinated bonds (PSBs)** of the bank in question.

2.10 Redemption terms

Eurobonds and UK domestic bonds can have a variety of redemption terms.

2.10.1 Bullets

Most bonds issued are still in the form of bullets with a single set redemption date. There has been a tendency to issue callable bonds, or indeed putable bonds, where the holder has the right to call for early redemption, but the complications involved in analysing these issues often dissuade investors from purchasing them. This shift away from unorthodox redemption patterns is particularly true for the next two potential repayment schemes that are now rarely used, namely **sinking funds** and **purchase funds**.

2.10.2 Sinking funds

With **sinking funds ('sinkers')**, there is a process whereby a proportion of the bonds in issue are redeemed each year.

Sinking funds can make a loan stock more attractive since they provide an assurance that positive steps are being taken to ensure the obligations of the company will be honoured.

- A **non-cumulative sinking fund** arises when funds are set aside each year to purchase other investments (for instance gilts with redemption dates around the same time as the loan stock). When the loan stock is due to be redeemed, there are adequate funds available for redemption.

- With a **cumulative sinking fund**, a set sum is generally put aside to cover repayment of loan interest and redemption of part of the capital. As time goes by, the fixed sum will redeem more and more capital, since the interest will diminish in line with the diminishing principal.

Sometimes the company purchases its own loan stock on the open market, whereas in other cases a proportion of the loan stock may be redeemed at par each year. When part is redeemed at par, the decision as to which loan stockholder is to be repaid will be made by ballot. When the market price is under par, the lucky stockholders will benefit, whereas when the market price is over par the stockholder whose stock is redeemed will lose out.

The precise terms of a cumulative sinking fund must be carefully studied, but companies will prefer open market purchase when stock is currently priced under par, and will prefer redemption at par when the market price exceeds nominal value.

Example: Sinking funds

$250 issue to be redeemed in four instalments

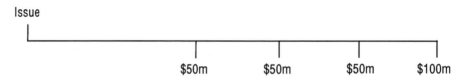

Issue

$50m $50m $50m $100m

The bonds to be redeemed in each year are selected by the process of 'drawing' the serial numbers. The serial numbers of the bonds drawn in this way are then published and the holders submit the bonds to the paying agent for redemption at par. The final repayment is normally larger than the others and is referred to as the balance or balloon repayment.

Sinking funds tend to come into operation towards the end of the bond's life and rarely start to redeem from the first coupon date.

Where a bond has a high coupon and is consequently priced above par, the existence of a sinking fund, where part of the issue is redeemed at par, will tend to depress the price. Where the bond has a low coupon and is priced below par, a sinking fund will tend to boost the price.

2.10.3 Purchase funds

A **purchase fund** buys back the bonds in the secondary market, and not at par. The obligation to repay is triggered by a condition specified in the offer document, normally the bond trading below par.

Purchase funds are found outside the Euromarkets. In the UK gilt-edged market, the 3½% Conversion 62 Aft has a purchase fund whereby 1% of the nominal is repurchased each year that the nominal value lies below 90.

The existence of a purchase fund tends to boost the price of a bond, since it creates artificial demand in the market. For example, the 3½% Conversion gilt referred to above has a higher price than other undated stocks, reflecting its purchase fund. This can be seen by referring to a gilts price list.

2.10.4 Serial notes

A serial note is one where a proportion of the capital is repaid each year along with the interest. An example outside the Euromarkets would be the Federal Agency stocks ('Fannie Maes') in the US.

2.10.5 Optional redemption

The option to redeem a bond can be given to either side of the deal. A call right would give the issuer the right to seek an earlier redemption. For example, the double-dated gilts in the UK market, where the Government has the right to redeem from the earlier of the two dates, but must redeem by the later date (e.g. 13½% Treasury 2004-2008).

The second form of option may be given to the bond holder in the form of a put right, giving the holder the right to redeem the bond normally at a premium to the face value.

2.11 Convertible loan stock

2.11.1 Overview

We introduced the topic of **convertible loan stock** in the previous chapter. Convertible loan stock may be either unsecured loan stock or debentures, which offer the option of conversion into ordinary shares at the redemption date as an alternative to cash.

2.11.2 Characteristics

By offering apparently favourable conversion terms, companies have been able to issue convertible stock with relatively low-coupon rates. The low rate of interest is compensated by the opportunity of a favourable return on conversion.

A conversion right will give the holder of the bond the right, at a date in the future, to convert the bond into shares at a specified rate. In effect, the purchaser of this bond receives two instruments.

- A low-coupon debt instrument
- An option to acquire equity

The cost of exercising the option is the loss of the debt instrument on conversion.

Conversion rights tend to be issued in the belief that they will be exercised. This makes sense from the point of view of the company issuing the debt, since if the conversion right is exercised, then there will be no need to refinance the loan when it matures, because it will be converted into shares.

The decision as to whether to convert is solely down to the holder and will only be undertaken if it is to the holder's advantage. There is no obligation on the part of the holder to convert.

In addition to the holder's right to convert, the issuer may also have the right to call (i.e. redeem) the issue if certain conditions are met. This characteristic of having multiple embedded options can make the evaluation of convertibles difficult.

Typically, a convertible will pay a **low coupon**, although this is compensated by the option to convert into shares at the conversion date. Convertibles are often subordinated, meaning that all 'senior' creditors must be settled in full before any payment can be made to holders in the event of insolvency.

Convertibles are often employed as a form of **deferred share**. Issuers expect them to be converted into shares at the conversion date. As a result, convertibles have some of the characteristics of bonds, responding to changes in interest rates, and some of the characteristics of shares, responding to share price movements.

The conversion right can be expressed in a number of ways. By convention, the right is normally to convert the debt into the Ordinary shares of the company in a given **conversion ratio**. For example, £100 nominal is converted into 25 shares (a conversion ratio of 25). The conversion right may exist for a period of time during the bond's life (the conversion window) or may only be available on maturity.

Additional terms may include the following.

- Different conversion ratios at different maturities of the bond.

- The holder of the bond may also be obliged to contribute additional capital on the conversion. For example, £100 nominal of the debt converts into 20 shares and the bondholder is obliged to contribute an additional £2.50 per share. Therefore, each share has an effective cost (assuming the bond is trading at par) of £100/20 = £5 + £2.50 = £7.50.

- Put rights enabling the holder of the bond to force an early redemption of the bond, normally at a premium to the par value.

- Call rights enabling the issuer to call the bond under certain conditions.

When establishing the terms of the convertible, the issuer will normally avoid unduly complicated terms, since this will confuse and thereby dissuade potential purchasers of the bond.

2.11.3 Reasons for a company to issue convertible loan stock

A company may consider the following reasons for issuing convertible loan stock.

- There is no immediate dilution of the interest of the current shareholders.

- If the company prospers, redemption of the convertible loan will be unnecessary since the stockholders will all exercise their conversion rights.

- The convertible can be issued at a lower coupon than that of a comparable 'straight' loan stock.

- Sometimes there are insufficient assets available to offer as security for a new issue of a fixed interest loan stock. The extra benefits from a conversion option may persuade otherwise reluctant investors to subscribe.

- A convertible loan can be an alternative to a rights issue. If the current share price is below nominal value, a company cannot make a rights issue as the subscription price must be at least equal to nominal value.

- Convertibles can be used as a means of financing long term projects. Subscribers would require a guaranteed income in the first few years whilst the profit levels were likely to be low. In later years, the investor could convert if the project had been as successful as had been anticipated.

- When a company wishes to take over another company, it may offer its own convertible loan stock in exchange for control of the shares of the company being bid for.

Such a stock can be very attractive to potential vendors of shares in the 'victim', since as we have seen convertibles can give the best of both worlds. In addition, the issue of a convertible loan stock defers equity dilution in the bidding company.

2.11.4 Disadvantage to the issuer

A **disadvantage** to the issuer is that if the company fails to perform, it is obliged to make the coupon payments, and ultimately redeem the bond for cash if the holder chooses not to convert. Therefore, the firm cannot be sure that they are issuing deferred share capital when they issue a convertible.

2.11.5 Advantages to the investor

The advantages to the investor of a convertible issue are as follows.

- The holder has the security of fixed income, offering downside protection if the shares fall in value, whilst at the same time offering the opportunity to benefit if the shares perform well.

- Convertibles rank above shares in the order of priority on liquidation.

- Convertibles tend to offer higher yields than the underlying shares.

- Convertible bonds tend to have good marketability compared to non-convertible issues.

2.11.6 Disadvantages to the investor

The disadvantages to the investor of a convertible issue are as follows.

- Though offering higher yields than the underlying shares, convertibles tend to offer lower yields than equivalent straight bonds.

- The attractiveness of a convertible may be reduced by issuer call options.

- If anticipated share growth is not achieved, the holder will have sacrificed yield for no benefit.

2.11.7 Premium put convertibles

During the bull market of the 1980s, a number of UK corporate issuers believed that there was a virtual guarantee that the conversion rights would be exercised, since their share prices were rising rapidly. However, in order to be able to justify an even lower coupon rate, they also gave the holder of the bond a second right. This right was the ability to put the bond back to the issuer at a premium over the par value.

The basic intention of this structure was to make the investor believe that he had a two-way option. If the share prices rose significantly, then the conversion right would be a valuable one. However, if the share price was to fall, the investor would always be able to put the bond back to the issuer, at the premium rate. The belief in the issuers' minds was that the conversion right would be used and there would therefore be no need to worry about the premium put.

After the crash of 1987, where equity markets tumbled by 20%, many conversion rights became unprofitable and consequently, those companies which had issued bonds with premium put features attached were obliged to redeem the bonds at considerably above par.

It appeared that investors were fully protected, since they stood to gain from conversion if the share price performed, but had cover through the premium put right. However, the risk that investors ran was that the company would be unable to refinance the debt and become insolvent. Saatchi & Saatchi was an example of a company that had severe problems meeting such a liability and had to enter into an arrangement with its creditors.

2.11.8 Debt plus warrants

Instead of being in conversion form, the 'equity kicker' may come in the form of a warrant. A warrant is a long-term call option, giving the holder the right to buy shares at a specified price up to a certain date in the future. The principal difference between a warrant and a conversion right is that a warrant may be split away from the bond and traded separately. Conversion rights, by their very nature, must always trade with the underlying bond.

3 MEASURING RETURNS

3.1 Yield calculations

The value of any investment will depend on the return that it generates and the risks inherent in those returns. In bond markets, the single most important measure of return is the **yield**. There are, however, several different yield measures that we may wish to calculate, each having its own uses and limitations.

For each of these measures, we need to know:

- How it is calculated
- Its uses
- Its limitations

3.2 Flat Yield

Calculation. The simplest measure of the return used in the market is the **flat (interest or running) yield**. This measure looks at the annual cash return (coupon) generated by an investment as a percentage of the cash price.

In simple terms, what is the regular annual return that you generate on the money that you invest?

Formula to learn

$$\text{Flat yield} = \frac{\text{Annual coupon rate}}{\text{Market price}}$$

Example: Flat yield

We hold 10% Loan stock (annual coupon) redeemable at par in four years. The current market price is £97.25. Calculate the flat yield.

Solution

The flat yield for the above would be

$$\text{Flat yield} = \frac{10.00}{97.25} = 0.10283 \text{ or } 10.283\%$$

Uses. The flat yield assesses the annual income return only and is most appropriate when either

- We are dealing with irredeemables, which pay no return other than a coupon into perpetuity, or
- Our priority is the short-term cash returns that the investment will generate

Limitations. This measure, while of some limited use (particularly in the short term), has three important drawbacks for the investment markets.

- In addition to the coupon flows, bonds may have returns in the form of the redemption moneys. Where the bond has been purchased at a price away from par, this will give rise to potential gains and losses, which are excluded from the calculation.

- The calculation completely ignores the timing of any cash flows and the time value of money.

- With some bonds (floating rate notes – FRNs), the return in any one period will vary with interest rates. If the coupon is not constant, then this measure is only of historic value unless the predicted return is used.

These limitations combine to make the flat yield of only marginal use.

3.3 Japanese Gross Redemption Yield

Calculation. The idea behind the **Japanese Gross Redemption Yield (GRY)** calculation is to overcome the first of the limitations of the flat yield noted above, specifically that any gains or losses to redemption are ignored. This measure recognises that the total return in any period is a combination of both income and capital components, i.e. the coupon received plus any gain (minus any loss) for the period.

The Japanese method for calculating the GRY is to take the flat yield and then add the average annual capital gain (or deduct the average annual loss) to redemption, stated as a percentage of the current market price. Thus, we can state the Japanese GRY as follows.

Formula to learn

$$\text{Japanese GRY} = \frac{\text{Annual coupon rate}}{\text{Market price}} + \frac{\text{Average annual capital gain to redemption}}{\text{Market price}}$$

Alternatively:

Formula to learn

$$\text{Japanese GRY} = \frac{\text{Annual coupon rate}}{\text{Market price}} + \frac{\frac{\text{Redemption price} - \text{Market price}}{\text{Years to redemption}}}{\text{Market price}}$$

Example: Japanese Gross Redemption Yield

We hold 10% Loan stock (annual coupon) redeemable at par in four years. The current market price is £97.25.

Calculate the Japanese GRY.

Solution

The Japanese GRY for the above would be:

$$\text{Japanese GRY} = \frac{10.00}{97.25} + \frac{\frac{100.00 - 97.25}{4}}{97.25}$$

$$= \frac{10.00}{97.25} + \frac{0.6875}{97.25}$$

$$= 0.10283 + 0.00707 = 0.10990 \text{ or } 10.99\%$$

Uses. The main use of this method is to provide a quick and easy way of assessing the GRY that takes into account all of the returns, income and capital.

This is not an absolutely accurate measure of return, since it assumes linear capital growth rather than the more realistic compound growth. As a result, it is liable to overstate the effects of any capital gain or loss. Furthermore, this inaccuracy increases the further away a bond is from maturity.

The measure does, however, serve as a useful tool in determining the true GRY as we illustrate below.

Limitations. While this method does overcome the first limitation of the flat yield, i.e. its failure to account for any capital gains or losses to redemption, it does not overcome the other noted drawbacks, specifically

- The calculation ignores the timing of any cash flows and the time value of money.
- With FRNs, the return in any one period will vary with interest rates. If the coupon is not constant, then the measure is only of historic value unless the predicted return is used.

The first of these limitations can only be overcome through the use of discounted cash flow techniques as illustrated below. The second is a valid limitation of all yield measures.

3.4 Gross Redemption Yield

Calculation. The gross redemption yield (GRY) resolves the issue of the redemption values **and** the time value of money by using more complex **discounted cash flow** techniques, which we will not go into further here.

The **gross redemption yield** is the **internal rate of return (IRR)** of:

- The dirty price paid to buy the bond
- The gross coupons received **to redemption**
- The final redemption proceeds

3.5 The yield curve

3.5.1 Introduction

The **yield curve** demonstrates the relationship between bond yields and their maturities. It is therefore closely linked to the **term structure of interest rates**, which refers to the different interest rates applying to assets with different terms to maturity.

3.5.2 The normal yield curve

The shape of the **'normal' yield curve** is as in the diagram below.

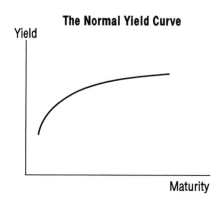

This curve demonstrates how longer maturity results in higher risk which, in turn, results in higher returns or yields.

One use of this relationship is in evaluating bond issues or trades by determining the yield to use for discounting its cash flows.

As we are aware, we may establish the market value of a bond by applying the relationship:

$$\text{Price} = \frac{C_1}{(1+r)} + \frac{C_2}{(1+r)^2} + \frac{C_3}{(1+r)^3} + \cdots + \frac{C_n + R}{(1+r)^n}$$

where r is the GRY of the bond.

If we can determine a suitable yield for a bond to use in this relationship, then we will be able to value it accurately. We will see, however, that this may not be as easy as it seems, and that there are other factors that need to be considered.

3.5.3 The inverted yield curve

However, the yield curve does not always follow the shape described above. Sometimes, it becomes **inverted**, with short-term yields exceeding longer term ones as shown below.

The Inverted Yield Curve

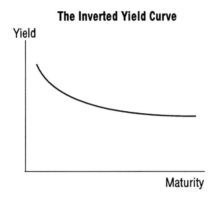

This **inverted yield curve** appears to contradict the fundamental idea that higher risk means higher return, one of the cornerstones of investment theory. Hence, we need to consider what factors determine the shape of this curve. There are clearly some other forces at work here in addition to the simple risk-return relationship that we have considered so far.

3.5.4 Shape of the yield curve

What, then, determines the shape of the yield curve? The risk/return relationship is one factor at work here but, as we noted earlier, there must be other, perhaps more, significant factors, otherwise we would never see an inverted yield curve.

Liquidity preference theory states that if an investor's money is invested in longer term (and therefore riskier) stocks, then they will require a greater return or **risk premium**. Short-term liquid stock carry a lower risk and therefore require a lower return.

As regards causality, this theory assumes that spot rates are established by the market from which forward rates and yields may be derived.

This risk premium gives rise to the normal upward sloping yield curve.

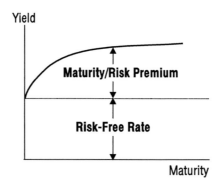

4 RISKS

4.1 Introduction

An investor in a fixed income security is exposed to a number of different risks, and a complete assessment of a bond will include consideration of these factors.

- **Interest rate risk** is probably the most important risk because of the powerful relationship between interest rates and bond prices. Duration and modified duration (volatility) are the means of measuring this risk. Convexity is the measure that is used to explain the variation away from the predicted return.

- **Credit risk** or **default risk** is the risk of the issuer defaulting on its obligations to pay coupons and repay the principal. The ratings by commercial rating companies can be used to help assess this risk (aka issuer risk).

- **Inflation risk** is linked to interest rate risk, as interest rates rise to compensate bondholders for inflation.

- **Liquidity risk** or **marketability risk** has to do with the ease with which an issue can be sold in the market. Smaller issues especially are subject to this risk. In certain markets, the volume of trading tends to concentrate into the 'benchmark' stocks, thereby rendering most other issues illiquid. Other bonds become subject to 'seasoning' as the initial liquidity dries up and the bonds are purchased by investors who wish to hold them to maturity.

- **Issue-specific risk** refers to factors specific to the issue, which tend to either increase or decrease the risk, e.g. issuer options such as the right to call for early redemption or possibly, holder options.

- **Fiscal risk** represents risk that withholding taxes will be increased. For foreign bonds, there would also be the risk of the imposition of capital controls locking your money into the market.

- **Currency risk** refers to the risk of adverse movements in exchange rates, which is relevant to investors purchasing overseas or international bonds.

4.2 Interest rate risk

Within bond markets, **interest rate risk** is sometimes referred to, somewhat confusingly, as the **volatility**.

The sensitivity of any bond to movements in the interest rate will be determined by a number of factors.

4.2.1 Sensitivity to maturity

Longer-dated bonds will be more sensitive to changes in the interest rate than shorter dated stocks, as illustrated by these prices for three 12% bonds of differing maturity subject to differing GRYs.

Coupon (%)	Maturity (years)	Price for a GRY of		
		8%	10%	12%
12	4	£113.24	£106.34	£100.00
12	7	£120 83	£109.74	£100.00
12	26	£143.23	£118.32	£100.00

In this example, it is the price of the 26-year bond which exhibits the greatest range as the yield alters (moving from £143.23 to par). The logic behind this is that the longer dated bond is more exposed to the movements of the yield, since it has longer to go to maturity.

4.2.2 Sensitivity to coupon

With regard to the level of coupon, it is the lower coupon stocks that demonstrate the greatest level of sensitivity to the yield.

Coupon (%)	Maturity (years)	Price for a GRY of		
		9%	10%	11%
5	15	£67.75	£61.97	£56.85
10	15	£108.06	£100.00	£92.81
15	15	£148.30	£138.03	£128.76

In this example, the price of the 5% bond moves from £61.97 when the GRY is 10% to 67.75 if GRY drops to 9% (a fall of 9%) to £56.85 if GRY rises to 11% (a fall of 8.2%). The other bonds whilst exhibiting the same overall relationship are not as responsive to the alteration in the GRY. The 10% bond rises by 8% and falls by 7.1%.

It should be noted that the relationship between the coupon and maturity and the price are not symmetrical (equal for both a rise or a fall in GRY). This is a relationship which is known as **convexity**.

The logic behind this relationship is that the lower coupon bonds have more of their value tied up in the terminal value. The ultimate low-coupon bond is, after all, the zero-coupon bond where the entire value is in the final payment.

4.2.3 The impact of yield

If **yields** are particularly high, then the flows in the future are worth relatively little and the sensitivity is diminished. Conversely, if the yield is low, then the present value of flows in the future is enhanced and the bond is more sensitive to the changing GRY.

Summary

Long dated > Short dated
Low coupon > High coupon
Low yields > High yields

Whilst these simple maxims are good indicators of the likely sensitivity to fluctuations in the rate of interest, they do not allow for two bonds to be compared.

For example, which of the following is likely to be the most sensitive to a rise in interest rates – a high-coupon long-dated stock or a low-coupon short-dated stock? It was for this reason that in the 1930s, a composite measure of interest rate risk was devised: the **duration**.

4.3 Evaluating risks

With government **gilts** (UK Government bonds), interest and inflation risk represent the greatest dangers to the investor: there is no significant possibility of default or liquidity problems. Government bonds can be considered a benchmark against which required yields for other bonds can be assessed.

The normal form of evaluation of non-government bonds is to judge them by virtue of such a benchmark government bond, establishing the required yield difference between the two stocks, and then investigating discrepancies which may be generated by the market.

Required yield	%
Yield on the equivalent benchmark gilt	X
Yield premium for additional credit risk	X
Yield premium on rights given to the issuer (calls)	X
Yield give up on option given to the holder (conversion and put premium rights)	(X)
Yield mark up for liquidity risk	X
Yield change for tax advantage/(disadvantage)	X
	X

The key reasons for a variance in the yield between a corporate issue and a government bond will be:

- Credit rating
- Name recognition
- Liquidity

In addition, the perceived security of the market place is important. In particular, government bond markets will attract money in volatile market places due to the **flight to quality**. The variety of other features that may be added to the bond may create uncertainty and therefore detract from the bond's value rather than add to it.

4.4 Bond credit ratings

All issues except those companies or corporations with high name recognition (household names) require a **credit rating** from one of the agencies. The credit rating gives an indication to potential investors of the level of security that they can find in a particular issue.

The three main agencies offering credit ratings are **Moody's, Standard & Poor's** and **Fitch**, whose rating systems are shown in the following Table.

BPP)))
LEARNING MEDIA

Investment grade (Prime)			Non-investment grade (Non-prime or Junk)		
Standard & Poor's	Moody's	Fitch	Standard & Poor's	Moody's	Fitch
AAA	Aaa	AAA	BB+	Ba1	BB+
AA+	Aa1	AA+	BB	Ba2	BB
AA	Aa2	AA	BB–	Ba3	BB–
AA–	Aa3	AA–	B+	B1	B+
A+	A1	A+	B	B2	B
A	A2	A	B–	B3	B–
A–	A3	A–	CCC	Caa	CCC
BBB+	Baa1	BBB+	CC	Ca	
BBB	Baa2	BBB	C	C	
BBB–	Baa3	BBB–	D		

4.4.1 Standard & Poor's ratings

The explanations below are based on **Standard & Poor's** ratings.

Within Standard & Poor's weighting system, the **plus (+)** and **minus (–)** sign indicates the relative standing of the debt within one of the major captions. The letter I indicates that the rating is implied. An implied rating will be given to a sovereign borrower who has not expressly asked for a rating to be produced.

AAA	Debt rated AAA has the highest rating assigned by Standard & Poor's. Capacity to pay interest and repay principal is extremely strong.
AA	Debt rated AA has a very strong capacity to pay interest and repay principal and differs from the higher rated issues only in small degree.
A	Debt rated A has a strong capacity to pay interest and repay principal although it is somewhat more susceptible to the adverse effects of changes in circumstances and economic conditions than debt in higher rated categories.
BBB	Debt rated BBB is regarded as having an adequate capacity to pay interest and repay principal. Adverse economic conditions or changing circumstances are more likely to lead to a weakened capacity to pay interest and repay principal for debt in this category than in higher rated categories. BBB and above are **investment grades**.
BB, B, CCC, CC, C	Debt rated BB, B, CCC, CC and C is regarded, on balance, as predominantly **speculative** with respect to capacity to pay interest and repay principal in accordance with the terms of the obligation. While such debt will likely have some quality and protective characteristics, these are outweighed by large uncertainties or major risk exposures to adverse conditions.
CI	The rating CI is reserved for income bonds on which no interest is being paid.
D	Debt rated D is in default, and payment of interest and/or repayment of principal is in arrears.

4.4.2 Other rating systems

In addition to the three main agencies mentioned above, **Duff, Phelps** and **NAIC** also provide credit ratings in various markets.

In 1978, the **Institute of Actuaries** set up a **bond rating system** that identified the following features as of importance.

- **Company status**
  - Market capitalisation
  - Upper limit of capital gearing ratio
  - Upper limit of income gearing ratio

- **Issue status**
  - Nature of security (fixed/floating/none)
  - Upper limit of capital priority (see below)
  - Borrowing limit as a percentage of capital and reserves
  - Provisions restricting the disposal of assets

5 BOND MARKET SECTORS

5.1 Introduction

There are two main ways of classifying bonds: by the **market** into which they are issued, and by their **structure** (or financial composition).

5.2 Domestic bond markets

Domestic bonds are sold in the issuer's own domestic market, denominated in the domestic currency. A typical domestic market has four sectors:

- Government sector
- Government agency sector
- Municipal sector
- Corporate sector

5.2.1 Domestic Government bonds

In descending order of size the four largest markets are the US, Japan, Germany, and the UK.
US Treasuries (T-Bills, T-Notes, and T-Bonds) are backed by the US Treasury and have been solely issued in non-callable form since 1989. Treasuries are exempt from State and local income taxes but subject to Federal taxes. JGBs (Japanese Government Bonds) are regarded as of equal quality to Treasuries, and are divided into medium term (2-4 years), long term (10 years), and super long term (15 and 20 years).

5.2.2 Government agency bonds

US agency issues are obligations issued through political subdivisions of the US Government. They account for about 25% of the US market. They are backed by the US Government, despite not being direct issues of the US Treasury. Examples are, the Government National Mortgage Association in the USA (GNMA known as **Ginnie Mae**) and the Federal National Mortgage Association (FNMA known as **Fannie Mae**). Some agency issues are taxable (unlike Treasuries).

Agency bonds account for approximately 15% of the Japanese market and 5% of the German. They do not exist in the UK.

5.2.3 Principal overseas government bonds

The principal bonds issued by overseas governments are summarised below.

- US Treasury Bonds – over 10 years
- US Treasury Notes – 2-10 years
- US Treasury Bills – under 1 year
- Japanese Government Bonds – 10 years
- Japanese Superlong Bonds – 20 years
- German Bunds – over 10 years
- German Bobl – 5 years
- German Schatze – 6 months – 2 years
- French OATs – 7, 10, 15 and 30 years
- French BTANs – 2-5 years

5.2.4 Municipal bonds (Munis)

Munis are bonds issued by political subdivisions of a country, such as states, counties and cities. They are principally a phenomenon in the US, where they carry tax advantages, although local authorities in the UK do issue bonds.

5.2.5 Corporate bonds

Corporate bonds are bonds issued by private companies/corporations. They are very important in the US, but small in Japan and very small in Germany and the UK (although the bank debenture market in Germany is of significant size, since most German companies finance themselves through bank loans).

The securities traded are listed securities and therefore go through the Stock Exchange's listing rules as set out in the Listing Rules (Yellow Book). The Stock Exchange acts as prime regulator for any issues, but the British Bankers Association (BBA) requires that issues over £20m are reported to it, and operates an unofficial queuing system to prevent two large issues hitting the market at the same time in order to prevent them reducing each others take up.

Corporate bonds are classified according to their credit rating. All European issues except those companies which are household names require a credit rating from one of the agencies. In practice all companies who issue debt will have a credit rating from at least one of the major rating agencies. The three main rating agencies are Moody's, Standard & Poor's and Fitch Ratings.

5.3 Foreign-issued bonds

Foreign-issued bonds are sold in a market that is not the issuer's domestic market, denominated in the currency of the issue market. For example, a Japanese corporation might raise dollars (possibly for the purposes of constructing a manufacturing facility in the US) by issuing dollar-denominated bonds in New York. An Italian company might issue Sterling bonds in London. The former would be referred to as **Yankee** bonds, while the latter are known as **Bulldogs**. Other varieties are **Samurai** (issued in Japan), and **Matador** (Spain). The issuer of a foreign bond has to follow the legal and regulatory requirements of the market of issue.

5.4 Eurobonds

Eurobonds are more difficult to define. One definition might be that they are bonds that are issued simultaneously in a number of financial centres or, if in just one centre, are issued in a currency which is not that centre's currency (called eurocurrency).

The market for Eurobonds has been in existence for over 30 years. The prefix **Euro** stems from an analogy with **Eurodollar** (the name given to deposits of dollars in Europe, a phenomenon that grew through the 1950s) but is now potentially misleading. After the Second World War, the US dollar became a quasi–international currency due to the reconstruction of Europe mainly being paid for in US dollars. This meant that investors were keen to hold US dollars and therefore a large overseas dollar holding began to build up.

The US bond market was open to all at the time whereas most other markets had some form of exchange controls. Therefore many companies were raising their funding in dollars. The US Government could not control dollars held outside the US. Consequently in the 1960s, the US Government introduced the Interest Equalisation Tax (IET) and exchange controls.

As a result of the dollars held outside of the US and the closure of the US market, the Eurobond market developed out of London. The Eurobond market was dominated by supranational organisations, governments and highly-rated corporate borrowers. Hence, the Eurobond market was born. While at least a third of Eurobond issues in Europe are dollar-denominated, and Europe (London and Luxembourg) continues to be the centre of Eurobond activity, almost all the major currencies have been used for Eurobond issues.

In essence, the Eurobond market is like any other fixed interest market place. The only real difference is that it is not constrained by any national barriers and is perhaps the only truly global market. The term 'Euro' in this sense is then somewhat misleading and should be replaced perhaps by international bonds.

The market is dominated by supranational organisations, governments and highly-rated corporate borrowers. The nature of the borrowers and the size of the market have encouraged innovation in the Euromarkets which then filters down into the domestic fixed interest markets.

5.4.1 Borrowers on Euromarkets

Access to the Euromarkets is limited to those institutions and companies with high credit ratings. Many governments fund a proportion of their debt through the Euromarkets along with the supranational bodies such as the World Bank and the European Investment Bank, which are the largest individual borrowers in the market.

In addition to governmental bodies, corporates also tap the market. However, as mentioned above, the ability to enter the Euromarkets is restricted to those companies with strong credit ratings and in particular, the markets tend towards those focused on banking and other financial services sectors. The key to launching a successful issue is the credit rating of the company.

5.4.2 Eurobond issues

A new Eurobond issue will be **lead managed** by a large international securities house. The lead manager (or **book runner**) is appointed by the issuer of the bond, and will organise a syndicate or selling group, the members of which will be responsible for selling tranches of the bond to their customers.

Although most Eurobond issues are listed on either the London or Luxembourg Stock Exchanges the trading is actually carried out over-the-counter, with and between the members of ICMA (International Capital Market Association, the Eurobond dealers' trade association). Market makers' books may be passed from Europe to North America to Japan and back to Europe in a 24-hour cycle. Transactions may be effected electronically, but are normally spoken agreements.

Market participants rely on Reuters, Bloomberg and other screen-based information systems for price information. The code of dealing in the secondary Eurobond market is regulated by the ICMA, which is a DIE (Designated Investment Exchange).

Transaction confirmation is via TRAX, an Automated Transaction Exchange System. Its objective is to provide a same-day, live, online comparison and confirmation system, principally for members of the

ICMA but also available to other professional participants in the international markets. It is designed as a trader/dealer front-line checking system.

Brokers conducting deals on the secondary market are able to input trade details onto a screen which is then automatically displayed and confirmed by the other party to the trade. Brokers are obliged to report trades within 30 minutes of trade time.

5.4.3 Settlement

Settlement in the Eurobond market takes place through two independent clearing houses, Euroclear and Clearstream. Both operate a three-day clearing cycle.

The majority of the bonds in the market are immobilised by the houses. In other words, they hold the bond certificates and move the ownership between member accounts electronically.

5.4.4 Legal form

Most Eurobonds issued are in bearer form. The only real exception to this are bonds which are issued to the US primary market, which due to the Tax Equity and Fiscal Responsibility Act (TEFRA), are obliged to be in registered form. Any new issues of bearer bonds are prevented from accessing the American markets, until the bond has **seasoned**, for a period of 40 days. Innovation in bonds issuance is strong in the Euromarkets and there are a variety of different issues which have taken place.

5.4.5 Redemption

Eurobonds (as with UK domestic bonds) can have a variety of redemption terms.

5.5 The major international bond markets

Over the course of the past decade, bond investment has become international, with a shift away from local markets. This has been matched by an increase in the number of issues and the availability of stocks.

**Relative Size of OECD Government Bond markets
Debt by Nominal Value @ December 2004**

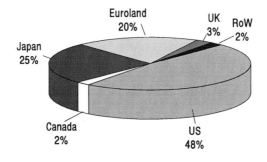

Public Debt as a Proportion of GDP 2005

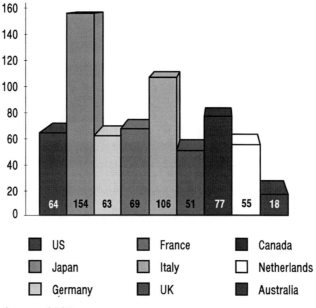

Source: OECD

6 BOND MARKETS OUTSIDE THE EURO ZONE

6.1 US bond markets

Segmentation of the US Bond Markets

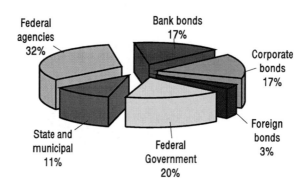

6.1.1 US Government bond market

The US Government bond market is the largest in the world. The market underwent rapid expansion in the 1980s. This size is evident in both the quantity of issuance in the primary market and volumes of activity in the secondary market.

The US Treasuries market is not dissimilar in structure from the UK gilts market. This is due to the UK reforms that have been designed to bring the two markets into line. Indeed, the general direction of all government bond markets has been towards greater '**fungibility**' or similarity, with the US being seen as the role model.

The key player in the market is the **Federal Reserve** (the 'Fed'). As the US central bank, it operates in much the same way as the Bank of England in the UK. It is the Fed which, through **open market operations**, manipulates liquidity to control US monetary policy. Unlike the Bank of England, the Fed is largely independent. The only political involvement comes in the appointment of the board. However, in many ways this possibility of political influence is more apparent than actual. For if a President were to try to 'rig' the Fed, then it is likely that the markets would react unfavourably and the benefits of credibility would be eroded very quickly.

The Fed's own publications summarise the objectives of the Board of Governors and the twelve Federal Reserve banks as follows.

- Conducting the nation's monetary policy by influencing money and credit conditions in the economy in pursuit of full employment and stable prices. However, the clear focus of policy is towards the latter of these two objectives in the belief that price stability is a prerequisite for higher levels of employment.

- Supervising and regulating banking institutions to ensure the safety and soundness of the nation's banking and financial system and to protect the credit rights of consumers.

- Maintaining the stability of the financial system and containing the systemic risk that may arise in financial markets.

- Providing certain financial services to the US Government, the public, financial institutions, and foreign official institutions, including playing a major role in operating the nation's payments system.

The **US Treasury** is part of government and responsible for the issuance of debt in order to fund the deficit.

Central to the operation of the market are the **primary dealers**. These firms are the market makers. They are authorised to conduct trades by the Fed and are obliged to make markets in all issues. As with the UK, there are inter-dealer brokers (IDBs) to facilitate the taking and unwinding of large positions. There are no money brokers, but there is a full repo market.

While the stocks are listed on the New York Stock Exchange, the market is effectively an over-the-counter market. The market operates 09:00 to 16:00 locally, but is perhaps the most truly global market. The market has deep liquidity across the maturity range and prices are quoted in decimals.

6.1.2 US Government bond instruments

There are three main types of instrument issued.

- **Treasury bills (T-bills)** – with a maturity of 3 - 12 months, at a discount to face value
- **Treasury notes (T-notes)** – coupon securities, issued with initial maturities of 2 -10 years
- **Treasury bonds (T-bonds)** – coupon securities, issued with an initial life of over 10 years

As with the Japanese markets, there is a tendency for the market to focus into the liquid issues referred to as the **'on-the-run bond' or 'hot runs'**. These benchmarks are normally the most recent issues. Other issues are referred to as 'trade by appointment'.

Treasury Inflation Protected Securities (TIPS)

In May 1996, the US Government decided to issue index-linked bonds for the first time. In part, this was seen as an unusual decision by the markets, who initially viewed it as a worrying sign with regard to the Government's commitment to low inflation. The justification is that, far from undermining the Government's commitment to low inflation, it actually reinforces it by ensuring that if inflation does take off, Government finance costs will likewise rise in nominal terms.

The first issue took place in 1997 and the format of the issues is in line with the Canadian model. The bonds are semi-annual paying with quotations on a dirty basis.

Other special issues

In addition, there have been specific issues in the past, such as Foreign-Targeted Notes. These are issues that pay annual coupons and are in bearer form, so as to mimic Eurobonds. Other issues have been in currency such as the DM 'Carter bonds' of 1979.

For both of the coupon bonds (T-bonds and T-notes), coupons are paid semi-annually. All bonds are traded on a clean price basis. The accrued interest is calculated using the following method.

Formula to learn

$$\frac{\text{Actual number of days from last payment to the day before settlement (inclusive)}}{\text{Actual number of days in the half year}} \times \tfrac{1}{2}\text{Coupon}$$

Settlement takes place predominantly through the Fed's wire (book entry system). Settlement is by convention for the next day, although same day settlement is possible.

There are no withholding taxes on US Government securities, which makes them particularly attractive to overseas investors.

There are a number of derivative contracts available on US Treasuries. These contracts have a variety of specifications and are available across the maturity range.

6.1.3 Issuance

The **US Treasury** is responsible for the **issuance** of new securities. Issuance takes place on a regular calendar with weekly issues of three or six-month Treasury bills, monthly issues of one-year bills and two and five-year notes, and quarterly issues in set cycles of longer dated stocks. These quarterly issues are referred to as the quarterly refunding. The quarterly refunding simply allows for the Treasury to clarify the current state of the Government's finances and to signal changes for the future. The extent of each auction is announced a week in advance of the auction. In 1998 and 1999, further reforms were introduced reducing the frequency of auctions, reflecting the Government's reduced financing requirements.

In 2001, the Government announced the cessation of issuance in the 30-year T-bond. Ostensibly this was designed to reflect the reduced funding needs of the state. However, by reducing the supply of extra long paper this has the effect of forcing the price up (and yield down). Consequently, the effect could be to stimulate longer term borrowing in the US by reducing the reference rate given by the yield curve. With the Federal deficit reaching $412 billion by 2004, the US Treasury re-introduced the 30-year T-bond in early 2006.

Timetable for issuance

In recent times, the US budget deficit has increased rapidly, thus causing a change in the issuance timetable. Currently, 2-year, 5-year and 10-year notes are being issued on a monthly cycle, however, this is only likely to be for the short-term. Even though there are no moves to reintroduce the 30-year T-bond, the US Treasury has recently issued a $12bn 20-year TIPS bond. It is likely that TIPS issuance will increase (both in nominal term and as a percentage of issuance) to cover medium to long-dated debt. Despite their continued poor liquidity in the secondary market, they have been very popular with investors who have tended to hold them for investment purposes. This strong demand for TIPS during the auction has kept their yields down.

A risk facing Treasuries is the high demand from overseas central banks, particularly Japanese and Chinese. To prevent their currencies from rising relative to the dollar, these banks have been intervening in the currency market, by buying the dollar. With these dollars they have been buying T-notes, particularly in the two to three-year maturity range, thus depressing yields. Whilst the demand for short-term yields persists, the monthly issuance can occur, with limited risk. However, the danger for the US Treasury (and investors) is, of course, the potential disruption that could be caused when this demand returns to normal levels. To prevent a sudden spike in short dated T-notes, a reduction in issuance may be required.

T-bonds are issued through competitive auction. Two and five-year T-notes are issued using a uniform price auction, or tender, where each bidder pays the highest accepted yield (i.e. the lowest accepted price).

6.1.4 The competitive auction

The competitive auction in the US is basically the system that was introduced into the UK in 1987. The principal differences are that, in the US, the primary dealers are obliged to bid for stock and bids are on a yield basis (rather than price in the UK).

Example: Competitive auction

Auction of $20bn ten-year T-bond

Non-competitive bids of $1bn are received. As in the UK, members of the public may submit non-competitive bids. This does not require them to estimate the price and they **will** be allocated stock at the average of the successful competitive bids.

Competitive bids received

$2bn @ 7.55%
$3bn @ 7.56%
$4bn @ 7.57%
$7bn @ 7.58%
$6bn @ 7.59%
$5bn @ 7.60%
$4bn @ 7.61%

The non-competitive bids will be allocated first at a price to be determined later. That leaves $19bn to be auctioned. The bids are allocated on a lowest yield (therefore highest price) first basis.

Therefore, the bidders who bid @ 7.55% will receive their full $2bn at the price that generates that yield. The coupon is only set by the Fed after the auction is complete. The coupon will be the average successful yield bid. Then the $3bn who bid @ 7.56% and so on. The issue will be exhausted by those investors bidding @ 7.59% and they will only receive half of the quantity that they bid for.

The non-competitive bids will be allocated at the average bid price of 7.57%.

The lowest accepted bid is known as the '**stop-out yield**' and the difference between this and the average price is the '**tail**'. The amount by which bids exceeded the issue is referred to as the '**cover**'.

6.1.5 The repo market

A **repo** is a **sale and repurchase agreement**. The basis of the transaction is that the holder of a bond is able to sell his holding of a particular bond in order to raise cash. Simultaneously, the holder enters into an agreement to repurchase the stock at a date in the future, at the same price plus interest.

Example: Repo

Leg 1. Bonds worth $200,000 are sold for $180,000. The size of this 'haircut' will depend on the securities to be repoed and the duration of the loan. The repo rate will be set at this point, let us say 6% for a 90-day repo.

Leg 2. The bonds are repurchased for $180,000 plus interest. The interest is worked out on a simple basis using the following formula.

$$\text{Interest} = \text{Principal amount} \times \text{Repo rate} \times \frac{\text{Days}}{360}$$

$$180{,}000 \times 0.06 \times \frac{90}{360} = \$2{,}700$$

Therefore, the sum due on repayment is \$182,700.

The end result is, in effect, a secured loan where one party borrows money on the surety of the US T-bonds that they own. Given the security of the loan, the rates can be extremely fine.

As well as repos, there are **reverse repos** that allow participants in the market to go short of stock. With a reverse repo an investor buys T-bonds now for cash. Simultaneously, he enters into an agreement to sell the bond back in the future. Again, the difference between the two deals represents the interest charged on the loan.

As a result of the reverse repo, the investor is able to 'borrow' stock now that can then be used to settle short trades. Eventually, the investor will be obliged to unwind his stock position and complete the repo by buying stock in the market and selling the stock back to the original owner with whom he entered into the repo agreement.

Whilst the market initially focused on short-term contracts (overnight, with any other contract being referred to as a **term repo**), the market is now liquid over a wide maturity range.

6.1.6 The strips market

The **strips market** developed in the US during the early 1980s. Initially run by individual investment houses, in 1984 the US Treasury created the **Separate Trading of Registered Interest and Principal of Securities (STRIPS)** programme.

The system takes an ordinary bond and breaks it down into its component parts. Each flow from a bond is converted into a zero-coupon bond.

For example, a five-year T-note with a semi-annual coupon of 6% would become 10 zero-coupon bonds, one for each of the individual coupon flows of \$3 (these are known as the **Tint**). These zero-coupon bonds range in maturity from six months to ten years. In addition, there is another zero-coupon bond formed out of the principal, known as the **TP**.

Given that the strips market is derived from the same market as the underlying bonds, then the possibility of arbitrage exists between the two to ensure that prices are consistent.

The yield derived from the strips market are the spot yields that can be derived from the GRYs. They will not tie up absolutely, since there is not perfect liquidity over the range of maturities in the market.

There will be substantial interest in the long end of the market, since by buying the strip the investor will be able to expose him to greater interest rate risk than by going through the conventional market. The 26-year bond may have a duration of ten years, however the TP (stripped zero based on the principal) will have a duration equal to the maturity, therefore 26 years.

The development of a full strips market has enabled the investors in the US Treasuries market to create highly structured strategies based on the movement of the yield curve.

A further advantage of trading through the strips market is that reinvestment is no longer a problem, since there is only one cash flow associated with a zero-coupon bond.

Strips markets have now been developed in most of the major government bond markets.

6.1.7 Federal agencies

These are quasi-governmental institutions established to fill gaps in the US financial markets. They are backed by the guarantee of the US Government via the Fed and are therefore riskless. However, they may well trade at a slight premium to the equivalent US Government securities principally due to lower liquidity.

The main Federal agencies

- Federal National Mortgage Association (FNMA or 'Fannie Mae')
- Government National Mortgage Association (GNMA or 'Ginnie Mae')
- Federal Home Loan Mortgage Corporation (FMLMC or 'Freddy Mac')
- Federal Home Loan Bank System (FMLB)
- Federal Guaranteed Student Loan Programme (GSL)
- Federal Farm Credit Bank (FFCB)

Unlike conventional government bonds, which are predominantly redeemed in bullet form, issues by these agenices repay a portion of the capital with each coupon payment. In addition to these quasi-governmental organisations, there are also municipal bonds (Munis) issued by state governments and districts. These obviously have a higher credit risk and are less liquid: yield spreads are consequently greater.

6.1.8 Domestic corporate bond markets

Unlike the UK, the US corporate sector has been able to borrow substantial sums via the issue of debt securities. In part, this has been forced upon them by the highly fragmented nature of the domestic banking market. Equally, however, investors are willing to hold corporate debt as part of their portfolios in a way in which UK investors are not. In the 1980s, a market in debt from speculative grade (BB and below) stocks was started by Drexels. This market (the junk bond market) represented a cross between debt and equity markets, and eventually collapsed.

6.1.9 Yankee bonds

Ever since 1945, the dollar has been the key international currency. Prior to the emergence of the Eurodollar market (and to a limited extent after this), there has been substantial interest from non-US firms in raising dollar finance.

A **Yankee bond** is a dollar-denominated bond issued in the US by an overseas borrower. Given that Eurodollar bonds may not be sold into the US markets until they have **seasoned** (a period of 40 days), there is still a divide between the Euromarket and the domestic market. Apart from the access to a different investor base, the market also allows issuers to raise longer term finance, since the American domestic investors are prepared to accept longer maturities.

These domestic and international bonds trade in a similar way to shares.

6.1.10 US private placement market

Overseas borrowers have often been constrained from entering the US market because of the high level of regulation imposed by the Securities and Exchange Commission (SEC). This was eased by the introduction in April 1990 of rule 144A. Under this rule, corporates are allowed to issue bonds into the private placement market without seeking full SEC registration. This access to the market is not restricted to overseas issuers, and the market is dominated by US domestic issuers who have chosen not to enter the public market.

The buy side of the market is restricted to certain institutional investors (primarily insurance companies) who are predominantly 'buy and hold' investors. The market is therefore less liquid than the full domestic market, since issues tend to be held to redemption, thereby limiting the secondary market. This thin secondary market is itself a discouragement to potential investors such as the mutual investment funds.

However, even this thin liquidity is an improvement on the previous private placement market, which made no allowance for trading at all.

Reflecting the nature of the market as in effect a one-to-one contract, new issue terms are negotiated between the issuer and the lender. This process can take up to eight weeks to complete. Equally, as a consequence, borrowers tend to have to pay a premium over the public market yields. However, they do not have the cost of seeking a rating, nor are they bound by the rules of the SEC.

6.2 UK Government bonds – Gilts

6.2.1 Characteristics

Governments, as a rule, spend more money in a year than they raise in revenue, resulting in the Public Sector Net Cash Requirement (PSNCR). Consequently, they are obliged to borrow money to cover the deficit. Due to their high credit rating, they are able to borrow substantial sums with a wide range of maturities. The combination of this high credit rating and the size of the issues attracts investors. Government debt markets are among the largest markets in the world in terms of activity.

Gilts are UK Government bonds. Historically, they were issued and managed by the Bank of England on behalf of the government; however, this role is now undertaken by the **Debt Management Office (DMO)**.

Let us take a typical issue and examine the key features.

Treasury	12½%	2007-9 @	126.56
Name	**Coupon**	**Maturity**	**Price**

Each stock bears a title. Treasury, Exchequer, Funding, Conversion, Consolidated (Consols), and War Loan are names used to indicate the Government department that issued the debt. The names are irrelevant, since all debt is the government's debt and ranks equally.

The **coupon** is the rate of interest that will be paid each year based on the nominal value of the stock. In the UK, the convention is for this coupon to be paid on a semi-annual basis, in equal instalments. However, the 2½% Consolidated stock pays on a quarterly basis.

Since April 1998, gilts have paid their coupons gross. This does not exempt holders from paying tax. It simply means that none has been paid yet. Indeed, if investors consider it most appropriate to do so for administrative reasons, they can elect to continue to receive the coupons net on any gilt.

The **maturity** date is the date on which the government has agreed to repay the debt. In this case, the government has issued debt with two dates. The Government has reserved its right to redeem the debt from 2007, but must redeem the stock by 2009. The decision on redemption will be taken with reference to the coupon. If the Government is able to replace the borrowing at a cheaper rate, then it will redeem the stock on the earlier of the two dates. Gilt-edged stocks are classified with respect to their maturity dates.

Official DMO definitions

- **Shorts** – gilts with 7 years or less to run
- **Mediums** – gilts with between 7 and 15 years until redemption
- **Longs** – gilts with over 15 years until redemption

Double-dated stocks are normally classified using the later of the two dates, since this is the point at which redemption has to take place.

In the past, the government has been able to issue some bonds without specifying a date on which redemption will take place. These **undated stocks** are all redeemable from a certain date. For example, the Treasury 3% 66 Aft has been redeemable since (or after) 1966: however, unlike double-dated stocks, there is no date by which the issue must be redeemed.

The **price** of a gilt is quoted in terms of the amount that an investor would have to pay in order to buy £100 nominal of the stock. Technically, an investor can buy as much as they want of a gilt. The market simply adopts this as a convention for the quote. The price is quoted in pounds and pence (decimal terms).

In the *Financial Times*, both the **flat yield** and the **gross redemption yield (GRY)** are published. By convention, the yield figures shown for gilts is twice the six-monthly yield, not the six-monthly yield compounded.

6.2.2 Types of gilt

Straight gilts. Our example above represents a straight gilt paying a fixed coupon at 12½% p.a. until maturity. The market value of such straight bonds may vary significantly as interest rates vary. This may however be expected since, as interest rates rise and fall, this coupon rate will become less or more attractive.

Variable coupon gilts. The advantage of a floating rate bond is that the coupon rate is always at a fair level regardless of interest rate movements, hence the price remains at or around par. Thus, a floating rate bond protects the nominal value of the investment. There are currently no variable coupon gilts in issue.

Index-linked gilts. Whilst a floating rate gilt may protect the nominal value of the investment, it cannot protect against the effects of inflation which, over time, eats into this value in real terms. This protection can, however, be achieved with index-linked bonds.

As inflation increases, the return demanded by investors, the yield, will also increase in order to maintain the real rate of return. Because inflation in the UK has been an issue over the past 20 years, the Government has issued a number of index-linked gilts which automatically compensate the investor for the impact of inflation. This compensation for inflation is applied to both the coupon and the capital repayment.

Convertible gilts. Convertible gilts are issued with an option to convert at a future date (or dates) into longer dated issues. The alternative course of action open to the holder is to allow the bond to mature and receive the redemption proceeds. There are currently no outstanding issues of convertible gilts.

Foreign currency debt issues. Over the past few years, the Government has issued some foreign currency gilts. The main purpose of these loans has been to finance the foreign currency reserves at the Bank of England. There are outstanding bonds in US dollars (straight) and euros.

These bonds are not like ordinary gilts. They trade like Eurobonds with the same conventions for accrued interest.

6.2.3 New issues of gilts

The **Debt Management Office (DMO)** has the prime responsibility of ensuring that the Government is able to borrow the money it requires to fund the Public Sector Net Cash Requirement (PSNCR). The most important source of financing open to the government is the gilts market.

The DMO controls the issue of gilts into the market place and uses a variety of methods depending upon the circumstances it faces at any time.

Issues by the DMO may be of an entirely new gilt with a coupon/maturity dissimilar to existing issues. Currently, the DMO believes that the range of issues in the market is, if anything, too large and may lead to excessive fragmentation of supply and demand.

In order to avoid the problem above, the DMO may issue a tranche of an existing stock. This entails issuing a given amount of nominal value on exactly similar terms to an existing gilt. The DMO refers to this as 'opening up an existing gilt'. The advantages of tranches are that they avoid adding further complexity to the gilt market and increase the liquidity of current issues. When a tranche is issued, it may be identified by the letter 'A' in order to indicate that when the tranche is issued a full coupon may not be paid on the next payment date to reflect the fact that the gilt has only been an issue for part of the coupon period.

A small tranche may be referred to as a **tranchette**.

6.2.4 Methods of issue

Tenders

Until 1987, gilts were primarily issued by means of **tenders**, also referred to as **Dutch auctions**.

In a tender, investors communicate to the DMO both the desired quantity and the price that they are willing to pay. The DMO accepts the applications at the highest prices sufficient to account for the nominal value being issued. All successful bidders receive the gilts at a common price: the lowest accepted bid price.

Auctions

From 1987, the primary issuance method became the **competitive auctions** system.

In a competitive auction, investors apply for gilts at a price they are prepared to pay. The DMO issues the gilts to those investors who apply at the highest prices. The key difference to a tender is that all successful applicants pay the price for which they bid. Thus, in an auction, all successful candidates do not pay the same price.

Currently, issuance by auction is the DMO's primary funding method. Either new issues or tranches of existing stock can be sold by way of an auction.

Running alongside each competitive auction are **non-competitive bids** where investors can apply for up to £500,000 of nominal value. Applicants through non-competitive bids will receive the gilts they applied for at a weighted average of accepted prices in the auction. The smaller investors can participate in the primary market for gilts, whilst avoiding the necessity of determining an appropriate price.

Taps

The Government's current principal method of funding is through regular competitive auctions. However, the Government may still wish to issue smaller quantities of stock to improve liquidity or improve market efficiency. In such situations, the DMO will sell smaller quantities of stock to investors via the **gilt-edged market makers (GEMMs)**.

When tapping stock into secondary markets in this way, it will often be a tranche of existing stock, or a tranchette if a relatively small amount. Alternatively, it could be as a result of a failed auction where the DMO has not received application sufficient to account for nominal value on offer. In such a situation, the remaining stock will be available on tap from the DMO.

Strips

Strips stand for Separately Traded Registered Interest and Principal of Securities, and a strips market was introduced for gilts from late 1997. This market facilitates the trading of individual gilt cash flows rather than the whole bond. Thus, each coupon payment and the final redemption proceeds can be traded as if they were Government-backed zero-coupon bonds.

6.2.5 The secondary market

As with the equities market, gilts used to be traded on the floor of the exchange, however, in 1986, they moved to a telephone-driven market supported by market makers.

The **DMO** is the lead regulator in the gilts market. Its objective is to ensure that the gilts market remains solvent, liquid and, above all, fair. The reason for this commitment is that the DMO is obliged to issue, on the Government's behalf, gilts to fund the Public Sector Net Cash Requirement (PSNCR). In order to do this, the DMO must have access to the markets. It is the DMO that allows participants to enter the gilts market and, thereafter, it is the DMO or the FSA that monitors their capital adequacy.

The **GEMMs** are the focus of the market place. Their role is to ensure that two-way quotes exist at all times for all gilts. GEMMs are allowed to enter the market by the DMO. Once accepted as a gilt-edged market maker, the firm is obliged to make a market in all conventional gilts at a size deemed appropriate by the DMO. There are 17 firms listed as GEMMs.

For index-linked stocks, because the market is less liquid, the DMO has authorised a more limited list of market makers.

Inter Dealer Brokers (IDBs) act as an escape valve for GEMMs. If a GEMM were to build up a large position in a particular stock and then decide to unwind it, it might be difficult to achieve without revealing to the rest of the market that he was long or short of a stock. This is obviously a dangerous position and would discourage GEMMs from taking substantial positions. The IDBs provide an anonymous dealing service, allowing GEMMs to unwind positions. IDBs are only accessible to market makers.

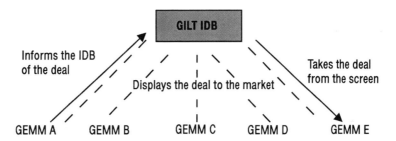

The repo market

The Bank of England introduced an open repo market in the UK in 1996. The opening of the repo market represented a culmination of several years of development, and brought the UK into line with the other major government bond markets in both America and Continental Europe.

We looked at repo transactions earlier in this Chapter. From the point of view of the lender, a repo is a simple loan transaction. They lend their surplus cash in return for interest, and have the support of collateral by the holding of the bond during the life of the contract.

As with any **collateralised loan**, there are two primary risks.

- **Counterparty and legal risk**. This is the risk of default at repurchase and the legal consequences that arise from such a default. This counterparty risk is, to some extent, minimised in the repo transaction by the passing of collateral and, in this sense, the lender then faces the second element of risk.

- **Market and collateral risk**. This risk arises from the fact that the underlying assets may deteriorate to such an extent that should the counterparty fail on the repayment date, then the lender would be left with insufficient collateral compared to the amount of the loan.

To cover this second risk element, repo arrangements allow for margin calls to be made against the borrower in the form of initial margin and variation margin.

- **Initial margin**. The initial margin or initial 'haircut' will be taken as a reduction in the amount of money lent against the bond. As a result, the amount lent will seldom be 100% of the value of the bond. The scale of this initial haircut will be influenced by such factors as the quality of the collateral, the quality of the counterparty and term of the repo.

- **Variation margin**. Variation margin will allow for the collateral to be marked to market throughout the term of the repo. This may be on a daily basis or it may be at specific dates throughout the term. Many agreements will specify a frequency of marking to market and within this, a minimum level of variation necessary to initiate the margin call. As a result, when the collateral falls in value by only a small amount, no additional margin is required to be put up, reducing the transaction costs.

The availability of variation margin obviously reduces the level of market risk that exists on repo transactions. Whilst there is still counterparty risk, the variation margin should ensure that the collateral more than repays the principal of the loan.

Stock Borrowing and Lending Intermediaries (SBLIs)

If market makers wish to take a short position in a stock, i.e. to sell more than they currently have on their books, they will need to have stock in order to settle the trade. The SBLIs provide access to large pools of unused stock. The institutional investors in the UK buy large blocks of gilt-edged securities and often hold these blocks for a number of years, possibly to redemption. The SBLIs borrow stock on behalf of market makers from these dormant positions. The stock is passed to the market maker who uses it to settle the trade and, in effect, to go short.

Eventually, the market maker will be obliged to buy stock to cover the short position, and this stock will then be passed back to the institutional investor. The SBLI charges commission on the trade of around ½%. This commission is split between the intermediaries and the institution. This is a facility available to all market participants and provides them with vital access to stock positions enabling them to go short. Since the introduction of the gilt repo market in 1996, activity of SBLIs in the gilts market has been minimal.

The fundamental difference between the **repo market** and **stocklending** is that under stocklending the institution does not have to do anything. They will simply receive a fee at the end of the process. Whereas, through the repo trade, they will have to take money on and lay it off into the market in order to make their return.

Settlement

Gilt settlement occurs on the business day following the transaction. Market professionals such as GEMMs or IDBs would settle electronically through CREST. In 2002, CREST announced its merger with Euroclear, and is now known as Euroclear UK & Ireland.

6.3 UK non-Government bonds

6.3.1 Elements

The UK non-Government bond market is made up of the following elements.

- Local authority debt
- Domestic corporate issues
- Overseas issuers of sterling debt – 'Bulldogs'

In addition, there is the eurosterling market.

Progressively, each of the three domestic areas have declined in importance over the last two decades as the eurosterling market has expanded.

In the case of local authorities, the decline has come through the control of their finances by central Government. This has meant no new issues into this market over the last few years.

With both domestic corporates and bulldogs, the growth of the eurosterling market has fundamentally undermined their issuer base. In the case of the domestic debt market, the issuance level was never strong, given the 'cult of the equity' which has dominated the UK markets since the 1950s and led to one of the largest equity markets, by number of stocks, in the world.

A further inhibitor of the growth of the market has been that, once a borrower has 'tapped' the Euromarket, it is unlikely to be able to re-enter the domestic market given the normal covenants included in the issues. Eurobonds are generally unsecured debt and most issues carry with them a negative pledge, assuring the lenders that no debt with a higher level of security will be issued. In the domestic markets, it is conventional for debt to carry security.

Much of the paper currently traded in the market is stock that was issued during the 1960s and 1970s, when the market was reasonably liquid. As these issues reach maturity, the market will contract further.

6.3.2 Local Authority debt

Unlike the Federal securities in the US market, UK local authority stocks carry a less explicit guarantee. If the authority defaults, there is only a 'moral' obligation on the part of the UK Government to support them.

Local authorities are able to issue a variety of stocks.

A **fixed loan** is, in effect, a mortgage and indeed, these instruments may be known as local authority bonds or mortgages. It is a loan arranged for a set maturity. During the period of the loan, interest is paid to the lender. **There is no secondary market** in this type of security. It is very much like a mortgage on a house.

Local Authority Negotiable Bonds (Yearlings) are short-term local authority debt. In essence, these are bonds like a gilt carrying a coupon. The maturity of yearlings will be either one or two years. The market in these bonds trades in set blocks, the size of a block being £1,000 nominal. Unlike fixed loans, there is a full secondary market in yearlings.

In essence, a **local authority stock** is similar to a **gilt**. It is a longer term bond carrying a coupon which pays semi-annually and there is a full secondary market in local authority stocks. The yield on local authority stocks will be slightly above the yield on gilts, reflecting the slight risk of default.

Local authority bonds, like gilts, are exempt from **capital gains tax**. Interest is paid half-yearly, net of 20% tax. With registration of HMRC Form R85, interest can be paid gross to a non-taxpayer. **Interest is taxable**, as savings income.

As mentioned above, the local authority debt market is gradually declining due to the absence of new issues. The majority of the stock in issue dates back to the 1960s. Local authority stocks are traded in line with the gilt-edged market representing lower credit versions of ordinary gilts.

Over the past decade, issuance in the market has dried up. Rather than allow the authorities to raise their own finance, the Local Authority Borrowing Requirement (LABR) has been subsumed into the PSNCR. The Government has then made some of the finance raised through the PSNCR available via the Public Works Loan Board (PWLB). This constraint has now been relaxed and Local Authorities are allowed to borrow again in their own right.

The **Private Finance Initiative** (PFI) was developed initially by the UK Government in 1992 to provide financial support for 'Public Private Partnerships' (PPPs) between the public and private sectors. This model has now been adopted by many other countries in North America, Europe and elsewhere. It was launched in the UK in order to encourage the use of private finance for major projects such as building bridges and hospitals. The logic behind this was that it was more efficient than the previous Government funding structure and would tap new areas of the investment community. This should particularly encourage the local community to invest in projects that have a direct bearing on their environment and welfare. This may represent an additional drain on the banking sector or alternatively may act as the catalyst for the development of a non-government debt market. These bonds will not carry the formal backing of the Government.

Large PFI projects are funded through the sale of corporate bonds issued by the company running the PFI. An essential feature is that these bonds are rated as BBB– by a credit rating agency (for example Standard and Poor's). BBB– is the lowest investment guide rating, any lower than that and the band receives speculative or 'junk' status. If a rating of better than BBB– is given then the government is likely to want to renegotiate the deal, to lower the unit price it pays for the scheme. Any lower than BBB– means that investors would be unlikely to take on the risk. So although bank rating typically affects the cost of borrowing for corporates, in the PFI case it effects the whole viability of the deal. The reason for the existence of the treasury team in the PFI supplying company is to gain an investment grade rating. A PFI firm will typically go to two of the three main credit rating agencies, sharing details of their financial model, concession contract and capital equipment solution.

The UK government has pledged to make it easier for projects to use the PFI and in time this should lead to far greater issuance in the UK non-government bond market.

6.3.3 Corporate debt

Until recently, the development of a **corporate bond market** in the UK has been stifled by the existence of a strong and solvent banking system. However, growing pressures on bank balance sheets and a more competitive atmosphere have led to the beginnings of a corporate debt market in the UK. EMU provides another dynamic to this process.

6.4 Canadian bond market

Segmentation of the Canadian Bond Market

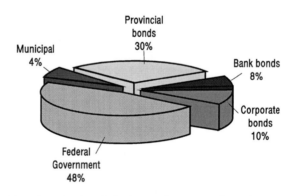

The Canadian Government bond market is relatively small compared to other members of the G7 group of nations, mainly because the Canadian system is largely decentralised. In essence, the provinces act as clearly distinct economic units with their own tax-raising and borrowing powers. Many analysts look to the Canadian example as a role model for the European government bond markets after EMU.

6.4.1 Primary market

Bonds are issued by auction, administered by the Bank of Canada on behalf of the Department of Finance. The issuance methods used in this market have now been reformed in order to bring them in line with the other major markets.

The Bank of Canada now uses an auction method of issuance. Bonds still work to an $^{Actual}/_{365}$ accrued interest convention.

There is an effective 14-day ex-coupon period. However, all trades are done on a cum coupon basis. Therefore, any seller of bonds during the ex-period must deliver not only the bond, but also a post-dated cheque for the coupon payment.

In line with many nations who have had a problem with inflation in the post-war era, the Canadian Government has issued Real Return (index-linked) bonds. These bonds track the Canadian CPI (Consumer Price Index), pay coupons semi-annually and trade on dirty prices. Unlike the UK ILG market, the time delay is not eight months but three months, making these bonds a more effective hedge against inflation.

6.4.2 Secondary market

Given the size of the outstanding market, the secondary market is perhaps surprisingly liquid. However, there is at present no exchange-traded derivative on offer.

6.4.3 Economic linkage to the US

In the past, the Canadian economy has been regarded as an adjunct to the US market. With the introduction of fiscal and monetary responsibility and the decrease in Canadian yields, the direct linkage has become less obvious in the past few years. However, given the size of the US economy and the strong trading links between the two economies, there will always tend to be a relatively high correlation.

6.4.4 Provincial debt

As mentioned above, a large proportion of finance for the Canadian state is raised by the quasi-autonomous provinces. Much of this has in the past been raised via the Euromarkets. In particular, the larger borrowers such as Quebec have issued global bonds that qualify as domestic and euro securities.

6.5 Japanese bond market

The Japanese bond market is dominated by Government bonds. This domination is not in terms of volume, where Japanese Government Bonds (JGBs) account for only half of the market, but in the secondary market where they account for over 80% of the secondary market trading. Within this, there tends to be a strong focus on the 'benchmark' bond. This has in the past caused wide discrepancies between the benchmark and other 'side issues'.

Segmentation of the Japanese Bond Market

6.5.1 Government bond market

The Japanese Government bond (**JGB**), with US$5.6 trillion of outstanding issues at the end of 2005, is the largest sovereign debt market in the world. The market is the second largest in the world. The market has grown from almost nothing in the early 1960s to its current size. Over the last ten years the deteriorating economic conditions in Japan made it necessary to borrow in order to finance fiscal injections into the economy. Previously, the market's growth was fuelled by the need to borrow to finance infrastructure investment.

Initially the market was dominated by domestic investors. Over the past decade, due both to the size of issuance and the growing importance of the yen, the market has attracted increasing numbers of overseas investors. To aid this internationalisation of the market the Government has introduced a number of liberalising measures. However, it is still impossible to settle and deliver JGBs outside Japan.

The Japanese market has in the past been regarded as one of the least developed and most 'investor unfriendly' markets amongst the major government bond markets. The Bank of Japan (**BoJ**) was until recently one of the least independent of all the central banks. However, steps have been taken recently in order to bring the market into line with the other major markets. These steps have included a greater level of say for the BoJ in the establishment of policy.

Many international investors still regard the Japanese market as a hostile environment and therefore tend to avoid it. Only around 5% of JGBs are owned by non-Japanese citizens.

6.5.2 Issuance

There are a variety of funding and monetary control instruments that can be used by the government.

- **Treasury bills**. Issued with three and six-month maturities, these are discount securities issued via public auction twice a month. The market is not active and external investors only have limited access.

- **Medium Term Notes**. These are two-year maturity notes that are issued via an auction every two months.

- **Government bonds**. These are conventional debt securities predominantly with a maturity of ten years. The Government does issue 'super longs' that have a maturity of 20 years. The Ministry of Finance has also placed a number of 30-year zero-coupon bonds in the past.

In 2004, Japan became the latest country to issue inflation-linked bonds (ten-year). They are structured similarly to UK ILGs, except for a shorter inflation lag (three months). They will not be available to overseas investors.

JGB categories

- **Construction** – Bonds used to finance infrastructure development
- **Refinancing** – Bonds issued to repay maturing debt
- **Deficit financing** – Bonds issued to cover a budget deficit

In essence, they are all the same semi-annual government bonds. The only difference is that the deficit financing stocks must be approved by the parliament. All new issues now pay their interest on set dates. JGBs can be in either registered or bearer form, and can be converted within two business days.

The **issue process** is more complex than the structure used in most markets with a monthly auction/syndicate issue. In Japan, the syndicate (still dominated by the large investment banks) is allocated 40% of the issue, with 60% sold via public auction. The terms of the issue are set by the Ministry of Finance having taken soundings in the market from the syndicate.

6.5.3 The secondary market

JGBs trade on both the Tokyo Stock Exchange (**TSE**) and the Broker-Broker (OTC) market. The market does tend to focus on the 'benchmark' issues, with occasionally 90% of the volume taking place in that stock. However, any issues that are deliverable into the JGB future will possess a fair degree of liquidity.

The benchmark stock will tend to be the most recent bond series in issue. For example, the authorities began to issue JGB No.182 maturing in 2005. Initially, the issue size was relatively small with only a limited amount of stock in existence. However, as progressively more stock was issued, the depth of the market in the stock grew. This was coupled with the previous benchmark moving progressively towards maturity and away from the ten-year benchmark status.

Once an indeterminate point has been reached, the four largest securities houses will decide to shift the benchmark status to JGB No.182. The yield difference that can result from this focus may be as much as 20bp under equivalent stocks.

Whilst a form of repo market ('Gensaki') does exist, it is not as liquid or as important as it is in other markets.

All prices are clean and accrued interest is calculated on the actual/365 convention, counting from the last payment date to the day before settlement inclusive. Whilst JGBs do not trade ex-dividend as such, it is not possible to settle in the 14 days prior to coupon payment dates.

TSE transactions settle after three days with the OTC taking nine days or more, following a complicated settlement timetable. Settlement is conducted through book entry systems. Withholding tax is levied at 20%. Recently, in an attempt to encourage more external participation, withholding taxes for overseas owners have been removed.

6.5.4 Other markets in Japan

In Japan, there are a number of important issuers other than the government. In the form of 'quasi-government' there are the agencies and municipal stocks (11%). As with Germany, the banks are large borrowers (19%), using the funds raised in this way to lend to their customers. The declining quality of the Japanese banking sector has led to some change with regard to corporate issuance. The inability of banks to lend money has now prompted larger corporates to issue bonds.

As the market in JGBs has become more international, some of this interest has filtered through to the other more domestically orientated markets.

International borrowers are able to access the domestic pool of savings through the issue of Samurai (publicly issued yen bonds) and Shibosai (yen bonds issued via private placement). This is not an important part of the market, with much more being issued in the form of euro-yen (for much the same reasons as the decline of the UK bulldog market).

In addition, there are Daimyo bonds, domestic bonds with the ability to settle through the normal Eurobond channels which are in effect a cross between the Samurai and the euro-yen. Trading in all of these markets is meagre compared with the volume and liquidity of the JGB market.

6.6 Australian bond markets

During the 1990s, greater fiscal responsibility led to a move in Australian Government finances away from deficit and into surplus. This surplus combined with a programme of privatisations to reduce the debt burden considerably. This reduction of the overall level of Government debt raises the prospect of a similar shortage of stock to that experienced in the UK.

A Government bond market with poor levels of liquidity is not the best foundation on which to develop a strong and vibrant corporate bond market. With this in mind, the authorities committed themselves to a minimum level of debt. Consequently, the Australian Office of Financial Management (AOFM) embarked on a series of asset purchases to offset the surplus.

As with most markets except the US, the Australian market is dominated by the government/quasi-Government bonds.

Commonwealth Government Bonds (CGBs) are issued by the Government to finance the central government deficit. By convention, the issues are non-callable with bullet maturities. Since 1982, all issues have been in registered form. By convention the coupon frequency is semi-annual and accrues on an Actual/Actual basis.

In addition to the conventional bonds, there are **Treasury Indexed Bonds (TIBs)**. These are capital indexed bonds. In this case, only the capital balance is affected by the actual indexation process. The coupon is simply then calculated on the basis of the set rate as applied to the adjusted capital value. These bonds pay their coupon quarterly. As with most index-linked markets, the liquidity is relatively low.

Segmentation of the Australian Bond Market

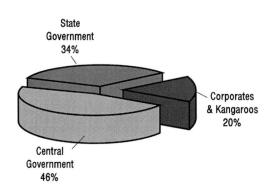

Source: Reserve Bank of Australia & Salomon Smith Barney

There are also **Treasury Adjustable Rate Bonds (TABs)**. These are floating-rate instruments and are issued normally with relatively short-dated maturities (three and five-year issues are conventional).

The debt is issued by way of **competitive tender** by periodic public auction. Whilst relatively frequent in the past, the number of these auctions is reducing due to the strength of the Government's fiscal position.

The **secondary market** is relatively unstructured with no formal market makers. Settlement is normally on a T + 3 basis. There is still a withholding tax of 10% applicable to overseas residents.

The Sydney Futures Exchange offers contracts into both three and ten-year CGBs. As in the UK, the introduction of a full repo market has diminished the level of activity in these contracts, which at one stage was greater than the cash market.

The **State Governments** are also significant borrowers in this market. The range of products that they use is very much the same as the Commonwealth Government, including the use of index-linked bonds. The States were the main instigators of the surge in asset-backed bonds in the 1980s as they used bonds to finance projects such as state housing schemes. Each state has its own Central Borrowing Authority or CBA. In addition to closed auctions (to a restricted panel of bidders), the debt is released by way of taps into the secondary markets and placements. The secondary market in these securities is relatively limited with only modest activity levels.

Thus far, the **corporate bond market** has remained relatively small in Australia. However, with the decline in the financing requirements of the Government there are signs of a resurgence in corporate bond issuance. In particular, there has been a buoyant market in asset-backed securities.

The Australian equivalent of Yankee bonds are called '**Kangaroos**'. These bonds are issued by non-Australian borrowers and are exclusively sold to Australian investors. **Matildas** are bonds issued by overseas borrowers into the Australian and international markets simultaneously – in essence, a global bond issue.

As a means of encouraging foreign ownership of corporate debt, the Australian Government removed a 10% withholding tax that previously applied. This more favourable tax treatment could further stimulate the market and thereby ease worries over the potential liquidity shortage.

7 EURO ZONE BOND MARKETS

7.1 Creation of the Euro zone

With effect from 1 January 1999, the separate bond markets of those nations participating in the first wave of European **Economic and Monetary Union (EMU)** effectively became one single **Euro Zone** market.

The Euro Zone market ranks as the third biggest market in the world.

Relative Shares of the Euroland Bond Market

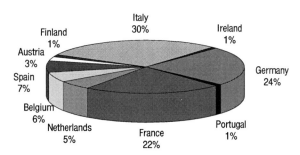

The immediate impact of **monetary union** was that debt previously denominated in individual currency units was redenominated into **euros**.

Initially, the markets have continued much as they had done before, although all of them share the same currency. Albeit this market will have a wider base given the creation of a pan-European pool of potential investors freed from the fears of currency risk.

Progressively, reforms will push the markets towards greater levels of harmonisation with regard to the structures of the individual markets. This has already begun with the move towards a consistent method for calculating accrued interest. All nations will move to the US T-bond convention of Actual/Actual. Some nations such as Belgium converted on day one, reconventioning their outstanding debt in much the same way as the UK did in 1998. Other nations such as Germany phased in the transition, converting existing debt on its next coupon payment date to the new convention.

Equally, many markets had hitherto established fixed block sizes in which to deal. The process of conversion into euro has required that those conventions be dropped and now all participating nations will reduce the minimum block size to one cent.

Other changes are likely to follow in the longer run, such as standardised issuance practices, coupon frequencies and common trading platforms.

7.2 The German bond market

The German bond market, including Government bonds, domestic bonds and Eurobonds, is the third largest in the world and one of the largest in Europe (the second largest after Italy), having tripled in size since 1985.

Unlike the UK, the Germans have a strong corporate debt market and a much weaker equity market. The bulk of finance for industry is provided through the banks, either as lenders or shareholders, with debt securities other than Eurobonds being less significant. Within the context of debt issuance, it is the banks that issue bonds and then lend on the money to the corporate sector.

Segmentation of the German Bond Market

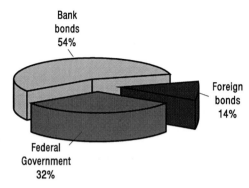

The key participant is the **Bundesbank**, the central bank of Germany. Unlike many other central banks, the Bundesbank (Buba) is totally outside political control. The role of Buba is to generate price and currency stability and the politicians have to operate within any constraints that this creates. The Bundesbank is obliged to support the overall direction of Federal Government policy to the extent that this does not conflict with price stability.

The German financial markets have undergone a process of liberalisation and modernisation. These have gradually removed the residual capital controls and allowed the development of a market in futures and options. In 1992, the final constraint on the EuroDM issues was removed when the German authorities no longer insisted that all bonds be listed on a German exchange. Since the adoption of the Euro, this growth has been strengthened by the emergence of the German bond market as the benchmark for Government bonds of the Eurozone.

Growth of public sector bonds was driven by the pressures of reunification, but also reflects a switch in the financing of Government. This occurred because in the past the German Government chose to finance a large proportion of its debt through the issue of loans referred to as **Schuldscheine**. These are simple promissory notes and used to form just under half of the outstanding debt of the public sector. In recent years, this has fallen from some 50% of debt to a current level of around 2½%.

The bulk of the banking sector bond issuance comes in the form of Pfandbriefe. These are effectively bonds collateralised against portfolios of loans. Offenliche Pfandbriefe are backed by loans to the public sector and Hypotheken Pfandbriefe are backed by mortgages. Traditionally, whilst being very secure, they have offered higher yields than bunds by virtue of their illiquidity. This is beginning to change.

7.2.1 Types of issue

There is a variety of types of issue.

- **Bunds (Bundesanleihen)**. These are the conventional bonds in the market, with normal maturities of ten years. Special bonds have been issued to fund the reunification process and are referred to as unity bonds. They are in all respects the same as bunds, as Bahns and Posts are the issues to fund the railways and the post office.

    At present, most Bunds pay annual coupons following the Euromarket conventions of 30-day months and a 360-day year. However, as of 1 January 1999, all new issues follow the Actual/Actual convention. In the course of 1999, all existing bonds converted to Actual/Actual on coupon dates. In 1993, the Bundesbank started to issue 30-year debt.

- **Bobls (Bundesobligationen)**. These are medium-term issues with lives of up to five years. Initially designed for the domestic market, they have been opened to foreign investment since 1989.

- **Bundesschatzanweisungen (Schatze) and Kassenobligationen**. A second type of medium-term finance, these were issued with maturities of between two and six years. Since May 1991, the maturity has been limited to four years. Both Schatz (which replaced the earlier Kassen) and Bobls are deliverable into the Euronext.liffe and Deutsche Terminborse (DTB) contracts. In common with the Bund, they pay annual coupons. These stocks are issued by way of tender on a regular basis.

- **BU-Bills**. In June 1996, Buba announced a change in the funding structure of the German market with the introduction of greater commitment to funding along the yield curve. There will now be regular auctions of these six-month bills (along with an enhanced cycle of two year Schatze). Both of these moves should strengthen the liquidity of the German market at the shorter end of the yield curve.

7.2.2 Issuance

Until May 1998, the primary market for Bunds had three elements. A tranche of each issue (20% to 30%) is retained by Buba and acts as their intervention funds. The remainder was split between a competitive auction and a 'konsortium' of banks. The consortium has now been dispensed with and issuance is through the auction. It is expected that the former consortium members will participate in the auction.

Buba undertakes to make a market in all Bunds. Initially, the objective was to place the bonds into the domestic market with private investors. With the large volume of issues over the last few years, the market has become increasingly internationalised. Approximately 30% of the market is currently held by overseas holders.

The primary market in Bobls is still restricted to domestic purchasers and takes the form of a **tap** directly into the secondary market. Once the stock has been listed, then the market is now (post-1989) open to all investors.

The domestic bank bonds are normally issued via placings. A substantial proportion of the market is comprised of Pfandbriefe (mortgage bonds) and Offentliche Pfandbriefe (municipal bonds). The yield spreads on these issues are more a reflection of the liquidity in the market than credit.

7.2.3 The secondary market

There are three main domestic routes for trading.

- The domestic stock exchanges (mainly Frankfurt)
- The over-the-counter market
- The domestic computerised market known as IBIS

The market is focused on those stocks that are deliverable into the futures contracts of Eurex (formerly the DTB). The importance of Euronext.liffe's Bund future contract has declined rapidly over the past 12 months.

In May 1997, the Bundesbank announced the introduction of a domestic strip facility with regard to the Bund market. In addition, the capital requirements with regard to the domestic repo market have been relaxed and wider participation is now likely.

Settlement date for domestic bond deals is three banking days after the day of dealing. This now matches to the Eurobond three-day settlement period, allowing Government or bank bonds held outside Germany to settle via Euroclear and Clearstream.

7.3 French bond market

The French bond market developed into one of the key international bond markets, mainly due to the economic transformation that took place since the introduction of the 'Franc fort' policy in 1985. The consequence of this strong commitment to inflation stability has been that the French economy and bond market have converged with the benchmark Germans.

In 1993, plans were announced to move towards a more independent central bank in line with the obligations of the Maastricht Treaty. This represents the continuation of the government's commitment to develop a transparent, liquid and technologically strong market. This commitment has made the French market the most efficient bond market within the first wave of EMU.

The development of MATIF (the French financial futures market, now part of Euronext) and the trading of the 'Notional' future into the French long bond were also a vital component in the reform of the market.

Segmentation of the French Bond Market

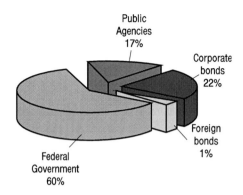

7.3.1 Types of issue

The French Government issues three types of bond, each with a different maturity.

■   **Bons du Trésor à Taux Fixe (BTFs)**. These are the French T-bills, issued at a discount to face value and with maturities of 13, 26 and 52 weeks.

■   **Bons du Trésor à Taux Fixe et Intéret Annuel (BTANs)**. These are fixed rate Treasury notes issued with maturities of between two and five years and an annual coupon. New issues are made on a six-monthly basis and, in between these new issues, existing issues are reopened on a monthly basis.

■   **Obligations Assimilables du Trésor (OATs)**. These are the conventional Government bonds that have become the key funding instruments used by the Government. They are issued with maturities of between seven and 30 years. Market activity tends to focus on the ten-year bond. Coupons are annual and based upon the Euromarket conventions. In common with BTANs, OATs are bullet issues. The yield convention in this market is Actual/Actual. Variable rate OATs are also available and these are linked to either long or short-term reference rates. Since the late 1990s the French have been issuing index-linked OATs, with a three-month delay in the indexation period.

All issues are now in book entry form with no physical delivery. The records are maintained either through RELIT, the domestic system, or Euroclear or Clearstream. Settlement is on a three-day basis.

7.3.2 Issuance

Debt is issued by way of monthly auctions to the public. There is, however, a syndicate of banks that the Government uses to underwrite issues in particular situations. Issuance takes place in accordance with a preset calendar.

■   **BTFs**. Auctioned on weekly basis. The issue is announced on Thursday and the auction takes place on Monday. All bids are on yield basis using a 30/360 basis.

■   **BTANs**. Auctions take place on the third working Thursday of the month. The stock to be offered is announced on the Monday preceding the issue. During a six-month period all issues are into the same two or five-year stock. These stocks are the benchmarks and attract the strongest liquidity. All bids are on a price basis (in basis points).

■   **OATs**. Auctions take place on the first Thursday of the month on much the same basis as BTANs. Settlement of the stock purchased in the auction takes place on the 25th of the month.

7.3.3 Trading

The market is focused around market makers who are obliged to make continuous two-way prices in all stock and participate in the auctions. Only the OATs are listed on the bourse. A substantial amount of trading takes place on the over-the-counter market. There are active repo and strips market in French Government debt. In addition, the French market has a liquid and efficient strips market.

Settlement is either cash or, for external holders of the bonds, follows the normal Euroclear and Clearstream timetable. Full facilities are available for investors to hold French Government debt through Clearstream and Euroclear. BTANs settle on the T + 1 basis for domestic holders.

7.3.4 Non-government bonds

As mentioned above, over half the market is made up of debt issues from the public corporations. These stocks are not, for the most part, guaranteed by the Government, but the corporations concerned do possess strong credit ratings. They have established their own market structure in order to facilitate trading in their stocks. All issues are by way of a placing through a syndicate of mainly local banks.

7.3.5 Taxation

There are no withholding taxes applicable to overseas investors for bonds purchased after 1987.

7.4 Italian bond market

Segmentation of the Italian Bond Market

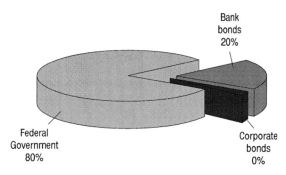

At the end of 1997, the Italian bond market was the fourth largest in the world. Of this total, 78% represented Government debt. Such a comparatively high level of debt has only been sustainable due to the high level of personal savings within the Italian economy. Household savings are funnelled into the Government debt market thanks to a series of favourable tax treatments of investments in these instruments. As a result, over 90% of the outstanding debt is held by Italian nationals.

Italian Government Bonds by Maturity

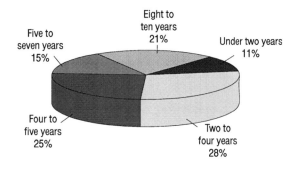

Historically, the bulk of funding has been drawn from the shorter maturity ranges in the market. This has been partly due to the high inflation risk within the economy and the consequent high long-term interest rates.

At the short end there are bills of exchange, **Buoni Ordinari del Tesoro (BOT)**, with maturities of three, six and twelve months.

Government bonds **(Buoni del Tesoro Poliennari (BTPs))** are most frequently issued into the five to seven-year maturity ranges, although some maturities of ten years have now been issued along with limited issuance at the 30-year mark.

The Government has also issued **Certificati di Credito del Tesoro (CCTs)**, which are in effect floating-rate notes. The coupon rate is established by adding a fixed margin to the BTP yield, as determined in the market. The normal maturity of these issues is between five and ten years.

Whilst the BTPs and CCTs are bullets, the Government has also issued Certificati del Tesoro con Opzione (CTOs), which are six-year bonds with an optional redemption after three years. The redemption is at par multiplied by the difference between 100 and the issue price.

In common with the UK, the Italian authorities have also issued index-linked CTRs. In 1995, the authorities commenced the issuance of zero-coupon bonds targeted primarily at the retail sector called **Certificati del Tesoro (CTZs)**.

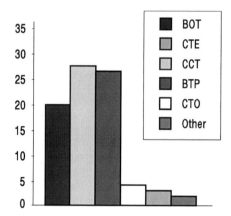

7.4.1 Issuance and trading

With such a volume of issuance to handle, it is important that the procedure is formalised into a set timetable. BOTs are auctioned twice monthly, at the middle and end of the month. The auction is run on a competitive basis, unlike the issue of BTEs, which is conducted through a Dutch auction.

The bonds are issued through monthly 'marginal' auctions that are in effect tenders.

Trading takes place through one of three markets. The Stock Exchange is by far the smallest of the three and lists the issues on call. In response to the inadequacy of the stock market, an OTC market was established using Reuters screens to display price information. This too has proved to be unsuccessful and now the market has switched to the Telematico market, where primary dealers focus the liquidity of the market. Maximum liquidity is generated in the new issues immediately post-issue.

Settlement takes place on the basis of three business days for domestically settled trades. Settlement takes place in book entry form through specified accounts held at the Bank of Italy. As with most European bond markets, settlement facilities are available through Euroclear and Clearstream on a T + 3 basis.

7.4.2 Withholding taxes

From 1997, withholding taxes on Italian Government bonds were removed.

7.4.3 Futures and options

There was for some time no official derivatives market in Italy – only an OTC market which offered a limited market place. Euronext offers a contract based upon the BTP. A more formalised local market in derivatives has commenced operation. The Mercato Italiano del Futures operates a screen-based system and offers a contract into the 12% notional ten-year BTP.

7.5 Netherlands bond market

Segmentation of the Dutch Bond Market

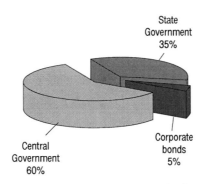

The Dutch Government bond market is the sixth largest amongst the Eurozone. The domestic market in bonds is dominated by the Government bond issues, which represent almost 70% of the total outstanding amount. Economically, the Dutch economy is very closely allied with Germany, operating a form of *de facto* monetary union.

Most state loans pay annual coupons, using the Eurobond convention of 30/360 (this was converted to Actual/Actual over the course of 1999). There is no withholding tax.

Maturity Profile of the Dutch State Loans

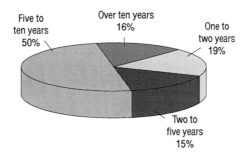

7.5.1 Trading and settlement

Dutch Government issues used to trade freely on both the Amsterdam Exchange (ASX) and the Amsterdam Interprofessional Market (AIM). Activity increasingly moved back to the Dutch markets following the liberalisation of the exchanges in the mid-1980s. However, the Dutch market was often regarded as insular and many overseas holders of the bonds preferred to trade in the London markets.

Today, after the formation of Euronext, and its 'take over' of the ASX, together with other reforms, the market has moved back to Amsterdam.

Although some cash bond trading is conducted through Euronext and cleared by LCH.Clearnet, the vast majority of the volume is executed on a very active regulated OTC market. Clearing and settlement is performed by Euroclear and the Dutch National Bank. The settlement convention is three business days with all stock being held in dematerialised form. Interest is paid on an annual basis on either the 1st or the 15th day of the month.

7.5.2 Primary markets

All new issues are in the form of bullets since 1986. Prior to that point, the Government used to issue bonds with sinking funds. In much the same way as the UK, the central bank uses a variety of issuance techniques to fund the borrowing requirement. This ranges from auctions and tenders to direct taps into the secondary market.

7.5.3 Quasi-government and corporates

Local Authorities are also substantial borrowers in the capital markets. In addition, the banks issue a variety of bonds into the debt market. These tend to dominate the non-Government bond market by virtue of their high credit rating. Whilst other corporates do issue bonds, they represent only a small proportion of the market.

7.5.4 Investor base

The institutional investors represent the most important element of the market. Pension fund portfolios normally contain a high proportion of fixed income securities (in the region of 70%), thereby creating an active and liquid secondary market.

7.5.5 Derivative products

The Euronext market operates a contract in the Government bond, using a notional 7% eight to ten-year bond.

7.6 Spanish bond markets

Segmentation of the Spanish Bond Markets

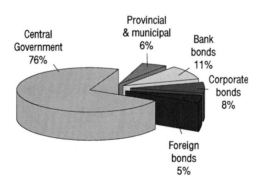

The development of the Spanish debt market began in the first half of the 1980s. The growing deficit and consequently larger outstanding debt volumes encouraged the Spanish Treasury and the Bank of Spain to set up an efficient, transparent and liquid secondary market for the management of its debt.

As Spain joined the EMU, the fiscal consideration process and debt management strategy implied a lower gross issuance but the activity on the secondary market kept on growing.

Given the important role of the public debt market and its special nature, the Spanish Government promoted its development via clear regulation, a high level of coordination among the different public entities involved and the following objectives.

- To satisfy government funding needs at the lowest possible long-term cost with acceptable risk
- To guarantee the integrity and efficiency of the primary and secondary government securities market
- To ensure its transparency and the protection of investors
- To promote the liquidity of the Spanish debt market

7.6.1 Government bonds

Over the past decade, the monetary authorities in Spain have been attempting to rationalise the financial management of the national debt, along with creating an open and liquid market in Government securities.

The Bank of Spain (BoS) has altered its approach to the market, shifting away from older, more unconventional forms of debt into securitised borrowing.

As in France, the debt has been formalised into set maturity bands to focus the liquidity of the market.

There are broadly types of instrument: short-term bills and longer term bonds.

- **Letras del Tesoro (Treasury bills)**. These form an important proportion of the Government's funding requirement. Whilst they are zero-coupon bonds issued at a discount to their face value with a maximum life of 18 months, to date they have only been issued with maturities of three and 12 months.

The longer term debt in the form of bonds is divided into two components.

- **Bonos del Estado (Bonos)**. These are bonds with lives of three to five years.

- **Obligaciones del Estado**. These are bonds with a maturity of ten years.

Both maturities are issued as bullets and are redeemable at par.

Spanish Government Bonds by Maturity

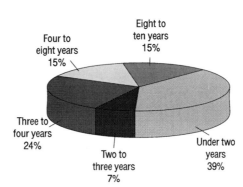

7.6.2 Issuance and trading

All bonds are now issued through monthly tenders. These issues take place on a set calendar announced at the start of the year. The coupon for the next three issues is announced prior to each auction. In line with most markets, issuance tends to focus on the reopening of existing bonds in order to deepen liquidity.

Bids are received and the issue amount is fixed, but not disclosed. Bids are then allocated on the basis from the highest price to the cut off or marginal price. Successful bids at above the average price pay the average price, whereas those who bid between the average price and the marginal price pay the price at which they bid.

If the bid has failed to meet the Treasury's funding target (a shortfall of more than 30% of the nominal value to be issued) they can then call a secondary phase, in which the primary dealers are obliged to submit bids for the remainder.

The secondary market functions around a market maker 'blind' (anonymous) system. There is a second level market that deals with smaller orders on a named basis.

7.6.3 Settlement

Settlement has been enhanced with the introduction of book entry settlement facilities at the BoS. In addition, Euroclear is also able to offer facilities for clearing and settling these transactions. It is the intention that this will move to a three-day basis which is the norm in the Euromarkets. Three-day settlement is available for those investors who hold their bonds in either Euroclear or Clearstream.

As a further inducement to enter the market, withholding taxes were removed in 1991.

Summary

	US T-Bond	German Bund	FrenchOAT	Italian BTP	UK Gilt	Japan (JGB)
Coupon frequency	Semi-annual	Annual	Annual	Semi-annual	Semi-annual	Semi-annual
Settlement	Same/next day	3 business days	3 business days	3 business days	Same/next day	3 business days
Registered or bearer?	R	R	R	R or B	R	R or B
Normal life	Life of over 10 years	Mostly 10 years	7 to 30 years	5 to 10 years	Varied	10 years, some 30 years
Quotation	1/32 converting to 1/100	1/100	1/100	1/100	1/100	1/100
Withholding tax	None	None	None	None	None	None
Medium-term debt	T-note life of 2 to 10 years	Bobls with lives of up to 5 years and Schatz with lives of 2 to 6 years	BTAN life of 2 to 5 years	CTOs with lives of up to 6 years	–	–
Settlement agencies	Federal Reserve	Euroclear, Clearstream	Relit, Euroclear France, Euroclear, Clearstream	Bank of Italy, Euroclear and Clearstream	CGO/Euroclear, Clearstream, RBNY	Tokyo Stock Exchange
Accrued interest convention	Actual / Actual	Actual / Actual	Actual / Actual	Actual / Actual	Actual / Actual	Actual / 365

CHAPTER ROUNDUP

- Bond is a general term for fixed interest securities which may be issued by governments, local authorities or companies.

- A bond may be sold 'cum dividend' or 'ex dividend'.

- The flat yield measures the 'coupon' (stated interest rate) as a percentage of the market price.

- The Gross Redemption Yield calculation uses discounted cash flow techniques to take account of gains or losses to redemption.

- The yield curve plots bond yields against their maturities.

- Characteristics of sources of finance, which will be specified in loan agreements, are: annual returns; capital repayment; security; influence; negotiability.

- Loan stock and debenture stock are secured or unsecured forms of borrowing by a company and usually carry a fixed coupon and redemption date.

- A sinking fund includes sums set aside from profits for future redemption of loan stock.

- Permanent Interest Bearing Shares are irredeemable fixed-interest securities issued by building societies.

- Convertible loan stock is fixed interest security carrying the right to convert into ordinary shares.

- There are various different types of risk associated with holding a bond: interest rate risk; credit (default) risk; inflation risk; liquidity / marketability risk; issue-specific risk; fiscal risk; currency risk.

- Bond credit ratings are assigned by Standard & Poor's, Moody's and Fitch.

- Bonds may be classified by the market into which they are issued or by their structure or financial composition.

- A typical domestic bond market includes: government sector; government agency sector; municipal sector; corporate sector.

- In the UK, domestic non-Government bonds have declined in importance as the Eurosterling market has expanded.

- As with UK domestic bonds, Eurobonds can have a variety of redemption terms.

TEST YOUR KNOWLEDGE

Check your knowledge of the Chapter here, without referring back to the text.

1   Distinguish between the 'clean price' and the 'dirty price' of a bond.

2   Fill in the blanks in the following with either 'cum-div' or 'ex-div', as appropriate.

A purchase made before the ex-dividend date is a .... bargain.

A purchase occurring after the ex-div date but before the coupon is paid is a .... bargain.

3   Which of the following *best* describes what is meant by a 'forward rate of interest'?

        A   A predicted spot rate of interest applying at a future date
        B   A rate of interest agreed now for a deposit or borrowing from one future date to another
        C   The current spot rate of interest adjusted for inflation to a future date
        D   A rate of interest fixed between now and a future date

4   Indicate which of the following values are represented by the terms A, B, C, D, E and F in the formula shown. A particular value may represent more than one of the terms.

        (a)   Market price
        (b)   Years to redemption
        (c)   Redemption price
        (d)   Annual coupon rate

Formula:

Japanese Gross Redemption Yield = $(A/B) + (((C - D)/E)/F)$

5   What is the highest credit rating given by (a) Standard & Poor's, (b) Moody's and (c) Fitch, respectively?

6   'Gilt' is a term commonly used to describe:

        A   Fixed interest securities in general
        B   Government bonds in general
        C   UK Government bonds in general
        D   UK Government bonds, except index-linked bonds

7   Official Debt Management Office definitions are as follows. *[Fill in the blanks.]*

Shorts: gilts with .... years or less to run
Mediums: gilts with between .... and .... years to run
Longs: gilts with over .... years to run

BPP)))
LEARNING MEDIA

3: INSTRUMENTS AND CHARACTERISTICS – FIXED INCOME

8   Which *one* of the following statements about company loan stock and ordinary (equity) shares is *incorrect*?

   A   Loans may be secured on company property while ordinary shares are never secured.

   B   Loan stock holders have a higher claim than equity shareholders in the event of winding-up of the company.

   C   Loan stock interest is payable even if there are no distributable profits in the year.

   D   Loan stock holders have stronger membership rights than equity shareholders.

TEST YOUR KNOWLEDGE: ANSWERS

1   Accrued daily interest is added at the time of the transaction to the 'clean price', to give the 'dirty price' that the buyer must pay. (See 1.4.1.)

2   A purchase made before the ex-dividend date is a cum-div bargain. A purchase occurring after the ex-div date but before the coupon is paid is an ex-div bargain. (See 1.4.2.)

3   A forward rate of interest is best described as a rate of interest agreed now for a deposit or borrowing from one future date to another. (See 1.7.)

4   The answers are as follows. (See 3.3.)

   A (d)
   B (a)
   C (c)
   D (a)
   E (b)
   F (a)

5   (a) AAA, (b) Aaa, (c) AAA. (See 4.4.)

6   The correct answer is C. (See 6.2.)

7   The definitions are as follows. (See 6.2.1)

   Shorts: gilts with 7 years or less to run
   Mediums: gilts with between 7 and 15 years to run
   Longs: gilts with over 15 years to run

8   The correct answer is D. Loan stock holders do not have membership rights. (See 2.8.)

4

Instruments and Characteristics
– Collective Investments

INTRODUCTION

'Funds' are vehicles for holding collective or 'pooled' investments, which enable the investor to hold, in a single product, a diversified holding in, for example, a market, a market sector or an index.

Unit trusts – which 'unitise' the value of underlying investments – have been well known on the UK investment scene for a long time. UK investment trusts, which also have a long history, are different in structure: they are public companies which make investments, and the investment trust's share price fluctuates according to demand and supply for their shares.

Open ended investment companies (OEICs) – also known as investment companies with variable capital (ICVCs) – are newer and have a type of structure which is more familiar to investors in Continental Europe. The index-tracking exchange-traded funds (ETFs) have risen to prominence even more recently.

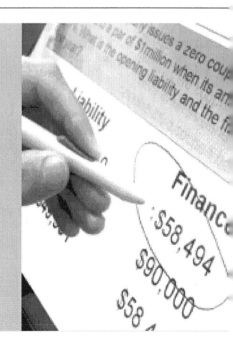

1 COLLECTIVE INVESTMENTS

1.1 Advantages and disadvantages of collective investments

A **collective** or **pooled** investment is a scheme by which the money of a large number of investors can be pooled to purchase shares or other securities. By participating in a collective investment, investors can participate in a pool of investments that would be more difficult to own directly as an individual. There are advantages and disadvantages of collective investment, as compared with direct investment.

Advantages of collective investments

- An individual can invest relatively small amounts, perhaps on a regular basis.

- The pooling of investments enables the fund to make purchases of securities at lower cost than would be possible for an individual.

- The time involved in directly managing one's own portfolio is saved.

- The funds are managed by professional fund managers. A fund manager with a good past performance record may be able to repeat the performance in the future.

- A wide diversification between different shares and sectors can be achieved: this can be impractical and costly in dealing charges for a small portfolio held by an individual.

- Risk is reduced by exposure to a widely diversified spread of investments in the underlying portfolio.

- Specialisation in particular sectors is possible.

- The investor can gain exposure to foreign stocks, which can be costly and inconvenient for an individual who holds shares directly.

- Different funds provide for different investment objectives, such as income or growth, or a combination of both.

Disadvantages of collective investments

- The individual can only choose baskets of investments selected by fund managers, not by himself, and this will not suit all investors.

- Although the investor does not have to pick individual securities, he still has to choose the fund manager, and different managers' performance can vary widely.

- Although 'star' fund managers can have a successful track record with a fund, such 'star' managers may switch jobs, making future management of the fund less certain.

- Larger collective funds find it more difficult to invest in shares of companies with a relatively small capitalisation, because of the small quantities of stock available.

- Successful collective funds investing in smaller companies can become a victim of their own success if more funds are brought in, as a greater fund size can make it more difficult for such a fund to follow their successful strategy.

1.2 Types of collective investment

The following are types of **collective investment:**

- Unit trusts
- Open Ended Investment Companies (OEICs)
- Investment trusts, including split capital investment trusts

Unit trusts and OEICs are often referred to using the general term '**funds**'. An OEIC is alternatively called an **Investment Company with Variable Capital (ICVCs)**.

1.3 Open-ended and closed-ended funds

Unit trusts and OEICs are **open-ended** funds. This means that the trust can create new units when new investors subscribe and it can cancel units when investors cash in their holdings.

This makes unit trusts and OEICs different from **investment trusts**, which are **closed-ended**: new investors buy investment trust shares from existing holders of the shares who wish to sell.

Open-ended funds	Closed-ended funds
• The price closely reflects the underlying net asset value (NAV) of the investment.	• The investments must be purchased from another investor. The price is subject to supply and demand and may not reflect the underlying value (NAV). High demand increases the price; low demand reduces the price. • Where the price is greater than the underlying value of the investment, it is said to be at a 'premium' to NAV, where it is below it is at a 'discount' to NAV.
• New investors can bring in new money, allowing the fund managers to invest in new opportunities.	• There is no new money coming in: fund managers must sell assets in order to make investments.
• When investors sell, assets must be sold to release cash to pay them possibly disrupting set policies and strategies.	• When investors sell, there is no need to sell assets as the total amount of money invested remains; the same set policies and strategies can be maintained.
• Unit trusts, OEICs and life assurance investments are open-ended, as are many offshore investment funds.	• Investment trusts and some offshore funds are closed-ended.

1.4 Limited issue funds

Under FSA rule changes introduced in 2001, unit trusts and OEICs are allowed to cap the number of units in issue. The introduction of such **limited issue funds** is intended to allow funds to be managed more efficiently, particularly in less liquid markets such as **smaller companies** and some **emerging markets**. The limited issue funds rules also help funds to structure products that offer some form of downside protection.

1.5 Structured investment funds

Structured products are available that link repayment of capital to the investor by a pre-determined formula to the performance on an index such as the FTSE 100 Index (most commonly), or to other factors or combinations of factors. Such structured funds may be located **offshore** (i.e. outside the UK mainland).

Some funds make use of derivatives in order to make a guarantee of a return of capital to the investor (which might be in the range 85% to 100% of the original investment, for example). A **fixed period** often applies to the investment. Returns may be specified in a proportion of the rise of an index. Many share price indices, including the normally quoted version of the FTSE 100 Index, do not reflect dividends paid out by companies. In making comparisons of the investment performance of structured products based on an index, this should be taken into account.

1.6 ISA and PEP wrappers

Fund managers and investment trust managers generally offer the facility for investment to be made through:

- The stocks and shares component of an Individual Savings Account (**ISA**), or

- An existing Personal Equity Plan (**PEP**) that can be transferred to the investment trust manager's scheme

The manager may make an additional flat rate or percentage charge for providing the ISA wrapper.

All **HMRC (s842) approved investment trusts** can now be held in an ISA or PEP.

Particularly after the removal of the **repayment of dividend tax credits** in ISAs with effect from 6 April 2004, the main appeal of ISA and PEP wrappers for investment trusts (and other equity investments) is to:

- Those who have a liability to pay **capital gains tax** because they have gains in excess of the annual allowance of **£9,200 (2007/08)**, and

- **Higher rate taxpayers**, who have to pay further tax on dividends they receive outside a tax-advantaged wrapper.

From **6 April 2008**, all **existing PEPs** become stocks and shares ISAs.

2 FUND TYPES

2.1 IMA categories

The **Investment Management Association (IMA)** publishes sector definitions to classify funds – i.e. unit trusts and OEICs. The groups correspond to different investment objectives.

- Some **income funds** principally target **immediate income**, while others aim to achieve **growing income**.

- **Growth funds** which mainly target **capital growth or total return** are distinguished from those that are designed for **capital protection**.

- **Specialist funds** form a fifth category.

Within the specified IMA categories of funds shown in the Table below are the following types of fund for which there is not a separate classification:

- **Index-tracking funds**, which mechanically 'shadow' a particular share index such as the FTSE 100 Index rather than being actively managed by fund managers (see below)

- **Ethical funds**, which fall mainly within the UK All Companies and Global Specialist sectors. (Ethical investing is discussed in a later chapter.)

As well as unit trusts and OEICs providing exposure to **equity** markets, there are the following types of fund available as well.

- **Bonds funds**, investing in fixed interest securities including government bonds, corporate bonds and convertibles.

- **Cash funds**, which enable the investor to have the advantage of wholesale rates on cash deposits. An investor might use a cash fund to hold money before it is switched into other funds.

Funds may be **UCITS schemes**, meaning that they conform to the European UCITS Directive and can be marketed throughout the European Economic Area (EEA).

UK fund classifications

Income funds		Growth funds		Specialist funds
Immediate income	Growing income	Capital protection	Capital growth/total return	
UK Gilts UK Index Linked Gilts UK Corporate Bond UK Other Bond Global Bonds UK Equity & Bond Income	UK Equity Income	Money Market Protected/Guaranteed Funds	UK All Companies UK Smaller Companies Japan Japanese Smaller Companies Asia Pacific including Japan Asia Pacific excluding Japan North America North American Smaller Companies Europe including UK Europe excluding UK European Smaller Companies Cautious Managed Balanced Managed Active Managed Global Growth Global Emerging Markets UK Zeros	Specialist Technology & Telecomm-unications Personal Pensions

2.2 Tracker funds

An **index tracker fund** is based on a simple concept. The tracker fund aims to match the performance of a particular index, such as the FTSE 100 Share Index, thus giving the investor an opportunity to benefit from positive movements in the overall market.

Tracking involves investing in the shares that make up the index, in the proportions in which those shares make up the index. Investors should note however that some quoted indices, such as the FTSE 100 Index are **price indices** rather than **total return indices**. A price index ignores dividends paid, while a total return index includes reinvested income (dividends). Data is often available on both bases for a particular index.

A tracker will not be able to match the total return from a **total return index** consistently, because of:

- Variations arising from **tracking errors** (see below)

- **Transaction costs** arising from buying and selling the shares held in the fund (spread and dealing commission)

- **Charges** levied by the manager of the tracker, to cover the manager's costs and profit

Management costs for tracker funds should be relatively low. The fund only requires **passive management** because there is no need for research to be undertaken as with an **actively managed** fund.

The **active** fund manager will analyse the investments and sectors in which a fund invests, and will base decisions about whether to buy or sell on this analysis. With **passive** index-tracking fund management, the criterion for inclusion of a particular stock in the fund portfolio is simply that a share forms part of the index.

Tracker funds can occur in various forms, including unit trusts, OEICs/ICVCs, investment trusts and exchange traded funds (ETFs).

2.3 Tracking methods

There are different ways in which a tracker fund can operate.

- **Full replication** is an approach whereby the fund attempts to mirror the index by holding shares in exactly the same proportions as in the index itself.

- **Stratified sampling** involves choosing investments that are representative of the index. For example, if a sector makes up 16% of the index, then 16% of shares in that sector will be held, even though the proportions of individual companies in the index may not be matched. The expectation is that with stratified sampling, overall the '**tracking error**' or departure from the index will be relatively low. The amount of trading of shares required should be lower than for full replication, since the fund will not need to track every change in capitalisation of a share. This should reduce transaction costs and therefore will help to avoid such costs eroding overall performance.

- **Optimisation** is a computer-based modelling technique which aims to approximate to the index through a complex statistical analysis based on past performance.

2.4 'Guaranteed' funds

Before 2001 rule changes, the word 'guaranteed' or other terms implying a degree of capital security were not allowed to be used in fund names. Now, funds are permitted to label themselves as 'guaranteed' if there is a separate full money back guarantee. Details of any guarantee must be disclosed in 'consumer facing material'.

2.5 Multi-manager schemes

Multi-manager schemes are increasingly popular and are now offered by most fund management groups. These schemes can give clients access to the investment management expertise of a number of investment houses within the framework of a single unit-linked life assurance or pension investment. The schemes often allow switches at low cost between funds, giving access to hundreds of different fund, sector and management options.

The switching feature of multi-manager arrangements is an advantage to the investor who is concerned about under-performance, since he or she can easily and cheaply switch to another manager. An investor may also want to switch easily between funds if his or her risk profile has changed. This type of flexibility is not available where a life office offers only its own funds, and can be a useful marketing tool.

2.6 Funds of funds

With **funds of funds**, a number of funds are packaged together within an overall '**umbrella' fund**. These may operate in two ways.

- A number of sub-funds (e.g. for equities, bonds or specific currencies) in which investors can spread their investments may be set up within the structure of the fund itself.

- Alternatively, the fund may offer a 'menu' of third party funds from which investors can make a selection. This can give investors pooled access to funds to which they would not be able to access individually.

A fund of funds is said to be '**fettered**' if it only invests in the funds of a particular management group. A fettered fund of funds might apply no annual charge on top of the fees charged for the underlying fund.

2.7 Manager of managers schemes

With a **manager of manager fund**, instead of choosing funds run by other fund managers as part of their collective fund, the fund manager passes sums of money to other managers directly to manage for them. These other managers are given strict investment objectives and can be replaced if they do not achieve them. These schemes still represent a two-tier management system and are therefore costly.

Funds of funds structures shelter investments from **capital gains tax**, since a switch between funds does not crystallise a capital gains tax liability. Capital gains tax taper relief will continue to accrue.

3 FSA REGULATIONS FOR FUNDS

Introduction

FSA regulations covering authorised unit trusts (AUTs) and OEICs/ICVCs are contained in the **Collective Investment Schemes Sourcebook** named '**COLL**', which came fully into effect on **13 February 2007**.

3.1 COLL Sourcebook

The Collective Investment Schemes Sourcebook (**COLL**) applies to ICVCs (ie, OEICs) and authorised unit trusts. COLL provides a regime for product regulation, with the objective of protecting the consumer, and also implements requirements of the UCITS Directive.

3.1.1 Types of scheme

COLL is designed as a two-tier approach, comprising:

- **Retail schemes**, which are promoted to the general public, and
- **Qualified investor schemes** (QIS), for institutions and expert private investors

Retail schemes are either **UCITS retail schemes** or **non-UCITS retail schemes**. However, there have been relatively few applications to set up non-UCITS retail schemes.

With **QIS**, fewer consumer protection rules apply than for retail schemes. QIS can invest in a very wide range of assets, with no significant limitation on the spread between buying and selling prices other than whatever is stated in the scheme documentation.

With regard to **gearing**, QIS are permitted to **borrow** up to 100% of the net asset value of the fund. QIS are also permitted to hold 'short' positions profiting from falls in prices and can charge performance fees. These possibilities make QIS very similar to **hedge funds**, which we discuss later in this Chapter.

3.1.2 Rules and limits

The scheme property of a **UCITS scheme** must normally consist only of any or all of:

- Transferable securities (which includes shares, debentures, government or public securities and warrants)

- Units in permitted collective investment schemes

- Approved money-market instruments

- Permitted derivatives and forward transactions

- Deposits

For an OEIC/ICVC, the scheme property may also include movable and immovable property that is necessary for the direct pursuit of the company's business.

For an authorised fund investing more than 35% in **government or public securities**, the following restrictions apply.

- A maximum of 30% of the fund may be in any one issue (e.g. of a gilt)
- The fund must hold at least six different issues

A retail UCITS scheme is very similar to existing UCITS schemes, with the following limits (based on percentage of the scheme's value) applying:

- 20% limit (of fund value) on investment in other collective investment schemes
- 10% limit (of fund value) on investment in unapproved (unlisted) securities
- Schemes cannot hold more than 25% of the units in a particular collective investment scheme

For UCITS and non-UCITS funds replicating ('tracking') an index, the **concentration** limit is raised under COLL rules to permit a holding of 20% in a particular share, and up to 35%, but only for one share and only in exceptional market conditions.

Under COLL rules, both UCITS and non-UCITS retail schemes can invest in a variety of types of instrument, including **warrants and derivatives**, within their overall investment objectives, provided that they apply a **risk management procedure**.

A **non-UCITS** retail scheme can invest in an even wider range of assets, including gold or 100% investment in immovable **property**.

Non-UCITS schemes may also **borrow** up to 10% of the fund value on a **permanent** basis, while UCITS retail schemes are only permitted to borrow on a **temporary** basis, again to 10% of the fund value.

Under COLL, there are the following investment limits for non-UCITS retail schemes.

- 35% limit for investing in other collective investment schemes

- If a scheme does invest in a second scheme, that second scheme must not itself have more than 15% of its value invested in other collective investment schemes

- 20% limit on aggregate investment in unapproved securities and unregulated schemes

Redemptions in non-UCITS retail schemes and QISs may be:

- Limited for up to six months in the case of property funds and in schemes offering a guaranteed return

- Deferred to the next valuation point if redemptions exceed 10% of the value of the fund, with proper disclosure to investors

COLL permits the **creation of units** on a **forward pricing basis** to take place up to **24 hours** after the relevant valuation point (previously, two hours).

COLL also allows fund managers to charge **performance-based fees**, either at fixed fee rates or based on the value of the fund.

Overall, the new COLL arrangements are designed to allow flexibility in product design by scheme providers, coupled with the retention of consumer protection based on the needs of different classes of investor.

3.2 Pricing of funds

The **COLL** pricing rules are intended to ensure that fund managers pay due regard to clients' interests and treat them fairly, in accordance with FSA *Principle for Businesses 6*.

To determine the price of units, the authorised fund manager must carry out a fair and accurate **valuation** of all the scheme property, which will include investments, cash held and income receivable, in accordance with the instrument constituting the scheme and the prospectus.

For each class of units in a **single-priced** authorised fund, a single price must be calculated at which units are to be issued and cancelled.

For a **dual-priced** authorised fund, each valuation of the scheme property must consist of two parts, carried out on an **issue basis** and a **cancellation basis** respectively.

3.2.1 Valuation points

The calculation of **buying** and **selling prices** will take place at the **valuation point**, which is typically at a particular time each day. The valuation point must be shown in the fund literature. A company can choose any time but most use mid-day.

Under COLL, an authorised fund must normally not have fewer than two regular **valuation points** in any month and if there are only two valuation points in any month, the regular valuation points must be at least two weeks apart. The buyer of units will not know how much he will pay until the next valuation point.

Schemes with special limited redemption arrangements (allowing redemptions less than twice monthly), the valuation points must be stated in the prospectus but must not be set more than six months apart.

Funds designated as **higher volatility funds** must have at least one valuation point every business day.

The authorised fund manager may determine to have an additional valuation point for an authorised fund as a result of market movement under **forward and historic pricing** (discussed later below).

3.2.2 Sale and redemption prices

The authorised fund manager of an authorised fund must not:

■ **Sell** a unit for more than the price of a unit of the relevant class at the valuation point, to which may be added any initial charge permitted (in the case of single-price funds) plus any provision for stamp duty reserve tax allowed for in the prospectus, and any dilution adjustment. (A **dilution levy** may be made to reflect additional dealing costs resulting from the issue and cancellation of units.)

■ **Redeem** a unit for less than the price of a unit of the relevant class at the relevant valuation point, less any redemption charge permitted and any deductions relating to an SDRT provision or dilution.

3.3 Prospectus and periodic reports

In addition to a **full prospectus**, the fund management company must publish a **simplified prospectus**. This, subject to some exceptions, must be provided to the customer before he completes the application for the scheme.

Reports and accounts must be prepared on a **half-yearly** and **annual** basis and the latest report must be supplied to investors free of charge on request.

3.4 Late trading and market timing

The FSA has investigated **stale price market timing.** This is a practice of trading in a fund which is valued by reference to out-of-date (stale) prices, e.g. a fund invested in US assets which has a valuation point of 12 noon will need to use the previous night's US closing prices. Publicly available information gives investors an indication of the direction and size of potential market movements when a market re-opens. A customer seeking to take advantage of a stale price effect is not in breach of FSA rules, however this activity operates to the detriment of long term holders who lose out as a result of the dilution of the fund. Hence the need for fund managers to manage conflicts of interest fairly, both between itself and its customers and between a customer and another client.

Late trading requires cooperation between a fund manager and its customer. The FSA has noted that this is the **wholly illegal** practice of permitting a customer to enter an order or withdraw an existing order in a collective investment scheme after a fund's valuation point, other than on justifiable administrative grounds. The counterparty would explicitly be provided with the ability to undertake trades at advantageous times and hence prices in a way which allows them to profit to the clear detriment of long term investors.

The FSA's 2004 investigation into market timing found no evidence of illegal late trading but did find some evidence of market timing in UK authorised collective investment schemes. The FSA took the view that market timing did not appear to have been a major source of detriment to long term investors.

The relationships between the UK fund managers concerned and the market timing clients appeared to be of a different nature to those uncovered in the US, where there had been evidence of significant financial benefit to fund managers as a result of their relationships. In the UK, deals are placed directly with the fund manager before valuation points, and an important control function is provided by the trustee in UK funds.

The FSA believes that its Principles and Rules provide sufficient tools to enable firms to manage the conflicts of interests posed by market timers. Among these tools are the ability to price underlying assets at a fair value and the ability to refuse to sell units to suspected market timers, as well as a number of measures to reduce dilution and to otherwise increase the cost (and so decrease the attractiveness) of market timing activity.

4 UNIT TRUSTS

4.1 Characteristics of unit trusts

A **unit trust** is a professionally managed **collective investment** fund.

- Investors can buy **units**, each of which represents a specified fraction of the trust.
- The trust holds a **portfolio** of securities.
- The assets of the trust are held by **trustees** and are invested by **managers**.
- The investor incurs **annual management charges** and possibly also an **initial charge**.

An authorised unit trust (AUT) must be constituted by a **trust deed** made between the manager and the trustee. Unit trusts have been available in the UK since the 1930s. Taking unit trusts together with **Open Ended Investment Companies (OEICs),** funds under management now exceed £200 billion.

The basic principle with AUTs is that there is a single type of undivided unit. This is modified where there are both **income units** (paying a distribution to unitholders) and **accumulation units** (rolling up income into the capital value of the units).

If the fund manager wishes to **market** the unit trust in **other Member States of the EU**, he may apply for certification under **UCITS** (Undertakings for Collective Investment in Transferable Securities).

4.2 The role of the trustee

Trustees of a unit trust must be FSA-authorised and **fully independent** of the trust manager. Trustees are required to have **capital** in excess of £4 million and, for this reason, will normally be a **large financial institution** such as a bank or insurance company. The primary duty of the trustees is to protect the interests of the unit holders.

The trustees must:

- Establish and maintain a **register** of unit holders listing their names and addresses and details of the numbers and types of units held

- Ensure that the manager is **acting in accordance** with the trust deed

- Ensure the manager is **not in breach** of rules set out by their regulators

- **Hold the investments** underlying the unit trust including any cash and income from investments (all purchases will be in the name of the trustees)

- **Replace the manager** if they believe that he is not acting in the investor's best interest, or if required to do so because of the manager not being able to continue (for example, by insolvency)

- Carry out the **proposals of a vote** by the majority of the unit holders (for example, to remove the fund manager)

It is part of the trustee's duty to ensure that at no time are there **certificates** in issue for more units than those for which he holds assets in the fund. So, when units are created, the trustee issues no certificates until he has received the money for the creation from the manager. When units are liquidated he does not pay the managers until endorsed certificates are lodged with him. When units are bought and resold by the manager, the trustee does not issue certificates to the new holders until he has endorsed certificates from other holders to an equivalent number of units. This protects the investor against the possibility of fraud by the manager when dealing in their units with the public. At any time, the number of units issued may be less than the number for which the trustee holds assets.

The **investor** in a unit trust owns the underlying value of shares based on the proportion of the units held. He is effectively the beneficiary of the trust.

The **trust deed** of each unit trust must clearly state its **investment objectives**, so that investors can determine the suitability of each trust. The limits and allowable investment areas for a unit trust fund are also laid out in the trust deed together with the investment objectives.

4.3 The role of the manager

The manager must also be **authorised** by the FSA and his role covers:

- **Marketing** the unit trust
- **Managing** the assets in accordance with the trust deed
- **Maintaining** a record of units for inspection by the trustees
- **Supplying** other information relating to the investments under the unit trust as requested
- **Informing** the FSA of any breaches of regulations while it is running the trust

Fund managers can perform these tasks themselves, or may **subcontract** them to a third party.

4.4 Buying and selling units

Unit trust **units** can be purchased in a number of ways: for example, via an intermediary, 'off the page' with a newspaper advertisement, over the phone or over the internet. These methods will generally require **payment with the order**, or some form of **guarantee of payment**. A **contract note** will be produced and sent to the investor as **evidence of the purchase**.

Investors can sell their units through the same source that they purchased them, or can contact the fund managers direct, for example by telephone. A **contract note** will be produced the next day. Where a **certificate** was issued, the investor will need to 'renounce' the units by signing the renunciation form on the back. The renunciation form will ask for details as to the number of units the investor wishes to sell, if he is not disposing of the whole holding. Payments should be issued within five business days and will be sent together with a balance certificate for any remaining units held.

4.5 Unit trust pricing

The **buying price** is the price that an investor will have to pay to buy units and the **selling price** is the price he will receive on selling.

Some fund managers use **single pricing**, in which case there is the same price quoted for buying and selling units, with any charges being separately disclosed.

4.6 The manager's box

Trust managers may keep units **repurchased** from unit holders to enable them to supply units to purchasers without creating new units. This will **increase liquidity** in the investment and will help the manager avoid having to create and cancel shares every day. It also saves considerable money on the **acquisition** and **disposal costs** of the underlying assets, as units are **recycled** rather than being created and destroyed. The trust manager can use this to make profits on the units sold **via the box**. In the right circumstances, the manager can effectively keep the **full spread**, representing a useful additional income stream that is not visible as a charge to the customer.

Once very significant in unit trusts, holding a large box is now not so common because of regulations introduced to reduce the scope of this practice.

4.7 Historic pricing and forward pricing

Prices can be set on a **historic** or **forward pricing** basis.

- Where the price the investor pays is based on the **previous valuation point**, the pricing is described as **historic**. All units purchased up to the valuation point on the following day will be at the same, previous price.

- Where the investor pays a price based on the **next valuation point**, it is called **forward pricing**. All units purchased up to next valuation point will be at that price.

With **historic pricing** the investor knows the price he will pay for units, but the value of the underlying securities may not be reflected in the price paid. This is good if prices have moved up, but bad if they have moved down. Investors find future pricing confusing, as it is not possible to determine in advance the price they will pay, but the price will be **more reflective** of the **underlying value** of the securities.

On an **historic pricing** basis, the manager creates units at the valuation point according to the amount of sales expected up to the next valuation point. If sales exceed expected levels, the manager must either move to forward pricing or risk loss of money for the fund if there is an unfavourable price movement.

On a **forward pricing** basis, the manager must create units at the valuation point sufficient to cover transactions since the last valuation point.

Under **COLL**, the manager must create units within **24 hours** of the valuation point, as noted earlier.

A manager using the historic pricing basis must move to a forward pricing basis if the value of the fund is believed to have changed by **2% or more** since the last valuation and if the investor requests forward pricing.

4.8 Charges

The **charges** on a unit trust must be explicit in the trust deed and documentation. They should give details of the current charges and the extent to which managers can change them.

Charges need to cover the following **costs.**

- Managing the fund
- Administration of the fund
- Marketing
- Regulation and compliance costs

- General administration
- Direct marketing costs
- Commissions for intermediaries

These charges can be taken in one or more of three ways, via an **initial charge**, an **exit charge** or through **annual management charges**.

4.8.1 Initial charges

The **initial charge** is added to the **buying price**. So, the buyer suffers both the bid/offer spread, and the initial charge. Managers might charge 3.0-6.5% on **equities**, and less on **fixed interest funds** (1-4%). Other funds with lower charges include **index tracker funds** and **cash/money market funds**, where the lower price reflects the lower burden of management. Where an initial charge is small or non-existent, there may be a further charge on exit.

Fund managers may offer discounts on the usual initial charge, particularly for direct sales or sales through '**fund supermarkets**'.

4.8.2 Exit charges

As an alternative to initial charges, a few trusts apply **exit charges**. These charges are typically invoked where the investor sells the investment within a set period of time, e.g. five years.

The **exit charge** levied will typically be on a **sliding scale**, for example varying from 5% if the investment is encashed in the first year and reducing by 1% for each subsequent year. After the fifth year, the exit charge will be zero, but the annual management charge will have been higher and the managers will have covered the cost of the initial charge. If the investment continues, they will still be getting their management charge at a higher rate.

4.8.3 Annual charges

An **annual charge** of around 0.5–1.5% of the underlying fund will generally be made to cover the ongoing cost of the investment management of the trust. In some cases part of the annual management charge is paid to intermediaries as **renewal commission**, typically at a rate of 0.5% per annum. The cost will vary with the level of management required on a fund. **Offshore funds** require more management and costs are likely to be **higher**. **Tracker funds** require less management and costs will be **lower**. Some funds will have several tiers of management and will allow access to a wide range of investment managers via a single management company. In this case, each tier of management will need to recoup its costs and, in these cases, annual management costs will be higher.

Management charges can be taken from income or capital, but historically has been taken from income. The main reason for this is that the charges could be offset against taxable income.

As noted earlier, **COLL** permits **performance-related charges**. These may be based on growth of the fund, or out-performance of the fund's standard benchmark. The basis of the charges must be disclosed in the fund prospectus and key features document.

4.9 Share exchange

Some fund groups offer the facility to use **existing shares** to fully or partly invest into unit trusts or OEICs. The fund manager can do this by **purchasing** the shares from the **investor** for inclusion into one or more of his own funds or sale if they are not required. In these circumstances, they will normally buy the shares at the **purchase price** rather than the **sale price**, giving the investor a **better return**. Alternatively, the manager can purchase the shares from the investor and sell them via their own dealer, usually with **less commission** being charged.

4.10 Taxation of unit trusts

Authorised unit trusts are **exempt from tax on gains** made within the fund, giving them an advantage, for instance, over life funds.

For a trust that has less than 60% of its funds in interest bearing securities, any income (other than dividend income from UK companies, which is not taxable) is taxed to corporation tax at **20%**. Foreign withholding tax on dividends will be offset against the tax charge, subject to double taxation treaties.

Management expenses can be offset against income from **non-UK equities.**

Unit trusts do not pay tax on gains from options or futures.

Since 1 April 2006, **Qualified Investor Scheme (QIS)** investors are made subject to a special annual income tax charge on movements in the capital value of their holding if they own more than 10% of the value of a QIS fund. This measure is intended to prevent QIS investors from taking advantage of a tax treatment intended for pooled investors, whilst possibly retaining some of the control that is a feature of direct investment.

The tax treatment of fund **distributions** parallels the tax treatment of direct holdings of equities and interest.

Under the 'bond fund test', if the trust holds 60% or more of its investments in **interest bearing securities**, the income is deemed to be interest and the distribution is made net of 20% tax, which can be reclaimed by non-taxpayers. 10% taxpayers can reclaim 10%, while basic rate taxpayers have no further liability. Higher rate taxpayers (and discretionary trusts) must pay additional tax at 20% of the gross amount.

For **equity unit trusts**, the distribution is made with a 10% tax credit, whether to **individuals** or **trustee** investors.

The tax treatment for different types of **individual taxpayer** is then as for dividends from shares held directly. The tax credit cannot be reclaimed by non-taxpayers. The tax credit satisfies the tax liability for a basic or lower (10%) rate taxpayer, but higher rate taxpayers (and discretionary trusts) will be liable to an additional 22.5% on the grossed-up figure. Non-taxpayers cannot reclaim the tax credit.

From **6 April 2007**, funds were able to pay interest distributions **gross** (ie, without deduction of tax) to **non-taxpayers** and those whose income falls below their personal allowance and other reliefs, in the same way as banks and building societies can pay interest gross, saving such investors the need to reclaim the tax deducted.

The investor is liable to **capital gains tax** on disposals of unit trust investments.

There is **no stamp duty** or **stamp duty reserve tax (SDRT)** to pay on purchases of UK unit trusts, but prices reflect the stamp duty/SDRT payable to purchase the underlying portfolio.

4.11 Unauthorised unit trusts

In order to be **marketed** to the public, a **unit trust** must be authorised by the FSA. This has a direct impact on the taxation of the fund, in that authorisation is a requirement for the trust to be treated as **exempt** from **capital gains tax**. **Unauthorised unit trusts** are used for specific applications such as **Enterprise Zone property** holdings, where they are not marketed directly to the public, and are subject to income tax and CGT within the fund. Investors are liable to any additional income tax and CGT on disposal. There is a further **exempt** type of **unauthorised unit trust** that may be used as investments for pensions and registered charities. **Exempt unit trusts** are free of CGT on disposals within the fund and are subject to income tax rather than corporation tax.

4.12 Income equalisation payments

Between distributions of income from a unit trust (or an OEIC – covered below), the unit price includes the value of any income received by its underlying assets since the previous distribution. On the first distribution of income after the purchase of units, the trust will pay out to the new unit holder the income which has accrued between the date of purchase of the units and the distribution date. In addition as the unit holder has paid for income accrued before he purchased the units this amount will be refunded to him as a capital payment. The total amount received by the unit holder should therefore be the same as the full dividend received by the original unit holders. The refund of capital, known as **income equalisation**, is not part of taxable income but should be deducted from the base cost for capital gains tax purposes.

The equalisation payment is treated as a **discount** on the **purchase price** of the units. This discount **reduces** the **acquisition cost** and effectively **increases** any **capital gains** that could result on disposal, potentially giving rise to a higher CGT charge.

5   OEICs

5.1 The OEIC framework

Open Ended Investment Companies (OEICs) are managed, pooled investment vehicles in the form of companies. They invest in securities with the objective of producing a profit for investors. Unlike unit trusts, the OEIC structure is recognised throughout Europe. The possible prospect of UK participation in economic and monetary union (EMU) and the single European Market helped to drive the UK to adopt this form of pooled investment, in addition to the unit trust. Regulations made under the European Communities Act brought OEICs into existence in the UK in 1997.

These Regulations provided for the incorporation in the UK of OEICs that fall within the scope of the **UCITS (Undertaking for Collective Investment in Transferable Securities)** Directive. This means they can invest only in **transferable securities** (for example, listed securities, other collective investment schemes, certificates of deposit). UCITS must be open-ended. UCITS certification allows the fund to be marketed throughout the European Economic Area (EEA). If it is marketed in the UK, an OEIC must be **authorised** by the Financial Services Authority (FSA).

With the implementation of the Financial Services and Markets Act 2000 (FSMA 2000), the range of UK authorised OEICs was extended to be similar to that of unit trusts, including money market funds and property funds for example, and (as we have seen) OEICs are now alternatively termed **Investment**

Companies with Variable Capital (ICVCs). Authorisation as an ICVC defines the regulations (i.e. the Treasury's ICVC Regulations, as well as further FSA Regulations) with which the fund must comply.

Unit trusts and OEICs are **Authorised Investment Funds (AIFs)**, and are often collectively referred to as **funds**.

The **COLL** rules, as mentioned earlier, apply to OEICs as well as unit trusts. OEICs can be set up as UCITS retail schemes or non-UCITS retail schemes, or QISs. The main COLL rules, which applies to all funds from 13 February 2007, were summarised earlier.

Both OEICs and unit trusts are types of **open-ended collective investments**. However, with a unit trust, the units held provide beneficial ownership of the underlying trust assets. A share in an OEIC entitles the holder to a share in the profits of the OEIC, but the value of the share will be determined by the value of the underlying investments. For example, if the underlying investments are valued at £125,000,000 and there are 100,000,000 shares in issue, the net asset value of each share is £1.25.

The holder of a share in an OEIC can sell back the share to the company in any period specified in the prospectus.

The various **permitted types of OEIC** are as for unit trusts, including for example futures and options funds and geared futures and options funds, except that OEICs cannot be feeder funds. (Feeder funds can only be used for pension purposes, and exist only for holding units in other funds.)

An OEIC may take the form of an **umbrella fund** with a number of separately priced **sub-funds** adopting different investment strategies or denominated in different currencies. Each sub-fund will have a separate client register and asset pool.

Classes of shares within an OEIC may include **income shares**, which pay a dividend, and **accumulation shares**, in which income is not paid out and all income received is added to net assets.

OEICs are similar to investment trusts in that both have **corporate structures**. The objective of the company in each case is to make a profit for shareholders by investing in the shares of other companies. They differ in that an investment trust is a **closed-ended investment** and an OEIC is **open-ended**. The open-ended nature of an OEIC means that it cannot trade at a discount to NAV.

5.2 The structure of OEICs

An OEIC has an **Authorised Corporate Director (ACD)**, who **may be the only Director**. The responsibilities of the **ACD** include the following.

- Day-to-day management of the fund
- Pricing of the fund
- Management of the investments
- Dealing in the underlying securities
- Preparation of accounts
- Compliance with OEIC regulatory requirements

In order to ensure that the **ACD** acts in the interests of **investor protection**, there is a **separate, independent** depository. The responsibility of the **depository** is similar to that of a trustee for a unit trust and covers the following.

- Overseeing the management of the investment company
- Protecting the interests of the investor
- Valuation and pricing of OEIC shares
- Dealing in shares for the OEIC
- The payment of income distributions
- Generally overseeing the ACD

- Ensuring that the ACD is acting in accordance with his investment powers
- Ensuring the ACD is acting in accordance with his borrowing powers

The ACD and the depository must be regulated by the FSA, and approved as **'authorised persons'**. FSA rules cover the sales and marketing of OEICs, and there are cancellation rules.

5.3 Pricing, buying and selling

The shares in the OEIC express the entitlement of the shareholders to the underlying fund which, like a unit trust, is valued on a net asset value basis. With equities, there are a limited number of shares available in each company and an individual must sell the share before another can buy. Because an OEIC is open-ended, the number of shares in issue can be **increased** or **reduced** to satisfy the demands of the investors.

OEICs are **single priced instruments**. The buying price reflects the value of the underlying shares, with any initial charge reflecting dealing costs and management expenses being disclosed separately. **Costs of creation** of the fund may be met by the fund.

As mentioned earlier, a further charge, known as a **dilution levy**, may be made at the discretion of the ACD. The **dilution levy** may be added to the single price, or deducted from the redemption price. The purpose of such a levy is to protect the interests of the shareholders in general and may be charged if the fund is in decline or is experiencing **exceptionally high levels of net sales or redemptions** relative to its size. This levy, if charged, is paid into the fund and not to the managers.

When the investor wishes to **sell** the **OEIC**, the **ACD** will **buy** it. The money value on sale will be based on the **single price** less a **deduction** for the **dealing charges**. The price may be further reduced by any **dilution levy**.

The **ACD** may choose to **run a box**. Shares sold back to the ACD will be **kept** and **reissued** to investors, reducing the need for creation and cancellation of shares.

The **register of shareholders** must be **updated daily** and include all shareholdings of the ACD and those held in the box (if there is one) as well as those of the investors.

5.4 Taxation of OEICs

OEICs themselves face a tax regime similar to that faced by **unit trusts**. Except for fixed interest funds, interest, rent and foreign dividends not taxed at source is subject to a 20% corporation tax charge. UK dividends received will suffer no further tax. Capital gains within an OEIC are exempt from CGT.

Distributions (dividends) paid to investors in an OEIC are taxable in the same way as the distributions from unit trusts.

- Equity fund dividends are paid with a **tax credit** of 10% that satisfies the **tax liability** for basic and lower rate taxpayers. **Higher rate taxpayers** are liable to an additional 22.5%.

- Fixed interest funds pay interest with 20% tax deducted, which satisfies the liability for basic rate taxpayers. Higher rate taxpayers and discretionary trusts must pay 20% more and starting rate taxpayers can reclaim 10%.

Non-taxpayers may **reclaim** tax on interest distributions, but not equity distributions.

For investors' OEIC holdings outside a tax-advantaged wrapper such as an ISA, **capital gains tax** will be chargeable on disposals. There is no UK **stamp duty / SDRT** to pay on purchases of OEICs, but the price reflects stamp duty / SDRT on the purchase of the underlying portfolio.

Where an OEIC is based **offshore**, the distributions will **not be taxed** internally. This will provide a **benefit** to non-taxpaying investors, and a cashflow benefit to tax-paying investors.

5.5 Advantages of OEICs for the investor

As for unit trusts, the general advantages of collective investment outlined at the beginning of this Chapter apply to OEICs. Like unit trusts, there is a wide range of types of fund available.

The introduction of OEICs was expected to lead to a **reduction in costs for the investor** and **transparency of charges**. At the same time, there is **no dilution** in **investor protection**.

The charges with **OEICs** may be lower than for unit trusts, particularly in respect of **cost of entry (setting up)** and **exit (encashing the investment)** due to single pricing. Annual management costs are not set out as a separate charge as with unit trusts. It is still possible to quantify the costs by looking at the **total expense ratio (TER)** of the company. Figures for this are available in the public domain, allowing investors to make valid comparisons between investment managers. There is further discussion of TERs in the next Chapter, in the context of investment trusts.

For the investment industry, an advantage of OEICs is that they are **widely recognised throughout Europe**.

6 OFFSHORE FUNDS AND HEDGE FUNDS

6.1 Introduction

The term **'offshore fund'** refers to a collective investment scheme domiciled in an offshore financial centre. These include the Channel Islands, the Isle of Man, the Cayman Islands, Hong Kong and Bermuda. In recent years, Luxembourg and Dublin have become more significant also, as 'tax havens' within the European Union. Offshore funds offer eligible investor significant tax benefits compared to many high tax jurisdictions, they are usually taxed at normal rates as foreign arising income. Many of these tax haven locations are considered investor-friendly and are internationally regarded as financially secure.

Many offshore funds are run by companies associated with large UK unit trust groups and most of the countries involved now have their own regulatory framework. Certain offshore funds receive recognition under sections 264, 270 and 272 of the **Financial Services and Markets Act 2000** (FSMA 2000).

Since 1979 when UK exchange controls were abolished, it has become relatively easy for the UK resident to invest his money abroad in equities, bonds or pooled investments such as bonds, UCITS (Undertakings for Collective Investments in Transferable Securities) and OEICs.

There may be income and capital gains tax advantages for **UK expatriates who are non-UK resident** and for **non-UK domiciled UK residents**. For non-UK domiciled persons, there may be inheritance tax advantages. However, investment in offshore funds may be not be as advantageous for **UK residents** as they think, particularly from a tax point of view.

In most cases, the tax benefit is limited to a possible **deferral of tax payments** resulting from income being paid gross.

There can be tax disadvantages, particularly if the offshore fund invests in UK shares.

Section 238(1) of FSMA 2000 prohibits any authorised person from promoting any collective investment scheme in the UK unless it is an authorised unit trust, an authorised OIEC, or a recognised scheme. The Financial Services Authority recognises the following **offshore pooled investments**.

(a)   Funds categorised as **Undertakings for Collective Investments in Transferable Securities (UCITS)** are constituted in other European Economic Area Member States. These funds are automatically recognised by the Financial Services Authority and can be marketed freely in the UK.

(b)   **Funds authorised in designated territories**, that is non-EU territories such as the Channel Islands, Bermuda and the Isle of Man. These funds may not be automatically recognised by the FSA.

However, the FSA recognises that certain countries in which investments are based offer a similar regulatory authority and investor protection to that afforded to the UK investor onshore. These regulatory authorities are as follows.

Bermuda	Bermuda Monetary Authority
Guernsey	Financial Services Commission
Isle of Man	Financial Supervision Commission
Jersey	Financial Services Department

(c) **Individually recognised overseas schemes funds**. The FSA also provides for the recognition of overseas schemes on an individual basis.

Non-regulated and non-recognised funds are subject to severe marketing restrictions in the UK. Prospectuses and details can only be forwarded to investment professionals such as stock brokers and Independent Financial Advisers (IFAs).

6.2 Offshore OEICs

OEICs (Investment Companies with Variable Capital – **ICVCs**) are the most common form of pooled investment in Europe. OEICs are based on the European type of ICVC known as **Société d'Investissement à Capital Variable** (**SICAV**). Unit trusts, in contrast, are more like what are known in Europe as **Fonds Commun de Placement** (**FCP**).

- The attraction of the OEIC is that it can issue any number of types of shares. As we saw earlier, an OEIC is 'open-ended', because the total amount invested in the scheme can be increased.

- The ability to offer a wide number of types of shares led to the concept of umbrella funds. In this type of fund, there are many types of share under one management (the umbrella). Each type of share can invest in a different international sector.

- There is a wider range of funds offered to the investor through an offshore OEIC than an onshore unit or investment trust. The funds include UK Equity, International Equity, International Emerging Markets, International Managed, America, Europe, Japan, Latin America, India, Korea, Hong Kong, Australia, Commodities and Currency funds (in all the major currencies) and Fixed Interest funds (in all the leading currencies: e.g. yen, sterling, euro, US$).

6.3 UCITS

Remember that **UCITS** are not a separate type of investment, but a classification for investments such as unit trusts and OEICs that can be marketed throughout the European Economic Area (EEA).

UCITS were created as a result of the UCITS Directive introduced by the Council for the European Communities in 1985 (updated by UCITS II and III). The idea of the Directive was that it would introduce a framework under which a fund management group could market a fund domiciled within one Member State to investors resident in another Member State.

Under the framework, a manager of a collective fund certified as a UCITS in its country of domicile may not be refused permission to market the fund in another Member State provided it complies with local marketing requirements.

The Directive covers funds investing in transferable securities (usually shares and bonds listed on a stock exchange or traded on a regulated market). The Directive does not cover **closed-ended funds** (such as UK investment trusts) and UCITS funds cannot hold **commodities** or **property**.

A fund is authorised by the regulatory authority of its domicile and it is granted a UCITS certificate. Application is then made to the regulatory authority of other Member States in which the provider wishes to market the fund. After two months the fund may be marketed.

6.4 Taxation of offshore funds

In general terms there will be no tax paid by an offshore fund. However, there may be withholding tax which may not be reclaimable by the fund. In addition, a fund may be subject to a small amount of local tax. Jersey funds are subject to a flat yearly corporation tax and Luxembourg funds to a tax on the asset value each year. The expenses of an offshore fund cannot be offset against its income.

6.5 Taxation of the individual

The taxation of the individual will depend upon the status of the fund whether it has **distributor** or **non-distributor** status.

- **Distributor status**. Distributor funds are those which are certified annually by HMRC as pursuing a policy of distribution of income. A fund will obtain this status if it distributes at least 85% of its net income after expenses. There is a concession for funds where the gross income in a year is very low and where the cost of distributing that income would be disproportionate to its value. The *de minimis* rule is set at 1% of the average value of the fund's assets. These funds are allowed to be certified as having distributor status.

  The distributions paid from such funds are paid gross. A UK resident will have to declare this income and pay tax. On encashment of the holding or transferring between classes of participating shares, should a capital gain arise, the investor may be liable to capital gains tax depending on his circumstances.

- **Non-distributor status**. This category of fund is often referred to as a **roll-up fund**. In this instance, all income is accumulated in the fund. If a fund is not certified with distributor status, on receipt of a distribution or on total encashment a charge to income tax arises. A charge to **income tax** on a gain rather than **capital gains tax** can be a **disadvantage**. As the charge is to income tax, there will be no annual CGT exemption to deduct and no indexation allowance or tapering allowance.

6.6 Uses of offshore funds

Offshore pooled investments may be useful for those who require a wider choice of funds than is available onshore. Offshore funds are particularly attractive to investors who wish to use **currency funds** or **hedge funds**.

A fixed interest fund with **distributor** status may be useful for a non-taxpayer. His money will be invested in a fixed interest fund which is rolling up tax-free and he will receive a gross dividend.

A **non-distributor** fund, the taxpayer would pay no tax while his income was rolling up. If a higher rate taxpayer can take encashment when he will be basic rate taxpayer later, this might work to his advantage.

The non-distributor fund may be useful for a UK resident who is anticipating retiring abroad. He can roll up his investment tax-free and encash it when he is no longer a UK resident and subject to UK tax. He should however check on the tax treatment of his investment in the country in which he is then resident.

6.7 Hedge funds

6.7.1 Overview

Most conventional collective investments are 'benchmarked' to a particular set of shares or investments, whose performance they aim to beat. This means that the performance of the benchmark – for example, a share price index – can be important as the skill of the fund manager. **Hedge funds** adopt a more flexible approach, adopting different investment strategies according to the manager's view of where markets are going.

Hedge funds are often based **offshore** and may be unauthorised. They may restrict their clientele to high net-worth individuals whom they can treat as expert private customers.

Hedge funds have wide freedom to invest in almost any type of financial instrument. For example, they might invest in gold, cocoa, currencies, interest rate futures or other derivatives.

Hedge funds also take advantage of the possibility of taking a **short position** in a stock or other investment, for example using **Contracts For Differences (CFDs)** or other derivatives. A fund that owns a stock is taking a long position in that stock: if the price rises, the fund gains. A fund that takes a short position is effectively betting on the stock falling in price: if the price of the stock falls, the fund gains.

Data on US hedge funds showed that hedge funds greatly **outperformed** the average US investment fund from 1988 to 2002. Hedge funds showed average annual gains of 17.0% compared with 8.2% for the average fund, and compared with annual performance by the Standard & Poor's 500 Stock Index of 11.1% over the period.

One such fund was George Soros' Quantum Fund, which was said to have gained $1 billion from speculating on the pound sterling at the time when the UK had to leave the European Exchange Rate Mechanism in 1992. Long-Term Capital Management was another hedge fund, which failed in 1998 with liabilities of $1.25 trillion.

6.7.2 Types

Hedge funds encompass the following types of fund.

- **Absolute return funds** aim to make, perhaps, 7% to 9% annually, irrespective of the state of the stock markets. They may use shorting, and **arbitrage**, which involves the simultaneous sale and purchase of securities to take advantage of pricing anomalies, for a known return.

- **Event-driven funds** take advantage of temporary pricing anomalies in shares, bonds or other investments.

- **Merger-arbitrage funds** seek to take advantage of opportunities that emerge during takeover bids.

- **Macro funds** try to exploit economic developments that could cause large asset price movements.

6.7.3 FSA rule changes

FSA rule changes have made it easier for hedge fund-style investments to be made available to investors.

- More funds are able to hold assets such as commercial property and commodities whose prices do not move in line with shares, and therefore diversify the risk of holding shares.

- Funds are allowed to charge performance-related annual fees, as hedge funds already do.

- Funds have greater freedom for funds to hold more of their money in cash: rather than having to stay almost fully invested even if they take the view that the market is likely to fall.

- QIS (Qualified Investor Schemes) are permitted to take short positions.

6.7.4 Operations

The attraction of this 'class' of security is the **lower cost of settlement** that use of the CREST settlement system provides.

Exam tip

> Operational and regulatory issues relating to hedge funds have become a commonly examined topic, with questions in both the Summer and Winter 2007 exams. Regulatory issues are explored further later in this Study Book.

Hedge fund **settlements** are non-standard in both liquidity and process compared with equities and retail funds such as unit trusts and OEICs. Settlement for subscriptions is typically monthly, with cash required five days before settlement. Redemptions may be quarterly, with 45 days' notice and cash settlement deferred for up to one month after settlement.

Hedge funds have some **unique features** such as performance fees and equalisation of performance fees through various series or equalisation credits. They are additionally subject to varied lock-up mechanisms with penalty fees for early redemption and for investing in 'side pocket' investments. These requirements will generally require specialist custody and administration, and possibly specialist in-house systems to track investments and the recruitment of specialist operations staff.

7 INVESTMENT TRUSTS

7.1 Overview

Investment trusts have a long history in the UK. The Foreign and Colonial Investment Trust was the first to be founded in 1868 with the aim of 'giving the investor of moderate means the same advantage as the large capitalist'. The investment trust provided a way for the small investor to have some exposure to investments in overseas stocks that it would have been impractical for the investor to buy individually. By mid-2003, there were 371 trusts in total, with total assets in the region of £50 billion.

Investment trusts are a form of **collective investment**, pooling the funds of many investors and spreading their investments across a diversified range of securities.

Investment trusts are managed by professional **fund managers** who select and manage the stocks in the trusts' portfolios. Investment trusts are generally accessible to the individual investor, although shares in investment trusts are also widely held by institutional investors such as pension funds.

Investment trusts are **public limited companies** (plcs) listed on the London Stock Exchange. Whereas other companies may make their profit from manufacturing or providing goods and services, an investment trust makes its profit solely from investments. The investor who buys shares in the investment trust hopes for **dividends** and **capital growth** in the value of the shares.

7.2 Comparison with unit trusts and OEICs

Investment trusts have wider investment freedom than unit trusts and OEICs/ICVCs. Investments trusts can:

- Invest in unquoted private companies as well as quoted companies
- Provide venture capital to new companies or companies requiring new funds for expansion

The corporate structure of an investment trust gives it a further advantage over unit trusts and OEICs because it can raise money more freely to help it to achieve its objectives. Unit trusts' and OEICs' powers to borrow are more limited. The ability to **borrow** allows an investment trust to 'gear up' returns for the investor. However, this **gearing** increases the volatility of returns.

Investment trusts are **closed-ended** investments. The number of shares in issue is not affected by the day-to-day purchases and sales by investors.

An advantage of the closed-ended capital structure is that it allows the managers to take a **long-term view** of the investments of the trust. With an open-ended scheme such as a unit trust or an OEIC, if there are more sales of units or shares by investors than purchases, the number of units is reducing and the fund must pay out cash. As a result, the managers may need to sell investments even though it may not be the best time to do so from a long-term viewpoint.

The **price of shares** of the investment trust **rises** and **falls** according to **demand** for and **supply** of the shares of the investment trust, and not directly in line with the values of the company's assets, i.e. **the underlying investments**. In this way, investment trust prices can have greater **volatility** than unit trusts and OEICs, whose unit prices are directly related to the market values of the underlying investments.

Because prices are **dependent on supply and demand**, the price of the shares can be **lower** than the **net asset value (NAV)** of the share. This can allow investors seeking income to **buy** investment trusts at a **discount**, while the **income** produced by the portfolio is based on the market value of the underlying investments. The income yield is therefore enhanced.

Charges incurred on investment trust holdings can be compared with the alternatives. Some **unit trusts and OEICs** have **initial charges** of around 5%. Initial charges may be much lower than this (at around 0.25%) for some investment trust savings schemes. However, there may be charges on selling investment trust holdings.

7.3 AIC and classification of investment trusts

The **Association of Investment Companies (AIC)** (formerly called the Association of Investment Trust Companies (AITC)) represents investment trusts, Venture Capital Trusts and closed-ended AIM investment companies.

The AITC classifies investment trusts into 38 sectors. The classification of each trust is based on a combination of the regional or industry focus of the portfolio and the investment objective of the trust.

7.4 Management

As a company, an investment trust has a **Board of Directors**. The **objective** of a company is to **invest** the money of the shareholders, so decisions on **investment strategy** are very important. These decisions might be made by the directors (in a **self-managed trust**), or may be delegated to an external fund management company. In all decisions, the directors of the company should act for the **benefit** of the shareholders.

Decisions made by the management of the company are open to scrutiny by shareholders, who may act if they are **not satisfied** with the performance. One sanction for shareholders is to **sell** their holding, which could affect the share price. If the share price falls significantly, the company could become a takeover target for other trusts or 'asset strippers' who may buy the shares in order to press for it being wound up.

Special resolutions, and those passed at the annual general meeting, will be subject to a vote by the shareholders. This will include **election of directors** and **appointment of professional advisers**. Some investment trusts also buy in other specialist services such as investment or registration services and the appointment of these will be subject to a shareholder vote.

7.5 Regulatory aspects

An **investment trust** is a listed company, governed by the Companies Act and Stock Exchange regulations. As with other companies, it is bound by the rules set out in its Memorandum and Articles of Association, which are set up when the company is formed. An investment trust is not a trust in the legal sense of that term.

The trust is also subject to the rules of the **Financial Services Authority**, the overall regulator of the financial services industry.

The following principles set down by the FSA apply to a company that seeks to apply for a listing as an investment trust.

- The investment managers must have adequate experience.

- An adequate spread of investment risk must be maintained.

- The investment trust must not control, seek to control or actively manage companies in which it invests.

- The investment trust must not deal in investments to a significant extent.

- The Board of the investment trust must be free to act independently of its management.

- The investment trust must seek **approval by HMRC** (under s842, Income and Corporation Taxes Act 1988 (ICTA 1988)).

Conditions must be met for HMRC approval.

The trust itself does not have direct dealings with the public. If the management company offers the shares of the trust for sale to the public through a savings scheme, then the company must be authorised by the FSA to carry on investment business under the **Financial Services and Markets Act 2000.**

7.6 Prices and dealing

The quotation of the price of investment trust shares is similar to that for equities generally, and a dealer will give two prices. In a price quote in a newspaper or website, a single price may be given: this will typically be the **mid-market price**, between the offer and bid prices. The difference between the offer price and the bid price is the **spread**.

Shares in investment trusts can be bought through a **stock broker**, who is likely to charge the same level of commission as for other equities. If the investor's agreement with the broker is **execution only** (without advice), then commission might be as low as 0.5%, or £10 per deal. Stamp duty will be payable at 0.5% of the purchase consideration.

If the broker is providing an **advisory service**, then commission will be higher, for example 1.5% or 2% of the purchase consideration. Some brokers provide **discretionary investment trust management services** for individuals with larger sums to invest. The broker will select trusts that meet the investor's investment objectives and will charge an annual management fee in addition to dealing charges.

An investor can usually **deal through the investment trust managers** instead of through a broker, and may incur lower charges by doing so. Small investors who do not have an account with a broker may prefer to deal through the managers. However, the managers may only deal on a daily basis, while a broker will be able to quote an up-to-the-minute price and a deal can be made instantly by telephone.

The major trust management groups also operate **regular savings schemes**, through which an investor can make monthly investments.

- **Dividend reinvestment** (in further shares) may be available as an option for investors who do not require income.

- A low cost **share exchange service** is offered by some investment trust groups, enabling investors to realise their existing equity investments and to be given investment trust shares in return.

7.7 Charges

Firstly, there are **internal charges** applied within the fund. These include funds' annual management charges, which generally range between 0.25% and 1.5% of the fund's total value.

Certain other costs, such as auditors' fees, custody fees, directors' remuneration, secretarial costs and marketing costs, may be charged in addition. They will normally be charged against the income of the trust, or in some cases against capital. Such charges will normally be disclosed in the investment trust company's annual report and accounts.

These various management expenses incurred within the fund over a year are totalled to give a **Total Expense Ratio (TER).** TERs for funds are calculated by a research company called Fitzrovia International plc. Fitzrovia aims to calculate TERs on a consistent basis to allow comparison across investment trusts and other funds. The TERs of investment trusts are often lower than those of unit trusts and OEICs, many of which fall in the range 1% to 1.5%.

There has been a growing trend for collective investment funds to introduce **performance-related fees** for fund managers. The basic principle is to reward outperformance against a selected benchmark, as specified by the Board of Directors.

There are various internal charges that are not reflected in the TER. The TER does not include the following costs included in the expenses section of the annual accounts: performance fees, restructuring costs and various other costs related to the investment transactions that the fund enters into. These transaction-related costs include stamp duty and brokers' commissions. Bank interest incurred, losses or gains on currency and the spreads incurred between buying and selling prices of investments made by the trust will also not be reflected in the TER.

7.8 Disclosures

Firms providing investment trust savings schemes and ISAs for investment trust investments must provide a **Key Features Document (KFD)** to the customer.

The Key Features Document gives general information about the investment trust and also must include a table illustrating the effect of charges and expenses over periods of 1, 5 and 10 years. The table must assume a standard investment growth rate of 6% for investment trust savings schemes and a rate of 7% for ISA schemes. (The rate is higher for ISAs to reflect broadly the effect of the differences in tax treatment.)

Using standard growth rates enables the investor to compare the products of different product providers of investment trust schemes. The investor can also make comparisons with other types of product, such as unit trusts, OEICs and insurance-based contracts, for which similar information must be made available by product providers.

7.9 Net asset value

An investment trust share is similar to any other equity, except that the specific objective of the company is to invest rather than to transact other forms of business. The **past performance** of the trust can be measured against standard **benchmarks** of performance such as **market indices** most closely covering the market sector in which the trust invests. Outperformance of market indices over a period of years can indicate skilled and successful investment management.

The **net asset value (NAV)** is the **net worth** of the company expressed in terms of the value of company assets per share.

The **net asset value** of an investment trust with assets worth £9 million, with liabilities of £3 million and 12 million ordinary shares would be 50p per share, i.e. (£9 million – £3 million) *divided* by £12 million. However, this figure is an **undiluted figure**. It does not make any allowances for any **warrants** in issue (which we discuss later in this Chapter).

In order to allow for the effects of **warrant holders** taking up their subscription, the subscription price is added as an asset and the new shares created are added to the total number of shares. The calculation for **diluted NAV** is therefore:

$$\frac{\text{Net assets (assets less liabilities) plus warrant subscriptions}}{\text{Shares in issue plus new shares in respect of warrants}}$$

7.10 Premium/discount to NAV

The share price at a particular time may be **greater** or **less** than the **NAV**. For example:

- If the NAV is 100 pence and the share price is 86 pence, then the shares are trading at a **discount** of 14%.

- If the NAV is 100 pence and the share price is 108 pence, then the shares are trading at a **premium** of 8%.

The *Financial Times* publishes figures for the **discount or premium to NAV** along with the share prices of investment trusts.

If shares in an investment trust are trading at a **premium to NAV**, this may reflect investors believing strongly in the management of the company and in their ability to make the **assets grow**.

The fact that a discount to net assets is common presents a problem in the initial **launch** of an investment trust, when the trust must raise enough money from new investors to make the trust viable. If investors foresee that a discount is likely, they will need some additional incentive to invest at the launch. Some investment trust companies arrange the capital structure of the company in order to ensure that the investment trust shares are marketable. One common way of doing this is to issue **warrants**, with for example one warrant being given away with every five shares issued – this is sometimes referred to as a '**sweetener**'. Another way is to split the capital of the company into several **different classes of share** each of which produce a different form of investment return.

7.11 Gearing

Gearing is a measure of the extent of borrowing by an investment trust and can be calculated as:

$$\frac{\text{Borrowings}}{\text{Capital and reserves}} \times 100$$

For example, if an investment trust has £100 million of total assets and £14 million of borrowings, shareholders' funds (capital and reserves) are £86 million. If the trust's total assets increase or fall by 10% to £110 million or £90 million respectively, and borrowings remain the same at £14 million, the shareholders' funds will have grown to £96 million or fallen to £76 million. This represents an increase or decrease in shareholders' funds of 11.6%, which in both cases is 16% more than the 10% increase or decrease in total assets.

We can say that the shareholders' funds are 16% geared ((14/86) x 100%), or we can express this as a **gearing ratio** of 116 (=(100/86) x 100%).

7.12 Buybacks of shares

If the discount to NAV becomes very wide, investment trust managers may decide to **buy back** some of the shares, thus reducing the excess supply and possibly narrowing the discount. As for other companies, a buyback by an investment trust of its own shares requires the permission of shareholders.

The following **FSA rules** apply to share buybacks.

- The approval of shareholders on one occasion can be to buy back up to 14.99% of the shares only. (Further approval would be needed to buy back more shares.)

- The trust must not pay more than 5% above the market price to buy back its own shares.

- The share buyback must be financed out of the investment capital of the trust.

Investment trusts are allowed to hold shares bought back (consisting of up to 10% of capital) '**in treasury**', rather than cancelling them. The shares could then be sold again at a later date. This mechanism can offer the trust a way of balancing supply and demand for its shares at different times.

7.13 Winding up an investment trust

Some investment trusts are set up with a **limited life.** Provision is made for shareholders to vote on whether to wind up the trust at the end of the specified period. As with all companies, the shareholders can in theory vote to wind up an investment trust at any time.

A reason for setting a limited life is to avoid a persistent wide discount developing. As the planned winding up date draws closer, the discount should narrow as investors are anticipating the sale of the net assets of the trust and distribution of the proceeds.

If a trust is wound up, shareholders will receive the NAV for their shares, after paying any prior charges and winding-up expenses.

7.14 Unitisation of an investment trust

Unitisation is the process whereby an investment trust could be converted into a unit trust. A possible benefit of this is that, if the shares in the investment trust are trading at a significant discount, the value of the units (determined by the value of the assets) will theoretically rise above the previous share price. However, should all unit holders try to realise their profit, the sales of units forced on the manager will probably result in unattractive prices being realised. In addition, the costs of the unitisation process will reduce the value of the fund. Unitisation will therefore only work in limited circumstances.

Shareholders may be better served if the investment trust is acquired by another trust or a pension fund which may be prepared to pay closer to the net asset value.

Unitisation procedures

- HMRC approval obtained to avoid adverse tax consequences
- Liquidator appointed for the investment trust
- Trustee appointed for the new unit trust
- FSA approval obtained for the new unit trust
- Shareholder approval obtained
- Repayment of loans, since unit trusts cannot borrow significant amounts of money
- Cancellation of shares and issue of units

7.15 Split capital investment trusts

A **split capital investment trust** is like other investment trusts in that it has a single portfolio of investments. A split capital trust, however, involves a number of different classes of share, with holders of the different classes having different entitlements to returns of capital or income from the trust.

A split capital trust has a limited life. The period of time remaining to the planned winding up of the trust is usually very significant in how the prices of the different classes of share move.

Split capital investment trusts allow trust managers to tailor returns to appeal to different investors with different strategies, circumstances and attitudes.

The **capital value** of all classes of share will vary up until the trust is wound up. At that stage, the amount of capital returned will depend on the class of share and the order of priority in which the trust is wound up.

7.16 Income shares

There are different types of **income share**. A financial adviser must be very clear about the terms of the different types of share, as some can result in substantial loss of capital.

Income shares pay regular dividends from surplus income on trust assets and have a predetermined maturity value, known as the redemption price (typically, the same as the issue price of £1). The redemption price is paid subject to there being sufficient assets remaining after debts and other preferred classes of share have been paid. The market price of these shares fluctuates above and below the redemption price, depending on dividend prospects and time to maturity.

Some income shares pay high income but have only a nominal redemption value, say 1p. Such shares may be attractive to an investor who has capital gains on other investments that can be set off against the capital loss.

7.17 Income and residual capital shares

Income and residual capital shares (also known as **ordinary income shares** or **highly geared ordinary income shares**) offer a high and rising income plus all the surplus assets of the trust at the winding-up date after other prior-ranking classes of shares have been repaid. They have no predetermined redemption value and are last in the order of priority.

If issued by a trust in **combination** with a **zero dividend preference share**, holders of such shares are entitled to all the income generated by the trust. If issued by a trust with a **stepped preference share**, the holders receive all excess revenue after the predetermined dividend payment to the other class of share has been made.

Income and residual capital shares offer the potential for **high dividends** and **capital returns**, although their high gearing does make them a relatively **high-risk investment**.

7.18 Capital shares

Capital shares do not pay dividends. Holders receive all of the capital remaining when the preference and income shareholders have been paid their maturity values. The absence of guarantees means that capital shares are inherently risky. When the trust matures, the capital shareholders are last in line; if there is nothing left, they could come away empty-handed. There is the potential for impressive growth, or significant losses, through **gearing**.

7.19 Stepped preference shares

Stepped preference shares are an unusual type of preference shares that pays a fixed dividend. Normal preference shares pay the same dividend but stepped preference shares offer dividends that step up in value during the life of the trust. They both pay a predetermined redemption value when the trust is wound up. Commitments to pay fixed amounts would make this category of share suitable for those with a low appetite for risk.

For example, a stepped preference share might pay a dividend at 5% in Year 1, 5.25% in Year 2, 5.5% in Year 3 etc.

7.20 Zero dividend preference shares

Zero dividend preference shares generate no dividend income but offer a fixed capital return or redemption value. The fact that they pay no income means they can be of particular interest for tax planning, especially if the annual capital gains tax allowance is used to shelter profits. For example, 'zeros' might be issued at £1, redeemable after ten years at £2, paying no dividend in the meantime. As low-risk investments that pay a set amount at a set time, they can be appropriate for investors needing capital at certain points. Zeros rank first in the winding up of the trust together with other preference shares.

Zeros should not be considered in the same **risk category** as cash investments. This fact came very clearly to light in 2002 as fears were rising that some 'zeros' would not provide their expected return. The fact that no 'zero' had failed to pay out its predetermined return made zeros popular.

The popularity created great demand for zeros and many new ones were issued. However, the risk reduction on this type of investment is provided by the other types of split in the structure of the trust. To meet the demand, zeros were set up without the supporting structure of the other share classes, simply by cross-holdings of other zeros. This has led to problems when markets have fallen in recent years. However, zeros that are based on a 'sound' split capital structure can still be a good low risk investment.

7.21 Winding up split capital investment trusts

At the predetermined date, shareholders will be asked to agree to **wind up** the trust according to the procedure laid down in its Articles of Association. They may also be given the option of **continuing** the life of the trust or of rolling their investment over into a new trust.

If the trust is **wound up**, the different classes of share are **repaid** in order of priority, after **repayment** of any loans or debentures, out of the **assets** and according to their entitlement after expenses have been deducted.

If there are **warrants**, these are ranked last and are paid after all other classes of share. Each share class follows in a particular order, both in respect of dividends, paid from the income earned by the trust during its life, and in respect of capital, paid from the assets of the trust at the winding-up date.

Although split capital trusts have a limited life (which may be extended if the shareholders vote in favour), shares are tradeable and can be sold at the prevailing market price at any time during the life of the trust. The price will reflect market conditions of demand and supply at the time.

7.22 C shares

C shares (conversion shares) are shares floated after the original issue of ordinary shares, usually to **raise additional capital**.

C shares are quoted separately from the ordinary shares until the capital raised through their issue is fully or substantially invested in the investment trust. At this time, they are converted into the ordinary shares at a set ratio based on their **net asset value**. They are used to allow a trust to increase the number of shares and the funds under management without diluting the value of the existing shares.

The issue of **C shares** provides an alternative to using a **rights issue** to raise capital.

7.23 S shares

S shares are used to issue new shares on the market without incurring the expense of launching a new investment trust company. They form a separate investment to the original share issue and, unlike C shares, the price of **S shares** will always be quoted separately.

7.24 Packaged units

The managers of some split capital trusts arrange for a combination of their shares to be traded together in what is known as a **packaged unit** (not to be confused with units issued by unit trusts). Such units usually comprise shares in the ratio at which those shares were originally issued.

Packaged units have similar characteristics to an ordinary share issued by a conventional investment trust, although in some cases the component classes of share can be separated out and traded as separate securities if required. The discount to NAV may be lower than it would otherwise be due to the increased demand created by the split capital structure.

Packaged units provide a benefit for the investment trust managers, who are effectively getting the best of both worlds. Splitting the units helps to reduce the discount on the shares and the recombination of them allows them to offer investors access to an investment with the more 'conventional' characteristics of an investment trust.

7.25 Taxation of investment trusts

If the investment trust is **approved by HMRC** under s842 ICTA 1988, the tax regime for the trust is similar to that of **unit trusts**.

- The trust pays **no tax on gains** made from selling investments in their portfolio.

- The trust is not liable to tax on dividends from UK companies (**franked investment income**).

- The trust is liable to corporation tax at 30% on **unfranked income** (which includes foreign dividends, gilts and bank interest, and underwriting commission). Interest paid on borrowings and management fees can be set against unfranked income, with the result that a trust may not have to pay any tax at all.

To obtain approval by HMRC, the investment trust must:

- Be a UK-resident company, with its ordinary shares quoted on the London Stock Exchange
- Not be a 'close' company (means broadly that it cannot be controlled by five or fewer persons)
- Get 75%+ of its income from shares and securities
- Have no more than 15% of its assets invested in one company
- Not distribute its capital gains (except for Venture Capital Trusts)
- Distribute ≥ 85% of its gross income from shares and securities

Some **offshore-registered** investment companies that are managed in the UK and listed on the London Stock Exchange have s842 ICTA 1988 approval.

7.26 Taxation of the investor

Investors are liable for **income tax** on **dividends** in the same way as they would be with shares in any other company, and will be liable for **capital gains tax (CGT)** on **disposal of shares**.

As with unit trusts and OEICs, CGT and additional (higher rate) income tax on dividends can be avoided where the shares are held in an **ISA** or **PEP**.

Stamp duty reserve tax (SDRT) of 0.5% is charged on purchases of shares in investment trusts, as for other equities.

7.27 Venture Capital Trusts

Venture capital trusts (VCTs) are listed companies that invest in unquoted trading companies and meet certain conditions. The VCT scheme differs from the Enterprise Investments Schemes (EIS) in that the individual investor may spread his risk over a number of higher-risk, unquoted companies. An individual investing in a VCT obtains the following tax benefits.

- A tax reduction of **30%** of the amount invested, in the year of making the investment (a 40% tax reduction applied in 2005/06)
- Dividends received from the VCT are exempt from further taxation
- Capital gains on the sale of shares in the VCT are exempt from CGT (and losses are not allowable)

Capital gains which the VCT itself makes on its investments are not chargeable gains, and so are not subject to corporation tax.

The above reliefs are not available if shares were acquired other than for *bona fide* commercial purposes or for the purpose of tax avoidance.

8 EXCHANGE-TRADED FUNDS

Exchange-traded funds (ETFs) are mainly **index tracking** funds and combine the ready-made diversification of unit trusts with the simplicity of shares. Like other types of index tracker, ETFs gain from the reduced costs involved in passively following an index. ETFs have some of the lowest annual charges of all collective investment schemes. First introduced to the UK in 2000, there are now various ETFs available, tracking equity and fixed income indices in the UK and around the world.

Providers are becoming increasingly inventive in the ETFs they offer: for example, the Clear Spin-Off Index ETF tracks stocks that are spin-offs from other companies, and the Ocean Tomo Index ETF tracks a portfolio of companies which own valuable patents.

ETFs are open-ended, which means that new units can be issued in response to demand. As a result, they trade at a price that is close to the net asset value of the fund.

ETFs are eligible for ISAs. There is no stamp duty on purchases of ETFs by the investor.

ETFs are traded on the London Stock Exchange. Prices are quoted in real time, and so they change throughout the trading day. In September 2006 the London Stock Exchange became the world's first exchange to offer a multi-currency trading service for ETFs giving investors a tax-efficient and currency risk-free alternative.

ETFs can help in a range of investment strategies:

- **Rebalance portfolios and steer investment strategy quickly and easily.** The flexibility that ETFs offer means that asset allocation decisions can be executed instantaneously and cheaply. An investor can achieve broad exposure to equity, bonds, the USA or Europe very easily. Subsequent rebalancing can take place with just a couple of trades. ETFs also allow even the smallest portfolios to achieve broad diversification.

- **Core / satellite approach.** No investor or even investment professionals can follow every instrument in every market. ETFs allow investors to build a core market portfolio while concentrating on those instruments they follow closely and add their stock picks for additional out performance. In this way, passive (tracker) funds can form part of a very successful active strategy.

- **Tactical investing in the short term.** Sometimes markets move very fast indeed and the ability to pick up the telephone, receive a real-time price and trade there and then can make all the difference. Unlike unit trusts, where one may not be able to deal for 24 hours and will not find out the price until afterwards, ETFs allow investors to both take advantage and avoid the pitfalls of fast markets.

9 US MUTUAL FUNDS AND 401(K) PLANS

9.1 The nature of mutual funds

The term '**mutual fund**' is used in the USA for collective investments which are similar to the open-ended funds available in the UK: unit trusts and OEICs.

US mutual funds began in 1924, five years before the stock market crash. The Securities Act 1933 and the Securities Exchange Act 1934 required mutual funds to be registered with the Securities and Exchange Commission (SEC) and to supply a prospectus to investors. Mutual funds must follow the provisions of the Investment Company Act 1940.

Mutual funds may invest in equities (generally referred to as 'stocks' in the USA), bonds, short-term money market instruments and other securities.

Stock funds investing in companies in a particular industry, such as pharmaceuticals or utilities, are known as **sector funds**.

9.2 Mutual funds and US retirement plans

Two types of retirement savings vehicles available in the US – **IRAs and 401(k) plans** – have greatly helped the **growth of the mutual funds industry** in the US.

- **Individual Retirement Accounts (IRAs)** allow US individuals to hold tax-advantaged retirement savings in addition to company pension plans, subject to annual limits.

- **Roth IRAs** receive after-tax contributions from the individual, while no tax is paid on investment gains within the Roth IRA nor on eventual distributions from them. Thus, Roth IRAs are similar to the Individual Savings Accounts available in the UK. For other (non-Roth) **IRAs**, tax is **deferred**, since eligible contributions to the IRA and investment income and gains are tax-free, but distributions are taxed, like pension income. Distributions are normally permitted from age 59½.

- A **401k plan**, named after the relevant section of the **US Internal Revenue Code,** is an employer-sponsored defined contribution retirement plan available to US persons. As with non-Roth IRA plans, a 401k plan offers the possibility of tax deferral, which may be attractive to higher rate tax payers who expect to be in a lower rate tax bracket in retirement.

9.3 401(k) plans

Although the 401(k) plan has been in existence for many years – since 1978 when the US Congress added Section 401(k) to the Internal Revenue Code – it has only recently become popular and accepted as the retirement benefit of choice in many organisations. This type of plan is also referred to as a '**cash or deferred arrangement**' (**CODA**) because it gives employees a choice between receiving cash currently or deferring the amount and having it contributed to the plan. In addition, many employers often match employee contributions, up to a certain percentage of salary. The CODA has become one of the most popular forms of qualified plans among both large and small employers.

The 401(k) plan must be part of a qualified profit-sharing plan, a stock bonus plan, a pre-ERISA money purchase pension plan, or a rural cooperative plan.

The ability of the employer to 'match contributions' has generated interest in the plans at all employee levels. This is important because 401(k) plans include non-discrimination tests that require lower paid employees to defer compensation under the plan, in proportion to highly paid employees – in accordance with one of several formulae. The minimum level of deferral for lower paid employees is determined under a statutory formula based on utilisation of the plan by highly compensated employees.

9.3.1 Features for the employee

The major benefit to employees is that they are not taxed currently on the portion of compensation that is placed in the plan. An employee has the option of choosing between cash or future benefits on a year-to-year basis. This protects an employee when faced with unexpected immediate financial needs.

A 401(k) plan is a qualified defined contribution plan. This means that an employee can elect to defer allocations. The contributions enjoy tax-free reinvestment of earnings and the opportunity to receive special tax treatment on certain plan distributions.

The 'employer matching' provision which many plans include encourages participation among employees at all levels.

A 401(k) plan is eligible for five-year averaging on distributions. However, if an early distribution is taken, the amount is subject to an additional 10% tax.

9.3.2 Advantages and drawbacks to the employer

Strict discrimination rules focus on highly compensated employees. They require that a business stimulate as much participation as possible, particularly from lower level employees, in order to avoid violating the rules and jeopardising the qualification of the plan.

Advantages

- A 401(k) plan can be a valuable way of triggering participation by employees, since it permits pre-tax contributions through salary reduction.

- A 401(k) plan permits a company to address employee demands for additional benefits without added cost and without jeopardising the retirement income security of employees.

Possible drawbacks

- A 401(k) plan's features can taint the need for employees to provide for their retirement because, under certain conditions, the money can be loaned or distributed in hardship situations.

- Such a plan should not be used *in lieu* of a thrift plan if its main purpose is to increase short-term capital accumulation. A 401(k) plan is not designed for frequent withdrawals.

- In an environment of primarily low-paid service employees, the attractiveness of a cash deferral plan is minimal.

- Record-keeping requirements are strict and costly.

9.3.3 Legal requirements

Because a 401(k) plan is a qualified plan, it is subject to the same rules imposed by the Internal Revenue Code and ERISA as are all other qualified plans. Therefore, it must be part of a written plan that is communicated to employees and established solely for the benefit of employees or their beneficiaries. A 401(k) plan must also meet these requirements.

- Certain **minimum funding rules**

- One of two **coverage tests**:

    - The **ratio percentage test**. The percentage of the non-highly compensated employees, benefiting under the CODA must be at least 70% of the percentage of highly compensated employees benefiting under the CODA, or

    - The **average benefits test**. In addition to meeting a non-discriminatory classification test, described below, the average benefits provided by the employer for non-highly compensated employees must be at least 70% of the average benefits provided for the highly compensated employees.

- The **minimum participation test**. The plan must cover no fewer than the lesser of 50 employees or 40% of all employees of the employer.

- **Eligibility restrictions**. No employee who is otherwise eligible can be required to complete more than one year of service as an eligibility requirement, even if 100% vested at all times.

- General **non-discrimination** tests.

- General **vesting** rules.

A 401(k) plan is also subject to the restrictions on the amount of pay that may be taken into account for contribution and benefits calculations.

9.3.4 Contributions

There are several different types of contributions that can be permitted in a 401(k) plan.

- **Elective contributions** – These are amounts a plan participant could have chosen to take in cash but has instead opted to defer.

- **Non-elective contributions** – Employer contributions (other than matching contributions) that are automatically paid to the plan; the employee may not elect cash instead of the plan contribution.

- **Qualified non-elective contributions** – These are a subset of non-elective contributions that

    - Are immediately non-forfeitable, and

    - Are subject to section 401(k) distribution restrictions; under those rules, the contributions cannot be withdrawn for purposes of hardship.

- **Employee contributions** – These are amounts contributed to the plan by an employee on a post-tax basis.

- **Matching contributions** – These are amounts made by an employer to a plan on account of employee contributions or elective contributions.

- **Qualified matching contributions** – These are subsets of matching contributions that are:

    - Immediately non-forfeitable, and

    - Subject to section 401(k) distribution restrictions. Under those rules, the contributions cannot be withdrawn for purposes of hardship.

9.3.5 Interaction with other plans

A 401(k) plan linked to a thrift or savings plan involves the deferral, throughout the year, of amounts employees would have otherwise received as taxable salary or wages. Consequently, such an arrangement is commonly known as a '**salary reduction plan**'.

9.3.6 Highly compensated employees

A qualified plan cannot discriminate in favour of **highly compensated employees (HCEs)**.

An HCE is any individual who, during the year or the preceding year:

- Was a 5% owner of the employer, or

- Received annual compensation in excess of the amount designated by the Internal Revenue Code (IRC), and (if so elected by the employer) ranked in the top 20% of employees (by compensation) in the prior year.

9.3.7 Tax consequences of withdrawals

Withdrawals made due to **hardship**, as defined in Inland Revenue Service rules, are subject to normal taxation of plan distributions and may be subject to a 10% tax for premature withdrawals. This additional tax can be avoided only if the distribution is made after the employee has reached age 59½, if the distribution is made in periodic payments, or if the hardship involves medical expenses and the distribution does not exceed the deductible medical expenses.

9.3.8 Plan loans

A 401(k) plan can also make funds available to participants by loan in a broader way, within specified limits, since a loan is not subject to the 'hardship rules'.

CHAPTER ROUNDUP

- The purchaser of units in a unit trust is the beneficiary of a trust fund and his interests are safeguarded by the fund trustee.

- A wide variety of types of unit trust fund is available to suit different investors' objectives, including: income funds; growth funds; balanced funds; specialised funds; index-trackers.

- A unit trust is an open-ended fund, meaning that the size of the fund and the number of units changes as units are created for purchases, or cancelled as a result of sales.

- The Financial Services Authority has the power to authorise unit trusts (which can be marketed to the general public) and to recognise offshore unit trusts.

- Investment trusts and venture capital trusts (VCTs) are public limited companies and may be geared.

- An investment trust is a closed-ended fund: its shares trade on the secondary market and a purchase on the secondary market is not add to the fund. The share price may be at a premium or discount to the investment trust's net asset value at any particular time.

- Open Ended Investment Companies (OEICs) are also referred to as Investment Companies with Variable Capital (ICVCs).

- An OEIC has a special company structure to enable it to continually issue or redeem its own shares as investors buy or sell the shares.

- The OEIC is governed by a Board, one of which is the Authorised Corporate Director. The investments of the OEIC are held by an independent FSA-authorised depository.

- Offshore fund are typically based in tax havens and may be structured as unit trusts or OEICs.

- Offshore funds may be marketed to UK investors if they are: UCITS funds, or based in designated territories, or individually approved by the FSA.

- Exchange-Traded Funds (ETFs) are open-ended funds. They comprise 'baskets' of securities that track a particular index and, unlike unit trusts and OEICs, trade on an exchange in real time.

- A 401(k) plan is a retirement savings plan for US employees through which tax is deferred until benefits are taken. The development of 401(k) plans and IRAs have helped boost the US funds industry, whose main products are called 'mutual funds'.

TEST YOUR KNOWLEDGE

Check your knowledge of the Chapter here, without referring back to the text.

1   Which one of the following is *not* a potential advantage of unit trusts?

    A   Unit trusts covering overseas stocks are available
    B   Unit trusts are closed-ended
    C   Unit trusts enable diversification of investment
    D   Unit trusts are professionally managed

2   What kind of funds is associated with the terms 'full replication' and 'optimisation'?

3   Which of the following cannot normally be a part of the scheme property of a unit trust that is a UCITS scheme?

    A   Immoveable property
    B   Transferable securities
    C   Derivatives
    D   Units in collective investment schemes

4   Which of the following is a role of the trustee of a unit trust?

    A   Calculating bid and offer prices
    B   Issuing certificates of ownership to unit holders
    C   Marketing the trust
    D   Investment of available funds

5   What is the name of the trade body for investment trusts?

6   Outline the steps involved in unitisation of an investment trust.

7   How often are prices set for an exchange-traded fund?

8   What is a '401(k) plan' and how did it get its name?

TEST YOUR KNOWLEDGE: ANSWERS

1   You should have chosen Option B: unit trusts are open-ended investment vehicles. (See 1.3.)

2   Index tracking funds. (See 2.3.)

3   The correct answer is A. Non-UCITS schemes can, however, hold immoveable property. (See 3.1.2.)

4   B is the correct answer. The other roles are functions of the manager of the trust. (See 4.2, 4.3.)

5   The Association of Investment Companies (AIC). (See 7.3.)

6   The unitisation process will involve the following steps. (See 7.14.)

- HMRC approval obtained to avoid adverse tax consequences
- Liquidator appointed for the investment trust
- Trustee appointed for the new unit trust
- FSA approval obtained for the new unit trust
- Shareholder approval obtained
- Repayment of loans, since unit trusts cannot borrow significant amounts of money
- Cancellation of shares and issue of units

7   Prices are quoted in real time, and so they change throughout the trading day. (See 8.)

8   A 401(k) plan is an employer-sponsored defined contribution retirement plan available to US persons and is named after the relevant section of the US Internal Revenue Code. (See 9.2.)

5

Instruments and Characteristics – Money Markets

INTRODUCTION

Money market instruments provide a short-term home for cash. Note the characteristics of the different types of instrument available.

There are various different interest rates, over different periods, which act as reference points to market participants.

At the end of this Chapter, we outline the main aspects of foreign exchange (currency) trading, for which London is the world's leading centre.

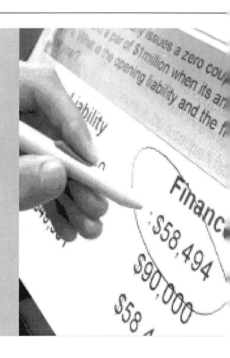

1 MONEY MARKET SECURITIES

The **money markets** are financial markets for lending and borrowing largely short-term capital.

The following types of money market security are available.

- **Time deposits**. A simple deposit of cash with a bank for a fixed term at a specified rate. Good for very short deposits of two weeks or less because the costs of issuing a security are saved. However, as this loan is not securitised, it cannot be sold on and there are punitive charges if the funds are required back early.

- **Money market funds**. Although often lower yielding than other securities, they can be a useful component of a balanced cash portfolio to provide the short-term liquidity requirements.

- **Repurchase agreements (repos)**. In a repo, the money is loaned to a bank for a short period in exchange for collateral in the form of negotiable bearer securities. The difference between the 'sell price' and the 'repurchase price' of the collateral is the interest earned (although ownership does not change unless the bank defaults).

- **Government securities**. Treasury Bills are short-term sovereign debt issued at a discount to par by comparative auction. Usually extremely liquid, although at significantly lower yields than other securities.

- **Euro Commercial Paper (ECP)**. A short-term negotiable bearer debt instrument issued under a specific continuously offered ECP programme. Issued by banks, corporations, supranationals and sovereign borrowers at a discount to par. ECP is issued in most currencies (unlike USCP, which in practice is only issued in USD).

- **Euro Certificates of Deposit**. Similar to ECP, but distinguished by usually being issued by commercial bank borrowers at par and paying a single coupon at maturity.

- **Auction rate securities**. Short-term instruments bought at par with a coupon that resets every 28 or 35 days. The coupon is reset via a 'Dutch auction' to establish a single rate that will apply to all investors. At the end of each period the security can be bought, sold or held at par, as another auction occurs to decide the new coupon.

- **Floating Rate Notes (FRNs)**. A bond with a coupon that is adjusted periodically against the interest rates of other widely quoted financial instruments (e.g. Libor). FRNs provide protection against rising interest rates, but pay lower yields than the equivalent fixed rate bonds.

- **Other corporate bonds**. When longer term bonds have less than a year to maturity, they can be viewed as secondary money market instruments. Greater yields are often obtainable for a given issuer, although with arguably less liquidity than in the primary money market.

2 TREASURY BILLS

A **Treasury bill** ('**T-bill**') is a **promissory note**. It is a promise made by the Treasury (via the Bank of England) to repay a set sum of money at a specified date in the future, normally not longer than 91 days.

T-bills are issued by way of a weekly auction and trade at a discount to their face value. Unlike gilts, they are not part of the Government's funding programme *per se*, but are much more an instrument of monetary policy. The principal use of T-bills is to drain liquidity from the market, thereby making it easier for the authorities to conduct their open market operations pursuant to establishing the interest rate.

The principal measures used to evaluate T-bills are as follows.

Formula to learn

$$\text{Discount rate} = \frac{100 - \text{Discounted value}}{100 \times \frac{\text{Days}}{365}} \times 100$$

$$\text{Discount rate} = \frac{100 - \text{Discounted value}}{100 \times \frac{\text{Days}}{365}} \times 100$$

$$\text{Interest rate or yield} = \frac{100 - \text{Discounted value}}{\text{Discounted value} \times \frac{\text{Days}}{365}} \times 100$$

The yield can also be arrived at through the discount rate.

Formula to learn

$$\text{Yield} = \frac{\text{Discount rate}}{1 - \left(\text{Discount rate} \times \frac{\text{Days}}{365}\right)}$$

Example: Treasury bills

91-day Treasury bill issued at 98.

The discount rate

$$\frac{100 - 98}{100 \times \frac{91}{365}} \times 100 = 8.02\%$$

The interest rate or yield

$$\frac{100 - 98}{98 \times \frac{91}{365}} \times 100 = 8.18\%$$

Alternatively, using the **discount rate**

$$\frac{0.0802}{1 - \left(0.0802 \times \frac{91}{365}\right)} \times 100 = 8.18\%$$

It is conventional for bills to trade on the discount rate and this requires the holder to convert to the yield in order to compare with other investments.

3 CERTIFICATES OF DEPOSIT

3.1 Introduction

A **certificate of deposit (CD)** is in effect a securitised bank deposit. Ideally, banks would like to be able to take deposits from customers on the understanding that these deposits would not be repayable within the short-term. However, investors are either unwilling to commit their funds for specified time periods (time deposits) or demand too high a premium.

The resolution to this dilemma came in the 1960s with the creation of certificates of a bank deposit that was committed for a period of time. Such certificates carry a fixed coupon rate and have a maturity of up to five years, more normally one year or less. Like any other security, the certificate can be traded enabling the deposit holder to realise the deposit through the sales proceeds and not by withdrawal.

Conventionally, CDs are issued by highly-rated banks and therefore carry a limited credit risk. Whilst, unlike the other money market instruments, they do carry a coupon, this is only paid on maturity. The exception to this is that any CD with a maturity of over one year will pay an annual coupon out to the holder.

Once issued, CDs trade on a yield basis. That is to say the amount that is to be paid for the CD means that, given the fixed coupon, the new purchaser will generate the yield at which it is trading.

3.2 Valuation of CDs

The simplest case is that of a CD where the maturity is less than one year, therefore there is only one flow, at the point of maturity.

Formula to learn

$$\text{Maturity value} = \text{Principal} + \left(\text{Principal} \times \frac{\text{Stated yield}}{100} \times \frac{\text{Life(Tenor)}}{365} \right)$$

The base in the sterling market is 365. In all other money markets, a base of 360 is used.

Example: Certificates of Deposit (1)

A £1,000,000 three-month (91-day) CD is issued with a stated yield or coupon of 8%.

$$\text{Maturity value} = \pounds1,000,000 + \left(\pounds1,000,000 \times \frac{8}{100} \times \frac{91}{365} \right)$$

$$= \pounds1,019,945.21$$

After 35 days, the CD is traded at a yield of 7¼%. The seller will receive the maturity proceeds discounted by the required yield.

Formula to learn

$$\text{Proceeds of sale} = \text{Maturity} \times \frac{1}{1 + \left(\text{Required yield} \times \frac{\text{No. of days remaining}}{365} \right)}$$

$$= \pounds1,019,945.21 \times \frac{1}{1 + \left(0.0725 \times \frac{56}{365} \right)}$$

$$= \pounds1,008,724.87$$

The proof of this is that £1,008,724.87 invested at 7¼% for 56 days will generate a settlement value of £1,019,945.21, the maturity value of the CD.

A CD with a maturity of over one year the position is complicated by the payment of coupons during the life of the certificate. However, in essence, the process is the same, with the flows arising from the CD being discounted back to their present value at the required yield.

Example: Certificates of Deposit (2)

A CD for £2,000,000 is issued for four years at a rate of 7%. After one year and 65 days, it is sold at a yield of 6½%. The original annual interest payments are as follows.

Year 1	£140,000
Year 2	£140,000
Year 3 (leap year)	£140,383.56
Year 4	£140,000

After one year and 65 days, the remaining cash flows arising from the CD are

£140,000   £140,383.56   £2,140,000

300 days   1 year   1 year

The value of the CD at the point of sale is the present value of these future cash flows discounted by the required yield of 6½%.

The first step is to take the value of the final flow and discount it back to the previous payment date.

$$£2,140,000 \times \frac{1}{1+0.065} = £2,009,389.67$$

This value represents the value of the flows at the end of the third year. The dividend at the end of Year 3 must be added to this and the total discounted back to the end of the second year.

$$(£2,009,389.67 + £140,383.56) \times \frac{1}{1+\left(0.065 \times \frac{366}{365}\right)} = £2,018,228.94$$

The final stage discounts the cumulative flows back to today's date. The overall effect of this process is to bring all of the flows that are occurring in the future back to today's value as determined by the required yield.

$$(£2,018,228.94 + £140,000) \times \frac{1}{1+\left(0.065 \times \frac{300}{365}\right)} = £2,048,773.90$$

Summary

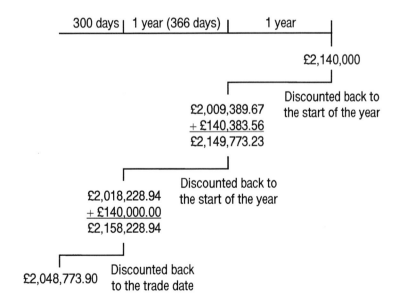

4 COMMERCIAL PAPER

A **Commercial paper (CP)** is another term for a promissory note issued by a commercial company in order to raise short-term funds.

Euro CP (ECP) usually have maturities of two to 180 days but can go up to 365 days, are unsecured and normally issued at a discount to face value in bearer form. Dollar issues are in US$100,000 lots.

Issuers obtain cheaper funds than through bank borrowing and flexibility.

The investor is only exposed to short-term credit risk, but during this time to changes in the credit status of the issuer. Smaller investors may find the denominations too large.

Issuers of **Sterling CP** must have a minimum net worth of £50m, have ordinary or preference share listed on the Stock Exchange. Maturities must be from 8 to 365 days with a minimum amount of £500,000.

5 DEPOSITS

5.1 Introduction

The simplest of all money market instruments is **cash**. In the deposits market, banks take and lay off deposits from each other.

The market is liquid over a wide range of maturities, although primarily less than one year.

Interest is computed on a simple basis, i.e. no compounding. For example, for a £1m deposit for three months (91 days) the interest at 10% would be

$$£1,000,000 \times \frac{10}{100} \times \frac{91}{365} = £24,931.51$$

In the UK, the day count convention is actual/365. Most other markets use the convention of actual/360. Note this is different from the accrued interest convention used in the bond markets.

5.2 Eurosterling

In the immediate post-World War II period, the dollar became established as a quasi-international currency, due to its central position within the Bretton Woods system. Investors were keen to hold the dollar, and large overseas holdings of dollars started to build up outside the US. This process was accelerated by the start of the 'Cold War' when the Eastern European countries repatriated their dollar assets.

The international or 'euro' dollar market gradually evolved from these deposits. London, by virtue of its position as an international banking centre between the two time zones, became the natural home for this market.

Whilst it is possible that there will be a discrepancy between the domestic and the euro rates, due to differences in supply and demand conditions in the markets, normally a process of arbitrage should alleviate relative surpluses and shortages.

With regard to sterling, and most other major currencies, due to the existence of tight exchange controls that prevented currency from leaving the UK, the development of a **Eurosterling market** was limited.

The removal of exchange controls in 1979 has meant that there is no real difference between domestic and international sterling and, consequently, the Eurosterling market remains small.

5.3 Interbank rates

It is from this, primarily interbank market, that key reference interest rates are produced. To date, the key reference rate has been the **London Interbank Offered Rate (LIBOR)**. Thus far, due to the dominance of London as an international banking centre, rate fixing has not been limited to sterling, extending to most internationally traded currencies. Consequently, many floating-rate deals have been priced off LIBOR rates set in London.

With the advent of the euro, this dominance has been under threat. This is particularly true with regard to the establishment of key euro reference rates. The key rival to euro LIBOR is **Euribor**, which is established on the basis of a wider range of quotes from a predominantly Eurozone pool of banks.

It remains to be seen which rate will be most popular as the basis for trading. However, Euribor starts with several key advantages.

	Euro LIBOR	EURIBOR
Panel	16 major banks active in the euro market in London	57 banks: 47 selected by national banking associations to represent the euro markets in the participating Member States; 10 international or 'pre-in' banks active in the euro market with an office in the euro zone
Calculation basis	Discard top and bottom 4 Average remainder	Discard top and bottom 15% Average remainder
Time of fixing	11:00 London time daily	11:00 CET daily
Fixing days	All TARGET days	
For value	Second TARGET day after fixing	
Fixing periods	1 week, 1 month to 12 months	

6 FOREIGN EXCHANGE

6.1 Spot rates

The **spot market** is the market for immediate currency trades. Delivery will take place two business days after the deal is made. The market has no formal market place and trading takes place via telephones with prices being quoted on screen services.

The spot market quotes bid/offer prices in the form of a spread, normally based against the US$. The main exceptions to this is £:$ (known as **'cable'**) and €:$, where the $ is quoted against the £ and € respectively.

Whichever currencies are involved, exchange rates are quoted as the number of units of one currency per single unit of another. For convenience, we will refer to these as the **secondary** and **primary** currencies, respectively. You may also hear them referred to as variable and fixed, or quoted and base – you should view these terms as interchangeable.

As we have just noted, most currencies are quoted against the US$.

- Any quote where the $ is the secondary or variable currency would be referred to as a **direct quote** (e.g. $ per £1)

- An **indirect quote** is where the exchange rate is stated with the US$ as the primary currency (e.g. £ per $1)

Example: £\$ spot rates

1.4275 – 1.4385

The $ buyer's rate   The $ seller's rate

£1 will get $1.4275 $1.4385 will get £1

Here, the dollar is the secondary currency and sterling is the primary currency.

To help remember which rate to use, remember that the bank always gives you the worse side. For example, if you want to buy dollars with £1, the bank will give you the least dollars it can, i.e. $1.4275 rather than $1.4385 in return. Alternatively, if you have dollars and want to buy £1, then the bank will charge you the most it can, i.e. $1.4385 rather than $1.4275.

6.2 Forward rates

The **forward market** is the market in currencies for delivery at an agreed date in the future. The exchange rate at which delivery takes place is agreed now.

Forward rates are quoted at either a **premium (pm)** or a **discount (dis)** to the spot rate. It is possible for rates to be quoted **at par**, in which case the spot and forward are the same.

The premium or discount is quoted in cents, whereas the spot rate is quoted in dollars.

A premium implies that the secondary currency is becoming more expensive relative to the primary one, i.e. in the above example, the dollar is strengthening against sterling and as a result, £1 will buy fewer dollars. Hence, to obtain the forward rate, the premium is **subtracted** from the spot rate. Similarly, the discount is **added**.

This same rule applies regardless of the nature of the quote, **direct or indirect**, since the premium or discount applies to the secondary currency, whichever is the primary one. The rule is that **premiums are subtracted** and **discounts are added**.

Example: £/$ forward rates

Spot   1.4275–1.4385
One-month forward 0.37–0.35c pm
Three-month forward 1.40–1.38c pm

Calculate the three-month forward rate.

Solution

Based on the above figures, the three-month forward rate is as follows.

Spot rate	1.4275-1.4385
Less: premium	0.0140-0.0138
	1.4135-1.4247

Exam tip

An important concept to remember is that forward rates do not necessarily reflect an expectation of what the spot rate will be in three, six or nine months' time. The differences between forward rates and spot rates reflect the difference in interest rates in the two countries: if this were not so, arbitrage would be possible and this would bring the rates back into line. The relationship between forward rates and spot rates is illustrated in the Example below.

Example: Forward rates and spot rates

In the previous example:

- Three-month sterling interest rates were 10%, meaning the interest rate for the three-month period is 2.5% ($10 \times 3/12$)

- Three-month dollar rates were 6%, meaning the interest rate for the three-month period is 1.5% ($6 \times 3/12$).

Spot rate			Three months forward rate	
£1,000	$\rightarrow$	@ 3-month £ rates at 2.5%	$\rightarrow$	£1,025
$\downarrow$				$\downarrow$
@ 1.4275				**Therefore @ 1.4136**
$\downarrow$				$\uparrow$
$1,427.50	$\rightarrow$	@ 3-month $ rates at 1.5%	$\rightarrow$	$1,448.91

The forward rate is calculated on the basis that the money is invested at the current rate of interest in the two countries. At the end of the period, the relationship between the value of the two deposits gives the forward rate.

$$\frac{1,448.91}{1,025} = 1.4136$$

If this relationship were not the case, then it would be possible to make an arbitrage profit by borrowing in one currency, converting it at today's spot rate into the other currency and placing this on deposit for, say, three months. At the same time, a forward contract could be taken out to reverse the original spot transaction, locking in a profit.

6.3 Interest rate parity

The link between exchange rates and interest rates can be worked through using first principles as above.

The link is summarised by the **interest rate parity** formula, which states that:

Formula to learn

$$\text{Forward rate} = \frac{1 + r_S}{1 + r_p} \times \text{Spot rate}$$

where:

r_s = interest rate for the secondary currency for the relevant period
r_p = interest rate for the primary currency for the relevant period

In the above example:

$$\text{Forward rate } = \frac{1.015}{1.025} \times 1.4275 = 1.4136$$

r_s and r_p are calculated based on the number of days in the period. For example, if dollar interest rates for a three-month (91-day) period are 8%, the relevant value for r_s is (8% × 91/360) 2.02%. If sterling interest rates for a three-month (91-day) period are 10%, then the relevant value for r_p is (10% × 91/365) 2.49%.

The use of a 360-day year for dollar interest rates and a 365-day year for sterling is market convention. When banks work out the yield they wish to pay or receive, they take this into account in their quote.

Exam tip

In the Summer 2006 exam, a 2-mark compulsory question asked for a calculation of the forward rate, given spot rate and interest rate information. Although the calculation is not complex, the examiner commented that very few candidates gave the right answer.

CHAPTER ROUNDUP

- A Treasury bill is a promise by the Treasury to repay a set sum of money at a date normally up to 91 days in the future.

- A certificate of deposit (CD) is a securitised form of bank deposit.

- 'Commercial paper' is a term for promissory notes issued by a commercial company to raise short-term funds.

- Many floating rates are priced relative to the London Inter-Bank Offered Rate (LIBOR). EURIBOR is a key euro reference rate.

- The market for immediate currency trades is the spot market. Forward rates are rates quoted now, for delivery of currencies at an agreed future date.

TEST YOUR KNOWLEDGE

Check your knowledge of the Chapter here, without referring back to the text.

1   What is Euro Commercial Paper?

2   Outline what a Treasury bill is.

3   Give two examples of key reference interest rates.

4   In the currency markets, what is meant by 'cable'?

5   If you know the spot rate between currencies A and B, which are freely floating, what information do you
     need to know to be able to calculate a 12-months forward rate?

TEST YOUR KNOWLEDGE: ANSWERS

1   It is a short-term negotiable bearer debt instrument issued under a specific continuously offered ECP programme. ECP is issued by banks, corporations, supranationals and sovereign borrowers at a discount to par. It is issued in most currencies. (See 1.)

2   A Treasury bill or 'T-bill' is a promissory note made by the Treasury via the Bank of England to repay a set sum of money at a specified date in the future, normally not longer than 91 days. (See 2.)

3   LIBOR (London Inter-Bank Offered Rate) and Euribor are key examples. (See 5.3.)

4   The £ sterling: US $ exchange rate is referred to as 'cable'. (See 6.1.)

5   You need to know the interest rate for 12-month deposits, in each currency. (See 6.2.)

6 Instruments and Characteristics – Financial Derivatives

INTRODUCTION

Financial derivatives are instruments which derive their price from the value of an underlying asset, which could be an equity or a commodity, for example.

Futures, options and swaps are major types of derivative, and we discuss these in turn. There is much special terminology relating to derivatives: we need to cover various terms if we are to understand how derivatives markets work.

A swap involves an exchange of cash flows between counterparties.

The level of knowledge you need of financial derivatives for the Global Operations Management exam is 'general', rather than detailed.

1 OVERVIEW

1.1 Introduction

In the minds of the general public, and indeed those of many people involved in the financial services industry, **futures** and **options** – two main types of financial derivative – are considered to be very complicated. They also seem to have little to do with the real world. Television coverage showing pictures of young traders in brightly coloured jackets shouting at each other in an apparent frenzy made it difficult to imagine that what they were engaged in might be of enormous value to the smooth functioning of the economy. Today much of this has migrated to electronic trading platforms.

At the heart of futures and options is the concept of **deferred delivery**. Both instruments allow you, albeit in slightly different ways, to agree **today** the price at which you will buy or sell an asset at sometime in the future. This approach differs from normal, everyday transactions. When we go to a supermarket, we pay our money and take immediate delivery of our goods. Why would someone wish to agree today a price for delivery at sometime in the future? The answer is **certainty**.

Imagine a farmer growing a crop of wheat. To grow such a crop costs money: money for seed, labour, fertiliser, etc. All this expenditure takes place with no certainty that when the crop is eventually harvested, the price at which the wheat is sold will cover these costs. This is obviously risky and many farmers will be unwilling to take on this burden. How can this uncertainty be avoided?

By using futures or options, the farmer will be able to agree **today** a price at which the crop will ultimately be sold, in maybe four or six months' time. This enables the farmer to achieve a minimum sale price for his crop. He is no longer subject to fluctuations in wheat prices. He knows what price his wheat will bring and can therefore plan his business accordingly.

From their origins in the 'commodities' of the agricultural world, futures and options have become available on a wide range of other assets, from metals and crude oil, to bonds and equities. To understand futures and options properly requires considerable application. There is the relevant terminology to master, and many definitions to be understood, but essentially, they are really quite simple. They are products that allow you to fix today the price at which assets may be bought or sold at a future date.

1.2 Over-the-counter (OTC) products

While futures are standardised exchange-traded products, derivatives such as forwards and swaps, as well as exotic options, are traded on the **Over-the-Counter (OTC) market**. This is not a formal market centred on an exchange, but rather a telephone and screen-based market with no administrative centre. Contracts are made on a bilateral basis with the terms negotiated separately for each transaction.

The following table summarises the differences between OTC and exchange-traded markets.

	Exchange-traded	OTC
Quantity	The quantity covered by each contract is determined by the Exchange. Only whole contracts may be traded.	Can be tailored to meet the need of the investor exactly.
Quality	Defined by the contract specification.	Can be varied according to need.
Delivery/ Expiry dates	Only allowed on dates fixed by the exchange.	Can be tailored to meet the customer's needs.
Liquidity	Generally good, but dependent upon the product.	May be limited; market may be made by just one firm.
Counterparty Risk	A central counterparty always exists so there is no counterparty risk to the clearing member once contract registered.	Risk exists of default, therefore credit rating of counterparty very important.
Margin	Margin will normally be required.	Normally, no margin.
Regulation	Subject to significant regulation as RIEs/DIEs.	Less actively regulated. May not be suitable for certain categories of customer.

1.3 ISDA

The **International Swaps and Derivatives Association (ISDA)** is a trade organisation for participants in the market for over-the-counter derivatives market. ISDA has created the **ISDA Master Agreement** – a standardised contract for derivatives transactions.

A key aspect of the ISDA Master Agreement is that the Master Agreement and all confirmations entered into under it form a single agreement. This allows parties to an ISDA Master Agreement to aggregate amounts owing by each of them under all of transactions outstanding under the Agreement and to net them off to a single amount payable by one party to the other.

Additionally, ISDA develops industry standards for derivatives and provides legal definitions of terms used in contracts.

1.4 Securities synthetics

The term '**synthetic**' refers to any combination of cash and derivative instruments which is designed to replicate the performance of another type of financial instrument. These include for example, synthetic calls, synthetic puts, synthetic bonds and synthetic floating rate notes.

A security synthetic is formed by repackaging an asset in the secondary market. An example might be if an interest rate swap and a fixed rate bond were combined to produce a synthetic floating rate payments flow. The terms of the new security might not otherwise have been available in the market so the resulting security is artificial and is termed 'synthetic'.

2 FUTURES

2.1 Terminology

2.1.1 Definition of a future

'A future is an agreement to buy or sell a standard quantity of a specified asset on a fixed future date at a price agreed today.'

There are two parties to a futures contract, a buyer and a seller, whose obligations are as follows.

- The buyer of a future enters into an **obligation** to buy on a specified date.
- The seller of a future is under an **obligation** to sell on a future date.

These obligations relate to a **standard quantity** of a **specified asset** on a **fixed future date** at a **price** agreed **today**.

2.1.2 Standard quantity

Exchange-traded futures are traded in standardised parcels known as **contracts**.

For example, a futures contract on lead might be for 25 tonnes of the metal, or a currency future might be for €125,000. The purpose of this standardisation is so that buyers and sellers are clear about the quantity that will be delivered. If you sold one lead future, you would know that you were obligated to sell 25 tonnes of lead.

Futures are only traded in whole numbers of contracts. So, if you wished to buy 50 tonnes of lead, you would buy two lead futures.

2.1.3 Specified asset

Imagine that you entered into a futures contract on a car (if such a contract were to exist). Let us say you buy one car futures contract that gives you the obligation to buy a car at a fixed price of £15,000, with delivery taking place in December.

It is obvious that something very important is missing from the contract, namely any detail about what type of car you are to buy. Most of us would be happy to pay £15,000 for a Porsche, but rather less happy if all our £15,000 bought was an old Citroen 2CV.

All futures contracts are governed by their contract specifications, and these legal documents set out in great detail the size of each contract, when delivery is to take place, and what exactly is to be delivered. It is not enough to know that a lead futures contract is for 25 tonnes of the metal. Users will want to know the level of purity and shape of the metal in which they are dealing.

2.1.4 Fixed future date

The delivery of futures contracts takes place on a specified date(s) known as **delivery day(s)**. This is when buyers exchange money for goods with sellers. Futures have finite lifespans so that once the **last trading day** is past, it is impossible to trade the futures for that date.

At any one time, a range of delivery months may be traded and as one delivery day passes, a new date is introduced.

2.1.5 Price agreed today

This final phrase in the definition is the most important of all. The reason why many people, from farmers to fund managers, like using futures is (as was explained in the first section of this Chapter) that they introduce certainty.

Imagine a farmer growing a crop of wheat. In the absence of a futures market, he has no idea whether he will make a profit or a loss when he plants the seeds in the ground. By the time he harvests his crop, the price of wheat may be so low that he will not be able to cover his costs. However, with a futures contract, he can fix a price for his wheat many months before harvest. If, six months before the harvest, he sells a wheat future, he enters into an obligation to sell wheat at that price on the stipulated delivery day. In other words, he knows what price his goods will fetch.

You might think that this is all well and good, but what happens if there is a drought or a frost that makes it impossible for the farmer to deliver his wheat?

Futures are tradable and so, although the contract obligates the buyer to buy and the seller to sell, these obligations can be **offset** by undertaking an equal and opposite trade in the market.

For example, let us suppose a farmer has sold 1 September wheat future at £120 per tonne. If, subsequently, the farmer decides he does not wish to sell his wheat, but would prefer to use the grain to feed his cattle, he simply buys 1 September future at the then prevailing price. His original sold position is now offset by a bought position, leaving him with no outstanding delivery obligations.

This offsetting is common in future markets: very few contracts run through to delivery.

2.2 Ticks

A **tick** is the smallest permitted price movement in a futures contract and is found in a legal document known as the contract specification.

For example, for the wheat future traded on Euronext.liffe, the tick is 5 pence per metric tonne. If the current quote were £120.00, the quote must change by at least 5 pence to £120.05 or £119.95. It could not change to £120.01, as this would be a movement of less than a tick. The reason for exchanges limiting the minimum amount by which prices may change is purely administrative – it avoids potentially huge numbers of trading prices.

Following on from tick size is the concept of **tick value**. Since each futures contract has a fixed size (e.g. for wheat this is 100 tonnes), the smallest price movement can be given a monetary value. In the case of the wheat future, this is 100 × 5p or £5.

Each tick will mean a difference of £5 in the cost of buying or selling 100 tonnes of wheat. By knowing the tick size and tick value, it becomes easy to calculate the resultant profits and losses from futures trades as we will see in the next section on futures usage.

2.3 Users of futures

Various sorts of people use futures. Some, like the wheat farmer, may use them to reduce risk, others to seek high returns and for this, be willing to take high risks. Futures markets are, in fact, wholesale markets in risk. They are markets in which risks are transferred from the cautious to those with more adventurous (or reckless) spirits.

The users fall into one of three categories: the **hedger**, the **speculator** and the **arbitrageur**.

- A **hedger** is seeking to reduce risk
- A **speculator** is a risk-taker, seeking profits
- An **arbitrageur** seeks riskless profits from exploiting market inefficiencies

In this section, we will look at **hedging** and **speculation**, starting with speculation.

2.4 Speculation: buying a future

Let us imagine a speculator thinks that the situation in the Middle East is becoming more dangerous and that war is imminent. If war takes place, he would expect oil supplies to become restricted and the price of oil to rise.

He therefore buys 1 July oil future at $60.50 per barrel. The cash price of oil is $59.00.

The contract size is 1,000 barrels, the tick size 1 cent. The tick value is $10, i.e. 1,000 × $0.01.

1 May – Action: Buy 1 July Oil Future at $60.50

Regrettably, the speculator's fears prove correct and the Middle East goes to war with oil prices rising accordingly. The **cash price** (that is, the price of oil for immediate delivery) rises to $69.

21 May – Action: Sell 1 July Oil Future at $70

To calculate the profit from this trade, we must first find out how many ticks the contract has moved, then multiply this by the tick value and further multiply it by the number of contracts involved.

Formula to learn

Ticks × Tick value × Contracts

How many ticks?

The contract has moved from $60.50 to $70. This is $9.50 or 950 ticks (a tick, remember, is one cent).

The tick value, we are told, is $10.

The number of contracts is 1.

Therefore

Ticks × Tick value × Contracts

950 × $10 × 1 = $9,500 profit

The reason the speculator has made a profit is that the futures market has risen in response to a rise in the cash market price of oil. Generally, futures prices can be expected to move at the same rate and to the same extent as cash market prices. This is a far from trivial observation. The cash market and the futures market in this example have both risen: the cash market from $59 to $69 – an increase of $10 per barrel; and the futures market from $60.50 to $70.00 – a rise of $9.50. Remember that the futures and cash markets, whilst related, are separate markets each subject to their own supply and demand pressures.

In the oil example above, the speculator bought a futures contract in anticipation of a rise in oil prices. A transaction in which a future is purchased to open a position is known as a **long position**. Thus, the purchase of the oil future would be described as 'going long of the future' or simply 'long'.

Conversely, when a future is sold to open a position, this is described as 'going short' or simply, **short**.

Before going on to consider a short futures position, let us summarise the risk of being long a future.

Long future

Risk	Reward
Almost unlimited. The maximum loss would occur if the future fell to zero. For our oil speculator, this would be if the July future fell from $60.50 to $0, i.e. a loss of $60.50.	Unlimited: as the futures price could rise to infinity, the profit is potentially unlimited.

2.5 Speculation: selling a future

Let us consider another example. If a speculator thinks that an asset price will fall, he will seek to make a profit by selling the future at the currently high price and subsequently buying it back at a low price. This is not an activity commonly undertaken in the cash markets and therefore needs explanation.

There are two ways of making profits – the first is to buy at a low price and sell at a high price. For example, we may buy a house at £80,000 and sell it at £100,000, making a £20,000 profit. In futures markets, it is equally easy to sell something at a high price and buy it back at a low price. If you thought the property market was going to fall, you could sell a house at £100,000 and buy it back at £80,000 again, realising a £20,000 profit. In the actual property market, it is not easy to go 'short' of a house, but in the futures market, in which deliveries are at some future date, it is straightforward.

Let us imagine that a speculator feels that the oil market is becoming oversupplied and that oil prices will fall.

1 July – Action: Sell 1 September Oil Future at $62.00

14 July – Action: Buy 1 September Oil Future at $60.00

By 14 July, the future price has fallen and the speculator 'buys back' his short futures position, thus extinguishing any delivery obligations.

The profit can be calculated by again multiplying:

$$\text{Tick movement} = \frac{22.00 - 20.00}{0.01^*} = 200$$

Ticks × Tick value × Contracts

200 × $10 × 1

= $2,000 profit

*1 cent or 1/100 of a dollar is the tick size.

Now we can summarise the risk of being short the future.

Short future

Risk	Reward
Unlimited	Limited, but large. The future can only fall to zero, giving in this example a gain of $62 per barrel.

2.6 Hedging

2.6.1 Protecting against a price fall

Speculators use futures to take on risks in the hope of large profits. **Hedgers** use futures to reduce the risk of existing cash market positions. **Hedging** is motivated by a need for certainty and security.

Consider the position of an oil producer. The producer's profitability will be determined largely by the price of crude oil. When times are good, and the demand for oil is high, he will make good profits. However, if oil prices fall, he may find that the market price for oil is so low that the price does not cover the costs of extracting the oil from the ground. It is in helping people such as this that futures have their most important application.

The following graph shows the oil producer's exposure to the price of oil.

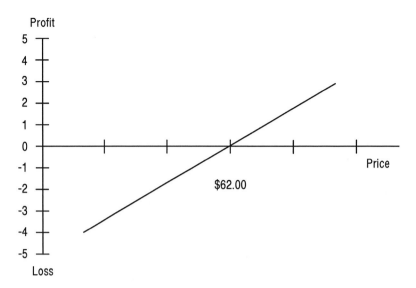

This shows that if prices go up, so do profits; if the price falls below a certain level, losses will emerge. This position is described as a **long position**.

How can the risk from a fall in price be reduced?

This can be done by selling futures and thereby entering into a contract that will obligate the futures seller to deliver oil at some time in the future at a price agreed today. Through this mechanism, the oil producer can establish a sale price for his, say, July production of oil some time in advance, without having to wait until July when the price may be much lower. When futures are sold to hedge a long cash market position, it is known as a **short hedge**.

The theory of futures hedging is based on the future's position producing profits or losses to offset the profits or losses in the cash market.

For example, an oil producer will have 100,000 barrels of crude oil available for delivery in July. He is nervous about the price of oil and expects it to fall sharply. On 1 May, the cash market price of oil is $62 a barrel, and the July future is trading at $63.

1 May – Action: Sell 100* July Oil Futures at $63

* 100 because each contract represents 1,000 barrels, and the producer is hedging 100,000 barrels.

The oil producer is now long in the physical market (that is, he has 100,000 barrels for July delivery). He is also short 100,000 barrels in the futures market.

By the middle of June, the oil price has fallen to $58 a barrel and the July future has fallen to $59 a barrel. The oil producer has managed to find a buyer for his July production at $58 and therefore buys back his futures contracts at $59.

15 June – Action: Buy 100 July Oil Futures at $59

The profit from the futures trade should, if we have constructed the hedge properly, compensate the producer for the fall in oil prices. Let us see if this is true by first calculating the futures profit and then calculating the oil market loss.

Futures profit

Ticks × Tick value × Contracts

$$\frac{23.00-19.00}{0.01} \times \$10 \times 100$$

= $400,000 profit

Cash market loss

58.00 – 62.00 × 100,000

= $400,000 loss

As you can see, the profit and loss net each other out, demonstrating that the fall in oil prices did not hurt the producer.

This is illustrated on the following graph.

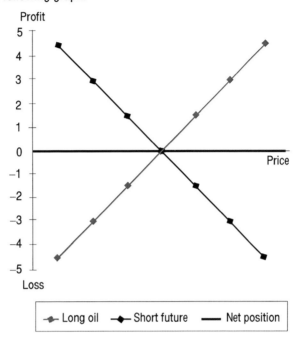

Whether the price of oil goes up or down, the producer need not worry as he has, by selling futures, 'locked in' a sale price for his oil.

The numbers in this example are slightly unrealistic, as there is a perfect offset between cash and futures markets. In the real world, futures do not always move precisely in line with the cash market.

In the example above, we have seen how futures can be used to protect the oil producer against a price fall with a short hedge.

Exam tip	Short hedge: Protects against a price fall.

2.6.2 Protecting against a price rise

Futures can also be used to hedge against a price rise.

Suppose that a chemical company, whose principal raw material is crude oil, is becoming nervous about a rise in oil prices. The current cash price of crude oil is $58.00 and the November future trades at $58.50 per barrel.

To protect itself against the possibility of a rise, the company could agree today the price it will pay for oil to be delivered in November. To guarantee the purchase price, the company can buy or go long in the futures contract.

If the price of oil does rise, the physical oil will now cost more to acquire, but the cost of purchase will be reduced by the futures profit.

Exam tip	Long hedge: Protects against a rise

3 OPTIONS

3.1 Definition of an option

> An option is a contract that confers the **right, but not the obligation**, to **buy or sell** an asset at a given **price** on or before a given **date**.

This lengthy sentence needs to be understood before moving on. A good way of understanding it is to think how a speculator hoping for a rise in the price of, say, cocoa, would use an option. The key phrase is, '**the right but not the obligation**'.

Conventionally, a speculator anticipating a rise in the price of cocoa would straightforwardly buy cocoa for immediate delivery and then store the goods, hoping to sell them for a profit once the price rose.

If we imagine that the price of cocoa is £600 per tonne and that the speculator buys just one tonne, the expenditure would be:

Cost × Quantity

£600 × 1 = £600

Another way of representing the hope of a rise in cocoa prices would be to buy a cocoa **option** – specifically, an option that would give the right, but not the obligation, to buy cocoa at a price of £600 per tonne – for a period of three months. The purchase of this option would cost, say, £5 a tonne. Remember that an option is a contract for a future delivery, so it would not be necessary to pay £600 in the first instance – the only money to be invested at this point is the £5.

If an option on one tonne of cocoa was bought, it would cost:

Cost × Quantity

£5 × 1 = £5.00

Suppose that, three months later, the price of cocoa has risen from £600 per tonne to £700 per tonne.

This is good news for both the conventional cocoa buyer and the cocoa options buyer.

First, let us look at the position of the speculator who bought physical cocoa.

Purchase price £600

Sale price £700

Profit £100

On an investment of £600, the investor has made a profit of £100 in just three months.

Let us now look at the profit for the options buyer. Three months ago, he entered into a contract that gave him the right, but not the obligation, to buy cocoa at £600. When purchased, that right cost just £5 per tonne. With cocoa now trading at £700, the right to buy at £600 must be worth £100 – the difference between the current price and the stated price in the contract.

Why is the option worth £100? Suppose that, given a market price of £700, the option to buy at £600 costs just £40. Any sensible investor would take up his right to buy at £600 and then immediately sell cocoa in the market at £700. The investor would have spent £640 and received £700 for no risk. Markets rarely, if ever, give money away without requiring people to take some risk, as arbitrageurs would move in to exploit the situation until prices come back into line. In an efficient market, the right to buy now at £600, with a market price of £700, must be worth £100.

Returning to our original options transaction, recall that the right to buy at £600 was purchased for £5. With the market price at £700 at the end of the option's life, the option will now be worth £100.

	£
Purchase price	5
Current value	100
Unrealised profit	**95**

On an investment of £5, a £95 profit has been achieved. In percentage terms, given the initial outlay of only £5, this profit is proportionately much greater than for someone buying and selling physical cocoa for cash.

Note that options are **tradable instruments**. It is not necessary for the underlying asset to be bought or sold. What more commonly occurs is that **options** are bought and sold. Thus, an option bought at £5 could be sold to the market at £100, realising a £95 profit with the investor never having an intention of taking delivery of the underlying asset (i.e., the cocoa).

3.2 Options terminology

In the definition of an option given earlier, an option was described as being the right, but not the obligation, to buy or sell something. Options giving the right to buy and the right to sell, respectively, are given different names.

- An option giving the right to buy is known as a **call option**
- An option giving the right to sell is known as a **put option**

The rights to buy (**call**) or sell (**put**) are held by the person buying the option, who is known as the option **holder**. The person selling an option is known as a **writer**.

The following diagram illustrates the relationship between option holders and option writers.

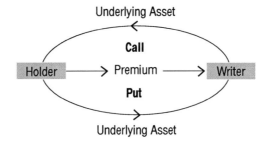

The first thing to understand is the flow of **premium**. Premium is the cost of an option. In our cocoa example, the premium was £5 and this is paid by the holder and received by the writer.

In return for receiving the premium, the writer agrees to fulfil the terms of the contract, which of course are different for **calls** and **puts**.

Call writers agree to deliver the asset underlying the contract if 'called' upon to do so. When options holders wish to take up their rights under the contract, they are said to **exercise** the contract. For a call, this means that the writer must deliver the underlying asset for which he will receive the fixed amount of cash stipulated in the original contract.

Therefore, for a cocoa call option that gives the holder the right, but not the obligation, to buy at £600, this would mean that the writer would be required to deliver cocoa to the holder at £600. The option's holder will only want to buy at £600 when it would be advantageous for him to do so, i.e. only when the real or market price is somewhat higher than £600. If the market price were less than £600, there would be no sense in paying more than the market price for the goods.

- **Call options writers** run great risks. In return for receiving the option's premium, they are committed to delivering the underlying asset at a fixed price. As the price of the asset could, in theory, rise infinitely, they could be forced to buy the underlying asset at a high price and to deliver it to the option's holder at a much lower value. The price at which an options contract gives the right to buy (call) or sell (put) is known as the **exercise price** or **strike price**.

- **Put options writers** are also run substantial risks. The writer of a put is obligated to pay the exercise price for assets that are delivered to him. Put options are only exercised when it is advantageous for the holders to do so. This will be when they can use the option to sell their assets at a higher price than would be otherwise available in the market.

To summarise, options writers, in return for receiving premium, run large risks. This is similar to the role undertaken by insurance companies. For a relatively modest premium, they are willing to insure your house against fire but, if your house burns down, they will be faced with a claim for many thousands of pounds. The reasons why insurers and options writers enter into such contracts are that houses don't often burn down, and markets don't often rise or fall substantially. If writers price options properly, they hope to make money in most instances. Option writing is not for the faint-hearted, nor for those without substantial resources. That said, many conservative users do write options as part of strategies involving the holding of the underlying asset. Such uses that are **covered** are much less risky and are discussed later.

When investors buy or hold options, the risk is limited to the option's premium. If the market moves against them, they can simply decide not to exercise their options and sacrifice the premium. Remember, options holders have the right, **but not the obligation**, to buy (call) or sell (put). If it does not make sense to buy or sell at the exercise price, the holder can decide to **abandon** the option.

3.3 Describing options

We have learnt so far that options come in two forms: **calls** and **puts**.

We have also learnt that the price paid for an option is known as the premium and that the price at which the option gives the right to buy or sell is known as the exercise price or strike price.

Another way in which options are described relates to their **maturity**. Options are instruments with limited life spans. The date on which an option comes to the end of its life is known as its **expiry date**. The expiry date is the last day on which the option may be exercised or traded. After this date, the option disappears and cannot be traded or exercised.

Options are available with different methods of **exercise**, which are specified when the options are traded.

- **'American style' options** can be exercised by the holder at any time after the option has been purchased
- **'European style' options** can only be exercised on its expiry date

There are many variations on the basic options described so far. These are commonly called exotics.

A person describing an option will need to specify:

- Underlying asset
- Expiry date
- Exercise price
- Call/Put

e.g.   Cocoa (Underlying asset)
       May   (Expiry date)
       600   (Exercise price)
       Call   (Call/Put)

The Table below shows prices of call options on the shares of a fictitious company, XYZ plc. The options give an entitlement to buy (call) the company's shares. The underlying price is 76.

XYZ Calls

Exercise price	January premium	April premium	July premium
60	23	28	33
70	12	18	23
80	5	8	12

Note that there are a range of exercise prices and expiry dates available. Normally, you would expect there to be exercise prices available both below and above the underlying price. As the underlying price fluctuates, new exercise prices are introduced.

There is also a range of expiry dates available. This allows investors a choice as to the maturity of their options. As one expiry date passes, a new expiry date is introduced, thus maintaining the choice of dates.

A similar range of exercise prices and expiry dates would be available in XYZ puts. The premiums quoted for calls and puts would however be different.

How much would you pay?

In the Table above, the premium quoted for the April 60 call is 28. To find out how much this would be, we must know two things: first, **how the product is quoted** and secondly, the **contract size**.

Options are traded on a wide variety of assets from currencies, bonds and shares to metals, oils and commodities. Each market has different conventions. For example, crude oil prices are normally quoted in US dollars per barrel, whilst share prices for UK companies are quoted in pence per share.

Governing the operation of options contracts are **contract specifications** that set out, amongst other things, rules specifying how they are quoted, expiry dates and when exercise prices are introduced. These documents are important because they enable everyone to understand the details of the contract.

Exchange-traded options, like futures contracts, are 'standardised', with the method of quotation and contract size being fixed. The only variable is the option's premium.

So, what does a quote of 28 for the April 60 call mean?

From the contract specification, we find out that the premium is quoted in pence per share. Thus, '28' means 28 pence per XYZ share.

To determine how much the option costs, we must consult the contract specification again to find out the contract size. This is given as 1,000 shares per contract.

All options, like futures, are traded in standardised lots or contracts. It is only possible to trade in whole numbers of contracts. You could not, for example, buy 1½ April 60 calls.

We know that the quote for XYZ options is in pence per share and that the contract size is 1,000 shares. Therefore, one XYZ April 60 call would cost:

28p × 1,000 = 28,000 pence, or £280.00

3.4 Simple uses of options

This section covers four basic strategies and uses of options.

The common perception of options is that they are invariably high-risk investments. This is not the case. Some positions may be high risk, whilst others may be considerably less risky than a holding in the underlying asset. It is vital that everyone involved in trading, administering or settling options understands the differences between high and low-risk strategies.

3.5 Buying a call

This strategy is motivated by a view that an asset's price will rise.

- **Risk** – The investor's risks are limited to the premium he pays for the options. So, if the 80 call could be bought for a premium of 5, the 5 is all he risks. The premium of the call option will only be a fraction of the cost of the underlying asset, so the option can be considered less risky than buying the asset itself. Even so, remember that the whole premium is at risk and one can lose 100% of the investment, albeit a relatively small amount of money.

- **Reward** – The rewards from buying a call are unlimited. As the contract gives the holder the right to buy at a fixed price, this right will become increasingly valuable as the asset price rises above the exercise price.

Suppose that an investor buys one XYZ call option, which gives him the right, but not the obligation, to buy the XYZ asset at a fixed price of 80 between now and the option's expiry date in January. The cost of this option is 5.

If the asset price rises to 120, the right to buy at 80 (i.e. the premium of the 80 call) must be worth at least 40. The net profit for the call would be 40 – 5 (the original cost of the option) = 35. Of course, if the price of XYZ falls below 80 at the option's expiry date, the 80 call will be worthless and 100% of the initial 5 invested will be lost. This loss occurs because no sensible person would want the right to buy at 80 if they could buy the asset more cheaply elsewhere.

By using a graph, we can show how much an option will be worth at expiry.

On the vertical axis of the graph is profit/loss and on the horizontal axis is the asset price.

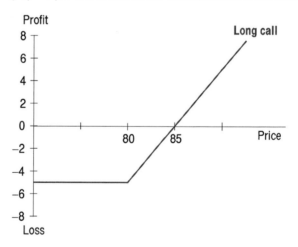

Holder of 1 XYZ January 80 Call – Premium 5

What the graph shows is that losses of 5 are made anywhere below 80, whilst profits emerge above 85. The **breakeven** point is represented by 85. This is the point at which the original investment is recouped and it is calculated by simply adding the premium to the exercise price, e.g. 80 + 5 = 85. The buying of a call to open a position is known as a 'long call'.

3.6 Selling a call

This is a risky strategy.

- **Risk** – Selling, or writing, a call without at the same time being in possession of the underlying asset is extremely risky. The **risk is unlimited** because the writer has a duty to deliver the asset at a fixed price regardless of the prevailing asset price. As the share price could, in theory, rise to infinity, the call writer assumes an unlimited risk. This strategy is sometimes called **naked** call writing and, as the term suggests, can leave you feeling very exposed.

- **Reward** – You might ask why someone would assume such an unlimited risk. The answer, of course, is the hope of a profit. The maximum profit the writer can make is the premium he receives. Let us look again at an 80 call with a premium of 5. The seller of this call will receive the 5 premium and, as long as the asset price at expiry is less than 80, no one will want to exercise the right to buy.

The graph of profit/loss against price for selling a call is set out below. You will see that it is the opposite of buying a call.

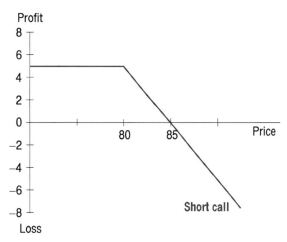

Writer of 1 XYZ January 80 Call – Premium 5

As the graph demonstrates, the call writer believes that the asset price is likely either to stay the same or fall. If this happens, the writer simply pockets the premium received and will not have to deliver the asset. The selling of a call to open a position is known as a 'short call'.

3.7 Buying a put

Now we summarise the risk and reward situation in buying a put.

- **Risk** – As when buying a call, the risk is limited to the premium paid. The motivation behind buying a put will be to profit from a fall in the asset's price. The holder of a put obtains the right, but not the obligation, to sell at a fixed price. The value of this right will become increasingly valuable as the asset price falls.

- **Reward** – The greatest profit that will arise from buying a put will be achieved if the asset price falls to zero.

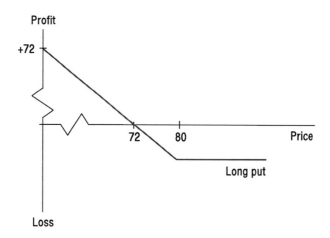

Holder of 1 XYZ July 80 Put – Premium 8

The breakeven point, and maximum profit, is calculated by deducting the premium from the exercise price, e.g. 80 – 8 = 72. Like the purchase of a call, the premium needs to be recovered before profits are made. The buying of a put to open a position is known as a '**long put**'.

3.8 Selling a put

Someone selling a put is taking on an obligation to buy an asset at a specified price.

- **Risk** – Selling a put is dangerous, as the writer enters into an obligation to purchase at a fixed price an asset whose may fall. If the market price of the asset falls, the put writer will end up paying a large amount of money for what could be a valueless asset. The worst case will arise when the asset price falls to zero. If this happens, the loss will be the exercise price less the premium received.

- **Reward** – The put option writer hopes that the put will not be exercised. This will occur if the asset has a price above the exercise price at expiry. The maximum reward is the premium received. The selling of a put to open a position is known as a 'short put'.

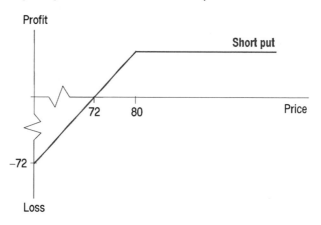

Writer of 1 XYZ July 80 Put – Premium 8

Exam tip

The **four basic strategies outlined above** form the building blocks of various more complicated option techniques.

You may wish to re-read the material so that you are clear about three things:

- What is the motivation behind each trade?
- What are the risks associated with them?
- What are the rewards?

3.9 Options on futures

The types of option discussed so far have been options which, upon exercise, result in the purchase or sale of a tangible underlying security such as a share.

More common than these types of option are **options on futures**. This apparently complex term simply describes options, the exercise of which results in a long or short futures position.

Thus:

- The exercise of a **long call** results in the holder establishing a **long futures** position
- The exercise of a **long put** results in the holder establishing a **short futures** position

4 GEARING AND RISK

4.1 Introduction

Clearly, the attributes of futures products and tangible assets are quite different. Two characteristics are worth highlighting, namely gearing and risk.

4.2 Gearing

One of the most attractive, but also dangerous attributes of futures and options, is that they can be used in a geared way.

Gearing describes the power of such products to control, for a low or nil cost, a relatively much more expensive asset. This has the effect of magnifying profits and losses.

To demonstrate how gearing works, let us look at an example using options.

Example: Gearing

An investor buys 1 XYZ January 70 call for 12.

The XYZ share price is 76.

XYZ's share price at expiry is 100 and the call is worth 30. From an investment of 12, a profit of 18 is made. In percentage terms, this is

$$\frac{\text{Profit}}{\text{Initial investment}} = \frac{18}{12} \times 100$$

= 150% profit

If the XYZ share had been bought at 76 and subsequently sold at 100, the figure would be

$$\frac{\text{Profit}}{\text{Initial investment}} = \frac{24}{76} \times 100$$

= 31.6% profit

As can be seen, the profit from the options trade is very much larger. However, if we imagine a fall in the shares to 70 at expiry, we can see that gearing works both ways.

Buy call at	12	
Call at expiry	0	
Loss	12	or 100%

If instead the stock had been bought at 76 and subsequently sold at 70 for a loss of 6, the percentage loss would be

$$\frac{6}{76} \times 100 = 7.9\% \, loss$$

Gearing needs be treated with great **caution** and only investors who understand this attribute should speculate with futures and options. It is very easy to lose your entire investment, or worse.

4.3 Summary of risks

Set out below is a table that broadly summarises the risks and rewards from the basic speculative futures and options positions described in this chapter.

Position	Risk	Reward
Long Call	Limited to premium	Unlimited
Long Put	Limited to premium	Almost unlimited*
Short Call	Unlimited	Limited
Short Put	Almost unlimited*	Limited
Long Future	Almost unlimited**	Unlimited
Short Future	Unlimited	Almost unlimited**

*   Asset cannot fall below zero
**   Future cannot fall below zero

5   SWAPS

5.1 Overview

Swaps are agreements under which counterparties agree to exchange (swap) specific future cash flows. For example, in an interest rate swap, the counterparties agree to exchange future interest payments.

Historically, these arrangements were first developed as corporate to corporate deals with any financial intermediary simply acting as a broker. Now, the financial intermediaries act as market makers. They execute swaps where there is no counterparty as yet, holding one side of the deal on their own account (warehousing one leg) until a counterparty can be found. In this way, they face the true risk of an intermediary.

There are five major types of swap arrangement to consider.

- Interest rate swaps
- Short-term currency swaps
- Long-term currency swaps
- Equity swaps
- Commodity swaps

Our aim in examining these is to analyse:

- The mechanics of the arrangement, i.e. the risks and rewards of their use
- The pricing/valuation of the arrangement

5.2 Interest rate swaps

5.2.1 Introduction

An **interest rate swap** is a contract which commits two counterparties to exchange, over an agreed period, two streams of interest payments, each calculated using a different interest rate index, but applied to a common notional principal amount.

Key points

- Only interest is exchanged in the swap; there is no exchange of principal. Interest rate swaps do not, therefore, impact on the balance sheet, only on the profit and loss account. They are therefore classed as '**off balance sheet instruments**'.

- Movements in the interest cash flow streams take place at intervals during the swap's life and are normally netted. For example, in a swap in which one side is paying a fixed rate and the other a floating rate, such as six-month LIBOR, only the cash difference is exchanged. This reduces credit risks between the counterparties.

5.2.2 A basic interest rate swap

The cash flows in a basic interest rate swap could be pictured as follows.

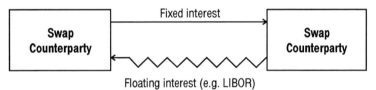

5.2.3 Terminology

- **Coupon swap.** A coupon swap involves the exchange of a fixed interest rate (e.g. the coupon payment on a bond) for the floating rate as measured by an index such as LIBOR. These are sometimes called fixed against floating or generic swaps.

- **Counterparties to a coupon swap**

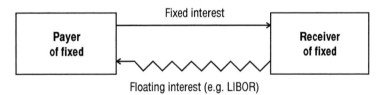

- **Counterparties – alternative terms**

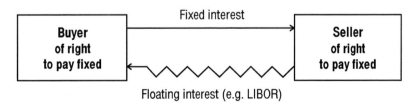

- **Basis swap.** It is possible to swap two interest streams which are both calculated using floating interest rates, e.g. three-month LIBOR vs six-month LIBOR.

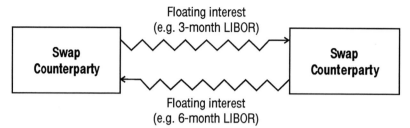

- **Counterparties to a basis swap**

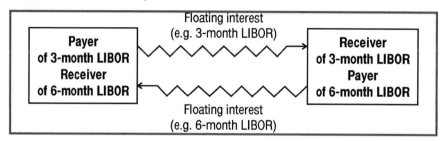

- **Asset swap.** When the interest streams being exchanged through an interest rate swap are funded with interest received on specific assets, the swap is called an asset swap. Asset swaps may also be **coupon** or **basis** swaps.

- **Term swap.** A swap with a lifespan of more than two years.

- **Money market swap.** A swap with up to two years of life when originally negotiated.

5.2.4 Dealing

Inception

The market in interest rate swaps is an over-the-counter (OTC) market. Trading is conducted over the telephone, and price information is disseminated through quote vendor systems, such as Reuters and Telerate.

In interest rate swaps, the floating rate in a coupon swap (the most common type of swap) is assumed to be six-month LIBOR. Negotiation therefore concentrates on the fixed rate, sometimes called the swap rate.

There are two methods of quoting the fixed rate: the all-in price, or as a swap spread on a benchmark rate.

All-in prices

A quote for a one-year swap may be given as 8.00%-7.85%. This is a two-way price in which the dealer would pay a fixed rate of 7.85% and would look to receive 8.00% fixed. The dealing spread of 15 basis points represents the dealer's profit.

Swap spreads

In more liquid interest rate swaps markets, such as the US, the use of all-in terms for quoting the fixed rates in coupon swaps has been replaced by the convention of quoting in two parts: a swap spread and a benchmark interest rate.

The benchmark interest rate is usually the yield on the 'on the run' (most actively traded) bond, with a remaining life similar to the swap. When the swap is agreed, the spread and the benchmark are fixed.

Example: Swap spread

	Swap spread	Bond yield
Two years	21/25	5.70-5.75

The spread is quoted bid/offer in basis, hence this quote corresponds to an all-in price of 5.91-6.00.

Termination and assignment

Termination and assignment are two methods by which counterparties can exit their swap positions. A third route, the reversal, in which an equal and opposite position is taken, is also available.

Termination is simply the mutual cancellation of the swap. Assignment is the process through which existing swaps are sold to new counterparties.

When a swap is terminated or assigned, it is valued and a cash compensation paid to the party that is in-the-money.

The termination value will be the NPV of the cash flows (see valuation below). Assignment values are calculated in the same way, although the pricing can be complicated by credit issues.

5.2.5 Uses of interest rate swaps

As with futures and options, there are three basic motivations: speculation, hedging and arbitrage.

Speculation

Interest rate swaps can be used to take risky positions independent of any underlying instruments. In a coupon swap:

- **The payer of fixed interest** is exposed to the risk of an interest rate fall but will benefit if rates rise, since he is in the same commercial position as an issuer of a fixed coupon bond or fixed rate mortgage borrower.

- **The receiver of fixed interest** is exposed to the risk of an interest rate rise but will benefit if rates fall, since he is in the same commercial position as an investor in a fixed coupon bond.

Hedging

Swap hedges work in a very similar way to futures hedges, in that swaps are used to establish an equal and opposite position.

For example, assume a bank has invested its assets in fixed rate bonds, but has liabilities (depositors) to whom it has to pay floating rates. The bank is exposed to rising rates which will increase its payments without the benefit of increased returns on its bonds.

This position could be hedged using swaps, and the cash flows for the hedged arrangement are illustrated below.

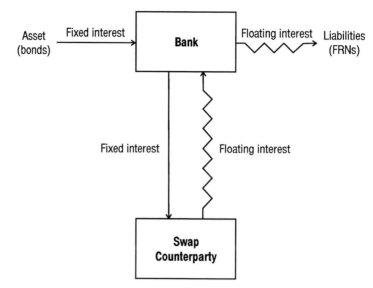

In this hedge, the bank:

Receives	Pays
Fixed interest from the bonds	Floating interest to depositors
Floating interest from the swap counterparty	Fixed interest to the swap counterparty

In this way, the mismatch between the asset and liability cash flows is overcome.

Example: Interest rate swap

An institution raises money by issuing a five-year bond at a yield of 8.75%, but would prefer floating rate funding. Five-year swaps are quoted at all-in rates of 8.95-9.075. How could the institution change its interest rate exposure to floating rates and what would be the all-in cost of its borrowing after swapping?

Solution

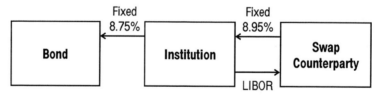

Summary of cash flows

Cost of bond	−8.75%
Fixed receipts via swap	+8.95%
Floating payments via swap	LIBOR
Net cost of borrowing	LIBOR − 20 basis points

Arbitrage

Another important use of interest rate swaps is arbitrage. Indeed, it was the driver behind the early development of the market. The arbitrage occurs because the fixed rate bond market and the floating rate banking markets have differing perceptions of an institution's credit risk.

The collaboration between two institutions that are viewed differently by the markets can result in an interesting example of financial alchemy. The following example illustrates this point.

5.3 Forward rate agreements

Interest rate swaps are usually appropriate for longer term interest rate exposures and are often used for maturities of between two and five years, possibly going out even further. **Forward rate agreements (FRAs)** are usually appropriate for shorter term hedging strategies. They enable a company to fix its interest rate for a particular future period, i.e. they allow a company to lock in to a relevant forward rate of interest for a specified future term.

An FRA is a contract between counterparties for a fixed interest rate on a notional principal sum with a specified value date (start date) and maturity (end date). Note that, as with an interest rate swap, there is no exchange of principal. Rather, this is an agreed notional sum on which the contract is based, and compensation is paid or received if the interest rate at the value date differs from the contracted FRA rate.

Example: Forward rate agreement

A company has borrowings of £100m, with interest payable quarterly at a rate of LIBOR + 1%. It is concerned that in three months' time, interest rates will rise, increasing its interest cost for the period from three months' time to six months' time. Accordingly, it buys a 3 v 6 FRA with a notional principal of £100m at an interest rate of 7%. This effectively locks it into a LIBOR rate of 7%, giving an overall cost for this future period of 8% (LIBOR + 1%).

At the value date in three months' time, LIBOR is 9%. Hence, the company's actual borrowing cost has risen to 10% (LIBOR + 1%). Under the FRA, however, it receives a compensating payment at a rate of 2%, being the difference between the prevailing LIBOR (9%) and the contracted FRA rate (7%) at the value date. Its net cost is therefore 8% for the three months (quoted on an annual basis).

Note that the actual receipt under the FRA will usually take place at the beginning of the period to which it relates (the value date), whereas interest is usually paid in arrears (maturity). As a result, the payment under the FRA is the discounted value of the difference, the discount rate being the appropriate market rate of interest.

Looking at this numerically gives:

	£'000
Actual interest cost payable at **maturity**	
– £100m × 2.5% $(10\% \times \frac{3}{12})$	2,500
Difference under the FRA at **maturity**	
– £100m × 0.5% $[(9\%-7\%) \times \frac{3}{12}]$	(500)
Net cost at maturity	2,000

The net cost clearly being 2% for the period, or 8% p.a.

The actual compensation payment received at the **value date** would be the present value of this £500,000 discounted at the prevailing LIBOR rate of 9% p.a. (2.25% for the three-month period), i.e. 500,000 × $\frac{1}{1.0225}$ = £488,998.

5.4 Valuation

In all swaps, there must be an equality between the value of the two legs at the inception date. The value of the swap at its start date is zero, with the net present value of one leg equalling the net present value of the other. If this were not the case, one party would be unable to rationalise entering into the swap, as they would immediately suffer a loss.

At any later date, the present value of the two legs may vary as spot rates change, and the swap may have a value being the difference between the present values of the two legs.

The value of the swap to either counterparty at any time will be given by

> Swap value = Difference between PV of cash flows swapped
> Swap value = PV of cash flows acquired − PV of cash flows sold

Approach

The clearest approach to evaluating a swap is to use bond-pricing ideas along with the ideas of arbitrage. Arbitrage ensures that if there are two different ways of achieving the same end result, then they must have the same value, and when it comes to swap cash flows, it is quite easy to replicate them with fairly simple instruments.

The cash flows that the payer of fixed interest (receiver of floating) would experience are identical to those that would be experienced if he borrowed with a fixed rate bond and invested the proceeds raised in a floating rate note (FRN). That is, throughout the term of the swap, he would pay fixed and receive floating, and at the termination date, the capital flows cancel with the capital received on the maturity of the FRN repaying the fixed borrowing.

As such, the value of a swap could be established as the difference between the value of a FRN and a fixed rate bond as follows.

Value of swap

Value to payer of fixed	£
Value of FRN asset	X
Value of fixed coupon bond liability	(Y)
Value of swap	Z

5.5 Short-term currency swaps

5.5.1 Definition

> A **short-term currency swap** is a contract that commits two parties to exchange pre-agreed foreign currency amounts now and re-exchange them back at a given future date (the maturity date). The flows are capital only; there is no direct interest payment involved.

5.5.2 Terminology

Primary currency. One currency is defined as the primary currency, and most deals are structured such that the nominal value of the primary currency exchanged on the two dates is equal.

Secondary currency. The other currency is the secondary currency, and the nominal value of this exchanged on the two dates is a function of the spot rate and the swap market forward rate.

Buyer and seller. The terms **buyer** and **seller** are a little awkward in relation to currency dealing, since each party is giving (selling) one currency and receiving (buying) the other.

The terms **buyer** and **seller** relate to these swap arrangements from the point of view of the primary currency cash flows at inception. The **buyer** is the person who, at inception, purchases the primary currency (selling the secondary currency). The **seller** is the individual who, at inception, sells the primary currency (buying the secondary currency).

Cash flows

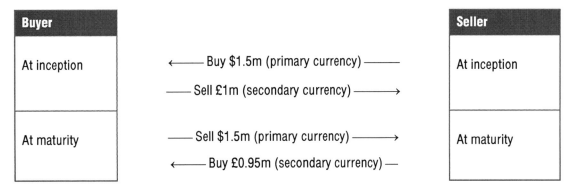

Buyer		Seller
At inception	⟵ Buy $1.5m (primary currency) ⸻ ⸻ Sell £1m (secondary currency) ⟶	At inception
At maturity	⸻ Sell $1.5m (primary currency) ⟶ ⟵ Buy £0.95m (secondary currency) ⸻	At maturity

Synthetic Agreement for Forward Exchange (SAFE)

A SAFE is a variation on the short-term currency swap, in which there is no actual exchange of principal at inception or at maturity, the arrangement being a contract for differences based on notional cash sums.

When the two parties agree to execute a SAFE, they agree the exchange rates at which the notional deals will be executed at inception and maturity. At maturity, one party pays to the other the difference in the value of the secondary currency between the rate originally contracted and the rate actually prevailing.

5.5.3 Dealing

The market in short-term currency swaps, as for interest rate swaps, is an OTC market. Trading is conducted over the telephone and price information is disseminated through quote vendor systems, such as Reuters and Telerate.

The quotes are as a swap spread on the current spot rate.

5.5.4 Using short-term currency swaps

Hedging

Short-term currency swaps provide an alternative to forward exchange rate agreements through simultaneously entering swap and spot deals. The arrangement may result in a better forward exchange rate being achieved as a result of differences between interest rates in swap and money markets.

The swap deal is chosen to achieve the correct cash flows at the maturity date, as could be achieved through the use of a forward exchange contract. The spot deal is undertaken to cancel the initiation leg of the swap so that the net position is that the only cash flow occurs at maturity. This is most easily seen with an example as follows.

Example: Short-term currency swap

$3m is to be received in three months from a US customer. The current spot rate is $1.733:£1 and three-month swap market interest rates are 10% in the UK and 4% in the US.

How can a swap arrangement be structured to translate this amount into sterling, and what will be the sterling receipt in three months?

Solution

The swap arrangement needs to be selling US dollars in three months, hence buying US dollars now. If the US dollar is the primary currency, we need to be the buyer of the swap.

Based on the information provided, the relevant exchange rates and corresponding secondary currency (sterling) values are

Now	spot rate = 1.7330	$\Rightarrow$ £1,731,102
3 months	forward rate = $1.7330 \times \dfrac{1.01}{1.025} = 1.7076$	$\Rightarrow$ £1,756,812

The whole deal can therefore be structured as set out below.

Spot Market	**Swap Market**	
	Now	**3 months**
Sell $3,000,000	Buy $3,000,000	Sell $3,000,000
Buy £1,731,102	Sell £1,731,102	Buy £1,756,812

These cancel out, resulting in a net zero cash flow at inception

Leaving the second leg as the only actual commercial cash flow

Speculation

Since short-term currency swaps reflect forward exchange rates and respond to interest rate differentials, a speculator may use them to speculate on:

- Future forward exchange rate spreads
- Changes in interest rate differentials

If, for example, a speculator believed that US rates were going to rise relative to UK rates in the near future, then the forward exchange rate on the US dollar would move to a lower premium. This would result in less pounds sterling being received per US dollar for forward exchange deals at that future date.

Entering a swap as in the above hedging example would, therefore, result in a gain to the speculator.

A buyer gains and a seller loses when the primary currency interest rate increases in relative terms.

5.6 Long-term currency swaps

5.6.1 Introduction

The long-term currency swap was the original swap product. In its contemporary form, it dates back to 1976, but it did not really take off until 1981, when a deal was done between IBM and the World Bank.

In terms of size, currency swap volume is now dwarfed by the single currency interest rate swap market.

5.6.2 Definition

A **long-term currency swap** is a contract that commits two counterparties to exchange, over an agreed period, two streams of interest payments in different currencies and, at the end of the period, to exchange the corresponding principal amounts at an exchange rate agreed at the start of the contract (there may or may not be an exchange of principal amounts at the start of the contract).

5.6.3 Key elements

Thus, broken down into its constituent parts, we might see:

- A UK corporate contracted to pay a US bank the interest payments on $15m at a rate agreed when the swap is negotiated.

- A US bank contracted to pay the UK corporate the interest payments on £10m at a rate agreed when the swap is negotiated.

- At the end of say, the three-year term of the swap, the principal amounts involved would be exchanged, with the UK corporate paying the US bank $15m and receiving £10m.

You will immediately notice two important differences between currency swaps and interest rate swaps.

- The cash flows involved take place in two currencies
- There is an exchange of principal amounts

As a result of these differences, the currency swap can help reduce, or increase, exposure to both currencies and interest rates.

As with interest rate swaps, there are many different structures that have developed from the simple currency swap outlined above. Some of the more important ones are listed below.

5.6.4 The currency swap

As with so much of the jargon of the financial industry, different practitioners often use the same term to mean different things but, strictly speaking, a currency swap is a swap involving the exchange of two fixed interest streams in different currencies with an exchange of principal at maturity.

This could be represented on a diagram as follows.

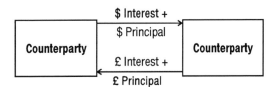

Some currency swaps may involve exchange of principals both at the beginning and end of the term. These are undertaken when the swap is associated with new borrowings by either or both of the counterparties. This form of currency swap was, in fact, the first manifestation of the product and was used to overcome some of the difficulties of back-to-back or parallel loans. These products are sometimes called cash swaps.

5.6.5 Cross-currency swaps

Cross-currency swaps involve an exchange of interest streams in different currencies, of which at least one is at a floating rate of interest.

These swaps could therefore include:

- **Cross-currency coupon swaps**, in which a fixed rate is exchanged for a floating rate, or
- **Cross-currency basis swaps**, in which two floating rates in different currencies are exchanged

5.6.6 Asset swaps

These are currency swaps in which the interest streams are backed by cash flows from **assets**.

5.6.7 Diff swaps

A **diff(erential)** or **quanto swap** is a special type of cross-currency basis swap, which does not involve any exchange of principal whatsoever. Both streams of interest payments through a diff are calculated with reference to the same notional principal amount of the same currency. For example, a $/€ diff swap would typically involve an exchange of six-month LIBOR € for a six-month US LIBOR. Both interest rate streams would be paid in euros.

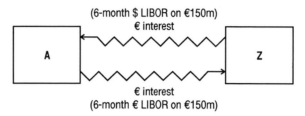

5.6.8 Circus swaps

A **circus swap** is a swap made up of a cross-currency coupon swap (fixed against floating) and a single-currency coupon swap. The purpose is to synthesise either a pure fixed against fixed currency swap or a cross-currency basis swap.

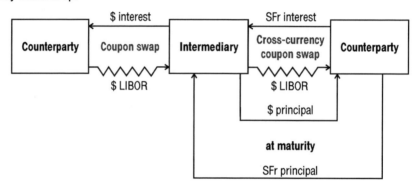

5.6.9 Dealing

It is conventional with interest rate coupon swaps to use six-month LIBOR as the standard index for the floating rate, thus leaving the fixed rate to be agreed. With currency swaps where a currency is also involved, the standard is to use six-month US dollar LIBOR.

Cross-currency basis swaps also use six-month US dollar LIBOR as a reference with the other floating rate (say, six-month UK LIBOR) being quoted as a margin over or under LIBOR in the non-dollar currency.

For example, a £/$ cross-currency basis swap might be quoted at +10, meaning the swap is between US dollar LIBOR on one hand and sterling LIBOR plus 10 basis points on the other.

Conventionally, currency swaps are quoted in terms of all-in prices, i.e. as absolute interest rates as two-way prices, e.g.

7.15%	7.25%
Receive 7.15% fixed	Pay 7.25% fixed

5.6.10 Uses of currency swaps

Speculation. Although currency swaps create exposures to both fluctuations in interest rates and exchange rates, they are not used as trading vehicles in the same way as futures. This is because of the credit risks involved in exchanging principals. Currency swaps are therefore used exclusively for hedging and arbitrage.

Hedging. Imagine a British pharmaceutical company that has issued a dollar bond to finance development. The company expects the dollar to appreciate and sterling interest rates to fall.

If this happens, the foreign currency liability (the bond) will increase in sterling terms, and the cost of servicing the bond begins to look increasingly unattractive. Which swap structure could be used to achieve the required end of accessing lower UK rates and fixing the sterling value of the liability?

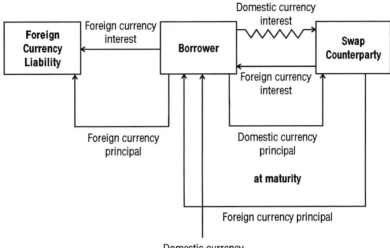

In the previous example, it was assumed that the British company could access the US bond market. In reality, the UK company might have a comparative advantage in its domestic corporate bond market and therefore raise funds there and swap the sterling into dollars at the start of the swap.

These are just two simple examples of swap hedges. There are, of course, many other potential uses.

Arbitrage. Currency swaps can be used in a similar way to interest rate swaps to arbitrage comparative advantage in different markets. It is also possible to arbitrage absolute advantage. For example, a Swiss company may be able to borrow dollars more cheaply than Swiss francs (perhaps, because the domestic Swiss market is already saturated with its paper), and a US company may be able to borrow Swiss francs more cheaply than dollars for the same reasons.

The appeal of new issue arbitrage using currency swaps is that borrowers can separate their funding decisions from risk management decisions about currency and interest rate risk.

5.6.11 Valuation

In order to initially justify the swap, the present value of the swapped future cash flows must be identical, hence the value of the swap is zero. The swap will attract a value if these present values change as a result of interest and foreign exchange rate movements.

To evaluate a long-term currency swap, as for all swaps, it would be necessary to evaluate the present values of the two legs and determine the differences between these amounts. However, the cash flows involved are identical to those for two bonds, this time in two different currencies. The bonds may be either fixed or floating rate. However, the problem again amounts to that of bond valuation.

If, for example, we have entered into a swap under which we pay sterling and receive dollars, then the cash flows are identical to those of borrowing in sterling and investing in dollars. Hence, the value of the swap to us could be calculated as follows.

Value to payer of Sterling	£
Value of dollar bond asset	X
Value of sterling bond liability	(Y)
Value of swap	Z

The approach is to evaluate each bond separately in its own currency based on the relevant currency cash flows and spot rates. These present values can then be translated into the same currency using the prevailing spot exchange rate and hence, the swap value, being the difference between these two values, can be determined in that currency.

5.7 Equity swaps

5.7.1 Definition

Equity swaps are similar in concept to **interest rate swaps**. The buyer pays the return on a money market deposit (e.g. LIBOR) and in exchange receives the total return on an equity investment (capital gains plus dividends). The two payments are usually netted and are generally exchanged between two and four times annually. As with interest rate swaps, no exchange of principal is involved.

Example: Equity swap

A fund manager enters into a one-year FTSE 100 index swap with a notional principal amount (NPA) of £20m and quarterly reset dates.

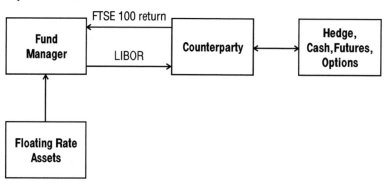

5.7.2 Uses of equity swaps

Speculation and hedging. Counterparties can use swaps to either gain or hedge their own exposure to physical equities.

The opportunities for swap counterparties to run a matched book in equity swaps are limited as whilst the index funds are naturally receivers of index returns, there are fewer people who would wish to pay equity returns other than over a short period of time (as they would for short futures).

There is therefore a fundamental disequilibrium that may limit further growth.

Arbitrage. There are opportunities for arbitrage profits where offsetting equity swaps and futures positions are taken, and futures trade away from their fair value.

Indexation. As a route to indexation, the equity swap may hold certain advantages over either a physically constructed fund or one synthesised using futures. The table below highlights the differences.

	Physical	Futures	Swaps
Settlement	Physical	Cash difference + Initial margin	Cash difference. No margin
Lifespan	Perpetual	Normally quarterly rollovers	Normally, up to 5 years
Tracking risk	Unless fully replicated, fund may not track	Subject to fair pricing of future	Guaranteed
Mark to market	No	Yes, daily (Thus, cash float must be maintained)	Yes, quarterly
Currency risk	Yes, if not in base currency	Yes, but only variation margin flows	Payments can take place in any negotiated currency
Yield enhancement	Stocklending	Low costs and tight bid/ offer spreads. May also be possible to buy future below fair value	Cash asset may yield better than LIBOR flat
Credit risk	None – once settled	None – at least for clearing members	Yes
Liquidity	Good	Best	Worst

5.7.3 Valuation

As with all swaps, the arrangement must have a zero present value at inception, but may attract a value later. The swap value will be the difference between the present value of the equity cash flow stream and the present value of the interest stream.

5.8 Commodity swaps

5.8.1 Introduction

The most recent addition to the stable of swap products is the **commodity swap**. These products are available on a wide variety of crude oils, refined products, non-ferrous metals and foodstuffs.

Commodity swaps overcome some of the limitations of exchange-traded futures in that they can be long dated and tailored to particular delivery points and grades.

5.8.2 Definition

In a commodity swap, the counterparty offers a series of cash-settled futures contracts to the hedger. The hedger is offered a single fixed price, at which he will notionally buy or sell on an agreed date. Cash settlement is calculated on the difference between the fixed price and the price of an agreed index for a stated notional amount of the underlying asset.

Commodity swaps enable users to immunise their price risk to a particular commodity for periods of up to ten years. Unlike interest rate swaps, they are predominantly hedging vehicles.

This idea is perhaps best illustrated with an example.

Example: Oil swap

Notional principal	1m barrels of Brent Crude
Start date	1 January
Reset dates	31 March, 30 June, 30 September, 31 December
Index	ICE Futures Brent Index
Fixed rate	$60.45 per barrel

Calculate the cash flows at the first reset date if the ICE Futures Index has moved to $58.50.

Swap structure

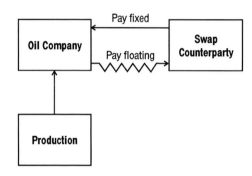

Solution

ICE Futures Index = $58.50

Oil Company			$m
Receives	$60.45 × 1m	=	60.45
Pays	$58.50 × 1m	=	(58.50)
Net			1.95

In this way, the oil producer has a fixed sale price of $60.45 per barrel for a production of one million barrels each quarter.

This simple structure could be refined to take account of differing production levels by adjusting the notional principal for each period.

5.8.3 Uses of commodity swaps

Speculation and hedging. Counterparties can use swaps to either gain or hedge their own exposure to commodities by dealing as illustrated above.

Arbitrage. There are opportunities for arbitrage profits where offsetting commodity swaps and futures positions are taken, and futures trade away from their fair value, as with equity swaps.

5.8.4 Valuation

In common with other swap structures, the swap counterparty will price the commodity swap by calculating the present value of a strip of futures contracts. However, the pricing of, for example, energy futures is not quite so straightforward as for financial futures.

While financial futures are priced in accordance with arbitrage conditions that take account of the cost of carry, energy futures prices are less amenable to arbitrage, as reverse cash and carries cannot be undertaken. In addition, energy futures prices may also include, particularly in near months, a convenience premium (i.e. a premium to fair value which consumers are willing to pay in order to guarantee supply).

As a consequence of this, commodity futures prices are more difficult to model, as their term structure is considerably less visible than that of the interest rate markets.

CHAPTER ROUNDUP

- A futures contract is an agreement to buy or sell a standard quantity of a specified asset on a fixed future date at a price agreed now.

- An option is a contract conferring the right but not the obligation to buy (call option) or sell (put option) an asset at a given price on (or, for American-style options, before) a given date.

- Options on futures are options whose exercise results in a long or short futures position.

- Futures and options offer the possibility of gearing, and may be used either for hedging or speculation.

- A security synthetic is formed by repackaging an asset in the secondary market, to replicate the performance of a financial instrument.

- With swaps, counterparties agree to exchange specific future cash flows, for example fixed and variable future interest payments.

TEST YOUR KNOWLEDGE

Check your knowledge of the Chapter here, without referring back to the text.

1 Define what is meant by a 'synthetic'.

2 What is a future?

3 What is a 'tick', in the context of futures?

4 What is an arbitrageur?

5 Define what is meant by an option.

6 What is the difference between an 'American style' option and a 'European style' option?

7 Explain why selling a call option exposes the seller to an unlimited risk.

8 What is an interest rate swap?

9 Outline what is meant by a cross-currency swap.

TEST YOUR KNOWLEDGE: ANSWERS

1   Any combination of cash and derivative instruments which is designed to replicate the performance of another type of financial instrument. (See 1.3.)

2   A future is an agreement to buy or sell a standard quantity of a specified asset on a fixed future date at a price agreed today. (See 2.1.1.)

3   A tick is the smallest permitted price movement. (See 2.2.)

4   An arbitrageur seeks riskless profits from exploiting market inefficiencies. (See 2.3.)

5   An option is a contract that confers the right, but not the obligation, to buy or sell an asset at a given price on or before a given date. (See 3.1.)

6   American style options can be exercised by the holder at any time after the option has been purchased. European style options can only be exercised on its expiry date. (See 3.3.)

7   The risk is unlimited because the writer has a duty to deliver the asset at a fixed price regardless of the prevailing asset price. As the share price could, in theory, rise to infinity, the call writer assumes an unlimited risk. (See 3.6.)

8   An interest rate swap is a contract which commits two counterparties to exchange, over an agreed period, two streams of interest payments, each calculated using a different interest rate index, but applied to a common notional principal amount. (See 5.2.)

9   Cross-currency swaps involve an exchange of interest streams in different currencies, of which at least one is at a floating rate of interest. These swaps could include:

  ■   Cross-currency coupon swaps, in which a fixed rate is exchanged for a floating rate, or

  ■   Cross-currency basis swaps, in which two floating rates in different currencies are exchanged (See 5.6.5.)

7 Trading and Dealing

INTRODUCTION

The global operations manager should have good general understanding of trading and dealing mechanisms. The cycle involved runs from the initial receipt of an order up to when a confirmation is issued. The syllabus calls for a general knowledge of trading.

In this chapter, we provide information on various types of market, both in the UK and in other countries, giving characteristics of the principal markets and also others. The syllabus highlights the LSE, NYSE Euronext.liffe, CME Globex (formerly CBOT) and Eurex.

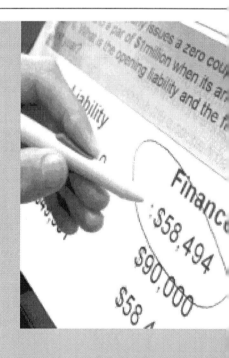

1 BACKGROUND

1.1 Brief history of the stock market

In the 16th and 17th centuries, entrepreneurs needed to raise money for trading expeditions to their countries' territories overseas. They did this by offering investors a share in the profits of the venture. The first company was The Muscovy Company, set up in 1553. As London and Holland were the major trading countries, with companies like the Hudson Bay Company and the East India Company, the stock markets grew in London and Amsterdam. The London Stock Exchange was formally established in 1773. The New York Stock Exchange opened in 1792.

During the Industrial Revolution, the need for a stock market and funding grew and at its height there were 20 regional exchanges throughout the UK.

In 1908 there was a move to regulate the stock market. In order to prevent unfair competition, fixed commission was introduced. To improve independence, single capacity was introduced. This meant that firms could either be brokers or market makers but not both.

In 1979, Margaret Thatcher and the Tories came to power. She wanted to promote the UK economy by making it easier for businesses to obtain funding and encouraging individuals to invest their spare cash.

The 'Big Bang' of 27 October 1986 revolutionised the London stock market with a fourfold impact.

- Fixed commissions were abolished, to make the market more competitive.

- The single capacity of the stock jobbers and brokers was abolished, also to encourage competition.

- A telephone trading quotation system was introduced through SEAQ and the floor was closed.

- Greater internationalisation of the London Stock Exchange membership was enabled, to allow overseas companies to locate in London.

Equity settlement was improved with CREST's introduction in 1996 (now Euroclear). The law changed to allow shares to be held electronically rather than as physical share certificates.

1.2 Types of company

A company is a separate legal entity whereby it is its own legal person, separate from the people who own it. In the UK, most companies are created, or incorporated, by registering with Companies House.

- **Unlimited liability companies.** Unlimited liability companies are rare. It means that upon liquidation, the shareholders would be responsible for meeting all liabilities to the extent of their entire personal fortune.

- **Companies limited by guarantee.** In a company limited by guarantee, the liability of the shareholders on winding up is limited by the amount they undertook to contribute on incorporation. Usually the amounts are very small, e.g. £1 for the Securities Institute Services.

- **Companies limited by shares.** This is the most common type of company. These companies must always include 'LTD', 'Ltd', or 'Limited' in their title. These companies are not allowed to issue their shares to the public. The liability of the shareholders is limited to the amount they agreed to pay for the shares. If the shares are 'fully paid' then there is no further liability. If the shares are partly paid, then the shareholder will have to pay the remaining share price upon liquidation.

- **Public limited companies.** Public limited companies (plcs) can issue their shares to the public and thus have more stringent requirements. All plcs must have allotted at least £50,000 shares and at least a quarter must have been paid up. These companies can issue shares to the public via PLUS Markets (formerly OFEX), AIM or by other means.

- **Listed companies**. In order to sell shares through the London Stock Exchange (LSE), a company must be **listed**. Differentiating it from the **Alternative Investment Market (AIM)**, the market in listed companies is sometimes called the **main market**. This means that it must comply with the more detailed **listing particulars** set out in the **Yellow Book**.

1.3 Listing on the LSE

1.3.1 UK Listing Authority (UKLA)

The Financial Services Authority (FSA) is appointed as the UK's 'competent authority' to decide on the admission of securities to the full list. The purpose of these Listing Rules is to ensure the following.

- A balance between providing issuers with ready access to the market and protecting investors
- Applicants are suitable for listing
- Securities are brought to market in an appropriate way that will ensure open and efficient trading
- Full and timely disclosure of relevant information by listed companies
- Confidence in the market
- Investors in a company have adequate opportunity to vote upon major changes in the company

A company will only gain admission to listing if it is considered to be suitable by the UKLA. Key points are as follows.

1.3.2 Public limited company

Private limited companies (Ltd) are not permitted to issue shares to the public. Therefore, a private company will need to re-register as a public limited company (plc) before it can apply for a listing. This means that it will have to have an issued share capital of at least £50,000, of which at least one quarter must be paid up.

1.3.3 Company history

It is important that there is evidence of a company's stability and likely future success. To this end, the company must have published accounts for the three years prior to the application for a listing, except in exceptional circumstances. The accounts must have been audited, though not necessarily with a qualified audit report, and comply in all material respects with acceptable accounting standards. Acceptable standards would be typically UK, US or International Standards.

The main business activity of the company should also have been carried on for the previous three years. In addition, there should have been continuity of management over the period.

1.3.4 Directors

The directors must have appropriate experience to run the business. They must be free of conflicts of interest, unless it can be demonstrated that these will be managed to avoid detriment to the company, thus avoiding Maxwell-type arrangements.

1.3.5 Working capital

The directors must be satisfied that the company has sufficient working capital for its needs and consequently, will not become insolvent in the near future.

1.3.6 Controlling shareholder

A controlling shareholder is a person who owns 30% or more of the voting rights in the company or who controls the board of directors. Such a shareholder would have a great deal of influence, if not effective control, over the company and this would lead to conflicts of interest between the controlling shareholder and other shareholders. A company must be able to demonstrate that all significant decisions are taken by directors independent of the controlling shareholder and there are arrangements in place to avoid detriment to other shareholders.

1.3.7 Transferability of securities

The shares must be freely transferable to be listed. This may mean that the company will have to change its Articles of Association. Many private companies will have a condition that shares may only be transferred with the approval of the board of directors. Alternatively, the Articles may say that shares must first be offered to existing shareholders prior to being made available to outsiders. Both of these conditions will prevent free transferability.

1.3.8 Market value of securities to be listed

In order to ensure that the securities to be listed for the first time are readily marketable, the minimum market value of shares to be listed is £700,000. The minimum value of any debt securities to be listed is £200,000.

These limits may be disapplied if the FSA is satisfied that securities of a lower market value would be adequately marketable. However, given the problems that arise with small company shares trading, it is unlikely that this will often be the case.

1.3.9 Marketability

Listed shares must be marketable, which will be assumed if 25% of the shares are made available to the public. A lower percentage may be permitted if the shares will be sufficiently marketable for a liquid market to develop.

1.4 The Alternative Investment Market (AIM)

1.4.1 Overview

The **Alternative Investment Market (AIM)** is a market where the shares of smaller, unlisted companies and smaller companies seeking funds for expansion may be traded. The types of company which may be traded on AIM include the following.

- Small, fast-growing companies
- Management buyouts
- Family businesses

The investor base should consist of professional or experienced investors who are aware of the risks and rewards of investing in such companies. It must be stressed that the level of regulation is deliberately low on AIM to reduce costs and encourage small companies to have their shares traded. Investors have to make their own judgements as to company prospects.

The market is run by the London Stock Exchange, and Stock Exchange facilities such as SETSqx, the Regulatory Information Service and market monitoring are available.

1.4.2 Entry requirements

There is no required level of market capitalisation, trading history or number of shares in public hands. The conditions that do need to be met are that the company must:

- Be a public limited company or its overseas equivalent
- Have published accounts conforming to UK, US or International Accounting Standards
- Ensure that its securities are freely transferable

- Adopt a code of share dealings for its directors and senior employees equivalent to that required by the UKLA for listed companies (the Model Code)

- Retain a nominated adviser and nominated broker

1.4.3 Nominated adviser

All companies on AIM are required to maintain a suitably qualified firm as their **nominated adviser (NOMAD)**, to assist them in complying with the rules and give assurance to investors. The nominated adviser will confirm in writing to the UKLA that the directors of the company have been advised and guided as to their responsibilities under the AIM rules and that the relevant rules have been complied with. A firm wishing to act as a nominated adviser must be on the register of nominated advisers held by the Stock Exchange. Such firms must be authorised under the Financial Services and Markets Act 2000.

1.4.4 Nominated broker

All companies on AIM must appoint a **nominated broker** to support trading in their shares. The nominated broker must be a member firm of the Stock Exchange and must use best endeavours to find matching business in a company's shares, unless a market maker registers in the stock. This means at least one firm will always trade or do its best to match bargains.

1.4.5 Company disclosure

On entering AIM, companies must disclose the following.

- A prospectus giving details of the company, its shares, financial information, management and future prospects

- Details of directors and their personal histories

- Names of substantial shareholders (holding 10% or more of the voting rights)

- A statement that the company has sufficient working capital for its needs

2 TRADING

2.1 Characteristics of an effective stock market

An effective stock market will have the following characteristics.

- **Cost efficiency** – in order to maximise volumes, the stock market needs to be cost effective. Electronic order systems should be the most cost effective and the middle man and timely telephones are removed.

- **Liquidity** – the ability to enter or exit the market at an acceptable price spread, creating only modest price distortion on a transaction of a reasonable size. Factors contributing to liquidity are effective and efficient IT and settlement systems, stock availability and stock lending facilities and a diverse membership.

- **Transparency** and **price discovery** – it is essential that the investor knows the price before, during and after a deal in order to be satisfied that he has a good deal.

2.2 Trading on a Stock Exchange

A person wishing to buy shares will normally approach a **member** of the relevant exchange (e.g. the London Stock Exchange (LSE)).

The member may then:

- Sell their own shares to the buyer: acting as **principal**, or
- Arrange a purchase of shares from another client: this is known as **agency cross**, or
- Arrange a purchase of shares from another member: acting as **agent**

The member will be rewarded by his profit on sale in (a) (his **turn**), or by commission in (b) and (c).

In (c) above, the purchase might be from a **market maker**, who has guaranteed to make available shares at all times in return for certain privileges. Market makers who are short of stock can purchase stock anonymously via an **inter-dealer broker** or borrow it via a **stock borrowing and lending intermediary**. For some shares there will be more than one market maker, ensuring competition in the market.

2.3 Some terminology

The **bid** is the price paid for the stock and the **offer** is the selling price. The **spread** or **turn** is the difference between the bid and the offer. The **tick size** is the minimum movement in a share price.

Whereas the term '**shares**' is commonly used for company shares in Britain, the term '**stocks**' is more commonly used in the US.

2.4 Quote- and order-driven market systems

Most European systems are **order-driven**. Thus a member will seek to find a seller for each buyer. More recently automated trading, such as the LSE's SETS system bypasses the need for a human intermediary. Large orders can present a problem, as the broker (or the system) struggles to find a counterparty at a suitable price. Various order types exist whereby orders may be presented to execute immediately at the prevailing market price or may be conditional orders depending on price and quantities to match before a trade is consummated.

Quote driven systems depend on the existence of market makers who are prepared to offer two-way quotes in shares at all times. This provides liquidity. Most shares on the LSE are traded via SEAQ, which is a quote-driven system. Market makers are prepared to take risks with large orders, and this encourages liquidity in the market. Even where the system is screen-based, a telephone call will be required to make the deal.

2.5 Screen trading and open outcry trading

In London, the LSE trading environments are exclusively **screen-based**, and the leading derivatives exchange NYSE Euronext.liffe (LIFFE) has now long completed the transition from **open outcry,** which involves traders communicating verbally or by non-verbal signals on a trading floor, to screen-based trading. It is argued that screen-based trading is open, auditable and economical, which improves the competitive nature of the market, since anyone, even non-members, can gain access to price information for each market maker.

Potential disadvantages of screen-based trading

- A tendency for market makers to chase each other's prices, particularly in a falling market
- A lack of instant information about prices for deals in larger sizes than displayed
- Any kind of power disruption can lead to severe problems

3 THE LONDON STOCK EXCHANGE

3.1 Permitted dealings

The securities which may be dealt in on the **London Stock Exchange (LSE)** are set out in Rule 2.1, and are as follows.

- Domestic equity market securities which are not the subject of a notice or order suspending the listing or admission to trading (including AIM securities)
- European equity market securities
- International equity market securities
- Gilt-edged securities, fixed interest securities, negotiated options and gilt warrants
- Traditional options

3.2 Prohibited dealings

The LSE may prohibit any transaction or class of transactions for any reason. The following are **specifically prohibited**.

(a) Transactions in securities

    (i)   Which are suspended from the Official List, or
    (ii)   In respect of which transactions are prohibited

(b) Special cum dividend transactions on or after the payment date

(c) Special ex-dividend transactions

    (i)   In a gilt-edged security

    (ii)   In a listed fixed interest non-convertible security issued by a UK incorporated company or maintained on a register in the UK earlier than seven calendar days before the ex-dividend date

    (iii) In a security registered in the UK other than a security falling within paragraph c (i) or (ii) before the tenth day before the ex-dividend date

(d) Traditional options for the put or call or both, in a security on an ex-dividend basis before the ex-dividend date of that security

(e) Transactions in prospective dividends

3.3 Dealing systems for UK equities

TradElect™ is the overall name for the London Stock Exchange's new world class trading system, designed to deliver enhanced levels of performance, reliability and scalability.

The revamped platform has increased capacity fivefold, allowing the LSE to handle 3000 messages per second. The time taken to process an order has been cut to about 10 milliseconds, from 140 milliseconds previously.

The LSE hopes that the new system will bring in more orders from hedge funds and investment banks running algorithmic trading systems. As well as being able to handle higher volumes, TradElect™ should be able to offer lower fees, and thus compete with new entrants such as the **Project Turquoise** group of investment banks (discussed later in this chapter).

The introduction of TradElect™ in June 2007 marked the final and most significant phase of the LSE's four-year system upgrade project – known as Technology Roadmap (TRM) – which was designed to deliver a range of key functional and technical enhancements including to:

- Increase the speed and efficiency of trading
- Provide the framework for the rapid development of new markets and asset classes
- Enhance the market structure to better support order routing, settlement and clearing
- Extend functionality for order handling, quote management and trade reporting

The following **systems** are currently in use.

- **SETS** (Stock Exchange Electronic Trading Service) for shares in 'liquid' stocks, and **SETSqx** for 'non-liquid' stocks

- **SEAQ** (Stock Exchange Automated Quotation System) for fixed interest and for AIM companies not traded on SETS or SETSqx

3.4 SETS

3.4.1 Overview

In October 1997, the LSE introduced the **SETS** system, initially for trading in shares of the FTSE 100 companies (i.e. the largest 100 listed UK companies by market capitalisation) and the two or three FTSE100 reserve stocks. The London Stock Exchange started 2006 with sizable increases in trading, most notably on SETS, its electronic order book. In January, the total value traded on SETS increased 33 per cent year on year to a record £156.5 billion. At the same time, the number of trades on SETS increased 61 per cent to 8.7 million. This was the highest number of trades ever recorded on the electronic order book in a single month. SETS provides an electronic order book which can only be accessed by members of the Exchange.

The strong growth in SETS trading is part of a long-term trend toward electronic trading on the Exchange's markets. As 2006 progressed, the Exchange rolled out electronic trading into mid-cap and AIM stocks using SETSmm (explained below). The average daily number of trades on SETS was up 54 per cent to 397,215, while the average daily value traded climbed 27 per cent to £7.1 billion. The average size of a SETS bargain during January was £17,874, a 17.7 per cent decrease on January 2006.

SETSmm had been launched in 2003 as the LSE's trading service for mid-cap FTSE 250 and liquid AIM securities. In October 2007, **SETSmm and SETS were amalgamated** to create a single platform for the trading of the constituents of the FTSE All Share Index and higher-traded AIM securities. The new service carries the name **SETS** and combines order-driven trading with integrated market making, guaranteeing two-way prices in all securities. It provides one approach (full execution including quotes) and one set of rules for trading of the more liquid UK securities. Order book trades in UK and Irish securities are covered by a central counterparty operated by the LCH.clearnet.

Under the new 2007 arrangements, SETS offers market making in all stocks including those deemed to be 'liquid' under the **Markets in Financial Instruments Directive (MiFID)**. This provides customers with an on-Exchange alternative to being a **Systematic Internaliser (SI)**. A Systematic Internaliser is an investment firm dealing on their own account by executing client orders outside a regulated market or MTF. This enhancement provides users with a two-tier market structure for the trading of all UKLA listed securities – **SETS** for 'liquid' stocks and **SETSqx** for 'non-liquid' stocks as defined under MiFID.

3.4.2 Timetable

The Order Book opens at 07:50, but the system can only be used to input orders in the ten minutes to 08:00. During this time, no execution takes place. At 08:00 an **uncrossing algorithm** is run. This determines the price at which the largest number of orders that have been input can be executed. These orders (input before 08:00) are then executed.

The uncrossing process takes an unspecified amount of time. Once completed and once the base price has been established, the process of automatic execution of orders commences and continues until 16:30. During the time from the end of uncrossing until 16.30 any of five different order types may be entered onto the system. Note that between 07:50 and 08:00 only one type of order, a limit order, may be input.

From 16:30 until 17:00 no automatic execution takes place, and any remaining limit orders that have not been executed may be deleted. During this time no orders may be added. At 17:00 the Order Book closes. From this time no automatic execution takes place, no orders may be added or deleted, and any expired orders are automatically deleted from the Order Book.

3.4.3 Orders

There are the following different types of order.

Limit	Limit orders are the only orders that remain on the order screen. They are entered with a specific quantity and a limit price (a 'no worse than' price). The customer or member whose order it is must be prepared for any unfilled part of the order to remain on the Order Book. However, he may add an expiry time or date. Upon reaching this, the system will automatically delete the order.
Execute and eliminate	These have a quantity and a limit price. Whatever proportion of the order that can be filled is filled, however, no remaining portion is left on the order book.
Fill or kill	Fill or kill orders are essentially 'do it all or don't bother' orders. They may have a limit price, in which case the order is to be done completely at that price or better or be abandoned. If there is no limit price then the order is only restricted by the volume depth of the Order Book.
At best	An at best order is simply one that is to be filled at the best possible price. The only restricting factor here is the volume that is on the Order Book. Any unfilled portion is rejected, i.e. it does not remain on the Order Book.
Market	The price at which products are selling and being bought. Hence, **at market** is the current price or rate.
Iceberg	An iceberg order is an order that can be partially hidden from market view. Upon entry of the order, the participant must therefore specify the total order size and the visible 'peak' size. The peak size is the maximum volume that will be shown to the market at any given instant. To maintain sufficient transparency in the market, a minimum peak size of 0.25 x Normal Market Size (NMS) has been set.

3.4.4 Order priority

Orders will have the following priority.

- Bids and offers with the best price will be executed first.

- If there are two bids (or offers) with the same price, the order that was input earlier will be executed first.

Orders may be deleted from the system, but they may not be amended. If an order is incorrect it has to be deleted and re-input. This will result in the order losing its place in the queue.

3.4.5 Reporting and publication

Trades executed through the Order Book will be reported automatically. Publication of these trades is immediate regardless of size.

3.4.6 Best execution

Orders executed through the Order Book are done at best price. This is because the orders on the Order Book must by definition contribute to best price. The price of the highest buy order is the best bid price, conversely the price of the lowest sell order is the best offer price. If there are no bids then the best bid price will be zero, and the mid-price is the best offer price. If there are no offers then the best offer price is zero and the best bid price becomes the mid-price.

Orders executed in the Order Book are by definition done at 'best execution' – remember that clients are entitled to expect best execution under FSA rules.

Member firms can also execute orders outside the Order Book, subject to the following requirements. Orders outside the Order Book that may be satisfied by the best bid or offer price (as appropriate) on the Order Book, must be executed at that price or better. Orders outside the Order Book that cannot be satisfied by the best bid or offer price (as appropriate) on the Order Book, must be executed at the volume weighted average price or better.

3.4.7 Order size

Minimum order size is one share. There is no maximum order size.

3.4.8 Interruptions to trading

- If a security's listing is suspended, no member firm may trade in that security without prior permission from the Exchange.

- A trading halt in a security usually occurs when the Exchange believes a disorderly market has occurred in that security.

- If a security moves more than 20% away (either up or down) from its base price, the Exchange will suspend automatic execution, normally for 10 minutes.

3.5 SETSqx

SETSqx (SETS 'quotes and crosses') is a trading platform for securities less liquid than those traded on SETS. SETSqx replaced SEATS Plus in June 2007.

Since 8 October 2007, all Main Market and EURM (EU Regulated Market) AIM equity securities not traded on a full order book are traded on SETSqx. They joined the Main Market and AIM securities with less than two market makers which were added in June 2007 following the replacement of SEATS Plus.

SETSqx combines a periodic electronic auction book with standalone quote driven market making. Uncrossings are scheduled at 08.00, 11.00, 15.00 and 16.35. Electronic orders can be named or anonymous and for the indicated securities order book executions will be centrally cleared.

3.6 SEAQ

3.6.1 Overview

The **SEAQ** system is the LSE's service for the fixed interest market and AIM securities that are not traded on either **SETS** or **SETSqx**.

SEAQ is a competing market maker system and would be described as a **quote-driven** system. Member firms can take on the responsibilities of market-making, obliging them to quote their prices to other members (alternatively known as broker/dealers) who then decide whether or not to respond to them.

These quotes are two-way prices, the lower of which is known as the bid price and is the price at which the market-makers will buy stock; the higher price is the offer (or ask price) and is the price at which they will sell stock.

3.6.2 Obligations of market makers

Only **market makers** are permitted to display prices on SEAQ. In return for this privilege, which is likely to generate business for them, they accept certain obligations, outlined below.

During the mandatory quote period (currently 8.00 a.m. to 4.30 p.m.) the market maker must display on SEAQ firm two-way prices in all SEAQ securities in which they are registered in not less than a specified minimum quantity of shares.

This minimum quote size (MQS) is currently set at 1 × NMS (normal market size). Each SEAQ security has an NMS level, which is fixed quarterly by the Exchange. There are 14 NMS levels, ranging from 100 up to 200,000. These levels represent, very approximately, the average size of an institutional deal in the relevant security.

If larger quantities are displayed by market makers, they must be prepared to deal in those quantities.

It should be noted that there is a system whereby market makers can apply to become 'reduced size market makers' and quote prices in only 50% of NMS. This designation is at the discretion of the Exchange.

Market makers displaying two-way prices on SEAQ must be prepared to deal at that price and in up to the size quoted, with all enquiring member firms who are acting on behalf of clients. However, the prices displayed only have indicative status if a member firm enquires to a market maker when acting on their own account.

If, however, the enquiring member firm is itself a market maker (or is part of a group which includes a market maker) who is registered in that security, the obligation is limited to dealing in up to the MQS.

Where reduced size market makers are enquiring, there is no obligation at all to deal with them, unless the firm receiving the enquiry is also a reduced size market maker. Here the obligation to deal is at the reduced size. Likewise a reduced size market maker receiving an enquiry from an ordinary market maker is under no obligation to deal.

A market maker who withdraws its quotation from SEAQ in respect of a security without the prior consent of the Exchange is required to justify its actions. Failure to do so may cause the registration in such security of the firm to be terminated. This is to avoid 'fair weather' traders, who only quote prices when convenient.

3.6.3 Privileges of market makers

Market makers have the following privileges over other broker/dealer members of the Exchange.

- They may display their prices on SEAQ.
- They do not pay stamp duty.
- They have pricing advantages under the best execution rule over non-market makers who wish to deal as principal. Non-market makers must beat the best price displayed by market makers in principal and agency cross transactions.

3.6.4 Registration of market makers

A member firm wishing to act as a market maker in a security must first register with the Stock Exchange. Provided application is made to the Exchange by 13:00, registration will normally become effective on the next business day.

Re-registration

- A member firm who wishes to cease acting as a market maker in a security shall instruct the Exchange to de-register it from that security.
- A member firm shall cease acting as a market maker in a security forthwith when instructed to do so by the Exchange.

■ A member firm shall not, without the prior consent of the Exchange, re-register as a market maker in any security in which its registration has been terminated by the Exchange.

■ Re-registration will not become effective for a period of three calendar months after the date of de-registration unless otherwise permitted by the Exchange.

3.6.5 SEAQ crosses

SEAQ crosses is a service which supplements the market maker quote driven system by providing an alternative anonymous execution mechanism. It applies to all quote driven FTSE 250 stocks. The execution price for the crosses is imported from the mid-price of market maker quotes at the time of each cross. There are three crosses each day with the final cross using the prices which form the official closing price. SEAQ crosses replaced the previous auction system, which was introduced in May 2000.

The system provides for anonymity, just like SETS, orders may be added or removed at any time of the trading day.

3.6.6 Reporting and publication of SEAQ deals

Trade reporting: transactions on SEAQ must be **reported** as follows.

Trades between 07:16 – 08:00   by 8:00 or within 3 minutes whichever is later

08:00 – 17:15   within 3 minutes or by 17:15 whichever is earlier

17:16 – 07:15 the next day   between 07:15 and 07:45

The period between 07:15 and 17:15 is known as the Trade Reporting Period (TRP).

The responsibility for reporting is dependent upon the parties to the transaction.

Transaction between	Who reports
Two market makers directly with each other or via an inter-dealer broker	The selling market maker
Market maker and a broker/dealer	The market maker
Two broker/dealers	The selling broker/dealer
One member and one non-member	The member firm
Two non-members (agency cross)	The member firm

While all bargains must be reported to SEAQ, the rules regarding **publication** of these deals vary.

(a) **For securities with an NMS above 1,000**

    (i)   All deals up to 6 × NMS are published immediately. This is known as the maximum publication level (MPL).

    (ii)   Deals in excess of the MPL are published after 60 minutes.

    (iii)   Deals larger than 75×NMS may be reported as **block trades**. They will then be published after the earlier of either five business days or upon the firm unwinding or hedging 90% of the original trade.

(b) **For securities with an NMS of 1,000 or 500**

    (i)   All deals up to the MPL are published immediately
    (ii)   Deals in excess of the MPL are published after 120 minutes
    (iii)   Deals larger than 50 × NMS are dealt with as at (a)(iii) above

(c)   **Other points to note**

(i)   Agency cross deals and transactions in takeover stocks are published immediately regardless of size.

(ii)   For securities with an NMS of less than 500, there will be no SEAQ publication, either online or delayed, of deals unless they fall under category (c)(i) above.

3.7 International equities

3.7.1 The International Order Book / International Bulletin Board

In 2001, the London Stock Exchange added the **International Order Book (IOB)** which led to the strong growth of depository receipt trading in emerging markets in London, particularly Russia. The International Order Book (IOB) provides a platform for trading in depository receipts, one of the most liquid sectors of overseas securities. The market is based on an electronic order book similar to SETS but with the added option for member firms to display their identity pre-trade by using Named Orders, offering greater visibility in the market.

In May 2004, another new service was introduced called the **International Bulletin Board (ITBB)** service. This allowed registered market makers to support liquidity in equities within a central limit order book structure. ITBB is part of the IOB.

In 2004, the remainder of the previous SEAQ International system was closed down. So today, all depository receipts are traded in the IOB and all equities on ITBB.

Both the IOB and the ITBB are open from 07.00 until 17.00 each business day. An auction call phase exists in both markets from 08.45 until 15.15.

All transactions conducted on the Order Book in IOB or ITBB are automatically reported to the exchange and published to the market immediately. Off-book trades in depository receipts must be reported to the exchange within 3 minutes of execution. ITBB equities trading on the ITBB need not be reported to the exchange irrespective of whether it was traded under the continuous market or auction market models.

As with all on-exchange trades, exchange members are required to transaction report all on-exchange trades conducted both on and away from the Order Book in all IOB and ITBB securities to the exchange by the end of the business day.

Settlement is in accordance with the rules of the home exchange.

3.7.2 EUROSETS™ – Dutch Trading Service

The LSE's Dutch Trading Service **EUROSETS** went live in 2004, signalling the first step in the London Stock Exchange's drive to open up competition across the European markets. The Dutch Trading Service enables Exchange members to trade in the most liquid Dutch securities that form the AEX and AMX indices via the SETS Order Book.

In October 2007, EUROSETS was enhanced to allow firms to be able to register as market makers in any EUROSETS security.

Whilst the LSE is not planning to make EUROSETS available for all EU Regulated Market (EURM) securities at present, it is 'assessing opportunities to extend our offering to provide a pan'European execution service as the market develops'.

3.7.3 European Quoting Service (EQS)

The **European Quoting Service (EQS)** is a new LSE service enabling clients to meet their pre-trade pan-European transparency obligations.

EQS is a quote-driven market making and trade reporting platform that supports all EU liquid securities (excluding those traded on the SETS, SETSqx, EUROSETS and ITBB services).

Initially, no electronic execution will be supported and market makers will enter non-electronically executable quotes during the Mandatory Quote Period (MQP). There will be no minimum number of market makers required per security.

3.8 Gilts (UK Government securities)

3.8.1 Introduction

Many aspects are the same as those which apply to quote driven trading of equities. The official participants in the gilt-edged market are all members of the Stock Exchange and the role of each is explained below.

3.8.2 Participants

Gilts market participants are as follows.

- **Broker/dealers** are essentially the same as for equities and are permitted to trade both as principal and agent.

- **Gilt-Edged Market Makers (GEMMs)**, also known as primary dealers, are firms which undertake to the UK Debt Management Office (DMO), an executive agency of HM Treasury, to make two-way prices to broker/dealers and people known directly to them (clients) in a range of securities in any trading conditions. In return, they are allowed direct access to the DMO's issuing department. Once registered with the DMO, GEMMs must report directly on a daily basis to the SFA regarding their financial stability. As for equities, only market makers are permitted to display prices on SEAQ, but, unlike with equities, they are under no obligation to do so. SEAQ is used very little in the gilts market. GEMMs' privileges are much the same as for equity market makers.

- **Stock Borrowing and Lending Intermediaries** are used by GEMMs to cover short positions. In addition, **repo trading** is allowed in the gilts market. A repo is a sale and repurchase agreement such that Party A sells gilts to Party B with a legally binding agreement to purchase equivalent securities from Party B for an agreed price at a specified future date, or on demand. Party B has unfettered title to the securities, and may use or dispose of them as it pleases, but it has an obligation to deliver equivalent securities to Party A at the end of the repo. The interest rate implied by the difference between the sale price and repurchase price is the repo rate.

  Repo trading is not just directed at GEMMs. All market participants are free to undertake gilt repo transactions with each other.

- **Inter-dealer brokers (IDBs)** must be set up as separate companies which can be subsidiaries of broker/dealers or completely independent organisations. Their function is to act as a matching agent for market makers who will be able to undo their positions with them, without revealing their position to their competitors. They may not take positions, but in order to protect the anonymity of the market makers involved, when matching trades between them the IDB will settle as principal. The prices displayed by them on their own computer screens must only be available to market makers and not to broker/dealers or clients.

3.8.3 Dealing

Since SEAQ is little used in the gilt market, a broker will need to phone around to establish the best price in the size in which he wishes to deal. For comparatively small transactions, i.e. purchases or sales of less than £1m nominal (known as **odd lots**), the size of the order must be made clear to the market maker before obtaining a quote.

In addition, when a firm which is not a GEMM either:

- Effects a principal transaction with a client, or
- Matches the order of one client with the order of another client,

it must take all reasonable steps to ensure that the transaction price is better than the best price available in a comparable size from a market maker registered in the security.

3.8.4 Reporting and publication

Details as for equities must be **trade reported**. Any transaction must be generally reported within three minutes of the transaction. **Transaction reporting** is via Euroclear by 20:00 hours on the same day.

Information is **published** (by subscription) only for retail size transactions – up to a consideration of £50,000.

3.8.5 Settlement

Settlement is normally on the business day following the business day of dealing. Formerly, transfer of title was usually through the **Central Gilts Office (CGO)**, but it is now handled by Euroclear. Computershare, which is the registrar for gilts, maintains a computer record in Euroclear and a book entry is made to transfer both the stock and the money for payment between accounts held at the Bank of England for that purpose. As it is a book entry transfer system, no certificates and no transfer forms are used. Many bargains settled through Euroclear are marked 'C.S.' for same day settlement.

3.9 Sterling fixed interest rates

The operation of the **fixed interest market** has some similarities to the gilts market and some to the equities market. Market makers are registered with the LSE and the dealing obligation imposed by the Exchange is to undertake to offer to buy and sell stock in a marketable quantity (as determined by the Board) at a named price. This obligation is only to fellow member firms, but excludes other market makers, inter-dealer brokers and stock borrowing and lending intermediaries.

Trade reporting follows the same rules as for domestic equities and gilts, and **transaction reporting** is via Euroclear by 20:00 the same day.

4 NYSE Euronext.liffe (LIFFE)

4.1 Introduction

The most important London market for futures and options is **NYSE Euronext.liffe** or **LIFFE (The London International Financial and Options Futures Exchange)**. It also is the umbrella name for all the Euronext derivative markets in both the UK and mainland Europe. It was established in September 1982 and at one time was the second largest derivatives exchange in the world. The combined Euronext exchange is the third largest derivatives market in the world by volume traded. It is a very important player in global terms, specialising in products which manage risk at the short-end of the euro yield curve. In the late 1990s, it faced a period of growing competition from Eurex, the automated German/Swiss derivatives exchange. This caused LIFFE to re-think its business strategy and to alter its trading systems completely. This two-year exercise was successfully managed and the exchange's 2001 and 2002 trading volumes surpassed their previous peak of 1997 following the downturns of the intervening years. The Exchange's share capital was purchased by Euronext in 2001 and **NYSE Euronext.liffe** was created. In 2007, the NYSE bought Euronext so the Liffe exchange is now called NYSE Euronext.liffe.

Prior to this, LIFFE had taken over two of London's other derivatives markets. The London Traded Options Market (LTOM), formed originally by the London Stock Exchange, was merged with LIFFE in 1992. One of London's oldest markets, the London Commodity Exchange (the LCE, formed in 1888) was taken over by LIFFE in 1996 and its name discontinued. This business now forms the non-financial contracts division of LIFFE.

All trading is performed on the LIFFE CONNECT® system. The role of the exchange is to provide an effective and efficient trading platform. It offers a very wide range of tradeable products covering financials, equities and non-financial contracts (agricultural and soft commodities). A separate clearing house structure is utilised to protect the financial integrity of the Exchange. Through this, trades are cleared and settled through LCH.Clearnet Ltd (LCH).

4.2 Trading methods

LIFFE used to have an open outcry method of trading with traders meeting face to face in a pit on a trading floor. This process was modelled on the style of the Chicago floor markets. Trading is now screen-based using LIFFE CONNECT®.

Does **open outcry** trading or **screen-based** trading provide a more effective and efficient trading system?

- **Cost**. Open outcry is costly in terms of labour and physical structure. At the height of LIFFE's floor trading days in 1997, there were plans to build a trading floor the size of two football pitches which would have been its third such home. Screen-based trading is expensive in terms of initial system development and hardware. However, settlement and supervision/surveillance are cheaper as straight-through processing reduces costs.

- **Liquidity**. Open outcry is a quotation-based method and has the advantage that traders will probably deal with each other if they see each other. In open outcry markets, the traders can 'smell fear' which creates volatility and thus a market. Screen-based trading is order driven and therefore dealers need to stimulate trades by placing orders.

- **Participants**. Open outcry is limited to the number of traders that can physically fit into the trading floor. Screen-based trading can easily be global and thus computer and network capacity is the only limit.

- **Transparency**. Open outcry markets are extremely transparent as all participants have access to the same information. Screen-based trading has transparency too but is also anonymous.

- **Regulation**. Open outcry is more difficult to police. It is hard for firms to oversee their traders' activities as they are on the floor rather than in the office. Trader turnover between firms is high and there is a danger that traders on the floor are doing trades for the benefit of their ego or their friends rather than the firm. Screen-based trading has the advantage that all the traders are in the building and thus easier to oversee.

  With open outcry, it is hard to prove best execution and timely execution. Various investigations into trading practices on LIFFE and the Chicago markets exposed front running orders, rigging trades, manipulating error accounts, colluding with locals and using bagmen. Screen-based trading automatically produces an audit trail and it is easy to check the time and price of every deal.

4.3 Central counterparty (CCP)

An exchange must protect its reputation for financial integrity. One way to do this is by assuring that all trades are honoured. A **central counterparty** ensures that all transactions are honoured and reduces the counterparty or credit risk for traders.

LCH.Clearnet (LCH) acts as a central counterparty on behalf of LIFFE for **all trades**. LCH receives a feed from LIFFE of trades from its LIFFE CONNECT® trading system. These are agreed trades and the Trade Registration System (TRS) and the Clearing Processing System (CPS) permit clearing members to confirm business into the correct clearing accounts.

The LCH then acts as principal to all trades which have been transacted. Hence every exchange member who buys or sells a contract ends up with a position with the LCH either directly, if they themselves are clearing members, or indirectly through the clearing member of the exchange who clears their trades. The LCH takes all the risk of counterparties' failing to honour obligations.

The LCH reduces its risk by requiring cash or collateral deposits (initial margins) for the clearing members' positions. The amount of initial margin is calculated using a portfolio algorithm such as SPAN. This uses an initial margin rate or 'scanning range' as one of its inputs. This rate set by the clearing house in consultation with the Exchange, will be a percentage of the face value of the contract. It generally varies between 0.1% and 6% depending on the historical price volatility of the underlying instrument. Futures and options are highly-geared products as, in order to buy/sell a future with a contract value exposure of a £1,000,000 sterling, a deposit – the only financial outlay – is the initial margin which can be a fraction of the overall exposure value.

LCH keeps detailed records of counterparties' transactions and the prices of contracts. Everyday LCH marks all positions to market (**'marking to market'**) and calculates daily profit and losses. If the future moves unfavourably, additional margin (**variation margin**) will be required. If the future moves favourably, the surplus cash can be withdrawn.

When a futures position is closed, the central counterparty will return:

- Initial margin
- *Plus* Variation margin
- *Plus* Profits
- *Minus* Losses
- *Minus* Cash withdrawals already made

Example: Central counterparty

A company bought five June sterling interest rate futures for 95.30. The initial margin was £2,000 and further variation margin of £1,200 was requested. The position was closed at 94.80. This was a fall of 50 ticks.

The overall loss was 5×50 ticks $\times £12.50 = £3,125$.

Cash returned by central counterparty:

$$£2,000 + £1,200 - £3,125 = £75$$

4.4 Participation in the LIFFE market

In order to trade on the facilities provided by the Exchange, a member must:

- Hold a permit issued by the Exchange, or
- Take a lease of a permit from an Exchange member, or
- Be granted a trading licence

Permits are issued, for example, in financial futures, financial options, equity options and commodity trading.

4.5 Membership criteria

In deciding whether to admit an applicant to membership of the market, the LIFFE Board determines whether the applicant satisfies the following criteria.

- That he is fit and proper

- That he enjoys the financial and business standing suitable for admission to membership

- That, where relevant, he is authorised, or otherwise licensed or permitted by the appropriate regulatory body to conduct business on the market

- That his staff are fit and proper with suitable qualifications and experience in order to implement and maintain adequate internal procedures and controls in relation to his intended business on the market, and

- Any other criteria (including criteria as to financial resources), which the Board may for the time being prescribe with regard to membership

4.6 Clearing arrangements

A member who is a futures member or an equity options member or a commodity member may become a clearing member upon application to the Clearing House and to the Board of LIFFE, provided that he satisfies the criteria (including criteria as to financial resources) which the Clearing House and the Board prescribe.

There are two types of clearing membership, a general clearing member (who may enter into clearing agreements with non-clearing members, and provide clearing of contracts for the non-clearing member) and individual clearing members who may not enter into clearing agreements with a non-clearing member. Clearing is the process of matching, guaranteeing and registering transactions. LIFFE trades are guaranteed against counterparty risk by LCH.

4.7 The LIFFE CONNECT® trading system

4.7.1 Overview

LIFFE CONNECT® is an electronic trading platform that has been designed by LIFFE for trading its range of individual equity option contracts, replacing the former open outcry method of trading for these products. Instead of traders meeting face-to-face in a pit on a trading floor, trading is conducted via PCs located at the premises of LIFFE member firms and other market participants.

Trading on LIFFE CONNECT® is conducted in an order driven rather than quote driven environment with buy and sell orders matched automatically in the virtual electronic market created between LIFFE and its market participants. In addition, the market operates anonymously with orders being matched on a strict price / time priority. Furthermore, two-way prices, visible on the screen, represent firm buy and sell orders instead of indicative quotes as existed in the open outcry market. It is also possible to automate more complex trades and structures.

A standard Applications Programme Interface (API) exists to which external independent service providers (ISVs) link their systems. These ISVs in turn link to end user traders. This is a competitive business with many participants. One of the reasons for the success of this approach is that the distribution of the market prices becomes greatly more successful with a much broader global reach.

LIFFE CONNECT® has been selected by Euronext for use across all its derivatives markets. The CME also selected this software in January 2003. LIFFE has also provided it to TIFFE in Tokyo.

4.7.2 Participants

There are a number of different roles in the market, as follows.

- **Market makers** (options only) – members who have agreed to fulfil certain market making obligations thus qualifying for defined benefits (party to a market making agreement)

- **Principal traders** – members who trade proprietary business

- **Brokers** – members who trade on behalf of clients

Member firms may choose to perform more than one of these roles. LIFFE members are simply dealers, brokers of broker/dealers. This classification is consistent across the whole of the Euronext group.

Members are required to register at least one **responsible person** with the Exchange.

A **responsible person** is assigned at least one Individual Trader Mnemonic (ITM), although they may have more than one, and will be ultimately responsible for all business submitted under any of their ITMs. The responsible person does not have to submit all business associated with their ITMs themselves, since other individuals within the member firm are permitted to trade using their ITMs.

4.7.3 Market making arrangements

There are two categories of market maker, **Category A** and **Category B**, each with different levels of commitment and benefits. The commitments are related to the making of continuous two-way prices and responding to Requests For Quotation (RFQs). The benefits are in the form of fee reductions and the ability to advertise.

4.7.4 Market control

A LIFFE market control function controls and monitors the operation of the electronic market. This is responsible, for example, for the following functions.

- Opening and closing markets

- Revoking the declaration of fast markets

- Suspending and reactivating price limits

- Disabling and re-enabling individual markets, for example to deal with stock events

- Locking out traders from the market if their actions are contrary to Trading Procedures or likely to adversely impact the integrity of the market, and

- Communicating significant events to market participants, either collectively or selectively

4.7.5 Trader qualification procedures

Only traders named on a member permit may have direct access to the electronic market via a secure log-on. All traders named on permits must complete a theory course and examination. In addition, traders using LIFFE-supplied Trading Applications will be required to complete a practical course and examination.

Where a member firm is employing its own or a third-party developed Trading Application, it will be the responsibility of the member/third party to provide a practical course in order to ensure its traders receive adequate training.

4.7.6 Market monitoring and audit

Market control and other exchange officials monitor trading in the futures market in order to identify and act upon any potential breaches of trading procedures, obligations or rules.

All events (e.g. orders submitted, revised, withdrawn, traded, traders logging on/off) are logged by the LIFFE CONNECT® system for audit (and possible investigation) purposes.

4.7.7 Equity derivatives services

- **Afirm**, **Bclear** and **Cscreen** form NYSE Euronext.liffe's unique new service for wholesale equity derivatives, introduced in 2005. These three services are fully integrated to provide **straight-through processing (STP)** from pre-trade price discovery to post-trade registration, administration and clearing.

- **Afirm** provides an efficient 'off-exchange' post-trade matching service offering affirmation or matching through to confirmation for OTC equity derivatives transactions. Afirm can be used as a stand-alone service or in conjunction with Cscreen, providing straight through processing (STP) from pre-trade price discovery to post-trade administration.

- **Bclear** provides a low cost means of registering, processing and clearing wholesale equity derivatives within the secure framework of an exchange and clearing house. Users can register OTC business as an exchange contract for futures and options on over 300 European blue-chip stocks and 12 indices. Bclear can be used as a stand-alone service or in conjunction with Cscreen.

- **Cscreen** is a dynamic application that enables brokers and traders to post and respond to 'Indications of Interest' (IOI) for wholesale equity derivatives. There are three versions of the Cscreen software available depending on the user's requirements.

5 THE INTERNATIONAL CAPITAL MARKETS ASSOCIATION

5.1 Overview

The International Securities Markets Association (ISMA) was the self-regulatory industry body and trade association for the international securities market. Initially it created rules for the Eurobond market. It merged in July 2005 with the International Primary Markets Association (IPMA), the professional association for institutions engaged in primary (new issues) markets for international securities, to form the **International Capital Market Association (ICMA)**. It has almost 800 members across over 50 countries.

ISMA, formerly the Association of International Bond Dealers (AIBD), was founded in 1969. Its original purpose was to standardise the wide variety of Euromarket payment and delivery methods. The ISMA issued rules and recommendations regarding trading and settlement, as well as rules governing good market conduct, disciplinary proceedings and procedures for the settlement of disputes through conciliation and arbitration. ISMA was originally recognised by the Secretary of State as the only international securities self-regulating organisation (ISRO) under the Financial Services Act 1986. ISMA had been recognised by the FSA as a **designated investment exchange (DIE)** for the purpose of conduct of business rules.

A **Eurobond** is commonly defined as being a bond issued by a borrower in a foreign country, denominated in a Eurocurrency (e.g. US Dollar, Canadian Dollar, Yen, Euro, Sterling, etc.), underwritten and sold by an international syndicate of financial institutions.

Most Eurobonds are listed on the Luxembourg Stock Exchange and the London Stock Exchange. However, most Eurobond trades are made over-the-counter (OTC). This describes a market in which trades are arranged by dealers by telephone rather than on the floor of an Exchange. Although the OTC market is generally not fettered by governmental restrictions, the advantages of standardisation mean that ICMA's rules, regulations and recommendations govern the trading and settlement of securities.

5.2 Dealer types

Broadly, three groups of dealers exist in the Euromarket.

- **Market makers:** dealers who carry a certain stock of Euromarket securities and quote bid and offer prices. These prices are transmitted to interested parties either on request or on a regular basis. The lead manager of an issue is expected also to be a market maker in that issue, not only finding interested parties as buyers or sellers but also maintaining an active market. In other words, supplying bonds when there is a demand and buying bonds when they are offered for sale.

- **Brokers:** agents acting for clients, dealing on their behalf with the market makers.

- **Reporting dealers:** market makers meeting certain criteria are registered as Reporting Dealers. The ICMA rules define a Reporting Dealer as any institution that makes a market in a representative number of securities in one sector or combination of market sectors.

5.3 Reporting dealer and inter-dealer broker obligations

Reporting Dealers have to follow the rules of conduct set by ICMA and have to comply with certain requirements, such as daily reporting of prices of transactions and furnishing of closing quotations for securities in which markets are made. Reporting Dealers are obliged to quote bid/offer prices to other Reporting Dealers rather than to any financial institutions.

The minimum round lot trade effected between ICMA members has been fixed by ICMA. Trading sizes are fixed individually by sub-committees comprising the Reporting Dealers in each specific market sector.

Confirmations of trades must be checked and the counterparty must advise any disagreement, error or omission immediately following receipt. In the event of such disagreement, error or omission, both parties must examine the matter and the party at fault must amend.

5.4 Transaction matching, reporting and confirmation

Reporting Dealers, inter-dealer brokers and UK ICMA members must use the **TRAX** system for trade matching, reporting and confirmation.

Required information

- Trade date
- Trade time
- Settlement date
- Counterparty
- Security code
- Quantity
- Price
- Purchase or sale

Transactions must be reported to ICMA within 30 minutes of the trade.

TRAX can automatically interface with both Clearstream and Euroclear to automate clearing and settlement as well as trade reporting. In addition to trade reporting for ICMA, TRAX can also report automatically to the FSA and the LSE.

5.5 Clearing system

Clearance and settlement of securities traded in the over-the-counter Euromarket is done mainly via Clearstream or Euroclear. Dealers are direct members of those clearing systems.

A **Bridge** exists between the systems if the clearance and settlement accounts of the dealers reside in opposite clearing systems. This system enables users of each service to be able to settle with each other. Euroclear Bank and Clearstream International in July 2003 jointly announced the development of a new, automated, daytime Bridge between the two international central securities depositories (ICSDs). The Bridge is an electronic communications link which facilitates the efficient settlement of securities transactions between counterparties in Clearstream Banking Luxembourg and Euroclear Bank. This new development supplemented the existing overnight electronic Bridge and replaced the manually operated daytime Bridge that previously linked the two ICSDs. The automated daytime Bridge substantially improved the existing infrastructure specifically by extending instruction deadlines, allowing same-day Bridge transactions. The launch was effected in two phases in June and November 2004 to ease implementation.

Phase 1 of the upgrade, achieved in June 2004, improved settlement efficiency of Bridge transactions in general. Clients were able to settle a wider range of securities transactions by being able to re-deliver securities from many more local markets across the Bridge during the day. The upgrade also allowed clients to reduce their financing costs by having more opportunities to settle Bridge transactions that failed during the overnight process. Also at this time, there was a reduction in and better control of the risk exposure between the ICSDs for Bridge transactions.

Phase 2, launched in November 2004, allowed same-day settlement of trades over the Bridge, and in particular, repo and securities financing transactions between ICSD counterparties. This phase extended Bridge instruction input deadlines into the daytime (from 20:30 the evening before settlement date to 13:30 on settlement date) and provided the means for same-day distribution of new issues during the daytime over the Bridge. This phase brought further cost and settlement efficiencies by enabling clients to repair previously unmatched instructions.

5.6 Settlement timing

ICMA has introduced settlement on a basis of T+3 to reduce risk. Of vital importance therefore is the definition of a business day which is 'a day when Clearstream, Euroclear and the cash market of the currency in which the relevant transaction is to be settled, are open for business'. Since Clearstream and Euroclear are only closed on December 25th, the problems only arise in the cash markets. Accordingly, ICMA publishes a calendar detailing all the bank holidays. Where there are one or more holidays in the cash market of the currency or the international clearing systems, the settlement date will be extended accordingly.

6 ICE FUTURES

6.1 Background

ICE Futures was previously the International Petroleum Exchange (IPE), until the name was changed in 2005. ICE Futures was established in 1980 when it started trading Gas Oil futures. Since then new contracts such as Brent crude, natural gas, electricity and unleaded gasoline futures have been introduced.

The market's foundation reflects the substantial price volatility of energy products since the 1970s and the emergence of significant European production in the North Sea. ICE Gas Oil has become one of the largest oil product futures contracts in the world and Brent crude is an industry benchmark.

The Exchange was acquired by the IntercontinentalExchange (ICE) of Atlanta, Georgia in June 2001. ICE is one of the world's largest electronic commodity and energy trading groups with particular emphasis upon the trading of OTC energy products.

6.2 Membership

There are a number of categories of membership. When the exchange took the decision to add electronic trading side by side with open outcry, it created some new membership classes known as participants (see table below). For a while members held more than one type of membership during the period that electronic trading ran in addition to the main floor operation. However when, in April 2005, it changed its trading approach to become fully electronic and closed the pits, the older membership classes including floor members were no longer relevant. In the list below the older floor-based classes are included in brackets for comparison purposes.

All trades must be carried out by a member. Non-members wishing to participate must use the broking services offered by many of the General Participant members.

- **General Participants** (previously Floor members) are similar to the 'clearing members' on NYSE Euronext.liffe – they must either be a member or have a clearing arrangement with a clearing member of LCH.Clearnet.

- **Individual Participants** (previously Locals) are individual traders who can only transact own account business. Since locals are not members of LCH.Clearnet, they will require a clearing arrangement to be in place with an LCH.Clearnet member.

- **Trade Participants** (previously Trade Associate members). This category includes companies that have an interest in the production, manufacture or distribution of physical energy products (for example, a natural gas distribution company). The trading associate member has trading rights for IPE products. They may be clearing members of LCH.Clearnet but, if not, they need to have a clearing arrangement in place with an LCH.Clearnet member.

6.3 Trading mechanism

Since 7 April 2005, all ICE Futures contracts have been traded electronically using a system known as **The Interchange**™, a system developed by the Exchange's parent company the Intercontinental Exchange (ICE®). It operates global market places for the trading of energy commodity futures and OTC contracts on its internet-based Interchange™ trading platform.

The Interchange™ is a fully electronic screen-based trade execution facility, providing instant access to the ICE Futures markets and through a web browser using industry standard data security and encryption technology.

Previously the market used an open outcry system with contracts traded in pits and then developed various electronic systems as an alternative to floor trading. Only qualified floor traders were allowed to enter the pits and make valid bid and offer prices.

6.4 Settlement types

ICE Futures operates the leading electronic regulated futures and options exchange for global energy markets. ICE's trading platform offers participants access to a wide range of energy futures products. Contracts include the Brent global crude benchmark contract, Gas Oil, Natural Gas, Electricity, and ECX carbon financial instruments.

Within the current ICE Futures product range, there are different methods of delivery. These are summarised in the following table.

Product	Type of settlement
Brent Crude Future	EFP delivery and cash settlement option
Gas Oil Future	Physical
Natural Gas Future	Physical
Electricity	Debit and credit of electricity
Carbon emissions	Physical

6.5 Options settlement

IPE-traded options are American style and can be exercised at any time up until expiry. The exercise of an option gives rise to a futures position. If long calls are exercised a long futures position results. If a long put is exercised a short futures position results.

Notice of exercise or declaration is made by submitting an exercise notice to the Clearing House subject to certain deadlines.

7 LONDON METAL EXCHANGE

7.1 Background

130 years old in 2007, the **London Metal Exchange (LME)** is the world's largest non-ferrous metals exchange. The LME commenced trading in 1877 when industrialisation in Britain led to the importing of large quantities of metals. The pricing and trading of these commodities was haphazard, sailing times were variable, information sparse and the merchant trade informal. Three factors changed the market into a more organised state. These were the development of the steamship, the opening of the Suez Canal and the introduction of the electric telegraph. Given the predictability of flows, traders now traded in cargoes for future arrival. By 1877 this trade was sufficiently well developed for an organised exchange to be established.

The LME is of great significance to London and the UK because of its unique global role and its continuing success and growth in activity. British Invisibles estimated in June 1999 that the Exchange was responsible for invisible earnings to the UK of about £250m a year. The daily value of contracts traded on the LME is about US$10 million. Annually, trading volume on the LME is consistently around 60 million lots. Volume of business has increased ten fold since 1990.

The LME's customers are not only drawn from those engaged in mining, smelting and metal fabrication and consumption. It is also used very extensively by fund managers, CTAs (commodity trading advisers) and other investment and trading interests.

The LME trades base metals. In the order of volume traded they are: aluminium, copper, zinc, nickel, lead, tin and aluminium alloy. Metals are traded for delivery on specific prompt dates. These are any business day. Most trades are executed for immediate delivery (spot) or for delivery in 3 months. There is also a substantial business in intermediate dates by way of borrowing and lending. It introduced its North American Special Aluminium Alloy contract in March 2002. LME plans to introduce steel futures in 2008 and launched two futures contracts in plastics in May 2005, both of which were subject to an effective re-launch in 2007.

Trades are settled via **LCH.Clearnet** as the central counterparty.

The terminology on the LME differs from other options markets as a option holder is a **taker**, an option writer is a **granter** and an expiry date is a **declaration day**. It is on the LME where the words contango and backwardation have special significance. If the futures price is higher than the spot price then it is known as **contango** market. If the futures price is lower than the spot price the market is said to be in a **backwardation**.

In 1997, Yasuo Hamanaka, a senior copper trader with the Sumitomo Corporation, caused losses in the region of US$2.7bn (far in excess of Barings' losses, following the actions of Nick Leeson). Although Sumitomo were not LME members, he managed to manipulate copper prices and thus called into question the operations of the LME, which led to a restructuring of its governance and operation.

In June 2000, following a report from a practitioners' committee the Board issued a consultation document containing proposals for the future strategic development of the Exchange. Amongst issues covered was the structure and governance of the Exchange including the recommendation to de-mutualise.

In January 2007 the exchange announced strategic plans to expand its business into ferrous metals and to embrace OTC transactions alongside its traditional exchange-based activities. They refer to this as their '2' by '2' growth strategy. To quote the strategy document released by the Exchange, 'This will see the LME developing two swathes of organic growth, from non-ferrous into ferrous and from futures into OTC trading. It is designed to double the volume of business at the LME within five years.

The London Metal Exchange (LME) launched small size, cash settled monthly futures contracts, traded electronically and via telephone market initially for copper, aluminium and zinc on 4 December 2006. These contracts are typically about a fifth the size of the standard contracts.

7.2 Membership

There are around 100 members (excluding individuals) of the LME and there are seven categories of membership.

- **Category 1 – Ring dealing members** are Clearing Members who enjoy all the privileges of membership including the right to issue client contracts and the exclusive right to trade in the Ring. There are only 12 firms in this category.

- **Category 2 – Associate broker clearing members** have all the privileges of Ring Dealing Members except that they may not trade in the Ring.

- **Category 3 – Associate trade clearing members** may not issue client contracts nor may they trade in the Ring but they are entitled to clear their own business.

- **Category 4 – Associate broker members** may issue client contracts but they are not Clearing Members and may not trade in the Ring.

- **Category 5 – Associate trade members** may not issue client contracts.

- **Categories 6 and 7 – Honorary and individual members** also have no trading rights.

7.3 Clearing arrangements

The LME is cleared by LCH.Clearnet Ltd (LCH). As it is a condition of ring membership to be a member of LCH all firms on the floor have a direct relationship with the Clearing House.

The LME has developed a trade matching system which covers both floor and inter-office trading. This system is similar to the Trade Registration System (TRS) used by other exchanges. Each trade is reported by the buyer and seller.

7.4 Trading mechanisms

LME has a '**ring and kerb**' method of trading. At 11:45 each day, the **ring** opens and each metal futures contract trades in turn for five minutes. At 12:20, when all metals have been traded once, there is a ten minute break and then the cycle starts again. There is also a 'kerb' session when all metals can be traded.

The LME operates two styles of trading: **open outcry** or **ring trading** and a **telephone and screen-based inter-office market**. During ring trading, each ring dealing member is entitled to have one dealer in the ring.

In April 2001, the LME introduced a new electronic trading platform known as LME Select in parallel to ring dealing methods. This system has now been upgraded. There is also a flourishing market in prices quoted by other electronic systems outside the Exchange including Reuters.

The LME trading system, incorporating as it does periods of open outcry trading, electronic trading as well as potentially 24-hour inter-office dealing is unique.

The focus of the day's activity are the open outcry ring sessions. Each of the metal futures contracts traded by the exchange is allocated four five-minute trading periods each day. Trading on the floor takes place in two sessions daily.

The two sessions are each broken down into two rings made up of five minutes trading in each contract. Each session is followed by a short period of open outcry dealing in all metals simultaneously known as '**kerb trading**'.

Trading in the ring is conducted by dealers calling out their bids and offers to the rest of the ring. There are no market makers making two-way prices, although dealers may, if they wish, make both a buying and a selling price.

Inter-office trading may take place 24 hours a day. Bargains made on the inter-office market are in every sense LME contracts as much as those traded during the ring session.

7.5 Official prices

As well as the LME's obvious role as a forum for trading futures contracts, it has worldwide significance in price setting. Many metals contracts are priced on the basis of LME official prices, or from an average of LME prices over a period.

Official prices are established after the second ring of the morning session by the quotation committee. The price committee confer amongst themselves and establish what was the last best bid and offer prevailing at the close of the ring. These are announced by the Exchange shortly afterwards as the prices of cash, three months and fifteen months metal – effectively world benchmark prices.

The last few moments of the second ring of the morning session are highly important and it is a feature of the market that trading activity and consequently noise are at their highest at the end of this session.

7.6 Prompt date

The delivery date of an LME futures contract is known as its 'prompt date'. By this time either the position must be closed or a delivery will take place. On the LME the final settlement price is in fact set two days before this prompt date for example for June 14th delivery the price will have been set on June 12th.

7.7 LME options

The LME trades options on all its products. The maximum life of the contracts are 27 months for copper, aluminium, nickel, silver and zinc and 15 months for lead, tin, and aluminium alloy. Expiry dates occur monthly, with the expiry day taking place two weeks prior to the underlying futures prompt date. Delivery is into an LME futures position.

7.8 Trading LME options

Options trading only takes place on an inter-office basis and is not part of the ring trading sessions. LME options are dealt in the same contract sizes as the futures contracts.

Trading can be conducted in any option up to the last business day before the declaration day, which is the first Wednesday in each month, with delivery in relation to the futures on the third Wednesday. By allowing two weeks between declaration of options and delivery, the LME management seek to avoid pressure on the futures prompt date.

8 EDX LONDON

8.1 Formation of EDX London

In December 2002, the London Stock Exchange plc and OM AB announced that they were to develop and provide derivatives market services specifically tailored for equity market participants through the creation of a new international equity derivatives business, **EDX London**.

EDX London attempts to combine the strength of London Stock Exchange's global equity market offering and expertise with OM's flexible technology and experience in equity derivatives. Initially, EDX London's business was built around the Scandinavian equity derivatives business of OM's London subsidiary, OM London Exchange. EDX London took responsibility for the operation of this business, expanded the product range and sought to create new business lines.

Part of EDX London's initial focus was on the development, in conjunction with LCH.Clearnet as its CCP, of an over-the-counter (OTC) equity derivatives trade confirmation and clearing service for wholesale market participants, which would provide capital and operational savings. This would reduce the cost and risk of conducting OTC business and was a facility not currently available at that time for the growing OTC equity derivatives market in London. This service was to be developed in close collaboration with the participants in this market.

Since the commencement of EDX London, other competitors in the OTC equity derivatives market have emerged in the shape of **Swapswire** and **DTTC**.

9 VIRT-X

9.1 Background

virt-x began trading on 25 June 2001 and in its second week of trading had total turnover of £7.2bn on 120,000 trades covering some 170m shares. It offers a single system that trades in the constituents of all the European blue chip indices bringing the total number of stocks traded on virt-x to over 600, representing approximately 80% of European market capitalisation.

virt-x Exchange Limited, a wholly owned subsidiary of virt-x plc, is a **Recognised Investment Exchange** supervised by the Financial Services Authority and is a regulated market under the Investment Services Directive. It also has been approved by the US SEC – the only European exchange so approved.

Based in London, virt-x was created in February 2001 through collaboration between Tradepoint Financial Networks plc (now renamed virt-x plc), the TP Consortium (TP Group LDC) and SWX Swiss Exchange to provide an efficient and cost-effective pan-European blue chip market.

The virt-x market is based on an integrated trading, clearing and settlement model intended to simplify the process of trading pan-European blue chips and to significantly reduce the costs associated with trading cross-border.

virt-x supports trading in the equities which comprise the major European blue chip indices. These are currently the 613 stocks that make up the AEX, CAC 40, DAX 30, Dow Jones STOXX 50, Dow Jones EURO STOXX 50, Dow Jones STOXX 600, FTSE 100, FTSE Eurotop 300, IBEX 35, MIB 30, MSCI Euro, MSCI Pan Euro, S&P Europe 350 and SMI.

9.2 Clearing and settlement

All order book trades settle on T+3. Where any settlement is due to take place on a day on which the central bank for that currency is closed, the settlement due date is adjusted to be the next 'open' day after the currency holiday.

virt-x trades can be settled in Euroclear and SIS. These are known as 'the **core CSDs**' (**Central Securities Depositories**). Members can choose to settle from one or more accounts within these core CSDs.

Currently settlement is between the trading counterparties although it was announced that from March 2007 a pan-European CCP would be offered giving members the option of linking via LCH or x-clear (the Swiss central counterparty). Both CCPs will clear the full range of stocks traded on virt-x.

Members have a choice of settlement accounts and, where counterparties have chosen different CSDs, settlement will be cross-border. Where the settlement is between the core CSDs, they have collaborated to make this as transparent as possible.

9.3 Trading

Rules at different times in the trading day

- **Pre-opening (05:00-08:00).** Addition and deletion of limit orders allowed. No automatic execution occurs. Submission of trade reports allowed.

- **Continuous trading (08:00-16:50).** An uncrossing algorithm is run (the 'opening auction'), after which the opening price is set (the price at which most business will execute) and automated execution begins. All types of orders can be entered and deleted from the time when automated execution begins.

- **Closing (16:50-17:00).** Automated execution stops. Addition and deletion of limit orders allowed. No automatic execution occurs. An uncrossing algorithm is run (the 'closing auction'), after which the closing price is set (the price at which most business will execute).

- **After hours trading (17:00-21:00).** Addition and deletion of limit orders allowed. No automatic execution occurs. Submission of trade reports allowed.

9.4 Reporting

Any transaction executed under the rules of virt-x must be reported. On order book executions are automatically reported by the trading system.

There are separate provisions for the delayed reporting of certain qualifying trades. Individual elements of Portfolio trades must be reported within one hour while Block Trades and Enlarged Risk Trades must be reported when the business is substantially (80%) complete, or by 18:00 (CET) on the day of trade, unless the Trade is agreed after 16:00 (CET), when the Trade must be reported by 18:00 (CET) the following business day. Block Trades and Enlarged Risk Trades are subject to minimum trade size criteria. All other transactions must be reported within three minutes.

10 PLUS MARKETS

10.1 Overview

PLUS Markets was formerly called **OFEX** and is London's third stock market after the LSE and AIM.

PLUS Markets is an off-exchange share matching and trading facility originally established by JP Jenkins Ltd to enable LSE member firms to deal in the securities of unlisted and unquoted companies. Securities traded on PLUS are not quoted, listed or dealt in on the LSE, nor are they subject to its rules.

Companies on this market have included Aberdeen Steak Houses, Arsenal Football Club, Rangers Football Club and Weetabix. The market is lightly regulated and was established to help smaller companies raise capital. However, it has struggled to attract listings thanks, in part, to the success of AIM. It has targeted smaller companies needing to raise between £2m (€2.8m) and £3m. The cost of raising finance is lower than on the AIM market. The market now has a number of brokers that make markets in shares of PLUS Markets companies.

10.2 Information provision

The PLUS Markets trading platform distributes PLUS price and company-related information to quote vendors such as Bloomberg, Primark, Reuters and FT Information.

10.3 Market makers

The market makers undertake to trade in the role of market maker in all PLUS securities and as such, undertake to quote a firm two-way price in a given quantity of stock for most PLUS Markets securities.

For less liquid or illiquid PLUS Markets securities, they will quote a basis price and seek to 'match' the trade with existing indicated business which has been previously noted.

The trading platform's role is to provide visibility for the trading activities of PLUS Markets by distributing all price and trading information as well as giving background information and news items for each company.

More information: www.plusmarketsgroup.com

11 RECENT INITIATIVES

11.1 Introduction

The November 2007 implementation of regulatory changes under the **Markets in Financial Instruments Directive (MiFID)**, which we discuss later in this Study Book, has encouraged the development of a number of new trading and reporting systems.

11.2 Project Turquoise

The concept of a pan-European trading and settlement system has been much debated over the past decade. **Project Turquoise** is the latest such initiative. Examples of initiatives that have not fully delivered in the past include Tradepoint, ITG Posit, JiWay and Liquidnet.

Project Turquoise is backed by some of the LSE's largest customers, and the Depository Trust & Clearing Corporation (DTCC). The founding group of banks – Goldman Sachs, Citigroup, Merrill Lynch, Morgan Stanley, UBS, Deutsche Bank and Credit Suisse – aims to create a user-owned Pan-European exchange offering lower trading costs. Project Turquoise is an example of a **Multilateral Trading Facility (MTF)**. MTFs are encouraged under MiFID. Originally planned for launch when MiFID took effect on 1 November 2007, Project Turquoise has been delayed beyond this date. Talks about a merger with Plus Markets ended in October 2007.

The Turquoise consortium expects that the system will be able to provide dealing services at a 50% discount to traditional exchanges. The project, based in London, is a hybrid system allowing trading both on and off traditional exchanges.

In April 2007, EuroCCP the European subsidiary of the US-based DTCC was appointed to provide clearing, settlement and risk management services to the group.

Some consider that the likelihood of failure is great, as history has shown how difficult it is to compete against the LSE. If the LSE were to match its low prices, then Project Turquoise could be in trouble.

Hurdles faced by Project Turquoise include:

- Incumbent vested interests and sovereignty issues
- Lack of interoperability of various platforms
- Different legal systems and languages for share issuance

The project's group of banks are essentially rivals in the commercial market place and will need to work to ensure that any conflicts of interests are resolved. Good leadership, commitment and innovative technology are needed to ensure success.

Although EuroCCP, is the European subsidiary of the DTCC, there were concerns about the DTCC's apparent lack of European infrastructure. It could however be questioned whether a substantial physical infrastructure is required, in a 'virtual' marketplace. By using the infrastructure of its parent company, EuroCCP could provide the necessary economies of scale.

The concept of Project Turquoise was seen to have evolved from **Project BOAT** (see below), as a way for banks to meet pre-trade and post-trade data requirements with the opportunity for a new trading system that would put more pressure on exchanges to lower prices. The founding banks of Project Turquoise account for about half of the equities trading in Europe, and more banks could join. The founding banks thus have financial strength, however most volume is controlled by their clients, such as hedge funds and other institutional traders.

Given best execution requirements, banks could divert trades from these clients to the new platform if they are able to offer the same or better quotes.

7: TRADING AND DEALING

Alternative revenue streams for the Project could arise from allowing transactions in 'dark liquidity' pools, whereby firms could buy and sell blocks of shares away from the public domain.

Exam tip

Keep up-to-date on developments in this current 'hot topic', which was examined in Summer 2007.

11.3 Project BOAT

Project BOAT led to the creation of Markit BOAT™, a price-reporting and display platform set up by a consortium of European banks to take advantage of MiFID by competing with exchange-based price display facilities.

BOAT enables investment firms to meet their pre-trade quoting and post-trade reporting obligations for all European OTC equity trades. The platform collects, collates, validates and stores OTC trade data and publishes it to the market in real-time.

With the support of over 22 investment houses, BOAT has the ability to capture and publish a majority of the daily volume of OTC trades in the EEA.

11.4 Instinet Chi-X

Aiming to provide clients with a fast, cheap and high-capacity alternative to trading on-exchange, Instinet's Chi-X is an order driven pan-European matching engine and central limit order book or MTF.

11.5 Equiduct

Equiduct, in which Börse Berlin holds a majority stake, aims to launch itself as a pan-European Regulated Market which will:

- Enable firms to meet their statutory commitments as defined by MiFID to provide best execution and transparency to clients in a Europe-wide single connection for trading services and execution

- Eliminate the need for financial institutions to become Systematic Internalisers

- Reduce the cost and time required for participant firms to achieve MiFID compliance

- Offer very low cost per transaction relative to other exchanges as well as settlement flexibility and guaranteed execution in a protected environment.

12 OVERSEAS EQUITY INVESTMENT

12.1 Advantages and disadvantages of overseas investment

Advantages

- Profits can be made in markets that are experiencing new growth that is not available to the UK market.

- Currency movements can generate higher profits when sterling falls against the overseas currency.

- It is possible to invest in areas that do not exist in the UK, or are very few and far between. Two examples of such areas have been gold and diamond mining although, in recent years, many mining stocks have become available on the AIM.

- An investor who puts his money purely into UK-based companies that have all or most of their profits arising in the UK loses out on the potential available in overseas markets.

Disadvantages

- Currency movements can work in favour of the investor or against him. A rise in the value of sterling against the particular currency could wipe out all the profits made. This is exchange risk or **currency risk**.

- There is a **political risk** involved in certain countries. Whilst a country may appear to be politically stable when an investment is made, changes may take place that wreck this stability.

- Overseas markets can be more volatile than the UK and a downturn will affect those markets to a greater extent.

- Whilst the UK does not have any exchange control regulations, other countries do have them or could introduce them. If this occurs, it may be impossible for an investor to remove his money from that country and no amount of profit made by that investment is of any use to the UK investor if it cannot be brought back to the UK.

- Although taxpayers can usually get a credit for tax suffered overseas under double taxation agreements, this may not be the case for non-taxpayers.

- Accounting policies and disclosure requirements abroad do not always match up to the UK standards. Where this is the case, an investor may not be aware of any adverse trends or unhealthy situations until it is too late.

- It can be difficult to obtain information about overseas companies from the UK press, and monitoring performance can be difficult.

12.2 Methods of investing in overseas equities

The LSE is renowned for its strength in international markets. It now offers several techniques for investors to trade in foreign securities

- **International Order Book (IOB)** is the market for trading liquid overseas securities. The market is based on an electronic order book similar to SETS but with the added option for member firms to display their identity pre-trade by using Named Orders. Developing markets depository receipts are traded on IOB. The Depository Receipts are issued by large companies from countries in Central and Eastern Europe, Asia and the Mediterranean. The IOB offers easy and cost efficient access for investors looking to invest in fast growing economies that are otherwise onerous or costly to access directly.

- **International Bulletin Board (ITBB)** offers bulletin board functionality for international securities secondary-listed on the London Stock Exchange. It is a screen-based service on which brokers can place buy and sell orders with a view to execution at the price stated. If a broker wishes to respond to an existing bid (buy) or offer (sell), the order can be executed by telephone or automatically through the service, using order-matching functionality. Once an on book transaction is agreed between the parties it is reported to the Exchange for regulatory and publication purposes.

- **International Retail Service (IRS)** provides UK retail investors access to trading in International Stocks. The service supports trading in major European and US blue chips, using sterling prices generated by market makers (Committed Principals or CPs).

12.3 Purchasing shares on an overseas Stock Exchange

A UK broker can make the necessary arrangements to purchase shares on an overseas stock exchange. This method of investing overseas carries all of the disadvantages mentioned, and can be an expensive operation because of high dealing costs. However, some discount brokers will deal in some foreign securities, with relatively low dealing costs.

This method of overseas investment may be most appropriate for institutional investors who have very large amounts to invest, and the necessary expertise available to monitor the risks involved.

12.4 Overseas stock markets

12.4.1 France

There is one stock market in France: Euronext. It operates a computerised order book known as the NSC. Settlement is on T+3 through the RELIT system and Euroclear France, the central securities depository.

12.4.2 Germany

The Deutsche Börse is a fierce competitor with the LSE. Trading takes place through a computerised order book called XETRA. Settlement is on T+2. Clearing, settlement and custody take place through Clearstream.

12.4.3 Japan

The Tokyo Stock Exchange is order driven through the CORES dealing system. Settlement is on T+3 by book entry transfer through the JSCC (Japanese Securities Clearing Corporation).

12.4.4 USA

The United States is home to the world's largest stock market with its constituent parts being the New York Stock Exchange, the American Stock Exchange, NASDAQ, the Philadelphia Stock Exchange, the Boston Stock Exchange, the Chicago Stock Exchange, the Cincinnati Stock Exchange and the Pacific Exchange.

The New York Stock Exchange was established in 1792 and is an order-driven floor dealing market. NASDAQ is a screen-based, quote driven market which is owned and operated by the National Association of Securities Dealers (NASD). The NASD is a self-regulatory organisation which is overseen by the Securities and Exchange Commission.

Settlement is on T+3. Clearing takes place though the **National Securities Clearing Corporation (NSCC)**. The NSCC is a wholly owned subsidiary of The Depository Trust and Clearing Corporation (DTCC). The NSCC guarantees the clearance on T+3. Institutional trades clear through the International Delivery (ID) system of the Depository Trust Company.

13 THE NEW YORK STOCK EXCHANGE

The **New York Stock Exchange (NYSE)**, which purchased the American Stock Exchange in 2007, is the largest securities market place in the world, is home to about 2,767 companies worth nearly US$21.2 trillion in global market capitalisation and trading about 1,602 million shares per day (2005 figures).

These companies include a cross-section of leading US companies, midsize and small capitalisation companies. Non-US issuers play an increasingly important role on the NYSE with non-US companies valued at nearly US$7.9 trillion.

A member firm is a company or individual that owns a seat on the trading floor. Only member firms are allowed to buy and sell securities on the floor. There are 1,392 members. To become a member firm, a company must meet rigorous professional standards set by the Exchange. Since 1953, the number of seats has remained constant at 1,366. Institutional investors are corporations that invest on behalf of individuals and companies. Institutions include pension funds, mutual funds, insurance companies and banks. The exchange uses Specialists and Floor Brokers on the trading floor.

Specialists are critical to the auction process. They maintain a fair and orderly market in the securities assigned to them. They manage the auction process, providing a conduit of information – electronically quoting and recording current bid and asked prices for the stocks assigned to them. This enables current price information to be transmitted worldwide, keeping all market participants informed of the total supply and demand for any particular NYSE-listed stock.

Each stock listed on the NYSE is allocated to a specialist, a broker who trades only in specific stocks at a designated location. All buying and selling of a stock occurs at that location called a trading post. Buyers and sellers – represented by the floor brokers – meet openly at the trading post to find the best price for a security.

The people who gather around the specialist's post are referred to as the trading crowd. Bids to buy and offers to sell are made by open outcry to provide interested parties with an opportunity to participate, enhancing the competitive determination of prices. When the highest bid meets the lowest offer, a trade is executed.

To a large degree the specialist is responsible for maintaining the market's fairness, competitiveness and efficiency. Specifically, the specialist performs five vital functions: they act as agents, catalysts, and auctioneers, stabilise prices and provide capital.

They provide capital as follows: if buy orders temporarily outpace sell orders in a stock (or if sell orders outpace buy orders) the specialist is required to use his firm's own capital to minimise the imbalance. This is done by buying or selling against the trend of the market, until a price is reached at which public supply and demand are once again in balance. In this role the specialist acts as a principal or dealer. Specialists participate in only about 10% of all shares traded. The rest of the time, public order meets public order, without specialist participation.

Examples of specialist firms are Spear, Leeds and Kellogg, LaBranche & Co. and Fleet Specialist Inc.

Brokers are agents representing customer orders to buy or sell. There are two main types of floor brokers, commission brokers and independent floor brokers.

Individual firms called brokerage houses that are members of the NYSE employ commission brokers. Operating quickly from booth to trading post, these brokers buy and sell securities for the general public. In return, they earn salaries and commissions. Independent floor brokers are brokers who work for themselves. They handle orders for brokerage houses that do not have full-time brokers or whose brokers are off the floor or too busy to handle specific orders. Independent floor brokers are often still referred to as 'two dollar brokers', a term coined back in the days when they received US$2 for every 100 shares they traded.

The public places its orders through sales personnel (or stockbrokers) of a brokerage house. These sales professionals are also called registered representatives, since they must pass a qualifying examination and are registered with the NYSE and the Securities and Exchange Commission. Investor orders are transmitted from a branch office of a brokerage house to the NYSE Trading Floor through sophisticated electronic communications and order-processing systems.

The New York Stock Exchange trading floor faces possible extinction. Once the 216-year-old institution finally bows to market pressures and allows unrestricted trading via computers, its biggest customers will be likely to execute most of their transactions without human intervention. Perhaps as little as 25% of the NYSE's business will be conducted on the floor after the change.

The NYSE's top 500 issues account for 80% of its trades. Furthermore, it is by no means certain that the NYSE will retain the lion's share of trading in its 2,300 other listed securities. Regulations introduced in 2006 will make it easier for struggling US regional exchanges to seize business from the NYSE if they post the best prices for stocks.

If investors turn *en masse* to electronic trading, the exchange will have little choice but to abandon the trading floor.

The NYSE converted to a for-profit publicly traded company after it acquired its former rival Archipelago in 2005.

14 THE EUREX MARKET

14.1 Overview

On the international derivatives exchange **Eurex**, a total of 1.526 billion contracts were traded and cleared in 2006, an increase of 22.2 percent on 2005. This corresponds to a daily average trading volume of 5.98 million contracts. With these trading figures, Eurex is recognised as the world's largest derivatives exchange. Open interest on Eurex consistently exceeds 100 million contracts.

Current membership has reached well over 700 locations from approaching 20 different countries. Its volumes leave its competitors in its wake, with the exception of the amazing KOSPI 200 index option on the Korea Stock Exchange which has recorded consistently soaring, largely domestic, volumes on its small denomination contract.

A fully electronic exchange, Eurex allows market participants decentralised and standardised access to its markets on a global scale. Providing access to benchmark products like the Bund future, Eurex has set a standard for a fast and secure global network. Its listed contracts are financial futures and options together with a range of equity options and index futures and options.

Eurex was created by Deutsche Börse AG and the Swiss Exchange in December 1996 and founded through the merger of DTB (Deutsche Terminbörse) and SOFFEX (the Swiss Options and Financial Futures Exchange). Both parties agreed to develop and implement a single platform for their derivatives markets and trade a harmonised product range. The operational and technical merger of the two markets was completed on 28 September 1998, when all DTB and SOFFEX participants united on a common trading and settlement platform and the newly established Eurex clearing house commenced its activities.

Trading on the fully computerised Eurex platform is distinctively different from trading on traditional open-outcry markets. It transcends borders and offers members technical access from any location, thereby creating a unique global liquidity network. Members are linked to the Eurex system via a dedicated wide-area communications network (WAN). To facilitate access to Eurex outside of Switzerland and Germany, access points have been installed in Amsterdam, Chicago, New York, Helsinki, London, Madrid, Paris, Hong Kong, Sydney and Tokyo.

Over 50% of all Eurex trades emanates from London.

14.2 Organisation and structure

Eurex is a public company and is owned in equal parts by Deutsche Börse AG and the Swiss Exchange. Aside from operating the electronic trading platform, Eurex provides an automated and integrated joint clearing house for products and participants, thereby achieving centralised, cross-border risk management. Through its structure, Eurex offers participants a comprehensive range of services from trading to final settlement via a single electronic system.

14.3 Eurex Clearing AG

The clearing house of the Eurex exchange is **Eurex Clearing AG**, wholly-owned subsidiary of Eurex Frankfurt AG founded in June 1998 under German law and registered in Frankfurt am Main.

With the expansion of the Eurex system to enable cross-border settlements and multi-currency clearing, Eurex Clearing AG clears and settles all transactions as the central counterparty. Transactions in German and Swiss securities are settled with delivery versus payment through SIS – SEGA Intersettle, the Swiss Central Security Depository, or Clearstream Banking Frankfurt.

Both central security depositories have set up omnibus accounts and established a "Cross Border DvP-Link" (DvP stands for **Delivery versus Payment**). In addition to securities, clearing and settlement facilities they also offer Clearing Members facilities for deposits of collateral (pledge accounts). Cross-border cash settlements by Eurex Clearing AG are processed through the Landeszentralbank (LZB) Hessen in Frankfurt/Main for Euro, the Swiss National Bank (SNB) in Zurich for CHF and Clearstream Banking Frankfurt for other currencies.

With the introduction of physically deliverable foreign currency products, a securities account will also have to be set up for the delivery of foreign securities. Eurex members will be provided with the information necessary for this before the individual products are launched.

Eurex Clearing assumed the responsibility for central counterparty requirements for the cash equity market on the Frankfurt Stock Exchange in 2003.

14.4 Eurex Clearing

14.4.1 Introduction

Every exchange participant admitted to trading at Eurex is required to participate in the clearing process of Eurex Clearing AG. The participant can choose to participate as a

- **General Clearing Member (GCM)**
- **Direct Clearing Member (DCM)**, or
- **Non-Clearing Member (NCM)**

GCMs and DCMs are both referred to as Clearing Members. NCMs are Exchange Participants without a clearing membership.

Every type of clearing membership entails different duties and requirements.

14.4.2 Clearing memberships

Clearing Members may be admitted either as General Clearing or Direct Clearing Members.

With a General Clearing Member (GCM) license, the exchange member concerned is authorised to clear its own transactions as well as those of its customers and those of Non-Clearing Members clearing through them. A Direct Clearing Member (DCM) license entitles the company or exchange member to carry out the clearing for its own transactions, those of its customers and of affiliated Non-Clearing Members.

General Clearing Members must have a minimum liable equity capital or own funds of €125m and pledge a third bank clearing guarantee in the amount of €5m. The minimum equity capital of Direct Clearing Members is €12.5m. They must pledge a guarantee amounting to €1m. Both GCM and DCM must maintain cash clearing accounts with Clearstream Banking AG, the Landeszentralbank Hessen (LZB) – the Regional Head Office of the Central Bank – and the Swiss National Bank (SNB) as well as a securities custody account with Clearstream Banking AG or SEGA/Intersettle (SIS), the Swiss Securities Clearing Corporation, respectively. Currently, banks domiciled in Germany or Switzerland are eligible for admission as Clearing Members.

The term '**Remote Clearing**' refers to General Clearing Members and Direct Clearing Members located outside Germany and Switzerland.

14.4.3 Eurex Remote Clearing

So-called Remote Clearing was introduced on 1 August 2000. Participants from every country in the EU and from Switzerland are not just able to participate in trading directly, they are also able to clear transactions themselves. Until that date they have had to clear their transactions through a General Clearing Member in Germany or Switzerland. The derivatives market is thus enhancing the flexibility of its participants in clearing substantially.

Their national supervisory authorities for deposit-taking business, lending operations and commission business must still license Eurex clearing members. A banking permit, however, is no longer required. An account with the Landeszentralbank Hessen (LZB) and with the Swiss National Bank (SNB) is necessary for cash settlements.

14.4.4 Eurex in North America

Eurex US entered the American derivatives marketplace in 2004. As a US registered exchange, Eurex US brought the Eurex business model to the US derivatives market, enabling access for all participants. Eurex bought the International Securities Exchange (ISE) in New York during 2007.

In response to market demand, Eurex US provided customers worldwide with easy and low cost electronic access to key benchmark US dollar-denominated fixed income futures and options on futures.

In a second phase, subject to the approval of the Commodity Futures Trading Commission (CFTC) – the American regulator for futures markets–, Eurex US hoped to provide access to Euro-denominated futures and options on futures as well as the most liquid European equity index products.

It competed head-to-head with the existing major American exchanges operating as a fully electronic market.

The Eurex US exchange in the USA used the services of the long-established Board of Trade Clearing Corporation (BOTCC), now renamed the Clearing Corporation. It is an independent corporation owned by 50 stockholder firms which trade on the Eurex US Exchange. The Clearing Corporation ensures the financial integrity of the futures and options contracts traded on the exchanges for which it clears.

See the BOTCC website at www.botcc.com

14.5 Membership: obtaining access to Eurex

Institutions wishing to trade at Eurex must be admitted as Eurex exchange members. Eurex does not permit personal memberships. However, once a company becomes a Eurex member, Eurex does not limit the number of traders that it registers on its behalf for exchange trading at Eurex. Companies may apply for admission subject to the following conditions.

- Conduct of derivatives trading in a commercial manner as well as evidence that the respective applicant is subject to proper banking or exchange regulation in its country of origin

- Admission and registration of at least one exchange trader (Trader Exam)

- Registration of at least one qualified back office staff member (Clearer Test)

- Minimum liable equity capital in line with the requirements for the class of clearing membership

- Payment of up-front and annual clearing fees

- Compliance with mandatory technical requirements for connection to the Eurex system

- Participation in the clearing process, either by signing an agreement with a General Clearing Member or with a Direct Clearing Member, provided the companies are 100% affiliated

Additionally, all exchange members may apply for a market maker licence for one or more products. Market makers are obliged to quote binding bid and offer prices at any time, upon request, in the products for which they hold a licence or licences. In turn, they are charged reduced transaction fees.

The US Futures Exchange (USFE) was launched in October 2006, following the acquisition of 70% of Eurex US by Man Group plc.

15 THE CHICAGO BOARD OF TRADE

15.1 Overview

The **Chicago Board of Trade (CBOT)**, established in 1848, is the world's oldest derivatives (futures and futures-options) exchange. More than 3,600 CBOT members trade 53 different futures and options products at the CBOT, resulting in an annual trading volume for 2003 of more than 454 million contracts. CBOT was bought by the Chicago Mercantile Exchange (CME) in 2007. The CME Group is now the biggest exchange company in the world.

Early, in its history, the CME listed for trading only agricultural instruments, such as wheat, corn and oats. In 1975, the CME expanded its offering to include financial contracts, initially the US Treasury Bond futures contract which is now one of the world's most actively traded. The CME listings expanded again in 1982, when options on futures contracts were introduced. In 1997, the CME made history again when it launched one of its most successful contracts—futures and futures-options on the Dow Jones Industrial Average. The current product mix extends across agriculturals, financials, equities, commodity indices and swaps. In February 2002, it introduced new X-Fund futures contracts which are based on an index of four underlying futures contracts, one of which links in an index the performance of interest rates (long and short dated) together with cattle and soybean oil.

For more than 145 years, the primary method of trading at the CME had been open outcry, during which traders meet face-to-face in trading pits to buy and sell futures contracts. Then, in 1994, the CME launched Project A, an electronic trading system. And then in the year 2000, the CME replaced Project A with the a/c/e electronic trading platform (alliance/CME/Eurex). In its first week, a/c/e had a trading volume of more than 280,000 contracts. The arrangement between the two exchanges was restructured in July 2002 to allow more flexibility for cross-listings. The a/c/e service was for a period an important electronic trading link between these two major derivatives exchanges.

The Chicago Board of Trade then entered into a licensing agreement to use the LIFFE CONNECT® electronic trading platform, e-cbot powered by LIFFE CONNECT® which replaced the existing platform at the end of November 2003.

Functionally, LIFFE CONNECT® provides enhanced trading capabilities, better reporting, flexible matching algorithms, and the ability to accommodate anticipated future trading needs. The choice of LIFFE CONNECT® illustrated the crucial importance for the CME to be able to compete against other principal global exchanges for the business of the global electronic trading community.

The CME's principal role is to provide contract markets for its members and customers and to oversee the integrity and cultivation of those markets. Its markets provide prices that result from trading in open auction or electronic platforms. The marketplace assimilates new information throughout the trading day, and through trading it translates this information into benchmark prices agreed upon by buyers and sellers.

The CME's markets also provide opportunities for risk management for users, including farmers, corporations, small business owners, and others. Risk management, in the form of hedging, is the practice of offsetting the price risk inherent in any cash market position by taking an equal but opposite position in the futures market. Hedgers use CME futures markets to protect their businesses from adverse price changes that could have a negative impact on their bottom line.

CME is a self-governing, self-regulated Delaware not-for-profit, non-stock corporation that serves individuals and member firms. There are several types of memberships within the CME, which allow access to all or some of the markets listed at the exchange. Of the CME's 3,600 members, 1,400 are full members who have trading access to all exchange contracts.

The governing body of the exchange consists of a Board of Directors that includes a Chairman, First Vice Chairman, Second Vice Chairman, 18 member directors, five public directors, and the President. An executive staff headed by the President and Chief Executive Officer administers the Exchange.

See the exchange website at www.cme.com

15.2 Clearing

For years immemorial, clearing for CME was conducted by the Board of Trade Clearing Corporation (BOTCC). This organisation was constituted separately from the Exchange. Under new arrangements, CME clearing has now been amalgamated with that of the Chicago Mercantile Exchange (CME) and is no longer linked to BOTCC or to The Clearing Corporation. This took effect fully at the beginning of 2004.

16 TRADE INPUT

16.1 Introduction

The **front office** executes trades or arranges the terms of the deal, e.g. buy/sell/lend/borrow the security or asset, the price, the quantity, the delivery or settlement date. It is the responsibility of the operations department to input the correct trade details into the settlement department, send out trade confirmations, match the trade to the counterparty, and ensure that the trade settles on time.

16.2 Deal capture

The dealers in the front office execute the trade. Each dealer will write the details of their trade in a log book. This is either a manual book or an electronic jotter. The log book gives the traders their own records.

All telephone calls are also recorded so that they can be played back in the case of a dispute. It is not uncommon for traders to telephone to confirm the details of very large transactions at the end of the day.

The dealers may also fill in a deal (or dealing) slip. The deal slip will contain (*inter alia*) the counterparty, the price, the quantity and the dealer's name. For agency trades, the dealer must also date/time stamp both the order and the execution time. The deal slip will either be manual or electronic. Often deal slips for buys and sells are different colours to reduce confusion. Also deal tickets are likely to be sequentially numbered so that it is easy for operations to check completeness. An electronic deal slip is the first step in straight-through processing.

Internet execution-only brokers can have an electronic dealing system whereby the customer enters the trade instructions on the internet and it flows into the trading system. Any unusual trades, e.g. large, rare stocks or high limit orders, will be flagged for manual intervention by the dealers. Otherwise, the IT systems will automatically route the trade to the dealing system and then the settlement system.

The terms of the trade, including the identity of the counterparty, must be reported to the London Stock Exchange. During the mandatory quote period (9 a.m. to 4.30 p.m.), the details must be transmitted within three minutes. The trading system will send the details to the LSE.

16.3 Trade input

The manual deal slip will then be passed to the back office to be re-keyed into the settlement system. Frequently it is 'double re-keyed' which means that it is input by two people and thus input errors can be easily identified – a form of verification checking.

The system should carry out validations to ensure the details are correctly input. Examples of such validity checks are to ensure that the trade and settlement date are business days, checking the prices to within a 10% tolerance against externally fed data, the system should go on to calculate commission and stamp duty.

Trades can either be settled directly with the counterparty or by the preferred route, through a settlement agency. The trade details must be sent to the settlement agency. Trade details are usually sent by file transfer to CREST.

Many firms use straight through processing (STP) whereby trades automatically flow from the trading system into the settlement system. STP is both cost effective and time efficient. The operations group will not need to re-key trades into the settlement system. This will reduce data capture errors and save both time and salary costs. The role of the trade input department would be to identify problems with the transfer of trades and perform reconciliations to ensure that trades are registered on both trading and settlement office systems.

16.4 Straight Through Processing (STP)

Straight Through Processing (STP) has been defined as '...the process of seamlessly passing financial information to all parties to the transaction process, spanning investment manager decision through to reconciliation, without manual handling or redundant processing'.

All the steps that are involved in a trade from the first order through to trade execution and subsequent settlement are referred to as the trade life cycle.

Elements of the trade life cycle

- Trade execution
- Trade capture
- Trade enrichment from static data
- Trade validation
- Transaction reporting

- Applying settlement instructions
- The custodian
- Pre-settlement date validation
- Settlement failure
- Final trade settlement

The term 'STP' describes the objective of managing trades throughout this life cycle automatically without the requirement for additional human intervention.

Potential benefits of STP

- Ability to manage the business better
- Reduced costs
- Better client service
- Minimised risk
- Improved throughput
- Enables management by exception

Note that STP applies both within a firm and beyond in respect of its external relationships with its clients, custodians and counterparties.

The **Global Straight Through Processing Association (GSTPA)**, an industry utility conceived, funded and developed during the boom times of the late 1990s, announced in November 2002 that its shareholders had voted to suspend operations and dissolve the business.

The GSTPA was focused on providing central matching of trade details between investment managers, broker/dealers and global custodians. The GSTPA system went live on 9 September 2002 but less than full commitment from investment managers, combined with an unwillingness on the part of shareholders to provide more funding, left the utility with little chance of survival.

Prior to its decision to close, GSTPA, whose 60 or so members were leading financial services firms, had focused its efforts on designing a model for the automated settlement of cross-border trades. This is typically a labour intensive process for brokers and one where the data can often be incomplete or in an incorrect format increasing the chance of trade failures. Consequently, this is where costs of settlement can be highest, and an obvious area for cost conscious management.

The solution suggested by the GSTPA was based on connectivity between all counterparties, from investment managers and broker/dealers through to global custodians and transparency of the trade settlement cycle. This was intended to be achieved through the use of a global network combined with a transaction flow manager (TFM), which acted as a hub for trade matching and processing. GSTPA went live with its TFM software in September 2002. Counterparties would have needed participant access modules to connect their internal systems to the TFM. While the GSTPA initiative was only one part of a potential solution to cross-border settlement issues, it demonstrated the increasing focus of the major players on reducing settlement risk.

Although its main competitor has closed, the news may not be completely positive for **Omgeo**, GSTPA's erstwhile chief rival. GSTPA's demise demonstrates a potential lack of overall enthusiasm for central matching, which means it is unclear whether Omgeo will achieve its return on investment for its Central Trade Manager service (CTM).

Both GSTPA and Omgeo had become known as 'virtual matching utilities' (VMUs). For the last few years GSTPA and VMUs were accepted by many in the securities industry as the most important solution to achieving settlement efficiencies to enable T + 1. Now that GSTPA has been consigned to history and T+1 has slipped, the industry is wondering what is the future for VMUs.

Various questions arise.

- Is the VMU concept dead along with GSTPA?
- Will Omgeo be a winner or loser in the new order?
- Does CTM become the solution or part of the problem?
- Does FIX provide the real answer to STP?
- What will be the cost to the industry of not developing STP initiatives?
- Is T+1 really unachievable without a VMU?
- What is the latest vision to achieving industry-wide STP?

16.5 Contract notes

Contract notes are required by the FSA to be produced for all transactions other than currency transactions, swaps, repos and stock borrowing and lending. These should be sent out as soon as possible. For private clients, mailed contract notes are perhaps the best although, if a customer has requested electronic contract notes and the firm can prove despatch, electronic contract notes are acceptable. For other member players, SWIFT or TRAX are used. SWIFT stands for Society Of Worldwide Interbank Financial Telecommunications. SWIFT transfers messages securely and quickly and in a standardised format. TRAX (Transaction Exchange System) is specifically designed for ICMA users which sends confirmations out thirty minutes after dealing.

The information that the FSA requires on a contract note is as follows.

(1)   The firm's name and a reference to it being regulated by the Financial Services Authority

(2)   The customer's name, account number or other identification

(3)   The date of the transaction, and either the time of execution or that the customer will be notified of that time on request

(4)   The security concerned, the size involved and whether the transaction was a sale or purchase

(5)   The unit price at which the transaction was executed or averaged, and the total consideration due from or to the customer, and a statement, if applicable, that the price is an averaged price

(6)   The settlement date

(7)   The amount of the firm's charges to the customer in connection with the transaction

(8)   The amount or basis of any remuneration which the firm has received or will receive from another person in connection with the transaction, or the fact that this will be made available on request

(9)   The amount or basis of any charges shared with another person who is not an associate, or the fact that this will be made available on request

(10)   If the transaction is a purchase of a unit in a collective investment scheme, the amount of any front-end loading

(11)   Whether the firm executed the transaction as principal, and whether the transaction was executed with or through an associate

(12)   A statement, if this is the case, that any dividend, bonus or other right which has been declared, but which has not been paid, allotted or otherwise becomes effective in respect of the relevant security, will not pass to the purchaser under the transaction

(13)   If any interest which has accrued or will accrue on the relevant security is accounted for separately from the transaction price, the amount of the interest which the purchaser will receive or the number of days for which they will receive interest

(14)   The amount of any costs, including transaction taxes, which are incidental to the transaction and which will not be paid by the firm out of the charges mentioned in (7) above

(15)   If the transaction involves, or will involve, the purchase of one currency with another, the rate of exchange involved or a statement that the rate will be supplied when the currency has been purchased

Contract notes for derivative instruments are called **confirmation notes**. A confirmation note should contain much the same information as a contract note, but would also include:

- The last exercise date and strike price in the case of an option, and
- The maturity date or expiry date of the derivative

A **difference account** is sent when a transaction in derivatives closes out an open position. It includes for each contract in the open position and for each contract by which it is closed out, all the information on a confirmation note.

An **exercise notice** is sent on exercise of an option.

16.5.1 Trade matching

The financial institution will be able to access the **Unmatched Report** from Euroclear or its equivalent from the appropriate settlement agency. This will show not only which trades have matched, i.e. the counterparty has agreed but also those which are **unmatched trades**.

In order to match, the following details must agree.

- ISIN (International Security Identification Number)
- Stock quantity
- Stock price
- Consideration
- Buy/sell
- Name of counterparties

Example: Matched/unmatched trade

Counterparty A		Counterparty B	
100 @ £8	Matched	100 @ £8	Matched
100 @ £8	Unmatched		Alleged
	Alleged	1,000 @ £8	Unmatched

If the details do not agree, the trade is '**unmatched**' or '**alleged**'. If counterparty A has a position which is not recognised by the market, the trade is 'unmatched' for A. If the market identifies a trade that the counterparty does not, it is said to be 'alleged'. One counterparty's alleged trade is another counterparty's unmatched trade.

16.5.2 Why might trades be unmatched/alleged?

There are a number of reasons why trades are alleged/unmatched. Below are the most common reasons

- The trader made a mistake, e.g.

    - **Deal direction**: the trader meant to buy but accidentally sold
    - **Wrong number of shares**: the trader bought e.g. 10,000 rather than 1,000
    - The trader bought the **wrong stock**, e.g. BT or BG, NEXT or NXT

- The wrong trade details were input, e.g.

    - **Wrong counterparty code / details**
    - **Typographical** or **transposition error**
    - **Missing instructions**
    - **Trade not recognised**

(The GSTPA estimated that 25% of manually input trades are incorrect and need to be re-entered.)

- Details not transmitted to Euroclear as there was a problem with the hub or the network

- The counterparty having the above problems

Most unmatched/alleged trades are just temporary problems due to input and processing errors. Real unmatched/alleged trades cause a greater and real risk.

16.6 Risks of genuine unmatched/alleged trades

The first course of action is to check the trade details and ascertain the cause of the problem. This can be done by talking to the dealers, the customers and the counterparties, reviewing the trader's log and the deal ticket and listening to the recordings of telephone calls. The deal can then be corrected. Occasionally the counterparty will allow a firm to cancel an erroneous trade on the grounds that everyone makes a mistake but it depends entirely on the discretion of the counterparties, the relationship and the size of the trade. Other counterparties allow firms to work the error by way of free commissions. Otherwise and most commonly, the firm who made the mistake will have to take the financial loss.

For a principal trader, the trader could decide the best course of action, e.g. either to sell or continue to hold the security. In an agency business, the firm would need to correct the trade for the customer so that the customer is in the same position as if the firm had transacted the trade correctly. The firm would need to suffer the trading loss and the associated stamp duty, dealing charges and commission.

16.7 Improving matching rates

Both straight through processing and the introduction of a central counterparty will increase the percentage of trades that match. Straight through processing reduces the risk of manual errors as there are no longer manual deal tickets and manual re-keying.

A central counterparty is beneficial as the central counterparty will input transactions quicker and more efficiently. It is easier to resolve problems as there is one contact at the central counterparty rather than at every counterparty.

Improved trade matching was a requisite for ensuring that the shortened settlement period in the UK market (T+3) from February 2001 would work.

CHAPTER ROUNDUP

- The dealing and trade cycle extends from receipt of order input to confirmation.

- Cost efficiency, liquidity and transparency are features of a properly working stock market.

- Rule 2.1 set out the types of dealing permitted on the London Stock Exchange.

- SETS and SETSqx are parts of the LSE's TradElect system for trading equities.

- The LSE's addition of the International Order Book has led to strong growth in trading of Depository Receipts.

- LSE members participating in the gilt-edged market are: broker/dealers, Gilt-edged Market Makers and Inter-Dealer Brokers.

- NYSE Euronext.liffe (LIFFE) is the most important London market for futures and options. Trading is now screen-based, using the LIFFE CONNECT® trading system.

- To join LIFFE, an applicant must satisfy certain criteria including being 'fit and proper'.

- Rules of the International Capital Markets Association (ICMA) govern trading and settlement on the Eurobond market.

- ICE Futures operates one of the leading electronic regulated futures and options exchange for global energy markets.

- The London Metal Exchange trades base metals, such as aluminium, copper and zinc, for delivery on specific prompt dates – generally, spot or for delivery in three months.

- EDX London, Swapswire and DTTC operate in the OTC equity derivatives market.

- virt-x enables trading in major European blue-chip equities using an integrated trading, clearing and settlement model.

- PLUS Markets (formerly OFEX) is London's third stock market, offering an off-exchange share matching and trading facility to enable Stock Exchange members to deal in securities of unlisted companies.

- Diversifying into overseas equities can bring new profit opportunities for the investor, as well as risks such as currency risk and political risk.

- Major overseas stock markets include those of France, Germany, Japan and the USA.

- The New York Stock Exchange (NYSE) is the largest securities market in the world.

- Eurex is an international derivatives exchange – the world's largest.

- The oldest derivatives exchange is the Chicago Mercantile Exchange (CME). CME has switched to electronic trading and now uses the LIFFE CONNECT® trading platform.

- The Operations Department is responsible for input of the correct trade details to the settlement system, sending out trade confirmations, matching the trade to the counterparty and ensuring that the trade settles on time.

- Project Turquoise, Project BOAT, Chi-X and Equiduct are new initiatives seeking to take advantage of post-MiFID opportunities.

Terminology

Exam tip

A question in Section A of the exam allocates ½ or 1 mark for defining words and names such as those below. The examiner often just uses an acronym. Familiarise yourself with as many meanings and definitions as you can. The list below is not exhaustive. (Some are explained later in this Study Book.)

A Shares	Active market	ADR
After-hours trading	Agency bargain	AGM
AIM	Alleged	Allocation
Allotment letter	AMEX	APCIMS
At best order	Backwardation	Bargain
Bear	Bear market	Bearer document
Beta	Bid/Offer spread	Big Bang
Blue chip	Broker	Brokerage
Bull	Bull market	CAC40
Call payments	Capitalisation	CME
CCP	Closing date	Commission
Common stock	CUSIP	Consideration
Corporate action	Cum dividend	Cumulative preference shares
Daily Official List (DOL)	DAX	Dematerialisation
Department for Business	Diversification	Dividend
Dilution	DTC	DTCC
Dow Jones Industrial Average	DvP	Earnings per share
ECB	ECSDA	Emerging markets
Exchange	Execution	Fill or kill
Final dividend	Flotation	FTSE
FTSE 100 Index	FTSE All-Share Index	Fully paid shares
Good for the day	Good till cancelled	Growth stock
Hybrid security	Index	Incorporated
ISD	ISIN	Issue price
Limit order	Liquidity	Listed company
Listing particulars	Listing Rules	Long
LSE	Making a price	Mandatory Quote Period
Market capitalisation	Market makers	Matching
Mid price	NASDAQ	Nikkei Dow Index
Nil paid shares	NMS	Nominal
NYSE	Offer	Offer for sale
Order Book	Order-driven	Ordinary shares
PIBS	plc	SEAQ
SEATS	SETS	STP
Unmatched trade	XETRA	

TEST YOUR KNOWLEDGE

Check your knowledge of the Chapter here, without referring back to the text.

1   State three qualities of a properly functioning stock market.

2   Define an 'agency cross'.

3   Explain how the 'uncrossing algorithm' works in the SETS system.

4   In relation to SEAQ, what do the initials 'MQS' and 'NMS' stand for?

5   Name the central counterparty for trades in NYSE Euronext.liffe and the London Metal Exchange.

6   Identify the different types of participant in ICE Futures trading.

7   Outline what is meant by the 'ring and kerb' method of trading.

8   The NYSE converted to a …………….. company after it acquired its former rival ……………… in 2005.
     [Fill in the blanks.]

9   Outline what Eurex is.

10   What is the world's oldest derivatives exchange, and with what other Exchange did it merge in 2006?

11   State six items of information that must be included on a contract note.

Test Your Knowledge: Answers

1   Cost efficiency, liquidity, and transparency or price discovery. (See 2.1.)

2   A transaction in a security is an agency cross where a broker matches orders between two of the broker's clients directly, instead of through the market. (See 2.2.)

3   The uncrossing algorithm is run at 8.00am daily. This determines the price at which the largest number of orders that have been input can be executed. These orders (input before 08:00) are then executed. (See 3.4.2.)

4   These are the Minimum Quote Size and Normal Market Size for a stock. (See 3.6.2.)

5   LCH.Clearnet acts as a central counterparty on behalf of LIFFE and LME trades. (See 4.3 and 7.1.)

6   General participants, individual participants and trade participants. (See 6.2.)

7   'Ring and kerb' trading takes place on the LME. At 11:45 each day, the ring opens and each metal futures contract trades in turn for five minutes. At 12:20, when all metals have been traded once, there is a ten minute break and then the cycle starts again. There is also a 'kerb' session when all metals can be traded. (See 7.4.)

8   The NYSE converted to a *for-profit publicly traded* company after it acquired its rival *Archipelago* in 2005. (See 13.)

9   Eurex is a fully electronic exchange allowing market participants decentralised and standardised access to its markets globally. Eurex's listed contracts are financial futures and options together with a range of equity options and index futures and options. (See 14.)

10   The oldest derivatives exchange is the Chicago Board of Trade (CME), which merged with the Chicago Mercantile Exchange in 2007. (See 15.1.)

11   The following is not an exhaustive list. (See 16.5.)

   - The firm's name and a reference to it being regulated by the Financial Services Authority
   - The customer's name and account number
   - The date of the transaction
   - The security concerned, the size and whether the transaction was a sale or purchase
   - The unit price at which the transaction was executed
   - The settlement date
   - The firm's charges, and the amount of any stamp duty charges

8

Settlement and Clearance

INTRODUCTION

Clearing and settlement are key topics in the syllabus, and you are expected to have a detailed knowledge. First of all, we explain the two processes. Then, we go on to look at the institutional arrangements involved.

We consider the UK system and also aspects of clearance and settlement in other principal markets around the world.

There have been moves towards international standards on settlement which we discuss later in the Chapter.

Finally, we outline Continuous Linked Settlement, which applies to the currency markets.

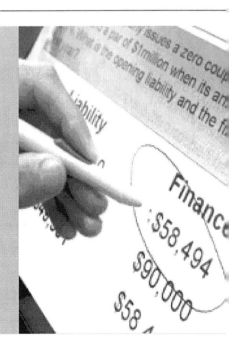

1 OVERVIEW OF CLEARING AND SETTLEMENT

1.1 The process

The terms **clearing** and **clearance** have exactly the same meaning. They refer to the practice post-trade and pre-settlement of defining settlement obligation and assigning responsibility for effecting settlement.

When the trade details have been confirmed, each counterparty submits trade instructions to a **clearing house**. This is an organisation that performs the gathering and matching of settlement instructions on behalf of market participants. The computerised system utilised for this purpose is called a **clearing system.**

Some exchanges act as their own clearing house, some depositories act as clearing houses and some clearing houses are entities separate from exchanges or depositories.

The clearing house will:

- Match delivery instructions with the corresponding receipt instruction, and
- Report the matched results to the participants

The clearing house matches both sides of the transaction. Trades that match are held in a pending file by the clearing house until settlement. If a trade does not match then it cannot settle and remedial action will be required. The problem must be resolved and the trade re-submitted to the clearing house for further matching.

A pre-settlement report will be sent to the counterparties. This will list those transactions that have matched and those that remain unmatched.

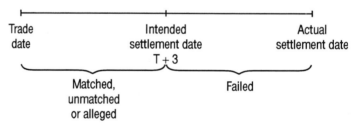

Trade date is the date when the counterparties 'do the deal'. This means that dealers agree the quantity and price of the stock and delivery date. All trades past trade date are known as 'open trades'.

Settlement date is when the stock and cash physically change hands. Intended settlement date takes place at T+3 for UK equities, e.g. a transaction executed on a Wednesday will settle the following Monday, assuming no public holidays intervene.

1.2 Matched trade confirmation

A **matched trade** is a trade where both counterparties agree the mandatory data, e.g. price, quantity, stock, and settlement date. Only matched trades can settle. The operations department must agree other details, e.g. bank account details and where the stock should be delivered prior to settlement date. These details might be part of standing data and set up when the account was opened or the operations department might need to coordinate and obtain the details.

Trade confirmation is the process of communicating the details of a trade from one party to its counterparty. Various methods of communication are used to achieve this. The objective is to achieve trade agreement whereby the two counterparties agree the details of a trade whether by electronic or manual means. Immediately a trade has been executed, certain procedures and checks must be undertaken before clearing and actual settlement can be performed. This is known as **pre-settlement**.

These activities will include the matching of trade instructions and investigation to verify that the seller has sufficient securities to deliver and that the purchaser has sufficient funds to cover the purchase cost. Securities trading firms always use limits to restrict the sizes of positions with clients and counterparties. Very often securities are held for clients in readiness for settlement and transaction parameters will be in place to govern the process.

1.3 Free Delivery and Delivery versus Payment

A **free delivery** or **free of payment** means that the stock changes hands first and then the cash, or *vice versa*. There is a risk that the counterparty might default after the cash has been delivered but before the stock is received.

DvP or **delivery versus payment** involves the simultaneous transfer of stock and cash and thus reduces the risk of default. The transaction will not settle until both counterparties have adequate stock or cash. Neither party is at risk to the late receipt or non-delivery of the asset or cash. Market, credit and counterparty risks are removed. The key test of **true** DvP is the **finality** of the delivery and payment. If payment 'clawback' is possible then it is not true DvP.

1.4 Settlement

Settlement can be regarded as the act of both buyer and seller (or their custodians) exchanging securities and cash in order to fulfil their contractual obligations. It is the process of transferring ownership of a security or other asset from the seller to the buyer in exchange for the equivalent value in cash. Ideally these two transfers occur simultaneously.

Settlement is the process whereby stock and cash change hands. Delivery versus payment (DvP) or **cash against documents (CAD)** means that the stock and cash transfer simultaneously so that neither party is short of either stock or cash. Free delivery or free payment means that the stock is transferred and then the cash and this increases the counterparty risk.

The use of a settlement agency or central counterparty reduces the risk as the counterparty can be trusted to deliver the stock or the cash.

2 SETTLEMENT CYCLES

2.1 Overview

The time between trade date and intended settlement date is known as the **settlement cycle**. In the UK, the settlement cycle used to take five business days although it was shortened to three days in 2001. This is known as T+3, settlement taking place three business days after the execution of the trade itself. This cycle varies between different world markets. Refer to the international standards tables contained in Chapter 10 of this Study Book, which summarises the salient features of some of the major markets.

Until 1994, the London Stock Exchange used to settle all transactions on every other Tuesday: this was known as **account settlement**. This meant that a trade could settle 14 days after execution. Although this increased risk, it meant that trades could be bought and sold and thus financed on one day. This aided investors' cashflow planning.

Rolling settlement was introduced in 1994. At first it was T+10 but was reduced to T+5 during 1995. T+5 is easy to remember and calculate, e.g. trade on a Thursday, settle the following Thursday. As indicated earlier, the UK cycle was reduced to T+3 in February 2001.

Benefits of shortening the settlement period

- Decreased counterparty risk
- Improved liquidity in the market
- Reduced funding costs for market participants
- Decreased operational risks (problems come to light and can be rectified sooner)
- Follows European equity trends, e.g. US wished to move to settle on T+1, Europe on T+3
- Similar to gilts which settle on T+1
- The settlement systems are technically competent to cope
- Most securities are dematerialised and thus easy to settle on T+1
- Improved STP

Difficulties of shortening the settlement period

- Pressure on computer and operation systems
- Historically it has been hard to settle some stocks within five days
- Very difficult for physical and bearer securities
- Hard for private customers who found T+5 difficult

A possibility would be to have a **two-tier settlement system**. The tiers could be either divided into institutional and private clients or into dematerialised and materialised share certificates. A two-tier system would give greater flexibility and it might increase the number of trades settling on intended settlement date and reduce counterparty risk. However, it might be confusing for both customers and operational systems.

2.2 Failed trades

Exam tip

> In Section B of the Winter 2007 exam, a question required candidates to write about the implications of failed trades.

In order for a trade to settle on the intended settlement date, both counterparties need the stock and the cash. On settlement date, if the counterparty has neither the stock nor the cash, the trade will not settle. This is known as a **failed trade**. (Note that an unmarked trade – or 'alleged' trade – cannot be a failed trade as it must first be recognised by both parties.)

Trades fail for a variety of reasons, such as the following.

- Non-matching settlement instructions

- Incorrect stock or cash account details, including collateral or credit lines

- In illiquid markets like emerging markets there is a shortage of stock

- The ADR market where securities have to be transferred into ADR form

- Counterparties are selling short as they have no stock to deliver

- Physical securities and bearer securities which require transfer forms to be completed and submitted to the registrar

- High volumes causing a backlog of transactions

Failed trades increase counterparty risk. If the price of the stock increased and the counterparty defaulted, the firm would have to buy the stock at the new market price.

A firm can issue a **buy in** notice whereby it can instruct the counterparty to deliver the stock two days later. The practice on various stock exchanges varies with respect to buy-in practice. The rules of the exchange will determine whether the practice is permitted and under what terms.

A firm may decide not to wait for a counterparty to produce the security or the cash. If buying in, the purchaser will buy from an alternative seller and any additional costs (the difference between the price paid on the buy in and the price agreed with the original seller) are passed on to the offending seller. When selling out the seller will sell to an alternative purchaser with the costs being passed on to the offending purchaser.

If a buyer or its clearing agent has caused the failure of settlement, the seller will normally make an interest claim for the loss of interest on the net amount that would have been received had settlement occurred on time.

3 REFERENCE DATA

The efficient use of reference data is a significant factor in enabling a firm to achieve **STP** (straight-through processing). The term **reference data** is commonly used to describe the information that is stored and is used to determine the appropriate actions that are necessary to achieve the successful processing of every trade.

Reference data is defined at six major levels.

- Internal trading companies/divisions within the firm
- Individual trading **books** within a trading company
- Counterparties of the firm
- Currencies
- Securities
- Security groups

Data items included are of the following four types.

- **Client data** – showing customers and counterparty details
- **Instrument data** – describing listed instruments and products including events and schedules
- **Market data** – details about prices, foreign exchange rates, corporate actions
- **Static data** – tax rules, currencies, markets, business days, holidays

The term **static data** clearly implies that this information does not change very frequently. Most data items can of course change and will be amended from time to time.

Firms must therefore organise themselves to be able to gather the necessary reference data, store it securely, update it accurately when necessary and to use the data appropriately within their systems.

Exam tip

> In the Winter 2006 exam, a compulsory 4-mark Section A question asked about the importance of static data to a securities firm, and required candidates to give three examples of static data.

As settlement cycles reduce in global markets, firms must operate within tighter deadlines in order to ensure that settlement occurs on time, that clients are provided with proper service and regulators receive their reports. Reference data plays an important role in helping to meet these deadlines.

4 SETTLEMENT AGENCIES

4.1 The function of a settlement agency

A **settlement agency** facilitates settlement. The role and mechanics of each settlement agency vary around the world but the underlying principles and basic services are the same.

The settlement agency will assist with the pre-matching stage by collating the information from the counterparties and producing matched/unmatched reports. In order to keep high standards in the market and ensure that trades settle on time, it is imperative that matching happens on a timely basis. The settlement agency might fine financial institutions for failing to meet matching targets.

Some settlement agencies will act as a **central counterparty**. Company A will transact with Company B but the trade will actually settle between Company A and the settlement agency and Company B and the settlement agency. This speeds up the matching process and assists the settlement process. It reduces risk as the central counterparty is more reliable than a counterparty. Derivatives exchanges for futures and options always use a clearing house as a central counterparty: examples are LCH.Clearnet Ltd. in the UK and the Options Clearing Corporation (OCC) in the United States.

Settlement agencies facilitate the securities movement because the securities are immobilised by the agency (DTCC and Euroclear) or the securities are electronic/dematerialised (Euroclear). The more sophisticated settlement agencies can resolve interdependent links and blockages to ensure that an optimum number of trades settle (the equivalent of a policeman directing traffic at a congested roundabout). This is known as **circles** within Euroclear.

Settlement agencies can provide additional functionality including stock borrowing/lending, processing corporate actions, collecting and paying taxes and performing reconciliations.

4.2 Euroclear in the UK

Euroclear is the UK equities settlement system. Over 98% of Euroclear trades settle on the intended settlement date. See the following chapter on Euroclear, for more detailed discussion.

Euroclear holds securities in a dematerialised format. The Euroclear system maintains a **Cash Memorandum Account** which keeps track of cash movements for each firm and the cash is held outside Euroclear by guarantee banks. At the end of the day, there is a net receipt or payment. Euroclear has a special function which runs a technical netting algorithm throughout the day to reduce settlement backlogs. Through Euroclear it is possible to reach 14 overseas CSDs using links that Euroclear has established via its Euroclear parent and via other relationships. The full country list is Austria, Belgium, Denmark, Finland, France, Germany, Italy, Netherlands, Norway, Portugal, Spain, Sweden, Switzerland and the USA.

It was announced in 2002 that Euroclear and CREST would merge their operations. This had a great potential impact upon the European cross-border settlement opportunities for investors and led to a greatly improved system.

In 2006, Euroclear launched the **Single Settlement Engine (SSE)**, which consolidated the settlement function of all Euroclear group entities. Euroclear has, in effect, two systems supporting the core processing of the UK and Irish markets: the 'legacy' Euroclear system and the new Euroclear SSE. In the short term, the impact for clients is fairly limited. Longer term, the SSE will provide the foundation for further consolidation of IT systems within the Euroclear group and the introduction of new group-wide services. Owing to the complexity of the project and risk controls, there has been a phased introduction across group markets. We discuss the SSE again in the next chapter of this Study Book.

The final switch to the **Single Platform** across all Euroclear group legacy systems will be completed by 2009.

4.3 Settlement in the USA

In the USA, there are two inter-related and coordinated automated clearance and settlement systems: one for dealer traders and the other for institutional customer transactions.

> The acronym **CUSIP** is used to refer to the 9-character alphanumeric security identifiers for all **North American securities** distributed by the Committee on Uniform Security Identification Procedures (CUSIP) to facilitate clearing and settlement of trades. In the 1980s there were moves to expand the CUSIP system to cover international securities. The resulting CINS (*CUSIP International Numbering System*) has however been little used as the truly international **ISIN** (International Securities identifying Number) system has been widely adopted.

4.3.1 National Securities Clearing Corporation (NSCC)

Part of the DTCC group, the main function of the NSCC is to act as a checking and clearing service for dealer-traders and members of the exchange. It creates the underlying records on which transactions are settled and, where appropriate, generates book entry transfer via the DTCC. The net balance of money due from or to a broker is settled daily by a single cheque with NSCC.

4.3.2 DTCC

DTCC operates similarly to Euroclear although the street players (equivalent to market counterparties and residing on Wall Street) guarantee that all trades will settle. Consequently, the US has fewer failed trades than the UK. DTCC works by immobilising the stock and having a book entry transfer system rather than the electronic holding.

Any securities not held in the DTCC tend to be registered in the name of a broker as nominee, these being referred to as 'street names'. It is always possible for an individual to insist on registration in their own name, but in practice it is a very rare occurrence.

5 CENTRAL COUNTERPARTY

The development of global financial markets demands an efficient and effective infrastructure for clearing and settlement. Global players face pressures of cost control, delivering enhanced shareholder value, product innovation and regulatory supervision.

In response, exchanges around the world have begun to adopt a **central counterparty (CCP)** approach. A global group of such organisations was formed in 2001 known as CCP12. Its members include DTCC, LCH.Clearnet, and OCC. It provides a vehicle for information sharing and industry development.

The CCP clearing model provides significant benefits of three fundamental types.

- **Enhancing trading liquidity**. In the years since the introduction of LCH's EquityClear as the CCP for the London Stock Exchange SETS market in February 2001, the average daily volume of trades has increased from around 50,000 to 250,000 and the SETS share of overall market trading has increased from 45% to over 60%. The secondary optional netting phase which came into effect in summer 2002 has brought about an increasing level of netting by members against the CCP from 44% to 72% of all trades received by LCH.Clearnet resulting in a netting rate of 99%.

- **Reducing risk and capital consumption**. By keeping all positions centrally with a low risk clearing house delivering the benefits of multilateral exposure netting, lower provisions for internal losses and the lowering of operational risk capital requirements.

- **Improving operational efficiency**. Fewer settlements owing to netting, the reduction of fails and errors and the ability to reduce the cost of operations.

Further principal reasons why exchanges have found the CCP approach attractive are as follows.

- Reduced risk of default – improved counterparty / credit risk

- Simplified risk management

- Counterparty risk management. The increased levels of cross-border business, involving a wider range of participants, requires the best possible protection against counterparty risk

- Reduced capital replacement risk

- Reduction in unproductive capital

- Reduced systemic risk

- Anonymity among participants is guaranteed: anonymous trading systems, e.g. SETS, followed by post-trade anonymity helps to protect price and position sensitivity

- Reduced operational risk

- Enables the netting of trades, reducing the cost of trading and maximising matching performance

- Encourages automatic trades, which is an advantage for the exchange

- Simplification of the settlement process, requiring fewer settlements and hence saving time leading to the lowering of industry costs

- Building confidence, which leads to increased participation, new business and tighter spreads and, as a result, liquidity on the exchange

- Increases attraction of exchange markets for existing customers

- Increases attraction of direct exchange trading for institutional investors

- Incentive to eliminate certificates

- Increases conformity across major markets

- Improves coordination of cross-border settlement

- Reduces costs to intermediaries and investors

- Competitive response to Electronic Communications Networks (ECNs)

- Positioning the exchange ahead of key competitors

- Responding to market demand

6 EUROCLEAR AND CLEARSTREAM

6.1 Overview

Euroclear and **Clearstream** both settle transactions in a large number of securities including all kinds of Eurobonds, domestic and foreign bonds, US Treasury and Agency bonds, short-term instruments (euro notes, CDs, bank bills, etc.) and international and domestic equities and American/Global Depository Receipts. Settlement is on a T+3 basis. Clearstream and Euroclear operate an **electronic bridge** between each other.

Within Euroclear and Clearstream, the stocks are physically immobilised within secure vaults, in comparison to CREST where the shares are held electronically. On settlement date there is a **book entry transfer** to move stock from one account to another.

6.2 Euroclear Bank

The core **Euroclear Bank** service is the settlement of cross-border securities transactions on behalf of Euroclear participants. Over 210,000 different securities are accepted for settlement through Euroclear, the majority of which are domestic securities from over 32 markets.

Settlement-related services such as wholesale custody, money transfer in over fifty currencies, and securities lending and borrowing meet the changing needs of securities professionals. Moreover, all services are seamlessly integrated within the settlement process.

Collateral management opportunities are offered to Euroclear participants to help them optimise their asset usage.

Euroclear is deemed to be the market leader and is forced by competition from Clearstream to keep pace with market changes and provide innovative responses to participants' needs and make steady investments in research and development for future services.

Added value comes from the provision of timely and accurate information, delivered through flexible and rapid means of communication at a competitive cost.

6.3 Euroclear France Services

Euroclear France has developed a competitive and flexible range of services, both in its original business as the French central depository (originally known as Sicovam) and in the management of clearing and settlement flows.

Euroclear France offers a variety of custody-related services.

- Custody services
- Securities numbering
- Administration of corporate actions
- Identification of shareholders
- Collateral management and cash transfers
- Access to counterparties in other countries

Euroclear Online offers Euroclear Participants an internet-based access to FundSettle, the online fund platform and eRGV, the workstation for all RGV/Relit+ transactions . It offers real-time access online and real-time access to all Euroclear services.

See the Euroclear website at: www.euroclear.com

6.4 Clearstream Services

Clearstream is part of the Deutsche Börse group. It has two divisions – Clearstream Banking Luxembourg (the International Central Securities Depository or ICSD) and Clearstream Banking Frankfurt – the German domestic CSD. Clearstream offers settlement and custody service to more than 2,500 customers in 94 global locations worldwide, covering over 150,000 domestic and internationally-traded bonds and equities. They settle half a million transactions daily across 40 markets. Acting as custodians, they take care of any rights attached to the securities that their customers keep with them.

Clearstream's core business is to ensure that cash and securities are promptly and effectively delivered against each other in clearing and settling market transactions.

Clearstream is now a settlement location for 22 trading platforms and Central Counterparties (CCP), in addition to the trading platforms and CCP run by the Deutsche Börse Group. These include a recent link with LCH.Clearnet and two similar relationships opened in late 2003 to BrokerTec and MTS Deutschland.

6.4.1 Clearing and settlement

Once they have executed trades on the market, customers send instructions to and receive reports from **Clearstream Banking** using connectivity tools. Cash and securities instructions are validated (with any errors reported back to the customer immediately), matched, checked for provision and released for settlement across a real-time transaction processing platform, called Creation. This straight-through, secure, high-performance transaction process brings to customers efficient, virtually risk-free settlement.

Once an instruction is sent, Clearstream Banking ensures that transactions settle on time by using a book-entry system in which cash and securities change hands simultaneously. This is Delivery versus Payment (DvP) settlement, a process that eliminates counterparty risk for customers.

6.4.2 Custody

With its custody services, Clearstream Banking reduces the administrative burden associated with new and existing issues and securities events such as exchanges and those associated with debt instruments, warrants, equities and depository receipts. When a coupon or a dividend is paid on a security, or a bond matures or is redeemed, Clearstream Banking collects the income proceeds and credits them to the customer's account on value date. When an income event involves a choice, Clearstream Banking provides the customer with timely information so that the appropriate decision can be taken.

Clearstream Banking customers may be eligible for a reduction or even a waiver of withholding tax at source, or for a refund of withholding tax after it has been paid, depending on tax status. In this case, customers can receive Clearstream's assistance in obtaining a withholding tax exemption and in reclaiming any excess tax paid.

With the Proxy Voting service, Clearstream Banking customers can participate in Annual General Meetings and Extraordinary General Meetings at companies in which they have a holding. Customers may also establish standing voting instructions that can be altered for any particular meeting.

6.4.3 Cash management and treasury services

Customers maintain both cash and securities accounts with Clearstream Banking for their buy and sell activities. Clearstream Banking promotes the efficient use of the cash component by providing:

- Cash investment services
- Same-day value withdrawal in 19 currencies
- Automatic currency conversion of income and residual balances

A range of foreign exchange services is available from Clearstream Banking on an automatic or a case-by-case basis. Clearstream Banking can arrange for flows from income proceeds and redemptions to be converted into a customer's preferred currency. The account the customer holds at Clearstream Banking is then automatically credited with the requested currency.

6.4.4 Financing, lending and borrowing

The cash financing service promotes settlement efficiency by helping customers borrow the cash required to fulfil their instructions to buy or release securities.

Clearstream's securities lending products have been designed to help transactions settle on time, and so reduce the cost of settlement failures. Automatic lending from Clearstream Banking enables customers to overcome any temporary lack of securities, to settle back-to-back transactions and to carry out cross-border transactions with a higher degree of confidence. Both borrowers and lenders benefit.

For the borrower, this reduces the costs due to failed instructions. The fee paid to lenders provides additional return on assets without loss to their value as collateral to back further transactions.

The Tripartite Collateral Management Service is a comprehensive service for the safekeeping and monitoring of securities used as collateral to back bilateral transactions and as an asset to support credit. This service helps Clearstream Banking customers monitor credit exposures and coverage throughout the duration of a deal efficiently and accurately.

6.4.5 Customer reporting

Clearstream Banking customers can receive reports of settled and unsettled trades hour by hour, throughout the day. Comprehensive reports are following overnight processing and daytime processing cycles. Instruction status updates are available throughout continuous daytime settlement processing.

For quick assimilation of information, delta reports are also available. They list only new transactions or those where the status has changed since the last report.

Portfolio valuations are available every day with details of the nominal and market values, by security, of the entire holding on a customer account.

A number of comprehensive Security Event notifications are provided to customers, depending on the timing of the announcement and the type of securities event. Advance notification of dividend payments, interest payments and redemptions is also made via Clearstream Banking reporting facilities.

7 OTHER PRINCIPAL MARKETS

7.1 South Africa

The Johannesburg Stock Exchange (JSE) has established the **STRATE** process. STRATE stands for Share Transaction Totally Electronic and was initiated during November 1999. The process of dematerialisation was scheduled to be conducted in four stages and was finalised in March 2001. STRATE was initiated following the surge in volume after the introduction of the JET system or Johannesburg Equities Trading during 1995. During 1999 on average, 53% of all trades did not settle on time every week and thus dematerialised settlement helped to improve settlement rates.

7.2 Japan

Settlement is handled by the **Japan Securities Clearing Corporation (JSCC)**. All quoted shares are in registered form and bonds can be either bearer or registered. Securities cannot be held outside Japan and therefore local safe custody facilities are obligatory for non-residents wishing to deal in Japanese securities. There are eight Stock Exchanges in different cities, the Tokyo Stock Exchange being the largest. Nearly all (99%) of transactions settle on T + 3 (regular settlement).

7.3 Hong Kong

Under **HKEx** in Hong Kong, all bargains are for two-day settlement and no more than one day's grace is likely to be granted before buying-in is instigated. All stocks are in registered form and the seller must therefore supply the documents with signed transfers on the day following the transaction. Overseas shareholders would use the services of a Hong Kong bank to ensure that the stock was available in time. Registration of transfer usually takes four to six weeks and during this period the shares cannot be sold. Most purchasers therefore do not register their own names, the majority of stock being registered is in banks' nominee names.

7.4 France

On the Euronext market, all bearer securities and the majority of registered securities never move in paper form but are held in safe custody by **Euroclear France** (previously known as Sicovam), the central depository. Euroclear France holds the securities from the issuer and subsequent trades are reflected in book entry transfer only. All financial intermediaries are eligible to participate in Euroclear France which adjusts its stock holding for each person and reflects cash movements accordingly.

Euroclear France, phased out *Règlement-Livraison de Titres* (RELIT) – the central matching, settlement, and account clearing system – to consolidate the settlement systems in the French market.

Previously, clearance and settlement had been organised around three different systems – RELIT, RELIT+ and RGV (*Relit Grande Vitesse*) – depending on the type of security settled and whether or not RTGS or end-of-day finality of settlement was required.

Since June 2001, equities, warrants, and rights have settled through RELIT+ (they previously settled through RELIT). Corporate and government fixed income instruments are still eligible to settle through RELIT+ at a participant's request. The phasing out of RELIT had no impact on *Relit Grande Vitesse* (RGV), Euroclear France's settlement system for all debt instruments.

Like RELIT, RELIT+ is a revocable system, with multi-batch securities settlement cycles and end-of-day finality after Banque de France's, the French central bank's, cash confirmation. RELIT+ offers a pre-matching functionality (similar to RGV) in which participants release trade instructions to RELIT+, allowing both parties to resolve any discrepancies before committing to settlement via the matching phase.

8 LCH.CLEARNET

In 2003, the London Clearing House and Clearnet sealed their merger to create Europe's leading clearing house, valued at €1.2bn (£830m). The merged entity is known as **LCH.Clearnet (LCH)**.

For contracts traded on Euronext.liffe (LIFFE), the London Metal Exchange (LME) and ICE Futures (formerly IPE), clearing takes place through the **LCH.CLearnet**. Trades on virt-x (previously known as Tradepoint) also settle through LCH.

Suppose, for example, that two members of LIFFE execute a contract. Assume that A buys a future from B. Once the transaction has been traded in the electronic trading system (LIFFE CONNECT), i.e. agreed by both parties, it is registered with LCH.CLearnet. The LIFFE market used to be an open outcry exchange and indeed was originally modelled much like those in Chicago. However, it followed the lead of the German market Eurex following huge competitive pressure and moved to an automated trading system over a two-year period between 1998 and 2000. Now all its trading is conducted via computers.

Upon registration, the contractual relationships are re-arranged so that the LCH replaces the original counterparty. Therefore A buys from LCH and B sells to LCH. The LCH is a central counterparty and thus reduces risk. The LCH essentially becomes the seller to every buyer and the buyer to every seller. The process of the legal substitution of LCH as counterparty is known as **novation**.

The LCH requires an **initial margin** to be paid. This will be a percentage of the face value of the contract. It varies between 1% and 6% depending on the price volatility of the underlying instrument. The rates of initial margin are set by LCH which consults with the exchanges.

All contracts are then marked-to-market by LCH on a daily basis. The profit or loss on that revaluation is the **variation margin**. If a loss has been made, an additional margin must be paid by the holder of the contract. Any profit is usually repaid. The payment of margins via LCH reduces credit risk for market participants.

At the time of final settlement of futures contracts upon maturity, **physical deliveries** of commodities may be required under the rules of the exchange. At that time the clearing house allocates buyers (long positions) on a random and impartial basis against its received notifications (known as **tenders**) of the intention to deliver from those with short positions. Delivery is conducted via LCH. Delivery of large quantities of some products is expensive and so some companies may specialise in this. As settlement date for a future draws near, counterparties using futures for speculative purposes will wish to close (or roll forward) their futures positions by trading with others who are prepared to deliver or take delivery of the underlying. This may lead to very heavy trading in the last few days of a future's life.

The vast majority of listed derivatives positions are **closed out** before the delivery date. This is achieved by taking an equal and opposite position so any loss or profit is crystallised and no further market risk remains.

Actual delivery of some assets would be most inconvenient (or impossibly impractical) so a process of **cash settlement** is used. For example, a futures contract on an index (a LIFFE FTSE 100 future would require delivery of a portfolio of 100 stocks) and interest rate futures (which would require one counterparty to make a loan to the other at the interest rate agreed in the deal) would be inconvenient to settle. Instead the portfolio is marked-to-market and the difference between the market value and the price originally contracted is actually paid. For most interest rate futures the interest rate is compared to the market interest rate, and the difference is calculated for the length and size of the loan (standard terms in the future).

LCH has developed further important additional central counterparty services:

- SwapClear (1999) – for interbank vanilla swaps
- RepoClear (1999) – for European bond repos
- EquityClear (2001) – the CCP for Euroclear
- EnClear (2002) – for OTC energy clearing

Visit the LCH website for further details at: www.*lchclearnet.com*

9 INTERNATIONAL SETTLEMENT STANDARDS

Much attention has been paid to ways of improving the quality of the industry by cooperating internationally. Examples of this include the work of ISSA (the International Securities Services Association), IOSCO (the International Organization of Securities Commissions), the European Securities Forum (ESF) and the European Union – see its Giovannini Report published in November 2001 and also the second Giovannini report of April 2003, addressing cross-border trading and settlement issues in the European Union and the Centre for European Policy Studies (CEPS) report published in December 2001.

9.1 The CPSS/IOSCO recommendations

In November 2001, the Committee on Payment and Settlement Systems (CPSS) and the Technical Committee of the IOSCO released a report entitled 'Recommendations for Securities Settlement Systems'. The report set out 19 recommendations that defined minimum standards for securities settlement systems worldwide, covering both domestic and cross-border transactions. National authorities responsible for the regulation and oversight of securities settlement system were expected to assess whether markets in their jurisdiction had implemented the recommendations, and to develop action plans for implementation where necessary. An assessment methodology was developed in 2002.

Several international initiatives completed in the past few years have the goal of maintaining financial stability by strengthening the financial infrastructure. IOSCO has developed the Objectives and Principles of Securities Regulation (IOSCO, 1998) and the Committee on Payment and Settlement Systems (CPSS) of the central banks of the Group of Ten countries has produced the Core Principles for Systemically

Important Payment Systems (BIS, 2001). Building on the previous work, the CPSS and the Technical Committee of IOSCO aim to contribute further to this process by jointly issuing these Recommendations for Securities Settlement Systems.

These CPSS/IOSCO recommendations were extended in November 2004 also to take into account the operations of Central Counterparty organisations, addressing resourcing, operations and approaches to a variety of risks. Resulting from this, several papers have been prepared examining and reporting upon the operational efficiency of CCP structure around Europe in the light of CPSS/IOSCO recommendations.

The 19 recommendations identify minimum standards that securities settlement systems (SSSs) should meet. The recommendations are designed to cover systems for all types of securities, for securities issued in both industrialised and developing countries, and for domestic as well as cross-border trades.

The high level list is as follows.

- Legal framework
- Trade confirmation
- Settlement cycles
- Central counterparties (CCPs)
- Securities lending
- Central securities depositories (CSDs)
- Delivery versus payment (DvP)
- Timing of settlement finality
- CSD risk controls to address participants' failures to settle
- Cash settlement assets
- Operational reliability
- Protection of customers' securities
- Governance
- Access
- Efficiency
- Communication procedures and standards
- Transparency
- Regulation and oversight
- Risks in cross-border links

9.2 The ISSA recommendations

There were nine key recommendations published by ISSA as long ago as 1989. They address the same fundamental points as shown in the above list. Their work still continues and it is possible through ISSA to check the preparedness of any nation's market from the organisation's website (www.issanet.com)

The revised recommendations published in 2000 are as follows.

- Securities Systems have a primary responsibility to their users and other stakeholders. They must provide effective low cost processing. Services should be priced equitably.

- Securities Systems must allow the option of network access on an interactive basis. They should cope with peak capacity without any service degradation, and have sufficient standby capabilities to recover operations in a reasonably short period within each processing day.

- The industry worldwide must satisfy the need for efficient, fast settlement by full adherence to the International Securities Numbering process (ISO 6166) and uniform usage of ISO 15022 standards for all securities messages. The industry should seek to introduce a global client and counterpart identification methodology (BIC – ISO 9362) to further facilitate straight through processing. Applications and programs should be structured in such a way as to facilitate open interaction between all parties.

- Each market must have clear rules assuring investor protection by safeguarding participants from the financial risks of failed settlement and ensuring that listed companies are required to follow sound policies on corporate governance, transfer of economic benefits and shareholder rights.

- The major risks in Securities Systems should be mitigated by five key measures, namely:

  - The implementation of real delivery versus payment

  - The adoption of a trade date plus one settlement cycle in a form that does not increase operational risk

  - The minimisation of funding and liquidity constraints by enabling stock lending and borrowing, broad-based cross-collateralisation, the use of repos and netting as appropriate

  - The enforcement of scripless settlement

  - The establishment of mandatory trade matching and settlement performance measures

- Convergence of Securities Systems, both within countries and across borders, should be encouraged where this eliminates operational risk, reduces cost and enhances market efficiency.

- Investor compliance with the laws and regulations in the home countries of their investments should be part of their regulators' due diligence process. Investors, in turn, should be treated equitably in the home country of their investments especially in respect to their rights to shareholder benefits and concessionary arrangements under double tax agreements.

- Local laws and regulations should ensure that there is segregation of client assets from the principal assets of their custodian and no possible claim on client assets in the event of custodian bankruptcy or a similar event. Regulators and markets, to further improve investor protection, should work:

  - To ensure clarity on the applicable law on cross border transaction

  - To seek international agreement on a legally enforceable definition of finality in a securities transaction

  - To ensure that local law fully protects the rights of beneficial owners

  - To strengthen securities laws both to secure the rights of the pledgee and the protection accorded to client assets held in Securities Systems

9.3 The G30 recommendations

These are the recommendations put forward by the **Group of 30** and published in January 2003.

- **Creating a strengthened, interoperable global network**

  (1) Eliminate paper and automate communication, data capture, and enrichment

  (2) Harmonise messaging standards and communication protocols

  (3) Develop and implement reference data standards

  (4) Synchronise timing between different clearing and settlement systems and associated payment and foreign-exchange systems

  (5) Automate and standardise institutional trade matching

  (6) Expand the use of central counterparties

  (7) Permit securities lending and borrowing to expedite settlement

  (8) Automate and standardise asset servicing processes, including corporate actions, tax relief arrangements, and restrictions on foreign ownership

- **Mitigating risk**

    – Ensure the financial integrity of providers of clearing and settlement services.

    – Reinforce the risk management practices of users of clearing and settlement service providers.

    – Ensure final, simultaneous transfer and availability of assets.

    – Ensure effective business continuity and disaster recovery planning.

    – Address the possibility of failure of a systemically important institution.

    – Strengthen assessment of the enforceability of contracts.

    – Advance legal certainty over rights to securities, cash or collateral.

    – Recognise and support improved valuation and closeout netting arrangements.

- **Improving governance**

    – Ensure appointment of appropriately experienced and senior board members.

    – Promote fair access to securities clearing and settlement networks.

    – Ensure equitable and effective attention to stakeholder interests.

    – Encourage consistent regulation and oversight of securities clearing and settlement service providers.

- **Operational benefits**

    – Every point above can by extension be translated into a benefit covering securities trading firms and investors

    – Streamlining of processes with the automation of communication and record keeping

    – Using ISO 15022 as the global standard for messaging will enable quicker, simpler communication processing globally

10 CONTINUOUS LINKED SETTLEMENT

10.1 What is Continuous Linked Settlement (CLS)?

The foreign exchange market is the largest in the world, by turnover: some US$ 2 trillion in currencies is traded daily. At the heart of the system lies a bank. The **CLS Bank** is a private initiative that began in 1996 supported by the largest **foreign exchange** banks – the Group of 20 (G20) – to eliminate settlement risk and reduce the systemic liquidity risk in the foreign exchange market. It started commercially in 2002. The system initially supported seven eligible currencies: the Australian, Canadian and US dollars, the euro, the Japanese yen, the Swiss franc and the UK pound sterling. Additional currencies were added – in 2003, the Danish krone, the Norwegian krone, the Singapore dollar and the Swedish krona, and in 2004 the South African rand, the Korean won, the Hong Kong dollar and the New Zealand dollar. The system today handles 15 currencies.

With an average daily turnover in global FX transactions of around US$2 trillion, the FX market has long needed an effective cross-currency settlement process. While transaction volumes have increased, the methods by which they are settled has stayed virtually the same for 300 years.

Before CLS, each side of a trade was paid separately. Taking time-zone differences into account, this heightened the risk of one party defaulting.

CLS represents a response to regulatory concern about systematic risk. It eliminates that "temporal" settlement risk, making same-day settlement both possible and final.

10.2 How does CLS work?

CLS is a real-time system that enables simultaneous settlement globally, irrespective of time zones.

CLS is an ongoing process of:

- **Submitting instructions** – receiving payments of specified currencies from customers
- **Funding** – settling pairs of instructions that satisfy all criteria
- **Execution** – making pay-outs in specified currencies

Settlement is final and irrevocable, or funds are returned same day.

Participating banks receive real-time settlement information that helps them to manage liquidity more efficiently, reduce credit risks and introduce operational efficiencies. This is all done within a five-hour window (three hours in Asia), which represents the overlapping business hours of the participating settlement systems.

10.3 Parties involved

CLS is only available through the unique and regulated relationship between CLS Bank, the central banks in whose currencies CLS settles, and members of CLS Bank.

The CLS process involves a number of different parties:

- Shareholders
- Settlement members
- User members
- Third parties

10.3.1 Shareholders

CLS Bank is owned by nearly 70 of the world's largest financial groups throughout the USA, Europe and Asia Pacific. Between them, these **shareholders** are responsible for more than half the value transferred in the world's FX market. Five CLS shareholders alone represent over 44% of this market. The shareholders have invested in CLS to develop CLS settlement. Each has purchased an equal shareholding in the CLS Group of companies and has the exclusive right to become a CLS Bank Settlement Member with direct access to the CLS system.

10.3.2 Settlement members

A **Settlement Member** must be a shareholder of CLS Group and must show that they have the financial and operational capability and sufficient liquidity to support their financial commitments to CLS. They can each submit settlement instructions directly to CLS Bank and receive information on the status of their instructions. Each Settlement Member has a multi-currency account with CLS Bank, with the ability to move funds. Settlement Members have direct access and input deals on their own behalf and on behalf of their customers. They can provide a branded CLS service to their third-party customers as part of their agreement with CLS Bank.

10.3.3 User members

User members can submit settlement instructions for themselves and their customers. However, user members do not have an account with CLS Bank. Instead they are sponsored by a Settlement Member who acts on their behalf. Each instruction submitted by a user member must be authorised by a designated Settlement Member. The instruction is then eligible for settlement through the account Settlement Member's account.

10.3.4 Third parties

Third parties are customers of settlement and user members and have no direct access to CLS. Settlement or user members must handle all instructions and financial flows, which are consolidated in CLS. The terms on which members can act on behalf of third parties are governed by private arrangement. These do not directly involve CLS Bank and third parties do not have any relationship with CLS Bank. Members may provide a trademarked CLS service to their third-party customers.

10.3.5 Nostro agents

Nostro agents:

- Receive payment instructions from Settlement Members

- May have multiple relationships with Settlement Members

- Must provide time-sensitive fund transfers to Settlement Members' accounts at CLS Bank

- Receive funds from CLS Bank, user members, third parties and others for credit to the Settlement Member account

10.4 Risks in foreign exchange

Herstatt risk is named after the Herstatt Bank (Bankhaus Herstatt) which was closed during the day in Germany by the Bundesbank on June 16th 1974 after FX losses. This left many who had dealt with Herstatt Bank with significant exposures due to the timing of clearing and settlement arrangements. These banks had paid out Deutschmarks to Herstatt Bank but the closure prevented them receiving US dollars in return. Overnight delivery risks from this kind of default are often known as **Herstatt risk**.

CLS seeks to eliminate these and other risks by enabling:

- Reduction in settlement risk
- The simultaneous exchange of currencies
- Safer, quicker and more efficient processing
- Improvement in the availability and flow of funds
- Working in real-time

CLS aims to improve operational efficiency, achieve settlement finality, introduce cost reduction and facilitate compliance with regulatory pressures.

CHAPTER ROUNDUP

- Detailed knowledge is needed of settlement and clearance, including RIEs, clearing houses, CSDs, ICSDs and CCPs.

- Post-trade and pre-settlement, clearing refers to defining settlement obligation and assigning responsibility for effecting settlement.

- The clearing house will match delivery instructions with the corresponding receipt instruction and report the matched result to the participants.

- With settlement, the buyer and seller (or their custodians) exchange securities and cash to fulfil their contractual obligations.

- The settlement cycle is the time between the trade date and the intended settlement date – now, generally three business days with T+3 settlement.

- Reference data – including client data, instrument data, market data and static data – is information stored and used to ensure successful processing of trades.

- A settlement agency performs various functions to facilitate settlement, such as collating information and possibly acting as a central counterparty.

- Euroclear UK + Ireland is the UK's equity settlement system, which holds securities in a dematerialised form.

- In the USA, DTCC operates similarly to Euroclear UK + Ireland.

- The CCP clearing model involves a central counterparty approach, which enhances trading liquidity and reduces risks.

- Euroclear and Clearstream – linked by an 'electronic bridge' – settle transactions including Eurobonds, domestic and foreign bonds, US Treasury bonds and international and domestic equities. In contrast to Euroclear where shares are held electronically, stocks are physically immobilised within secure vaults.

- Other major stock exchanges have their settlement arragements: STRATE in Johannesburg; JSCC in Japan; HKEx in Hong Kong; Euroclear France in France.

- LCH.Clearnet was formed as a merger between the London Clearing House, which provides clearing for contracts traded on LIFFE, LME and ICE Futures, and Clearnet, which still operates autonomously as a central counterparty clearing house, chiefly from Paris.

- Moves towards developing international standards on settlement have included the 2001 CPSS/IOSCO recommendations and the 2003 G30 recommendations.

- The Continuous Linked Settlement (CLS) system is centred on a bank and was set up in 1996 to eliminate settlement risk and reduce systematic liquidity risk in the currency markets.

8: SETTLEMENT AND CLEARANCE

TEST YOUR KNOWLEDGE

Check your knowledge of the Chapter here, without referring back to the text.

1   What is DvP? What is its chief advantage?

2   Give four reasons why failed trades may occur.

3   What are the four types of reference data? Give examples of each.

4   State three areas in which a Central Counterparty approach presents significant benefits.

5   With (a) Euroclear Bank, (b) Clearstream and (c) Euroclear, how are instruments normally stored?

6   Explain the difference between 'initial margin' and 'variation margin' in respect of futures contracts.

7   Explain briefly Continuous Linked Settlement.

TEST YOUR KNOWLEDGE: ANSWERS

1   DvP or delivery versus payment involves the simultaneous transfer of stock and cash. This reduces the risk of default. (See 1.3.)

2   Your answers might be on the following list. (See 2.2.)

- Non-matching settlement instructions
- Incorrect stock or cash account details
- In illiquid markets, a shortage of stock
- Securities having to be transferred into ADR form
- Counterparties selling short as they have no stock to deliver
- Physical securities and bearer securities requiring transfer forms submitted to the registrar
- High volumes causing a backlog of transactions

3   Data items are of the following four types. (See 3.)

- Client data – showing customers and counterparty details
- Instrument data – describing listed instruments and products including events and schedules
- Market data – details about prices, foreign exchange rates, corporate actions
- Static data – tax rules, currencies, markets, business days, holidays

4   Three important areas are as follows, although there are many other possible answers. (See 5.)

- Enhancing trading liquidity
- Reducing risk and capital consumption
- Improving operational efficiency

5   With Euroclear Bank and Clearstream, they are stored physically in a vault. With Euroclear, stocks are in electronic de-materialised form. (See 6.)

6   The initial margin, as required by the LCH, will be a percentage of the face value of the contract. The initial margin varies between 1% and 6% depending on the price volatility of the underlying instrument.

All contracts are then marked-to-market by LCH on a daily basis. The profit or loss on that revaluation is the variation margin. If a loss has been made, an additional margin must be paid by the holder of the contract, while any profit is usually repaid. The payment of margins via LCH is intended to reduce credit risk for market participants. (See 8.)

7   The CLS (Continuous Linked Settlement) Bank is a private initiative that began in 1996 supported by the largest foreign exchange banks – the Group of 20 – to eliminate settlement risk and reduce the systemic liquidity risk in the foreign exchange market. (See 10.1)

9

Euroclear UK & Ireland

INTRODUCTION

As mentioned in the previous chapter, the Diploma syllabus calls for a detailed knowledge of settlement and clearance.

The UK settlement agency Euroclear UK & Ireland has various aspects that you should know for the examination.

Euroclear has important roles in enabling the holding of dematerialised stock and settlement. Study the detail carefully.

Euroclear is the Central Securities Depository for the UK and Ireland, and is regulated by the FSA.

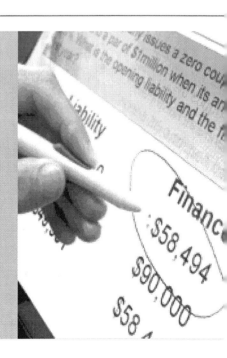

1 EUROCLEAR AND ITS SERVICES

1.1 Overview

Euroclear UK & Ireland Limited (formerly EuroclearCo Ltd) is the Central Securities Depository (CSD) for the UK and Ireland, and operates the Euroclear system. It provides advanced, low-cost settlement facilities for a wide range of corporate and government securities, including those traded on the London and Irish Stock Exchanges and virt-x. Euroclear also settles money market instruments and funds, plus a variety of international securities.

Euroclear started service in 1996 as a result of an initiative by the Bank of England to improve the settlement mechanism for the London market. This followed the 1993 Taurus debacle, a huge development project by the London Stock Exchange which attempted to implement a new leading-edge, world class clearing and settlement system for the London market yet cost the exchange and its members a fortune without really achieving anything.

In 2002, it was announced that Euroclear would merge with Euroclear. The merger created Europe's premier securities settlement system and has a vision for changing the face of European securities settlement by implementing a new 'Single Settlement Engine' for Europe. Stage one of the project was completed towards the end of 2004, and the second and final stage followed in 2006. This implementation will be followed by the establishment of a Common Communications Interface (CCI) across the Euroclear group of companies. This in turn will be overtaken in 2009 by a new Single Application Platform (SAP) for Euroclear. When this occurs, the Euroclear system will have been replaced and will cease to exist.

Euroclear UK & Ireland Limited is regulated by the UK's Financial Services Authority. Membership of Euroclear is available to firms and for individuals. There are over 38,000 corporate and individual members of Euroclear.

During 2006, Euroclear settled over 258,000 transactions every business day. The value of securities settled was £2,532bn. Settlement rates are measured both by value and by volume. Both sets are impressive with. 95.9% of CCP securities by value settling on the intended settlement date (ISD). Some £614bn moves each day in cash payments generated by Euroclear activity. Statistics on Euroclear performance are available from the Euroclear monthly newsletters.

Euroclear is open to stockbrokers, custodians, fund managers, market makers and all forms of intermediaries - as well as payment banks, registrars and receiving agents. A wide range of brokers, international banks, custodians and investment houses connect directly to Euroclear. Through these institutions, access to Euroclear is provided for retail investors and companies that wish to hold and settle shares electronically, but do not wish to maintain a direct connection.

Euroclear UK & Ireland Limited also offers private investors a variety of options for holding their UK, Irish and international securities. As an electronic settlement system, Euroclear offers all investors the opportunity to hold their securities in secure electronic form and take advantage of dealing and settling in the same short timescales as the wholesale market.

1.2 Asset servicing

Euroclear offers full corporate action services, as well as a range of services for registration and new issues, including:

- Automated production of market claims

- Automatic transformations of open transactions during company reorganisations and buyer protection for all relevant events, and

- The possibility for users to electronically appoint and instruct proxies at company meetings

- Facility to distribute income payments and associated dematerialised tax vouchers

- Calculation and collection of stamp duty from members on behalf of HM Revenue & Customs and the Irish Revenue Commissioners

- Tax assistance, including a foreign withholding tax reclaim service – available as part of the international service

1.3 Central Moneymarkets Office

The **Central Moneymarkets Office (CMO)** provides efficient settlement and safe-keeping services for a wide range of euro and sterling money market instruments, including Treasury bills, bank bills, trade bills, certificates of deposit and commercial paper.

Euroclear has owned CMO since 1999 and fully integrated money market instruments into the Euroclear system in 2003.

1.4 Key functions of Euroclear

Euroclear has three key functions:

- Holding dematerialised stock
- Facilitating settlement
- Enabling effective DvP settlement throughout the day

At present, Euroclear operates a real-time delivery versus payment (DvP) dematerialised settlement system and settles transactions in UK and Irish equities, government stocks and corporate loan stocks either free of payment or DvP against sterling, dollars and euros.

Firms with the hardware and software to connect directly to the Euroclear system are known as **users**. A firm can also connect through a user as a **sponsored member**.

Users can communicate via any of the three currently accredited networks to exchange electronic messages.

Users can access the system via:

- File transfer or MQSeries messaging, using standard ISO 15022 or Euroclear proprietary messaging

- A PC-based Graphical User Interface (GUI) software, which gives access to the full range of Euroclear functionality, or

- Their own back-office systems with interfaces developed by themselves or commercial software providers.

Euroclear has continued to introduce new initiatives, as follows.

(a)   **Settlement on T+3** from 5 February 2001: a rolling settlement environment.

(b)   A **central counterparty service** (CCP) with LCH.Clearnet from February 2001. This was extended to include optional netting in July 2002. The netting service is being used by over 50 firms and approximately 70% of SETS trades are netted.

This central counterparty service for electronically executed trades on SETS and SEAQ Crosses is operated by Euroclear together with LCH.Clearnet and the London Stock Exchange. It delivers full counterparty anonymity and improved counterparty risk protection by introducing LCH.Clearnet as the central counterparty to the market. A similar central counterparty service is available for virt-x trades in UK securities.

The Euroclear CCP services are currently used in three electronic markets:

- In co-operation with LCH.Clearnet and the London Stock Exchange, Euroclear UK & Ireland Limited operates a CCP service for electronically executed trades on the SETS platform and SEAQ Crosses

- In co-operation with virt-x, LCH.Clearnet and SIS x-clear, Euroclear UK & Ireland operates a CCP service for virt-x order book trades in UK and Irish securities

- In co-operation with Eurex Clearing AG and the Irish Stock Exchange, Euroclear UK & Ireland operates a CCP service for securities traded on the ISE Xetra order book of the Irish Stock Exchange

(c)   In November 2001, Euroclear introduced two new services which delivered **full Delivery versus Payment (DvP)** for London securities markets. The introduction of **Electronic Transfer of Title (ETT)** now provides buyers with immediate and irrevocable legal title to dematerialised securities, at the point of transfer in Euroclear. Payment in central bank money ensures the final and irrevocable transfer of central bank money, in sterling or euros, between payment banks for all transactions.

(d)   In July 2002, Euroclear introduced **optional settlement netting** for transactions executed on the London Stock Exchange's Electronic Trading System (SETS) and cleared through the London Clearing House. Simultaneously, Euroclear introduced direct input allowing members' transactions to be created from an exchange trade feed without Euroclear receiving explicit instructions from the member. Introduction of netting within Euroclear permitted effective leverage off the central counterparty facilities introduced in 2001 to reduce the cost of development. It offers members close integration of the netting process with members' existing systems as well as sophisticated facilities to handle corporate actions across the central counterparty.

Some 50% of eligible transactions are currently netted with greater than 98% efficiency in the reduction of trades for settlement and reducing Euroclear's load by an average of 130,000 transactions per day. Customers benefit from improved straight through processing, capacity savings in their systems and tariff benefits.

In September 2002, Euroclear enhanced its link to SegaInterSettle (SIS) in Switzerland to offer delivery versus payment in sterling, euro and US dollars. At the same time, Euroclear automated the confirmation process to those third party CSDs that Euroclear accesses through SIS.

(e)   In January 2003 an **electronic proxy voting service** was introduced enabling Euroclear users to receive information about company meetings and to cast their votes electronically.

(f)   From 1 April 2008, Euroclear UK & Ireland plans to deliver record-breaking fee reductions of £11.8 million to its clients. This represents overall savings to clients of about 10% and follows rebates of £7.5 million provided in 2007.

1.5 Holding dematerialised stock

Investors can hold their shares in a dematerialised form within Euroclear. Following the **Uncertificated Securities Regulations 1995**, the law was changed to allow share certificates to be held electronically. Euroclear reconciles its holdings to the company registrar on a daily basis. During working hours, customers can view their holdings over the Euroclear GUI (Graphical User Interface).

Euroclear can still settle physical share certificates (known as residual or certificated stock).

1.6 Facilitating settlement

Euroclear provides real-time settlement (on trade date if required) allowing users to monitor and manage their transactions throughout the day.

Delivery versus payment (DvP) in central bank money is provided, with simultaneous and irrevocable transfer of cash and securities (this is recognised as DvP model 1).

Full legal title is transferred at the point of settlement for all UK registered shares and government bonds.

Credit facilities are provided by a range of commercial payment banks, and multiple currencies are supported – currently sterling, euros and US dollars.

Optional settlement netting is available for trades executed through the London Stock Exchange's SETS platform, cleared through the LCH.Clearnet service, and settled in Euroclear. The same service is also available for virt-x trades in UK securities.

Direct links to US and European settlement systems allow settlement in 18 international markets.

Euroclear further offers settlement services for UK and Irish unit trusts and open-ended investment companies (OEICs). The service provides the product provider with a secure and highly reliable means of receiving funds from Euroclear members investing in their products, and much improved reconciliation mechanisms.

Euroclear also offers dematerialised settlement for a range of Exchange Traded Funds (ETFs).

Euroclear facilitates settlement by:

- Authenticating and matching instructions from parties who wish to settle the transaction
- Providing reports of unmatched trades on a daily basis
- Recording payment obligations and records of stock holdings
- Providing information and instructions to settlement banks
- Updating the registrars, who have an agreement to update within two hours if instructed
- Reconciling and checking that settlement has occurred correctly

1.7 DvP settlement throughout the day

Euroclear settles stock against cash throughout the day. However, cash is actually held outside the Euroclear system by twenty guarantee banks and Euroclear just keeps a tally of cash transactions in the Cash Memorandum Account (CMA). At the end of the day, each member's guarantee bank makes a net payment or receipt so that the CMA balance is reduced to zero. Thus it is 'effective DvP' rather than 'actual' **DvP**.

2 STOCK AND CASH ACCOUNTS

2.1 Stock accounts

Stock accounts are created and removed as necessary. There is a separate stock account for each stock held by each member, e.g. Brown's BT account, Brown's Vodafone account, etc.

Within the stock account, there are three types of account – available, deposit link and escrow.

- The **available** stock is a listing of all stock that the member has and can sell.

- The **deposit link** is used for the physical receipt and delivery of stock. A buy and a sell transaction can be linked together.

- The **escrow** account is used for stock in the process of a takeover. Although the member owns the stock they have assigned it to the bidder until the time when the deal goes unconditional.

2.2 Cash accounts

Cash is kept outside the Euroclear system. Instead Euroclear members have CMAs (**Cash Memorandum Accounts**) within Euroclear. The CMA shows their cash balances.

The underlying payment banks have an agreement with Euroclear to pay the balance on the CMA accounts. The CMA starts the day at zero. The balance shows a running total of the cash obligations arising from the purchases and sales throughout the day. At the end of the day, the underlying payment banks pay the balance so that the CMA starts the following day at zero. The actual cash movement occurs outside Euroclear through accounts held by the various banks at the Bank of England.

The payment banks are obliged under a trilateral agreement with Euroclear and the member to guarantee payment for all securities delivered to their customers through Euroclear. The payment banks will impose caps or credit limits for each member so that they can only purchase a certain amount of stock. The difference between the CMA balance and the cap is known as '**headroom**'.

Payment banks maintain separate sums of liquidity with the RTGS system operated by the Bank of England in order to settle their customers' transactions in Euroclear. These discrete elements exist for both sterling and euro payments. At the start of a Euroclear settlement cycle the separate element of liquidity for each bank is ring-fenced for Euroclear settlement purposes so that it is not available for any other purpose. For each payment bank, Euroclear records the balance of liquidity that has been reserved or set aside on a **Liquidity Memorandum Account (LMA)**.

3   THE MECHANICS OF EUROCLEAR

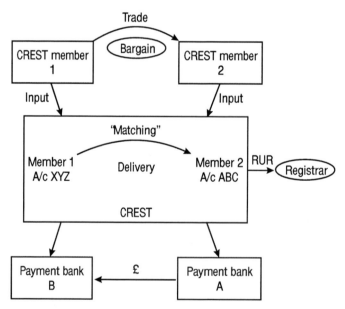

The Euroclear process operates as follows.

- Following the trade execution, both counterparties input the trade details into Euroclear. The standardised instruction is a delivery instruction or a DEL. The following must be input – transaction reference number, intended settlement date, inputting/counterparty ID, security code (ISIN), quantity and consideration. Other fields are optional.

- Euroclear authenticates and attempts to match the transaction. If the trade does not agree it will appear on the urgent unmatched trade report the following day. An unmatched transaction is marked 'not complete'.

- A user can attempt to correct the transaction at any time and eventually it will be matched. The trade will be cancelled if it is unmatched for 60 days.

- A matched transaction is marked 'not ready' before settlement date and 'ready to action' on settlement date. Once a transaction is matched, both parties would have to send deletion instructions to cancel the trade.

- On settlement day, Euroclear checks the seller has sufficient stock in their stock account and that the purchaser has sufficient credit in their CMA.

- The stock is then moved between the stock accounts and the CMA reflects the movement.

- Euroclear notifies the Registrar via a RUR (Registrar Update Request) to reflect the change in ownership. This occurs immediately.

- At the end of the day, the payment banks pay or receive the balance on the CMA accounts.

4 EUROCLEAR FEATURES

4.1 Circles

As mentioned earlier, Euroclear has a processing function known as **circles**. Frequently, jams are caused by mutual interdependencies whereby Customer A cannot purchase stock X from Customer B until A receives the cash from selling stock Y to Customer C whilst Customer B cannot sell stock X to A until he receives it from Customer C and so on. Euroclear runs the circles algorithms once a day at around 7.30 a.m. to identify which trades can settle. Circles create settlement efficiency. The process is perhaps the equivalent of a policeman directing traffic at a congested roundabout. The circles concept will be replaced under the SSE with an approach called **technical netting**.

4.2 Queues

Euroclear members can alter the priority of transactions so that certain trades settle prior to other trades. Trades can have a priority from 0-100. Only Euroclear can use 90-100. Trades are set at 50 by default but can be moved to a higher or lower priority to speed up/delay settlement.

4.3 Communications

Users communicate to Euroclear by both file transfer or by using a standard, interactive screen known as the Graphical User Interface (GUI). File transfer is used for sending settlement instructions and amendments whilst the GUI is used for looking at exceptional items. The GUI reports cannot be integrated with other computer systems.

Euroclear does not provide accounting or control reports. All information must be extracted from Euroclear and formatted appropriately.

4.4 Shaping

One party to a trade may want to change its shape into a series of smaller quantities. For example, a fund manager will buy a share and allocate it according a number of funds. Within Euroclear, each side of the trade can be split into 60 parts. Each split can also be split into a further 60 trades if necessary. Each split will have a unique Euroclear ID number and will be referenced back to the original instruction. Euroclear will make sure that the sum of shapes equals the original matched quantity and the original unit price.

4.5 Paperless office

Euroclear is working towards a **paperless office**. All reports are sent electronically. Euroclear will not send out paper statements – not even at the year-end for audit confirmation purposes.

4.6 Stock borrowing and lending

Financing is available from third parties using transactions known as Deliveries by Value (DBVs). A full and flexible stock borrowing and repo functionality is offered.

Same-day settlement is handled, allowing firms to arrange, execute and settle their borrowing needs within a matter of minutes. Daily stock lending and settlement performance data is available on the Euroclear UK & Ireland Limited website as a subscription service.

Members are able to obtain reports on open positions and liquidity projections.

Euroclear facilitates stock borrowing and lending. It provides functions for the transfer of stock and cash, automatically creates stock loan instructions (SLO, SLD, SLR), re-values on a daily basis, and enables borrowers to collateralise their borrowing by means of DBVs, which can also be used to borrow cash overnight. In December 2004, equity net stock borrowing was in excess of £94bn per day.

Both sides of the party input SLO instructions which are matched. There is a 5% default margin on the cash side. Every night, Euroclear revalues the stock and creates a cash-only revaluation transaction (SLD). This ensures that the cash always equals the stock value plus the agreed margin. Euroclear automatically creates the stock loan return SLR. Where appropriate Euroclear will also generate claims.

A DBV is a dual input transaction where a package of securities are assembled by Euroclear from a member's account and passed to another member in return for cash. In December 2004, DBVs issued per day amounted to over £77bn by value. There are two types of DBV – those which limit the concentration of any one stock type and those that have no concentration limits. Instructions must be input by midday.

4.7 Corporate actions

Corporate actions is the generic term given to stock situations and benefit distributions ranging from dividend payments to complicated capital reconstructions. Euroclear deals with both the cash and the stock and calculates and settles the dividend claims.

Euroclear's approach is based around four tenets.

- It is optional for issuing firms and receiving agents to use Euroclear for corporate actions.

- Euroclear can deal with all stock events but there is only a minimum specialised functionality. There are only five Euroclear commands.

- Euroclear only stores the information it needs – detailed information like prospectuses and voting

- Euroclear raises benefit claims for all parties shown on the register at the record date.

Five out of the nineteen Euroclear commands relate to corporate actions.

Unmatched Stock Event (USE)	These are transactions which do not need to be matched by the recipient, e.g. stock and cash distributions.
Many to Many (MTM)	This transaction type enables two cash movements and four stock movements to take place at one time, e.g. new nil paid rights.
Registrar Adjustment (REG)	This changes the details at the registrar, e.g. a bonus issue.

Transfer to Escrow (TTE)	For takeovers, Euroclear uses the escrow accounts where stock can be passed to a third party (an escrow agent), without transferring ownership of the stock.
Transfer from Escrow (TFE)	If the takeover is unsuccessful, the stock will be moved back into the 'available' account.

Euroclear automatically raises a claim transaction (CLA) which is cross-referenced to the underlying trade. It is given a zero priority which must be raised and matched by both parties.

4.8 Stamp Duty Reserve Tax

Euroclear automatically calculates the **stamp duty reserve tax (SDRT)** payable on purchases. Euroclear collects the money and pays it over to HM Revenue & Customs (HMRC). It fulfils a similar role for the Irish Revenue Commissioners in respect of Irish stamp duty on Irish securities.

4.9 Trade reporting

Euroclear reports trades to the LSE in order to comply with trade reporting requirements.

4.10 Electronic transfer of title

We have mentioned the introduction of **electronic transfer of title (ETT)**, which occurred in 2001. This required HM Treasury to draft new regulations which were passed by Parliament. Under these regulations, at the point of transfer within Euroclear, the transferee (buyer) receives immediate and irrevocable legal title to the dematerialised securities. The Euroclear records are the register for these dematerialised securities. This change removed the extremely remote risk that a buyer of stock might discover that his interest in the stock could not be registered after settlement.

4.11 Performance monitoring

Euroclear monitors the performance of members against matching and settlement targets. Depending on the type of firm, they are put into league tables. Firms failing to reach their targets are fined.

4.12 International links

Euroclear has direct ICSD links with 18 international markets. These include the United States (via the DTCC), Switzerland (via SegaInterSettle – SIS) and various European countries (via Euroclear Bank). These offer members cross-border settlement, custody and tax services.

5 CERTIFICATED SETTLEMENT

Thousands of private individuals use Euroclear's electronic settlement. As Euroclear offers all investors the opportunity of holding their shares in secure electronic form, they can take advantage of dealing and settling in the same short timescales as the wholesale market. If holding stock securely in electronic form does not appeal, then investors can continue to retain their physical share certificates in physical form outside Euroclear. Settlement is still possible, but clients' stockbrokers may advise them to trade for longer-dated settlement **(normally T+10)**.

Euroclear can facilitate the settlement of certificated stocks by taking care of the delivery to the registrar via the CCSS (Euroclear Courier and Sorting Service). The CCSS provides, operates and manages the recording, processing and sorting of physical share certificates from sites located in London, Birmingham, Manchester, Glasgow, Dublin and Leeds. The advantage of using Euroclear is to take advantage of the Euroclear cap.

A customer will place an order to sell a certificated stock through a broker who will execute it in the market. The broker inputs the order into Euroclear in exactly the same way as for a uncertificated trade except that it will be marked for the **deposit link account**.

The customer submits a signed Euroclear transfer form (CTF) and delivers the physical shares to the broker. The broker will then create a stock deposit transaction (STD). The broker writes the Stock Deposit Reference Number (SDRN) on the CTF and sends the package to the CCSS. The SDRN is also given a barcode. The CCSS checks the details and sends the deposit set to the registrar.

On receipt of the deposit set, the registrar has 27 hours to reject or register the delivery. If the deposit is registered, then Euroclear will credit the members' account with the shares. If the deposit is rejected it will be returned to the customer via the broker.

To withdraw the stock, the broker will submit a stock withdrawal transaction (STW). The process is similar to the deposit transaction.

6 EUROCLEAR USERS

6.1 Participants

Anyone who has a formal relationship with Euroclear is known as a **participant**. Participants can use the services of other operations to access Euroclear systems. Participants include members and sponsored members, registrars, receiving agents, payment banks, regulators, HMRC and information providers.

6.2 Users

Users are organisations who can communicate with Euroclear via a gateway over the BT Syntegra or S.W.I.F.T. networks.

6.3 Members

A Euroclear member is a participant who holds stock in accounts within the system and whose name appears on the company register as the legal owner of the securities. A Euroclear member could be a broker, an institutional investor, custodian or market maker.

In order to become a member, a participant must:

- Have a contract with a payment bank to say that the payment bank has an irrevocable obligation to pay Euroclear

- Have the technical capacity to interface with Euroclear (e.g. be a user)

- Accept the terms and conditions of Euroclear

6.4 Sponsored members

Sponsored members hold securities in accounts with Euroclear and appear on the share register as the legal owners. They have the responsibilities of membership but rely on the technical capacities of the member to interface with Euroclear. A sponsored member has a trilateral membership contract with Euroclear and the sponsor as well as an assured payment arrangement with the bank. Nominee companies are frequently sponsored members.

6.5 Designated accounts

Each member and sponsored member can set up a number of different identities (**designations**) called **member accounts**. The stock register reflects the name on the member accounts. Member accounts are used so that individuals can hold stock individually.

7 DELIVERY VERSUS PAYMENT IN CENTRAL BANK MONEY

Real-time settlement in **central bank money** for all sterling and euro payments through Euroclear was introduced on November 2001. These revised payment arrangements followed completion of testing and trials of the interface between Euroclear and RTGS (Real-Time Gross Settlement, the inter-bank payments system operated by the Bank of England). At the point of settlement in Euroclear, the Euroclear payment – which discharges the buyer's obligation on the seller – is accompanied by a simultaneous payment from the buyer's settlement bank to the seller's. Consequently, from the moment of settlement in Euroclear, the purchaser is solely exposed to risk on their chosen settlement bank with no exposure to their counterparty's settlement bank. This applies to all £800bn (the November 2007 level) and €800m payments currently arising from Euroclear each day, irrespective of the size of individual payments.

Real-time settlement in central bank money requires settlement banks to maintain sufficient funds at the Bank of England ('liquidity') to support their customers' payments throughout each day. As part of this development, Euroclear and the Bank of England have introduced self-collateralising repo arrangements whereby a member may use eligible securities (i.e. gilts) in the course of settlement to generate intra-day sterling liquidity for its settlement bank. Such arrangements are appropriate to Gilt Edged Market Makers, intermediaries, banks' own treasuries and other principal gilts dealers. At inauguration, 28 firms participated in the self-collateralisation process generating significant values of intra-day sterling liquidity. These reduce the banks' provision of proprietary liquidity (and the prime collateral necessary to support this) and allow efficient liquidity management whilst maintaining the high levels of Euroclear settlement performance.

Under these arrangements, irrevocable and final inter-bank payment in central bank funds is simultaneous, with irrevocable transfer of full legal title. Euroclear members therefore benefit from the highest quality of transfer and elimination of settlement risk within Euroclear.

8 CENTRAL COUNTERPARTY AND SETTLEMENT NETTING

The London Stock Exchange (LSE), LCH.Clearnet Ltd. (LCH) and Euroclear jointly introduced a central counterparty (CCP) service for electronically executed trades on SETS and SEAQ Crosses in February 2001. This delivered full counterparty anonymity and improved counterparty risk protection by introducing LCH as the central counterparty to the market.

It was recognised that the service should be enhanced to deliver optional Settlement Netting and Euroclear, LCH and the LSE introduced this second phase of the project on 1 July 2002. From the start some 45% of SETS market volume was netted. This has consistently risen.

9 THE SINGLE SETTLEMENT ENGINE

Following the merger of EuroclearCo and Euroclear in 2002, the process of consolidating all Euroclear group systems and harmonising all Euroclear group services was initiated. The first concrete result of this consolidation is the introduction of the **Single Settlement Engine (SSE)**. The SSE is at the heart of the Euroclear Business Model to deliver a domestic market for Europe.

In the longer term, it will provide the basic infrastructure for transactions between all Euroclear group clients to be settled as internal book entries (as opposed to cross-system settlement), irrespective of which group (International) Central Securities Depository ((I)CSD) the counterparties use.

The objectives of the SSE are threefold:

- A single settlement processor for all group (I)CSDs

- A common interface between the group (I)CSDs and the SSE, allowing synergies in future development work and eliminating duplication of investment, and

- Implementation of group services within the SSE

In the first stage, the SSE will bring the settlement systems of the group (I)CSDs together on to a single platform, and will interface with each (I)CSD's non settlement-related legacy systems. Clients will continue to input and receive reports through their existing infrastructure directly, or indirectly through an intermediary. In due course, the (I)CSDs' legacy systems will be progressively integrated on to the single platform. This will take place in parallel with the introduction of a Common Communication Interface (CCI), which will replace each of the (I)CSD's current client interfaces.

Over time, the single platform will deliver significant benefits to clients. It will progressively allow:

- Seamless access to counterparties in all group (I)CSDs

- Significant improvements in the settlement efficiency of transactions that were previously processed between two different systems

- Considerable tariff reductions from the current high cross-border, cross-system levels, as a result of the large volumes that will settle through the SSE, achieving significant economies of scale, and

- Reduced risk by enabling previously free-of-payment cross-system transactions to become Delivery versus Payment (DvP) transactions

The SSE itself was implemented in two phases to mitigate any risk.

- **Release 1**, which went live in December 2004, allows the SSE to receive reference data, such as security and participant information, from Euroclear, as well as from the Euroclear Bank and Euroclear France systems. This release does not affect Euroclear UK & Ireland clients. All settlement activity for the markets served by Euroclear UK & Ireland Limited (formerly EuroclearCo) continues to take place entirely on the Euroclear system.

  Release 1 permits the relationship between Euroclear UK & Ireland operations and SSE operations to be developed in a non-critical environment, prior to release 2.

- **Release 2** allows the SSE and Euroclear, Euroclear Bank and Euroclear France to interact fully, with settlement activity taking place at the SSE. For Euroclear UK & Ireland clients, the technical launch of this release went live on 7 August 2006; with settlement continuing to take place within Euroclear. The full launch, which allows settlement activity to take place at the SSE, went live on 31 August 2006.

The actual migration of each (I)CSD's version of the SSE to the final single SSE platform took place in November 2006, when the SSE was launched at Euroclear Bank. It was anticipated that this synchronisation phase would be an internal development for Euroclear and would therefore not affect members.

Whilst settlement activity is being transferred to the SSE, each (I)CSD's transactions and related reference data will be completely segregated so there will be no possibility for one (I)CSD's data to be used by another.

Euroclear will enter the final phase of consolidating all Euroclear legacy systems on to a single platform serving all Euroclear group markets. Starting with custody-related processing in late 2008, all key components of the Single Application Platform are scheduled to be completed by 2009.

Exam tip

In the Winter 2006 paper, a 25-mark Section C question asked candidates to compare the different approaches of the Single Settlement Engine (SSE) and TARGET2–Securities, and discuss the benefits and disadvantages of each approach from the perspective of a market participant. We discuss the development of TARGET2–Securities in Chapter 15.

CHAPTER ROUNDUP

- Detailed knowledge is needed of the UK settlement agency, Euroclear.

- Euroclear is operated by the Central Securities Depository for the UK and Ireland (Euroclear UK & Ireland Limited), which is regulated by the FSA.

- Euroclear has the key functions of: holding dematerialised stock; facilitating settlement; and enabling effective DvP (delivery versus payment) settlement throughout the day.

- There are three different types of account within the stock account: the available stock; the deposit link; and the escrow account.

- Cash is kept outside the Euroclear system and Euroclear members have Cash Memorandum Accounts (CMA) within Euroclear.

- Following execution of a trade, details are input to Euroclear by both counterparties. Euroclear then authenticates and matches transactions. Stock is moved between stock accounts, and the cash movement is reflected in the CMAs, with CMA balances being settled through payment banks. Euroclear notifies the Registrar immediately.

- The 'circles' function in Euroclear will be replaced under the SSE by 'technical netting'.

- All Euroclear reports and statements are sent electronically, not on paper.

- Investors may choose to hold physical share certificates, but this may necessitate trading for T+10 settlement.

- Euroclear 'participants' include members and sponsored members, registrars, receiving agents, payment banks, regulators, HMRC and information providers.

- Euroclear users are organisations that can communicate with Euroclear via a gateway over the BT Synegra or SWIFT networks.

- A Euroclear member could be a broker, an institutional investor, a custodian or a market maker.

- The Central Moneymarkets Office (CMO) provides settlement and safekeeping services for euro and sterling money market instruments.

- Euroclear provides for real-time settlement in central bank money for all sterling and euro payments.

- At the point of transfer within Euroclear, the buyer (transferee) receives immediate and irrevocable legal title to the dematerialised securities – this is Electronic Transfer of Title.

- There is a central counterparty service for electronically executed trades on SETS and SEAQ crosses, and the service is enhanced by optional Settlement Netting.

- The Single Settlement Engine (SSE) is at the heart of the Euroclear business model to deliver a domestic market for Europe.

TEST YOUR KNOWLEDGE

Check your knowledge of the Chapter here, without referring back to the text.

1   Euroclear UK & Ireland Limited is regulated by the UK's Financial Services Authority. *True* or *False*?

2   State three key functions of Euroclear.

3   What is 'headroom' in the context of Euroclear?

4   (a) Explain briefly what is meant by 'circles' in the context of Euroclear.

     (b) What replaces 'circles' under the SSE?

5   Outline briefly how electronic transfer of title is effected.

6   What is the normal settlement period for certificated settlement?

7   What three aspects are there to the aims of the SSE?

TEST YOUR KNOWLEDGE: ANSWERS

1   True. (See 1.1.)

2   The following are key functions of Euroclear. (See 1.4.)

- Holding dematerialised stock
- Facilitating settlement
- Enabling effective DvP settlement throughout the day

3   'Headroom' is the difference between the Cash Memorandum Account balance and the 'cap', which is the member's credit limit. (See 2.2.)

4   'Circles' is an algorithm that is run daily at around 7.30 a.m. to identify which trades can settle. Circles enhances settlement efficiency. The circles concept will be replaced under the SSE by 'technical netting'. (See 4.1.)

5   At the point of transfer within Euroclear, the transferee (buyer) receives immediate and irrevocable legal title to the dematerialised securities. The Euroclear records are the register for these dematerialised securities. (See 4.10.)

6   T + 10. (See 5.)

7   The objectives of the SSE have the following aspects. (see 9.)

- A single settlement processor for all group (I)CSDs

- A common interface between the group (I)CSDs and the SSE, allowing synergies in future development work and eliminating duplication of investment, and

- Implementation of group services within the SSE

10

International Clearing and Settlement Conventions

INTRODUCTION

You should have a broad knowledge of international clearing and settlement.

Key markets we will be covering in this chapter include those of the US, Europe, Singapore and Japan.

Settlement periods and other features of clearing and settlement in different international markets are compared in a table towards the end of the chapter.

BPP
LEARNING MEDIA

1 THE NEW YORK STOCK EXCHANGE

The primary exchange in the United States is the **New York Stock Exchange**, which became a for-profit public company following its merger with Archipelago in 2006. It now trades as the NYSE Group. NYSE now owns Euronext and the American Stock Exchange.

	Main features	Comment
Central Counterparty	**National Securities Clearing Corporation (NSCC)** Provides trade guarantee and netting services Regulated by Securities & Exchange Commission Other market-owned clearing corporations exist for specific instruments, e.g. GSCC for government securities	NSCC ownership: An operating subsidiary of Depository Trust & Clearing Corporation (DTCC), which is owned by its principal members, and is an autonomous, not-for-profit organisation. DTCC also owns DTC, the securities depository.
Central Securities Depository	Depository Trust Company (DTC) Book entry Securities eligible for DTC settlement and custody services include equities, government and corporate debt Additionally, the Federal Reserve Bank runs a depository – FBE – for government securities and money-market instruments	
Settlement period	Equities, corporate bonds and ADRs: T+3 Government debt: TD	The market was planning to move to T+1 settlement for equities in 2004, although this date has now been deferred. It may come back on the agenda.
Fail rate	N/A	
Trade affirmation/ matching	Via commercial vendors The SDA rate (same day affirmation) was 12%	In 2001, DTCC entered into a joint venture with Thomson Financial ESG, called Omgeo, which now owns and operates the DTCC's trade affirmation, processing and management services (formerly known as TradeSuite) as well as Thomson's Intelligent Trade Management products (e.g. Oasys, Alert).
Netting	Via NSCC's Continuous Net Settlement system or through other clearing agencies	
DvP	Yes	
Paper	DTCC operates on an immobilised basis, usually holding jumbo/global certificates. All US Treasuries are dematerialised and are held in the Federal Book Entry system (FBE).	

BPP
LEARNING MEDIA

2 THE LONDON STOCK EXCHANGE

The primary UK exchange is the **London Stock Exchange (LSE)**. In early 2007, the London Stock Exchange plc successfully defended itself against a takeover bid from NASDAQ.

The UK's infrastructure providers are all independent from one another. Before the Euroclear merger, the LSE owned 3% of CRESTCo Ltd and had no board representation. Tradepoint (now part of virt-x) owned under 1% with no board representation. LCH.Clearnet (LCH) owns no shares in Euroclear. Euroclear UK + Ireland owns no shares in LCH or the LSE.

	Main features	Comment
Central Counterparty	**LCH.Clearnet Ltd (LCH)** Formed by merger in December 2003 Acts as CCP for trades executed on London Stock Exchange's electronic order matching system, SETS x-clear was added in 2007.	45.1% of LCH.Clearnet is owned by exchanges and 45.1% by members, with the balance held by Euroclear. This balanced share ownership was effected by the offer of a 7.6% stake in LCH.Clearnet by Euronext to member shareholders. Euronext remains the largest individual shareholder, with a 41.5% stake, but its voting rights are limited to 24.9%. An autonomous, not-for-profit organisation.
Central Securities Depository	CRESTCo Ltd (now Euroclear) Which operates two main systems: Euroclear for equities, government debt (Gilts) and corporate debt. The Central Moneymarkets Office for money market instruments. It also provides a central settlement service for Irish equities and corporate debt. It is regulated by the FSA.	Ownership: Was private limited company with 97 shareholders. Now owned by Euroclear.
Settlement period	Equities: T+3 Fixed Income (Gilts): T+1 Money-market: T+0	
Fail rate	Euroclear settlement rates are around 97-98%	
Trade affirmation/ matching	Via commercial vendors	
Netting	Introduced in July 2002	
DvP	In November 2001, Euroclear moved to BIS Model 1 DvP with finality of stock and cash movements at the point of settlement.	
Paper	Technically, Euroclear is not a depository, as it does not hold any physical securities. Share certificates are therefore held by custodians externally.	

3 THE FRANKFURT STOCK EXCHANGE

The **Frankfurt Stock Exchange (FWB)** is the largest of the eight German stock exchanges. FWB is managed by Deutsche Börse AG, which also owns and manages Clearstream and Eurex, the German derivatives exchange. Some of the other regional stock exchanges also use Deutsche Börse's systems.

The Deutsche Börse's ownership is divided between German banks (with a 72% stake), German branches or subsidiaries of foreign banks (10%), Deutsche Börsen Beteiligungsgesellschaft mbH (an amalgamation of the supporting authorities of the regional stock exchanges, 10%) and official and unofficial brokers (8%).

	Main features	Comment
Central Counterparty	Eurex Clearing Introduced on 27 March 2003.	Deutsche Börse has introduced netting and a CCP for equities via Eurex Clearing, which is jointly owned by the Swiss Exchange and Deutsche Börse.
Central Securities Depository	Clearstream Banking Frankfurt (CBF) Provides facilities for domestic equities, bonds, warrants, certificates and money market instruments, as well as international securities. Regulated by BaFin, the German supervisory authority.	Ownership originally equally split between Deutsche Börse and Cedel (via Clearstream International). In April 2002, Deutsche Börse obtained agreement from Cedel shareholders to acquire their 50% stake. Full integration of Clearstream into the Deutsche Börse group was achieved in 2003.
Settlement Period	Equities and bonds: T+2	
Fail rate	Less than 10%.	
Trade affirmation/matching	Pre-settlement matching between broker and custodians is available through Cascade (Central Application for Settlement Clearing and Depository Expansion).	
Netting	Included within CCP launch.	
DvP	CBF offers both Model 1 and Model 2 settlement.	
Paper	About 98% of all securities transactions are settled via book entry transfer.	

4   EURONEXT

The primary exchange for France, the Netherlands, Belgium and Portugal, **Euronext** is the result of the merger of the former Paris, Amsterdam and Brussels bourses to which Lisbon subsequently joined.

Euronext is a public listed company incorporated in the Netherlands and now owned by the New York Stock Exchange.

	Main features	Comment
Central Counterparty	LCH.Clearnet S.A. (since merger in December 2003) Acts as CCP for transactions conducted on Euronext's cash and derivatives markets. Provides such services for OTC transactions in financial instruments such as French, German, Dutch and Belgian bonds, for buying, selling and repo operations carried out on a designated gateway.	45.1% of LCH.Clearnet is owned by exchanges and 45.1% by members, with the balance held by Euroclear. This balanced share ownership was effected by the offer of a 7.6% stake in LCH.Clearnet by Euronext to member shareholders. Euronext remains the largest individual shareholder, with a 41.5% stake, but its voting rights are limited to 24.9%. An autonomous, not-for-profit organisation. Although the Euronext trading and clearing mechanisms are linked, it is not a fully vertical silo, as there is almost no ownership or control of the settlement function (3% of Euroclear Bank through Euronext).
Central Securities Depository	Euroclear France Euroclear Bank (ISCD) Euroclear Nederland Euroclear Belgium	The French Central Securities Depository (Sicovam) merged with Euroclear in January 2001 to create Euroclear France. The consolidation of CIK and Necigef into the Euroclear group and the acquisition by Euroclear of a 20% stake in Clearnet took place by means of a share exchange between Euroclear plc and Euronext. Euronext has a 3% stake in Euroclear plc.
Settlement Period	Equities and Bonds: T+3	
Fail rate	Less than 1%	
Trade affirmation/ matching	Via commercial vendors	
Netting	Yes	
DvP	Yes (Euroclear France offers settlement in central bank money)	
Paper	All three markets are largely dematerialised.	

5 VIRT-X

The primary exchange in Switzerland is **virt-x**, which is owned by SWX Swiss Exchange, TP Consortium and virt-x (formerly Tradepoint Financial Networks).

	Main features	Comment
Central Counterparty	Since May 2003, there have been two choices for users: LCH.Clearnet (LCH) x-clear	See notes for UK and Euronext markets for LCH.Clearnet ownership. x-clear is a subsidiary of SIS Swiss Financial Services Group Ltd.
Central Securities Depository	CRESTCo Ltd Euroclear SegaInterSettle	Members have a choice of settlement accounts, facilitated by links built between the three CSDs. Once the CCP is in place, all settlements are treated as local, regardless of the counterparties' choice of CSD.
Settlement period	Equities: T+3 Bonds: Varies by market	
Fail rate	N/A	
Trade affirmation/ matching	Via commercial vendors	
Netting	Both CCPs offer settlement netting	
DvP	Yes	
Paper	Largely dematerialised	

6 THE SINGAPORE EXCHANGE

The primary exchange in Singapore is the **Singapore Exchange (SGX)**, which is a public listed company.

Singapore's infrastructure is vertically integrated, with the Exchange owning the depository and also operating the central counterparty.

	Main features	Comment
Central Counterparty	Central Depository (Pte) Ltd (CDP) Acts as CCP for equities trades executed on Singapore Exchange Securities Trading system (SGX-ST). Is regulated by the Monetary Authority of Singapore.	Owned by SGX.
Central Securities Depository	CDP Equities and corporate debt Monetary Authority of Singapore Government debt	
Settlement period	Equities: T+3 Government debt: T+1 Corporate debt: T+3 (varies)	Retail equity trades are already T+1 and SGX intends to enable all institutional equity trades for T+1.
Fail rate	N/A	
Trade affirmation/ matching	Via Institutional Delivery & Affirmation System (IDAS)	Automatic pre-settlement matching for institutional trades is in place.
Netting	Yes	Netting is performed on the money settlement but not on securities settlement.
DvP	Yes	
Paper	Immobilised at CDP. A small proportion of physical shares are held with local custodians.	

7 THE TOKYO STOCK EXCHANGE

The primary exchange in Japan is the **Tokyo Stock Exchange (TSE)**.

	Main features	Comment
Central Counterparty	TSE	
Central Securities Depository	Japan Securities Depository Center Inc. (Jasdec) (Equities) Bank of Japan (Government bonds) Jasdec is the sole equity depository; eligible securities are domestic securities, including stocks, convertible bonds beneficiary certificates of exchange-traded funds, certificates of real estate investment trust and preferred investment bonds of financial institutions established by co-operative associations, which are listed on stock exchanges or registered with the Japan Securities Dealers Association (JSDA).	Jasdec is owned by over 200 shareholders. It started operations again in June 2002, after restructuring. It is regulated by the Financial Services Agency and the Ministry of Justice.
Settlement period	Equities and bonds: T+3	The market was expected to move to T+1 at the same time as the US. Date now deferred.
Fail rate	N/A	
Trade affirmation/ matching	Jasdec launched stage 1 of the Pre-Settlement Matching System (PSMS) in September 2001, offering a post-trade, pre-settlement reconciliation service for institutional investors' trading in Japan.	Further stages remain to be added to provide additional product coverage.
Netting	Via Jasdec for exchange trades	
DvP	Introduced in May 2001. Extended to non-exchange transactions from end 2003.	
Paper	Equities are in registered form and can be either immobilised or dematerialised.	

8 MARKET COMPARISONS

8.1 Clearing and settlement

Stock Exchange	Countries
The New York Stock Exchange	USA
The London Stock Exchange	UK
The Frankfurt Stock Exchange	Germany
Euronext	France, Netherlands, Belgium, Portugal
virt-x	Switzerland and UK
The Singapore Stock Exchange	Singapore
The Tokyo Stock Exchange	Japan

	NYSE	LSE	Frankfurt SE	Euronext	virt-x	Singapore Exchange	Tokyo SE
Equities: standard settlement period	T + 3	T + 3	T + 2	T + 3	T + 3	T + 3	T + 3
Govt. bonds: standard settlement Period	T + 0	T + 1	T + 2	T + 3	N/A	T + 1	T + 3
Netting	Yes	Yes	Yes	Yes	Yes	Yes	Yes
Delivery versus Payment	Yes	Yes	Yes	Yes	Yes	Yes	Yes
Central Counterparty	Yes	Yes	Yes	Yes	Yes	Yes	Yes
Separation of ownership	Partial	Yes	No	Yes	Yes	No	No
Holdings at CSD*	I	D	D	D	D	I	Both

*Immobilised (I), Dematerialised (D)

8.2 The process of globalisation

Companies are tending more and more to take a global view of business. The process of **globalisation** in various areas has been accelerated by improvements in communications, including the expansion and falling cost of air travel; the development of Internet-based systems; and improvements in telecommunications generally.

Capital markets of various countries have become internationally integrated – 'globalised'. The process of integration is facilitated by improved telecommunications and the deregulation of markets in many countries. Securities issued in one country can now be traded in capital markets around the world. This trend can only increase as stock exchanges are linked electronically.

8.3 The UK's position in the world

The financial services industry is a key sector of the UK economy.

With a long history going back to the time of merchant adventurers who sought finance for world-wide overseas trading, the 'Square Mile' of the **City of London** is the centre for the UK financial services industry. The City is the largest centre for many international financial markets, such as the currency markets. The UK has the world's largest share in the metals market (95%), Eurobond trade (70%), the foreign equity market (58%), derivatives markets (36%) and insurance (22%).

8.4 London as a financial centre

At the time of the introduction of the euro as a common European currency, it was suggested by many that London could lose its strong position as a leading world financial centre and might lose out to competing European centres such as Frankfurt.

There are a number of aspects favouring London as a financial centre.

- Its location in time zones: able to deal with US and Asian markets at either end of the day
- A workforce that is English-speaking – the international business language
- A varied pool of relatively well-educated labour
- Non-business activities making the City an attractive place to work
- Transport links (including air) and infrastructure
- A trend towards an increasingly cosmopolitan business environment
- The historical legacy and long tradition of supporting commerce
- Diversity in financial products available and traded
- Market transparency
- 'Fairness' of business environment, with relatively low incidence of corruption
- Government generally responsive to business needs
- Relatively 'light touch' regulatory environment

Against these potentially positive factors, it could be argued that London's institutional financial markets have a generally wholesale mentality.

There are other threats, as well as opportunities, affecting London's future.

- The potential for outsourcing operations to other countries has increased due to technological advances as well as some relaxation in regulatory regimes.
- Financial markets are showing increasing **virtuality**, so that with electronic communication, physical location becomes less significant.
- There are continuing trends towards consolidation in exchanges, clearing houses and central securities depositories.
- Firms are becoming increasingly likely to relocate processing centres and head offices wherever it is most beneficial.

Exam tip

In the Summer 2007 exam, a Section C question asked about the future challenges and opportunities that continued expansion of China might pose for London as an established financial centre.

BPP LEARNING MEDIA

8.5 China

With a population of around 1.3 billion, China comprises approximately 20% of the world population, and so – with continued economic growth – represents substantial buying potential over the longer term. China will come to represent a significant pool of consumers of services as time goes on.

- In 2006, China's Gross Domestic Product (GDP) was broadly equivalent to that of the UK, at US$ 2.5 trillion.

- China's economic growth (increase in GDP) has been around 10% annually every year since 1978 – which is approximately four times the UK's growth rate over the same period.

- There is increasing foreign investment in China, particularly by European investment funds.

- In recent years, foreign banks and financial institutions have been able to establish a foothold in China through cash and share ownership, in spite of China's traditionally protectionist stance.

In a similar way to India and Malaysia in recent years, China could become a cost-effective focus for service provision in the financial sector. The experience of outsourcing into other emerging markets in recent years shows how security and reliability are key to the expansion of such service provision.

Against these factors in China's favour, it is likely to take some more time for China to build up to the 'critical mass' of other major world financial centres.

CHAPTER ROUNDUP

- The New York Stock Exchange (NYSE) is a listed public company.

- The UK's infrastructure providers are all independent from one another.

- The Frankfurt Stock Exchange, FWB, is the largest of the eight stock exchanges in Germany and is managed by Deutsche Börse AG.

- Euronext, a public listed company incorporated in the Netherlands, is the primary exchange for France, the Netherlands, Belgium and Portugal.

- virt-x trades pan-European stocks.

- Singapore's infrastructure is vertically integrated, with the Singapore Exchange (SGX) operating the central counterparty as well as owning the depository.

- A comparison can be made of settlement periods and other features of the key stock markets.

- There are various reasons why London has been able to maintain its position as a major world financial centre.

BPP LEARNING MEDIA

TEST YOUR KNOWLEDGE

Check your knowledge of the Chapter here, without referring back to the text.

1   Which organisation regulates the New York Stock Exchange?

2   Why is Euroclear technically not a depository?

3   What is BaFin?

4   For which countries is Euronext the primary exchange?

5   In which country is virt-x the primary exchange?

6   What is Jasdec?

7   What is the standard equities settlement period on (a) NYSE, (b) LSE, (c) Euronext and (d) virt-x?

8   Which exchange uses a T + 2 standard settlement period for equities?

TEST YOUR KNOWLEDGE: ANSWERS

1   The Securities & Exchange Commission. (See 1.)

2   It does not hold securities in physical form. (See 2.)

3   BaFin is the Federal Supervisory Authority of Germany and regulates the Frankfurt Stock Exchange.
    (See 3.)

4   France, the Netherlands, Belgium and Portugal. (See 4.)

5   Switzerland. (See 5.)

6   Jasdec is Japan Securities Depository Center Inc., the central securities depository for equities on the
    Tokyo Stock Exchange. (See 7.)

7   T + 3 in each case. (See 8.1.)

8   Frankfurt. (See 8.1.)

BPP
LEARNING MEDIA

11

The Regulatory Framework

INTRODUCTION

The current system of regulation for the UK financial services industry was set up with the establishment of the Financial Services Authority (FSA) as the statutory regulator in 2001.

The FSA Handbook is continuing to evolve and recent moves from 'rules-based' regulation to 'principles-based' regulation are intended to lead to a reduction in the volume of detailed rules.

We set out the SII's Code of Conduct in this chapter.

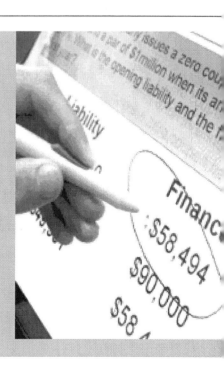

1 THE FSA AND UNDERLYING PRINCIPLES

1.1 Reform of the regulatory system

Exam tip

> On regulatory topics, it is common to be asked about recent changes. When answering such exam questions, address the changes and do not focus unnecessarily on historical aspects as this would not gain additional marks.

When the Labour Party gained power in 1997, it wanted to change the regulation of financial services. The late 1990s saw a radical reform of the financial services system with the unification of most aspects of financial services regulation under a **single statutory regulator**, the **Financial Services Authority (FSA)**. The process took place in two phases.

First, the Bank of England's responsibility for banking supervision was transferred to the **Financial Services Authority (FSA)** as part of the **Bank of England Act 1998**. Despite losing responsibility for banking supervision, the **Bank of England** ('the Bank') gained the role in 1998 of **setting official UK interest rates**.

The Bank is also responsible for maintaining stability in the financial system by analysing and promoting initiatives to strengthen the financial system. It is also the financial system's **'lender of last resort'**, being ready to provide funds in exceptional circumstances.

The **second phase** of reforms consisted of a new Act covering financial services which would repeal the main provisions of the Financial Services Act 1986 and some other legislation. The earlier 'patchwork quilt' of regulation would be swept away and the FSA would regulate investment business, insurance business, banking, building societies, Friendly Societies, mortgages and Lloyd's.

On 30 November 2001, the new Act – the **Financial Services and Markets Act 2000 (FSMA 2000)** – came into force, to create a system of **statutory regulation**. While practitioners and consumers are actively consulted, it is the FSA that co-ordinates the regulation of the industry.

1.1.1 Responding to regulatory failures

The new regime seeks to learn from many of the **regulatory failures** that occurred during the 1980s and 1990s, such as the following.

- The **Bank of Credit and Commerce International** (**BCCI**), an important international bank with many UK offices and customers, was the subject of an £8 billion fraud. This led to the FSA taking on regulatory responsibility for banks and increased regulation in the field of money laundering.

- The **Barings Bank** crisis was caused by the actions of a single rogue trader, Nick Leeson, whose unauthorised trading, coupled with the inadequacy of controls, led to the collapse of the bank. This has led to a big drive towards ensuring that senior management take their responsibilities seriously and ensure that systems and controls are adequate.

- In a further instance, world copper prices were manipulated by the unauthorised trading of Mr Hamanaka of **Sumitomo**, with much of his trading taking place on the London Metal Exchange. As a result, the new regime introduces more stringent rules to deal with market abuse.

The regulation of the UK financial services industry continues to evolve, and may need to react to new circumstances as they develop.

1.2 FSA as the UK statutory regulator

The creation of the FSA as the UK's **single statutory regulator** for the industry brought together regulation of investment, insurance and banking.

With the implementation of FSMA 2000 at date 'N2' in 2001, the FSA took over responsibility for:

- Prudential supervision of all firms, which involves monitoring the adequacy of their management, financial resources and internal systems and controls, and

- Conduct of business regulations of those firms doing investment business. This involves overseeing firms' dealings with investors to ensure, for example, that information provided is clear and not misleading

Arguably, the FSA's role as **legislator** has been diminished by the requirements of EU Single Market Directives – in particular, the far-reaching **Markets in Financial Instruments Directive (MiFID)**, implemented on 1 November 2007 – as the FSA has increasingly needed to apply rules which have been formulated at the **European level**.

1.3 The FSA's statutory objectives

Section 2 of the Financial Services and Markets Act (FSMA 2000) spells out the purpose of regulation by specifying the FSA's four **statutory objectives**.

The FSA's statutory objectives

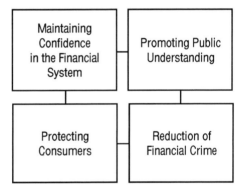

1.4 Status of the FSA

The FSA is not a government agency. Its members, officers and staff are not Crown servants nor civil servants. It is a private company limited by guarantee, with HM Treasury as the guarantor. The FSA is financed by the financial services industry. The Board of the FSA is appointed by the Treasury and the Chancellor of the Exchequer is ultimately responsible for the regulatory system for financial services under FSMA 2000.

HM Treasury, to which the FSA is accountable, will judge the FSA against the requirements laid down in FSMA 2000 which includes a requirement to ensure that the burdens imposed on the regulated community are **proportionate** to the benefits it will provide. In delivering against this, the FSA has undertaken a cost/benefit analysis whenever it has increased the burden of a rule.

HM Treasury also requires that the FSA submit an **annual report** covering such matters as the discharge of its functions and the extent to which the four regulatory objectives have been met. HM Treasury also has powers to commission and publish an independent review of the FSA's use of resources and commission official enquiries into serious regulatory failures.

1.5 Functions of the FSA

The FSA's **principal powers** are as follows.

- Granting **authorisation** and permission to firms to undertake regulated activities

- **Approving** individuals to perform controlled functions

- The right to issue under **S138 FSMA 2000:**

    - General rules (such as the *Conduct of Business* rules) for authorised firms which appear to be necessary or expedient to protect the interests of consumers

    - Principles (such as the *Principles for Businesses*)

    - Codes of conduct (such as the *Code of Practice for Approved Persons*)

    - Evidential provisions and guidance

- The right to **investigate** authorised firms or approved persons

- The right to take **enforcement** action against authorised firms and approved persons

- The right to **discipline** authorised firms and approved persons

- The power to take action against any person for **market abuse**

- The power to **recognise** investment exchanges and clearing houses

- As the **UK Listing Authority**, approval of companies for stock exchange listings in the UK

Note that the term **'firm'** is used generally in the FSA regulations to apply to an authorised person, whether the person is an individual, a partnership or a corporate body.

1.6 Regulatory bodies in other countries

You should have a general awareness of regulatory bodies in other countries, some of which, such as the **US** Securities & Exchange Commission (SEC) and Federal Reserve, come up in other parts of this Study Book.

In **Hong Kong**, the Hong Kong Securities and Futures Commission (SFC) is responsible for administering the laws governing the securities and futures markets in Hong Kong and facilitating and encouraging the development of these markets. The Hong Kong Monetary Authority (HKMA) is the government authority in Hong Kong responsible for maintaining monetary and banking stability.

1.6.1 Irish Financial Services Regulatory Authority

The Irish Financial Regulator is the IFSRA which is responsible for the development of codes of conduct and other requirements applicable to regulated entities authorised by or registered with the Financial Regulator.

In March 2004 the Financial Regulator started a review of existing codes in order to unify and develop the conduct of business requirements of these codes under one **Consumer Protection Code** (the Code). The Code was published on 25 July 2006.

The Code's principal aims are to:

- Ensure a consumer-focussed standard of protection for buyers of financial products and services

- Ensure that there is the same level of protection for consumers regardless of the type of regulated entity they choose to deal with, and

- Facilitate competition by contributing to a level playing field

The Financial Regulator also engaged in public consultations on minimum competency requirements in April 2004. The minimum competency requirements were published in July 2006.

1.7 The Principles for Businesses

1.7.1 Overview

The **Principles for Businesses (PRIN)** state firms' fundamental obligations under the regulatory system. They are formulated to require honest, fair and professional conduct from firms.

The Principles are drafted by the FSA and derive authority from the FSA's rulemaking powers under FSMA 2000 and from the FSA's **statutory objectives**, and they also include provisions which implement the EU Single Market Directives.

The Principles for Businesses apply in whole or in part to every **authorised firm** carrying out a regulated activity. (Approved persons are not covered by these principles, but are instead subject to a separate set of principles, known as **Statements of Principle**, which we shall look at later).

While the Principles for Businesses apply to regulated activities generally, with respect to the activities of accepting deposits, general insurance and long-term pure protection policies (i.e. that have no surrender value and are payable upon death), they apply only in a 'prudential context'. This means the FSA will only proceed where the contravention is a serious or persistent violation of a principle that has an impact on confidence in the financial system, the fitness and propriety of the firm or the adequacy of the firm's financial resources.

As we shall see, the implementation of **MiFID** – the EU **Markets in Financial Instruments Directive** – (with effect from **1 November 2007**) has had a significant impact on various aspects of FSA rules. The application of the Principles is modified for firms conducting MiFID business (including investment services and activities, and ancillary services, where relevant), and for EEA firms with the right (often referred to as a '**passport**') to do business in the UK.

1.8 Breaches of the Principles

The consequence of breaching a Principle makes the firm liable to **enforcement or disciplinary sanctions**. The FSA may bring these sanctions where it can show that the firm has been at fault in some way. The definition of 'fault' will depend upon the Principle referred to.

S150 FSMA 2000 creates a right of action in damages for a '**private person**' who suffers loss as a result of a contravention of certain **rules** by an authorised firm. However, a 'private person' may not sue a firm under s150 FSMA 2000 for the breach of a **Principle**.

1.9 The Principles

The **eleven Principles for Businesses** are as follows. A brief description is given of the activity each relates to.

Principles for Businesses	
1.	**Integrity** A firm must conduct its business with integrity.
2.	**Skill, care and diligence** A firm must conduct its business with due skill, care and diligence.
3.	**Management and control** A firm must take reasonable care to organise and control its affairs responsibly and effectively, with adequate risk management systems.
4.	**Financial prudence** A firm must maintain adequate financial resources.
5.	**Market conduct** A firm must observe proper standards of market conduct.
6.	**Customers' interests** A firm must pay due regard to the interests of its customers and treat them fairly.
7.	**Communications with clients** For customers – A firm must pay due regard to the information needs and communicate information to them in a way that is clear, fair and not misleading. For eligible counterparties – A firm must communicate information in a way that is not misleading.
8.	**Conflicts of interest** A firm must manage conflicts of interest fairly, both between itself and its customers and between a customer and another client.
9.	**Customers: relationships of trust** A firm must take reasonable care to ensure the suitability of its advice and discretionary decisions for any customer who is entitled to rely upon its judgement.
10.	**Clients' assets** A firm must arrange adequate protection for clients' assets when it is responsible for those assets.
11.	**Relations with regulators** A firm must deal with its regulators in an open and co-operative way and must disclose to the FSA appropriately anything relating to the firm of which the FSA would reasonably expect notice.

1.10 Scope of the Principles

Some of the Principles (such as Principle 10) refer to **clients**, while others (such as Principle 9) refer to **customers**. This difference affects the scope of the relevant Principles.

- 'Client' is an all-encompassing term that includes everyone from the smallest retail customer through to the largest investment firm. It therefore includes, under the terminology of MiFID, eligible counterparties, professional customers and retail customers.

- 'Customer' is a more restricted term that includes professional and retail clients but excludes 'eligible counterparties'. 'Customers' are thus clients who are not **eligible counterparties**. (Eligible counterparties are discussed in Chapter 13.) Principles 6, 8 and 9, and parts of Principle 7, apply only to **customers**.

In line with MiFID, a firm will not be subject to a Principle to the extent that it is contrary to the EU Single Market Directives. Principles 1, 2, 6 and 9 may be disapplied for this reason, in the case of:

- Eligible counterparty business

- Transactions on a regulated market (e.g. the London Stock Exchange), and member transactions under a **multilateral trading facility** – a system that enables parties (e.g. retail investors or other investment firms) to buy and sell financial instruments

Note that Principle 3 would not be considered breached if the firm failed to prevent **unforeseeable** risks.

1.11 FSA's approach to regulation

After the establishment of the FSA, there were concerns about the extensive nature of regulation, and the volume of regulatory material which firms were having to follow.

A 'twin approach' was heralded by the FSA, combining 'risk-based' and 'principles-based' aspects.

- The FSA's **risk-based approach** means that it focuses attention on those institutions and activities that are likely to pose the greatest risk to consumers and markets. The FSA considers it both impossible and undesirable to remove all risk from the financial system.

- The 'principles-based' approach implies that, rather than formulate detailed rules to cover the varied circumstances firms are involved in, the Authority would expect firms to carry more responsibility in making their own judgement about how to apply the regulatory Principles and Statements of Principle to their business. The FSA's initiative on **'Treating Customers Fairly' (TCF)** is an example of the Authority's emphasis on principles.

The FSA does not define **treating customers fairly (TCF)** in a way that applies in all circumstances. By adopting a **'Principles-based approach'** to TCF through Principle 6, the FSA puts the onus on firms to determine what is fair in each particular set of circumstances. Firms therefore need to make their own assessment of what TCF means for them, taking into account the nature of their business.

1.12 Principles-based regulation

In its **2006/07 Business Plan**, the FSA signalled its intention to shift, through time, towards more reliance on **higher-level principles**, with fewer detailed rules and thus potentially a slimmer Handbook in future. This focus was re-emphasised in the FSA's **2007/08 Business Plan**, and there has been progress towards reduction in the volume of detailed rules. The incorporation of new **MiFID** rules has helped this process, because the MiFID Directive is generally less wordy and less detailed than the previous FSA rules which have been replaced.

The impact of principles-based regulation has also been seen in **enforcement cases**, where the FSA has relied on its expectation that firms would follow higher-level principles, even where there might not have been breaches of detailed rules. The FSA is deliberately shifting responsibility on to firms to decide what higher level principles mean for them.

1.13 The client's best interests rule

The **Conduct of Business Rules** require that firms must act honestly, fairly and professionally in accordance with the **best interests of the client**. This rule applies to designated investment business for a retail client or, in relation to MiFID business, for any other client.

In communications relating to designated investment business, a firm must not seek to exclude or restrict any duty or liability it may have under the regulatory system. If the client is a retail client, any other exclusion or restriction of duties or liabilities must meet the 'clients' best interests rule' test above. (The general law, including **Unfair Terms Regulations**, also limits a firm's scope for excluding or restricting duties or liabilities to a consumer.)

1.14 Supervision

The FSA's approach to supervision is designed to reflect a number of important concepts.

- The FSA's four **regulatory objectives**.

- The responsibility of **senior management** to ensure that it takes reasonable care to organise and control the affairs of the firm effectively and develops and maintains adequate risk management systems. It is the responsibility of the management to ensure the firm complies with its regulatory requirements.

- The principle that the burden or restriction on firms should be **proportionate** to the benefits to be provided.

The FSA's policy on supervision is grouped under the following **four** headings.

- Diagnostic
- Monitoring
- Preventative
- Remedial

The FSA's overall approach is one of risk-based supervision. The Authority has developed a system known as the **A**djusted **R**isk **R**eturn **O**perating Frame**w**ork ('**ARROW**'), which involves the FSA looking at particular risks posed by individual firms and also risks to consumers and to the industry as a whole.

ARROW II is a revised model introduced in 2006 and designed to allow FSA supervisors more accurately to reflect their assessment of risk in individual firms or through cross-firm 'thematic' work.

The aim is to focus the FSA's resources in the most efficient and economic way. The FSA will therefore undertake an **impact and probability** assessment on each firm to determine the risks that the firm poses to the four regulatory objectives. In terms of impact, this looks primarily at the impact on the four regulatory objectives. In terms of probability, this is assessed in terms of **risk groups** arising from the firm's strategy, business risks, financial soundness, type of customers, systems and controls and organisation of the firm. The FSA will place firms into risk categories and communicate with them the outcome of the assessment.

The general procedure for this categorisation is as follows.

1. **Preliminary assessment** of the firm's impact on the regulatory objectives
2. **Probability assessment** – the detail will depend on the impact rating and complexity of the firm
3. A sample of various firm's categorisations are then reviewed by a **validation panel**
4. A **letter** is sent to the firm outlining category
5. The FSA ensures **ongoing review** of risk assessment

In terms of the supervisory process, the FSA will use a broad range of tools, including:

- Desk-based reviews
- Meetings with the firm
- On-site inspections
- Issuing public statements
- Imposing requirements on the firm

1.15 Whistleblowing

Part of the FSA Handbook relating to Senior Management Arrangements, Systems and Controls covers procedures relating to '**whistleblowing**'.

The FSA rules and guidance serve to:

- Remind firms that there is legislation covering whistleblowing which applies to authorised firms (**Public Interest Disclosure Act 1998**, '**PIDA**')
- Encourage firms to adopt and communicate procedures for employees to raise concerns about the risk management arrangements of the firm

Whistleblowing is the process whereby a worker seeks to make a **protected disclosure** to a regulator or law enforcement agency outside the firm, in good faith, of information which tends to show that one or more of the following activities is, or is likely, to be committed or is being deliberately concealed by their employer.

- A criminal offence
- A failure to comply with a legal obligation
- A miscarriage of justice
- A breach of health and safety rules
- Damage to the environment

A firm cannot include a clause in the employee's contract preventing the employee from making such a disclosure, i.e. from 'blowing the whistle' on their employer's practices. The rules apply even if the activity listed above occurs outside the UK.

In addition, if the firm or member of staff of an authorised firm were to discriminate against an employee who made a disclosure in any way, the FSA would regard this as a serious matter. In particular the FSA would question the firm's '**suitability**' under **Threshold Condition 5** and the individual's **fitness and propriety**. In serious cases, the FSA could withdraw the firm's authorisation and an individual's approval.

1.16 Statements of Principle for Approved Persons

FSA *Statements of Principle* apply generally to all **approved persons** (i.e. relevant employees of FSA firms) when they are performing a **controlled function**. The scope of 'controlled' functions is covered later in this Chapter.

Section 59 FSMA 2000 states that a person (an individual) cannot carry out certain **controlled functions** unless that individual has been approved by the FSA. This requirement gives rise to the term '**approved person**', and the FSA's Supervision Manual (SUP) covers the approval process.

The Statements of Principle will not apply where it would be contrary to the UK's obligations under EU Single Market Directives. Under **MiFID** rules, the requirement to employ personnel with the necessary knowledge, skills and expertise is reserved to the firm's **Home State**. As a result, the FSA does not have a role in assessing individuals' competence and capability in performing a controlled function in relation to an **incoming EEA firm** providing MiFID investment services.

There are **seven Statements of Principle**. The first four Principles apply to all approved persons (which includes those doing a **significant influence function** as well as those not doing a significant influence function). As noted in the Table below, the final three Principles only apply to approved persons performing a significant influence function.

Statements of Principle for Approved Persons	
1 Integrity	Apply to all approved persons
2 Skill, care and diligence	
3 Proper standard of market conduct	
4 Deal with the regulator in an open way	
5 Proper organisation of business	Apply only to those doing a significant influence function
6 Skill, care and diligence in management	
7 Comply with regulatory requirements	

We now look at the **seven Statements of Principle** in detail taking into account the treatment of each by the Code.

Statement of Principle 1

An approved person must act with integrity in carrying out his controlled functions.

The *Code* provides examples of behaviour that would not comply with this Statement of Principle. These include an approved person:

- **Deliberately misleading clients**, his firm or the FSA, or

- **Deliberately failing to inform** a customer, his firm, or the FSA, that their understanding of a material issue is incorrect.

Statement of Principle 2

An approved person must act with due skill, care and diligence in carrying out his controlled function.

Examples of non-compliant behaviour under Statement of Principle 2 include failing to inform a **customer,** or his firm, of material information or failing to control client assets.

The coverage of Statement of Principle 2 is similar to Principle 1. The difference is that Principle 1 states that each act needs to be **deliberate**. Principle 2 may be breached by acts which, whilst not deliberate wrongdoing, are **negligent**.

Statement of Principle 3

An approved person must observe proper standards of market conduct in carrying out his controlled function.

Examples of non-compliant behaviour under Statement of Principle 3 include:

- A breach of market codes and exchange rules

- A breach of the *Code of Market Conduct*

The FSA expects all approved persons to meet proper standards, whether they are participating in organised markets such as exchanges, or trading in less formal over-the-counter markets.

Statement of Principle 4

An approved person must deal with the FSA and with other regulators in an open and co-operative way and must disclose appropriately any information of which the FSA would reasonably expect notice.

This Statement of Principle concerns the requirement to co-operate, not only with the FSA, but also with other bodies such as an overseas regulator or an exchange.

Approved persons do not have a duty to report concerns directly to the FSA unless they are responsible for such reports. The obligation on most approved persons is to report concerns of **'material significance'** in accordance with the firm's **internal procedures**. If no such procedures exist, the report should be made direct to the FSA.

It would also be a breach of this Statement of Principle if an approved person did not attend an interview or meeting with the FSA, answer questions or produce documents when requested to do so and within the time limit specified.

Statement of Principle 5

> An approved person performing a significant influence function must take reasonable steps to ensure that the business of the firm for which he is responsible in his controlled function is organised so that it can be controlled effectively.

As stated above, Principles 5 to 7 relate only to those approved persons performing a significant influence function. This Principle requires those performing a significant influence function to **delegate** responsibilities responsibly and effectively. Paramount to this is a requirement that they should delegate only where it is to a suitable person. In addition, they must provide those persons with proper reporting lines, authorisation levels and job descriptions. Clearly, all of these factors (and in particular the suitability requirement) should be regularly reviewed.

Principle 5 will be particularly relevant to the person whose responsibility it is to ensure appropriate apportionment of responsibilities under the Senior Management Arrangements, Systems and Controls (SYSC) section of the FSA Handbook.

Statement of Principle 6

> An approved person performing a significant influence function must exercise due skill, care and diligence in managing the business of the firm for which he is responsible in his controlled function.

This Principle requires those performing a significant influence function to inform themselves about the affairs of the business for which they are responsible. They should not permit transactions or an expansion of the business unless they fully **understand the risks** involved. They must also take care when monitoring highly profitable or unusual transactions and in those or other cases, must never accept implausible or unsatisfactory explanations from subordinates.

This Principle links to Principle 5 as it makes it clear that **delegation is not an abdication** of responsibility. Therefore, where delegation has been made, a person must still monitor and control that part of the business and, therefore, should require progress reports and question those reports where appropriate.

Statement of Principle 7

> An approved person performing a significant influence function must take reasonable steps to ensure that the business of the firm for which he is responsible in his controlled function complies with the relevant requirements and standards of the regulatory system.

This has a clear link to Principle 3 of the Principles for Businesses – Management and Control. Those exerting a significant influence on the firm must take reasonable steps to ensure that the requirements set out therein are implemented within their firm. They should also review the improvement of such systems and controls, especially where there has been a breach of the regulatory requirements. Principle 7 will be particularly relevant to the person whose responsibility it is to ensure appropriate apportionment of responsibilities under the Senior Management Arrangements, Systems and Controls section of the FSA Handbook.

1.17 The Code of Practice for Approved Persons

FSMA 2000 requires the FSA to issue a code of practice to help approved persons to determine whether or not their conduct complies with the Statements of Principle. The FSA has complied with this obligation by issuing the **Code of Practice for Approved Persons (The Code)**. This sets out descriptions of conduct which, in the FSA's opinion, does not comply with any of the statements, and factors which will be taken into account in determining whether or not an approved person's conduct does comply with the Statements of Principle. These descriptions have the status of **evidential provisions**.

The Code is not conclusive – it is only evidential towards indicating that a Statement of Principle has been breached. Account will be taken of the context in which the course of conduct was undertaken. In determining whether there has been a breach of Principles 5 to 7, account will be taken of the nature and complexity of the business, the role and responsibilities of the approved person, and the knowledge that the approved person had (or should have had) of the regulatory concerns arising in the business under their control. The examples in the Code that would breach a principle are not exhaustive.

In addition, the Code may be amended from time to time and the current published version at the time of the approved person's conduct will be the relevant Code that the FSA will look to in determining whether or not there has been a breach. The FSA will examine all the circumstances of a particular matter and will only determine that there has been a breach where the individual is **'personally culpable'**, i.e. deliberate conduct or conduct below the reasonable standard expected of that person in the circumstances.

2 THE SECURITIES AND INVESTMENT INSTITUTE'S CODE OF CONDUCT

Professionals within the securities and investment industry owe important **duties to their clients**, to the market, the industry and to society at large. Where these duties are set out in law or in regulation, the professional must always comply with the requirements in an open and transparent manner.

Membership of the Securities and Investment Institute (SII) **requires** members to meet the standards set out within the Institute's Principles. These Principles impose upon members an obligation to act in a way that moves beyond mere compliance and supports the underlying values of the Institute.

A **material breach** of the Principles would be incompatible with continuing membership of the Securities and Investment Institute.

Members who find themselves in a position, which might require them to act in a manner contrary to the Principles, are encouraged to:

1.   Discuss their concerns with their line manager

2.   Seek advice from their internal compliance department

3.   Approach their firm's non-executive directors or audit committee

4.   If unable to resolve their concerns and, having exhausted all internal avenues, to contact the Securities and Investment Institute for advice (email: principles@sii.org.uk)

Principles	Stakeholder
1. To act honestly and fairly at all times when dealing with clients, customers and counterparties and to be a good steward of their interests, taking into account the nature of the business relationship with each of them, the nature of the service to be provided to them and the individual mandates given by them	Client
2. To act with integrity in fulfilling the responsibilities of your appointment and seek to avoid any acts or omissions or business practices which damage the reputation of your organisation or which are deceitful, oppressive or improper and to promote high standards of conduct throughout your organisation	Firm
3. To observe applicable law, regulations and professional conduct standards when carrying out financial service activities and to interpret and apply them to the best of your ability according to principles rooted in trust, honesty and integrity	Regulator
4. When executing transactions or engaging in any form of market dealings, to observe the standards of market integrity, good practice and conduct required by, or expected of participants in that market	Market participant
5. To manage fairly and effectively and to the best of your ability any relevant conflict of interest, including making any disclosure of its existence where disclosure is required by law or regulation or by your employing organisation	Conflict of interest
6. To obtain and actively maintain a level of professional competence appropriate to your responsibilities and commit to continued learning and the development of others	Self
7. To strive to uphold the highest personal standards including rejecting short-term profits which may jeopardise your reputation and that of your employer, the Institute and the industry	Self

3   SENIOR MANAGEMENT RESPONSIBILITIES

3.1 Introduction

The FSA has drafted a large amount of guidance on **PRIN 3** (Principle for Businesses 3). You may recall that this Principle is as follows.

Management and control
A firm must take reasonable care to organise and control its affairs responsibly and effectively, with adequate risk management systems. Note: it would not be a breach of this Principle if the firm failed to prevent unforeseeable risks.

This emphasis comes from a desire to avoid a repetition of the collapse of Barings Bank, where it was clear that management methods and the control environment were deficient.

The FSA suggests that, in order to comply with its obligation to maintain appropriate systems, a firm should carry out a regular review of the above factors.

There is a section of the FSA Handbook called '**Senior Management Arrangements, Systems and Controls**'. As the name suggests, the main purpose of this part of the FSA Handbook is to encourage directors and senior managers of authorised firms to take appropriate responsibility for their firm's arrangements and to ensure they know what those obligations are.

3.2 SYSC requirements

A significant requirement of SYSC is the need for the Chief Executive to apportion duties among senior management and to monitor their performance. Beyond this, the main issues that a firm is expected to consider in establishing compliance with Principle 3 are as follows.

- Organisation and reporting lines
- Compliance
- Risk assessment
- Suitable employees and agents
- Audit committee
- Remuneration policies

There is a rule regarding apportionment of significant responsibilities, which requires firms to make clear who has particular responsibility and to ensure that the business of the firm can be adequately monitored and controlled by the directors, senior management and the firm's governing body. Details of apportionment and allocation of responsibilities must be recorded and kept up-to-date.

Under non-MiFID rules, record-keeping requirement is for records to be kept for **six years** from the date they are replaced by a more up-to-date record. MiFID requires firms to keep transaction records for **five years**.

Under **SYSC**, the firm has a general obligation to take reasonable care to establish and maintain systems and controls that are appropriate to its business. MiFID firms are required to **monitor and regularly evaluate** the adequacy of its systems, internal control mechanisms and arrangements established to comply with the above. Firms are likely to have to keep additional documentation to meet fully this requirement.

Furthermore, the **compliance function** must be designed for the purpose of complying with regulatory requirements and to counter the risk that the firm may be used to further financial crime.

Depending on the nature, scale and complexity of the business, it may be appropriate for the firm to have a separate compliance function although this is not an absolute requirement. The organisation and responsibilities of the compliance department should be properly recorded and documented and it should be staffed by an **appropriate number of persons** who are sufficiently **independent** to perform their duties objectively. The compliance function should have unfettered access to relevant records and to the governing body of the firm. The MiFID requirements here are broadly in line with the FSA's existing rules.

4 REGULATORY INFRASTRUCTURE

4.1 The Office of Fair Trading (OFT)

4.1.1 The role of the OFT

The **Office of Fair Trading (OFT)** has the goal of helping make markets work well for consumers. Markets work well, the OFT states, 'when fair-dealing businesses are in open and vigorous competition with each other for custom'.

The OFT offers advice, support and guidance to businesses on competition issues and on consumer legislation. It also seeks to promote good practice in business by granting 'approved status' to Consumer Codes of Practice meeting set criteria. The OFT will pursue businesses that rig prices or use unfair terms in contracts.

Under the **Control of Misleading Advertising Regulations**, the OFT works with bodies including the Advertising Standards Authority in exercising its powers to seek injunctions to stop advertising that is deceptive or misleading.

The OFT also regulates the consumer credit market with the aim of ensuring fair dealing by businesses in the market. It operates a **licensing system** through which checks are carried out on consumer credit businesses and it issues guidelines on how the law will be enforced.

4.1.2 The OFT and the FSA

The OFT has specific responsibilities under FSMA 2000.

It is part of the role of the OFT to keep under review the activities and rules of the FSA with respect to competition issues.

If the OFT believes that FSA rules will impact adversely on competition, then it will report this to the FSA, the Treasury and the **Competition Commission (CC).** The CC is required to report on the matter to the Treasury, the FSA and the OFT. The Treasury must then decide on any further action, which could include requiring the FSA to change the rules concerned.

4.2 Recognised Investment Exchanges (RIEs)

The act of running an investment exchange is, in itself, a regulated activity (arranging deals in investments) and therefore requires regulatory approval. However, **Recognised Investment Exchange** status exempts an exchange from the requirement. This status assures any parties using the exchange that there are reasonable rules protecting them.

Membership of an RIE does not confer authorisation to conduct regulated activities. Many firms are members of an RIE and also required to be authorised and regulated by the FSA. Membership of an RIE merely gives the member privileges of membership associated with the exchange, such as the ability to use the exchange's systems.

Exchanges with RIE status

- London Stock Exchange (LSE)
- PLUS Markets plc
- LIFFE Administration and Management
- London Metal Exchange (LME)
- ICE Futures
- virt-x Exchange
- EDX London

4.3 Recognised Overseas Investment Exchanges (ROIEs)

As well as the above UK exchanges that are permitted to operate under the RIE status, certain **Recognised Overseas Investment Exchanges (ROIEs)** are permitted to operate in the UK.

Recognised Overseas Investment Exchanges examples:

- NASDAQ
- Chicago Mercantile Exchange (CME)
- New York Mercantile Exchange (NYMEX)
- EUREX

A ROIE is also granted recognition by the FSA.

4.4 Recognised Clearing Houses (RCHs)

This recognition permits the organisation to carry out the clearing and settlement functions for an exchange.

At present there are two **RCHs**:

- Euroclear UK & Ireland Limited (formerly CRESTCo)
- LCH.Clearnet Limited

4.5 Designated Investment Exchanges (DIEs)

In addition to those RIEs in the UK and overseas which the FSA recognises as being effectively run, there are also overseas exchanges that have been given a form of approval yet are unable to conduct regulated activities in the UK.

Designated Investment Exchange (DIE) status assures any UK user of the overseas market that the FSA believes there are appropriate forms of local regulation that guarantee the investor's rights.

The term 'designated' does *not* mean exempt from the requirement to seek authorisation.

Designated Investment Exchanges include, for example:

- Tokyo Stock Exchange
- Toronto Stock Exchange
- New York Futures Exchange
- New York Stock Exchange

4.6 Multilateral Trading Facilities (MTFs)

A **Multilateral Trading Facility (MTF)** is a system that brings together multiple parties (e.g. retail investors, or other investment firms) who want to buy and sell financial instruments, and enables them to do so.

MTFs may be crossing networks or matching engines that are operated by an investment firm or a market operator. Instruments traded on a MTF may include shares, bonds and derivatives.

Changes to FSA rules brought the rules into line with MiFID requirements from 1 November 2007. MiFID requires operators of MTFs to ensure their markets operate on a fair and orderly basis. It aims to ensure this by placing requirements on MTF operators regarding how they organise their markets and the information they give to users.

Additionally, MiFID provides for the operators of MTFs to **passport their services** across borders.

4.7 The Financial Services and Markets Tribunal

FSMA 2000 makes provision for an independent body accountable to the Ministry of Justice (previously the Department for Constitutional Affairs) (known as the **Financial Services and Markets Tribunal**) which is established under the Financial Services and Markets Tribunal Rules 2001. This provides for a complete rehearing of FSA enforcement and authorisation cases where the firm or individual and the FSA have not been able to agree the outcome. Therefore, if a firm or individual receives a decision notice or supervisory notice or is refused authorisation or approval it may refer this to the Tribunal. The Tribunal will determine what appropriate action the FSA should take and in doing so can consider any new evidence which has come to light since the original decision was made.

4.8 The Financial Services Compensation Scheme (FSCS)

The **Financial Services Compensation Scheme (FSCS)** is designed to compensate **eligible claimants** where a relevant firm is unable or likely to be unable to meet claims against it. Generally speaking, therefore, the scheme will only apply where the firm is declared **insolvent or bankrupt**.

The compensation scheme is independent, but accountable, to the FSA and HM Treasury for its operations and works in partnership with the FSA in delivering the FSA's objectives, particularly that of consumer protection. FSCS is funded by levies on firms authorised by the FSA.

4.8.1 Compensation limits

Maximum compensation levels per claim are summarised in the Table below. (The most important scheme for our purposes is that relating to **investments**.)

	Limit
Protected investments	£48,000 (100% of the first £30,000 and 90% of the next £20,000)
Protected deposits	£35,000 (100% of the first £35,000)
Long-term insurance	100% of first £2,000, plus 90% of remaining value (unlimited)

The compensation limit for deposits has applied since 1 October 2007: the previous limits were less generous. The limits are per claim, and not per account or contract held.

5   THE FSA HANDBOOK

5.1 Overview

The FSA Handbook comprises a final set of rules, principles and guidance that an authorised firm must adhere to. The FSA derives its power to make rules in the FSA Handbook from FSMA 2000. Therefore, it includes Principles for Businesses and various rules contained in the Conduct of Business Sourcebook.

Given the range of financial services activities covered, it is hardly surprising that the *FSA Handbook* is a lengthy document. However, as already mentioned, the Handbook is undergoing a process of simplification, in line with the move towards principles-based regulation. This process is partly being carried out in conjunction with the implementation of the MiFID, which has resulted in major changes to the content of the Handbook with effect from 1 November 2007.

5.2 Structure of the FSA Handbook

The FSA Handbook is split into seven main blocks.

High Level Standards	Prudential Standards
Principles for Businesses (PRIN)	General Prudential Sourcebook (GENPRU)
Statements of Principle and the Code of Practice for Approved Persons (APER)	Prudential Sourcebooks for Banks, Building Societies and Investment Firms (BIPRU), for Insurers (INSPRU), for UCITS Firms (UPRU) and for Mortgage and Home Finance Firms and Insurance Intermediaries (MIPRU)
Threshold Conditions (COND)	
Senior Management Arrangements, Systems and Controls (SYSC)	
Fit & Proper Test for Approved Persons (FIT)	Interim Prudential Sourcebooks (for Banks, Building Societies, Friendly Societies, Insurers and Investment Business) (IPRU)
General Provisions (GEN)	
Fees Manual (FEES)	

Business Standards
Conduct of Business (COBS)
Insurance: Conduct of Business (ICOB)
Mortgages: Conduct of Business (MCOB)
Client Assets (CASS)
Market Conduct (MAR)
Training & Competence (TC)

Regulatory Processes	Redress
Supervision (SUP)	Dispute Resolution: Complaints (DISP)
Decision Procedure and Penalties Manual (DEPP)	Compensation (COMP)
	Complaints against FSA (COAF)

Specialist Sourcebooks
New Collective Investment Schemes (COLL)
Credit Unions (CRED)
Electronic Money (ELM)
Professional Firms (PROF)
Recognised Investment Exchanges and Recognised Clearing Houses (REC)

Listing, Prospectus and Disclosure
Listing Rules (LR)
Prospectus Rules (PR)
Disclosure and Transparency Rules (DTR)

5.3 Handbook guides

Handbook Guides point particular kinds of firm in the direction of material relevant to them in the Handbook. These include guides for Energy Market Participants, Oil Market Participants, Service Companies, Small IFA Firms and Small Mortgage and Insurance Intermediaries.

5.4 Design of the FSA Handbook

The FSA Handbook contains a number of different kinds of provisions – including rules, evidential provisions and guidance as follows.

R	This indicates that the corresponding paragraph is a **rule** and means that it places a binding duty on a firm. Most rules are also used to give **private persons** a right of action under **s150**.
E	This indicates that the corresponding paragraph is an **evidential provision**. If a firm complies with an evidential provision, this will tend to establish compliance with the linked rule. If a firm breaches an evidential provision, this will tend to establish that a breach of the linked rule has occurred.
G	This indicates that the corresponding paragraph is **guidance**. Guidance is not binding on a firm but it is used to flesh out particular issues arising from rules.

6 REGULATED AND PROHIBITED ACTIVITIES

6.1 The general prohibition

Section 19 FSMA 2000 contains what is known as the **general prohibition**. The general prohibition states that no person can carry on a regulated activity in the UK, nor purport to do so, unless they are either **authorised or exempt**.

The definition of person here includes both **companies and individuals**. The list of exemptions and exclusions are set out in the regulations. There is no right to apply for an exemption from s19 if you do not fall into the existing categories.

The sanctions for breaching s19 are fairly severe, namely: criminal sanctions, unenforceability of agreements, compensation, and actions by the FSA to restrain such activity.

Breach of the general prohibition is an offence punishable in a court of law. The courts have a lower level, known as a Magistrates' Court, where summary offences are heard, and a higher level with a judge and jury, known as the Crown Court, where indictable offences are heard.

The maximum penalties for conducting unauthorised regulated activities are set out in s23 FSMA 2000:

- **Magistrates' Court:** six months' imprisonment and/or a £5,000 fine
- **Crown Court:** two years' imprisonment and/or an unlimited fine

It is a **defence** for a person to show that all reasonable precautions were taken and all due diligence exercised, to avoid committing the offence.

6.2 Unenforceable agreements

As a consequence of the general prohibition, an agreement made by an **unauthorised** firm will be **unenforceable** against the other party.

FSMA 2000 makes it clear that agreements are not illegal or invalid as a result of a contravention of the general prohibition: they are merely '**voidable**'. This ensures that the innocent party to the agreement may still be able to enforce the agreement against the other party, even though the performance may be a criminal offence.

The innocent party will be entitled to recover **compensation** for any loss sustained if the agreement is made unenforceable.

6.3 Injunctions and restitution orders

The FSA may seek **injunctions** and **restitution orders** to restrain the contravention of the general prohibition and seek to remove the profits from offenders.

6.4 The requirement for authorisation

As stated above, no person can carry on a regulated activity in the UK, nor purport to do so, unless they are either **authorised** or **exempt**.

The **Perimeter Guidance Manual (PERG)** in the FSA Handbook gives guidance about the circumstances in which authorisation is required, or exempt person status is available, including guidance on the activities which are regulated under FSMA 2000 and the exclusions which are available.

6.5 Exempt persons

The following are the types of person that are **exempt** from the requirement to seek authorisation under FSMA 2000.

- **Appointed representative.** In markets such as life assurance, the bulk of sales takes place through self-employed individuals who act on behalf of the companies. As the companies do not employ them, if this exemption were not in place, such persons would need separate authorisation. The exemption removes them from the scope of authorisation so long as they act solely on behalf of one firm and that firm takes complete responsibility for their actions.

- **Members of professions.** Solicitors, accountants and actuaries have been giving investment advice for many years. As long as giving such advice does not constitute a major proportion of their business (i.e. is incidental) and they are not separately paid for those activities, they are exempt from the requirement to seek authorisation. However, they will still be governed by their professional bodies (e.g. the Law Society, for solicitors). These professional bodies are known as **Designated Professional Bodies (DPBs)** and are subject to scrutiny by the FSA.

- **Certain persons listed in the Financial Services and Markets Act (Exemption) Order 2001**, including supranational bodies, municipal banks, local authorities, housing associations, the national grid, trade unions, the Treasury Taskforce, the English Tourist Board, government organisations (such as Bank of England, other central banks, an enterprise scheme, the International Monetary Fund and the UK's National Savings & Investments). In addition, charities and the Student Loans Company are exempt in respect of deposit-taking activities. The Financial Services and Markets Act (Exemption) Order 2001 is written by HM Treasury under powers set out in s38 FSMA 2000.

- **Members of Lloyd's**. The requirement to seek authorisation is disapplied for members of Lloyd's writing insurance contracts. The Society of Lloyd's, however, is required to be authorised. This exemption covers **being** a Lloyd's member but does not cover the activities of **advising** on Lloyd's syndicate participation or **managing** underwriting activities.

- **Recognised Investment Exchanges (RIEs), Recognised Overseas Investment Exchanges (ROIEs)** and **Recognised Clearing Houses (RCHs)**.

Exam tip

> The word **APRIL** can be used to help learn the five types of exempt persons.
>
> **A**ppointed representatives
> **P**rofessional people, e.g. solicitors, accountants and actuaries
> **R**IE, ROIEs and RCHs
> **I**nstitutions who are exempt, e.g. the Bank of England
> **L**loyd's members

6.6 Misleading statements and practices

Under s397 FSMA 2000 'Misleading Statements and Practices', each of the following is an offence.

- Mislead the market either through a **statement, promise or forecast**. Misleading statements that are intended to make individuals or the market move in a particular direction will constitute an offence if they are made recklessly or with dishonest intent. It is a defence if the statement was made in accordance with the price stabilisation rules.

- Engage in a **course of conduct** which creates a false or misleading impression as to the market, price or value of investments and that is intended to make individuals or the market move in a particular direction. It is a defence if the statement was made in accordance with the price stabilisation rules or the offender reasonably believed a false or misleading impression would not be created by their conduct.

- Dishonestly **conceal** material facts, which may make individuals or the market move in a particular direction.

This is a matter of criminal law which applies to all persons and can be brought to justice either through a Magistrates' Court or through a Crown Court.

7 ENFORCEMENT AND REDRESS

7.1 Regulatory Decisions Committee (RDC)

The FSA's **Enforcement Division** investigates when firms breach FSA rules or the provisions of FSMA 2000. Enforcement staff prepare and recommend action in individual cases. For more significant decisions (called **statutory notice decisions**) the FSA passes the case to another body which is a separate Committee of the FSA, called the **Regulatory Decisions Committee (RDC)**.

The RDC will look at the case and decide whether or not to take action. This would cover the giving of fines, censures, restitution orders, and withdrawing, varying or refusing authorisation or approval. For less serious disciplinary actions, e.g. requesting the firm to provide reports, the FSA may act itself under its 'executive procedures'.

The RDC is appointed by the FSA Board to exercise certain regulatory powers on its behalf. It is accountable to the board of the FSA for the decisions. However, the RDC is outside the FSA management structure and apart from the Chairman of the RDC, none of the RDC's members are FSA employees. The RDC members comprise practitioners and suitable individuals representing the public interest.

If the RDC decide to take action:

- A **Warning Notice** will be sent, containing details of the proposed action. The person concerned then has access to the material which FSA is relying on and may make **oral or written representations** to the RDC.

- The RDC will then issue a **Decision Notice** detailing the reasons for the decision, proposed sanction and a notice of the right to refer the matter to the Financial Services and Markets Tribunal, which undertakes a complete rehearing of the case.

- When a decision notice is accepted, or appeals finalised, a **final notice** is sent to the person.

A Final Notice only contains FSA/RDC/Tribunal discipline, not any disciplinary action the firm has taken itself internally. The process is summarised in the following diagram.

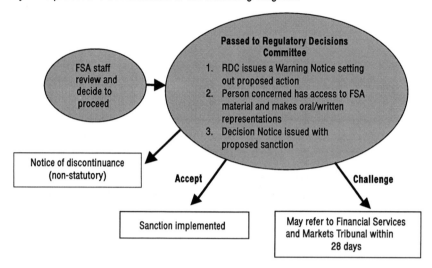

Under Part V of FSMA 2000, the FSA must commence disciplinary action within **two years** of first being aware of the misconduct.

7.2 Disciplinary processes

Disciplinary measures are one of the regulatory tools available to the FSA. The FSA must be proportionate in its use of disciplinary measures: 'the punishment must fit the crime'. The disciplinary process has been designed to ensure that it is compliant with human rights legislation. Therefore, while FSA staff will investigate the matter and decide whether they feel enforcement action is appropriate, they will not take the final decision on matters of such regulatory significance.

The FSA can take decisions themselves under their own **executive procedures** for matters of lesser regulatory impact to the firms, such as imposing a requirement on a firm to submit regular reports covering activities such a trading, complaints or management accounts. As we have seen, more significant decisions are made by the **RDC** (Regulatory Decisions Committee).

If the FSA think it would be beneficial for the approved person or firm to know that they were close to being the subject of formal proceedings, then the FSA can issue a **Private Warning**.

7.3 FSA powers

The FSA may discipline authorised firms or approved persons for acts of misconduct in order to pursue its regulatory objectives. The detail is contained in the **Enforcement Guide** of the FSA Handbook.

Disciplinary measures against approved persons and authorised firms include the following.

- **Public censure and statements of misconduct**

  The FSA may issue a public censure to a firm where the firm has contravened a requirement imposed under FSMA 2000. The FSA may issue a public statement of misconduct to an approved person where the approved person is guilty of **'misconduct'**. Misconduct means breaching a Statement of

Principle or being knowingly concerned in the contravention of a regulatory requirement by their firm. The FSA will issue a **Warning Notice** of its intention to censure in this way.

- **Financial penalties, i.e. unlimited fines**

  The FSA will impose a financial penalty on a firm where the firm has contravened a requirement imposed under FSMA 2000. The FSA may impose a financial penalty on an approved person where the approved person is guilty of 'misconduct' (as defined earlier). The FSA can also impose a financial penalty on any person who has committed market abuse and also on an applicant for listing or an issuer of listed securities where the UKLA listing rules have been breached. In determining the **size of the penalty** the FSA must have regard to:

  - The seriousness of the misconduct
  - The extent to which the misconduct was deliberate or reckless
  - Whether the person on whom the penalty is to be imposed is an individual

  To impose a financial penalty, the FSA must give the individual a **Warning Notice** followed by a **Decision Notice** and a **Final Notice** and the individual must be able to refer the matter to the **Financial Services and Markets Tribunal**. Financial penalties are normally published via a press release unless it would be unfair on the person to whom the penalty is imposed or prejudicial to the interests of consumers.

- **Restitution order/redress**

  Where a person (whether authorised or not) has breached a relevant requirement the FSA has powers to require that person to effect restitution on the affected consumers (i.e. **restore them in the pre-breach situation**). In determining whether to exercise its powers, the FSA will have regard to the circumstances of the case and also other facts, including other ways the consumer might get redress and whether it would be more effective or cost effective for the FSA to require redress.

  In addition to the disciplinary measures mentioned above, the FSA can take the following **preventative or remedial action**.

- **Cancellation or variation of authorisation or approval**

  Under FSMA 2000, the FSA may **vary** a Part IV permission where:

  - The firm is failing or likely to fail to meet the threshold conditions for one or more of the regulated activities in respect of which it has Part IV permission

  - The firm has not carried out a regulated activity for which it has a Part IV permission for at least 12 months, or

  - It is desirable to protect consumers

  The FSA will consider **cancelling** a firm's Part IV permission where:

  - It has very serious concerns about a firm or the way its business has been conducted, or

  - The firm's regulated activities have come to an end and it has not applied for its permissions to be cancelled

As we shall see later, individuals must be **approved** by the FSA to perform specified **controlled functions**.

Approval may be removed if the individual is no longer fit and proper to conduct that controlled function. To withdraw approval the FSA must give the individual a warning notice followed by a Decision Notice and the individual must be able to refer the matter to the Financial Services and Markets Tribunal.

Furthermore, **s56 FSMA 2000** allows the FSA to prohibit individuals from carrying out specified functions in relation to regulated activities within the investment industry. This is called a **Prohibition Order** and may be issued in respect of anyone whether they are approved or not.

The FSA will exercise its power to make a Prohibition Order where it determines that the individual represents a risk to consumers or confidence in the market generally and is not fit and proper to carry out that function.

A Prohibition Order is much wider than the withdrawal of approval. If the FSA wishes to discipline an approved person, they can use either the withdrawal of approval route or issue a Prohibition Order. However, the FSA will only issue a Prohibition Order if the degree of risk to consumers or confidence in the financial system cannot be addressed by simply withdrawing approval for the relevant controlled function.

7.4 Rights of private persons

As mentioned earlier, **Section 150** FSMA 2000 creates a right of action, in damages, for a '**private person**' who suffers loss as a result of a contravention of certain rules by an authorised firm. A **private person** means individuals not doing a regulated activity, and businesses, in very limited circumstances (where the loss does not arise from their business activities, e.g. setting up an occupational pension scheme for their employees).

This right exists in addition to common law actions, such as negligence or misrepresentation. However, s150 provides a privileged right of action since there is no need to prove negligence. It is sufficient that there has been a **rule breach** leading to **loss**.

Section 59 FSMA 2000 states that a person cannot carry out a **controlled function** in a firm unless that individual has been **approved** by the FSA. Note that we are now referring to the individual members of staff of an authorised firm.

If a person is performing a controlled function and is not approved, this is known as a **breach of statutory duty** and a private person has the right to sue their firm for damages if they have suffered loss, using **s71** FSMA 2000, just as they have for a breach of rules under s150.

7.5 FSA powers to require information

Under **s165** FSMA 2000, the FSA may, by written notice, require an authorised firm (or any person connected with it) or certain other persons (e.g. RIEs) to produce specified information or documents, which it reasonably requires. The FSA can require the information or documents to be provided within a specified, reasonable timescale and at a specified place. The FSA may also require that the information provided is verified and documents are authenticated.

The FSA may require access to an authorised firm's premises on demand: **no notice** need be given.

The FSA may launch an investigation on a number of grounds, including:

- (For an authorised firm) where it has good reason to do so
- Where any person has contravened specific provisions of the regulatory regime (e.g. market abuse)
- At the request of an overseas regulator

The FSA may also require a report from a skilled person (e.g. an accountant).

7.6 Dispute resolution: complaints

7.6.1 General points

Firms carrying on regulated activities may receive **complaints** from their clients about the way the firm has provided financial services or in respect of failure to provide a financial service. This could include allegations of financial loss whether or not such losses have actually yet occurred: for example, in the case of a mis-sold pension contract, future losses may be involved. Under the FSA's rules, a firm must have **procedures** to ensure complaints from eligible complainants are properly handled.

A **complaint** is defined as 'any **oral or written** expression of dissatisfaction, whether justified or not, from, or on behalf of, a person about the provision of, or failure to provide, a financial service, which alleges that the complainant has suffered (or may suffer) financial loss, material distress or material inconvenience'.

DISP 1 includes various complaints handling rules which we outline below, and which apply generally to authorised firms. However, there are some exceptions, as follows.

The rules do not apply to **authorised professional firms** (such as firms of accountants or solicitors) in respect of their **non-mainstream regulated activities**.

For **MiFID business**, DISP 1 applies to:

- Complaints from **retail clients**, but **not** those who are not retail clients

- Activities carried on from a **branch** of a UK firm in another EEA State, but **not** to activities carried on from a branch of an EEA firm in the UK

7.6.2 Eligible complainants

The rules (in DISP within the FSA Handbook) on how firms must handle complaints apply to **eligible complainants**. An eligible complainant is a person eligible to have a complaint considered under the Financial Ombudsman Service.

Eligible complainants comprise: private **individuals**, **businesses** with a group annual turnover of less than £1m, **charities** with an annual income of less than £1m or trusts with net asset value of less than £1m (other than those who are properly classified as **professional clients or eligible counterparties**) who are customers or potential customers of the firm.

7.6.3 Complaints handling (DISP 1.3)

Firms, and UK firms' branches in the EEA, must establish procedures for the reasonable handling of complaints which:

- Are effective and transparent

- Allow complaints to be made by any reasonable means (which might include email messages, or telephone calls, for example)

- Recognise complaints as requiring resolution

In respect of non-MiFID business, firms must ensure that they identify any **recurring or systemic problems** revealed by complaints. For MiFID business, the requirement is that firms must use complaints information to detect and minimise risk of '**compliance failures**'.

7.6.4 Complaints resolution (DISP 1.4)

For all complaints received, the firm must:

- Investigate the complaint **competently, diligently and impartially**

- Assess **fairly, consistently and promptly**:
  - whether the complaint should be upheld
  - what remedial action and/or redress may be appropriate
  - whether another respondent may be responsible for the matter (in which case, by the **complaints forwarding rule**, the complaint may be **forwarded** to that other firm, promptly and with notification of the reasons to the client)

- Offer any redress or remedial action

- Explain the firm's assessment of the complaint to the client, its decision, including any offer of redress or remedial action made – in a fair, clear and not misleading way

7.6.5 Complaints resolved the next day (DISP 1.5)

Complaints **time limit, forwarding and reporting rules** do not apply to complaints which are **resolved by the next business day** after the complaint is made.

7.6.6 Time limit rules (DISP 1.6)

On receiving a complaint, the firm must:

- Send to the complainant a prompt written acknowledgement providing 'early reassurance' that it has received the complaint and is dealing with it, and

- Ensure the complainant is kept informed of progress on the complaint's resolution thereafter.

By the end of **eight weeks** after receiving a complaint which remains unresolved, the firm must send:

- A final response, or

- A holding response, which explains why a final response cannot be made and gives the expected time it will be provided, informs the complainant of his right to complain directly to the FOS if he is not satisfied with the delay, and encloses a copy of the Financial Ombudsman Service explanatory leaflet

The FSA expects that, within eight weeks of their receipt, almost all complaints will have been substantively addressed.

7.6.7 Firms with a two-stage complaints procedure (DISP 1.6)

Some firms operate a **two-stage complaints procedure** that provides for a complainant who is still not satisfied with the firm's initial response to refer the matter back to the firm or to its head office.

These firms are subject to the time limits set out above, but the rules recognise that some complainants may never respond to the initial reply or may take a long time to do so. Therefore, where the firm sends a response to the complainant offering redress or explaining why they do not propose to give redress and setting out how the complainant can pursue the claim further within the firm or apply to the FOS, it is permissible for the firm to regard the matter as closed if the firm does not get a reply within eight weeks.

If the complainant does reply indicating that they remain dissatisfied, then the general time limits will resume. However, the firm can discount any time in excess of a week taken by the complainant to reply.

7.6.8 Time barring (DISP 1.8)

Complaints received outside the FOS **time limits** (see below) may be rejected without considering their merits in a final response, but this response should state that the FOS may waive this requirement in exceptional circumstances.

7.6.9 Complaints reporting (DISP 1.10)

Firms must provide a complete **report to the FSA** on complaints received **twice a year**.

7.7 The Financial Ombudsman Service (FOS)

7.7.1 Overview

The **Financial Ombudsman Service (FOS)** was set up by Parliament to help settle individual disputes between businesses providing financial services and their customers.

Additionally, the **Consumer Credit Act 2006** has amended FSMA 2000, giving the FOS power to make rules to resolve certain disputes against holders of licences issued by the Office of Fair Trading under the Consumer Credit Act 1974.

FSMA 2000 sets out the roles and responsibilities of the FSA and the FOS. Both organisations are concerned with protecting consumers, but within this overall objective they have distinct and separate responsibilities.

A **complainant** must first go to the authorised firm against which the complaint is being made. If the authorised firm does not resolve the complaint to his satisfaction, the complainant may refer it to the **Financial Ombudsman Service (FOS)**.

The purpose of the Ombudsman scheme under **FSMA 2000** is to provide for the resolution of 'certain disputes' quickly and with minimum formality by an independent person (s225(1)). The scheme is to be administered by a body corporate with further direction being provided with regard to jurisdiction and operation in Part XVI and Schedule 17 FSMA.

The Ombudsman scheme is generally dealt with under the Dispute Resolution: Complaints Sourcebook (DISP).

7.7.2 Powers of the FOS

The FOS is a body set up by statute and, whilst its Board is appointed by the FSA, it is **independent** from the FSA and authorised firms. The FOS is, however, accountable to the FSA and is required to make an annual report to the FSA on its activities. Jurisdiction of the FOS is covered under **s226-227 FSMA 2000** and **DISP 2**.

The FOS can consider a complaint against an authorised firm for an act or omission in carrying out any of the firm's regulated activities together with any ancillary activities that firm does. This is known as the **Compulsory Jurisdiction** of the FOS.

In addition to the Compulsory Jurisdiction, the FOS can consider a complaint under its **'Voluntary Jurisdiction'**. Firms or businesses can choose to submit to the voluntary jurisdiction of the FOS by entering into a contract with the FOS. This is available, for example, to unauthorised firms, and can cover activities such as credit and debit card transactions and ancillary activities carried on by that voluntary participant where they are not regulated activities.

A further **Consumer Credit Jurisdiction** applies under the **Consumer Credit Act 2006**, which gives to the FOS powers to resolve certain disputes regarding loans against holders of licences issued by the Office of Fair Trading under the **Consumer Credit Act 1974**.

7.7.3 Eligible complainants and referral to FOS

Only **eligible complainants** who have been customers of authorised firms or of firms which have voluntarily agreed to abide by the FOS rules may use the FOS. The scope of what is meant by 'eligible complainants' was explained earlier.

Where an eligible complainant refers a matter to the Ombudsman, a firm has no definitive right to block the matter being referred, but may dispute the eligibility of the complaint or the complainant. In such circumstances, the Ombudsman will seek representations from the parties. The Ombudsman may investigate the merits of the case and may also convene a hearing if necessary.

7.7.4 Ombudsman's power to require information

S231 FSMA 2000 allows the Ombudsman to require a party to the complaint to provide information which it considers necessary for determination of the complaint.

7.7.5 Outcome of FOS findings

Where the Ombudsman finds in favour of the complainant, it can force the firm to take appropriate steps to remedy the position including to pay up to **£100,000** plus reasonable **costs** (although awards of costs are not common). This figure will normally represent the financial loss the eligible complainant has suffered but can also cover any pain and suffering, damage to their reputation and any distress or inconvenience caused. If the Ombudsman considers that a sum greater than £100,000 would be fair, he can recommend that the firm pays the balance, although he cannot force the firm to pay this excess.

Awards and the **costs** rule are covered in ss229-230 FSMA 2000.

Once the Ombudsman has given a decision, the complainant may decide whether to accept or reject that decision.

- If the complainant **accepts** the Ombudsman's decision, **the authorised firm is bound** by it
- If the complainant **rejects** the decision, they can pursue the matter further through the **Courts**

7.8 Complaints against the FSA (COAF)

One of the sources of the FSA's accountability is an independent **Complaints Commissioner**. The COAF Sourcebook in the FSA Handbook sets the role of the Complaints Commissioner and the procedure for lodging a complaint against the FSA.

The process is designed to address allegations of misconduct or negligence by the FSA, including:

- Mistakes and lack of care
- Unreasonable delay
- Unprofessional behaviour
- Bias
- Lack of integrity

The Commissioner is not concerned with complaints regarding contractual or commercial disputes.

Complaints should initially be made to the **FSA**, which will conduct an initial investigation and respond. If the complainant is unhappy with the FSA response, he can refer the matter to the Complaints Commissioner.

8   REGULATED ACTIVITIES AND AUTHORISATION

8.1 List of activities regulated

What range of activities are **regulated activities**? The activities regulated by FSMA 2000 are set out in the **Regulated Activities Order** (as amended).

- **Accepting deposits.** These must be accepted by way of business to be covered.

- **Issuing electronic money.** Some banks and building societies issue 'e-money' which is a form of electronic money that can be used (like notes and coins) to pay for goods and services.

- **Effecting and carrying out contracts of insurance.** After date 'N2' (30 November 2001), the FSA took responsibility for regulating all insurers for capital adequacy purposes and life insurance firms for Conduct of Business Rules. Since January 2005, the FSA has regulated the sales and administration of general insurance as well as life insurance.

- **Dealing in investments as principal or agent.** This covers buying, selling, subscribing or underwriting investments.

- **Arranging deals in investments and arranging regulated mortgages.** This covers making, offering or agreeing to make any arrangements with a view to another person buying, selling, subscribing or underwriting investments. It also covers most mortgages, but generally does not cover buy-to-let or second charge loans. The FSA started to regulate mortgages in October 2004.

- **Operating a Multilateral Trading Facility (MTF).** As mentioned earlier, an MTF is a system which may be operated by an investment firm that enables parties, who might typically be retail investors or other investment firms, to buy and sell financial instruments.

- **Managing investments.**

- **Assisting in the administration and performance of a contract of insurance** (see above).

- **Safeguarding and administering investments** or arranging such activities.

- **Sending dematerialised instructions.** This relates to the use of computer-based systems for giving instructions for investments to be transferred.

- **Establishing a collective investment scheme or stakeholder pension.** This would include the roles of the trustee and the depository of these schemes.

- **Advising on investments, regulated mortgage contracts, or home finance contracts.**

- **Lloyd's market-related activities.** Lloyd's is the UK's largest insurance market.

- **Providing funeral plan contracts.**

- **Entering into and administering a regulated mortgage contract or home finance contract.** Initially, the FSA regulated mortgage lending only, but since 31 October 2004 the FSA has regulated mortgage advice and administration, in addition to mortgage lending.

- **Agreeing to carry on most regulated activities.** This is itself a regulated activity and so a firm must get the appropriate authorisation before agreeing to do business such as dealing or arranging for clients.

As you can see from the above list, the activities regulated cover the investment industry, banking, insurance and mortgage lending industries, and Lloyd's.

8.2 Activities carried on by way of business

Note that the regulated activity must be carried on **'by way of business'** for the Regulations to apply. Whether something is carried on by way of business is, ultimately, a question of judgement: in general terms it will depend on the degree of continuity and profit. HM Treasury has also (via secondary legislation) made explicit provisions for certain activities, such as accepting deposits. This will not be regarded as carried on by way of business if a person does not hold himself out as doing so on a day-to-day basis, i.e. he only accepts deposits on particular occasions. An example of this would be a car salesman accepting a down payment on the purchase of a car.

8.3 Excluded activities

As set out in PERG, the following activities are **excluded** from the requirement for authorisation.

- **Dealing as principal where the person is not holding themselves out to the market as willing to deal.** The requirement to seek authorisation does not apply to the personal dealings of unauthorised individuals for their own account, i.e. as customers of an authorised firm. It would also exclude companies issuing their own shares.

- **Trustees, nominees and personal representatives.** These persons, so long as they do not hold themselves out to the general public as providing the service and are not separately remunerated for the regulated activity, are excluded from the requirement to seek authorisation.

- **Employee share schemes.** This exclusion applies to activities which further an employee share scheme.

- **Media**, e.g. TV, radio and newspapers. Many newspapers and other media give investment advice. However, provided this is not the primary purpose of the newspaper, then under the exceptions granted within FSMA 2000, it need not seek formal authorisation. On the other hand, the publication of '**tip sheets**' (written recommendations of investments) will require authorisation.

- **Overseas persons.** Overseas persons are firms which do not carry on regulated activity from a permanent place within the UK. This exception covers two broad categories: first, where the activity requires the direct involvement of an authorised or exempt firm and, second, where the activity is carried on as a result of an unsolicited approach by a UK individual. Thus, if a UK individual asks a fund manager in Tokyo to buy a portfolio of Asian equities for them, the Japanese firm does not need to be authorised under FSMA 2000.

Exam tip

> Use the word **DEMOTE** to help you to learn the five excluded activities.
>
> **D**ealing as principal, where the person is not holding themselves out to the market as willing to deal
> **E**mployee share schemes
> **M**edia
> **O**verseas persons
> **T**rustees
> Nomin**E**es and personal representatives

8.4 Specified investments

Only activities relating to **specified investments** are covered by FSMA 2000. Specified investments are also defined in the **Regulated Activities Order** (as amended). In general terms, these are as follows.

- **Deposits.** Simply defined, this is a sum of money paid by one person to another under the terms that it will be repaid on a specified event (e.g. on demand).

- **Electronic money.** This is defined as monetary value, as represented by a claim on the issuer, which is stored on an electronic device, is issued on receipt of funds and is accepted as a means of payment by persons other than the issuer.

- **Contracts of insurance.** Included in this category are general insurance contracts (such as motor insurance, accident or sickness), long-term insurance contracts (such as life and annuity) and other insurance contracts (such as funeral expense contracts).

- **Shares** or stock in the capital of a company wherever the company is based.

- **Debentures, loan stock and similar instruments**, e.g. certificate of deposit, Treasury bills of exchange, floating rate notes, bulldog bonds and unsecured loan stock (but not cheques or other bill of exchange, banker's drafts, letters of credit, trade bills or Premium Bonds).

- **Government and public securities**, e.g. gilts, US Treasury bonds (not National Savings & Investments products, such as Premium Bonds and National Savings Certificates).

- **Warrants.** A warrant gives the right to buy a new share in a company.

- **Certificates representing certain securities**, e.g. American Depository Receipts.

- **Units in Collective Investment Schemes** including shares in, or securities of, an Open-Ended Investment Company (OEIC). A collective investment scheme is a specified investment whatever underlying property the scheme invests in.

- **Rights over a stakeholder pension.**

- **Options** to acquire or dispose of any specified investment or currencies, gold, silver, platinum or palladium.

- **Futures** on anything for investment purposes. This differs from the treatment of options as it will cover all futures regardless of the underlying investment, provided it is **for investment purposes**.

  The definition of 'investment purposes' is complex. In general terms, any futures contract traded either on an exchange, or in an over-the-counter market or form similar to that traded on an exchange, will constitute an investment. The type of future, in effect, excluded by this definition would be a short-term contract between a producer and a consumer of a good to purchase that good in the future, e.g. a wheat buyer buying from a farmer. This can sometimes be referred to as a 'commercial purpose future'.

- **Contracts for differences (CFDs).** A contract for a difference is a contract whose price tracks the price of an underlying asset, while the CFD holder does not take ownership of the asset. The underlying asset might be a company's shares, a bond, a currency, a commodity or an index. Investors can use CFDs to take a short position – and thus gain from price declines, but lose if the price rises.

- **Lloyd's syndicate capacity and membership.** Lloyd's is an insurance institution specialising in risks such as aviation and marine insurance. Insurance is provided by members and syndicates.

- **Funeral plan contracts.** These are contracts whereby someone pays for their funeral before their death.

- **Regulated mortgages.** Note that not all mortgages are covered, only regulated mortgages. In a regulated mortgage the loan is secured by a first legal mortgage or property located in the UK, which will be occupied (at least 40% of the time) by the borrower or their family.

- **Rights to or interests in specified investments.** 'Repos' (sale and repurchase agreements) in relation to specified investments (e.g. a government bond) are specified investments.

- **Personal pensions.** This is a pension plan which is not a stakeholder scheme and is not an employment-based (occupational) scheme.

- **Home finance.** This covers types of personal mortgage finance.

Spot currency ('forex') trades, general loans (e.g. car loans), property deals and National Savings & Investments products are *not* specified investments.

When applying for authorisation to carry out a regulated activity regarding a specified investment, the firm will specify on the application form which regulated activities relating to which specified investments it wishes to conduct.

8.5 Authorisation routes

A firm may be authorised by one of two main routes:

- Authorisation by the FSA
- Passporting

The concept of a '**passport**' enables a firm to conduct business throughout the EEA.

8.6 Authorisation by the FSA

By far the most common route to authorisation is to obtain permission from the FSA to carry out one or more regulated activities.

The permission that a firm receives will play a crucial role in defining the firm's business scope. This permission is sometimes referred to as **Part IV permission** as it is set out in Part IV of FSMA 2000.

Where a firm obtains permission to do one or more regulated activities, it is then authorised to do those activities. In the application, the applicant must set out which regulated activities and specified investments it requires permission for. The permission will set out what activities and investments are covered and any limitations and requirements that the FSA wishes to impose.

It is not a criminal offence for a firm to go beyond its permission but doing so may give rise to claims from consumers. Furthermore, the FSA will be able to use the full range of disciplinary sanctions, such as cancelling or varying permission.

8.7 Threshold conditions

Before it grants permission, the FSA must be satisfied that the firm is **fit and proper**. In accordance with FSMA 2000, the firm must meet and continue to satisfy the **'threshold conditions'** for the activity concerned in order to be deemed fit and proper. These link closely with the statutory objective of protecting consumers in that they all go towards ensuring that the business will be operated effectively and supervised by the FSA.

There are five Threshold Conditions (set out in the **COND** part of the FSA Handbook) as follows.

- **Condition 1** sets out the **legal status** that the applicant must have to carry on certain regulated activities, i.e. the legal structure of the business.

- **Condition 2** relates to the **location of the offices** of the applicant. If the applicant is a UK company, its head and registered offices must be located in the UK. For an applicant that is not a company, if it has its head office in the UK, then it must carry on business in the UK.

- **Condition 3** relates to the effect of **close links** of the applicant with other entities, e.g. other members of the same group.

- **Condition 4** requires that the applicant for authorisation must have **adequate resources** for the activities they seek to undertake. Such resources would not only include capital, but also non-financial resources such as personnel.

- **Condition 5.** The final condition relates to the **suitability** of the applicant. The firm must be considered to be 'fit and proper', i.e. it must have integrity, be competent and have appropriate procedures in place to comply with regulations. The management and staff of the firm must also be **competent**.

Exam tip

Use the word **CALLS** to help you to learn the five Threshold Conditions.

Close links
Adequate resources
Legal status
Location of offices
Suitability

The FSA provides guidance on the Threshold Conditions in the FSA Handbook. The guidance is unsurprisingly very general, as satisfaction of the Threshold Conditions is considered on a case-by-case basis in relation to each regulated activity that the firm wishes to carry on.

Note that suitability to carry on **one** regulated activity does not mean that the applicant is suitable to carry on **all** regulated activities.

In determining whether the applicant satisfies and will continue to satisfy the Threshold Conditions under FSMA 2000, the FSA will consider whether the applicant can demonstrate that the firm is ready, willing and organised to comply with the regulatory obligations that will apply if it is given permission to conduct those regulated activities.

Linking closely to Condition 4 is the requirement that the firm demonstrates that it has adequate **financial resources** to meet the financial resources requirement for its type of firm.

8.8 Procedure for obtaining approval

Certain **individuals** within an authorised firm will require **approval** from the FSA because they carry out **controlled functions**. We explain what the controlled functions are below.

It is important to appreciate that the process of an **individual** obtaining **approved person** status is different from the process of a **firm** obtaining **authorisation**.

To obtain approval, a person must satisfy the FSA that they are **fit and proper** to carry out the controlled function. The suitability of a member of staff who performs a controlled function is covered in the **Fit and Proper Test for Approved Persons** (part of the High Level Standards section of the FSA Handbook).

The most important considerations are as follows.

- **Honesty, integrity and reputation.** The FSA will examine whether the person's reputation might have an adverse impact on the firm for whom they are performing a controlled function. This will include looking at a number of factors including whether they have had any criminal convictions, civil claims, previous disciplinary proceedings, censure or investigations by any regulator, exchange, governing body or court; any other previous contraventions of regulations; any complaints which have been upheld; any connection with any body which has previously been refused a registration, authorisation or licence or had such registrations, authorisations or licences revoked or been expelled by a regulatory or governmental body; whether they have had any management role within any entities which have gone into liquidation; whether they have been dismissed or asked to resign from a similar position or position of trust; any disqualifications as a director, and finally whether they have been candid and truthful in their dealings with all regulatory bodies and demonstrated a willingness to comply with the regulatory and legal standards applicable to them. When looking at previous convictions, even old (i.e. spent) convictions, as defined in the Rehabilitation of Offenders Act 1974, can be taken into account.

- **Competence and capability.** The FSA will examine whether the Training and Competence requirements in the FSA Handbook have been complied with and whether they have demonstrated by training and experience that they are able to perform the controlled function. If a person has been convicted of, or dismissed or suspended from employment due to drug or alcohol abuse this will be considered in relation only to their continuing ability to perform that function. In addition, s61 FSMA 2000 emphasises that the fit and proper test for approved persons includes assessing qualifications, training and competence. It is not a requirement that a person has experience in order to be approved.

- **Financial soundness.** The FSA will look at whether the applicant has any outstanding judgement debts, has filed for bankruptcy or been involved in any similar proceedings. The fact that a person is of limited financial resources will not in itself affect their suitability to perform a controlled function.

8.9 Controlled functions

Section 59 FSMA 2000 and the **Supervision Manual (SUP)** states that a person cannot carry out a controlled function in a firm unless that individual has been **approved** by the FSA.

As we saw earlier, when a person (individual) is performing a controlled function and is not approved, there is a breach of statutory duty and a private person has the right to sue their firm for damages if they have suffered loss, using **s71** FSMA 2000.

The FSA may specify a function as a **controlled function** if the individual performing it is:

- Exerting a significant influence on the conduct of the firm's affairs
- Dealing directly with customers
- Dealing with the property of customers

The FSA Handbook (specifically, the **Supervision Manual**) has identified specific controlled functions which are split into the following groups. (The numbering is discontinuous because of re-categorisation of functions.)

Group	Function
Governing functions	1. Director function 2. Non-executive director function 3. Chief executive function 4. Partner function 5. Director of an unincorporated association function 6. Small Friendly Society function
Required functions	8. Apportionment and oversight function 9. EEA investment business oversight function 10. Compliance oversight function 11. Money Laundering Reporting Officer function 12. Actuarial function 12A. With-profits actuary function 12B. Lloyd's actuary function
Systems and controls function	28. Systems and controls function
Significant management function	29. Significant management function
Customer functions	30. Customer function

Individuals who fall within all of the above categories **except** customer functions would be considered to be exerting a **significant influence** on the conduct of the firm's affairs.

9 TRAINING AND COMPETENCE

9.1 Overview

Principle 3 of the **Principles for Businesses** requires firms to take reasonable care to organise and control its affairs responsibly and effectively, with adequate risk management systems. This implies having appropriate systems of control, including ensuring employees maintain and enhance competence.

SYSC states that a firm's systems and controls should enable it to satisfy itself of the suitability of anyone who acts for it. A requirement under **MiFID** is that firms must employ personnel with the skills, knowledge and expertise necessary for the discharge of the responsibilities allocated to them.

Requirements relating to Training and Competence (TC) for employees are set out in the FSA Handbook, as summarised below.

A contravention of the TC rules does not give rise to a right of action by a private person under s150 of FSMA 2000.

9.2 The competent employees rule

Competence means having the skills, knowledge and expertise needed to discharge the responsibilities of an employee's role. This includes achieving a good standard of **ethical behaviour**.

- The **competent employees rule** is now the main Handbook requirement relating to the competence of employees. The purpose of the TC Sourcebook is to support the FSA's supervisory function by supplementing the competent employees rule for **retail activities**.

- The **competent employees rule** is that firms must employ personnel with the skills, knowledge and expertise necessary for the discharge of the responsibilities allocated to them. This rule applies to non-MiFID firms as well as **MiFID** firms.

9.3 Assessment of competence and supervision

Appropriate examination requirements apply to **designated investment business** carried on for a **retail client**, except that they do not apply to providing basic advice on non-deposit-based stakeholder products. There are also appropriate examination requirements for **regulated mortgage activity**, and home reversion schemes, carried on for customers.

Employees must not carry out these activities without first passing the relevant **regulatory module** of an appropriate examination.

Firms may choose to impose time limits on the time by which examinations must be passed, or on the number of times examinations can be attempted.

In respect of these activities, firms must not allow employees to carry them on without **appropriate supervision**.

The **level and intensity** of supervision should be significantly greater in the period before the firm has assessed the employee as competent, than after. A firm should, therefore, have clear criteria and procedures relating to the **specific point** at which the employee is **assessed as competent** in order to be able to demonstrate when and why a reduced level of supervision may be considered appropriate. At all stages, firms should consider the **level of relevant experience** of an employee when determining the level of supervision required.

Those providing the supervision should have the necessary **coaching and assessment skills**, as well as **technical knowledge**. Firms should consider whether supervisors should themselves pass **appropriate examinations**.

Employees' **training needs** should be assessed at the outset and at regular intervals, including when their role changes. Firms must review employees' competence on a regular and frequent basis, and should take action to ensure that they **remain competent** in their role, taking into account:

- Technical knowledge and its application
- Skills and expertise
- Changes in markets, products, legislation and regulation

9.4 Appropriate examinations

The FSA maintains a list of **appropriate examinations**, for the activities for which they are required, from which firms may choose. Although a firm may set its own examinations, choosing examinations from the FSA list may be relied on as 'tending to establish compliance' with the TC rules.

An employee with three years of 'up-to-date' **relevant experience outside the UK** may be exempted from modules of an appropriate examination, but the regulatory module must still be taken. However, this type of exemption will not apply to those advising retail clients on packaged products, broker fund advising, advising on syndicate participation at Lloyd's or acting as a pension transfer specialist.

9.5 T&C record-keeping

A firm must make appropriate records to demonstrate compliance with the rules in TC and keep them for the following periods after an employee stops carrying on the activity:

- At least five years for MiFID business
- Three years for non-MiFID business, and
- Indefinitely for a pension transfer specialist

9.6 Why does Training and Competence matter?

The FSA places great emphasis upon senior management responsibility and training and competence (T&C) throughout the regulated firms. Added to this is its desire to ensure that firms treat customers fairly. These two objectives interrelate and FSA visits are designed to examine how firms are responding to their duties.

In 2004 and 2005, the FSA cited T&C in relation to eight cases of fines against regulated firms. T&C is a regulatory requirement and firms' schemes for T&C are rarely as robust as they believe them to be.

The following quotations reflect the FSA's view

"Training and Competence is a litmus test of a firm's overall compliance culture."

Sir Howard Davies, Chairman, Financial Services Authority

"For all sorts of reasons, apart from regulation, training is absolutely key. Your staff are the custodians of your personal reputation and livelihood; they protect your brand and drive customer satisfaction. Therefore, having appropriately trained staff who operate within this framework is absolutely vital to everything we do as managers of businesses."

David Kenmir, Financial Services Authority

Training and competence is seen as being the key to providing a professional service to customers. It is increasingly under the regulator's spotlight.

A firm's T&C scheme is thought to be an indicator of its overall compliance. It also helps to protect the firm's brand and drive customer satisfaction. Senior management is responsible for putting in place a proper compliance culture, suitable training and standards of competence.

9.7 T&C rules and operations management

Operations Managers must recognise that these FSA rules impact upon their own activities such that their teams are being assessed and audited in respect of the following.

- **Recruitment** – The standards for training and competence encompass the hiring and recruitment of all staff.

- **Training** – Staff members must be trained and knowledgeable in respect of their job responsibilities.

- **Attainment of competence** – Programmes of training and building expertise must be in place throughout the team.

- **Maintenance of competence** – It is just as important to remain competent as it is to become competent in the first place.

- **Supervising competence** – Firms must ensure appropriate supervision for the employee and recognition of the importance of appropriate supervision in the quality control of employees' work.

- **Examinations** – Managers must be aware of appropriate examinations for staff functions.

- **Record keeping** – Firms must be able to demonstrate that staff have been trained and possess the ability to prove and demonstrate the attainments of team members over the prescribed periods of time.

Operations Managers must ensure that as well as their staff being competent, it must be possible to demonstrate compliance with training and competence requirements. This could include organigrams, records (of recruitment, employment, training appraisal etc), job descriptions, supervisors in place and maintaining knowledge of job roles.

10 HEDGE FUNDS: REGULATORY ISSUES

10.1 Introduction

The 'problems' posed by **hedge funds** can be hard to address. The difficulties stem from three sources:

- Uncertainty about what hedge funds are
- The near impossibility of applying global regulation, and
- The fact that the problem is leverage (or 'gearing') rather than the hedge fund industry *per se*

10.2 The nature of hedge funds

Long-Term Capital Management (LTCM) was a highly leveraged hedge fund whose collapse in 2000 threatened financial markets. In the aftermath of the LTCM collapse, it was inevitable that politicians and regulators would respond with demands for tougher restrictions or an outright ban. Hedge funds, such as LTCM, are part of an eclectic family of funds that are recognisable most easily by what they are not.

How do **hedge funds** operate? Such funds eschew the buy and hold, long-side only techniques of classic fund managers. Their focus is on absolute returns, as opposed to relative returns and they contemplate using arbitrage, short selling, spread trading and derivatives to secure superior risk-adjusted returns. A constant feature of hedge funds, regardless of their trading methodology, is the use of leverage.

However, if leverage is the problem, it would be inappropriate to limit any regulatory response to hedge funds alone, but if the regulators wish to address the systemic risk posed by leverage more broadly, they risk constraining economic growth. Many individuals, most companies and all banks use leverage. Indeed, investment banks themselves are arguably like limited liability hedge funds. Thus, while policing hedge funds alone might deliver a politically satisfying conclusion, it would somewhat miss the point.

10.3 How to regulate?

Notwithstanding the difficulties outlined above, the inappropriate and extravagant use of leverage is a major cause of **systemic risk** in the global economy and therefore needs controlling. While such control is difficult for regulators to exert, it is relatively easy for banks to manage. At the heart of the LTCM problem are some surprisingly traditional banking errors. Hedge funds need to borrow to leverage their positions; banks therefore make credit decisions in determining the loans they extend.

In its original **Discussion Paper** on hedge funds (DP 16, August 2002), the **FSA** set out its approach to the **regulation of hedge funds**: in particular the selling and marketing of hedge funds in the UK and the regulation of UK-based hedge fund managers. The Authority's focus was perhaps more on the risks to consumers than the larger systemic issues involved. Regarding marketing, the FSA emphasised that hedge funds do not have special rules and broadly, as unregulated collective investment schemes, they can only be sold to intermediate customers, market counterparties or those for whom it is suitable. They cannot be promoted to most private customers. In view of this, the FSA saw no real need to alter their existing rules.

The FSA has however considered the potential impact of their restrictive marketing rules on product choice and portfolio diversification if these products cannot be sold to the retail sector. Research and responses to DP16 showed little appetite for hedge funds amongst retail investors.

The UK is not a popular place for hedge funds to be set up because the funds usually attract corporation tax on income and capital gains. However, many offshore funds do have onshore fund managers who provide investment advice and strategy to those funds. To the extent that these fund managers are carrying on **regulated activities**, they must be authorised by the FSA.

Two further issues affecting all funds (whether hedge funds or otherwise) have been the various debates surrounding **short selling** and **market timing** issues. In Discussion Paper 17, as we noted earlier, the FSA reiterated the FSA's view that short selling is a valid investment activity supporting efficient markets. However, they were concerned about the risks of disorderly trading, short-term volatility and settlement risks caused by large amounts of short selling. The FSA suggested providing disclosure mechanisms to give valuable data to the market on the extent of short selling. The agreed mechanism now in place is that CRESTCo publishes stock lending data to the market. As short selling is normally backed by borrowing the underlying asset, this provides a useful indicator of levels of shorting.

The market timing issue, like many current conflict-based issues, originated in the US. The practice involves short-term arbitrage of retail funds to take advantage of changes in the value of underlying stocks before the valuation point of the fund. While not illegal, it is considered poor practice as it affects long-term fund value and requires the fund manager to maintain higher liquidity than they would prefer. At the worst end of the spectrum has been 'late trading' where fund managers have colluded with market professionals to allow trades to occur after the close of trading. The problem is less prevalent in the UK where rules require forward pricing of funds. In the UK these practices would also be prohibited by PRIN 6 *Customers' interests* and PRIN 8 *Conflicts of interest*.

Following on from their original work, the FSA published feedback to its Discussion Paper 05/4. This paper looked at the impact of hedge funds in the UK's wholesale market.

Two main risks identified by the FSA became the subject of supervisory focus.

- **Asset valuations**. Hedge fund managers may be exposed to conflicts of interest as their remuneration is based on performance and assets under management. This may create an incentive to overstate the valuations it provides to administrators, who may not be able to challenge them. Themed visits are currently being carried out in this area and the findings will be known in the third quarter of 2006. The FSA has also sponsored an IOSCO project on valuing complex and illiquid assets in hedge funds.

- **Side letters**. The failure by hedge fund managers to disclose that side letters have been granted to certain clients may result in some investors receiving more information and preferential treatment to other investors in the same share class. The FSA expects managers to ensure that all investors understand that a side letter has been granted and that conflicts may arise.

In 2006, the FSA made a statement a consultation on widening the range of funds that can be marketed to retail investors to potentially include new authorised **funds of hedge funds**.

10.4 FSA comment: hedge fund risk areas

In September 2006, Hector Sants, Managing Director, Wholesale & Institutional Markets at the FSA, commented that the five key risk areas with hedge funds are as follows.

1. **Serious market disruption and erosion of confidence.** The failure of a large and highly exposed hedge fund or a cluster of medium-sized hedge funds with significant and concentrated exposures could cause serious market disruption. It could also erode confidence in the financial strength of other hedge funds or of firms which are counterparties to hedge funds.

2. **Market abuse / insider trading and manipulation.** Some hedge funds might be testing the boundaries of acceptable practice with respect to insider trading and market manipulation. In addition, given their payment of significant commissions and close relations with counterparties, they may create incentives for others to commit market abuse.

3. **Control and operational issues.** The recent rapid growth of the sector has been challenging for some hedge fund managers, with problems such as late trade confirmations, non-notified trade assignments and novations adding significantly to market-wide operational and credit risk levels.

4. **Mis-valuation of complex illiquid instruments/fraud.** Conflicts of interest arise when managers provide valuations of complex illiquid instruments to administrators, in particular where performance has been poor, the pressure on managers to provide overstated valuations is greatest.

5. **Preferential treatment of investors.** Some hedge funds are issuing undisclosed side letters which offer enhanced liquidity and other preferential benefits to selected investors, to the potential detriment of other investors in the fund.

10.5 Future proposals on FAIFs

In November 2007, the FSA issued an update on proposals to allow **UK retail consumers** to invest in funds of hedge funds and other alternative investments sold by firms authorised in the UK.

The FSA had planned to issue a policy statement and final rules towards the end of 2007 to allow the development of **Funds of Alternative Investment Funds (FAIFs)**, including funds of hedge funds, within the **retail market**.

However, the FSA found that there were a number of taxation issues, for consideration by HM Treasury, in operating such a regime. Therefore, the FSA is delaying publication of its proposals, probably until early 2008.

CHAPTER ROUNDUP

- The Financial Services Authority became the single statutory regulator for the industry in 2001. The Financial Services and Markets Act (FSMA) 2000 provides for a system of statutory regulation of the financial services industry.

- Four statutory objectives of the FSA regulatory system are set out in FSMA 2000.

- The FSA has wide powers, including approval of individuals to perform controlled functions, and authorisation of firms. The Authority can issue rules and codes of conduct, can investigate authorised firms or approved persons, and can take discipline and enforcement action.

- The Principles for Businesses (PRIN) state firms' fundamental obligations under the regulatory system, and require honest, fair and professional conduct from firms. The FSA emphasises the principle of Treating Customers Fairly (TCF).

- FSA Statements of Principle apply generally to all approved persons (i.e. relevant employees of FSA firms) when they are performing a controlled function. The Code of Practice for Approved Persons sets out types of conduct breaching the Statements of Principle.

- The Securities and Investment Institute's Code of Conduct includes seven core Principles. If a member encounters a conflict of interest (SII Principle 5), then the member may decide to decline to act.

- The SYSC manual in the FSA Handbook encourages directors and senior managers of authorised firms to take appropriate responsibility for their firm's arrangements and to ensure they know what those obligations are.

- No-one may carry on a regulated activity, unless either authorised, or exempt from authorisation. Some activities (e.g. media coverage, but not tipsheets) are excluded from the authorisation requirement.

- Disciplinary measures include public censure, unlimited fines, restitution orders and cancellation of authorisation or approval. Various Statutory Notices may be issued in cases involving the FSA's Regulatory Decisions Committee.

- The FSA has wide powers to visit firms' premises without notice and to require documents to be produced.

- The Regulated Activities Order specifies the list of regulated activities, and the specified investments covered by FSMA 2000.

- A firm may be authorised through obtaining 'Part IV permission' or, for EEA firms, through passporting. Five threshold conditions must be met for authorisation, which is specific to the types of activities the firm carries out.

- Those carrying out a controlled function need to meet a 'fit and proper' test to be approved persons. This test covers honesty, integrity and reputation; competence and capability; and financial soundness.

- Controlled functions include exerting significant influence on the firm, and dealing with customers or their property.

- A firm is responsible for ensuring that there is appropriate training for employees and that employees remain competent.

- A 'whistleblowing' employee can make a protected disclosure to a regulator or law enforcement agency of wrongdoing.

TEST YOUR KNOWLEDGE

Check your knowledge of the Chapter here, without referring back to the text.

1   What are the four regulatory/statutory objectives of the FSA?

2   List six of the FSA Principles for Businesses.

3   What is 'ARROW II'?

4   What term would apply to a crossing network operated by a group of investment firms to enable investors to buy and sell financial instruments?

5   Can you name the seven blocks of the FSA Handbook?

6   Can you name three types of exempt persons?

7   What does s397 FSMA 2000 cover?

8   Can you name three excluded activities?

9   Can you name three threshold conditions?

10   What is the difference between authorisation and approval?

TEST YOUR KNOWLEDGE: ANSWERS

1   Maintaining confidence, promoting public understanding, protecting consumers, reduction of financial crime. (See 1.3.)

2   You could have listed any six of the following: Integrity, Skill, Care & Diligence, Management and Control, Financial Prudence, Market Conduct, Customers' Interests, Communications with Clients, Conflicts of Interest, Customers: Relationships of Trust, Clients' Assets, Relations with Regulators. (See 1.9.)

3   ARROW is the risk-based supervision model which involves the FSA looking at particular risks posed by individual firms and also at risks to consumers and to the industry as a whole. ARROW II is a revised model which is designed to allow FSA supervisors more accurately to reflect their assessment of risk in individual firms or through cross-firm 'thematic' work. (See 1.14.)

4   Multilateral Trading Facility (MTF). (See 4.6.)

5   The seven blocks of the FSA Handbook are: High Level Standards, Prudential Standards, Business Standards, Regulatory Processes, Redress, Specialist Sourcebooks and Listing, Prospectus and Disclosure. (See 5.2.)

6   You could have mentioned any three of the following (mnemonic: **April**): **A**ppointed Representatives, **P**rofessional people, **R**IEs, **R**OIEs, **R**CHs, **I**nstitutions, e.g. the Bank of England and **L**loyd's members. (See 6.5.)

7   Section 397 FSMA 2000 relates to Misleading Statements and Practices. It covers dishonestly or recklessly making false or misleading statements, dishonestly concealing material facts and engaging in a course of conduct which gives a false or misleading impression. (See 6.6.)

8   Recall the word **Demote**: **D**ealing as principal where the person is not holding themselves out to the market as willing to deal, **E**mployee share schemes, **M**edia, **O**verseas persons, **T**rustees, nomin**E**es and personal representatives. You could have mentioned any three. (See 8.3.)

9   You could have mentioned any three of: legal status, location of offices, close links, adequate resources and suitability. (See 8.7.)

10 A firm needs to be authorised under s19 FSMA 2000 if it is carrying out regulated activities by way of business in the UK. An individual requires approval under s59 FSMA 2000 if he/she is undertaking one of the FSA's controlled functions e.g. as director, or compliance oversight. (See 8.8.)

12

EU Directives and Other Provisions

INTRODUCTION

The date for implementation of the far-reaching Markets in Financial Instruments Directive (MiFID) was 1 November 2007. The FSA has made substantial revisions to its Handbook to comply with MiFID. To a substantial degree, this has been achieved by 'copying out' MiFID provisions.

There are other EU Directives we also look at in this Chapter.

There are various measures designed to deal with crimes relating to the financial services sector as well as to financial transactions generally. It is important to know the law so that one does not inadvertently breach it, as ignorance of the law is not a defence. It is also important to know how legislation and regulations require those working in the financial sector to contribute to the detection and investigation of crime.

We also review in this chapter the provisions relating to data protection.

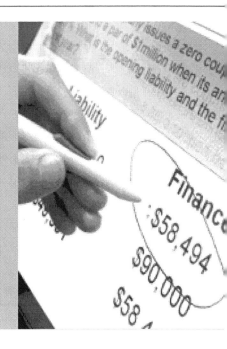

1 EUROPEAN FINANCIAL SERVICES REGULATION

1.1 Overview

One of the key objectives of the EU is to create a **common market** that allows for free and unencumbered trade. To this end, a large number of EU Directives have been agreed amongst the Member States and have subsequently been transposed into domestic legislation. These Directives seek to 'harmonise' regulations in order to create an open and competitive market place.

Since the creation of the EU (formerly known as the European Community), a number of important Directives relating to financial services have been implemented, including the following. (**UCITS** stands for Undertakings for Collective Investments in Transferable Securities.)

Directive	Date	Summary
First UCITS Directive	1985	Created the ability to sell certain unit trust style products freely throughout Europe via a European passport. This covered funds largely investing in listed shares and bonds.
Investment Services Directive (ISD)	1996	Created a single market for investment firms to transact business throughout Europe via a European passport.
Capital Adequacy Directive (CAD)	Various	CAD aims to create a harmonised set of financial regulations for banks and investment firms who are passporting.
Banking Consolidation Directive (BCD)	2001	This updated various earlier banking Directives and is the primary Directive providing the rights of credit institutions to passport that business. Banks have been able to passport since the mid-1990s.
UCITS Product Directive	2002	Expanded the coverage of the UCITS passport to include funds investing in other products such as money market instruments, deposits, financial derivatives and funds of funds.
UCITS Management Directive	2002	Allows UCITS Management Companies, i.e. those providing services relating to funds, to passport that business.
Markets in Financial Instruments Directive (MiFID)	2004	Updates the original ISD and allows a wider range of activities to be passported, e.g. including Multilateral Trading Facilities (MTFs) – came into force in member states: 1 November 2007.
Capital Requirements Directive (CRD)	2005	CRD amends the BCD and CAD – implementation date: 1 January 2007.

1.2 Ongoing issues in the creation of a single market

As we shall see later, **passporting** is an important concept in the creation of the single market but is only one of various tools in trying to encourage cross-border activities. In recognition of the need for a co-ordinated approach to the creation of a single market in Europe, the EU convened the Lisbon Conference which led, in 1999, to the announcement of the aim of creating a single market in financial services, they had hoped, by 2005. This process is known as the **Financial Services Action Plan (FSAP)**.

The stated aims of the FSAP are to create a single wholesale market, an open and secure retail financial services market and state-of-the-art prudential rules and regulation. The longer-term aim is that Europe will be the world's most competitive economy by 2010.

In order to achieve this, a committee of 'wise men' was set up, chaired by Alexandre Lamfalussy who is a senior European academic and adviser. This committee was charged with identifying targets for completing the single market for the investment industry by making the implementation of Directives more efficient and effective.

The committee's preliminary report was published in November 2000, and it had a rallying tone.

> 'The European Union has a great opportunity to strengthen its economy, improve its long-run competitiveness and investor returns for all citizens, if it can create a single financial market in the next few years. But this can only happen if the European regulatory system is made more efficient and decisions are taken in a timely way, at the right level. We can no longer afford the luxury of regulatory inefficiency in the instantaneous internet age. Financial markets are changing by the week – and European regulation is simply not up to speed.'

The preliminary suggestion of the wise men was to use a four-level approach.

- **Level 1:** Legislation, in the form of **Regulations and Directives** is proposed by the European Commission following consultation with the European Parliament and European Council. Legislation should be based on broad framework principles and the detailed technical implementing measures should be decided at Level 2.

- **Level 2:** The **European Securities Committee (ESC)** assists the European Commission in adopting technical implementing measures. The ESC is made up of policy makers from the Member States. Representatives from HM Treasury sit on the ESC.

- **Level 3:** The **Committee of European Securities Regulators (CESR)**, which has the objective of improving the consistent implementation of Level 1 and Level 2 legislation across Member States, aims to ensure best practices and a consistent regulatory approach is taken and to provide technical advice to the Level 2 process. The CESR is made up of regulators from the Member States, including representatives from the UK's FSA.

- **Level 4:** The European Commission, Member States and supervisory authorities work to ensure the implementation and enforcement of EU law.

The FSAP consists of 42 new legislative measures. Some of the more debated Directives are as follows.

- The **Market Abuse Directive** sought to harmonise rules on abusive practices, such as insider dealing and market manipulation, covered later in this chapter.

- The **Takeover Directive** aimed to harmonise the rules relating to takeovers within the EU. The experiences gleaned from the Takeover Directive are a very good example of political, cultural and economic divergence of views throughout the EU. Twelve versions of the Directive were tabled and rejected. In 2004 agreement was finally reached but in order to obtain agreement many important provisions (such as those relating to frustrating action) were made optional in order to reach a consensus. Thus the effectiveness of the Directive is questionable, as it does not truly harmonise EU takeover practices.

- The **Markets in Financial Instruments Directive (MiFID)**, sometimes known as **Investment Services Directive II (ISD II)**, has expanded the reach of cross-border investment activity, which was limited under the first Directive (see later). There were fierce debates about the ability of Multilateral Trading Facilities (MTFs) to passport due, in part, to some Member States wishing to maintain the dominant position of their domestic markets.

- The **Distance Marketing Directive** extended the requirement to provide cancellation rights and certain documentation to retail customers dealt with at a distance. Under the FSA's original rules, cancellation rights were only generally provided where private customers purchased packaged products such as life policies. Under the new Directive, cancellation rights and documentation must be provided in a wider range of cases such as for securities broking services provided at a distance. This required UK firms to significantly alter their documentation and cancellation procedures. These rules came into force in late 2004.

While the aims of Lamfalussy are to be applauded, the practicalities of creating a complete single market remain questionable. Arguably a large number of barriers have stood in the way of full and meaningful integration, including the following.

- Lack of proper implementation of Directives by some Member States

- Delay in implementation of Directives by some Member States

- Lack of real censures for non-compliant Member States

- Too great a focus on meeting the now out-of-date 2005 FSAP deadline rather than producing good legislation

- Lack of consumer desire to deal with foreign service providers

- Lack of integration of cross-border settlement and clearing services

- Lack of full coverage of the FSAP measures

- A protectionist attitude of some Member States to their domestic markets: for example, in some Member States, market-makers must still have a local presence

- Differences in law, language and culture throughout the EU

- Lack of a clear view as to what a single market might ultimately look like

However, there have been some positive achievements.

- All of the 42 FSAP measures have been adopted by the EU.

- The two committees (ESC and CESR) created by the Lamfalussy process have been largely a success. Indeed this committee structure has since been implemented in the sphere of banking and insurance regulation. In the sphere of banking regulation, the committees are called the European Banking Committee (EBC) and Committee of European Banking Regulators (CEBR) respectively.

More information on the FSAP is available at the FSA's website and at www.europa.eu.int.

2 MARKETS IN FINANCIAL INSTRUMENTS DIRECTIVE

2.1 Introduction

The **Markets in Financial Instruments Directive (MiFID)** was adopted by the European Council in April 2004 and is part of the European **Financial Services Action Plan**. MiFID was originally due for implementation in April 2006. However, due to the number of changes that MiFID requires the industry to make, the deadline was deferred twice, delaying its effective date until **1 November 2007**.

MiFID replaces the previous Investment Services Directive (ISD), and it applies to all **investment firms**, e.g. investment and retail banks, brokers, assets managers, securities and futures firms, securities issuers and hedge funds.

2.2 Implementation of MiFID

The MiFID **Level 1** Directive sets out a number of specific conduct of business 'principles' and a requirement that the European Commission impose more specific 'Level 2' requirements which flesh out the principles.

The MiFID **Level 2** Directive – similar to secondary legislation in the UK – was formally adopted in September 2006 and covers technical implementation measures in the form of **organisational requirements** and **operating conditions**. In addition, the European Commission aims to adopt 'Regulations' which deal with 'market' issues, e.g. transaction reporting and transparency, which will be directly applicable to the UK.

The provisions of the Level 1 and Level 2 Directives are being implemented in the UK through changes to UK law and FSA rules.

New regulation has been required on the basis of **'maximum harmonisation'**, which means that Member States should not be able to add rules of their own or make amendments to the original text, a process called **'gold plating'**. The FSA has been accused of 'gold plating' in the past whilst implementing other European Directives.

The European Commission and the Committee of European Securities Regulators (CESR) has been focusing more recently on the delivery of convergent implementation of the MiFID requirements across Member States – this is **Level 3**.

2.3 Passporting within the EEA

The idea of a **'passport'**, which already existed under the ISD, enables firms to use their domestic authorisation to operate not only in their **home state**, but also in other **host states** within the **European Economic Area** (EEA) (EU plus Norway, Iceland and Liechtenstein).

An important aspect of MiFID is that, to make cross-border business easier, the home country principle has been extended. Under MiFID, investment firms which carry out specified investment services and activities (a wider range than under the ISD, as detailed below) are authorised by the Member State in which they their registered office is located (the **home state**).

Where a **branch** is set up, **host state** rules will continue to apply. A **tied agent** established in the EEA will be able to act on behalf of a firm instead of the firm needing to set up a branch. (A **'tied agent'**, similarly to an **appointed representative** under FSMA 2000, acts on behalf of and under the authority of an investment firm and as a result does not require authorisation.)

Firms which have an **ISD** 'passport' should automatically be given a MiFID passport.

2.4 Scope of MiFID

MiFID applies to a specified range of 'core' **investment services and activities** in relation to specified categories of **financial instruments**, as summarised below.

- **Investment firms** are firms which provide such services or engage in such activities.

- Investment firms are also regulated in respect of various 'non-core' **ancillary services** they may provide (also listed below).

Investment services and activities

- Receiving and transmitting orders
- Execution of orders on behalf of clients
- Dealing on own account
- Managing portfolios on a discretionary basis
- Investment advice
- Underwriting of financial instruments
- Placing of financial instruments
- Operating a Multilateral Trading Facility (MTF)

Financial instruments covered by MiFID

- Transferable securities, e.g. shares and bonds

- Money market instruments

- Units in collective investment undertakings

- Derivatives relating to securities, currencies, interest rates and yields, financial indices and financial measures settled either physically or in cash, including: options, futures, swaps and forward rate agreements

- Commodity derivatives capable of being settled in cash, commodity derivatives capable of being physically settled on a regulated market or multilateral trading facility, and certain other commodity derivatives which are not for commercial purposes

- Derivative instruments for transferring credit risk

- Financial contracts for differences (CfDs)

- Derivatives relating to climatic variables, freight rates, emission allowances, inflation rates or other official economic statistics capable of being settled in cash

Ancillary services

- Safekeeping and administration of financial instruments, including: custodianship; collateral and cash management

- Granting credit or loans to an investor to enable him to carry out a transaction in which the firm is involved

- Advising undertakings on capital structure, industrial strategy

- Advising on mergers and acquisitions

- Foreign exchange services connected with providing investment services

- Investment research, financial analysis or other general recommendations relating to transactions in financial instruments

2.5 MiFID exclusions

Although MiFID has extended regulation beyond what was regulated under the ISD, there are a number of exclusions. These exclusions mean that a significant part of the retail financial services sector falls outside the scope of MiFID.

MiFID's overall scope is narrower than the UK regulatory regime. However, a UK exclusion (in the Regulated Activities Order) will not apply if it conflicts with MiFID.

The **exclusions** are as follows.

- MiFID applies to **EEA-domiciled firms** only. (However, the FSA rules extend MiFID requirements to **'MiFID equivalent activities of third country firms'**.)

- **Credit institutions** (banks and building societies, in the UK) are regulated instead by the Banking Consolidation Directive. However most MiFID provisions will apply to these institutions when they engage in activities within MiFID's scope.

- MiFID does not apply to **insurance companies**.

- MiFID does not apply to **collective investment schemes** nor to their managers, although UCITS managers who provide advice or discretionary management to clients who are not funds will generally be subject to MiFID requirements.

- MiFID **Article 3** allows Member States to **exclude** from MiFID the activities of firms whose investment services are limited to receiving and transmitting orders in transferable securities or collective investment schemes, plus related advice. Such firms may not hold client money or securities, nor put themselves in debit to the client. Orders must be transmitted only to investment firms, credit institutions, EEA-regulated collective investment schemes or closed-ended funds traded on a-regulated market in the EEA. Many firms of financial advisers and other retail investment product distributors will meet these criteria, and the UK has enabled them to be excluded from MiFID regulation. Such firms may alternatively opt in, in order to benefit from **passporting**.

2.6 The 'common platform'

The organisational and systems and controls requirements of **MiFID** and the **Capital Requirements Directive (CRD)** are being implemented through a single set of high level rules: this is known as the '**common platform**', since it applies to firms commonly, whichever of the Directives they are subject to.

- Firms subject to both **MiFID and CRD** include most banks and investment firms.

- Firms subject to **MiFID only** are those authorised to provide investment advice and/or receive and transmit orders without having permission to hold client money or securities.

- Firms subject to **CRD only** include banks that do not perform any investment services or other activities within the scope of MiFID.

The implementation of MiFID has led to the introduction of a new **Conduct of Business Sourcebook (COBS),** whose rules are shorter than the previous COB Sourcebook. Various other changes to the FSA Handbook have also been necessary.

2.7 Multilateral Trading Facilities and Systematic Internalisers

MiFID introduces the ability to passport **Multilateral Trading Facilities (MTFs)** as a 'core' investment service. MTFs are systems where firms provide services similar to those of exchanges by matching client orders. A firm taking proprietary positions with a client is not running an MTF. There has been debate about the requirements to be imposed on MTFs. The Committee of European Securities Regulators (CESR) has published standards they expect to be met by MTFs, including notifying the home state regulator of activities, fair and orderly trading, price transparency, clarity of systems and reduction of financial crime.

A **Systematic Internaliser** is an investment firm which deals on its own account by executing client orders outside a regulated market or a MTF. MiFID will require such firms to publish firm quotes in liquid shares (for orders below 'standard market size') and to maintain those quotes on a regular and continuous basis during normal business hours.

3 OTHER EU DIRECTIVES

3.1 Capital Requirements Directive

3.1.1 Overview

The overall aim of capital requirements rules is to ensure that firms remain solvent by having greater assets at their command than they will need to cover their positions. In general, a firm must maintain, at all times, financial resources in excess of its financial resources requirement.

As a result of the implementation of the Capital Adequacy Directive (CAD), the FSA rules have incorporated two distinct sets of rules relating to capital adequacy, found in the **Interim Prudential Sourcebook (IPRU)** of the FSA Handbook.

Before 1 January 2007, the **Interim Prudential Sourcebook for Investment Businesses (IPRU (INV))** was the part of the Handbook that dealt with capital requirements for investment firms subject to the position risk requirements of the previous version of the Capital Adequacy Directive. Now, however, investment firms which are subject to the risk-based capital requirements of the Capital Adequacy Directive are subject to the **General Prudential sourcebook (GENPRU)** and the **Prudential sourcebook for Banks, Building Societies and Investment Firms (BIPRU)**.

3.1.2 Basel II and the Capital Requirements Directive

The UK financial resources requirements are based on the Basel Capital Accord known as '**Basel II**'. Basel II is implemented in the European Union via the **Capital Requirements Directive (CRD)** for credit institutions and investment firms. It directly affects banks, building societies and certain types of investment firm in the UK. CRD amends the two existing directives: the **Capital Adequacy Directive (CAD)** and the **Banking Consolidation Directive (BCD)**.

The **Basel Committee on Banking Supervision** does not have legal powers but creates common standards and guidelines of best practice with the aim that individual states will implement these in their own law. The Committee has tried to reduce divergences in international supervisory standards. They seek to ensure that all foreign banking establishments are actually supervised by someone and that supervision is adequate.

The revised Basel Capital Accord, referred to as Basel II (the full formal title is *International convergence of capital measurement and capital standards - a revised framework*), is reflected in EU law via the **Capital Requirements Directive** whose implementation date was 1 January 2007.

3.1.3 Key aspects of Basel II

Basel II is a revision of the existing prudential framework and aims to make the framework more risk-sensitive and more representative of modern banks' risk management practices. The new framework aims to leave the overall level of capital held by banks collectively broadly unchanged.

The **capital adequacy framework** is intended to reduce the probability of consumer loss or market disruption as a result of prudential failure. It does so by seeking to ensure that the financial resources held by a firm are commensurate with the risks associated with the business profile and the control environment within the firm.

3.1.4 The three pillars

The framework consists of three '**pillars**'.

- **Pillar 1** sets out the minimum capital requirements firms will be required to meet for credit, market and operational risk. There is a two-stage process to determine a firm's minimum capital requirement reflecting market, credit and operational risk. The first stage involves assessing the category of the firm. The second stage is to establish the method for calculating the minimum capital requirement.

- **Pillar 2:** firms and FSA supervisors have to take a view on whether a firm should hold additional capital against risks not covered in Pillar 1 and must take action accordingly. Under Pillar 2 a firm will, amongst other things, have to assess regularly the amount of internal capital it considers adequate to cover all of the risks to which it is exposed within the context of its overall risk management framework. BIPRU provides guidance on some of those risks.

- **Pillar 3** aims to improve market discipline by requiring firms to publish certain details of their risks, capital and risk management. This is intended to allow market participants to assess key pieces of information on a firm's capital, risk exposures and risk assessment processes.

3.2 Electronic Commerce Directive

3.2.1 Purpose and scope

The Electronic Commerce Directive has been implemented in the UK and aims to provide freedom for EEA firms to carry out Electronic Commerce Activity (ECA) freely into other EEA states. The Directive simplified previous rules so that an EEA firm doing ECA generally only has to comply with its **home state** conduct of business rules, therefore introducing a **country of origin** approach to regulation.

Electronic Commerce Activity (ECA) is defined as any electronic financial service which would be a regulated activity if it were provided by non-electronic means, e.g. the provision of electronic broking services.

The rules apply to three types of ECA provider:

- Incoming
- Outgoing
- Domestic

3.2.2 Incoming ECA providers

An **incoming ECA provider** is an EEA firm (other than a UK firm) carrying out ECA with or for a UK consumer. This would, for example, cover a French firm providing ECA to a UK consumer.

An incoming ECA provider has to comply with the applicable laws in the country of origin (home state) from which the service is provided, e.g. France, and not FSMA 2000 or the FSA Handbook.

This makes it easier for firms to provide cross-border services, but the general rule is subject to certain derogations. These derogations would allow the host State, in our example the UK, to impose certain 'host State' (i.e. UK) requirements. These derogations are allowed as the host state has continuing responsibility for consumer protection and include requirements to provide basic terms and conditions in English. Therefore subject to certain derogations set out in FSA regulations, the FSA Handbook and FSMA 2000 do not apply to incoming ECA providers.

3.2.3 Outgoing ECA providers

An **outgoing ECA provider** is one which carries on electronic commerce activity with an EEA recipient (other than a UK recipient) from a UK establishment, whether or not the recipient is a consumer. This would, for example, cover a UK firm providing ECA to a French consumer.

There are minimum information requirements on outgoing ECA providers such as information about the firm. These requirements are in addition to the requirements otherwise applicable to firms when they carry on regulated activities in the UK as set out in FSMA 2000 and the FSA Handbook, e.g. conduct of business rules.

The electronic commerce rules relate to all regulated firms in relation to a financial promotion which is an outgoing electronic commerce communication. An outgoing electronic commerce communication is one which is made from an establishment in the United Kingdom to a person in an EEA State (other than the UK). This would, for example, cover a UK firm marketing their services to a French consumer. The rules require the firm to comply with Chapter 4 of the Conduct of Business (COB) rules on financial promotions as if the person to whom the communication is made or directed was in the UK.

3.2.4 Domestic ECA providers

From the UK perspective, a **domestic ECA provider** is an FSA-authorised firm which provides ECA from an establishment which it has in the United Kingdom, with or for a UK recipient or a recipient outside the EEA. This would, for example, cover a UK firm providing ECA to a UK or a Canadian consumer.

In the first scenario, not surprisingly, UK rules apply to the relationship. In the second scenario, the UK firm would have to comply with Canadian rules as the recipient is not in the EEA. So the rules revert to a 'host State' position. However, as well as considering the host state rules, the UK firm is required to supply certain minimum information requirements to the ECA recipient regardless of the recipient's location.

3.3 EU provisions on collective investment schemes

3.3.1 UCITS Directives

The EU has enacted a number of Directives relevant to collective investment schemes. These are known as the **UCITS Directives**. **UCITS** stands for **Undertakings for Collective Investment in Transferable Securities**.

The aim of UCITS was to create a type of passport throughout the EEA for collective investment schemes that meet the UCITS criteria. The idea was to promote the free movement of services in the same way as the ISD allows investment firms to passport their services throughout the EEA.

The CIS must be authorised in its home State and receive confirmation from its home State regulator that the CIS complies with UCITS criteria. That confirmation is then provided to the host State regulator, who the fund manager notifies that they wish to market the fund in that EEA state. Although UCITS aims to make cross-border sales of CIS easier, the CIS must comply with the marketing rules of the host state and the documentation requirements of the Directive.

UCITS was updated in 2002 by the **UCITS III Product Directive,** which expanded the range of assets which UCITS funds are able to invest. It also made provision for a single UCITS scheme to replace all of the previous categories of fund which had separate rules.

3.3.2 UCITS schemes

As a result of the **UCITS Product Directive**, UCITS schemes are able to invest in the following types of **permitted investment**.

- Transferable securities (see below)
- Money market instruments
- Forward contracts and financial derivatives
- Deposits
- Units in other Collective Investment Schemes

Transferable securities comprise of shares, instruments creating or acknowledging indebtedness (e.g. debentures, loan stock, bonds, government and public securities) and certificates representing certain securities.

Although **commodity derivatives** are excluded, it would appear that derivatives based on commodity indices could be eligible as financial derivatives.

3.3.3 UCITS and non-UCITS schemes

Under FSA Handbook (COLL) rules, both UCITS and non-UCITS retail schemes can invest in a variety of types of instrument, including warrants and financial derivatives, within their overall investment objectives, provided that they apply a risk management procedure. A non-UCITS retail scheme can invest in an even wider range of assets, including gold or 100% investment in immovable property.

Non-UCITS schemes may also **borrow** up to 10% of the fund value on a **permanent** basis, while UCITS retail schemes are only permitted to borrow on a **temporary** basis, again to 10% of the fund value.

3.4 European Savings Directive

The main aim of the EU Savings Directive is to **reduce tax evasion** by allowing EU Member State tax authorities to easily identify whether taxpayers have not reported savings income that they have received. This Directive requires EU Member States to exchange information automatically on the financial affairs of residents of other EU countries, or to levy a withholding tax.

The home state tax authority then has the obligation to share this information with the taxpayer's local tax authority – known as '**automatic exchange of information**'. This enables each Member State's tax authority to be able to check that the correct amount of tax has been paid.

The European Savings Directive affects EU citizens who hold investments offshore within the EU, or in Switzerland, a country that remains outside the EU and has been well known for having a banking system offering high levels of secrecy to account holders.

Two different mechanisms came into effect on 1 July 2005.

- There is **automatic exchange of information** between respective tax authorities, For most EU countries, including the UK. Information about payment of savings income is required to be reported by **paying agents** (such as banks/building societies and bond issuers paying interest to bondholders) to their own home state tax authority.

- Switzerland together with the three EU members Belgium, Luxembourg and Austria have instead introduced a **withholding tax** on cross-border interest payments via banks and paying agents responsible for crediting interest. The tax retained will increase in steps from 15% in 2005 to 20% in 2008 and 35% in 2011.

The rules do not cover interest payments originating outside the EU and Switzerland, and they cover individuals but not **legal entities**.

The Directive covers bank accounts, interest bearing investments including investment funds whose assets are made up of at least 40% of bonds, money market instruments, government securities or corporate debt. Investments that pay a dividend or capital gains, such as shares, are currently exempt.

3.5 The Prospectus Directive and cross-border prospectuses

The **Prospectus Directive** is an EU Directive which came into force in December 2003. It was implemented in the UK with effect from 1 July 2005 by the Prospectus Regulations 2005, which amended Part IV FSMA 2000, and by the Prospectus Rules in the FSA Handbook.

The Directive requires that a prospectus is produced whenever there is a public offer of securities or where securities are admitted to trading on a regulated market. The Directive specifies the content of prospectuses and requires that they are approved by the relevant **competent authority** – in the UK, this is the **FSA**.

These requirements are designed to increase protection of investors by ensuring the quality of prospectuses and to enhance international market efficiency through the issue of single approved prospectuses for use throughout the EEA.

The Directive identifies two types of situation where prospectuses are required:

- An offer of securities to the general public
- Admission of securities to trading on a regulated market

Under the Prospectus Directive, there is a **'single passport'** for issuers, with the result that a prospectus approved by one competent authority can be used across the EEA without any further approval or burdensome administrative procedures in other Member States. If the competent authority in the relevant Member State approves the prospectus, it will be accepted throughout the EEA.

A prospectus is required on admission of a company's transferable securities to a **regulated market** in the EEA: the London Stock Exchange is such a regulated market.

London's **Alternative Investment Market (AIM)** was deregulated in October 2004, and there are some exemptions which may apply to AIM IPOs (Initial Public Offers), takeovers and fund raising.

The overall position is that a prospectus is required in the case of an offer of transferable securities to the public in the EEA, unless an exemption applies. An 'offer' is defined broadly and covers any communication in any form and by any means which presents sufficient information about the terms of the offer and the securities offered such as to enable an investor to decide to buy or subscribe to those securities.

The main **exemptions** are as follows.

- Offers made only to qualified investors, which includes regulated institutions and investment companies, as well as some UK-resident persons and small and medium-sized enterprises who meet specified criteria and are registered as qualified investors with the FSA

- Cases where the total consideration for the offer over a 12-month period is less than €2,900,000

- Offers made to fewer than 100 persons per EEA state other than qualified investors

- Documents where securities are offered in connection with a takeover or merger, if they contain information similar to that in a prospectus: such documents will not require formal approval

4 MARKET MANIPULATION

4.1 The offence

Section 397 FSMA 2000 makes it a criminal offence to manipulate a market (usually by misleading the market).

The offences in s397 FSMA 2000 apply to natural as well as legal persons, so an individual, company or authorised firm could be guilty of the offences. The provisions of s397 are summarised below.

Section 397 (1), (2)

Any person who:

- Dishonestly or recklessly makes a **statement, promise or forecast** that is misleading, false or deceptive, **or**

- Dishonestly **conceals** any material facts

is guilty of an offence if he makes the statement, promise or forecast or conceals the facts for the purpose of inducing (or is reckless as to whether he may induce) another person to enter into an **investment agreement**.

In the context of this section of FSMA 2000, it does not matter whether the individual who entered into the investment agreement was the person to whom the statement was made, merely the act of making the statement is an offence.

Section 397 (3)

This offence covers any person who commits any act, or engages in any **course of conduct**, which creates a false or misleading impression as to the market in, or the price or value of, any investment. They will be guilty of the offence if their conduct is for the purpose of creating an impression and thereby inducing another person to acquire, dispose of, subscribe for or underwrite those investments or refrain from any such act.

4.2 Securities covered

Section 397 FSMA 2000 covers any '**relevant investment**'. This means all specified investments as defined in the Regulated Activities Order (as amended from time to time).

4.3 Defences

There are **general defences** to s397 to cover acts done in accordance with UK, Japanese, Hong Kong or US price stabilisation rules.

Regarding **misleading conduct and practices**, an acceptable defence would also be that the individual **reasonably believed** that their act or conduct would not create an impression that was false or misleading.

4.4 Territorial scope and sanctions

The s397 offences do not apply unless one of the following applies.

- The statement, promise or forecast is made, or the facts concealed, in or from, the UK
- The person on whom the inducement is intended to, or may have effect on, is from the UK
- The agreement is or would be entered into, or the rights are or would be exercised, in the UK
- The act or course of conduct is conducted in the UK
- The false or misleading impression is created in the UK

Note that there is no requirement for the recipient to have **acted** in line with the inducement, merely that the statement was made or the practice undertaken.

Section 397 is a **criminal offence** and the penalties available depend on the method of prosecution.

- **Magistrates' Court** – maximum of six months' imprisonment and a £5,000 fine
- **Crown Court** – maximum of seven years' imprisonment and an unlimited fine

There are no automatic civil sanctions contained in s397. In addition, no contract is automatically void or unenforceable by reason only that it is the result of a breach of s397.

5 INSIDER DEALING

5.1 Introduction

Insider dealing is the offence of acting with information that is not freely and openly available to all other participants in the market place. This became an offence in 1980 but the current legislation making it a criminal offence is found in **Part V** of the **Criminal Justice Act 1993**.

The Act makes it a **criminal offence** for connected persons who receive inside information to act on that information.

The legislation (Schedule 2) covers the following instruments.

- Shares
- Debt securities issued by the private or public sector
- Warrants
- Depository Receipts
- Options, futures or contracts for difference on any of the above

5.2 Insider

An insider is defined under CJA 1993 as an individual who has **information** in his possession that he **knows** is **inside information** and **knows** is from an **inside source**.

Inside information in this context refers to **unpublished price-sensitive information** that is **specific or precise** and **relates to a security or its issuer**.

What is **published** information? The following information is deemed to be 'published'.

- Information published via a regulated market, e.g. an RIE
- Information contained in public records
- Information which can otherwise be readily acquired by market users, e.g. in the financial press
- Information derived from public information
- Information which can only be acquired by expertise or by payment of a fee
- Information which is published only to a section of the public, rather than the public in general, or published outside the UK
- Information which can be acquired by observation, e.g. a factory burning down

An inside source is **an individual** and would include a **director, employee** or **shareholder** of an issuer of securities or a person having access to the information by virtue of their employment, office or profession.

A person will also be an inside source if he receives the information directly or indirectly from one of the above and satisfies the general definition above.

5.3 Offences

If a person satisfies the definition of an insider, it is an offence for that person to:

- **Deal** in the affected securities either on a regulated market or through a professional intermediary
- **Encourage another** person to deal with reasonable cause to believe that dealing would take place on a regulated market or through a professional intermediary
- **Disclose the information** to another person other than in the proper performance of their duties

5.4 General defences

An individual is not guilty of insider **dealing** if he can show that:

- He did not, at the time, expect the dealing to result in a profit attributable to the fact that the information was price sensitive

- At the time, he believed on reasonable grounds that the information had been disclosed widely enough to ensure that none of those taking part in the dealing would be prejudiced by not having the information

- He would have done what he did even if he had not had the information

A similar series of defences are available to the charge of **encouraging** another to deal in price-affected securities.

An individual is not guilty of insider dealing by virtue of a **disclosure** of information if he shows that:

- He did not, at the time, expect any person, because of the disclosure, to deal in securities either through a regulated market or via a professional intermediary

- Although he had such an expectation at the time, he did not expect the dealing to result in a profit attributable to the fact that the information was price sensitive in relation to the securities

5.5 Special defences

5.5.1 Market makers

A market maker is a person who holds himself out at all normal times in compliance with the rules of a RIE as willing to acquire or dispose of securities and is required to do so under those rules. An individual is not guilty of insider dealing by virtue of dealing in securities or encouraging another to deal if he can show that he acted in **good faith** in the course of market making.

5.5.2 Market information

An individual is not guilty of an offence under the Act if he can show that the information which he had as an insider was **market information** (information concerning transactions in securities that either have been or are about to be undertaken) and that it was reasonable for an individual in his position to have acted in that manner when in possession of inside information. Consideration will be taken as to the content of the information, the circumstances of receiving the information and the capacity in which the recipient acts, to determine whether it is reasonable.

This defence will also cover the **facilitation of takeover bids**.

5.5.3 Price stabilisation

An individual is not guilty of an offence under the Act by virtue of dealing in securities or encouraging another person to deal if he can show that he acted in conformity with the **price stabilisation rules**.

5.6 Prosecution by the FSA

The FSA has powers under s401 and s402 FSMA 2000 to prosecute a range of criminal offences, including **insider dealing**, in England, Wales and Northern Ireland.

While the Department of Business, Enterprise and Regulatory Reform (formerly the Department of Trade and Industry) retain their powers to prosecute, since 2001 the **FSA** will now normally prosecute insider dealing. Accordingly, the London Stock Exchange (as the person who often initiates an investigation) will pass information directly to the FSA.

5.7 The Model Code on Directors' Dealings

In addition to the formal regulation of insider dealing through statute, the FSA, in its role as the **UK Listing Authority (UKLA)**, imposes additional regulations on directors of listed companies in the form of the **Model Code**, which appears as an Annex to the Listing Rules.

The purpose of the Model Code is to maintain confidence in the markets by ensuring directors and others with senior management responsibilities are acting in the best interests of the company as a whole and its shareholders. This is as required by directors' fiduciary obligations. The Model Code is not part of the law and breach of the Code does not constitute a criminal offence.

Main provisions of the Model Code affecting directors

- Directors must not deal in securities in their own company nor any contract for difference or other contract designed to make a profit or loss in movements in the price of the company's securities, without seeking **approval** from a senior member of the board, usually the Chairman. If the Chairman or Chief Executive wish to deal, they should seek approval from each other.

- Directors' deals should not be made for the **short term.**

- No trades should be undertaken in the 60 days before publication of the annual report or, if shorter, the period from the end of the financial year up to publication. This is known as a **close period**. The close period before publication of the half-yearly report is from the end of the six-month period up to publication. For quarterly results, the close period is one month prior to the announcement. If, as provided by the **Disclosure and Transparency Rules**, Interim Management Statements are issued instead of quarterly reports, there is no close period and companies must exercise discretion.

A breach of the Model Code will result in disciplinary action being taken by the UKLA. This action may be taken against the individual or the company.

6 MARKET ABUSE

6.1 Introduction

Market abuse is a **civil offence** under **s118 FSMA 2000,** which provides an alternative civil regime for enforcing the criminal prohibitions on insider dealing and misleading statements/practices.

The UK market abuse rules conform with the **EU Market Abuse Directive**.

The **territorial scope** of market abuse is very wide. It covers everyone, not just authorised firms and approved persons. Firms or persons outside the UK are also covered by the offence.

As market abuse is a **civil offence**, the FSA must prove, on the balance of probabilities, that a person:

- Engaged in market abuse, or
- By taking or refraining from action, required or encouraged another person to engage in market abuse

As shown in the following diagram, there are seven types of behaviour that can amount to market abuse.

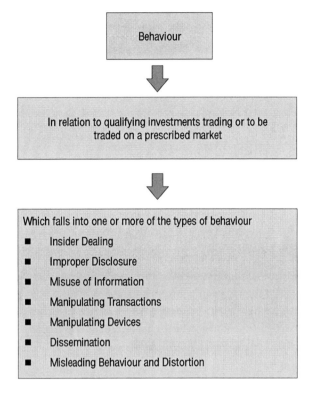

6.2 Requiring and encouraging

Section 123(1)(b) FSMA 2000 allows the FSA to impose penalties on a person who, by taking or refraining from taking any action, has required or encouraged another person or persons to engage in behaviour, which if engaged in by A, would amount to market abuse.

The following are **examples** of behaviour that might fall within the scope of section 123(1)(b).

- A director of a company, while in possession of inside information, instructs an employee of that company to deal in qualifying investments or related investments in respect of which the information is inside information. (This could amount to **requiring**.)

- A person recommends or advises a friend to engage in behaviour which, if he himself engaged in it, would amount to market abuse. (This could be **encouraging** market abuse.)

6.3 The regular market user test

A regular user is a **hypothetical reasonable person** who regularly deals on that market in investments of the kind in question. The **regular market user test** then determines in light of the circumstances whether an offence has been committed.

Since the implementation of the Market Abuse Directive, the regular market user is only used to determine whether market abuse has occurred in relation to the behaviours 'Misuse of Information', 'Misleading Behaviour' and 'Distortion'.

Therefore, the regular market user decides:

- Whether information that is not generally available would be relevant when deciding which transactions in qualifying investments or related investments should be undertaken, and

- Whether behaviour is below the expected standard, or creates a false or misleading impression or distorts the market

6.4 Qualifying investments and prescribed markets

Behaviour will only constitute market abuse if it occurs **in the UK or in relation to qualifying investments traded on a prescribed market**. The term 'behaviour' is specifically mentioned as the offence of market abuse can cover both action and inaction.

A **prescribed market** means any UK RIE, and any regulated market. **Qualifying investment** thus means any investment traded on a UK RIE or a regulated market. **Regulated markets** comprise the main EEA exchanges.

The definition of prescribed market and qualifying investment are amended slightly with reference to the offences of '**Misuse of Information**', '**Misleading Behaviour**' and '**Distortion**'. Here, a prescribed market means any UK RIE. Qualifying investment thus means any investment traded on a UK RIE. Therefore, these offences are only relevant to the UK markets.

In addition, the rules confirm that a prescribed market accessible electronically in the UK would be treated as operating in the UK.

As behaviour must be **in relation to** qualifying investments, the regime is not limited to on-market dealings. A transaction in an OTC (Over The Counter) derivative contract on a traded security or commodity would be covered by the regime. In addition, abusive trades on foreign exchanges could constitute market abuse if the underlying instrument also trades on a prescribed market. This makes the regime much wider than the criminal law offences.

6.5 The definition of market abuse

Market abuse is behaviour, whether by one person alone or by two or more persons jointly or in concert, which occurs in relation to:

- Qualifying investments admitted to trading on a prescribed market, or

- Qualifying investments in respect of which a request for admission to trading on a prescribed market has been made, or

- Related investments of a qualifying investment (strictly, this is only relevant to the offences of 'Insider Dealing' and 'Improper Disclosure' – see below)

and falls within one or more of the offences below.

6.6 The seven types of market abuse offence

The seven types of behaviour that can constitute market abuse are as follows.

1   **Insider Dealing**. This is where an insider deals, or attempts to deal, in a qualifying investment or related investment on the basis of **inside information**.

2   **Improper Disclosure**. This is where an insider discloses **inside information** to another person otherwise than in the proper course of the exercise of his employment, profession or duties.

3   **Misuse of Information**. This fills gaps in '1' or '2' above and is where the behaviour is

   –   Based on information which is not generally available to those using the market but which, if available to a regular user of the market, would be regarded by him as relevant when deciding the terms on which transactions in qualifying investments should be effected, and

   –   Likely to be regarded by a regular user of the market as a failure on the part of the person concerned to observe the standard of behaviour reasonably expected of a person in his position.

4   **Manipulating Transactions**. This consists of effecting transactions or orders to trade (otherwise than for legitimate reasons and in conformity with accepted market practices) which

–   Give, or are likely to give a false or misleading impression as to the supply, demand or price of one or more qualifying investments, or

–   Secure the price of one or more such investments at an abnormal or artificial level.

5   **Manipulating Devices**. This consists of effecting transactions or orders to trade which employ fictitious devices or any other form of deception.

6   **Dissemination**. This consists of the dissemination of information by any means which gives, or is likely to give, a false or misleading impression as to a qualifying investment by a person who knew or could reasonably be expected to have known that the information was false or misleading.

7   **Misleading Behaviour** and **Distortion**. This fills any gaps in '4', '5' and '6' above and is where the behaviour

–   Is likely to give a regular user of the market a false or misleading impression as to the supply of, demand for, or price or value of, qualifying investments, or

–   Would be regarded by a regular user of the market as behaviour that would distort the market in such an investment and is likely to be regarded by a regular user of the market as a failure on the part of the person concerned to observe the standard of behaviour reasonably expected of a person in his position.

6.7 Intention

The market abuse regime is **effects based** rather than 'intent based'. Thus, whether the perpetrator intended to abuse the market is largely irrelevant – the key question is whether the action **did** abuse the market.

6.8 Code of Market Conduct

While the law is set out in FSMA, the FSA also has a duty to draft a **Code of Market Conduct**.

The main provisions of the Code of Market Conduct are that it sets out:

■   Descriptions of behaviour that, in the opinion of the FSA, do or do not amount to market abuse. Descriptions of behaviour which do not amount to market abuse are called '**safe harbours**'

■   Descriptions of behaviour that are or are not **accepted market practices** in relation to one or more identified markets

■   Factors that, in the opinion of the FSA, are to be taken into account in determining whether or not behaviour amounts to market abuse

The Code does not exhaustively describe all types of behaviour that may or may not amount to market abuse.

6.9 Enforcement and penalties

The FSA may impose one or more of the following **penalties** on those found to have committed market abuse.

■   An unlimited **fine**

■   Issue a **public statement**

■   Apply to the court to seek an **injunction** or **restitution order**

- ■ Where an authorised/approved person is guilty of market abuse, they will also be guilty of a breach of the FSA's Principles and they could, in addition to the above penalties, have disciplinary proceedings brought against them, which may result in withdrawal of authorisation/approval.

The case of Paul Davidson ('The Plumber') has led to change in perceptions about how market abuse may be treated. The current position is that a **civil standard of proof** (on the balance of probabilities) of the appropriate degree can still be used by the FSA in market abuse cases. However, even when the punishment (in accordance with s123 FSMA 2000) is treated as **civil** for domestic law purposes, market abuse is a **criminal** charge (with a standard of proof 'beyond reasonable doubt') for the purposes of the European Convention on Human Rights, and someone committing it is subject to possible criminal prosecution.

In addition to being able to impose penalties for market abuse, the FSA is given criminal prosecution powers to enforce insider dealing and s397. The FSA has indicated that it will not pursue both the civil and criminal regime. In terms of the enforcement process for market abuse, this is the same as FSA's disciplinary process.

6.10 Safe harbours

If a person is within one of the **safe harbours** set out in the **Code of Market Conduct** they are not committing market abuse. These are indicated by the letter **C** in the Handbook.

Generally, there are no rules in the Takeover Code that permit or require a person to behave in a way which amounts to market abuse.

However, the following rules provide a **safe harbour** meaning that behaviour conforming with that rule does not amount to market abuse.

6.10.1 FSA rules

Behaviour caused by the proper operation of a Chinese wall or behaviour that relates to the timing, dissemination or content to a disclosure under the Listing Rules will not amount to market abuse.

6.10.2 Takeover Code

Behaviour conforming with any of the rules of the Takeover Code about the timing, dissemination or content of a disclosure does not, of itself, amount to market abuse. This is subject to the behaviour being expressly required or permitted by a rule and provided it conforms to the General Principles of the Takeover Code.

6.10.3 Buy-back programmes and stabilisation

Behaviour which conforms with the **Buy-Back and Stabilisation Regulation** (in the Market Conduct Sourcebook of the FSA's Handbook) will not amount to market abuse.

However, buy-back programmes which do not follow the Buy-Back and Stabilisation Regulation are not automatically seen as market abuse, but do not have an automatic safe harbour.

6.11 Due diligence defence

Under section 123 FSMA 2000, the FSA may not impose a financial penalty in relation to market abuse where it is satisfied that the person believed, on reasonable grounds, that his behaviour did not amount to market abuse or he took all reasonable precautions and exercised all **due diligence** to avoid engaging in market abuse.

6.12 Notification of suspicious transactions by firms

The FSA's Supervision manual (**SUP**) stipulates that an authorised **firm** which:

- Arranges or executes a transaction with or for a client in a qualifying investment admitted to trading on a prescribed market, and

- Has reasonable grounds to suspect that the transaction might constitute market abuse

must **notify the FSA** without delay.

7 MONEY LAUNDERING

7.1 Introduction

Money laundering is the process by which money and other property from criminal conduct is made to appear legally derived. By a variety of methods, the nature, source and ownership of those criminal proceeds are concealed.

Criminal conduct is any crime that constitutes an offence in the UK, or any act abroad that would constitute an offence if it had occurred in the UK.

Property is criminal property if it constitutes a person's benefit from criminal conduct and the alleged offender knows or suspects that it constitutes this benefit.

This means that UK Money Laundering legislation applies to the proceeds of all crimes no matter how small.

The three stages of money laundering can be broken down as follows.

- **Placement** – the investment of the proceeds of criminal activity
- **Layering** – the mingling of the money from an illegal source with that from a legitimate source
- **Integration** – the withdrawal and usage of the now undetectable proceeds of criminal activity

The consequence is that the origin of and entitlement to the money are disguised and the money can again be used to benefit the criminal and/or his associates.

In recognition of the scale and impact of money laundering internationally various national governments have in recent years collaborated on an international scale to combat money laundering. Action taken has concentrated not only on the law enforcement process but also on recommendations to banks and financial institutions to put in place practices and procedures which will assist in the detection of money laundering activity.

7.2 Money Laundering Directives

In 1991, the European Union adopted Council Directive 91/308 on prevention of the use of the financial system for the purpose of money laundering. This Directive was implemented by all Member States. The **European Union Money Laundering Directive** stipulates that EU Member States should ensure that all financial and credit institutions located within the national Member States should implement certain **internal procedures** and controls and also ensure that it is a **criminal offence** for individuals to assist money laundering.

In 2001, a **second EU Money Laundering Directive** was adopted to cure some of the deficiencies in the first Directive. A **third EU Money Laundering Directive** was implemented in **15 December 2007**.

In the UK, the requirements have been implemented by passing the Money Laundering Regulations (MLR) 1993, 2001, 2003 and – the Regulations that now apply – MLR 2007. MLR 2007 implements the third ML Directive.

The aims of those internal procedures are threefold.

- **Deterrence** – to prevent credit and financial institutions being used for money laundering purposes

- **Co-operation** – to ensure that there is co-operation between credit and financial institutions and law enforcement agencies

- **Detection** – to establish customer identification and record-keeping procedures within all financial and credit institutions that will assist the law enforcement agencies in detecting, tracing and prosecuting money launderers

The main changes brought about by the Third Directive are as follows.

- The term **'occasional transaction'** (with a monetary limit) is now used, instead of 'one-off' transaction as in the earlier Regulations, but such transactions are excluded from the Regulations altogether

- A **risk-based approach** is now mandatory, in respect of risk management generally, and in applying customer due diligence

- There is detailed coverage of **customer due diligence** in the 2007 Regulations, with substantial guidance on how firms should meet their obligation of identifying customers, and mandatory monitoring of customer relationships

- There is **enhanced** due diligence on a **risk-sensitive basis**, including for 'politically exposed persons' ('PEPs')

- There is additional scope for **relying on other appropriately qualified regulated firms**, although the 'relying firm' retains ultimate responsibility for meeting the obligations under the Regulations

7.3 'Know Your Customer' (KYC)

Firms are expected to 'know their customers'. **Know Your Customer (KYC)** requirements:

- Help the firm, at the time customer due diligence is carried out, to be reasonably satisfied that customers are who they say they are, to know whether they are acting on behalf of others, whether there are any government sanctions against serving the customer, and

- Assist law enforcement with information on customers or activities under investigation.

Anti-money laundering (AML) /counter-terrorism financing (CTF) procedures provide that, based on an **assessment of the money laundering / terrorist financing risk** that each customer presents, the firm will need to:

- **Verify the customer's identity (ID)** – determining exactly who the customer is

- **Collect additional 'KYC' information**, and keep such information **current and valid** – to understand the customer's circumstances and business, and (where appropriate) the sources of funds or wealth, or the purpose of specific transactions

Thus, not only does the institution need to verify identity, but it should also establish the nature of the business to be undertaken. The **additional KYC information** to be obtained at the **start of a customer relationship** could include:

- Purpose/reason for establishing relationship
- Anticipated nature and level of activity
- Relationships of signatories and underlying beneficial owners
- Expected origin of funds

The firm will need to exercise judgement as to what is required in the circumstances. KYC information could be crucial in determining whether a pattern of activity or trade is suspicious.

Regulators focus on KYC because:

- The FSA has **statutory objectives** of maintaining confidence in the financial system and preventing financial crime, and focusing on KYC helps meet these objectives

- **Acts of terrorism** have brought a fresh impetus to the task of detecting crime through the financial system

- There is increased legislation on risks, business methods and products (such as **FSMA 2000** and the legislation on the proceeds of crime and money laundering)

Exam tip

> In the Summer 2006 *Global Operations Management* exam, a 25-mark Section B question was based around the topic of KYC. The scenario was that, in the Accounts Opening Section, a Supervisor has identified that the KYC procedures has potentially been circumvented in the Accounts Opening Section of an organisation.
>
> The question asked: what are the personal implications and what should the Supervisor do? What measures does a firm need to consider implementing, to ensure that it is fully compliant with anti-money laundering legislation? And: why is KYC a particular focus of the regulators?

7.4 Individual liability – Proceeds of Crime Act 2002

The Money Laundering Directives have required that there be legislation applicable to individuals. The **Proceeds of Crime Act 2002 (POCA 2002)** consolidated and updated the original money laundering requirements which applied to individuals and is now the main legislation covering individual liability.

The three main offences under POCA 2002

- Assistance
- Failure to report
- Tipping off

7.4.1 Assistance (POCA S327, S328, S329)

The offence

If any person knowingly helps another person to launder the proceeds of criminal conduct, he or she will be committing an offence. This covers obtaining, concealing, disguising, transferring, acquiring, possessing, investing or using the proceeds of crime. The legislation historically covered the laundering of the proceeds of **serious crime**, however as a result of the POCA it now covers the proceeds of **all crimes**, no matter how small. This could include evasion of tax.

The possible defences

- It is a defence to the above offence that a person **disclosed** his knowledge or belief concerning the origins of the property either to the police or to the appropriate officer in his firm.

- Under changes made by the **Serious Organised Crime and Police Act 2005 (SOCPA)**, there may also be a defence if the person knew or believed on reasonable grounds that the relevant criminal conduct occurred outside the UK and the conduct was not at the time unlawful in the overseas jurisdiction.

The penalty

The maximum penalties for any offence of assisting a money launderer are **14 years' imprisonment and/or an unlimited fine**.

7.4.2 Failure to report (ss330–332 POCA 2002)

The offence

If a person discovers information during the course of his employment that makes him **believe or suspect** money laundering is occurring, he must inform the police or the appropriate officer (usually the Money Laundering Reporting Officer (MLRO)) of the firm as soon as possible. If he fails to make the report as soon as is reasonably practicable, he commits a criminal offence.

For those working in the **regulated sector** (for an authorised firm), this offence covers not only where the person had actual suspicion of laundering (i.e. subjective suspicions) but also where there were **reasonable grounds for being suspicious**. The grounds are when a hypothetical **reasonable person** would in the circumstances have been suspicious (i.e. **objective suspicions**).

The possible defences

The only defences to this charge are if a person charged can prove one of the following.

- He had a **reasonable excuse** for failing to disclose this information. Whether an excuse is reasonable will depend on the circumstances of the case, but it is noteworthy that the person charged has the burden of proving that he had a reasonable excuse for his failure to disclose.

- Where the person had no subjective suspicion but is deemed to have objective suspicions, they had not been provided by their employer with appropriate **training** to recognise and report suspicions.

- Under changes made by the Serious Organised Crime and Police Act 2005 (SOCPA), there may also be a defence if the person knew or believed on reasonable grounds that the relevant criminal conduct occurred outside the UK and the conduct was not at the time unlawful in the overseas jurisdiction.

The relevant legislation specifically provides that any person making a disclosure of this kind will not be in breach of any **duty of confidentiality** owed to a customer.

The penalty

This offence is punishable with a maximum of **five years' imprisonment** and/or an **unlimited fine**.

7.4.3 Tipping off (POCA S333)

The offence

If a person either knows or believes that the police are or will be investigating the laundering of the proceeds of criminal conduct that person **must not disclose to any third party** any information which might prejudice such an investigation. If he does, he will commit the offence of tipping off. This covers the proceeds of **all** crimes no matter how small.

The possible defence

It is a defence to this offence if the person charged can prove that he neither knew nor suspected that the disclosure would prejudice an investigation.

Again, the burden of proving the defence rests upon the person who has been charged with an offence.

The penalty

Tipping off is punishable with a maximum of **five years' imprisonment** and/or an **unlimited fine**.

7.4.4 Serious Organised Crime and Police Act 2005 (SOCPA 2005)

There are a number of provisions in the **Serious Organised Crime and Police Act 2005 (SOCPA 2005)** which amend the existing POCA 2002, most of which came into effect on 1 July 2005. A summary of the key changes is given below.

BPP)))
LEARNING MEDIA

- SOCPA 2005 established a new agency, the Serious Organised Crime Agency (SOCA), in April 2006. This replaced the National Criminal Intelligence Service (NCIS) and the National Crime Squad.

- Conduct overseas may no longer count as a criminal offence under POCA 2002 if it is not a criminal offence in the jurisdiction in which it occurs. This is therefore a change to the so called 'bull fighting' offence. There is now an additional defence to the assistance and failure to report offences in relation to legal conduct outside the UK which would be illegal in the UK, e.g. bull fighting in Spain. This defence can be used where:

    - The person knew or believed on reasonable grounds that the relevant 'criminal' conduct occurred outside the UK, and

    - That conduct was not, at the time it occurred, unlawful in the overseas jurisdiction, and

    - The conduct is not of a description prescribed by statutory instrument

- No SOCA report needs to be made where this is likely to be of no practical use to the authorities, e.g. where the identity of the offender and whereabouts of the criminal property is not known and the information to be reported would not assist in an investigation

- The use of a standard disclosure form is mandatory when reporting to the Serious Organised Crime Agency

- There is much needed clarification that lawyers can seek advice about potentially suspicious cases from MLROs outside of privileged circumstances without the MLRO needing to report to SOCA

- Deposit takers can administer accounts below a threshold of £250 without fear of being prosecuted under the assistance offence even if the account is used in connection with criminal property

7.5 Application of MLR 2007

Under MLR 2007, there are a number of **supervising agencies** with whom businesses of different types are required to register. For the purposes of the Regulations, the FSA is responsible for the supervision of FSA-authorised firms and also certain other firms including leasing companies, commercial finance providers and safe custody services.

MLR 2007 applies *inter alia* to:

- The regulated activities of all financial sector firms, i.e.:

    - Banks, building societies and other credit institutions

    - Individuals and firms engaging in regulated investment activities under FSMA 2000

    - Issuers of electronic money

    - Insurance companies undertaking long-term life business, including the life business of Lloyd's of London

- *Bureaux de change*, cheque encashment centres and money transmission services (money service businesses)

- Trust and company service providers

- Casinos

- Dealers in high-value goods (including auctioneers) who accept payment in cash of €15,000 or more (either single or linked transactions)

- Lawyers and accountants, when undertaking relevant business

7.6 Institutional liability – MLR 2007

The **Money Laundering Regulations 2007 (MLR 2007)** relate to institutional liability generally. They require internal systems and procedures to be implemented to deter criminals from using certain institutions to launder money. They also aim to enable money laundering to be more easily detected and prosecuted by the law enforcement agencies.

The following 'risk-sensitive' policies and procedures must be established.

- Customer due diligence measures and ongoing monitoring

- Internal reporting

- Record-keeping procedures (for five-year period)

- Internal control

- Risk assessment and management

- Compliance monitoring, management and communication of the policies and procedures

- Recognition of suspicious transactions and reporting procedures (including appointing a Money Laundering Reporting Officer)

- Staff training programmes

Failure to implement these measures is a criminal offence. The **FSA** may institute proceedings (other than in Scotland) for money laundering regulation breaches. This power is not limited to firms or persons regulated by the FSA. Whether a breach of the Money Laundering Regulations has occurred is not dependent on whether money laundering has taken place: firms may be sanctioned for not having adequate **anti-money laundering (AML) /counter-terrorism financing (CTF)** systems. Failure to comply with any of the requirements of the ML Regulations constitutes an offence punishable by a maximum of two years' imprisonment, or a fine, or both.

Note that, where a UK business **outsources** certain operations to an overseas jurisdiction, the business is still effectively carried on in the UK. For example, if an investment bank moved its call centre to India, it would still have to comply with money laundering requirements and staff in India would need proper training.

In addition to the substantive law contained in POCA 2002 and MLR 2003, interpretation and guidance is given in the **Guidance Notes** (referenced here as **JMLSG**) issued by the **Joint Money Laundering Steering Group**. The JMLSG is made up of representatives of trade bodies such as the British Bankers Association. The purpose of the guidance notes is to outline the requirements of the UK money laundering legislation, provide a practical interpretation of the MLR 2007 and provide a base from which management can develop tailored policies and procedures that are appropriate to their business.

The latest **2007 version** of the JMLSG Guidance Notes enables the UK financial services industry to take the required **risk-based approach** to the international fight against crime.

JMLSG guidance is approved by HM Treasury and a court must take account of whether such guidance has been followed in determining a breach of the regulations.

7.7 Internal reporting procedures

All institutions must appoint an 'appropriate person' within the organisation, generally known as the **Money Laundering Reporting Officer (MLRO)**. The MLRO must then decide whether to report these on to the Serious Organised Crime Agency (SOCA), formerly the National Criminal Intelligence Service (NCIS).

The functions of the MLRO are as follows.

- To receive reports of transactions giving rise to knowledge or suspicion of money laundering activities from employees of the institution

- To determine whether the report of a suspicious transaction from the employee, considered together with all other relevant information, does actually give rise to knowledge or suspicion of money laundering

- If, after consideration, he knows or suspects that money laundering is taking place, to report those suspicions to the appropriate law enforcement agency

For the purpose of each individual employee, making a report made to the MLRO concerning a transaction means that the employee has fulfilled his statutory obligations and will have **no criminal liability** in relation to any money laundering offence in respect of the reported transaction.

7.8 FSA senior management arrangements, systems and controls (SYSC)

7.8.1 Systems and controls in relation to compliance, financial crime and money laundering

A firm must take reasonable care to establish and maintain effective systems and controls for compliance with applicable regulations and for countering the risk that the firm might be used to further financial crime. Applicable regulations include the Proceeds of Crime Act 2002, the Money Laundering Regulations 2003 and the Terrorism Act 2000.

The **principles-based approach to regulation**, as we have seen, implies that, instead of formulating very detailed rules, the FSA expects firms to work out for themselves how the Principles for Businesses can be given effect in the firm's business.

The systems and controls laid down should enable the firm to identify, assess, monitor and manage **money laundering risk**, which is, the risk that a firm may be used to further money laundering. In addition, the systems and controls should be **comprehensive** and **proportionate** to the **nature**, **scale** and **complexity** of its activities and be regularly assessed to ensure they remain adequate. Failure by a firm to manage money laundering risk will effectively increase the risk to society of crime and terrorism.

In identifying its **money laundering risk** and in establishing the nature of the systems and controls required, a firm should consider a range of factors, including:

- Its customer, product and activity profiles
- Its distribution channels
- The complexity and volume of its transactions
- Its processes and systems
- Its operating environment

7.8.2 The Money Laundering Reporting Officer (MLRO)

The MLRO which each authorised firm must appoint has responsibility for oversight of its compliance with the FSA's SYSC rules on money laundering.

The MLRO:

- Must act as the focal point for all activity within the firm relating to anti-money laundering
- Must have a level of authority and independence within the firm
- Must have access to sufficient resources and information to enable them to carry out that responsibility
- Should be based in the UK

7.8.3 The nominated officer

A **nominated officer** is someone who has been nominated by their employer to receive reports of suspected money laundering. In practice this will be the **Money Laundering Reporting Officer (MLRO)** or **his deputy**.

Employers will have reporting processes in place for staff with suspicions to disclose to the MLRO. The nominated officer will act as a filter for reporting, and is placed under a duty to disclose to the **Serious Organised Crime Agency (SOCA)**, if he knows or suspects, or has reasonable grounds to suspect, that another person is engaged in money laundering.

7.8.4 The compliance function

Depending on the nature, scale and complexity of its business, it may be appropriate for a firm to have a separate **compliance function**. The organisation and responsibilities of the compliance function should be documented.

The compliance function should:

- Be staffed by an appropriate number of competent staff who are sufficiently independent to perform their duties objectively

- Have unrestricted access to the firm's relevant records

- Have ultimate recourse to its governing body

A firm which carries on designated investment business with or for customers must allocate to a director or senior manager the function of having responsibility for oversight of the firm's compliance and reporting to the governing body in respect of that responsibility. This will be the person carrying out the controlled function '**Compliance oversight**' under the FSA's approved persons regime. As a minimum, this individual will have to oversee compliance with COB, CASS and COLL, however, firms are free to give additional responsibilities to this person.

7.9 Rationale of the risk-based approach

To assist the overall objective to prevent money laundering and terrorist financing, a risk-based approach:

- Recognises that the money laundering/terrorist financing threat to firms varies across customers, jurisdictions, products and delivery channels

- Allows management to differentiate between their customers in a way that matches the risk in their particular business

- Allows senior management to apply its own approach to the firm's procedures, systems and controls, and arrangements in particular circumstances, and

- Helps to produce a more cost effective system. (JMLSG Pt I, 4.4)

7.10 Sanctions and the Consolidated List

There are certain customers and organisations who may not be dealt with and whose assets must be frozen, as specified in anti-terrorism legislation and sanctions. A **Consolidated List** of all targets to whom financial sanctions apply is maintained by HM Treasury, and includes all individuals and entities that are subject to financial sanctions in the UK. This list is at:www.hm-treasury.gov.uk/financialsanctions. There is a range of **financial sanctions** applying against specific **countries or regimes**. HM Treasury directions can be found on the Treasury and JMLSG websites. The obligations under the UK financial sanctions regime apply to all firms, and not just to banks.

7.11 Customer Due Diligence

As already mentioned, the MLR 2007 require detailed **customer due diligence (CDD)** procedures and these are explained in **JMLSG Chapter 5**.

CDD involves:

- Identifying the customer and verifying his identity

- Identifying the beneficial owner (taking measures to understand the ownership and control structure, in the case of a company or trust) and verifying his identity

- Obtaining information on the purpose and intended nature of the business relationship

CDD may be:

- **Enhanced due diligence (EDD)** – for higher risk situations, customers not physically present when identities are verified, correspondent banking and politically exposed persons (**PEPs**)

- **Simplified due diligence (SDD)** – generally, in other cases

Firms' information demands from customers need to be '**proportionate, appropriate and discriminating**', and to be able to be **justified to customers**.

7.12 Enhanced Due Diligence

EDD measures when a customer is not present include obtaining additional documents, data or information to those specified below, requiring certification by a financial services firm, and ensuring that an initial payment is from a bank account in the customer's name.

Prominent 'politically exposed persons' (PEPs), which includes members of parliaments, can pose a higher risk because their position may make them vulnerable to corruption. PEPs include immediate family members and close associates of prominent persons. Senior management approval (from an immediate superior) should be sought for establishing a business relationship with such a customer and adequate measures should be taken to establish sources of wealth and of funds.

7.13 Simplified Due Diligence

SDD means not having to apply CDD measures. In practice, this means not having to identify the customer, or to verify the customer's identity, or, where relevant, that of a beneficial owner, nor having to obtain information on the purpose or intended nature of the business relationship. Firms must have reasonable grounds for believing that the customer, transaction or product relating to such transaction falls within one of the categories set out in the Regulations, and may have to demonstrate this to their supervisory authority (the FSA, for FSA-regulated firms).

7.14 CDD and ongoing monitoring

As an obligation separate from CDD, firms must conduct ongoing **monitoring of the business relationship**, even where SDD applies. Ongoing monitoring of a business relationship includes scrutiny of transactions undertaken including, where necessary, sources of funds.

CDD and **monitoring** is intended to make it more difficult for the financial services industry to be used for money laundering or terrorist financing, but also helps firms guard against fraud, including impersonation fraud.

7.15 Applying CDD

7.15.1 General points

A firm must apply CDD when it:

- Establishes a business relationship
- Carries out an occasional transaction, of €15,000 or more
- Suspects money laundering or terrorist financing
- Doubts the veracity of identification or verification documents

Applying CDD measures involves a number of steps, as follows.

7.15.2 Identification and verification of the customer

The firm **identifies** the customer by obtaining a range of information about him, and **verifies** the identity against documents, data or information from a reliable and independent source.

7.15.3 Identification and verification of a beneficial owner

A **beneficial owner** is normally an individual who ultimately owns or controls the customer or on whose behalf a transaction or activity is being conducted.

The obligation to verify the identity of a beneficial owner is for the firm to take 'risk-based and adequate' measures so that it is satisfied that it knows who the beneficial owner is. There is no specific requirement to have regard to particular types of evidence.

7.15.4 Customers already having business relationship on 15 December 2007

Firms must apply CDD measures at appropriate times to its existing customers on a 'risk-sensitive' basis.

7.15.5 Taking over another firm or a portfolio of customers

On taking over another firm or a portfolio of customers, identities do not need to be re-verified provided that all customer records are acquired, or a warranty is given that customers' identities have previously been verified. The acquiring firm's due diligence enquiries should however include some sample testing.

7.16 Standard identification evidence: private individuals

For **private individuals**, the firm should obtain full name, residential address and date of birth of the personal customer. Verification of the information obtained should be based either on a document or documents provided by the customer, or electronically by the firm, or by a combination of both. Where business is conducted face-to-face, firms should request the original documents. Customers should be discouraged from sending original valuable documents by post.

7.17 Standard identification evidence: corporates

The structure, ownership, purpose and activities of many corporates will be clear and understandable. However, corporate customers can use complex ownership structures, which can increase the steps that need to be taken to be reasonably satisfied as to their identities. The use of complex structures without an obvious legitimate commercial purpose may, however, give rise to concern and increase the risk of money laundering or terrorist financing.

Firms should therefore obtain the following in relation to **corporate clients**:

- Full name
- Registered number
- Registered office in country of incorporation
- Business address

In addition, for private companies:

- Names of all directors (or equivalent)
- Names of beneficial owners holding over 25%

The firm should verify the identity of the corporate from:

- A search of the relevant company registry, or
- Confirmation of the company's listing on a regulated market, or
- A copy of the company's Certificate of Incorporation

Higher risk corporate customers may include smaller and more opaque entities, with little industry profile and those in 'less transparent jurisdictions'. In such cases, Enhanced Due Diligence (EDD) may be considered appropriate.

The information below provides further guidance on steps that may be applied.

7.18 Publicly quoted companies

Corporate customers that are listed on a regulated market are publicly owned and generally accountable.

Simplified Due Diligence (SDD) only will be required where the applicant is:

- A company listed on a regulated market subject to public disclosure rules, or
- A majority-owned and consolidated subsidiary or such a publicly listed company

7.19 Private companies

Private companies are subject to a lower level of public disclosure than public companies. However, the structure, ownership, purposes and activities of many private companies will be clear and understandable.

In the UK, a company registry search will confirm that the applicant company has not been, or is not in the process of being dissolved, struck off or wound up.

7.20 Other financial services firms

SDD may generally be applied in the case of other financial services firms subject to MLR 2007 or an equivalent, and which are regulated by the FSA, or in the EU or an equivalent jurisdiction, by an equivalent regulator.

7.21 Reliance on third parties

The ML Regulations expressly permit a firm to rely on another person to apply any or all of the CDD measures, provided that the other person is listed in MLR 2007, Regulation 17(2), and that **consent** to being relied on has been given. The relying firm, however, retains responsibility for any failure to comply with a requirement of the Regulations, as this responsibility cannot be delegated.

In this context (MLR 2007, 17(2)), the other person must be:

- An FSA-authorised credit or financial institution, or

- An auditor, insolvency practitioner, external accountant, tax adviser or independent legal professional, who is (for UK businesses) supervised under the ML Regulations or (for the EEA) ML Directive or (for businesses outside the EEA) equivalent requirements

Where customers are introduced between different parts of the same financial sector **group**, entities that are part of the group are able to rely on identification procedures conducted by that part of the group which first dealt with the customer.

7.22 Approach to training

The firm's approach to training should be built around ensuring that the content and frequency of training reflects the risk assessment of the products and services of the firm and the specific role of the individual.

Selected or relevant employees should be given regular appropriate training in order to be aware of:

- The criminal law relating to money laundering and terrorist financing

- The ML Regulations

- FSA rules

- Industry guidance

- The risks money laundering and terrorist financing pose to the business

- The vulnerabilities of the firm's products and services, and

- The firm's policies and procedures in relation to the prevention of money laundering and terrorist financing

Relevant employees should also be made aware of the particular circumstances of customers who present a **higher risk** of money laundering or terrorist financing, or who are **financially excluded** (for example, people with less documentation to prove their identity). Training should include how identity should be verified in such cases, what additional steps should be taken, and/or what local checks can be made.

8 TERRORISM

8.1 Terrorist activities

Acts of terrorism committed since 2001 have led to an increase in international efforts to locate and cut off funding for terrorists and their organisations. Terrorists are using increasingly sophisticated methods to transfer funds and often require the services of bankers, accountants and lawyers.

There is a considerable overlap between the movement of terrorist funds and the laundering of criminal assets. Terrorist groups are also known to have well-established links with organised criminal activity. However, there are two major differences between terrorist and criminal funds.

BPP
LEARNING MEDIA

- Often only small amounts are required to commit a terrorist atrocity, therefore increasing the difficulty of tracking the funds.

- Whereas money laundering relates to the proceeds of crime, terrorists can be funded from legitimately obtained income.

The **Terrorism Act 2000** defines **terrorism** in the UK as the use or threat of action wherever it occurs, designed to influence a government or to intimidate the public for the purpose of advancing a political, religious or ideological cause where the action:

- Involves serious violence against a person, or

- Involves serious damage to property, or

- Endangers a person's life, or

- Creates a serious risk to the health or safety of the public, or

- Is designed seriously to interfere with, or seriously to disrupt an electronic system, e.g. a computer virus

8.2 Offences

The Terrorism Act 2000 sets out the following terrorist offences.

- **Fund raising**, which covers inviting another to provide money or other property to fund terrorism

- **Use and possession**, which covers using money or other property for the purposes of terrorism

- **Funding arrangements**, which covers involvement in funding arrangements as a result of which money or other property is made available for terrorism

- **Money laundering**, which covers any arrangement which facilitates the retention or control by any person of terrorist property by means of concealment, removal from the jurisdiction, transfer to nominees or in any other way

An offence will be committed if the action or possession of terrorist funds occurs in the UK. It will also be an offence if the action or possession occurs outside the UK but would have constituted an offence in the UK if it had occurred here.

8.3 Terrorist property

Terrorist property is defined as money or other property which is likely to be used for the purposes of terrorism, proceeds of the commission of acts of terrorism and proceeds of acts carried out for the purposes of terrorism.

8.4 Preventative measures

The risk of terrorist funding entering the financial system can be reduced if firms apply satisfactory money laundering strategies and, in particular, know your customer procedures. Firms should assess which countries carry the highest risks and should conduct careful scrutiny of transactions from countries known to be a source of terrorist financing.

In some countries, public information about known or suspected terrorists is available. For example, terrorist names are listed on the US Treasury website.

The **Financial Sanctions Unit** of the Bank of England acts as the agent of the Treasury for the purpose of administering financial sanctions in the UK. **Sanctions lists** are available online within the Publications section of the **Bank of England** website www.bankofengland.co.uk .

8.5 Duty to report terrorism

A **duty to report** occurs where a person believes or suspects that another person has committed a terrorist offence and where the belief or suspicion has arisen in the course of a trade, profession, business or employment.

An individual commits an offence of failing to report if he does not disclose the suspicion and the information on which it is based to a constable (i.e. the police) as soon as is reasonably practicable.

The following are possible defences to the offence of the failure to report.

- The firm has an established procedure for making disclosures, and the individual properly disclosed the matters in accordance with this procedure.

- The person had a reasonable excuse for not making the disclosure.

A person guilty of failing to report will face a **maximum penalty** of **six months in jail** and/or **£5,000 fine** in the **Magistrates' Court** and **five years in jail** and/or an **unlimited fine** in the **Crown Court**.

8.6 Failure to disclose: regulated sector

The Anti-Terrorism, Crime and Security Act 2001 contains additional more onerous legislation applicable to the regulated sector. The definition of the regulated sector is wider than just FSA-authorised firms and includes, for example, *bureaux de change*.

8.6.1 The offence

Where a person knows or suspects, or has **reasonable grounds** for knowing or suspecting, that another person has committed a terrorist offence and the information came to him in the course of a business in the regulated sector he must report the information to a nominated officer or the police as soon as practicable. Otherwise, that person is committing the offence of failure to disclose.

A nominated officer is the individual in a firm who has been nominated to receive disclosures and is normally the firm's Money Laundering Reporting Officer (MLRO). The disclosure must be made in the course of employment and in accordance with the procedure set out by the firm.

In deciding whether a person has committed an offence under this section of the Anti-Terrorism, Crime and Security Act 2001 a court must consider whether any of the following guidance has been followed.

- Guidance issued by a supervisory authority (e.g. the FSA) or any other appropriate body (e.g. the Investment Management Association 'IMA').

- Guidance approved by the Treasury.

- Whether the guidance was published in such a manner that it is available to persons likely to be affected by it.

8.6.2 Defences

A person has a defence against failure to disclose under this section of the Anti-Terrorism, Crime and Security Act 2001 if he/she has a reasonable excuse for not disclosing the information.

8.6.3 The penalty

A person guilty of failing to disclose will face a **maximum penalty** of **six months in jail** and/or **£5,000 fine** in the **Magistrates' Court** and **five years in jail** and/or an **unlimited fine** in the **Crown Court**.

8.7 Protected disclosures

There is clearly a concern that where a disclosure is made in accordance with the above requirements the client may claim this is a breach of client confidentiality. However, the rules state that where disclosures are made in accordance with the reporting rules there will not be a breach of client confidentiality.

9 DATA PROTECTION AND RECORD KEEPING

9.1 Data Protection Act 1998

Under the **Data Protection Act 1998 (DPA 1998)**, where persons process personal data, whether electronically or manually, they must (unless exempt) be registered with the **Information Commissioner** (who maintains a **public registry of data controllers**) and must comply with the DPA provisions. The requirements apply to most organisations and cover all personal data whether it relates to clients, employees, suppliers or any other person. In essence, to comply with DPA 1998, firms should be open with individuals about information held about them and very careful about passing that information to third parties.

9.2 Data Protection Principles

Under DPA 1998, there are **eight Data Protection Principles** (sometimes called the principles of good information handling) with which those controlling personal data must comply.

- **Principle 1** – Personal data shall be **processed fairly and lawfully**. This requires that data shall not be processed unless consent has been obtained from the subject of the data, or the processing is necessary to comply with legal obligations or to protect the vital interests of the subject of the data. Protection of vital interests could be where medical details need to be passed as a result of an accident. Also, where the data is 'sensitive personal data' (e.g. regarding ethnic origin, religion, health, or criminal record) additional requirements are imposed to handle such data.

- **Principle 2** – Personal data shall be obtained only for specified and lawful purposes and shall only be processed in a manner that is compatible with those purposes.

- **Principle 3** – Personal data shall be **adequate, relevant and not excessive** in relation to the purpose or purposes for which they are processed. This is to ensure no more data is held on a person than is strictly required in the circumstances.

- **Principle 4** – Personal data shall be **accurate** and, where necessary, kept up-to-date. This requires reasonable steps to be taken to ensure the accuracy of the data.

- **Principle 5** – Personal data processed for any purpose(s) shall **not be kept for longer** than is necessary for that purpose(s). Data should be reviewed regularly to determine whether it can be deleted.

- **Principle 6** – Personal data shall only be processed in accordance with data subjects, i.e. in accordance with the wishes of those individuals who are the subjects of the data.

- **Principle 7** – Appropriate **technical and organisational measures** shall be taken against unauthorised or unlawful processing of personal data and against accidental loss or destruction of, or damage to, personal data. Consideration should therefore be taken as to those members of staff accessing data and the technology used to store such data.

- **Principle 8** – Personal data shall **not be transferred** to a country or territory outside the **EEA**, unless that country or territory ensures an adequate level of protection of the rights and freedoms of data subjects in relation to the processing of personal data. Guidance as to which countries comply with these requirements can be obtained from the Information Commissioner.

9.3 Breaches of the Principles

Where breaches occur, the **Information Commissioner** has **wide powers** to issue enforcement notices requiring the data controller to take certain action to remedy any breaches.

- Breaches of the DPA 1998 requirements are punishable by a maximum fine of **£5,000** in the **Magistrates' Court** and **unlimited fines** in the **Crown Court**.

- There are also powers to enter premises and seize documents with a court warrant.

9.4 Record keeping: general rules for firms

As a general rule, a firm must arrange for orderly records to be kept of its business and internal organisation, including all of its services and transactions, which must be sufficient to enable the FSA or another competent authority under MiFID to monitor the firm's compliance with the requirements under the regulatory system, and in particular the firm's compliance with all obligations with respect to client.

A firm must retain all records kept by it in relation to its **MiFID business** for a period of **at least five years**.

In relation to its **MiFID business**, a **common platform firm** must retain records in a medium that allows the storage of information in a way accessible, so that the following conditions are met.

- The FSA or any other relevant competent authority under MiFID must be able to access them readily and to reconstitute each key stage of the processing of each transaction

- It must be possible for any corrections or other amendments to be easily ascertained

- It must not be possible for the records otherwise to be manipulated or altered

Records required under the **FSA Handbook** should generally be capable of being reproduced in the **English** language on **paper**, or a firm should be able to provide a translation to English. For business carried on outside the UK, an official language of that country may be used instead.

For **non-MiFID business**, firms should have appropriate security systems and controls. The general principle is that records should be **retained** for **as long as is relevant for the purposes for which they are made**.

9.5 Record keeping and DPA 1998

As a result of DPA 1998, authorised firms should be aware that **records** required to be obtained and kept under FSA rules (including money laundering identification requirements) must also comply with the requirements of DPA 1998.

CHAPTER ROUNDUP

- The Markets in Financial Instruments Directive (MiFID) replaces the Investment Services Directive (ISD), with effect from 1 November 2007. MiFID applies to all 'investment firms', including investment banks, securities dealers and portfolio managers.

- Under MiFID, firms which carry out specified investment services and activities (a wider range than under the ISD) are authorised by the member state in which they their registered office is located. Where a branch is set up, host state rules will continue to apply. 'Passporting' enables them to operate throughout the EEA.

- The MiFID regime does not apply to credit institutions, which are regulated by the Banking Consolidation Directive. Nor does it apply to insurance companies or collective investment schemes. Many firms of financial advisers are also excluded if they do not hold client money. Such firms may 'opt in', to take advantage of passporting.

- The Capital Requirements Directive seeks to ensure that firms remain solvent and are able to cover their positions at all times.

- UCITS Directives enable passporting for collective investment schemes which meet UCITS criteria, in the interests of facilitating cross-border financial services within Europe. The scheme must be regulated or authorised in its home state, and the home state regulator will confirm that the scheme complies with UCITS criteria.

- A Prospectus which is formally approved in one EEA Member State can be used across the EEA without further approval: this is referred to as the 'single passport' for issuers.

- To act on information not freely available to the market is to commit the criminal offence of insider dealing.

- Various types of behaviour, including insider dealing and manipulation of transactions, can constitute market abuse. The FSA's Code of Market Conduct describes behaviours that amount to market abuse, but not exhaustively.

- Money laundering has three stages: placement, layering, integration. Those in the financial services industry must keep alert to possible offences relating to the proceeds of any crime.

- Joint Money Laundering Steering Group guidance emphasises the need for firms to assess risks when implementing money laundering precautions. The 'Know Your Customer' principle implies that firms should, where appropriate, take steps to find out about the customer's circumstances and business.

- It is a criminal offence to assist laundering the proceeds of crime, to fail to report it satisfactorily, or to tip off someone laundering the proceeds of crime.

- The Money Laundering Regulations apply to all authorised firms and individuals. Each firm must have a Nominated Officer, who will decide whether to report suspicions to the Serious Organised Crime Agency.

- Fund raising, use and possession, funding arrangements and money laundering are offences under the Terrorism Act 2000. There is a duty to report suspected terrorism to the police.

- Those who process personal data must be registered with the Information Commissioner.

- The Data Protection Act 1998 sets out eight Data Protection Principles with which data controllers must comply. The Principles are designed to ensure that firms are open with individuals about the information they hold about them, and should be careful about passing it on.

TEST YOUR KNOWLEDGE

Check your knowledge of the Chapter here, without referring back to the text.

1   What is meant by 'gold plating'?

2   Outline how 'home state' and 'host state' rules apply under MiFID.

3   Which of the following financial instruments are normally covered by MiFID:

   (a) Cocoa futures
   (b) Contracts for differences
   (c) Forward rate agreements?

4   What is the significance of 'ancillary services' within the MiFID framework?

5   What is the overall purpose of capital requirements rules?

6   What criminal legislation covers insider dealing?

7   What restrictions does the Model Code for Directors Dealings impose?

8   What are the maximum penalties for market abuse?

9   What are the three stages of money laundering?

10   Explain what is meant by the 'Nominated Officer' in money laundering prevention provisions.

11   Which body maintains a register of data controllers under the Data Protection Act 1998?

TEST YOUR KNOWLEDGE: ANSWERS

1   'Gold plating' refers to the process of adding further rules when implementing a Directive. (See 2.2.)

2   Under MiFID, investment firms are authorised by the Member State in which their registered office is located and home state rules will apply. Where a branch is set up, host state rules will, however, apply. (See 2.3.)

3   All of these instruments are covered by MiFID. Cocoa futures are a type of commodity derivative. (See 2.4.)

4   MiFID regulated firms are also regulated in respect of ancillary services they provide. (See 2.4.)

5   Capital requirements rules seek to ensure that firms remain solvent by having greater assets at their command than they will need to cover their positions. In general, a firm must maintain, at all times, financial resources in excess of its financial resources requirement. (See 3.1.)

6   The Criminal Justice Act 1993. (See 5.1.)

7   The Code restricts directors from dealing without permission (normally from the Chairman of the company), dealing for the short-term, i.e. speculating and dealing in the two months, prior to the announcement of interim (six-monthly) or final (annual) results. (See 5.7.)

8   An unlimited fine. Other sanctions also include a public statement, an injunction or restitution order, and possible disciplinary proceedings. (See 6.9.)

9   Placement, layering and integration. (See 7.1.)

10   The nominated officer is someone who has been nominated by their employer to receive reports of suspected money laundering. In practice this will be the Money Laundering Reporting Officer (MLRO) or his deputy. (See 7.8.3.)

11   The Information Commissioner. (See 9.1.)

13

Conduct of Business and Client Assets Rules

INTRODUCTION

The FSA Principles for Businesses are central to the 'principles-based' approach to regulation. Recall that protection of consumers is one of the FSA's four statutory objectives. The FSA has made detailed rules in the 'Conduct of Business Sourcebook' (COBS) which are aimed largely at providing such protection.

The COBS rules cover a wide range of operational areas, and have been substantially revised in 2007 following the implementation of the Markets in Financial Instruments Directive (MiFID). This underlines the fact that regulation is increasingly being determined at the European level.

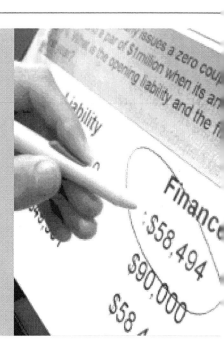

1 COBS: APPLICATION AND GENERAL PROVISIONS

1.1 COBS

The FSA includes various rules in a large section of its Handbook called the **Conduct of Business Sourcebook**. The Conduct of Business Rules have been revised extensively, and shortened, with the implementation of the Markets in Financial Instruments Directive (MiFID), with effect from November 2007. The new Sourcebook has sometimes been referred to as 'NEWCOB', but is now referred to by the abbreviation '**COBS**'. (The version which COBS replaced had the abbreviation 'COB'.)

1.2 General application rule

The **general application rule** is that **COBS** applies to an authorised **firm** in respect of the following activities when carried out from one of its (or its **appointed representative's**) **UK** establishments.

- Accepting deposits
- Designated investment business
- Long-term life insurance business

Many rules (except the financial promotion rules) only apply when the firm is doing **designated investment business** with customers.

The term '**designated investment business**' has a narrower meaning than the concept of '**regulated activities**' by excluding activities relating to Lloyd's business, deposits, funeral plans, mortgages, pure protection policies and general insurance contracts. Following the implementation of MiFID, operating a **multilateral trading facility (MTF)** is designated investment business.

There are **modifications** to the general application rule. Only some of the COBS rules apply to **eligible counterparty business** which is MiFID or equivalent third country (that is, **non-EEA**) business. The term 'eligible counterparty' is explained later in this chapter. The following COBS rules **do not** apply to such business.

- Conduct of business obligations, except 'Agent as client' and 'Reliance on others' rules
- Communicating with clients (including financial promotions rules)
- Rules on information about the firm and its services
- Client agreements
- Appropriateness rules (for non-advised sales)
- Best execution, client order handling and use of dealing commission
- Information about designated investments
- Reporting information to clients

1.3 Further general provisions

The **territorial scope** of COBS is modified to ensure compatibility with European law: this is called the '**EEA territorial scope rule**'. One of the effects of the EEA territorial scope rule is to override the application of COBS to the overseas establishments of EEA firms in a number of cases, including circumstances covered by MiFID, the Distance Marketing Directive or the Electronic Commerce Directive. In some circumstances, the rules on financial promotions and other communications will apply to communications made by UK firms to persons located outside the United Kingdom and will not apply to communications made to persons inside the United Kingdom by EEA firms.

For a UK **MiFID investment firm**, COBS rules within the scope of MiFID generally apply to its MiFID business carried on from a **UK branch or establishment**. COBS also applies to EEA MiFID investment firms carrying out business from a UK establishment. However, certain provisions (on investment research, non-independent research and on personal transactions) apply on a **'Home State' basis**: those rules will apply to all establishments in the EEA for the UK firm, and will not apply to a non-UK EEA firm.

COBS provisions on **client limit orders** do not apply to transactions between the operator of a MTF and its members, for MiFID or equivalent third country business. Members or participants in a **regulated market** do not have to apply client limit orders rules to each other, again for MiFID or equivalent third country business. However, in both cases, these rules must be applied if the members are executing orders on behalf of **clients**.

1.4 Communications by electronic media

Where a rule requires a notice to be delivered in writing, a firm may comply using **electronic media**. The COBS rules often specify that communication must be in a **durable medium**.

Durable medium means:

- Paper, or

- Any instrument (e.g. an email message) which enables the recipient to store information addressed personally to him in a way accessible for future reference for a period of time adequate for the purposes of the information and which allows the unchanged reproduction of the information stored. This will include the recipient's computer hard drive or other storage devices on which the electronic mail is stored, but not internet websites unless they fulfil the criteria in this definition.

Some communications are allowed to be delivered either in a durable medium or via a website, where the **website conditions** are satisfied.

The **website conditions** are specified as follows.

(1)   The provision of the information in that medium must be appropriate to the context in which the business between the firm and the client is, or is to be, carried on (i.e. there is evidence that the client has regular access to the internet, such as the provision by the client of an email address).

(2)   The client must specifically consent to the provision of that information in that form.

(3)   The client must be notified electronically of the address of the website, and the place on the website where the information may be accessed.

(4)   The information must be up-to-date.

(5)   The information must be accessible continuously by means of that website for such period of time as the client may reasonably need to inspect it.

1.5 Reliance on others

Suppose that a firm (**F1**) carrying out MiFID or equivalent third country business receives an instruction from an investment firm (**F2**) to perform an investment or ancillary service on behalf of a client (**C**).

F1 may rely on:

- Information about the client **C** which firm **F2** provides
- Recommendations about the service provided to **C** by **F2**

F2 remains responsible for the completeness and accuracy of information provided and the appropriateness of its advice.

More generally, a firm is taken to be in **compliance with COBS** rules which require it to obtain information, if it can show it was **reasonable** for it to rely on information provided by others in writing. It is reasonable to rely on written information provided by another where that person is **competent** and **not connected** with the firm.

This rule links with Principle 2 *Skill, Care and Diligence*. Note that this rule has no impact on the requirements laid down in the Money Laundering Regulations, which require a firm to identify its clients for money laundering purposes.

2 CLIENT CATEGORISATION

2.1 Levels of protection

Within any cost-effective regulatory system, protection provided ought to be **proportionate** to the need for protection. This is because there is not only a cost element to protection but also an inverse relationship with freedom. It is desirable that those who do not require high protection are given more freedom to trade without the restrictions that the rules inevitably bring.

The **size** and **financial awareness** of **clients** will determine the level of protection. As the size/knowledge increases, protection will decrease. A system of categorising clients can help determine that the level of protection is appropriate to the client.

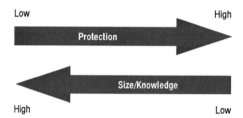

While this would ideally be a continuous process, gradually moving from full protection to no protection, in practical terms this is an impossibility.

2.2 Client categories

The terms used to classify clients has changed following the implementation of **MiFID** and the introduction of the new COBS.

Firms (unless they are providing only the special level of **basic advice** on a **stakeholder product**) are obliged to classify all clients who are undertaking **designated investment business,** before doing such business.

MiFID creates three client categories:

- **Eligible counterparties** – who are either *per se* or **elective** eligible counterparties
- **Professional clients** – who are either *per se* or **elective** professional clients
- **Retail clients**

As well as setting up criteria to classify clients into these categories, MiFID provides for clients to **change** their initial classification, on request.

2.2.1 Clients

A **client** is a person to whom an authorised **firm** provides a service in the course of carrying on a **regulated activity** or, in the case of MiFID or equivalent third country business, a person to whom a firm provides an **ancillary service**.

2.2.2 Retail clients

Retail clients are defined as those clients who are not professional clients or eligible counterparties.

2.2.3 Professional clients

Some undertakings are automatically recognised as **professional clients**. Accordingly, these entities may be referred to as *per se* professional clients. (An **undertaking** is a company, partnership or unincorporated association.)

Clients who are *per se* **professional clients** are as follows.

- Entities that **require authorisation or regulation** to operate in the financial markets, including: credit institutions, investment firms, other financial institutions, insurance companies, collective investment schemes and pension funds and their management companies, commodity and commodity derivatives dealers, 'local' derivatives dealing firms, and other institutional investors

- In relation to **MiFID** or equivalent third country business, a **large undertaking** – meaning one that meets two of the following size requirements:

    - €20,000,000 balance sheet total
    - €40,000,000 net turnover
    - €2,000,000 own funds

- In relation to business that is not **MiFID** or equivalent third country business, a **large undertaking** meeting **either** of the following requirements:

    - Called up share capital of at least £10,000,000 or equivalent, or

    - Two of the three following size tests:

        (i)   €12,500,000 balance sheet total
        (ii)   €25,000,000 net turnover
        (iii)   250 average number of employees in the year

- Central banks, international institutions, and national and regional government bodies

- Institutional investors whose main activity is to invest in financial instruments

A firm may treat a retail client as an **elective professional client** if the following tests are met.

- **Qualitative test.** The firm assesses adequately the client's **expertise**, **experience** and **knowledge** and thereby gains reasonable assurance that, for the transactions or services envisaged, the client is capable of making his own investment decisions and understanding the risks involved.

- **Quantitative test.** In the case of **MiFID** or equivalent third country business, at least **two** of the following three criteria must apply.

    - The client has carried out at least ten 'significant' transactions per quarter on the relevant market, over the last four quarters

    - The client's portfolio, including cash deposits, exceeds €500,000

    - The client has knowledge of the transactions envisaged from at least one year's professional work in the financial sector

Additionally, for professional client status to apply:

- The client must agree in writing to be treated as a professional client

- The firm must give written warning of the protections and compensation rights which may be lost

- The client must state in writing, separately from the contract, that it is aware of the consequences of losing protections

It is the responsibility of the professional client to keep the firm informed about changes (e.g. in portfolio size or company size) which could affect their categorisation.

COBS states that an elective professional client should not be presumed to have market knowledge and experience comparable to a *per se* professional client.

2.2.4 Eligible counterparties

In relation to MiFID or equivalent third country business, a client can only be an eligible counterparty in relation to eligible counterparty business.

The following, and their non-EEA equivalents, are ***per se* eligible counterparties** (i.e. they are automatically recognised as eligible counterparties).

■ Investment firms
■ Credit institutions
■ Insurance companies
■ UCITS collective investment schemes, and their management companies
■ Pension funds, and their management companies
■ Other financial institutions authorised or regulated under the law of the EU or an EEA state
■ Certain own-account commodity derivatives dealers and 'local' derivatives firms
■ National governments
■ Central banks
■ Supranational organisations

A firm may treat an undertaking as an **elective eligible counterparty** if the client:

■ Is a *per se* professional client (unless it is such by virtue of being an institutional investor), or

■ Is an elective professional client and requests the categorisation, but only in respect of the transactions and services for which it counts as a professional client, and

■ In the case of MiFID or equivalent third country business, provides 'express confirmation' of their agreement (which may be for a specific transaction or may be general) to be treated as an eligible counterparty

If the prospective counterparty is established in another EEA state, for MiFID business the firm should defer to the status determined by the law of that other state.

2.3 Agent as client

One area that has proved complicated in the past is where a firm is dealing with an **agent**. For example, suppose that a solicitor is acting for his client and approaches a firm to sell bonds on his client's behalf. Clearly, it is important that the firm establish whether it owes duties to the solicitor or to the solicitor's client.

The agent is the client of the firm, unless an agreement in writing treats the other person as the client.

The relevant COBS rule applies to designated investment business and ancillary services. The rule states that the firm may treat the agent as its client if the agent is another authorised firm or an overseas financial services institution **or** if the agent is another person, provided that the arrangement is not to avoid duties which the firm would otherwise owe to the agent's clients.

An agreement may however be made, in writing, to treat the other person (in the above example, the solicitor's client) as the firm's client.

2.4 Providing a higher level of protection to clients

Firms must allow **professional clients** and **eligible counterparties** to re-categorise in order to get more protection. Such clients are themselves responsible for asking for higher protection if they deem themselves to be **unable** to assess properly or manage the risks involved.

Either on its own initiative or following a client request or written agreement:

- A *per se* **eligible counterparty** may be re-categorised as a **professional client** or **retail client**
- A *per se* **professional client** may be re-categorised as a **retail client**

The **higher level of protection** may be provided through re-categorisation:

- On a general basis
- Trade by trade
- In respect of specified rules
- In respect of particular services, transactions, transaction types or product types

The client should (of course) be notified of a re-categorisation.

Firms must have written internal policies and procedures to categorise clients.

3   CLIENT AGREEMENTS AND INFORMATION PROVISION

3.1 Client agreements: designated investment business

If a firm carries on **designated investment business**, other than advising on investments, for a **new retail client,** the firm must enter into a **basic agreement** with the client. Although little guidance is given in the rules as to the contents, the agreement will set out the essential rights and obligations of the firm, and must be in writing – on paper or other durable medium. For a **professional client**, there is no requirement for an agreement, although most firms will wish there to be one.

In good time, normally **before** the client is bound by any agreement relating to designated investment business or ancillary services, the firm must provide to the retail client – either in a durable medium or on a website, if the website conditions are satisfied:

- The terms of the agreement

- Information about **the firm and its services** (see below), including information on communications, conflicts of interest and authorised status

The agreement and information may be provided **immediately after** the client is bound by the agreement if the agreement was concluded using a means of distance communication (e.g. telephone).

Relevant material changes to the information provided must be notified to the client in **good time**.

3.2 Information disclosure before providing services

A firm must provide to clients appropriate information in a comprehensible form about:

- The **firm and its services**

- Designated investments and proposed investment strategies, including guidance and warnings on **risks** associated with designated investments and investment strategies

- Execution venues

- Costs and associated charges

The information on designated investments and proposed investment strategies must be provided for MiFID business, and also for non-MiFID designated investment business in relation to **derivatives, warrants** and **stock lending activity**.

3.3 Information about a firm and its services

Information about a firm and its services which must be provided to a **retail client** comprises the following general information:

- The firm's **name and address**, and **contact details** which allow effective communication

- For MiFID and equivalent third country business, the **languages** the firm uses for documents and other communication

- **Methods of communication with clients** which are used by the firm, including those for sending and receiving orders where relevant

- Statement that the firm is **authorised**, and the name of the authorising **competent authority** (e.g. the FSA) – with the authority's contact address, in the case of MiFID business

- If the firm is acting through an **appointed representative or tied agent**, a statement of this fact specifying the EEA state in which the representative/agent is registered

- The nature, frequency and timing of **performance reports** provided by the firm (in accordance with rules on reporting to clients)

- For a common platform firm or a third country (non-EEA) investment firm, the firm's **conflicts of interest policy** (or a summary of it)

- For non-common platform firms, details of **how the firm will ensure fair treatment** of clients when material interests or conflicts of interest arise

3.4 Information about designated investments

The provisions in this section apply to **MiFID** and equivalent third country business, and also to the **following regulated activities** when they involve a **retail client**.

- Making a personal recommendation about a designated investment
- Managing designated investments
- Arranging or executing a deal in warrants or derivatives
- Stock lending activity

Firms must provide to clients a **general description of the nature and risks** of the type of designated investments involved, taking into account the client's categorisation as a **retail** or **professional** client.

4 COMMUNICATING WITH CLIENTS

4.1 Introduction

A **financial promotion** is an **invitation** or **inducement** to engage in investment activity. The term therefore describes most forms and methods of marketing financial services. It covers traditional advertising, most website content, telephone sales campaigns and face-to-face meetings. The term is extended to cover **marketing communications** by MiFID.

The purpose of regulation in this area is to create a regime where the quality of financial promotions is scrutinised by an authorised firm who must then comply with rules to ensure that their promotions are **clear, fair and not misleading** (Principle 7) and that customers are treated **fairly** (Principle 6).

4.2 Application of the financial promotions rules

The **financial promotions rules** within COBS apply to a firm:

- Communicating with a **client** in relation to **designated investment business**
- **Communicating** or **approving** a **financial promotion** (with some exceptions in respect of: credit promotions, home purchase plans, home reversion schemes, non-investment insurance contracts and unregulated collective investment schemes)

Firms must also apply the rules to promotions issued by their **appointed representatives**.

4.3 Territorial scope

For financial promotions, the **general application rule** applies. This indicates that the rules apply to a firm in respect of designated investment business carried out from an establishment maintained by the firm or its appointed representative in the UK. Additionally, in general the rules apply to firms carrying on business with a client in the UK from an establishment overseas.

The financial promotions rules also apply to:

- Promotions communicated to a person in the UK
- Cold (unsolicited) calling to someone outside the UK, if the call is from within the UK or is in respect of UK business

4.4 Fair, clear and not misleading

A firm must ensure that a communication or financial promotion is **fair, clear and not misleading**, as is **appropriate** and **proportionate** considering the means of communication and the information to be conveyed.

This rule applies to **communications** in relation to designated investment business other than a third party prospectus.

It applies to **financial promotions** approved by the firm, and to financial promotions communicated by the firm which are not non-retail, or excluded and are not a third party prospectus.

Note that additionally **s397 FSMA 2000** creates a criminal offence relating to **certain misleading statements and practices**, as explained earlier in this Study Book.

The **fair, clear and not misleading rule** is specifically interpreted in COBS as it applies to financial promotions in some aspects, as follows.

- If a product or service places a client's capital at risk, this should be made clear
- Any yield figure quoted should give a balanced impression of both short-term and long-term prospects for the investment
- Sufficient information must be provided to explain any complex charging arrangements, taking into account recipients' needs
- The regulator (FSA) should be named, and any non-regulated aspects made clear

- A fair, clear and not misleading impression should be given of the producer for any packaged or stakeholder products not produced by the firm

The British Bankers' Association / Building Societies Association **Code of Conduct for the Advertising of Interest Bearing Accounts** is also relevant in the case of financial promotions relating to deposits.

4.5 Identifying promotions as such

A firm must ensure that a **financial promotion** addressed to a **client** is clearly **identifiable as such**.

- This rule does not apply to a third party prospectus in respect of **MiFID** (or equivalent third country) business.

- There are also some exceptions in respect of **non-MiFID** business, including prospectus advertisements, image advertising, non-retail communications, deposits and pure protection long-term care insurance (LTCI) products.

4.6 Exceptions

The **financial promotions rules** in COBS do **not apply** to promotions of qualifying credit, home purchase plans, home reversion schemes, non-investment insurance contracts, and certain unregulated collective investment schemes whose promotions firms may not communicate or approve.

Except in regard to disclosure of compensation arrangements, the COBS rules on communications (including financial promotions) do **not** apply when a firm communicates with an **eligible counterparty**.

The financial promotions rules also do **not** apply to incoming communications in relation to **MiFID business** of an investment firm **from another EEA state** that are, in its home state, regulated under MiFID.

4.7 Excluded communications

A firm may rely on one or more of the following aspects which make a communication into an **excluded communication** for the purposes of the rules.

- A financial promotion that would benefit from an exemption in the Financial Promotion Order (see below) if it were communicated by an unauthorised person, or which originates outside the UK and has no effect in the UK

- A financial promotion from outside the UK that would be exempt under Articles 30, 31, 32 or 33 of the Financial Promotion Order (Overseas communicators) if the office from which the financial promotion is communicated were a separate unauthorised person

- A financial promotion that is subject to, or exempted from, the Takeover Code or to the requirements relating to takeovers or related operations in another EEA state

- A personal quotation or illustration form

- A **'one-off' financial promotion** that is not a cold call. The following conditions indicate that the promotion is a 'one-off', but they need not necessarily be present for a promotion to be considered as 'one-off'.

  (i)   The financial promotion is communicated only to one recipient or only to one group of recipients in the expectation that they would engage in any investment activity jointly

  (ii)   The identity of the product or service to which the financial promotion relates has been determined having regard to the particular circumstances of the recipient

  (iii) The financial promotion is not part of an organised marketing campaign

4.8 Financial Promotions Order

Section 21 FSMA 2000 makes it a criminal offence for someone to undertake a financial promotion, i.e. invite or induce another to engage in investment activity, unless they are either:

- An **authorised firm** (i.e. **issuing the financial promotion**), or
- The content of the communication is **approved** by an authorised firm

Contravention of section 21 is punishable by up to **two** years in jail and an **unlimited** fine.

There are a number of exemptions from s21 set out in the **Financial Promotions Order**. The effect of being an **exemption** is that the promotion would **not** need to be issued or approved by an authorised firm. It would therefore not have to comply with the detailed financial promotion rules.

The main examples are as follows. (Other exemptions cover certain one-off and purely factual promotions.)

Exemption	Comments
1. Investment professional	A communication to an authorised or exempt person.
2. Deposits and insurance	Very limited application of COBS.
3. Certified high net worth individuals	Anyone may promote **unlisted securities** to persons who hold certificates of high net worth (normally signed by their accountant or employer, however, these can now be self-certified by an individual) and who have agreed to be classified as such. Requirements for a certificate are that a person must have a net income of £100,000 or more, or net assets (excluding principal property) of £250,000 or more. Note that, if applicable, the financial promotion should not invite or induce the recipient to engage in business with the firm that signed the certificate of high net worth.
4. Associations of high net worth individuals	Anyone can promote non-derivative products to associations of high net worth investors.
5. Sophisticated investors	Anyone can promote products to a person who holds a certificate indicating that they are knowledgeable in a particular stock (normally signed by an authorised firm, however, individuals can now self-certify themselves as sophisticated in relation to unlisted securities) and who have signed a statement agreeing to be such. Note that the financial promotion should not invite or induce the recipient to engage in business with the authorised firm that signed the certificate.
6. Takeover Code	Promotions subject to the Takeover Code.

4.9 Approving financial promotions

The rules in **SYSC** require that a firm which communicates with a client regarding designated investment business, or communicates or approves a financial promotion, puts in place **systems and controls** or **policies and procedures** in order to comply with the COBS rules.

Section 21(1) FSMA 2000 prohibits an unauthorised person from communicating a financial promotion, unless either an exemption applies or the financial promotion is approved by an authorised firm.

Approval of a financial promotion by an **authorised firm** enables it to be communicated by an **unauthorised firm**.

5 ADVISING AND SELLING

5.1 Assessing suitability

Suitability rules apply when a firm makes a **personal recommendation** in relation to a **designated investment** (but not if the firm makes use of the rules on basic scripted advice for stakeholder products).

The firm has obligations regarding the assessment of **suitability**: the firm must take reasonable steps to ensure that, in respect of designated investments, a personal recommendation or a decision to trade is **suitable for its client**.

A **transaction** may be **unsuitable** for a client because of:

- The risks of the designated investments involved
- The type of transaction
- The characteristics of the order
- The frequency of trading
- It resulting in an unsuitable portfolio (in the case of **managing investments**)

For non-MiFID business, these rules apply to business with **retail clients**. When making personal recommendations or managing investments for **professional clients**, in the course of MiFID or equivalent third country business, a firm is entitled to assume that the client has the necessary experience and knowledge, in relation to products and services for which the professional client is so classified.

5.2 Advising on packaged products

'**Packaged products**' relates to products that can be bought 'off-the-shelf', with the terms and conditions and price identical for all potential investors. These are typically products sold through an intermediary, for example an Independent Financial Adviser (IFA).

A **packaged product** is defined as one of the following:

- A life policy
- A unit in a regulated collective investment scheme
- An interest in an investment trust savings scheme
- A stakeholder pension scheme
- A personal pension scheme

whether or not (in the case of the first three types listed above) it is held within a PEP, an ISA or a Child Trust Fund (CTF) and whether or not the packaged product is also a stakeholder product.

When advising on **packaged products**, the firm's disclosures should indicate whether it expects its scope to be:

- The whole of the market or market sector
- Limited to several product providers
- Limited to a single product provider

What is meant by the **scope** and **range** of a firm's advice?

- The **scope** relates to the **product providers** whose products it sells
- The **range** relates to which **products** from those providers it sells

A firm must maintain an up-to-date **record** of the **scopes and ranges** it uses, and must keep the records for at least **five years**.

5.3 Appropriateness

The **appropriateness** rules we outline here apply to a firm providing **investment services** in the course of **MiFID** or equivalent third country business, **other than** making a personal recommendation and managing investments. The rules thus apply to '**execution only**' services which are available in the UK, where transactions are undertaken at the initiative of the customer without advice having been given. (Note that, as we have seen, the **suitability** rules apply where there is a personal recommendation.) One firm may rely on another MiFID firm's assessment of appropriateness, in line with the general rule on reliance on other investment firms.

The rules apply to arranging or dealing in **derivatives** or **warrants** for a **retail client**, when in response to a **direct offer financial promotion**.

To **assess appropriateness**, the firm must ask the client to provide information on his knowledge and experience in the relevant investment field, to enable the assessment to be made.

The firm will then:

- Determine whether the client has the necessary **experience and knowledge** to understand the **risks** involved in the product/service (including the following aspects: nature and extent of service with which client is familiar; complexity; risks involved; extent of client's transactions in designated investments; level of client's education and profession or former profession)

- Be entitled to assume that a **professional client** has such experience and knowledge, for products/services for which it is classified as 'professional'

If the firm is satisfied about the client's experience and knowledge, there is **no duty to communicate** this to the client. If, in doing so, it is making a personal recommendation, it must comply with the **suitability** rules. But if the firm concludes that the product or service is **not appropriate** to the client, it must **warn** the client. The warning may be in a standardised format.

5.4 When is an assessment of appropriateness not needed?

A firm does **not** need to seek information from the client or assess appropriateness if:

- The service consists only of execution and receiving / transmitting client orders for particular **financial instruments** (see below), provided at the initiative of the client

- The client has been informed clearly that in providing this service the firm is not required to assess suitability and that therefore he does not receive protection from the suitability rules, and

- The firm complies with obligations regarding conflicts of interest

The particular **financial instruments** are:

- Shares on a regulated or equivalent third country market

- Money market instruments, bonds and other forms of securitised debt (excluding bonds and securitised debt which embed a derivative)

- Units in a UCITS scheme

- Other non-complex financial instruments (among the requirements to qualify as 'non-complex' are that they cannot lead the investor to lose more than they invested, adequate information is freely available, there is a market for them with prices made available independently of the issuer, and they do not give rise to cash settlement in the way that many derivatives do)

A firm need not assess appropriateness if it is receiving or transmitting an order for which it has assessed **suitability** under the COBS suitability rules (covered above). Also, a firm may not need to assess appropriateness if it is able to rely on a recommendation made by a **different investment firm**.

6 DEALING AND MANAGING

6.1 Application of rules

COBS includes rules on **dealing and managing**. These rules (except for the rules on personal account dealing – see below) apply to **MiFID business** carried out by a **MiFID investment firm**, and to equivalent third country business.

The provisions on **personal account dealing** apply to designated investment business carried on from a UK establishment. They also apply to passported activities carried on by a UK MiFID investment firm from a branch in another EEA state, but not to the UK branch of an EEA MiFID investment firm in relation to its MiFID business.

6.2 Conflicts of interest

6.2.1 Principle 8

Inevitably, authorised firms, particularly where they act in dual capacity (both broker and dealing for the firm itself), are faced with **conflicts** between the firm and customers or between one customer and another.

Principle 8 of the Principles for Businesses states: 'A firm must manage conflicts of interest fairly, both between itself and its customers and between a customer and another client'.

Principle 8 thus requires that authorised firms should seek to ensure that when **conflicts of interest** do arise, the firm **manages** the conflicts to ensure that customers are treated **fairly**.

6.2.2 SYSC 10

SYSC 10 applies to **common platform firms** carrying on regulated activities and ancillary activities or providing MiFID ancillary services, where a service is provided, to any category of client.

The common platform firm must take all **reasonable steps** to **identify conflicts of interest** between the firm, its managers, employees and appointed representatives or tied agents, or between clients, which may arise in providing a service.

The firm must take into account, as a minimum, likely financial gains, or avoidance of losses, at the expense of a client, interests in the outcome of a service which are different from the client's interest, financial incentives to favour some clients or groups of client, and whether the firm carries on the same business as the client, or receives inducements in the form of monies, goods and services other than the standard commission or fee for that service.

Regularly updated records must be kept of where conflicts of interest have or may arise.

The firm must maintain and operate effective **organisational and administrative arrangements** to prevent conflicts of interest from giving rise to material risk of damage to clients' interests.

Where conflicts are not preventable, the firm must disclose them to clients – in a durable medium, in sufficient detail for the client to take an informed decision – before undertaking business.

Common platform firms should aim to **identify** and **manage** conflicts under a **comprehensive conflicts of interest policy**. That firms actively manage conflicts is important: 'over-reliance of disclosure' without adequate consideration of how to manage conflicts is not permitted.

6.2.3 Conflicts policy

A **common platform firm** must maintain an effective **conflicts of interest policy**, in **writing** and appropriate to the size and type of firm and its business.

The conflicts of interest policy must:

- Identify circumstances constituting or potentially giving rise to conflicts materially affecting clients
- Specify procedures and measures to manage the conflicts

The procedures and measures must:

- Be designed to ensure that activities are carried on an appropriate **level of independence**

- As and where necessary, include procedures to **prevent and control exchange of information** between persons involved, to **supervise persons separately**, to remove **links in remuneration** producing possible conflicts, to prevent exercise of **inappropriate influence**, and to **prevent and control simultaneous and sequential involvement** of persons in separate services or activities

In drawing up its conflicts policy, the firm must pay **special attention** to the following **activities** (in particular, where persons perform a combination of activities): investment research and advice, proprietary trading, portfolio management and corporate finance business, including underwriting or selling in an offer of securities, and advising on mergers and acquisitions.

In management of an **offering of securities**, the firm might wish to consider agreeing:

- Relevant aspects of the offering process with the corporate finance client at an early stage

- Allocation and pricing objectives with the corporate finance client, inviting the client to participate actively in the allocation process, making the initial recommendation for allocation to retail clients as a single block and not on a named basis and disclosing to the issuer the allocations actually made

6.2.4 'Chinese walls'

Chinese walls are administrative and physical barriers and other internal arrangements, designed to contain **sensitive information**. Most commonly, they are used around the corporate finance departments of firms that often have confidential, sometimes inside, information.

Chinese walls **do not have to be used** by firms, but if they are, this rule becomes relevant.

Where a common platform firm establishes and maintains a Chinese wall, it allows the persons on one side of the wall, e.g. corporate finance, to withhold information from persons on the other side of the wall, e.g. equity research, but only to the extent that one of the parts involves carrying on **regulated activities, ancillary activities** or **MiFID ancillary services**.

A firm will not be guilty of the offences of **Misleading Statements and Practices** (s397 FSMA 2000), **market abuse** (S 118A(5)(a)) or be liable to a lawsuit under **s150** where the failure arises from the operation of a Chinese wall.

The **effect** of the Chinese walls rule above is that a corporate finance department may have plans for a company that will change the valuation of that company's shares. The equity salesman on the other side of the 'wall' should have no knowledge of these plans; consequently his inability to pass this knowledge on to clients is not seen as a failure of his duty to them.

6.3 Investment research and conflicts of interest

6.3.1 Introduction

There have been concerns that analysts have been encouraged to write favourable research on companies in order to attract lucrative investment banking work. There have also been concerns about firm's employees recommending particular securities while privately trading contrary to the recommendation.

COBS rules on investment research apply to MiFID business carried on by a MiFID investment firm. Rules on disclosure of research recommendations apply to all firms.

6.3.2 Investment research

The rules cover investment research which is intended or likely to be disseminated to clients or to the public.

Firms must ensure that its measures for **managing conflicts of interest** cover the **financial analysts** who produce its investment research, and any other relevant staff.

The firm's arrangements must ensure that:

- The financial analysts and other staff involved do not undertake personal transactions or trade on behalf of other persons, including the firm (unless they are acting as a market maker in good faith), in financial instruments to which unpublished investment research relates, until the **recipients** of the research have had a **reasonable opportunity** to act on it

- In other circumstances, personal transactions by financial analysts and other staff in financial instruments related to investment research they are producing which is **contrary to current recommendations** must only occur in **exceptional circumstances** and with **prior approval** of the firm's legal or compliance function

- The firm and its staff must not **accept inducements** from those with a material interest in the subject matter of investment research, and they must not **promise issuers favourable research coverage**

- Issuers and persons other than financial analysts must not be allowed to **review pre-publication drafts** of investment research for any purpose **other than to verify compliance** with the firm's legal obligations, if the draft includes a recommendation or a target price

There is an exemption from the rules outlined above where a firm distributes investment research **produced by a third party** which is not in the firm's group, provided that the firm does not alter the recommendations and does not present the research as produced by the firm. The firm is required to verify that the independent producer of the research has equivalent arrangements in place to avoid conflicts of interest.

6.3.3 Non-independent research

Investment research is research which Is described as investment research or in similar terms, or is otherwise presented as an objective or independent explanation of the matters contained in the recommendation. Research not meeting this requirement falls within the definition of **non-independent research**.

Non-independent research must:

- Be clearly identified as a **marketing communication**

- Contain a clear and prominent statement that it does not follow the requirements of independent research and is not subject to prohibitions on dealing ahead of dissemination of research

Financial promotions rules apply to non-independent research as if it were a marketing communication.

6.3.4 Research recommendations: standards and disclosures

The **identity** (name, job title, name of firm, competent authority) of the person responsible for the research should be disclosed clearly and prominently.

The research should meet certain **general standards** for example to ensure that facts are distinguished from interpretations or opinions. Projections should be labelled as such. Reliable sources should be used, and any doubts about reliability clearly indicated. The substance of the recommendations should be possible to be substantiated by the FSA on request. The firm must take reasonable care to ensure **fair presentation**.

Firms must make **disclosures** in research recommendations broadly covering the following areas.

- All **relationships and circumstances** (including those of affiliated companies) that may reasonably be expected to impair the objectivity of the recommendation (especially, financial interests in any relevant investment, and a conflict of interest regarding the issuer)

- Whether employees involved have **remuneration** tied to investment banking transactions

- **Shareholdings** held by the firm (or an affiliated company) of over 5% of the share capital of the issuer

- **Shareholdings** held by the issuer of over 5% of the share capital of the firm (or an affiliated company)

- Other **significant financial interests**

- Statements about the **role of the firm** as market maker, lead manager of previous offers of the issuer in the last year, provider of investment banking services

- Statements about **arrangements** to prevent and avoid conflicts of interest, prices and dates at which employees involved acquired shares

- **Data** on the proportions of the firm's **recommendations** in different categories (e.g. 'buy', 'sell', 'hold'), on a quarterly basis, with the proportions of relevant investments issued by issuers who were investment banking clients of the firm during the last year

- Identification of a **third party** who produced the research, if applicable, describing also any alteration of third party recommendations and ensuring that any summary of third party research is fair, clear and not misleading

For shorter recommendations, firms can make reference to many of the relevant disclosures, e.g. by providing a website link.

6.4 Inducements

A firm must **not** pay or accept any fee or commission, or provide or receive any non-monetary benefit, in relation to designated investment business, or an ancillary service in the case of MiFID or equivalent third country business, other than:

- Fees, commissions and non-monetary benefits paid or provided to or by the client or a person on their behalf

- Fees, commissions and non-monetary benefits paid or provided to or by a third party or a person acting on their behalf, if the firm's duty to act in the best interests of the client is not impaired, and (for MiFID and equivalent business, and where there is a personal recommendation of a packaged product, but not for 'basic advice') clear, comprehensive, accurate, understandable disclosure (except of 'reasonable non-monetary benefits', listed later) is made to the client before the service is provided (Thus, the rule on inducements does not apply to discloseable commissions.)

This rule supplements Principles 1 and 6 of the Principles for Businesses. It deals with the delicate area of inducements and seeks to ensure that firms do not conduct business under arrangements that may give rise to conflicts of interest.

Inducements could mean anything from gifts to entertainment to bribery. The rules provide a test to help judge whether or not something is acceptable.

Where commissions must be disclosed in relation to packaged products, the firm should not enter into:

- Volume overrides, if commission on several transactions is more than a simple multiple of the commission for one transaction
- Agreements to indemnify payment of commission which might give an additional financial benefit to the recipient if the commission becomes repayable

If the firm selling packaged products enters into an agreement under which it receives commission more than that disclosed to the client, rules on disclosure of charges and inducements are likely to have been breached.

In the case of packaged products business with retail clients, there are rules to prevent a product provider from taking a **holding of capital** in the firm or providing **credit** to a firm unless stringent terms are met, including a condition requiring the holding or credit to be on commercial terms.

If a product provider makes benefits available to one firm but not another, this is more likely to impair compliance with the **client's best interests rule**.

Most firms deliver against the inducements requirements by drafting detailed '**gifts policies**' (although the rule does **not** explicitly require firms to have a gifts policy). These contain internal rules regarding disclosure, limits and clearance procedures for gifts.

6.5 Use of dealing commission

The practice of **using dealing commission** (previously called **soft commission**) dates back many years. The practice developed from brokers effectively **rebating** part of the commission paid by large fund management clients, to be used to cover the costs of services such as equity research. The effect was to reduce the 'real' commission paid for the execution of the trade. It is deemed necessary to control these arrangements to ensure that customers who ultimately pay the commissions, namely the fund managers' clients, are protected from abuse.

The rules on the use of dealing commission aim to ensure that an investment manager's arrangements, in relation to dealing commissions spent on acquiring services in addition to execution, are transparent and demonstrate accountability to customers so that customers are treated fairly.

The rules therefore help to ensure firms comply with Principle 1 (Integrity), Principle 6 (Customers' Interests) and Principle 8 (Conflicts of Interest).

The rules on the use of dealing commission apply to investment managers when executing customer orders through a broker or another person in shares or other investments which relate to shares, e.g. warrants, hybrids (ADRs and options) and rights to, or interests in, investments relating to shares.

When the investment manager passes on the broker's or other person's charges (whether commission or otherwise) to its customers and in return arranges to receive goods or services **the rules require the investment manager to be satisfied that the goods or services:**

- Relate to the execution of trades, or
- Comprise the provision of research

This is subject to a clause that the goods or services will reasonably assist the investment manager in the provision of services to its customers and do not impair compliance with the duty of the investment manager to act in the best interests of its customers.

In relation to **goods or services** relating to the execution of trades, the FSA have confirmed that post-trade analytics, e.g. performance measurement, is not going to be an acceptable use of dealing commission. Where the goods or services relate to research, the investment manager will have to be satisfied that the research:

- Is capable of **adding value** to the investment or trading decisions by providing **new insights** that inform the investment manager when making such decisions about its customers' portfolios

- In whatever form its output takes, represents **original thought**, in the critical and careful consideration and assessment of new and existing facts, and does not merely repeat or repackage what has been presented before

- Has **intellectual rigour** and does not merely state what is commonplace or self-evident, and

- Involves analysis or manipulation of data to reach **meaningful conclusions**

Examples of goods or services that relate to the execution of trades or the provision of research that are **not** going to be **acceptable** to the FSA include the following.

- Services relating to the valuation or performance measurement of portfolios
- Computer hardware
- Dedicated telephone lines and other connectivity services
- Seminar fees
- Subscriptions for publications
- Travel, accommodation or entertainment costs
- Order and execution management systems
- Office administration computer software, e.g. for word processing or accounting
- Membership fees to professional associations
- Purchase or rental of standard office equipment or ancillary facilities
- Employees' salaries
- Direct money payments
- Publicly available information
- Custody services relating to designated investments belonging to, or managed for, customers other than those services that are incidental to the execution of trades

Investment managers must make **adequate prior disclosure** to customers about receipt of goods and services that relate to the execution of trades or the provision of research. This should form part of the summary form disclosure under the rule on inducements. **Periodic disclosures** made on an annual basis are recommended.

6.6 Best execution

The basic COBS rule of **best execution** is as follows.

A firm must take all reasonable steps to obtain, when executing orders, the best possible result for its clients taking into account the execution factors.

When a firm is **dealing on own account with clients**, this is considered to be execution of client orders, and is therefore subject to the best execution rule.

If a firm provides a best quote to a client, it is acceptable for the quote to be executed after the client accepts it, provided the quote is not manifestly out of date.

The obligation to obtain best execution needs to be interpreted according to the particular type of financial instrument involved, but the rule applies to **all types of financial instrument**.

The **best execution criteria** are that the firm must take into account **characteristics of**:

- The client, including categorisation as retail or professional
- The client order
- The financial instruments
- The execution venues

The '**best possible result**' must be determined in terms of **total consideration** – taking into account any costs, including the firm's own commissions in the case of competing execution venues, and not just quoted prices. (However, the firm is not expected to compare the result with that of clients of other firms.) Commissions structure must not discriminate between execution venues.

6.7 Order execution policy

6.7.1 Policy requirements

The firm must establish and implement an **order execution policy**, and it must monitor its effectiveness regularly.

The policy must include, for each class of financial instruments, information on different execution venues used by the firm, and the factors affecting choice of execution venue.

The firm should choose venues that enable it to obtain on a consistent basis the best possible result for execution of client orders. For each client order, the firm should apply its execution policy with a view to achieving the best possible result for the client.

If orders may be executed outside a regulated market or Multilateral Trading Facility, this must be disclosed, and clients must give prior express consent.

A firm must be able to demonstrate to clients, on request, that it has followed its execution policy.

6.7.2 Client consent and clients' specific instructions

The firm must provide a **retail client** with details on its execution policy before providing the service, covering the relative importance the firm assigns to execution factors, a list of execution venues on which the firm relies, and a clear and prominent warning that **specific instructions** by the client could prevent the firm from following its execution policy steps fully.

If the client gives **specific instructions**, the firm has met its best execution obligation if it obtains the best result in following those instructions. The firm should not induce a client to gives such instructions, if they could prevent best execution from being obtained. However, the firm may invite the client to choose between execution venues.

The firm must obtain the **prior consent** of clients to its execution policy, and the policy must be **reviewed annually** and whenever there is a material change in the firm's ability to achieve the best possible result consistently from execution venues.

6.7.3 Portfolio management and order reception and transmission services

Firms who act as **portfolio managers** must comply with the **clients' best interests rule** when placing orders with other entities. Firms who provide a service of **receiving and transmitting orders** must do the same when transmitting orders to other entities for execution. Such firms must:

- Take all reasonable steps to obtain the best possible result for clients

- Establish and maintain a policy to enable it to do so, and monitor its effectiveness

- Provide appropriate information to clients on the policy

- Review the policy annually or whenever there is a material change affecting the firm's ability to continue to obtain the best possible result for clients

6.8 Client order handling

The general rule on **client order handling** is that firms must implement procedures and arrangements which provide for the prompt, fair and expeditious execution of client orders, relative to other orders or the trading interests of the firm.

These procedures and arrangements must allow for the execution of otherwise comparable orders in accordance with the time of their reception by the firm.

When carrying out **client orders**, firms must:

- Ensure that orders are promptly and accurately recorded and allocated

- Carry out otherwise comparable orders sequentially and promptly, unless this is impracticable or not in clients' interests

- Inform a retail client about any material difficulty in carrying out orders promptly, on becoming aware of it

Where it is not practicable to treat orders sequentially e.g. because they are received by different media, they should not be treated as 'otherwise comparable'.

Firms must not allow the **misuse of information** relating to pending client orders. Any use of such information to deal on own account should be considered a misuse of the information.

When overseeing or arranging **settlement**, a firm must take reasonable steps to ensure that instruments or funds due are delivered to the client account promptly and correctly.

6.9 Aggregation and allocation

Aggregation (grouping together) of client orders with other client orders or a transaction for own account is not permitted unless:

- It is unlikely to work to the disadvantage to any of the clients

- It is disclosed to each client that the effect of aggregation may work to its disadvantage

- An **order allocation policy** is established and implemented, covering the fair allocation of aggregated orders, including how the volume and price of orders determines allocations, and the treatment of partial executions

The order allocation policy must prevent reallocation of transactions on own account executed in combination with client orders, in a way that is detrimental to the client (e.g. if unfair precedence is given to the firm or another person).

If a firm aggregates a client order with a transaction on own account, and the aggregated order is partially executed, it must allocate the related trades **to the client in priority** to the firm, although if it can demonstrate that the aggregation enabled advantageous terms to be obtained, it may allocate the transaction proportionally.

6.10 Client limit orders

A **limit order** specifies a limit at or below which a client agrees to buy, or at or above which a client agrees to sell.

Unless the client expressly instructs otherwise, a firm has an obligation to make unexecuted client limit orders (for shares on a regulated market) public, to facilitate the earliest possible execution. The order may be made public by transmitting it to a regulated market or Multilateral Trading Facility.

For **eligible counterparties**, this obligation to disclose applies only where the counterparty is explicitly sending a limit order to a firm for its execution.

The obligation to make public will not apply to a limit order that is **large** in scale compared with the **normal market size** for the share.

6.11 Personal account dealing

Personal account dealing relates to trades undertaken by the staff of a regulated business for themselves. Such trades can create **conflicts of interest** between staff and customers.

A firm conducting **designated investment business** must establish, implement and maintain adequate **arrangements** aimed at preventing employees who are involved in activities where a conflict of interest could occur, or who has access to inside information, from:

■ Entering into a transaction which is prohibited under the **Market Abuse Directive**, or which involves misuse or improper disclosure of confidential information, or conflicts with an obligation of the firm to a customer under the regulatory system

■ Except in the course of his job, advising or procuring anyone else to enter into such a transaction

■ Except in the course of his job, disclosing any information or opinion to another person if the person disclosing it should know that, as a result, the other person would be likely to enter into such a transaction or advise or procure another to enter into such a transaction

The **firm's arrangements** under these provisions must be designed to ensure that:

■ All relevant persons (staff involved) are aware of the personal dealing restrictions

■ The firm is informed promptly of any personal transaction

■ A service provider to whom activities are outsourced maintain a record of personal transactions and provides it to the firm promptly on request

■ A record is kept of personal transactions notified to the firm or identified by it, including any related authorisation or prohibition

The rule on personal account dealing is **disapplied** for personal transactions:

■ Under a discretionary portfolio management service where there has been no prior communication between the portfolio manager and the person for whom the transaction is executed

■ In UCITS collective undertakings (e.g. OEICs and unit trusts) where the person is not involved in its management

■ In life policies

■ For successive personal transactions where there were prior instructions in force, nor to the termination of the instruction provided that no financial instruments are sold at the same time

6.12 Churning and switching

Churning and switching are similar wrongs. They involve the cynical **overtrading** of customer accounts for the purpose of generating commission. This would clearly contravene the **client's best interests rule**.

The difference between the two lies in the **different products** in which the transactions are undertaken.

- **Churning** relates to investments generally
- **Switching** describes overtrading within and between packaged products

Churning or switching will often be difficult to isolate, unless blatant. Much would depend upon the market conditions prevailing at the time of dealing.

The **COBS rules** on churning and switching state that:

- A series of transactions that are each suitable when viewed in isolation may be unsuitable if the recommendations or the decisions to trade are made with a frequency that is not in the best interests of the client

- A firm should have regard to the client's agreed investment strategy in determining the frequency of transactions. This would include, for example, the need to switch within or between packaged products

7 REPORTING TO CLIENTS

7.1 Reporting executions

In respect of **MiFID** and equivalent third country business, a firm must ensure that clients receive **adequate reports** on the services provided to it by the firm and their costs.

A firm must provide promptly in a durable medium the **essential information** on **execution of orders** to clients in the course of **designated investment business**, when it is not managing the investments. The information may be sent to an agent of the client, nominated by the client in writing.

For retail clients, a notice confirming execution must be sent as soon as possible and no later than the first business day following receipt of confirmation from the third party.

Firms must supply information about the **status of a client's order** on request.

For **series of orders** to buy units or shares in a collective undertaking (such as a **regular savings plan**), after the initial report, further reports must be provided at least at six-monthly intervals.

Where an order is executed in tranches, the firm may supply the price for each tranche or an average price. The price for each tranche must be made available on the request of a retail client.

For business that is not MiFID or equivalent third country business, confirmations need **not** be supplied if:

- The client has agreed not to receive them (with informed written consent, in the case of retail clients), or

- The designated investment is a life policy or a personal pension scheme (other than a SIPP), or

- The designated investment is held in a CTF and the information is contained in the annual statement

Copies of confirmations dispatched must be **kept** for at least **five years**, for MiFID and equivalent third country business, and for at least **three years** in other cases.

Information to be included in trade confirmations to a retail client

- Reporting firm identification

- Name / designation of client

- Trading day and time

- Order type (e.g. limit order / market order)

- Venue identification

- Instrument identification

- Buy / sell indicator (or nature of order, if not buy/sell)

- Quantity

- Unit price

- Total consideration

- Total commissions and expenses charged with, if requested, itemised breakdown

- Currency exchange rate, where relevant

- Client's responsibilities regarding settlement, including time limit for payment or delivery, and appropriate account details where not previously notified

- Details if the client's counterparty was in the firm's group or was another client, unless trading was anonymous

7.2 Periodic reporting

A firm **managing investments** on behalf of a client must provide a periodic statement to the client in a durable medium, unless such a statement is provided by another person. The statement may be sent to an agent nominated by the client in writing.

Information to be included in a periodic report

- Name of the firm

- Name / designation of retail client's account

- Statement of contents and valuation of portfolio, including details of:
    - Each designated investment held, its market value or, if unavailable, its fair value
    - Cash balance at beginning and end of reporting period
    - Performance of portfolio during reporting period

- Total fees and charges, itemising total management fees and total execution costs

- Comparison of period performance with any agreed investment performance benchmark

- Total dividends, interest and other payments received in the period

- Information about other corporate actions giving rights to designated investments held

For a **retail client**, the **periodic statement** should be provided once every **six months**, except that:

- In the case of a leveraged portfolio, it should be provided at least **once a month**

- It should be provided every **three months** if the client requests it (The firm must inform clients of this right.)

- If the retail client elects to receive information on a transaction-by-transaction basis and there are no transactions in derivatives or similar instruments giving rise to a cash settlement, the periodic statement must be supplied at least once every **twelve months**

A firm managing investments (or operating a retail client account that includes an uncovered open position in a contingent liability transaction – involving a potential liability in excess of the cost) must report to the client any **losses** exceeding any **predetermined threshold** agreed with the client.

Periodic statements for **contingent liability transactions** may include information on the **collateral value** and **option account valuations** in respect of each option written by the client in the portfolio at the end of the relevant period.

For **non-MiFID business**, a firm need not provide a periodic statement to a client habitually resident outside the UK if the client does not wish to receive it, nor in respect of a **CTF** if the annual statement contains the periodic information.

8 CLIENT ASSETS RULES

8.1 Introduction

The rules in this section link to Principle 10 of the Principles for Businesses. The rules aim to restrict the commingling of client's and firm's assets and minimise the risk of client's investments being used by the firm without the client's agreement or contrary to the client's wishes, or being treated as the firm's assets in the event of its **insolvency**. The focus therefore, is on two main issues, namely custody of investments, and client money.

The client assets rules have a broader coverage than the rules contained in COBS, the Conduct of Business Sourcebook, in that they afford protection not only to retail and professional clients, but also to **eligible counterparties**.

Under MiFID, client assets are regulated by the **home state**. Therefore, for example, if a French firm is **passporting** into the UK, it will adhere to French client assets rules.

The implementation of MiFID has resulted in more onerous requirements on firms in respect of custody of client assets and client money.

- Except in the case of credit institutions, firms may not use client funds for their own account in any circumstances.

- Sub-custodians and depositaries must be selected in accordance with specified rules.

- There are rules specifying that client funds be held with particular types of bank and (if the client does not object) certain money market funds meeting specified criteria.

- One of the most significant impacts of MiFID implementation on the existing client money regime is that MiFID firms will no longer be able to allow professional clients to 'opt-out' of the client money rules, for MiFID business.

The **Client Assets (CASS)** section of the FSA Handbook includes custody rules for **custody** and **client money** which apply to a firm which holds financial instruments belonging to a client in the course of the firm's **MiFID business**.

Separate '**Non-directive custody rules**' in CASS apply to other firms which receive money from clients, or hold money for them, in the course of **designated investment business** other than MiFID business. Firms subject to the non-Directive custody rules may opt in to the MiFID custody rules if they elect (and keep a written record of the election) to do so. Under the non-Directive custody rules for designated investment business, 'opt out' rules allow a firm to enable a professional client or an eligible counterparty to choose whether their money is subject to the client money rules. However, there is no such 'opt out' in respect of MiFID business, as noted above.

You are expected to have knowledge of the **custody and client money rules for MiFID business** and these rules are covered below.

8.2 Holding client assets

Firms sometimes hold investments on behalf of clients in physical form, e.g. bearer bonds, or may be responsible for the assets but not physically holding them as they are held elsewhere, e.g. with another custodian or via CREST.

Firms which hold financial instruments belonging to clients must make arrangements to **safeguard clients' ownership rights**, especially in the event of the firm's insolvency. Firms are not permitted to use financial instruments which are held for clients **for their own account** unless they have the express consent of the client.

The firm must have **adequate organisational arrangements** to minimise risk of loss or diminution of clients' financial instruments or of rights over them resulting from misuse, fraud, poor administration, inadequate record-keeping or other negligence.

As far as practicable, the firm must effect registration or recording of legal title to financial instruments, normally in the name of:

- The client, or
- A nominee company

For nominee companies controlled by the firm, the firm has the same level of responsibility to the client regarding custody of the assets.

In the case of **overseas financial instruments**, where it is in the client's best interests, the instruments may be held by:

- Any other party, in which case the client must be notified in writing

- The firm, subject to written consent (if a retail client) or notification of the client (for professional clients)

8.3 Requirement to protect client money

A firm must make adequate arrangements to safeguard clients' rights over **client money** the firm holds, and to prevent the use of client money for the firm's own account.

As with financial instruments, the firm must have **adequate organisational arrangements** to minimise risk of loss or diminution of clients' money or of rights over such money resulting from misuse, fraud, poor administration, inadequate record-keeping or other negligence.

If a firm leaves some of its own money in a client money account, this will be referred to as a '**pollution of trust**' and, if the firm fails, the liquidator will be able to seize all the money held in the client account for the general creditors of the firm.

8.4 Client bank accounts

Client money must be deposited with:

- A central bank
- An EEA credit institution
- A bank authorised in a third country, or
- A qualifying money market fund

8.5 Financial instruments: reconciliations with external records

The firm should ensure that any **third party** holding clients' **financial instruments** provides regular statements.

To ensure accuracy of its records, the firm must carry out regular reconciliations between its own records and those of such third parties:

- As regularly as is necessary, and
- As soon as possible after the date to which the reconciliation relates

The person, who may be an employee of the firm, carrying out the reconciliation should, whenever possible, be someone who is independent of the process of producing and maintaining the records. (This type of control is called **segregation of duties**.)

If a firm has not complied with the reconciliation requirements 'in any material respect', then it must inform the FSA without delay.

8.6 Financial instruments: reconciliation discrepancies

Any **discrepancies** revealed in the reconciliations – including items recorded in a suspense or error account – must be corrected promptly.

Any unreconciled shortfall must be made good, if there are reasonable grounds for concluding that the firm is responsible. If the firm concludes that someone else is responsible, steps should be taken to resolve the position with that other person.

If a firm has not made good an unreconciled shortfall 'in any material respect', then it must inform the FSA without delay.

8.7 Client money: reconciliations with external records

Broadly, if a firm holds money that belongs to someone else, then that money is client money.

As with financial instruments, to ensure accuracy of its records, the firm must carry out regular reconciliations between its own client money records and those of third parties, such as a bank, holding **client money**:

- As regularly as is necessary, and
- As soon as possible after the date to which the reconciliation relates

In determining the **frequency** of reconciliations, the firm should **consider relevant risks**, such as the nature, volume and complexity of the business, and where the client money is held.

The FSA recommends that reconciliations should compare and identify discrepancies between:

- The balance of each **client bank account** as recorded by the firm, *and* the balance shown on the bank's statement, and

- The balance as shown in the firm's records, currency by currency, on each **client transaction account** – for **contingent liability investments**, which includes certain derivatives, spot forex trades, spread bets and contracts for difference (CfDs) – *and* the balance shown in the third party's records.

Any **approved collateral** held must be included in the reconciliation.

8.8 Client money: reconciliation discrepancies

The **reason** for any **discrepancy** must be identified, unless it arises solely from timing differences between a third party's accounting systems and those of the firm.

Any **shortfall** must be paid into (or any **excess** withdrawn from) the client bank account by the close of business on the day the reconciliation is performed.

If a firm cannot resolve a difference between its internal records and those of a third party holding client money, the firm must pay its own money into a relevant account to make up any difference, until the matter is resolved.

As with financial instruments held, If a firm has not complied with the reconciliation requirements in respect of client money 'in any material respect', then it must inform the FSA without delay.

8.9 Statutory trust

Section 139(1) FSMA 2000 provides for creation of a fiduciary relationship (a **statutory trust**) between the firm and its client, under which client money is in the legal ownership of the firm but remains in the beneficial ownership of the client. In the event of failure of the firm, costs relating to the distribution of client money may have to be borne by the trust.

8.10 Exemptions from CASS rules

There are some circumstances in which the client money rules do not apply.

8.10.1 Credit institutions

The client money rules do not apply to **Banking Consolidation Directive (BCD) credit institutions** in respect of deposits. Institutions whose business is to receive deposits from the public are credit institutions.

8.10.2 Coins held for intrinsic value

Client money rules do not apply to **coins** held on behalf of a client, if the firm and client have agreed that the money is to be held by the firm for the **intrinsic value** of the **metal** in the coin.

8.10.3 DVP transactions

Money arising through **delivery versus payment (DVP) transactions** through a commercial settlement system need not be treated as client money, if it is intended that:

- Money from the client, in respect of a client's purchase, will be due to the firm within one business day, on fulfilment of a delivery obligation, or

- Money is due to the client, in respect of a client's sale, within one business day following the client's fulfilment of a delivery obligation

8.10.4 Discharge of fiduciary duty

Money **ceases to be client money** if it is paid:

- To the client or his authorised representative

- Into a bank account of the client

- To the firm itself, when it is due and payable to the firm, or is an excess in the client bank account

- To a third party, on the client's instruction, unless it is transferred to a third party to effect a transaction – for example, a payment to an intermediate broker as initial or variation margin on behalf of a client who has a position in derivatives. In these circumstances, the firm remains responsible for that client's equity balance held at the intermediate broker until the contract is terminated and all of that client's positions at that broker closed

CHAPTER ROUNDUP

- The Conduct of Business Sourcebook (COBS) generally applies to authorised firms engaged in designated investment business carried out from their (or their appointed representatives') UK establishments. Some COB rules do not apply to eligible counterparty business.

- Designated investment business' is business involving regulated activities, except mortgages, deposits, pure protection policies, general insurance, Lloyd's business and funeral plans.

- The level of protection given to clients by the regulatory system depends on their classification, with retail clients being protected the most. Professional clients and eligible counterparties may both be either *per se* or elective. Both professional clients and eligible counterparties can re-categorise to get more protection.

- Firms doing designated investment business, except advising, must set out a basic client agreement. Firms must provide to clients appropriate information about the firm and its services, designated investments and their risks, execution venues and costs. Firms managing investments must establish a performance benchmark and must provide information about valuations and management objectives.

- A financial promotion inviting someone to engage in investment activity must be issued by or approved by an authorised firm. Communications must be fair, clear and not misleading. Prospectus advertisements must clearly indicate that they are not a prospectus.

- Rules on assessing suitability of the recommendation apply when a firm makes a personal recommendation in relation to a designated investment.

- There are obligations to assess 'appropriateness' – based on information about the client's experience and knowledge – for MiFID business other than making a personal recommendation and managing investments.

- Firms must seek to ensure fair treatment if there could be a conflict of interest. Common platform firms must maintain an effective conflicts of interest policy. Conflicts of interest policies must cover financial analysts producing investment research.

- Inducements must not be given if they conflict with acting in the best interests of clients, and there are controls on the use of dealing commission.

- A firm must in general take all reasonable steps to obtain, when executing orders, the best possible result for its clients. This is the requirement of best execution. There must be arrangements for prompt, fair and expeditious client order handling, and a fair order allocation policy. Unexecuted client limit orders must normally be made public, to facilitate early execution.

- Firms must establish arrangements designed to prevent employees entering into personal transactions which are prohibited forms of market abuse. Staff must be made aware of the personal dealing restrictions.

- Churning (investments generally) and switching (packaged products) forms of unsuitable overtrading of customer accounts in order to generate commission.

- There are requirements to send out confirmation notes promptly, and periodic statements (valuations) regularly.

- Client assets rules aim to restrict the commingling of client's and firm's assets and to prevent misuse of client's investments by the firm without the client's agreement, or being treated as the firm's assets in the event of the firm's insolvency.

TEST YOUR KNOWLEDGE

Check your knowledge of the Chapter here, without referring back to the text.

1   Name the three main categories of client.

2   Name three types of *per se* eligible counterparty.

3   A firm's communications and financial promotions must be ' ….., ….. and not …'. *Fill in the blanks.*

4   What information will the firm need to obtain from the client to enable it to assess the appropriateness of a product or service to the client?

5   What is the name for administrative and physical barriers and other internal arrangements, designed to contain sensitive information?

6   What does the rule on best execution require?

7   What is the effect of a statutory trust created under section 139(1) FSMA 2000?

TEST YOUR KNOWLEDGE: ANSWERS

1   Eligible counterparties, professional clients and retail clients. (See 2.2.)

2   Investment firms, national governments and central banks are all examples. (See 2.2.4.)

3   Fair, clear and not misleading. (See 4.4.)

4   The firm will need to ask the client for information about his knowledge and experience in the relevant investment field, so that it can assess whether the client understands the risks involved. (See 5.3.)

5   'Chinese walls'. (See 6.2.4.)

6   The best execution rule requires a firm to take all reasonable steps to obtain, when executing orders, the best possible result for its clients, taking into account the execution factors. (See 6.6.)

7   Section 139(1) FSMA 2000 provides for creation of a fiduciary relationship (a statutory trust) between the firm and its client, under which client money is in the legal ownership of the firm but remains in the beneficial ownership of the client. (See 8.9.)

14

Risks and Controls

INTRODUCTION

The possibility of an unfavourable outcome can be called a 'risk'. For the examination, you are expected to be able to show knowledge and understanding of the types of risk encountered in the financial services industry.

You should ensure that you have a general knowledge of types of risk and a detailed knowledge of ways of controlling risks and audit measures.

CHAPTER CONTENTS

1 TYPES OF RISK

1.1 Overview

Risk is defined in the *Oxford English Dictionary* as: (1) a situation involving exposure to danger; (2) the possibility that something unpleasant will happen; and (3) a person or thing causing a risk or regarded in relation to risk.

Managing risk is fundamental in the financial markets and associated industries.

Types of risk faced by financial institutions include:

- **Market risk** (or **principal risk**)
- **Credit risk** (or **counterparty risk**)
- **Liquidity risk**
- **Operational risk**

We also discuss in this section **country risk** (**sovereign risk**) and **linked** or **systemic risk**.

1.2 Market risk

Market risk or principal risk is the risk that changes in market conditions will have a negative impact on an institution's profitability.

Examples of **changing market conditions** include changes in:

- Interest rates, referred to as interest rate risk

- Foreign exchange rates, referred to as foreign exchange risk or currency risk

- The market value of investments held by the institution, which is sometimes referred to as price risk or equity position risk (in the case of equities)

Factors affecting market risk

- Length of time the position is held: the longer the period, the greater is the possibility of an adverse market price movement

- Liquidity or ease of resale when the level of risk becomes unacceptable for the holder: the longer it takes to find a buyer/seller, the greater is the risk of price movement

- Volatility of price fluctuations: for example, some emerging market equities have fluctuating prices, whereas many gilts have relatively stable prices

- Sensitivity of the price to underlying factors: derivatives prices move far more than the price of the underlying equity

To evaluate its exposure to market risks, a financial institution should evaluate the market value of its positions on a daily basis. Financial institutions should also compare this exposure to established market risk limits.

Methods of measuring and monitoring market risk

- **Value at risk (VAR) models** use probability-based methodologies to measure the institution's potential loss under certain market conditions. VAR is a statistical measurement of the maximum likely loss on a portfolio due to adverse market price movements. It calculates the loss if the price moves by two standard deviations or 95%. It uses historical price movements to identify the probability of future adverse price movements.

- **Stress testing** involves the application of extreme market movements that may arise as a result of hypothetical political or economic upheavals to a portfolio of investments.

- **Marking to market** all short positions at the bid price and all long positions at the offer price enables the firm to monitor its daily profit or loss. The mark to market value can be refined to take account of liquidity or settlement risk. In mark to market operations sometimes a single price is used to revalue positions, in listed derivatives for example.

- **Sensitivity analysis** measures the degree to which the values of trading positions are vulnerable to changes in interest rates. Every future cash flow is discounted by the time value of money to give a net present value (NPV). The sensitivity calculation is usually expressed as the change in NPV of the portfolio produced by a one basis point movement in interest rates across the whole cash flow portfolio.

1.3 Market liquidity risk

Market liquidity risk is the risk of loss through not being able to trade in a market or obtain a price on a desired product when required. This type of risk can arise when large positions in individual instruments or exposures reach more than a certain percentage of the market. This can mean they are not capable of being replaced or hedged without influencing the market price.

1.4 Credit risk or counterparty risk

Credit risk is the risk that a customer will fail to complete a financial transaction according to the terms of the contract, resulting in a loss to the financial institution.

Settlement risk is a sub-category of credit risk and relates to risks occurring within the settlement cycle. It is the risk that the transaction will not settle properly, will deliver 'bad' stock, will settle late, or one counterparty will default on their obligation.

Settlement risk is greatest in free deliveries and **foreign exchange** transactions. With foreign exchange transactions, there is a risk of non-receipt of the purchased currency after irrevocable instructions have been passed to deliver the sold currency. This is further exacerbated by banks operating in different time zones and over public holidays and weekends.

Settlement risk is increased by the 'chain effect' as there are frequently many interdependent transactions. For example, Customer A cannot buy stock X from B until they have sold stock Y to Customer C. Customer C cannot buy stock from Customer A until they have sold stock Z to Customer B and so on. CREST runs a 'circles' algorithm to resolve inter-dependencies.

Financial institutions need to measure their credit risk and compare their exposure to predetermined counterparty limits. Credit risk measurements should reflect the impact of changing market conditions on the current and future ability of customers to meet contractual obligations. **DvP** settlement of trades should be used as often as possible.

Today **counterparty risk** is further mitigated by the advent of the **Central Counterparty (CCP)** for securities settlement. LCH.Clearnet group provides a CCP for transactions on the London Stock Exchange through CREST and on Euronext respectively.

Exam tip

> It is important to study the introduction of and the role of the CCP as it has a major impact on the operational workflow.

The evaluation of customer and counterparty creditworthiness, as well as the setting of individual credit limits, should be the responsibility of an independent credit department. Help is available in the shape of the credit ratings agencies.

A broad measure of a firm's credit risk is its external credit rating, which is an assessment of its credit-worthiness. It is used by investors in public issues of debt capital as a guide to managing their credit exposure.

An independent rating agency will assign a credit rating based on its analysis of the company's financial statements. This is usually done with a short- and long-term outlook. Different agencies assign different terminologies to their ratings.

For example, Moody's Investors Services use ratings for long-term credit that range from Aaa, representing the highest quality investments, to C for firms more likely to default.

Leading agencies supplying ratings

- Moody's Investor Services
- Standard & Poor's
- Fitch Ratings

1.5 Liquidity risk

Liquidity risk encompasses two risks.

- Firstly, **liquidity risk** is the risk of not being able to sell or buy a security at a given time or at an acceptable price. This may be because of a lack of market participants (a thin market) or due to technical or operational disruptions in the market place. A prime example was the Stock Market crash in October 1987.

- Secondly, there is also **funding liquidity risk**, where a firm's cash flow is insufficient to meet its payment obligations on settlement dates or margin calls. (One man's funding liquidity risk is another man's counterparty risk.) In February 1995, trader Nick Leeson had severe problems meeting Simex margin calls after the Kobe earthquake made the futures prices move even more unfavourably.

Systemic risk is the ultimate liquidity risk, whereby the default by one firm will cause further firms to default leading to further firms defaulting until the whole system collapses like a set of dominoes, e.g. the Wall Street Crash of 1929. The Bank of England must consider this when it decides whether to step in to save banks, for example, in the cases of Barings, BCCI and, in 2007, Northern Rock.

1.6 Operational risk

1.6.1 Overview

Operational risk was originally defined by the Basel Committee on Banking Supervision in 2001 as 'the risk of direct or indirect loss resulting from inadequate or failed internal processes, people and systems or from external events'.

This focus on operational risk was generally welcomed, although concerns were expressed about the exact meaning of 'direct or indirect loss'. The words 'direct' or 'indirect' have now been omitted from their definition. In the work preparing for the Basel II Capital Accord, for the purposes of a Pillar 1 capital charge, strategic and reputational risks are not included, and it is not the intention for the capital charge to cover all indirect losses or opportunity costs. As a result, reference to 'direct or indirect' in the overall definition has been dropped. By directly defining the types of loss events that should be recorded in internal loss data, the Basel Risk Management Group (RMG) can give much clearer guidance on which losses are relevant for regulatory capital purposes.

This leads to a slightly revised current definition, as follows: **'the risk of loss resulting from inadequate or failed internal processes, people and systems or from external events'**.

The RMG confirms that this definition does not include systemic risk and the Basel II operational risk charge will be calibrated accordingly.

Operational risk can be broken down into further sub-categories such as **reporting risk**, **malicious risk**, **legal risk** and **regulatory risk**.

Exam tip

> A 25-mark Section C question in Summer 2006 asked for a discussion of the potential impact of operational risk, the major causes of operational risk and the benefits of an operational risk framework, including the internal implications if operational risk is not effectively managed.

1.6.2 Human error

Examples of human error include inputting trade details incorrectly e.g. a buy rather than a sell, 10 rather than 100, entering trades twice, running reports at the wrong time, forgetting to start IT processes and failing to back up. The premise, 'What can go wrong, will go wrong' is frequently true.

Human error is exacerbated by overstretched staff in periods of high volume, staff absence due to illness and holidays, inexperienced staff and lack of clear written procedures.

1.6.3 Systems failures

IT and system problems can range from **program failure**, e.g. system bugs or incorrect codes to complete system failures, when no trades can be input or processes can be run. Such problems are aggravated by either new systems which experience teething problems or old systems which have problems coping with the volumes and complexity of the business. In addition, IT problems are exacerbated if a financial institution has many different systems and applications.

1.6.4 Inadequate procedures and controls

If a financial institution does not have written **procedures** and clearly defined organisational charts, it is easy for processes to be missed. These problems are aggravated if there are frequent organisational or process changes.

1.6.5 Information risk or reporting risk

Information risk or **reporting risk** is the risk that the reports and sources of information that management use to make their decisions contain incorrect or misleading information. Incorrect and misleading information can lead management to make wrong policy decisions and to make corrective action in the wrong direction. Misleading, distorted or delayed information can lead to trends or mistakes not being identified and, thus, ignored. Badly produced reports can lead to the incorrect amount of client money being segregated.

1.6.6 Strategic risk

Strategic risk is risk of loss due to a sub-optimal business strategy being employed and is associated with the way the institution is managed. For instance, a new product strategy may be employed that fails to maximise the return on the investment made.

1.6.7 Business risk

Business risk is commonly understood as being the risk of loss due to an adverse external environment such as high inflation affecting labour costs; an over-competitive market reducing margins; or legal, tax or regulatory changes in the markets.

1.6.8 Regulatory risk

Regulatory risk is the risk that a firm breaches the regulator's rules or codes of conduct. In this way it is perhaps the most important of risks as any other operational risk has the potential to manifest itself as a regulatory risk.

- The **FSA's Conduct of Business (COBS) rules** set how to classify customers and thus what investments are suitable. The COBS rules set out requirements on customer agreements, contract notes, the content of advertising etc.

- The **client money** and safe custody rules set out how client money must be segregated and separately identified at all times. Segregated money is held 'in trust' and due to the trust rules, the exact client money must be segregated.

- The **financial resources** rules set out how much capital buffer an institution must have to protect it from unforeseeable losses.

- The **Money Laundering Regulations** set out what steps a financial institution must undertake to prevent and identify money laundering. There are severe penalties for not complying with these procedures.

1.6.9 Reputational risk

Reputational risk is more important than people sometimes realise and can lead to the rapid decline of a company, e.g. Ratners Jewellers and Arthur Andersen. This is particularly the case with companies that have strong brand names, are in highly competitive markets, or new, up and coming companies such as the internet stockbroking companies.

The Peter Young case at Morgan Grenfell in the mid-1990s provides another good example of the impact on a firm's reputation. The fiasco cost Morgan Grenfell an estimated £400m, including compensation to some 80,000 investors for money lost due to trading irregularities. The damage to Morgan Grenfell's reputation was no doubt even more costly.

A recent case was the flight of the customers and counterparties of Refco, the US capital market and futures broker in late 2005 following revelations about the misappropriation of funds by the Chief Executive. **Regulatory censure** will almost certainly lead to lead to reputational risk.

1.6.10 Legal risk

Legal risk is the risk that contracts are not legally enforceable (*ultra vires,* meaning literally 'beyond the powers') or documented incorrectly, leading to a loss for the firm.

An example of legal risk involves the London borough of Hammersmith and Fulham. Between 1986 and 1989, the local government was extremely active in sterling swaps, suggesting speculation rather than hedging. The speculation was unsuccessful, and in 1991 the House of Lords ruled that the transactions were *ultra vires*, and therefore beyond the scope of the powers of the borough. Consequently, swap agreements between more than 130 councils and 75 major banks were also rendered *ultra vires*, and counterparties lost an estimated US$1 billion.

Another example of legal risk is Orange County's *ultra vires* claim in its lawsuit against Merrill Lynch following its bankruptcy in 1994. Robert Citron, Orange County's Treasurer, had invested US$7.5 billion of the county's money into a risky, and eventually costly, portfolio of mostly interest-based securities. When US interest rates rose shortly thereafter, Citron found himself a victim of a liquidity trap, and the county was forced to declare bankruptcy. In the hope of nullifying the US$1.5 billion owed, Orange County claimed Merrill Lynch should have known that their contract violated several provisions of the California constitution.

1.6.11 Malicious risk

All companies face the risk of fraud and theft, of **malicious** intervention in the firm's systems by both employees, disgruntled ex-employees, competitors and outsiders. There are also an increasing number of computer hackers and other outsiders who may seek to ruin a company. The press contains numerous articles and frequently contains names of large established companies who have been targeted e.g. Amazon, CNN, Ebay.

This is further evidenced by demonstrations such as the environmentalists and the 'Stop The City' demonstrations that have hit cities such as London and Seattle.

A further threat highlighted by the 11 September 2001 terrorist attacks in New York and Washington is the sudden complete **shutdown of operations**. Such a situation has prompted companies to examine their disaster recovery procedures and **business continuity planning (BCP)**, **business continuity management (BCM)** and **business availability management (BAM)** – all of which have slightly different emphases.

1.7 Causes of operational risk

Operational risk results from **process**, **people**, **technology**, **environment** or **events**.

Common process causes

- Lack of effective procedures and/or procedural documentation
- Lack of capacity
- Volume sensitivity
- Lack of effective controls and/or control documentation
- Failure to review controls when processes change

Common people causes

- Human error
- Staff acting in an unauthorised manner
- Lack of accountability for operational risk management
- Dishonesty or poor integrity
- Lack of customer care
- Lack of skills and/or insufficient training
- Poor communication
- Concentration of expertise
- Lack of an effective control culture
- Lack of appropriate supervision

Technological causes: examples

- **Operational system failure**, caused by poor design or inadequate security can leave systems vulnerable to hacking, unauthorised access, sabotage and attack by computer viruses, power failures and vulnerability to the forces of nature such as earthquakes, lightning strikes, fire and floods.

- **Lack of system integrity**. If systems do not automatically pass on information, there is a need for manual re-keying between systems and reconciliations between systems.

- **Inadequate control functionality.** This is a growing concern as the pace of change and pressure for operational areas to become revenue generators increases. This may lead to a greater emphasis for technology to deliver cost reductions rather than ensure control integrity.

- **Inadequate testing of systems** in their development stage may lead to later production problems.

- **Lack of a strategic approach to system design**. Symptoms of this lack of strategy might be: a preponderance of 'tactical' system solutions; the uncontrolled use of business critical spreadsheets; or a lack of integration of systems across functional areas.

- High system complexity means that there can be a **lack of understanding of functionality** and it can be difficult to predict the knock-on effects of any major changes.

Causes from changes in environment (either internal and external)

- Change in technology and over-reliance on certain systems with little or no back-up
- Risk of error when processing consistently higher volumes than the systems and staff can handle
- Changes in tax structures and the need to modify procedures by the due date
- Changes to worker employment laws leading to non-availability of staff
- Political environment leading to terrorist action

Causes resulting from events

- Incorrect data
- Delayed processing and documentary omissions
- Regulatory non-compliance
- Project mismanagement
- Client dissatisfaction
- Fraud and theft
- Litigation

1.8 Country risk (sovereign risk)

International investment and trading portfolios will carry numerous products that provide good opportunities for profit. Equally, many of those products may be issued and traded in emerging markets or markets where volatility is high. **Emerging market** or **country risk** is an important issue as there are likely to be heightened risk implications, particularly for operations.

Typical country risks

- Market open to manipulation
- Rapid expansion of newly listed securities caused by the dash for growth
- Volatile trading activity
- Conflicting and ineffective (by mature market standards) regulatory environment and structures
- Lack of and poor quality information
- Physical share certificates
- Lack of automated settlement processes
- Fraud
- Low liquidity

Given that emerging markets present trading and investment opportunities, it is inevitable that operations teams must overcome the settlement problems associated with such business.

Operations Managers must familiarise themselves with the potential risks associated with each country and implement the necessary processes and controls to manage such business efficiently and safely.

An example of the kind of problem that might arise is the action taken by Malaysia in September 1998 to protect its currency from speculators. By freezing any movement of capital from the country, profits on investment and trading were effectively frozen and were also at risk from any fluctuation in the value of the Ringgit (Malaysian dollar).

Among countries, the term **BRIC** has been used to refer to the combination of Brazil, Russia, India and China. In a 2003 Goldman Sachs article, it was recognised that the BRIC countries had changed their political systems to embrace world capitalism. Goldman Sachs predicted that by 2050, China and India respectively would be the dominant global suppliers of manufactured goods and services while Brazil and Russia would become dominant suppliers of raw materials.

1.9 Linked or systemic risk

Risk rarely remains confined to one specific area or category. A risk may arise in one area but its severe impact may be felt in another. Thus the ability of the Operations Manager to identify source, cause and impact of operational risk is vitally important in the overall risk management process

An uncontrolled **'linked' risk** can ultimately create a disaster by becoming **systemic** and impacting elsewhere in an organisation.

The case of **Barings Bank** provides an example of this where the failure to deal with operational risk issues – segregation of duties, reconciliations and payment validation – ultimately led to the bank going bust.

In global operations, standards and practices may vary across different parts of an organisation. Controls and procedures must be robust enough to recognise this.

Systemic risk affects an **entire financial market or system**, and not just specific participants. It is the risk that an unexpected event originating from either inside or outside the financial sector could cause damage to the wider economy and the health of the financial system as a whole. Systemic risk is often described as a chain reaction or domino effect, whereby one system or organisation crashes and fails to meet its obligations, bringing down other organisations who as a result also default.

1.10 Risk – preparing for the exam

Exam tip

> A good way to understand risks is to read disaster stories, in books and on the internet, of what happens when it goes badly wrong. By doing this you can try to identify why cases went wrong and how they could have been prevented. Was it market risk? Credit risk? Operational risk? Or a combination of all three?

Various references are available is at the following website address:

http://www.erisk.com/Learning/CaseStudies.asp

Some major cases

- Barings (Nick Leeson), 1995
- Yasuo Hamanaka at Sumitomo Corporation, 1996
- Star bond trader (Joseph Jett *aka* 'Jet') at Kidder Peabody, 1994
- London Borough of Hammersmith and Fulham interest rate swaps, 1986-89
- BCCI, 1991
- Daiwa Bank, 1983-95
- Long Term Capital Management, 1998
- Griffin Trading, 1998
- Metallgesellschaft, 1993
- Peter Young at Morgan Grenfell, 1995-97
- Orange County (Robert Citron), 1991-94

- NatWest Markets, 1997
- James Archer and the 'Flaming Ferraris', 1998
- John Rusnak of Allfirst, Allied Irish Bank's US subsidiary, 1997-2002
- Enron Corporation, to 2001
- Worldcom, 2002
- The HealthSouth Corporation, 2003
- National Australia Bank, 2004
- China Aviation Oil (Singapore) Corporation, 2004
- Refco, 2005
- Societe Generale

2 STRATEGIC RISK CONTROLS

Exam tip

> This section on risk controls is to enable you to develop the required knowledge and understanding of the techniques and measures which may be employed by market practitioners in the management of risk.

A financial institution needs **adequate controls** in place to monitor and manage risk. A good internal control environment would have the aspects outlined below.

2.1 Organisational structure

All firms must have a clear **organisational and reporting structure** so that all employees know whom they report to. All employees should know the tasks for which they are responsible. When jobs are divided, there must be a clear allocation of duties.

While managing risks is important throughout an institution, specific responsibility for risk management falls to:

- The Board of Directors
- Executive Committee
- Risk Management Unit
- Internal Audit
- Compliance Department
- Controller's Department

The responsibility for understanding an institution's risks (and of ensuring they are appropriately managed) is placed clearly with the **Board of Directors**. The Board of Directors must approve risk management strategies, but will delegate authority for day-to-day decisions to an executive committee so that risk can be effectively managed in the institution.

The Board, through the executive committee, should identify and assess the institution's risks and develop a firm-wide risk management strategy to cover those risks. It should put structures in place to manage the quantifiable risks and to control the non-quantifiable risks.

Responsibility for capital allocation to business units/divisions also lies with the Board. In the process, they should make use of an independent Risk Management unit to ensure that risks undertaken are within the institution's risk tolerance. The **Executive Committee** should maintain continuous and demonstrable compliance with applicable capital requirements.

The Executive Committee should evaluate the independence and overall effectiveness of the institution's control and risk management infrastructure on a regular basis. The executive committee should also initiate and maintain a set of risk limits to manage and restrict the maximum amount of risk across business units. This set of limits (e.g. capital at risk or value at risk limits) should be approved by the Board. In addition, the institution's organisational structure should have clear reporting lines and responsibilities to enable the executive committee to monitor and control activities.

The **Risk Management Unit** should be independent with clearly defined responsibilities, reporting directly to the Board or a special sub-committee.

An **Internal Audit** function should be set up by the Board to examine, evaluate and report on accounting and other controls over operations. Internal audit should be specifically charged with assessing, for each area it examines, the adequacy of the information technology and other systems in operation, in relation to the risk management strategy adopted.

The Board should also ensure that a fully staffed **Compliance Department** has been established, charged with managing the institution's compliance with financial and business conduct regulations on a global basis. In addition, the Board should ensure that the activities of the institution are subject to frequent review by regulatory experts, so the business should not be exposed to material risk of loss due to breaches of regulations or failure to anticipate regulatory changes and issues.

Lastly, the institution should ensure that all management, trading, operations, risk management and auditing activities are undertaken by professionals in sufficient number, and with appropriate experience, skill levels and degree of specialisation.

This commitment by senior management to provide leadership and to engender the right corporate culture and environment is essential if the firm is to be successful in combating operational risk. Risk awareness is a collective responsibility across the whole firm. Operational risk is cross-functional in its nature. The important points to remember are that operational risk occurs throughout the lifecycle of a transaction and is embedded in all of an institution's functions. This makes its management difficult because it too must cross all functional boundaries. For this reason, operational risk must be managed in a structured manner and an integrated approach must be employed. This integrated, firm-wide approach can be extended to financial risk in general.

2.2 Management responsibility

The FSA has moved towards a culture of giving senior management more responsibility. These proposals were originally set out in Consultation Paper 35 (CP35, 1999) on *Senior Management Arrangements, Systems and Controls.*

Many regulated firms are using, or moving to, forms of **risk-based compliance** in order to focus most effectively on scarce resources on the key business issues. In CP35, the FSA made it clear that it will look to the senior management of regulated firms to prove that they have allocated responsibilities appropriately and put in place adequate control systems and procedures.

CP35 amplified FSA Principle 3, which states that: 'A firm must take reasonable care to organise and control its affairs responsibly and effectively, with adequate risk management systems'. Firms are therefore obliged to allocate responsibilities among the directors and senior managers and to ensure that the operations of the firm can be adequately monitored and controlled both by the senior managers and its governing body. Firms must take reasonable care to ensure that appropriate systems and controls are established and maintained.

This early work on CP35 resulted in the publication of two Sourcebooks, APER – which defines the Statements and Code of Practice for Approved Persons under the Approved Persons Regime, and T&C – which describes the Training and Competence requirements. These were published and took effect from N2 on 30 November 2001.

In terms of accountability, the FSA makes it clear that it 'would not institute disciplinary proceedings against a firm's Chief Executive, or equivalent, simply because a breach of the regulatory requirements has occurred in an area for which he or she is responsible'. The FSA would take disciplinary action only where the Chief Executive was considered to be in deliberate breach, or his or her actions fell short of the requisite standard of care. Following the Barings case, the regulators have sought not to allow management to avoid responsibilities, leading some to speculate that 'ignorance is not, and never will be, a defence – directors will be judged not on what they know, but on what they should have known'. (Institute of Directors).

2.3 Role of risk management

The creation of operational risk management programmes has been driven by:

- Management commitment
- The need for an understanding of enterprise-wide risks
- A perceived increase in exposure to operational risk and risk events, and
- Regulatory interest

To manage risk, a financial institution must consider the following aspects.

- **Strategy**. Risk management begins with the determination of the overall strategies and objectives of the institution and the subsequent goals for individual business units, products, or managers. Once strategies and objectives are determined, the institution can identify the associated inherent risks in its strategy and objectives. Both hazards (negative events such as a major loss that would have a significant impact on earnings) and opportunities (such as new products that depend on taking operational risk) are considered. A firm is then able to set a risk appetite. Specifically, it can determine what risks the company understands, will take, and will manage, versus those that should be transferred to others or eliminated. It is the basis for decision making and a reference point for the organisation.

- **Risk policies**. Operational risk management policies are a formal communication to the entire organisation about the company's approach to operational risk management. Policies typically include a definition of operational risk, the organisational approach and related roles and responsibilities, key principles for management, and a high-level discussion of information and related technology.

- **Risk management process**. This process defines the overall procedures for operational risk management, which includes:

  - **Controls**: Definition of internal controls, or selection of alternate mitigation strategy, such as insurance, for identified risks.

  - **Assessment**: Programmes to ensure that controls and policies are being followed and to determine the level of severity. These may include process flows, self-assessment programs, and audit programmes.

  - **Measurement**: A combination of financial measures (e.g. to quantify the '**value at risk**') and non-financial measures, risk indicators and escalation triggers to determine current risk levels and progress toward goals.

  - **Reporting**: Information for management to increase awareness and prioritise resources.

- **Risk mitigation**. These are specific controls or programmes designed to reduce the exposure, frequency, or severity of an event. The controls can also eliminate or transfer an element of operational risk. Examples include business continuity planning, IT security, compliance reviews, project management, and merger integration and insurance.

- **Risk acceptance.** This means doing nothing – typically when the quantified value of the risk is within the firm's stated risk appetite range.

- **Risk avoidance.** Making changes so that the adverse event will not occur (for example, relocating a business away from an area prone to flooding).

- **Operations management**. The day-to-day processes of operations management, such as front and back-office functions, technology, performance improvement, management reporting, and people management, have a component of operational risk management embedded in them.

- **Culture**. There is always a balance between formal policies and culture, or the values of the people in the organisation. In operational risk, cultural aspects such as communication, the 'tone at the top', clear ownership of each objective, training, performance measurement, and knowledge sharing, all help set the expectations for sound decision making.

  In addition, the integration with market and credit risk in an enterprise-wide risk management framework is noted, as well as alignment with the needs of the stakeholders – for example, customers, employees, suppliers, regulators, and shareholders.

- **Using risk indicators**. By identifying and assessing the severity of risks and properly understanding the chain of events, objective measurement criteria can be chosen to measure ongoing risk status. These measures are called risk indicators. They are a 'health check' on the performance of the business and are used by all functions to ensure that risk is satisfactorily controlled. They usually measure the effects (rather than the cause) of risk at set control points in the business and act as early warning signals or forward looking measures to alert management to problem areas.

  The term **Key Risk Indicators (KRIs)** is sometimes used. An extension of this concept is the use of objective Key Performance Indicators (KPIs). Mapping KRIs against KPIs enables a firm's risk managers to assess performance and to manage risk against proper benchmarks.

  Risk indicators can be thought of in terms of process related indicators (which tend to relate directly to performance) and non-process indicators (which incorporate other important measures of control, especially relating to people).

  Levels of **acceptable risk** can be established by attaching limits or thresholds of acceptability to the indicators. These allow the firm to set its risk appetite and give its managers the autonomy to make business decisions within specified boundaries.

Examples of process related indicators

- The number of settlement failures occurring over a given time period
- The number of times a trader exceeds agreed credit limits
- The average length of time a confirmation remains unsigned
- The mark-to-market value of transactions with confirmations unsigned
- The number of times funding deadlines are missed in a given time period
- The number and value of cash (*nostro*) or position (*depot*) reconciliation breaks over a given time period
- The number of reconciliation breaks between front office and back office systems over a given time period
- The value of interest claims incurred over a given time period, and
- The volume/number of transactions per head

Examples of non-process related indicators

- Staff turnover
- Percentage of temporary staff to permanent staff
- Amount of overtime
- Percentage of staff with an agreed training plan
- Period of time to review departmental plans, and
- Response and resolution times to line problems

Summary: advantages of using indicators

- Allow trends to be monitored and can therefore be used to anticipate problems

- Allow limits of acceptability to be established

- Provide a basis for objective performance measurement. Performance measurement can be used to encourage staff to become more risk-aware, especially where performance targets, expressed in terms of key indicators, are linked to compensation

- Act as early warning signals to alert management to problem areas

Summary: disadvantages of using indicators

- Can be misleading if used in isolation
- Are difficult to obtain automatically
- Are prone to manipulation

2.3.1 Risk management departments

Companies have evolved in their operational risk management practices in a variety of ways depending on the culture and the organisation's operational risk event history.

One survey outlined **five stages of development**

- **Stage I – Traditional baseline**. Operational risks have always existed and are managed by focusing primarily on internal controls. They are the responsibility of individual managers in the business and specialist functions, with periodic objective review by Internal Audit. Traditionally, there is not a formal operational risk management framework, like that discussed in this report.

- **Stage II – Awareness**. Senior management must take an active role in increasing the understanding of operational risk in the organisation, and they must appoint someone to be responsible for it. To gain awareness, a common understanding and assessment of operational risks must exist. This assessment begins with the formulation of an operational risk policy, a definition, and development of common tools. The tools in this stage usually include self-assessment and risk process map. In addition, early indicators of operational risk levels and collection of loss events are beginning to be developed. These provide a common framework for risk identification, definition of controls, and prioritisation of issues and mitigation programmes. However, the most important factor in this stage is gaining senior management commitment and the buy-in of ownership of operational risk at the business unit level.

- **Stage III – Monitor**. After identifying all of the operational risks, it is important to understand their implications to the business. The focus then becomes tracking the current level of operational risk and the effectiveness of the management functions. Risk indicators (both quantitative and qualitative) and escalation criteria, which are goals or limits, are established to monitor performance. Measures are consolidated into an operational risk scorecard along with other relevant issues for senior management. About this time, the business will realise that operational risk management process is valuable and assign dedicated staff to analyse processes and monitor activity. An operational risk programmes may be introduced.

- **Stage IV – Quantify**. With a better understanding of the current situation, it is time to focus on quantifying the relative risks and predict what will happen. More analytic tools, based on actual data, are required to determine the financial impact of operational risk on the organisation and provide data to conduct empirical analysis on causes and mitigating factors. Operational risk management is developing a comprehensive set of tools for the identification and assessment of operational risk, as follows.

- Self- or risk assessment
- Risk mapping
- Risk indicators
- Escalation triggers
- Loss event database

■ **Stage V – Integrate**. Recognising the value of lessons learned by each business unit and the complementary nature of the individual tools, management focuses on integrating and implementing processes and solutions. It balances business and corporate values, qualitative versus quantitative and different levels of management needs. Risk quantification is now fully integrated into the economic capital processes and linked to compensation. Quantification is also applied to make better cost/benefit decisions on investments and insurance programmes. However, this integration goes beyond the processes and tools. In leading companies, operational risk management is being linked to the strategic planning process and quality initiatives. When this link is established, the relationship between operational risk management and shareholder value is more directly understood.

A new organisational model is emerging, with a new position – a **Head of Operational Risk**, reporting to the **Chief Risk Officer**. The role is to develop and implement the operational risk framework and consult to the lines of business. The business units are primarily responsible for managing operational risk on a day-to-day basis. Other risk-related functions (e.g. IT, Legal, Compliance, Human Resources) have responsibility for specific operational risk issues. While the trend for market risk and credit risk is towards increasing centralisation, operational risk, by its nature, is decentralised. In operational risk there is no position to report, few approvals to request, or hard policy limits to measure against. The businesses have this risk whether they like it or not, and cannot transfer the responsibility for management of it.

The culture of the organisation, rather than the type of institution, determine the risk management approach, but three types of structure have appeared:

■ A **head office** operational risk function
■ A dedicated but **decentralised** support, and
■ **Internal audit** playing a lead role in operational risk management

2.4 Audit Committee

An **Audit Committee** establishes processes and procedures and creates monitoring to ensure all processes and procedures across the financial institution are followed. The Audit Committee typically acts independently of management and has oversight responsibilities.

In some countries, institutions are required to have an independent Audit Committee made up entirely of outside directors, independent of management. They are charged with reviewing the policies, procedures and financial reports with management and the independent accountants. Certain country regulations require audit committees to possess both banking and management expertise to offer the best guidance and oversight to the organisation.

2.5 Internal audit

The role of **internal audit** is to perform various services for management, including performing tests of operating, financial and regulatory controls, reviewing operating practices to promote increased efficiency and economy, and to carry out special projects and inquiries at management's discretion. Many times the professional in-charge of internal audit reports to management and to the Independent Audit Committee.

3 CONTROLS OVER STAFF

3.1 Registration of approved persons

As we saw earlier in this Study Book, the FSA operates prior approval individual 'approved person' registration procedures which covers those working in **controlled functions** all businesses regulated by the FSA (and therefore, for the first time, banks, insurance companies and building societies).

The FSA has the power to regulate those carrying out specified controlled functions if one of the following applies.

- The person carrying out the function is likely to be able to exercise a significant influence on the conduct of the firm's affairs.

- Employees have dealings with the actual or potential consumers of a firm's services (e.g. advisers).

- Individuals who deal with the property of customers whilst carrying on a regulated activity (e.g. fund managers). The FSA regulates those who manage funds on behalf of customers, or who act in a management capacity as custodian. This regime applies to fund managers (and so on) carrying out controlled functions in the UK even if the firm is incorporated outside the UK, provided the FSA is the prudential regulator.

When firms sub-contract regulated functions, those to whom the functions are delegated must also be individually registered, and so firms are not allowed to sub-contract to unauthorised firms. (In any case, the unauthorised firm would probably need authorisation to carry out the delegated function.)

3.2 Staff training

One of senior management's greatest sources of comfort in relying on their staff is the knowledge that they are well trained, not just in terms of the firm's procedures but also their general understanding of market practice. The provision of high quality training to staff encourages their loyalty to the firm at the same time as giving them skills which are ultimately transferable.

While in the past the training spotlight has focused on the front office, many firms have realised that the formal training of back office staff brings just as much to the firm in terms of efficiency of processing and the integrity of management controls. An often quoted saying is 'revenue is taken in the front office, but profits are made or lost in the back'. Following IMRO's lead of several years ago, it is also an area of growing interest at the FSA in terms of incorporation of operational training requirements into the ongoing Training and Competence regime.

3.3 Staff resources

There must be **adequate staff resources** to ensure that tasks are correctly performed and not omitted due to time pressure. The resourcing must take account of holidays, sickness and increases in volume. The use of temporary staff or secondments can aid temporary resources deficiencies. The recruitment procedures should be thorough, with all references and CVs checked for validity and accuracy. The disciplinary and dismissal procedures need to be adequately documented and followed.

Exam tip

> Because the international approach to risk is constantly being changed and modified, it is a good idea to research the approach to risk taken by the FSA as well as other overseas regulatory bodies such as the Securities and Exchange Commission (SEC) in the United States and the Japanese Financial Services Agency. It is also sensible to research the comments, papers and guidelines issued by industry bodies such as the Bank for International Settlement, The Futures Industry Association, ISSA, and ISMA.

4 DAY-TO-DAY CONTROL PROCEDURES

The likelihood of operational risk losses can be reduced through the use of operational controls. Operational controls are activities that are inserted into a process to protect it against specific operational risks. Controls do not generally add value to processing in direct terms (i.e. by moving the process forward from one state to another), but they can add value in indirect terms by protecting against error and consequential loss.

For instance, a procedural control might be set up to protect against the risk of a member of staff diverting funds to a personal bank account when making a payment (i.e. committing fraud). This procedure might ensure that one person prepares the documentation to send a payment and another person physically sends it. This action doesn't directly make the process any quicker or cheaper (in fact in might make it slower and more costly), but it is necessary to protect the firm against fraudulent activity, in order to save money in the longer term.

Potential risks should be anticipated and evaluated when the process is first designed and the necessary controls embedded within it. There are two main types of control – **preventive** and **detective** controls.

Preventive controls are those that prevent errors occurring in the first place. They attempt to tackle the root causes of risk and are most effective when incorporated within processes at the outset by anticipating a risky outcome. Technology solutions are often used as a key means of implementing such controls.

A key preventive control is the **segregation of duties**. This means the separation of trading, operation and control, financial reporting and risk management functions. The aim of segregating these functions is to prevent too much responsibility and authority being concentrated in the hands of specific individuals. In turn, this prevents the possibility of the internal control structure being compromised and the risk of fraud arising. The lack of appropriate segregation of duties is one of the major process causes of operational risk.

From the transaction processing perspective, another important area is in the maintenance of data integrity in systems. For instance, the incorrect capture of a transaction's details in a firm's systems due to errors in manual input needs to be avoided. If the process was designed so that the transaction was captured once at the point of execution and this data then flowed automatically into the downstream systems, the risk of manual errors would disappear (being replaced by the system risks, which are generally considered to be smaller).

Other examples of preventive controls

- Setting up and maintenance of good procedures to prevent unauthorised actions and errors
- Use of training to reduce the likelihood of human errors arising from a lack of expertise
- Well-designed systems automating processes and controls to eliminate risk due to human error

Detective controls detect errors once they have occurred. They are less ideal than preventive controls but can still be effective in reducing risk. They can be further split into two sub-categories – internal and external detection.

- **Internal detection controls** detect errors after they have occurred but before a potential loss is realised in the outside world; that is, they detect the risk event in order to prevent the effect. Any checking activities fall under this category. For instance, checking the legal terms of a contract before it is signed is a control that may detect errors in the terms and conditions of the contract. These errors would then be rectified and the contract sent out at no loss to the firm. If the control did not exist, the potential for legal risk to be realised would increase.

- **External detection controls** are those that detect errors and losses once they have been realised. They detect the effects. Post-settlement checks such as statement-to-ledger reconciliations fall under this category. If a problem is found, for instance, if a counterparty has not been paid on time, loss due to a compensation claim for lost interest will occur. If the detective control is effective, the problem will be resolved quickly and the loss effect limited. External detective controls are important because they can limit the direct and indirect losses to the firm. External detective controls are really concerned with reducing the impact of loss, rather than reducing the likelihood (because the loss has already occurred).

4.1 Segregation of duties

Segregation of duties is vital as lack of segregation can lead to problems being covered up accidentally or purposefully. Segregation should occur at both a macro level between front and back office and a micro level. Examples might include one person banking the money, with another person maintaining the cashbook and a third performing reconciliations.

4.2 Procedures manual

An up-to-date **procedures manual** is vital for staff and management to know what processes are supposed to happen at what time. The regulators believe that an out-of-date procedures manual is as bad as not having a procedures manual. If a firm does not follow its written procedures, it can be deemed as negligent.

4.3 Programmes and checklists

The use of programmes and checklists can promote thought, monitor progress and ensure that vital information or procedures are not omitted.

There must be in-built controls to ensure that transactions and entries are input correctly. The use of hash totals and check digits are good controls.

4.4 Supervision and review

There must be adequate reviews to identify any mistakes and to highlight and correct trends. Reviewers should sign and date schedules to evidence their review.

4.5 Reconciliations

Exam tip

A 25-mark question in Section B of the Winter 2006 paper was on the topic of reconciliations. Note the FSA regulations on client money reconciliations, which we covered in Chapter 13 of this Study Book.

The process of proving that a firm's books and records are accurate is commonly known as **reconciliation**. Reconciliations are a vital management control to ensure that two systems are in agreement or that the firm agrees to external information sources so that it remains in control of its assets and liabilities. Any discrepancy that is highlighted will require investigation and resolution.

Each major component of a company's securities and cash positions must be reconciled in its own right. These will cover trading positions, cash accounts, stock depot positions, margin accounts (where applicable) and collateral accounts. Checks will be carried out to ensure first that the firm's records agree internally, and second that the records agree with external sources such as counterparties, custodians, clearing houses, CSDs and CCPs.

At a more detailed level the firm will need to undertake the following.

- **Trade by trade reconciliation** – to prove that all trades transacted by the traders have been successfully captured within the settlement system.

- **Trading position reconciliation** – by comparing the trading book, individual securities and the trading position to prove that the trade dated securities positions (by security and trading book) are in agreement with the equivalent positions calculated by the settlement system.

- **Open trades reconciliation** – to prove that open trades (not yet settled) are in reality open at the relevant custodian.

- **Custodian (depot) position reconciliation** – to prove that the settled securities positions held within internal books agree with the equivalent positions as advised by the custodian(s).

- **Settlement system integrity reconciliation** – to prove that the settlement system remains in balance, i.e. that the total of the securities owned is equal to the sum of the parts in their various locations.

- **Safe custody reconciliation** – to prove that every aspect of the securities position agrees with the clients records. The securities trading firm will normally hold client accounts at the custodian. The reconciliation exercise will check that the sum of the client's holdings is mirrored at the custodian and is segregated from the firm's own proprietary dealing records. Both the client's and the custodian's positions will need to be checked.

- **Cash reconciliations** – in addition to trades and positions, cash must also be reconciled. This will embrace net settlement value checks, cash values pertaining to open trades and *nostro* accounts with custodians and agent banks. Cash may be checked from the perspective of open trades with counterparties, balances at custodians and profit and loss.

- **Inter-company and inter-account reconciliations** – additional internal checks to ensure that temporary cash accounts do in fact clear to zero and that inter-company dealings are correctly booked.

Methods of reconciliation are either a snapshot without any kind of opening and closing balance or they are of the form where an opening balance is taken and movements applied to derive a closing balance. The information sources required will be the firm's own settlements systems and, for the outside world, a combination of the firm's own trading system and the custodian-supplied *depot* and *nostro* information.

Steps in the reconciliation process

- Conduct a comparison of statement information
- Identify items which agree
- Identify internal and external discrepancies
- Investigate those discrepancies
- Rectify discrepancies

Manual reconciliation is traditional but does have major drawbacks in that it is prone to error, is very time consuming and often means that discrepancy rectification is not achieved in good time. **Automation** of the reconciliation process is possible today. Specialist **software** products have been developed to make the required comparisons of the detail contained within files from various sources. The biggest advantage is the ability to derive and begin the resolution of discrepancies within minutes rather than hours (or days). This leads to a true ability to **manage by exception** and to handle greater volumes.

It is best to keep the reconciliation function totally independent of other operations groups, for example the settlement department. This is a strong example of the need for segregation of duties.

In most cases reconciliations should be performed on a daily basis. Failure to do so will prevent the firm from knowing that it is in control of its assets.

Benefits of reconciliation

- Traders may execute new trades knowing that their trading positions are complete.

- Similarly, repo traders may execute new trades with the full knowledge that their decisions are based upon reconciled trading positions, securities positions with custodians and outstanding trades with counterparties.

- The securities lending and borrowing teams (if present) may undertake further transactions without risk as their information on stock balances at custodians is up-to-date.

- Credit managers within the firm know that they can check counterparty risk situations with clarity.

- Operations management may attend to settlement of truly open trades.

- The accounting department can calculate profit and loss figures accurately.

- Corporate actions teams are able to calculate entitlements to dividends and coupon payments with accuracy.

In conclusion, errors will sometimes be made and that the instances of fraud do occur from time to time within the financial markets. As the size of positions and the sheer monetary values involved continue to increase, a firm will take a huge risk if it fails to address essential reconciliation disciplines, on a daily basis. The FSA has substantial powers to punish UK-regulated firms whose reconciliations fall short of the mark.

5 MANAGEMENT REPORTING

Risk reporting is the process mechanism of communicating the losses, exposure and risks to the right level of management in the firm.

Functions of risk reporting

- To provide transparency of risk status and issues
- To aid communication
- To reduce uncertainty
- To escalate issues and recommendations
- To allow early, decisive action to address

It is necessary to report risk **internally** (across and up through the organisation) **and externally** (to regulators, auditors and analysts).

5.1 Exception reporting

Exception reporting can be used to identify unusual trades or items that fall outside pre-determined limits. These can include unidentified bank credits exceeding £1m or trades that have failed for more than ten days. Exception reporting alerts management to concerns.

5.2 Status reports

Status reports are used to give management regular feedback on the status of various items. Status reports can be used for reporting on the number and size of reconciling items, and the age and size of failed trades.

5.3 Key performance indicators (KPIs)

Many firms use **KPIs** to report statistics to management and are required to ensure that these statistics fall within certain limits.

6 IT CONTROLS

It is important to have a well controlled information technology (IT) environment.

There should be controls over:

- Input, processing and output of data
- Physical security
- File security

These controls can be categorised into:

- Application controls over data processing
- General controls of the system and its development

6.1 Application controls over data processing

The aim of the controls is to ensure that correct information is input and processed. It is necessary to ensure that every transaction or document is present so sequential numbering or 'checks in total' will help. To ensure that correct information has been input, there can be computerised reasonableness checking by tolerances (i.e. flagging trades where price is US$5 different), computerised calculation (of stamp duty, commission), use of hash totals and batch control totals.

Manual processes such as double re-keying information, signing and initialling reviews or input and reviewing logs of amendments can help to identify problems.

Checks on processing can include monitoring the time taken to fulfil procedures compared to usual time taken, reviewing completion logs, error messages and exception reports. Process output can be checked on a sample basis, control totals and the number of items can be reviewed. Printed reports should state 'end of report'.

6.2 General controls of the system and its development

General controls over the IT environment ensure that only authorised users can input authorised data and make changes or interrupt processes.

General controls include the following.

- Passwords which are changed periodically
- Hierarchical access, e.g. read only
- User acceptance testing
- Regular back up (both on and off-site)
- Log of all errors
- Review of amendments
- Clear file labelling
- Virus checks and fire walls
- Limited access to computer room
- Environmental controls in the computer room (e.g. dust, temperature, humidity)
- IT Policy for all employees

- 24/7 IT Support team
- Contingency and back up

In summary, there are many causes, events and effects as well as multiple dependencies in the world of operational risk. The relationship between the processes, the people performing them and the enabling technology are complex, interrelated and difficult to control in isolation. As a result, operational losses often derive from multiple points of failure. There must therefore be a strategic approach to risk management that cuts across the traditional boundaries and functions of financial institutions.

7 AUDIT

7.1 Overview

Exam tip

> For the examination, you need to be able to demonstrate a knowledge and understanding of the types of audit controls necessary within the financial services industry to control data and prevent fraud. This section explains the importance of internal and external audit.

An **audit** is an independent review of the functions, procedures and controls within an organisation.

- An **internal audit** is performed by an internal department solely for the purposes of senior management. The subject, depth and scope of the internal audit is chosen by the management. The audit findings are then reported to management.

- An **external audit** is performed by an external registered auditor. The scope and the methodology is in accordance with Companies Act and Auditing Standards. The aim is to report to the members (shareholders) on whether the financial statements give a 'true and fair' view and are in accordance with applicable accounting standards.

Internal audit plays an important role in the risk control framework. It provides an independent, internal assessment of the effectiveness of the firm's controls and procedures. It also independently assesses the effectiveness of the risk management process.

The independent periodic review of all transaction lifecycle activities is an indispensable safeguard for senior management in ensuring the integrity of the internal control structure. It also ensures that **management information systems (MIS)** are operating effectively.

By performing reviews, internal audit assesses control strength, questioning whether an institution's processes and procedures are:

- Adequately controlled
- Up-to-date
- Practised in accordance with manuals and documentation

Internal audit also acts as a 'dry run' for external audits and regulatory examiners.

Internal auditors must have an unrestricted mandate to review all aspects of the transaction life cycle and be totally independent of senior managers and their departments who are subject to the review.

There is a crossover with the operational risk management process in that both involve the identification of risk issues. However, auditing is aimed more at checking the control environment on a 'snapshot' basis (e.g. once every six months), highlighting issues (audit points) but leaving 'cause-effect' analysis and solution implementation to the business. Operational risk management on the other hand, monitors risk on a continuous, day-to-day basis as part of the process allowing more dynamic and strategic management. Audit information should therefore be used as an input to operational risk management. Audit points can also be used as risk indicators.

Both internal and external audits can be a powerful enabler of change. As part of the cultural change to a more risk aware outlook, the political will to clear audit issues can significantly raise the profile of the need for effective risk management.

7.2 Internal audit

The scope and objectives of **internal audit** vary. They are decided by the senior management of the company and can cover the following areas.

- Review the design of the accounting and internal control systems, monitoring their operation and recommending improvements

- Examine financial and operating information such as the means used to identify, measure, classify and report information and specific enquiry into individual items including detailed testing of transactions, balances and procedures

- Review of non-financial controls such as economy, efficiency and effectiveness

- Review of compliance with regulatory, tax, employment and environmental laws, regulations and other external requirements

- Review of segregation of duties

- Special investigations such as suspected fraud

7.3 Effectiveness of internal audit

Factors relevant to internal audit effectiveness

- **Organisational status** – The internal audit department should report directly to the Board, rather than indirectly via the finance, compliance or legal department. The internal audit department should be seen as both important and independent from the other departments.

- **Technical competence** – Internal audit must be competent. They must have adequate technical training and must fully understand the complexities of the business.

- **Due professional care** – Internal audit work should be properly planned, supervised, reviewed and documented. There should be adequate audit manuals, work programmes and working papers.

- **Reporting and follow-up** – Internal auditors should ensure that findings, conclusions and recommendations arising from each internal audit assignment are communicated promptly to the appropriate level of management. All the points should have a management response and action plan. Internal audit should revisit the area six months later to ensure that the recommendations have been put in place.

7.4 External audits

External auditors report to the members/shareholders of the firm being audited. The auditors give an **opinion** as to whether the financial statements give a '**true and fair**' view and are properly prepared in accordance with the Companies Act.

A 'clean' audit opinion means that the auditors believe the financial statements to be correct, whereas a 'qualified' opinion means that the auditors cannot give an opinion that the financial statements are 'true and fair'.

The phrase 'true and fair' does not have official definitions. 'True' means that the financial statements are **materially** accurate. This means that the turnover and profits are correct and the assets and liabilities are shown at a realistic value, within the bounds of what is significant or 'material'. 'Fair' means that the financial statements give the reader an accurate reflection of the company and they are not misleading. This means, for instance, that the company does not appear in the financial statements to be profitable when it is not.

'Properly prepared' means that the company keeps adequate accounting records. Adequate accounting records enable a firm to identify its assets and liabilities at any time.

Auditing is guided from the following sources.

- **Companies Act 1985** and subsequent amendments

- The **Auditing Practices Board** who produce Auditing Standards, and the **Accounting Standards Board** who produce Financial Reporting Statements and Statements of Standard Accounting Practice: both are operating bodies of the **Financial Reporting Council** (FRC).

It is a common misconception known as the '**expectations gap**' that auditors identify 'fraud and other irregularities'. Auditors check that the financial statements are true and fair to within materiality limits – a process which may fail to identify some instances of fraud.

Materiality is the concept of 'when a balance actually matters', e.g. if a balance should be £100,000 and it is £100,010 or £100,100, it is likely to be immaterial, whereas if it was £50,000 or £200,000 it would be material. Materiality is subjective, as a balance of £90,000 or £120,000 could be material depending on the situation.

7.5 The external audit approach

Historically, audits used to be 'substantive' exercises where all balances were 'ticked' and agreed to supporting evidence. As businesses became more complex the risk of fraud or misstatement became greater. The increasing size of organisations, the sophistication of computer systems and the globalisation of business meant that substantive approaches were less appropriate.

Auditing is now typically controls- and risk-based.

- In a **'controls-based' audit**, the auditors gain assurance that the numbers are accurate by testing that the controls are adequately designed and reviewed, e.g. that there is segregation of duties and that limits cannot be exceeded.

- In a **'risk-based' audit**, the auditors identify the risky areas and concentrate on those areas.

7.6 Stages of an external audit

7.6.1 Planning

The first stage in any audit should be **planning**. The auditors need to identify the risk areas via discussions with management. A **letter of engagement** must always be signed before the audit work starts.

7.6.2 Identifying the systems and internal controls

This is a fact-finding exercise to identify the internal controls by discussing the accounting system and document flow with all the relevant departments, including typically, sales, purchases, cash, inventory and accounts personnel. These controls are documented.

7.6.3 Testing controls

The auditors check that the controls documented function as they are supposed to. The auditors select a random sample of transactions and 'walk through' the systems. The auditors will review reports and reconciling items.

The conclusion drawn from the results of a test of controls may be either

- That the controls are effective, in which case the auditors will only need to carry out restricted substantive procedures, or

- That the controls are ineffective in practice, although they had appeared strong on paper, in which case the auditors will need to carry out more extensive substantive procedures.

7.6.4 Substantive testing

Substantive testing involves checking a large number of transactions to backing information. It is timely and repetitive. If errors are found the sample size is increased. Errors are then extrapolated to the whole population to identify the potential size of the misstatement.

7.6.5 Producing the financial statements

The financial statements have to be prepared in accordance with the prescribed disclosures set out in Companies Acts and the FRSs. The form of the income statement and balance sheet is set out in Schedule 4. Insurance companies and banks use Schedule 9. The director and the audit partner should sign the financial statements on the same day.

7.6.6 Regulatory work

The auditors then concentrate on the regulatory work. This falls into three sections: reviewing client money and safe custody; reviewing prudential returns including the calculation of the financial resources requirement; and thirdly checking whether the accounting records are adequate for regulatory purposes.

7.6.7 Feedback

At the end of every audit, the auditors and the management have a meeting to discuss their findings. This can be a formal audit committee meeting or a more informal clearance meeting. The auditors also write a management letter identifying potential weaknesses and recommending improvements.

8 OTHER SERVICES PROVIDED BY AUDIT FIRMS

External audit firms typically provide a range of other services, such as the following.

Corporation tax	Advising on corporate tax efficient structures and optimising tax efficiency
Indirect tax advice	Advising on VAT and related topics
Company Secretarial	Filing Companies House returns
Treasury	Advising on a firm's treasury function, including use of derivatives
Project management	Helping firms install new systems
Computer solutions	Offering technical IT advice
Risk management	Reviewing the firm's procedures or identifying risk
Corporate finance	Assisting firms in takeovers and mergers
Corporate recovery	Helping firms restructure efficiently
E-business	Giving practical guidance to firms developing e-commerce

CHAPTER ROUNDUP

- Market risk (or principal risk) is the risk that changes in market conditions will impact negatively on an institution's profitability.

- Credit risk (or counterparty risk) is the risk that a financial transaction will fail to be completed by the customer.

- Liquidity risk is the risk of not being able to sell or buy a security at a given time. Funding liquidity risk is the risk of a firm's cash flow being insufficient to meet payment obligations on the settlement date, or margin calls.

- Operational risk is the risk of loss resulting from inadequate or failed internal processes, people, systems or external events. It can be broken down into sub-categories, including regulatory risk, legal risk and malicious risk.

- Country risk (or sovereign risk) can be significant for operations.

- Systemic risk affects an entire financial system or market – not only specific participants.

- Cases of different types of risk can be analysed by following accounts of actual events.

- A financial institution should have adequate controls in place to monitor and manage risk, within a clear organisational structure.

- The independent audit committee establishes procedures and processes, and creates monitoring arrangements.

- The FSA operates an individual registration procedure for staff carrying out specified functions in all regulated businesses. A business must provide adequate staff resources, and appropriate training.

- Operational controls protect against specific operational risks. The main types of control are preventive controls and detective controls.

- Risk reporting communicates losses, exposure and risks to the appropriate level of management.

- IT controls should include controls over input, processing and output of data, physical security and file security. Such controls comprise application controls over data processing, and general controls over the system and its development.

- An audit is an independent review of the functions, procedures and controls within an organisation.

- The scope and objectives of internal audit are decided by senior management. External auditors report to the shareholders of a firm.

TEST YOUR KNOWLEDGE

Check your knowledge of the Chapter here, without referring back to the text.

1   Define 'credit risk'.

2   Give three examples of how operational risk can arise from processes.

3   Give five examples of typical types of country risk.

4   Outline the role of internal audit function in an organisation.

5   In an organisation, one person banking the money, another maintains the cashbook and a third performs reconciliations. What is the name given to this form of control?

6   Outline the steps on the reconciliation process.

7   What is the central objective of an external audit?

TEST YOUR KNOWLEDGE: ANSWERS

1 Credit risk is the risk that a customer will fail to complete a financial transaction according to the terms of the contract, resulting in a loss to the financial institution. (See 1.4.)

2 Here is a list of examples. (See 1.7.)

- Lack of effective procedures and/or procedural documentation
- Lack of capacity
- Volume sensitivity
- Lack of effective controls and/or control documentation
- Failure to review controls when processes change

3 Your answers may be on this list. (See 1.8.)

- Market open to manipulation
- Excessively rapid expansion of newly listed securities
- Volatile trading activity
- Conflicting and ineffective regulatory environment and structures
- Lack of and poor quality information
- Physical share certificates
- Lack of automated settlement processes
- Fraud
- Low liquidity

4 To perform various services for management, including performing tests of operating, financial and regulatory controls, reviewing operating practices to promote increased efficiency and economy and to carry out special projects and inquiries at management's discretion. (See 2.4.)

5 Segregation of duties. (see 4.1.)

6 Steps in the reconciliation process are as follows. (See 4.5.)

- Conduct a comparison of statement information
- Identify items which agree
- Identify internal and external discrepancies
- Investigate those discrepancies
- Rectify discrepancies

7 The aim is to report to the shareholders on whether the financial statements give a true and fair view and are in accordance with applicable accounting standards. (See 7.1.)

15

Custody

INTRODUCTION

This chapter provides the coverage you need to be able to demonstrate knowledge and understanding of the custody environment and its services and practices. In the area of asset servicing and custody, you need detailed knowledge of collection of dividend income.

As you work through the chapter, note the different ways in which securities can be held.

Withholding tax, a type of tax which is levied by various countries on dividends, is covered at the end of the chapter.

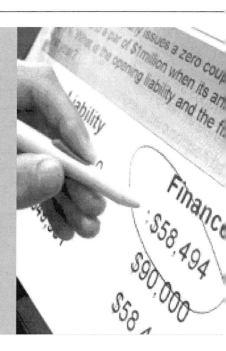

BPP LEARNING MEDIA

1 CERTIFICATED V DEMATERIALISED SECURITIES

Securities can be held in either paper (**certificated**) or electronic (**dematerialised**) form.

1.1 Bearer documents

A **bearer document** is one where there is no specified owner's name on the document. The holder is therefore the owner of the certificate, which states 'for the benefit of the bearer'. An example is of a bearer bond. If the share certificate is lost, the record of ownership is lost and thus the value of the share is lost. Bearer documents are prone to counterfeiting. The Listing Rules set down standards for UK share certificates to meet. These standards are adopted throughout the industry, e.g. most share certificates are 9' by 8' in size.

In the United States many bearer documents are held in 'street names'.

1.2 Lost certificates

If the share certificate is lost, the owner can send a letter of indemnity to the Registrar and the Registrar will issue a replacement share certificate. The letter of indemnity states that the owner will not use the original share certificate if he finds it. The replacement share certificate will have the words 'DUPLICATE' clearly marked.

1.3 Registered documents

Registered stock is stock where the owner is recorded on a central register. The central register can be kept by the company issuing the stock or by an appointed Registrar. The share certificate shows the name of the shareholder but the Registrar also keeps a record. When the owner sells the shares, the share certificate together with a stock transfer form is sent to the Registrar.

Every UK company is required by s352 Companies Act 1985 to keep a Register of Members, which shows:

- The name and address of each member

- The date on which he/she entered as a member and the eventual date on which he/she ceased to be a member

- The number, and class of shares he/she holds, and the amount paid on each share in the case of an IPO

As the Registrar provides *prima facie* evidence of membership it is important that it is kept correct and up-to-date. All entries and amendments to the Registrar require prior approval of the Board, and any changes in the particulars required to be entered in the Register must be registered as soon as the company is aware of them.

To make any changes the Registrar needs to see the original share certificate (unless it is dematerialised) and the following information.

1.4 Dematerialised shares

Electronic shares (also known as **dematerialised**) are shares which do not exist in paper form. The Unlisted Securities Regulations 1995 allowed UK securities to be held electronically. The Electronic Transfer of Title (ETT) increases the flexibility of electronic share ownership.

The Registrar just keeps a record of the share owners. This aids the quick and efficient transfer of stock between buyers and sellers thus speeding up the settlement process. Dematerialised securities also reduce the risk of fraud and 'bad certificates'. Dematerialised shares (all within Euroclear) now account for 85% of the shares in the UK and for securities to be settled via the Euroclear service, they must be dematerialised.

So-called '**demat accounts**' (dematerialised accounts) have become popular in **India**. Demat accounts are bank accounts through which dematerialised shares can be held. The Securities and Exchange Board of India (SEBI) mandates a demat account for share trading above 500 shares.

Problems with dematerialisation

- One hurdle in the dematerialisation process concerns security. In India, it has become compulsory since the start of 2007 for the holder of a demat account to have a Permanent Account Number (PAN).

- Another hurdle concerns acceptance by private investors, who may need to be informed that their rights as shareholders on the register are unaffected.

1.5 Death

On a member's death, an original copy of the **death certificate** is required. If the person had a valid will, there will be a grant of probate giving the personal representative/administrator responsibility to act according to the will. The Registrar will need to see the **grant of probate** before moving the shares into either their name or the name on the will. If the person died intestate (without a will), then the court will issue a Letter of Administration.

1.6 Power of attorney

A **power of attorney** is the written appointment of an agent and could be used, for example, when the member goes abroad for a long time.

A **Lasting Power of Attorney** under the Mental Capacity Act 2005 (formerly called an Enduring Power of Attorney) can be used by an elderly person who is mentally capable of making decisions in preparation for a time when he may be incapable of making decisions.

The Registrar needs the original of the document or a copy that has been certified as a true copy. There can only be one of these.

1.7 Mental incapacity of a member

Under the Mental Health Act 1983, the **Court of Protection** may appoint a receiver with clearly defined powers over the estate of the mentally disordered person. The powers will be clearly defined, thus the Registrar will need to review the document to ascertain that share transfers are acceptable.

1.8 Bankruptcy or insolvency

Individual insolvency is regulated by the Insolvency Act 1986. A member becomes bankrupt when the court makes a **bankruptcy order** against him. The court will issue a Letter of Request to the Trustee.

Corporate liquidations are either compulsory via a Court Order or voluntary via a Special Resolution. The company will need to review either document to prove the validity of the liquidator.

1.9 Change of name

The most frequent **change of name** is as a result of marriage and the Registrar will need either the original certificate or a photocopy certified by a solicitor.

A formal name change not occurring on marriage would normally involve a deed poll and a notice in the *London Gazette*. The company needs to see either document.

For an informal name change, the member needs to give the firm a written statutory declaration of identity of both the old and new names.

For a corporate change of name, the company would need to see either a copy of the resolution or the change of name certificate. They would also need to have a copy of the list of appointed directors.

1.10 Change of address

The company needs to receive a signed request from the member. As addresses are not usually shown on the share certificate, the certificate does not need to be altered.

2   WHERE ARE SECURITIES HELD?

2.1 Registrar

In the UK, the company's **Registrar** keeps the legal records of the identities of the shareholders on behalf of the issuing companies. The Registrar can either be an internal function of the corporation or an external specialist body. There are just a few major specialist registrars now in the UK including Capita and Computershare. External bodies are used when there are frequent changes in ownership. In addition to maintaining the legal records, the Registrar might send out certificates as evidence of ownership. When there is a change of ownership, the Registrar would re-issue the share certificate.

2.2 Depository

A '**depository**' is a warehouse where securities are immobilised. '**Immobilised**' means that the securities are being physically held in the vault of the depository. A depository is usually provided by a clearing house or settlement agency whose primary role is to facilitate settlement. Settlement delays are often caused by the time it takes for securities to be moved between counterparties and thus time can be reduced if the securities are held in one place. When there is a transfer between these customers, the settlement agency will simply amend its records by book entry rather than physically move the securities between customers. The change in ownership is achieved by debiting/crediting the customer accounts, which is known as book entry transfer. The term immobilised reflects the fact that the securities themselves do not move despite the change in ownership. The securities will only physically move if they are sold to someone who is not a member of the settlement agency and the securities have to be moved out of the vault.

DTCC, Euroclear and Clearstream are examples of depositories. Euroclear is **not** a depository. With electronic/dematerialised securities, there is no need for a depository as there are no physical securities to hold in safekeeping or to move.

2.3 Legal and beneficial ownership

For registered securities, legal ownership is determined by the name that appears on the company register. For individuals (private investors) who do not use the services of a custodian, their shares are held in their own name and they are the registered owners.

If custodians were to arrange for all of their clients to appear as registered owners of the shares held, this would ensure that they were readily identified as the legal owners. However, such an arrangement would be impractical from an administrative point of view as custodians would require their clients to sign transfer forms every time they wished to sell all or part of a holding. Additionally, if the clients were on the registers, they would receive the dividends and corporate action communications directly from the issuing company and not via the custodian.

In order to manage its clients' holdings efficiently, a custodian arranges for their registrable securities to be registered into a nominee fund for that purpose. Once in the nominee, the custodian is able to transfer the securities on instructions from their client, without necessitating a transfer form signed by the client.

In the case of a nominee's name, the beneficial owner is the underlying investor, as shown in the following table.

Name on Register	Legal ownership	Beneficial ownership
Investor	Investor	Investor
Nominee	Nominee	Investor

As there are no certificates for book-entry securities, these are reflected by entries on a computerised system or ledger statement.

The nominee company becomes the legal owner of the investments and its name appears on the issuing company's register. Beneficial ownership is implied in this situation and it is the custodian's responsibility to maintain accurate records reflecting the identity of the underlying beneficial owners.

There are two different approaches to the management of nominee holdings, both of which can provide a secure and effective custody environment, as long as the custodian operates proper and continuous controls – the pooled omnibus account and the individual account.

2.4 Pooling or individual designation

Under the **pooling** (or omnibus) system, all investors' holdings are registered in the same nominee name (e.g. ABC Nominees Ltd), and the entries on the share register and the certificates do not identify the actual beneficial owners.

Advantages of pooling

- Administration is simplified and risk of clerical error reduced.

- The settlement process is made easier as any certificate(s) may be delivered from the pool so long as the total does not exceed the number of shares actually held for the shareholder at the time of delivery.

- There is only one holding for the custodian to reconcile in respect of each issue (although there must be a subsequent reconciliation of this holding to the records of the underlying investors).

- It reduces the number of names that need to be maintained by the Registrar on the company register.

- It provides anonymity for the investors except in cases where disclosure is required in accordance with the Companies Act 1985 s212.

Disadvantages of pooling

- Although it is prohibited, there is the risk that a custodian with poor controls might use the shares of one investor to settle trades of another when there are delays in the settlement system.

- It is difficult to establish beneficial ownership in the absence of comprehensive and up-to-date records.

- More time is required *inter alia* to allocate dividends and to manage corporate actions and proxy voting to individual investors.

Under a system of **individual designation** within a nominee name, individual beneficial owners are identified by the addition of a designation. This designation, which can be a unique reference rather than a name (the tax status of client can also be used) will also be reflected in the issuing company's register.

Advantages of individual designation

- Beneficial owners are more easily identifiable from the company register and the share certificates.
- Reconciliation of share holdings to investors' balances is more straightforward.
- Time spent on such activities as allocating dividends is reduced.
- Risk of using the balance of one investor to settle the trades of another is reduced.
- Individual designation will facilitate establishing claims for securities in a default situation.

Disadvantages of individual designation

- There is the risk that the holdings of one investor might be incorrectly designated under the designation of another investor.

- It might be unsuitable for a custodian with many holdings over a wide client base. This would make the administration of such a client base difficult to manage and costly to operate.

2.5 Shareholder limits and restrictions

In a number of countries, there are limits and restrictions on the amount of a company's equity that may be in non-resident ownership. Purchases of securities, whether for residents or non-residents, will be notified to the company so that the shareholder register can be updated. Once the limit has been reached for the non-residents, all further registration is blocked.

The following table gives examples of non-resident shareholding limits and other restrictions.

Country	Non-resident restrictions
Australia	The individual foreign ownership level for equities is 15% and the aggregate is 40%. However, there are specific restrictions for media, telecommunications, banking, airports, shipping and casino shares.
France	There are no foreign ownership limits in France. However, foreign investors must obtain authorisation from the Ministry of Finance prior to investing in sensitive sectors (e.g. defence industry and public health sector).
Hong Kong	There are no restrictions to foreign ownership of Hong Kong shares, except for companies that hold television licences. No single non-resident can own more than 10% of the television broadcast company without the Broadcasting Authority's approval, and the aggregate foreign ownership limit is 49%.
Hungary	Although there are no restrictions concerning foreign ownership in Hungarian companies, individual issuers can impose various regulations regarding shareholder concentration, registration and ownership ceilings.

Country	Non-resident restrictions
Japan	Foreign ownership of Japanese stocks is largely unrestricted, with the exception of selected airline, communications and broadcasting companies, which set limits unique to them. The Japan Securities Depository Center (JASDEC) does not track foreign ownership.
Malaysia	Foreign investors can generally own up to between 30-49% of any listed or unlisted companies. For financial institution stocks, the limit for foreign interest in local companies is generally 30%.
Thailand	There is a non-resident shareholding limit of 49% (25% for commercial banks and finance companies). Some companies may have lower limits in their Articles of Association.
United Kingdom	Some companies (e.g. industries of national importance, shipping companies, mass communications, air transportation) have limits on the percentage of foreign ownership. Prior to registration, the domicile and/or identity of the new beneficial owner has to be disclosed by the completion of a nationality declaration.

2.6 Custodian

Custodians provide a specialist service in the safe keeping of assets on behalf of other financial institutions and customers. A custodian specialises in looking after both physical and electronic/dematerialised stock and thus performs all the necessary reconciliations. What was once a quiet, backroom service has grown into a highly competitive business involving large sophisticated customers and non-stop, global trading. Today, the custody market is dominated by a few global players, primarily because the costs needed to compete require economies of scale to generate profitability.

The global custodians offer additional services such as performance reporting, collecting income from corporate actions, record-keeping, cash management and stock lending. A domestic custodian operates in one local country, whilst a global custodian exists in all countries around the world. A global custodian might use a network of local sub-custodians.

2.7 Custodian and depository compared

A **custodian** is a financial institution which provide a 'safe keeping service' for customers. A **depository** is a clearing house or settlement agency whose primary role is to facilitate settlement. Settlement delays are often caused by the time it takes for securities to be moved between counterparties. The settlement agency might therefore reduce these delays by holding the securities on behalf of customers. These securities will be held in the vault of the depository. This means that transfers between these customers are easy because the settlement agency will just amend the records. The securities only move if they are sold to someone who is not a member of the settlement agency.

2.8 Storage in a safe

Physical share certificates can be stored by the financial institution in their safe. There should be adequate controls over access to that safe.

2.9 Held by another counterparty

With collateralised transactions and repo-transactions, the securities are temporarily lent between counterparties. Although the accounting records will show the movement, the securities will not actually move. Therefore the financial institution might hold stock on behalf of counterparties and *vice versa*.

2.10 Company's power to request information on shareholders

Section 793 Companies Act 2006 states that where a public company knows or has reasonable cause to believe that someone has at any time in the previous three years had an interest in the company's share capital, then they can send a notice to the person requiring them to confirm whether or not this is the case. (This section replaces the previous s212 Companies Act 1985.)

If the person has had an interest in the shares, then the notice can also require him to disclose details of his holding, whether it is part of a **concert party** holding and to whom he sold the interest, if relevant.

The person should reply within the time limit set by the notice, which should be reasonable. If he fails to do so then the company can suspend the shares' voting and other rights (s794 CA 2006).

Once the company has obtained information in this manner, it should enter the details on its share register.

Shareholders of the company holding at least 10% of the voting rights can require a company to use its powers under s793 Companies Act 2006 to identify another shareholder.

3 CENTRAL SECURITIES DEPOSITORIES AND CUSTODY

In 1989, the Group of 30 (G30) recommended that each domestic market should establish a **Central Securities Depository (CSD)** to hold securities. The fundamental objectives for the establishment of a CSD are for gains in efficiencies and for reduction in risk. Efficiency gains are achieved through the elimination of manual errors, lower costs and increased speed of processing through automation, which all translate into lower risks. Most markets that did not already have established CSDs in 1989 have organised one or more CSDs and centralised local settlement through them. Almost all countries have some form of central depository where the securities are either immobilised or dematerialised.

In a 'dematerialised' system, there is no document which physically embodies the claim. The system relies on a collection of securities accounts, instructions to financial institutions which maintain those accounts, and confirmations of account entries.

Immobilisation is common in markets that previously relied on physical share certificates, but the certificates are now immobilised in a depository, which is the holder of record in the register. Access by investors to the depository is typically through financial institutions which are members of the depository.

Through the establishment of CSDs, investors are able to reduce risks of loss, theft and illiquidity costs substantially by holding securities through one or more tiers of financial intermediaries such as banks or brokers. This has led to multi-tiered securities holding systems. There can be several types of holding systems. For example, some professional investors and financial intermediaries have direct contractual relationships with CSDs. They hold interests in securities through accounts on the records of the CSDs. Other investors, particularly retail investors, generally hold their interests through brokers or other financial intermediaries at a lower tier in the multi-tiered structure.

A direct holding system is one where the investor appears as the named owner in the issuer's records. The issuer therefore knows who its investors are, as the issuer's shareholder accounts are the same as the accounts which reflect the investor's ownership. An indirect holding system is one where the investor holds his securities through accounts maintained by one or more tiers of intermediaries. The person who appears as the registered owner of the securities in the accounts of the issuer in an indirect holding system is the top-tier intermediary through which the investor holds the shares.

In an indirect holding system, the functions of the holding system are performed by different institutions:

- **Custodian** – with which an investor deposits securities
- **Central depository** – where custodian deposits securities of customers, and
- **Issuer's registrar** – which reflects the central depository as the owner of securities held through the depository and its custodian members

To maximise the efficiencies of the multi-tiered structure, most CSDs and other financial intermediaries have adopted the practice of holding physical securities in fungible pools and of holding interests in dematerialised or registered physical securities through accounts in the name of the CSD or other financial intermediary (nominee name) with the issuer or its agent. The ultimate investor's ownership interest may not be shown on the books of the issuer, the CSD or other financial intermediary, except the particular intermediary with which it has a direct contractual relationship. The investor's direct intermediary will typically hold interests in the security in an omnibus account with the CSD or other intermediary at the next level up the multi-tiered structure.

There are some systems that have combined the advantageous features of both direct and indirect holding systems, resulting in a **'hybrid' holding system**. In those systems, the 'custodian' function in an indirect holding system is replaced with an 'account administrator' or 'sponsor' for direct investor accounts. The account administrator will deal with all communications to and from the registrars for securities which the investor owns. This helps to reduce the risks involved of having the investors' securities held in the name of custodians or brokers that may go bankrupt.

Most countries that have introduced immobilisation or dematerialisation have had to use some form of indirect holding systems.

Advantages of an indirect holding system

- The investor only has to deal with one institution, the custodian, for purposes of receiving securities, authorising transfer of securities, delivering securities etc.
- Brokers would know, prior to entering sell orders that the investor owns the securities and that they are positioned for delivery. In a direct holding system, the broker would need to take extra precautions to ensure that the investor will be able to deliver the securities for settlement.
- The transfer of securities is by book entry and there are no physical movements of securities and no accounting entries made on the books of the issuer or its agent.
- It reduces the traditional loss, theft and illiquidity costs and risks associated with holding, transferring and pledging securities.

However, in order for indirect holding systems to work well, there are several legal issues which have to be addressed.

4 ICSDs and CSDs

The principal **International Central Securities Depositories (ICSDs)** – **Euroclear** and **Clearstream** – have traditionally provided clearance and custody of Eurobonds and other Euromarket instruments. In recent years however they have increasingly become involved in settlement and custody of international equities.

The ICSDs have established linkages with several domestic **CSDs** and have created a sub-custodian network.

In summary, the main roles of ICSDs and CSDs are as follows.

ICSDs	CSDs
International client base	Domestic/local client base
Cross-border activity	Domestic activity only
All securities	Local securities only
Settlement	Settlement
Custody	Custody
Collateral management	
Other services	
Securities lending	

5 GLOBAL CUSTODY

5.1 Introduction

5.1.1 Growth in custody services

The recent high growth rate in **global custody services** is expected to continue, driven by a combination of global trends.

- Investors are demonstrating a growing appetite for cross-border assets, for emerging and exotic markets and for a wider range of financial instruments.

- Investment managers and banks are making increasing use of global custodians to replace their own network of local custodians.

- In many countries, the state is retreating from its role of primary pension provider, causing citizens to invest in defined contribution pensions and mutual funds in record numbers, with custody banks serving the pension and mutual funds, their money managers and the banks acting for high net worth individuals.

5.1.2 Overview

In short, global custody is about processing cross-border securities trades, keeping financial assets safe and servicing the associated portfolios.

The term 'global custody' describes both a major international industry and a set of services relating to the administration of investments, including processing cross-border securities trades and keeping safe those financial assets made outside the country where the investor is located.

Investors use global custodians to:

- Provide safe keeping services in multiple jurisdictions

- Make the necessary arrangements for the receipt and delivery of securities and cash in settlement of purchases and sales (under the instruction of the customer or its investment manager)

- Report details of securities held to the customer

A global custodian generally delivers its services through a customer service centre in the jurisdiction of the customer. Securities and information processing is usually conducted by a single operations hub, typically based in the United Kingdom or another Western European location. In each jurisdiction where the securities are safe-kept, the global custodian may conduct local custody activities through its own branch (if it has one in the jurisdiction concerned), or may appoint a sub-custodian to deal with matters locally.

Customers can benefit from economies of scale offered by a global custodian from the consolidation of holdings of securities for various customers, and from their technical expertise.

5.1.3 Future industry growth

Global custodians are entrusted with the safe keeping and processing of huge volumes of securities. Recent years have seen a dramatic growth in the value of assets under custody. This high growth rate is expected to continue, driven by a combination of global trends in addition to the retail brokerage industry driving demand for clearing and custody services.

5.2 Investors

Investors fall into three principal categories.

- **Institutional investors** who include pension funds, mutual funds, insurance companies and hedge funds. These will manage their investments either directly or through one or more investment companies. If directly, the institutional investor will be the customer of the global custodian; if indirectly, the investment manager will be the customer acting on behalf of the investor.
- **Direct market participants** such as broker/dealers, market-makers and banks who principally deal for their own account.
- **Investment (or portfolio) managers** acting for institutional investors, corporate entities and private client brokers acting for high net-worth individuals.

5.3 Suppliers of custody services

Suppliers of a domestic custody service will usually be based in the country of their client. Suppliers of global custody services are based in whichever country best suits their needs and those of their clients.

Domestic global custody suppliers are either independent custodians (banks and trust companies) or investment management companies. The former group additionally provide normal banking services such as trade finance, lending and foreign exchange. Examples of the leading suppliers of global custody services are Bank of New York, J P Morgan Investor Services and State Street Bank and Trust Company. Investment management companies provide their clients with a full range of investment/custody services. These include well-known investment banks.

5.4 Services

5.4.1 Overview

Once a dealer has executed a transaction on behalf of an investor the clearing, settlement and safe keeping processes begin. There are three main functions or stages – validation of the trade, clearing and settlement, and custody.

The custody services include the following.

- Safe keeping securities in a vault (where appropriate)
- Pre-advice of dividend announcements and early redemptions
- Reporting on dividend collection, receipt of interest and principal proceeds
- Providing statements of holdings and valuations
- Reporting and executing clients' instructions of corporate actions and entitlements
- Proxy voting, tax-withholding/reclamation and securities lending/borrowing services

- Foreign exchange and hedging services
- Regulatory reporting

Through access to sophisticated computer systems and a worldwide network of sub-custodians, global custodians are in a position to deliver a variety of services to their clients which are referred to as either **core services** or **value added services**.

- Core services are those which are so standardised that there is not a great deal of scope for any particular global custodian to differentiate its service from that of another global custodian. Any fundamental changes and improvements will affect the industry as a whole.

- Value-added services, on the other hand, provide global custodians with the opportunity to offer a markedly better service to their clients, and in so doing, enhance their standing within the market place and improve their fee-earning capabilities.

- The global custody business has moved beyond securities processing and core services of safe keeping and settlement. Investor or securities services is an increasingly popular term to describe custodians' activities, covering as it does, derivatives, cash, foreign exchange and third party mutual funds, in addition to the sort of 'data-enriched' information custodians now seek to provide across all asset classes.

Range of services

- Safe keeping of securities
- Maintenance of multi-currency securities and funds accounts
- Settlement of securities trades in domestic and foreign markets, free of or against payment
- Collection of dividends, interest and principal due for redemption on due date
- Exercise or sale of subscription rights
- Attending to other corporate actions as well as pending fails
- Reporting of transactions completed and periodical delivery of hardcopy statements of account
- Contractual or actual settlement date accounting
- Contractual or actual income collection
- Computer links to pass on instructions and retrieve client information from custodian's database
- Customised multi-currency reporting and performance information
- Securities borrowing and lending
- Assistance with withholding tax claims
- Handling/settlement of derivatives
- Briefings on specific countries, in particular on emerging markets
- Cash projection and cash management
- Ensuring that physical certificates and associated documentation are in good order

5.4.2 Core services

The typical core service requirements of client investors including banks, pension funds, insurance companies and asset managers are as follows.

- Settlement
- Safe keeping
- Corporate actions
- Proxy voting
- Foreign exchange
- Cash management
- Reporting

5.4.3 Settlement conventions

The process of achieving timely and accurate settlement of a securities transaction is very much the same the world over. The execution of a trade is followed by a pre-settlement phase of confirmation, and matching is followed by the actual settlement consisting of a delivery of securities and a payment of the cash consideration.

In practice, however, there are almost as many methods of achieving settlement as there are number of countries which support trading in investments.

5.4.4 Trade confirmation

The two counterparties to a trade will confirm details with each other by telephone, fax, telex, mail or a combination of these.

5.4.5 Trade matching

The next stage in the settlement process is matching of the trade within the local clearing house. This is the process by which pre-defined sets of information about the trade are sent to the clearing house which will expect the same details from the other counterparty. Mail or electronic communication can effect this and the settlement staff may generate the information automatically from the counterparty's computer system, or manually.

5.4.6 Securities delivery

Delivery of certificated securities can be delayed for the following reasons.

- Certificates in the course of registration for a previous purchase can take several weeks to process and will delay a sale due for settlement during that time.

- Bearer certificates, such as cash, are not replaceable in the event of loss or theft (although there have been notable cases where the certificates have been stopped by the issuer, effectively preventing the thieves from negotiating the certificates through normal market channels).

5.4.7 Cash payment

The effective transmission of cash does not in itself present any real problem; it is the way in which the payment is linked to the underlying securities transaction that is the issue.

5.4.8 Cross-border investment

The term **cross-border investment** is generally accepted to refer to the investment in securities quoted on the local stock exchange of one country by investors based in another country.

The trading of overseas securities can take place either locally between two participants, or cross-border between the local participant and the overseas participant.

Whilst the actual trading of cross-border securities is relatively straightforward, the investing institution is confronted with settlement and safe keeping issues which are not found in their local environment.

5.4.9 Time zones

Time zone differences create an issue for the custodian in order to be able to meet deadlines for settlement in different parts of the world, whilst at the same time being able to confirm instructions with clients, counterparties, other custodians and CSDs, who may all operate from different locations. Daylight exposure risks are also a direct result of time zone differences.

5.4.10 Real-time settlement

Real-time settlement became a hot topic in the custody industry in the 1990s and enormous amounts of capital were, and continue to be, invested in the process. A Real-Time Gross Settlement (RTGS) system ensures payment instructions are transmitted on a transaction-by-transaction basis between direct members of the system and are settled individually across central bank accounts in real time. Any intra-day central bank credit given to participating banks is fully collateralised in order to eliminate settlement risk. There is the risk, present in alternative net end-of-day settlement systems, that losses might arise through a bank failing during the day and so not being able to honour the payment messages already sent.

All EU member countries are developing RTGS systems as a means of reducing interbank settlement risk between members. Most often these systems have replaced, or sit alongside, electronic net settlement systems. Many of the payments put through RTGS systems are not time-critical within the day and the development of these systems does not affect the speed with which a payment needs to be made.

Since 1998, Euroclear has operated real-time settlement. It offers participants quicker processing, greater flexibility and less risk in managing their settlement transactions because Euroclear will extend deadlines for inputting instructions and same-day settlement for repo transactions. (A repo is a repurchase agreement – a short-term contract – frequently overnight, that is used to finance government and money market positions by agreeing to sell and subsequently repurchase securities at a specific date and price.) The current overnight batch process has a 7.45 p.m. cut-off time and the daytime cycle has a deadline of 1.30 p.m.

Euroclear offers real-time settlement for daytime processing to allow its members worldwide to settle cross-border trades on a real-time basis with as many counterparties in different time zones as they wish.

5.4.11 Cross-currency settlements

With cross-currency settlement, securities trading organisations and custodians need access to FX and payments systems. The need to settle cross-currency may result from an organisation executing a trade with a counterparty who wishes to pay or receive cash in a currency other than the usual base currency in which the security is normally traded.

If the company decides to trade say a euro-dominated security in a currency other than euros, it will assume an FX position and the attendant risk. Any FX transaction is an outright position which is subject to market risk. This risk could offset the profit made on the transaction and therefore the FX risk must be mitigated immediately. The exchange rates could move sharply; they are always beyond the control of the company. For this reason it is normal practice for trading firms to cover FX risks at the same time as the trade execution.

5.4.12 Euro payment systems

TARGET (Trans-European Automated Real-time Gross Settlement Express Transfer System) is the biggest payment system in Europe, and indeed the world. **TARGET2** is the second version of it, which is designed to be more efficient, less costly and more user-friendly, and opened in November 2007. Following on from this, **TARGET2-Securities** is a project which would make use of or link with the TARGET2 platform to settle the cash legs of securities transactions. The objective of TARGET2-Securities is to maximise safety and efficiency in the settlement of euro-denominated securities transactions.

In preparing the design of the second generation of TARGET, the European Central Bank (ECB) has indicated that: first, the accounts of the banks will continue to be maintained by the national central banks rather than the ECB; and second, that the services offered by TARGET to its users will evolve. Users have, for example, requested a single communication interface and more sophisticated liquidity management. In one model of TARGET, the 16 existing IT platforms would be replaced by a single one, which would offer the same functionality to all TARGET participants (like Fedwire in the USA). Another model would maintain multiple platforms, but achieve a much greater degree of technical harmonisation between RTGS systems, including some common elements.

The European Central Bank's proposals to create a single settlement platform for euro-based securities in the form of **TARGET2-Securities** are controversial.

TARGET2-Securities would split the settlement process from custody. As proposed, Target2-Securities would use the Eurosystem platform TARGET2. It would settle the cash legs of securities transactions and provide a single platform for settlement of central bank money for all euro-denominated securities and for all central securities depositaries (CSDs) in the euro zone.

The European Central Bank (ECB) says that safety would be optimised by using the delivery versus payment (DvP) mechanism. Efficiency would be enhanced by settling cash and securities on the same IT platform.

Unlike the **Fedwire-Securities** system of the US, which acts as a full CSD for government securities, TARGET2-Securities would be only a settlement platform and not a CSD. The Eurosystem would not deal with issuers or manage corporate events. Securities accounts would not be opened for users. Custody activity would take place at the local CSDs, however the CSDs would not have to maintain settlement links.

5.4.13 Securities reconciliation

This is a control function, which seeks to establish that balances of assets beneficially owned by one party agree with the balances of the same assets held on behalf of the beneficial owner by another party (the Registrar).

In the UK it is a regulatory requirement that safe custody holdings are reconciled at least twice every 12 months at intervals of approximately six months. Reconciliation may be done on a rolling basis rather than at two points in time, providing that the following conditions are met.

- Confirmation from an auditor that there are adequate internal controls
- Additional records reflecting clients' entitlements from an issuer's perspective

Positions that do not reconcile are queried in order to establish the reasons why. These can include clerical errors, unsettled trades and unauthorised use of fraudulent misappropriation of the assets.

The actual process of reconciling two sets of records has traditionally been performed manually. This is not only a time-consuming exercise and open to error, but in addition, serious problems may not be highlighted and corrected until it is too late.

In recognition of this problem, global custodians and their investors can automatically perform the reconciliation by electronically matching their respective securities balances, outstanding trades and corporate action events and in so doing produce an exception report highlighting only those securities which require remedial action.

5.4.14 Reporting requirements

These form an important part of the core services as both investor and global custodian require statements of holdings, which can be available in hard copy format or from the custodian's software.

The information on the asset listings usually indicates the following.

- Investor account number and name
- Security name and description (e.g. Ordinary shares)
- International Security Identification Number (ISIN)
- Quantity of securities (ledger and settled balances/outstanding receipts/deliveries balances)
- Name of depository in which the security is held
- Market price
- Valuation in currency of security
- Valuation in base currency of investor

5.4.15 Settlement date

This is the date on which securities and payment are exchanged and credited to proper accounts. If securities are debited from the seller's account one or more days prior to being credited to the buyer's account, or if securities and cash move at different times, then settlement date is commonly perceived as the date on which securities are received by the buyer, which in most cases is also the value date of the payment. In general, the term refers to the contractual settlement date. The actual settlement date, as opposed to the contractual settlement date, may be delayed in the settlement process.

The global custodians have approached this problem by making a commitment to the investor that funds will be debited or credited for good value (in this case on the original settlement date). This is known as **Contractual Settlement Date Accounting (CSDA)**. It enables the investor to operate in the certain knowledge that the cash accounts will reflect the expected entries and balances.

In terms of settlement accounting, global custodians would credit sale proceeds and debit purchase costs on whatever date the trade actually settled. This is known as **Actual Settlement Date Accounting (ASDA)**. The application of ASDA works in favour of purchasers as they will have the use of their funds for an extra few days and perhaps have the opportunity either to earn interest or place the funds on deposit for that period. The actual settlement date may be different from the **Intended Settlement Date (ISD)**.

ASDA presents a disadvantage to sellers who will be unable to use the funds until received on settlement. This can cause a knock-on problem if the expected funds were committed for other purposes on the original settlement date.

In one or more of the following circumstances the global custodian will protect himself from risk of non-performance of the trade by insisting on variations in its contractual commitments to the investor.

- CSDA is not offered in those countries which the global custodians consider to have a sub-standard settlement infrastructure.

- Investors' settlement instructions, which have missed a deadline, will be considered received the following day by some global custodians. Therefore, either the CSDA value will be applied on a later date or ASDA will be applied.

- Global custodians retain the right to reverse cash entries in the event that trades remain unsettled after a particular length of time.

- CSDA on a sale will not be provided if there are insufficient securities to satisfy the delivery.

Whichever accounting practice is used, it is in the global custodian's interests (and the investor's if ASDA is used) to apply pressure on the local stock markets and authorities to improve the settlement environment.

5.5 Payment systems

5.5.1 CHIPS

In the United States the **Clearing House Interbank Payments System (CHIPS)** is a computerised network for the transfer of dollar payments. CHIPS links over 100 depository institutions that have offices or subsidiary companies in New York City. CHIPS operates on a multilateral netting basis and enables banks to settle dollar payments by electronic transfer.

5.5.2 CHAPS

The UK's system, **Clearing House Automated Payment System (CHAPS)**, was introduced in 1984. CHAPS is an electronic credit transfer system for sending same-day value sterling payments from one CHAPS member settlement bank to another. CHAPS currently has 15 sterling, 19 euro members and around 400 participating institutions, which include all of the world's major banks.

CHAPS Sterling provides its members and participants with a RTGS system, whereby each payment is settled in real-time across Bank of England settlement accounts. Every CHAPS payment is unconditional, guaranteed and cannot be recalled.

Since 4 January 1999, the CHAPS Clearing Company has provided a CHAPS Euro service alongside CHAPS Sterling. Instead of using the CHAPS Sterling network, CHAPS Euro utilises the SWIFT network. This means the system will combine the efficiency and robustness of CHAPS and the ease of access of SWIFT. CHAPS Euro is linked into the TARGET system (see below) for cross-border payments.

5.5.3 TARGET

Trans-European Automated Real-time Gross Settlement Express Transfer (TARGET) has already been mentioned and is the real-time gross settlement system for the euro. TARGET consists of the 15 real-time gross settlement systems of the EU members and the European Central Bank (ECB) payment mechanism which are interlinked to provide a uniform platform for the processing of cross-border payments.

5.5.4 Fedwire

Fedwire is the Federal Reserve's electronic transfer of funds system. It is a real-time gross settlement system in which more than 9,000 depository institutions initiate funds transfers that are immediate, final, and irrevocable when processed. It allows member banks to transfer funds on their own behalf, or on behalf of their customers. Payments are processed through the Federal Reserve Bank of New York.

5.6 Netting

It is common to net cash (and to co-mingle it with other cash sums being paid) but less common to net securities.

Netting occurs when trading partners agree to offset their positions or obligations. By so doing they reduce a large number of individual positions or obligations to a smaller number of positions or obligations. Hence it is on this netted position that the two trading partners settle their outstanding obligations. Besides reducing transaction costs and communication expenses, netting is important because it reduces credit and liquidity risks.

On the credit risk side, if a counterparty goes into liquidation and cannot meet its obligations, the net obligations will be lower than the individual obligations. As an example, imagine a firm owed a counterparty US$800,000, and that the same counterparty owed the firm US$600,000. On the day of settlement, the firm pays out the US$800,000 but the counterparty cannot meet its obligations and pays nothing. The US$600,000 will have to be reclaimed from the administrators. At best, there will be a delay before it is received and at worst, little or none of the amount will be reclaimed. If the figure is netted, this loss is avoided as only US$200,000 is paid.

On the liquidity risk side, it reduces requirements for a particular stock. Imagine a similar scenario where US$800,000 and US$600,000 worth of shares were to be exchanged. Both counterparties would have to have that amount of stock, and may need to go out and borrow it, just so that they can receive a similar amount. Netting reduces this requirement. This is particularly important when the stock is illiquid making it difficult and expensive to secure.

Netting can be **bilateral** or **multilateral**.

Bilateral	Multilateral
Trades between the same two counterparties in the same security are set off or netted off so that there is only one transfer	Extends bilateral netting to cover all trades in the same security by any number of counterparties
This can be in respect of cash and securities or just cash	For each security traded this will result in each counterparty making only one transfer of cash or securities normally to the central clearing system
In respect of cash only there is only one cash transfer but each securities transfer is carried out separately	Handles only trades due for settlement on the same day. It does not deal with settlements outstanding from previous days (unsettled positions do roll forward in some markets – e.g. Hong Kong and USA)
Separate netting agreements must be in place with each counterparty	Requires the use of a central clearance system to establish the cash and securities position of each counterparty, to calculate the most efficient netting off and to process the resulting transfers

5.7 CLS Bank International

Continuous Linked Settlement (CLS) is a real-time system enabling simultaneous settlement globally in the foreign exchange market.

At the heart of the CLS system lies a bank. The CLS bank is a private initiative that began in 1996 supported by the largest FX banks – the Group of 20 (G20), to eliminate settlement risk and reduce the systemic liquidity risk in the foreign exchange market. It started commercially in 2002. The system initially supported seven eligible currencies: the Australian, Canadian and US dollars, the euro, the Japanese yen, the Swiss franc and the UK pound sterling. The list now contains 15 currencies the inclusion mainly of additional European and Asia Pacific currencies. These are the Hong Kong, Singaporean and New Zealand dollars, the Korean won, the Danish and Norwegian krone, the Swedish krona and the South African rand.

With the average daily turnover in December 2006 in global FX transactions in excess of US$3.3 trillion, the FX market has long needed an effective cross-currency settlement process. On 16 January 2007 a new record was set for the volume of payment instructions settled in one day. 705,582 payment instructions were settled with a gross value of US$5.22 trillion. While transaction volumes have increased, the methods by which they are settled have stayed virtually the same for 300 years.

Before CLS, each side of a trade was paid separately. Taking time-zone differences into account, this heightened the risk of one party defaulting.

CLS represents a response to regulatory concern about systematic risk. It eliminates that 'temporal' settlement risk, making same-day settlement both possible and final. It is a real-time system that enables simultaneous settlement globally, irrespective of time zones.

Effectively, CLS is an ongoing process of:

- **Submitting instructions** – receiving payments of specified currencies from customers
- **Funding** – settling pairs of instructions that satisfy all criteria
- **Execution** – making pay-outs in specified currencies

Settlement is final and irrevocable or funds are returned on the same day.

Participating banks receive real-time settlement information that helps them to manage liquidity more efficiently, reduce credit risks and introduce operational efficiencies. This is all done within a five-hour window (three hours in Asia), which represents the overlapping business hours of the participating settlement systems.

Herstatt risk is a name given to **overnight delivery risk**, as mentioned earlier in this Study Book. Herstatt Bank was closed by the German Bundesbank in 1974 after FX losses. Many banks had paid out Deutschmarks to Herstatt Bank but the closure prevented them receiving US dollars in return.

CLS seeks to eliminate these and other risks by enabling:

- Reduction in settlement risk
- The simultaneous exchange of currencies
- Safer, quicker and more efficient processing
- Improvement in the availability and flow of funds
- Working in real-time

It aims to improve operational efficiency, achieve settlement finality, introduce cost reduction and facilitate compliance with regulatory pressures.

A total of 56 member banks are today settling payment instructions associated with foreign exchange trades through CLS Bank, with over 120 customers of members also live. CLS Bank is now settling on average over 130,000 instructions each day, with a gross value in excess of US$ 1.4 trillion.

5.8 Cash management

5.8.1 Overview

Cash management is financial management used by corporate treasurers to accelerate the collection of receivables, control payments to trade creditors, and efficiently manage cash. Large corporations collect funds into a single concentration account and invest excess funds in the money market. The local accounts are frequently drawn down to zero-funds every day. In disbursing payments to trade creditors, treasurers attempt to control the outflow of funds by timing payments with receipts of invoices from trade creditors.

The optimum management of cash assets is important in global custody in that it controls receivables and payments across all currencies pertaining to the securities held. The prediction of cash requirements (funding) and the movement of the cash itself by the custodians ensures that control is kept over cash balances and payments/receipts together with interest rate and foreign exchange exposure reporting. This helps to monitor future settlement activities, dividend income and interest receipts together with projected cash balances.

Single-currency accounts are more appropriate to those clients who operate in one currency. Multi-currency accounts would better suit those investors whose activities typically generate cash flows in foreign currencies. The global custodians will provide whichever service is required including the additional foreign exchange conversions that single-currency accounts may involve. They will also maximise the interest-bearing element by utilising interest bearing accounts and cash sweeps whereby at the end of each day uncommitted cash balances will be removed from non-interest accounts into interest bearing ones. Pooling balances by currency can also be offered to provide the client with more advantageous interest earning opportunities.

5.8.2 Importance of cash management

The movement of securities and in particular, the settlement of securities trades, is linked to the movement of the corresponding countervalue of cash. Cash must be found to cover purchases; proceeds of sales and income payments may be reinvested in some way or another.

The prediction of cash requirements (funding) and the movement of cash itself are known as cash management.

The performance of an investor's portfolio is made up of:

- Profit (or loss) on trading activity
- Yield of the portfolio through receipt of income

If little attention is paid to cash management then, together with poor settlement performance, the overall performance of the securities portfolio will be affected.

Global custodians can provide their clients with a number of multi-currency payment and banking facilities designed to ensure that control is kept over cash balances and payments/receipts, together with interest rate and foreign exchange exposure reporting. Global custodians also have the ability to monitor future settlement activities, dividend income and interest receipts, and projected cash balances.

5.8.3 Cash management techniques

The problems that would be created should a global custodian fall into receivership need to be considered.

It has recently been established that the ways in which global custodians hold clients' non-cash assets are sufficient for the liquidator to identify separately those assets which are beneficially owned by the clients, and those which belong to the global custodian.

The position for cash assets is not so secure; owners of cash are considered by the liquidator to be unsecured creditors in the accounts of the bank (deposit taker, borrower or global custodian).

The global custodians are aware of the problems involved and constantly seek new ways to keep the client's cash related business in-house.

5.8.4 Single-currency accounts

Clients whose business generates cash in one currency, and who wish to enter into cross-border trading, might prefer to operate with cash accounts in a single currency.

They will arrange for all purchase costs, sale proceeds and income receipts to be exchanged (an FX trade) into their base currency as and when the need arises.

Advantages for the investor

- Exposure to adverse exchange rate movements is removed once the FX trade has been executed
- Funding requirement calculations are simplified
- They are free to obtain the most advantageous exchange rates from the FX market place
- Cash reconciliation and control processes are more straightforward

Disadvantages for the investor

- There will be extra FX trading charges over and above the securities trading commissions.

- Securities trade settlements will no longer be on a DvP basis as the currency movements will take place separately from the securities movements.

- FX trades dealt with counterparties other than the global custodian will require instructions for cash and securities settlement separately.

Implications for the global custodian

- Income receipts are changed into the base currency.

- The global custodian will not necessarily be responsible for exchanging the purchase and sale amounts as the investor will search the market for the best FX rates.

- The global custodian will continue to settle trades in the relevant currency on a DvP basis.

5.8.5 Multi-currency accounts

Multi-currency banking will suit those investors whose ordinary business activities generate cash flows in foreign currencies and/or who prefer to settle the securities trades on a DvP basis in the foreign currency. The cash funding requirements will be undertaken as a separate process.

Advantages for the investor

- Securities trades benefit from DvP settlement
- The ability to take advantage of the global custodian's settlement service
- The options available in terms of subsequent use of the foreign currency balances

Disadvantage for the investor

- Increased controls and administrative burden as a result of operating different currency accounts

Implications for the global custodian

- Rounded custody and banking service can be provided to the client.

- The need to exchange all income into the base currency is removed, reducing the number of relatively small-value FX trades that must be executed.

5.8.6 Interest bearing accounts

Investors who actively manage their cash balances wish to reduce or eliminate the time that un-invested or uncommitted cash balances remain in non-interest bearing accounts. Cash balances will be transferred to deposit accounts or other financial products.

Although this achieves the objective, it increases the administrative burden and becomes expensive to operate.

The global custodians now provide interest on various currency accounts and thus help to cut down the number of cash movements across the accounts.

5.8.7 Cash sweeping

Global custodians may offer to transfer automatically (or sweep) un-invested and uncommitted balances overnight from non-interest bearing accounts into interest bearing deposit accounts. This ensures that customer's cash balances are being used in the most efficient manner.

5.8.8 Cash pooling

Global custodians hold different accounts for their clients

- Accounts in the same currency, and/or
- Multi-currency accounts for their clients

For interest calculations only, the custodians can pool the balances by currency into one larger balance in order to attract a higher rate of interest or reduce the effect of some accounts being overdrawn.

5.9 Banking services

Global custodians are continually able to offer an ever-increasing range of banking services which can include the following.

- **Funds transmission systems** – enable the client to transfer electronically funds covering clean payments (i.e. those not directly connected to a securities trade)

- **Treasury services** – provide dealing facilities to purchase and sell foreign currency and place funds on deposit

- **Screen-based dealing systems** – some global custodians have made available facilities which allow clients to execute their smaller FX deals without reference to a bank dealer. Clients are able to accept or reject the rates offered on the screen and, should the rate be acceptable, the transaction is immediately confirmed.

As part of their overall service to their clients, custodians will from time to time be engaged in the following activities, each of which may require the custodian to engage in money market activities.

- Investment of income and capital repayments
- Management of excess cash
- Maintenance of multi-currency securities and funds accounts
- Management of cash received as a result of securities settlements or sale of rights
- Securities borrowing and lending plus the collateral requirements in parallel
- Derivatives transactions

5.10 Proxy voting

Proxy voting is the exercise of the voting right(s) of an investor in shares, bonds and similar instruments through a third party, based on a legally valid authorisation and in conformity with the investor's instructions.

Depending on the country in which the 'proxy' is being exercised, the third party can be:

- A bank
- A person designated by the company
- Another shareholder
- The Chairman of the shareholders' meeting

Proxy voting generally takes place at shareholders' meetings of companies (Annual General Meetings (AGM) and Extraordinary General Meetings (EGM)) for the purpose of approving or rejecting certain resolutions such as the following.

- The election of new board directors and/or re-election of existing board directors
- The approval/adoption of the annual accounts
- The proposed payment of a dividend
- Takeover bids
- Issuing equity capital for cash other than to existing equity shareholders (pre-emptive rights)
- Level of auditors' remuneration
- Resolutions put before the AGM/EGM by the shareholders themselves

Proxy voting can be subject to more or less stringent restrictions depending on national legislation and company by-laws. In each case, therefore, the legal aspects must be examined carefully.

Though automation has now reached most sectors of the securities market, from trading through to settlement, the business of proxy voting (the process by which pension funds and asset managers vote their shares in a company) remains firmly in the paper age.

Institutional investors have a catalogue of bungled voting instructions and of voting deadlines being missed which have caused increasing concern, particularly in the UK. The fear is that global custodians and Registrars are failing to cope with the increasing demand among investors to use their votes.

The UK system allows three weeks between information on annual meetings and its agenda leaving the company to the deadline for voting. In between those two dates, the annual report containing the information is typically sent to the Registrar and then to the custodian before arriving at the investment house. One solution to the problem is to move to electronic voting.

The International Securities Services Association (ISSA) recommended in 1992 that:

'Standard messages be used and standard time frames be developed for various corporate actions. Distinctions need to be made between those requiring timely reaction by the client and those which involve a simple notification and no response.

'That the information must be provided electronically as well as in hard-copy form. A central body, either public or private and accessible to domestic and international bodies, must be designated as the official carrier of the data in each market.

'That international issues should be communicated in English as well as the local language.'

5.11 Cross-border and time zone issues

In recent years, there has been a rapid increase in **cross-border portfolio investing**, in particular by institutional investors. Global custodians through their sub-custodians in the respective domestic markets are holding foreign securities with an estimated value of several hundred billion pounds.

With communication in a foreign language, possibly across different time zones, there is a danger that companies are not able to inform their shareholders in time to cast their votes or react to news about corporate actions concerning their securities.

It is now universally accepted that all shareholders should have an opportunity to exercise their **voting rights**, even though many of them may not actually wish to cast their votes. Indeed, there are some countries which are now beginning to encourage a more proactive participation by shareholders in the affairs of the companies.

In Japan, for example, most shareholder meetings are scheduled at the same time on the same date to prevent members of organised crime from disrupting these meetings. In Argentina, split voting is complex and allowed conditionally. In the Czech Republic, split voting is permitted in principle, but there is no practical method by which to do it.

Proxy voting is not normally a widely debated issue and only in isolated cases (e.g. if there is an outside attempt to gain control of a company) does the subject get coverage in the press.

As a result of increased shareholding by large institutional investors, investment and pension fund managers have shown a new interest in exercising their voting rights. This is partly in response to expectations expressed by the various regulatory bodies and partly an apparent underlying desire to influence a company's business or information policy.

Large cross-border investments are reinforcing this trend and there is a call for a mechanism that will permit the exercise of cross-border voting rights with the same ease as is found in the investor's home country.

As a consequence, and with few exceptions, custodian banks do not advise their clients of forthcoming general meetings abroad. Therefore, holdings of non-resident investors are as a rule not represented at these meetings, unless standing proxy instructions are permitted and have actually been given.

In the long term, this may prove harmful to the functioning of the democratic principles in a free market economy. The system should enable all shareholders, whether domestic or foreign, to vote if they want to.

5.12 Value-added services

The core custody services existed unchanged for many years. With developments over recent years in the custody business, the role of a custodian is becoming that of an information processor and provider. Their clients are expecting the custodian to save them money, reduce risk, improve control and increase returns. Clients are becoming more sophisticated in their requirements. The custodians have responded by seeking to differentiate themselves from their competitors through **value-added services**.

Banks are building on their basic custody package to offer a range of additional services such as fund administration, collateral management and risk management. Securities lending in particular has been a significant area of growth with an increase in demand for this service.

5.12.1 Securities lending

Securities lending occurs when authorised institutions lend their assets and, when permitted, those of their clients, to market makers or other institutions through a network of intermediaries in exchange for a fee.

Legal title to the securities passes from the lender to the borrower but the lender retains the benefits of ownership. This means that the lender continues to receive income and retains the right to sell the securities in the open market. The lender, however, loses the right to vote. Income will not be paid direct to the lender, as the name will have been removed from the company's register. Instead the income is claimed from and paid by the borrower.

Securities lending and borrowing provides liquidity to the market and has been recognised by the Group of 30 (G30) in their Recommendation 8, which stated that:

> 'Securities lending and borrowing should be encouraged as a method of expediting the settlement of securities transactions. Existing regulatory and taxation barriers that inhibit the practice of lending securities should be removed'.

Market participants borrow for a variety of reasons, including:

- To cover settlement failures where participants do not have sufficient securities to settle a delivery
- To cover short positions where participants sell securities that they do not hold
- To support a derivatives activity where exercising options may require the delivery of the security

Firms lend securities for one purpose only and that is to earn fee income, which has two benefits.

- Fee income enhances the investment performance of a securities portfolio.

- Securities lending decreases the size of the portfolio and with it a corresponding reduction in safe keeping charges results.

Lending and borrowing policy must be determined. This will either be negotiated where rates will be subject to the market supply and demand, or non-negotiated where rates stay the same regardless of the type of securities and length of loan. Formal agreements and managed securities lending programmes will be defined. The global custodians and the ICSDs both act as intermediaries or conduits in the process, each helping to provide liquidity to the market.

Precautions and controls must be established to ensure that the lender will receive back the safe return of the securities. A borrower may default, the return of the securities may be delayed owing to settlement and securities liquidity problems, or there may be settlement inefficiencies or infrastructure collapse within the local market. It is customary therefore for collateral to be provided in the form of cash or acceptable collateral in the form of other securities to protect the lender. Non-cash collateral would need to exceed the market value of the loaned securities. There are various disadvantages and advantages of accepting cash/securities as collateral.

5.13 Investment accounting

Accounting will take the form of the provision of a full range of reports that show the client their portfolio at both detailed and summary levels, including:

- Pricing and evaluation reporting
- Investment analysis
- Investment performance
- Investment income tracking
- Consolidation reporting

5.14 Withholding tax

Withholding tax is deducted from payments to non-residents, usually in the form of a standard rate of tax applied to dividends or other payments by companies. It may be reclaimable under double taxation agreements. The tax authorities of the country in which the company is based determine the rate of the tax. Global custodians will provide the collection and reporting service for their clients in respect of all securities to which withholding tax applies.

5.15 Performance measurement

The investor will seek to discover many aspects of the efficiency and performance of the portfolio. Performance measurement provides the investor with detailed information about the actual performance of the funds that the custodian is handling on the investor's behalf.

These measures can apply to the following.

- **Settlement** – deadlines, efficiency, accuracy, failures etc

- **Safe keeping** – collection timeliness, market claim activity, corporate action notification, corporate action entitlement, proxy voting information, position reconciliation and reconciliation of accruals

- **Reporting** – accuracy and timeliness

- **Client service** – numbers of enquiries, acknowledgement, responsibilities and timeliness of problem resolution

- **Cash management** – interest paid and balance calculations

- **Fees** – reliability, accuracy and billing timeliness

5.16 Master custody

Master custody is the name of the overall product offering provided by global custodians which encompasses both 'vanilla' custody together with all the typical value-added service areas of asset servicing, pricing, portfolio performance measurement and securities lending.

It is a comprehensive series of services available to clients who maintain several relationships with investment managers or advisers and who seek the benefits of an agent to serve as the centralised collection point for information regarding portfolio growth, activity etc. Acting on behalf of the client, the custodian interacts with the investment adviser(s), securities depositories, brokers, and other agents on all matters relating to the client's investments from the settlement of any portfolio changes to the collection of all income generated by the portfolio.

The primary value-added service that a master custodian provides is the collection of the enormous amount of detail generated by the investment process and the presentation of information that can be easily accessed and efficiently used by the client.

5.17 Consolidated reporting

Investors might use two or more fund managers because each has a particular specialist investment skill. If the fund managers use their own global custodian, the investors have the problem of consolidating a range of reports from the fund managers and their global custodians into one combined set of reports.

To save the investors time and effort in making the consolidation, one global custodian acts as recipient for the reports generated by the other global custodians and prepares the consolidated set of reports.

5.18 Custodian network structures

Global custodians manage the settlement and custody of their clients' non-domestic securities by using a network of banks known as sub-custodians, who provide domestic custody in their own country.

Custodians will therefore structure their networks either to utilise their own branches or subsidiaries in local markets, or to choose the best agent bank within each market. The model chosen may use elements of global, regional and/or direct access to particular countries.

Key issues in selecting a sub-custodian centre

- Cash management
- Risk
- Pricing
- Credit rating
- Technology
- Vigilance

Irrespective of the quality of service that the global custodian itself is able to provide, the sub-custodians are a potential weak link in the chain (i.e. a source of risk). It is therefore important that only the best sub-custodian is chosen. Clients therefore take the quality of a global custodian's sub-custodian network into consideration when making their custody selection.

5.19 Global custodian selection

From time to time investors will wish to appoint a new custodian. This may be as a result of unsatisfactory performance of the existing provider, the unsatisfactory performance of an investment management house, or the desire to change the model to a multi-custodian arrangement. It may also occur following a change in credit policy to move to custodians with a higher rating than the incumbents.

The selection process will typically involve the drawing up of a **Request For Proposal (RFP)** document, which will act as a yardstick in defining and benchmarking the services required against those available. It will also serve as a method of finding out whether the bank can indeed provide the level of service required. It is not, in itself, a decision making document, rather it is a means to that end.

When formulating a RFP document clients should take care that they have defined their business requirements/priorities and that the questions contained in the RFP are pertinent to the firm's business needs. The document should be unambiguous and be so written that the recipient (the potential global custody service provider) can understand the customer and its business. The answers to the RFP will form the basis for decision making in due course.

The RFP is likely to contain topics such as the following.

- **Background information about the custodian** – credit standing, commitment, personnel, experience, references, regulatory compliance

- **Settlement capability** – deadlines, mechanisms, capacity

- **Safe keeping** – security, income collection mechanisms, tax reclaims, corporate action processing, proxy voting

- **Cash management and foreign exchange** – interest rate policy, instruction deadlines, mechanisms for the automatic conversions into base currency, cash sweeps procedures

- **Client reporting** – sample reports, statements, currencies, production frequency, delivery mechanisms

- **Technology** – system platform, investment, customer interfaces, contingency plans for system failure and disaster backup, SWIFT compatibility, training and support, future development plans and so on

- **Sub-custodian network** – list of sub-custodians, communication methods, network management procedures, draft agreements

- **Pricing structure** – breakdown of detailed transaction charges, custody fees and sub-custodian costs, billing frequency, query procedure

5.20 Global custody risks

5.20.1 Overview

There is, as you might expect, a range of **risks** associated with global custody. In safe keeping securities on a global basis using a global custodian and/or a sub-custodian network, there are many sources of risk whereby an asset can fail to earn the rate of return expected or whereby a loss may occur. These include **credit risk, delivery risk, foreign exchange risk** (or **currency risk**), **operational risk, political risk** and **settlement risk**.

Risk can be present through any area of activity including tax, staff, counterparties, clearing and settlement, clients, data communications, safe keeping and emerging markets.

Other risks include **country risk, issuer risk, investment risk, systemic risk, counterparty** and **credit risk**.

Thus the global custodians must demonstrate a commitment to be aware of and to manage risk in their businesses. With clients' assets measured in tens of trillions of US dollars and the cross-border element a significant, say 25%, of that sum there is a need for investors to be vigilant and to possess a comprehensive knowledge of the operating environment and market infrastructure in which their investments are made.

- **Risk reviews** are necessary and will vary in depth of detail. Generally speaking, a customer's assets should not be invested until a full analysis of the payment system, clearing house, CSD and agent bank has been completed.

- **Risk audits** will concentrate upon service-related risks, relationship risks and communication risks.

5.20.2 Service-related risks

These would cover the risk issues emerging from trade and settlement activities, safe keeping and all operational risks including theft, fraud and money laundering.

5.20.3 Relationship risks

Legally binding agreements will link the participants together. Global custodians will face relationship risk with three outside groups – clients, sub-custodians and fund managers.

With clients there must always be a complete and unambiguous custody agreement in place, documentation must be maintained accurately and kept up-to-date. A service level agreement (SLA) may be applicable.

With sub-custodians there exists the question as to what extent the global custodian is prepared to protect against fraud, negligence and default, those client assets held in the sub-custodian network, especially in emerging markets.

The fund manager acts either as a principal in respect of the assets being managed or as a third party on behalf of its clients. With the former, the contractual relationship and agreements are directly between the fund manager and the custodian. In the latter, the custodial contractual relationship is between client and custodian.

The various parties, whether client, global custodian, local sub-custodian or CSD, all enter into legally binding agreements with one or more of the entities. Many of the exposures in this type of risk relate to liability in contract and/or claims for damages.

Relationship risk for the global custodians can be divided into three categories.

- **Clients** – There must always be a complete and unambiguous custody agreement in place. Special attention must be paid when entering into agreements with foreign sub-custodians, given the intricacies of the market in question. Custodians should maintain up-to-date and accurate client documents (Certificates of Incorporation, Memoranda and Articles of Incorporation, signature cards, etc.). A detailed Service Level Agreement (SLA) may be applicable.

- **Fund managers** – The fund manager acts as either a principal in respect of the assets being managed, or as a third party on behalf of its own clients. In the former case, the contractual relationships and agreements are directly between fund manager and custodian. In the latter case, the custodial contractual relationship is between client and custodian.

- **Sub-custodians** – Apart from ensuring that the sub-custodians are selected with care and due diligence, there is the question of the extent to which the global custodian is prepared to protect those clients' assets held in the sub-custodial network, especially in the emerging markets. Clients are keen to obtain guarantees against the risk of sub-custodial negligence, default and fraud.

In terms of relationship management, the global custodian is, in some jurisdictions, obliged to undertake regular site visits (usually annually) and to carry out an in-depth review of the relationship. This could include an audit and reconciliation and inspection of operational procedures to ensure that the contracted standards are maintained. At the same time, the opportunity should be taken to communicate with other players within the local market infrastructure, including the relevant regulatory bodies.

5.20.4 Communication risks

Every medium of communication between clients and their custodians presents a mix of benefits and risks – whether communication is performed by post, e-mail, fax, telephone, telex, the custodian's proprietary software, or via a network such as SWIFT.

5.20.5 Systemic risk

Systemic risk is the risk that the disruption (at a company, in a market segment, at a central clearing entity or central securities depository) causes widespread difficulties for other companies, in other market segments or in the financial system as a whole, i.e. it sets up an adverse chain reaction. This risk represents one manifestation of a *force majeure*.

5.20.6 Country (or sovereign) risk

Country risk or **sovereign risk** is the risk of holding assets in a foreign country and incorporates political, economic, fiscal and legal changes and gaps in supervisory coverage. Country risk also includes the risks generated by local market practice, the local clearing system and currency transfer risk.

5.20.7 Currency risk

This arises from market price fluctuation (volatility) of currencies.

5.20.8 Market risk

Market risk arises from market price fluctuation (volatility) of securities from the time of trade execution to eventual settlement.

5.20.9 Issuer risk or investment risk

This is the risk that the issuer defaults. For example, in the case of a bond or other traded debt instrument, it is the amount at risk if the issuer fails to meet their obligation to pay interest and principal on the bond. The exposure in economic terms potentially amounts to the full market price of the instrument plus accrued interest; it also includes the cash deposit risk.

5.20.10 Settlement risk

Although it may be caused by a number of factors, this is simply the risk that a party will default on one or more delivery or payment obligation to its counterparties or to a settlement agent.

5.20.11 Counterparty credit risk

Counterparty credit risk refers to the risk that a counterparty will not settle its obligation for the full value, either when due or at any time.

The issues of risk management shifts the focus to operations and, consequently, to custody operations. The issues raised by the FSA for custodians to address included the following.

- A firm should be made contractually responsible for losses in its nominee companies. This would provide added certainty that if the firm was to default, a private investor could make a claim through the Investors Compensation Scheme.

- A firm should make its customers aware of the risks attendant to custody.

- A firm should not use its customers' investments for its own (or other customers') account without obtaining clear and express consent.

- A firm should consider the effect of a third party custodian becoming insolvent.

5.20.12 Importance of risk reviews

Typically, the custodian network management function has had the responsibility for investigating the global securities markets, with legal opinion being sought prior to the global custodian entering into an agreement with a sub-custodian to open an account in the market.

The depth of these reviews varies from bank to bank, but typically the custodians do not focus much attention on market infrastructure and how the sub-custodian interacts with that infrastructure.

It is generally accepted that clients' assets should not be invested in a market until a full analysis of the payment system, clearing house, CSD and agent bank has been completed.

When assessing the safety of CSDs and clearing houses, assumptions should not be made as to the ownership of the CSD, the extent to which the guarantee fund is supported by the government, or the fact that the local Central Bank, as owner of the payment system, ensures DvP.

To assess the safety of a CSD and clearing house, a thorough analysis must be performed. In a clearing house review, this would typically include the following areas.

- Ownership and guarantor
- Regulation
- Participation criteria
- Clearing fund
- Margin on open position
- Capacity of entity
- Loss sharing provisions and adequacy of capital support
- Access to stock loans

Similarly, a CSD review would assess:

- Ownership
- Participation criteria
- Finality assurance
- Real-time gross settlement of cash and securities
- Guarantor/guarantee funds
- Asset commitment periods (cash/securities)
- Insurance
- Settlement type
- Segregation of client assets
- Securities interests/liens
- Registration of securities in client name

Many market participants are concerned to find the CSDs with whom much of their trust and securities are held have varying levels of support, capital and insurance.

The research of Thomas Murray (an independent research-based management consultancy) has shown that only about 60% of CSDs have insurance to cover the loss or theft of securities held in safe custody and damage from fire, while a mere 40% have a compensation fund to cover losses which might take place during business operation. Only 56% are legally required to compensate for the loss of missing deposited securities. The problem is not diminishing as the number of CSDs worldwide grows at a significant rate. In 1990 there were 32 CSDs in operation, in 1997 there were 91, in 2000 there were 120 and today approximately 150 are operational.

The evaluation of local market agent banks is an area in which the custodians have a substantial amount of expertise. When evaluating an agent bank's capabilities, the primary area of focus are its credentials and profile, its quality of service, its systems and communications and its fees and expenses. This is a more conventional assessment than, for instance, a CSD or clearing house review at the initial level, but the real importance of such a review of the agent bank's capabilities is the way the bank interacts with the local market infrastructure.

This means that if the local market practice is that cash and securities are locked into a settlement process for, say 10 hours, does the bank extend that time unnecessarily to, say 15 hours, to allow them time to prepare for the settlement or receive the proceeds back into the client's account? Holding the client's cash and securities in the settlement system obviously exposes the client to additional risk, so the shorter the period, the less exposed the assets.

5.20.13 Consequences of inadequate asset protection

The primary purpose in reviewing an agent bank's capabilities is to ensure that the client's assets benefit from the most competitive asset safety and risk minimisation opportunities in the markets. The main factors are the bank's credit rating, strength of balance sheet and overall commitment to the business, as well as its willingness to take on the responsibility for the loss of value to the client through actions or omissions. The standards offered, surprisingly, vary quite significantly from bank to bank, and market to market. Identifying local market best practice for CSDs, clearing houses and agent banks is a critical component of a review if the clients are to benefit from the process. Some best practice recommendations are shown below.

From the client's perspective, minimising risk in global markets is relatively simple if certain procedures are followed and the risks are properly identified. As a first step, the infrastructure must be researched thoroughly, by taking comprehensive legal opinions and gaining an understanding as to how the market works from a settlement/processing perspective.

The relationship that the agent has with the local market infrastructure is critical. In at least one market, if the bank appoints the CSD, no lien (charge) is exercisable over the client securities. If, however, the client makes the appointment themselves, they in effect give a lien over their assets. Investors need to act with caution.

Investors must at all times have confidence that they know where and how their cash and securities are held. Once the risks have been identified, agent banks with strong credit ratings should be appointed. They should have sound balance sheets and be willing and able to take responsibility for losses. Part of that process will necessarily involve securing clear and precise legal terms. The overall arrangements should be reviewed on a regular basis to ensure market best practice has not changed and that the service being offered to the client has not become less competitive as the market evolves.

Asset protection is part of the foundation of the securities industry. Without it, ongoing initiatives, such as the amalgamation of exchanges, the proliferation of CSDs and the implementation of straight-through processing cannot be implemented effectively.

5.20.14 Risk countermeasures

ISSA considered the various causes of these risk types in the trade, settlements and other operational areas and suggested appropriate countermeasures.

Situation 1

Failure to notify or process a corporate action exposes the client to market risk. The following countermeasures, if used on a regular and monitored basis, will reduce the chances of failure.

- Using more than one source of information
- Instructing sub-custodians to give timely advice on all corporate actions
- Regular review of relevant press, newsletters, bulletins etc

Situation 2

The inability to cope with variable and cyclical volumes can lead to losses due to work overload, penalty interest claims, and exposure to market risk and FX risk. A stable and experienced work force will help to absorb sudden increases and a higher degree of automation will provide more flexibility with respect to changing workload.

Situation 3

Prolonged service disruption of the custodian or sub-custodian through any number of causes can lead to market, systemic and FX risk, debit interest charges and claims for damages unless:

- Contingency plans are put in place and regularly rehearsed to ensure that service disruption is kept to a minimum.

- Uninterrupted power sources and computer systems sites are available.

- Third-party service providers have contingency plans in place.

Situation 4

If the custodian acts on an invalid instruction, it is exposed to a claim for damages.

Countermeasures include the following.

- Client's documentation must include who is authorised to act on the client's behalf, by what means and to what extent. Ensure the documentation is updated on a regular basis to reflect changes in personnel.

- Client's representatives must have the legal capacity to contract.

- Proper standards of care should be taken concerning arrangements for telex test keys and third parties who are authorised to act on the client's behalf in custodian relationships.

- The articles of association/incorporation, containing the objectives of corporate clients, must be known by the custodian in case there is any conflict with the practice of due care by the custodian in its operations on behalf of the client and on the type of service that can be offered to the client.

6 CORPORATE ACTIONS

6.1 Overview

Effectively part of asset servicing, the term '**corporate action**' is given to any action taken by a company which distributes cash, stock or a combination to shareholders or stockholders, usually in proportion to the investor's holding (i.e. **a benefit or entitlement distribution**), or which changes the nature or description of a company's stock (i.e. **a stock event**). Corporate actions include, *inter alia*, dividends, rights issues, redemptions, consolidations and placings. Sometimes a decision has to be made by the investor (e.g. a takeover situation) and sometimes the investor will either receive (e.g. dividend) or have to pay additional money (e.g. in the case of a rights issue) as a result of the corporate action. Usually the corporate action will have some time criticality.

Corporate actions apply both to equity and fixed income products. A receiving agent is an organisation appointed by a company to handle the processing of documents and payments in connection with a corporate action. A receiving agent would be responsible for both rights issues and takeover scenarios.

Typically, a corporate action will result in an investor having to make a choice and possibly making an additional payment. The investor's custodian will probably provide the necessary support services to achieve this. Time is likely to be critical as there will always be deadlines involved and possibly difficulty in reaching the beneficiaries concerned in order to obtain their decisions.

Corporate actions also affect derivatives where, for example, a stock future or traded stock option is based upon an underlying share upon which a corporate action event occurs. The derivatives exchange or the counterparties (in the case of an OTC deal) will need to define what changes are to be applied to the contract specification and the effective date for them. Exchanges such as Euronext.liffe are extremely careful to stipulate precise and practical arrangements. They will always be published on the relevant websites.

Although traditionally corporate actions have been paper-intensive exercises, in recent years the application of better and more effective software has been possible which has seen the emergence of improved technology and a reduction of operational risk in corporate action processing. The optimum manner for the application of automation will vary between different types of market user – custodians, banks, stockbrokers and fund managers.

If and when an issuer of an existing security distributes benefits to shareholders or bondholders, or chooses to change the security's structure, such events are commonly known as corporate actions. A corporate action is any action involving a company's issued security other than market trading. Corporate actions can be initiated by the company (dividends, debt repayments) or by the security holder (exercise of a warrant into equity).

For global custodians there are a number of issues that have to be taken into consideration when dealing with events that require the investor either to make a decision or take no action at all.

All corporate action events can be classified as mandatory or voluntary (optional) where:

- Participation by the owner in mandatory events is compulsory, but the owner may or may not be given an option to select its form, and

- Participation by the owner in voluntary events is initiated by the owner.

6.2 Entitlement distributions

Entitlement distribution is a distribution made by a company to its shareholders in the form of cash, securities or a combination of both in cases where entitlement is a fraction of a share. Distributions are usually made in proportion to the investor's holding at the record date.

6.3 Dividends on shares

A **dividend** is a cash payment, reflecting the company's decision to distribute a portion of the company's profit to its shareholders. The rate of distribution will vary, although the timing will usually be regular, whether annually, semi-annually or quarterly.

The speed with which the dividends are paid once the payment date has been announced varies considerably throughout the world. The investor expects to be able to utilise the cash as soon as possible, but is uncertain as to exactly when.

6.4 Contractual income collection: equities

Global custodians are increasingly in a position to offer a **contractual income collection** service. Investors' cash accounts are credited with good value on a pre-determined number of days after the intended payment date, a delay which reflects the ability of the local market to make payment. Whilst there is no standardised time lag per country amongst the global custodians, in many countries the timeliness of income receipt has become more certain.

Hence global custodians can give a contractual (guaranteed) income collection service whether in the local currency or converted back into the investor's base currency.

Contractual income is generally offered in most countries, including the following.

Australia	Denmark	Hong Kong	Malaysia	Portugal	Sweden
Austria	Finland	Ireland	Netherlands	Singapore	Switzerland
Belgium	France	Italy	New Zealand	South Africa	UK
Canada	Germany	Japan	Norway	Spain	USA

6.5 Interest payments

An interest payment is a cash payment made to holders of debt securities including:

- Eurobonds (fixed interest and floating rate)
- Foreign bonds
- Convertible bonds

The rate of interest (the coupon) and the frequency of payment are determined within the original terms of issue. As the company's principal and sub-paying agents pay the interest on the dates specified by these terms (also printed on the coupon), there is more certainty of value for both the global custodian and the investor.

6.6 Repayment of capital

A capital repayment is a partial repayment of a company's issued capital. The company pays each shareholder a proportion of the value of the shares at the current market price. Whilst the number of shares issued remains the same, the nominal value of each share is reduced by the amount of the capital repayment per share.

6.7 Timing

A trade that fails to settle on time will eventually settle. There might be penalty interest to pay and possible delays in other related trades; the trade nevertheless still stands.

With corporate actions however, the overriding factor in cases that require a proactive approach in order to benefit from the corporate action is for all parties in the information chain to deliver instructions before the deadline expires. A missed corporate action is irretrievable and internal controls must be in place to address this possibility.

6.8 Sources of information

Global custodians must have a reliable, comprehensive source of information on forthcoming corporate actions. This usually comprises a combination of their sub-custodian network and multiple third party securities data vendors. Information should be matched across two independent sources (subject to the availability of multiple reliable sources). Validated events data must be matched to a client's holding and each event tracked through to confirmation that the resulting entitlement has been received for the client and settled. The process should include pre-matching of entitlements (whether or not this is standard market practice) with exceptions pursued vigorously as the settlement date approaches. Ideally, the entire process should be automated, with manual effort focussed on resolving exceptions. Events must be notified to clients, and event status reported, with clarity and timeliness, preferably in real-time.

The prime source of information covering registered securities is the issuing company or its agent. The global custodian has to rely on his sub-custodian network to gather this information and pass it on to the client with a minimum of delay. (The transmission of information may also include translation into English.)

Secondary sources of information are the numerous information vendors such as Extel, Reuters, Telekurs, *Financial Times*, *Wall Street Journal* and the domestic financial press.

However, these secondary sources, by providing information on equities (dates for shareholder meetings, dividends etc), become primary sources for holders of bearer securities if the issuing companies are unable to communicate directly with their bond shareholders.

If possible, the information needs to be re-confirmed as the quality and sources of the information may be poor; language problems and time delays are the main problems experienced.

6.9 Entitlements at record date

Calendar date is used by bond issuers in determining eligibility to collect future payments of principal and interest. It is also a date on which owners of a company's shares are declared by the board of directors as eligible to receive dividends at a specific date in the future or vote on corporate issues, such as rights issues.

The amount of interest due to an investor is determined by reference to the quantity of shares each investor holds on a **record date**. The issuing company announces this record date. The local market will usually establish a date (ex date) which is used to determine whether the buyer or seller of shares is entitled to receive the dividend.

Problems arise when a purchaser buys shares before the ex date (i.e. is entitled to receive the dividend) and does not have his name recorded on the register before the record date. The Registrar is unable to recognise the new shareholder and the dividend is paid to the previous shareholder (seller) even though it is due to the new shareholder.

The global custodian's job is to make sure that entitlements are received on a timely basis to avoid lost opportunities in trading. Therefore, there needs to be a mechanism in place to ensure that the correct entitlements are received and, if not, claimed from the seller.

6.10 Information to investor

It is the global custodian's responsibility to provide as much information as possible to enable the client to make the necessary decisions, to ensure that the information is accurate and to allow enough time for the client's instructions, if appropriate, to be relayed back to the company.

As there are a variety of information types, it has not been easy for the global custodians to translate them into electronic message formats for the client. Instead, information on corporate actions has tended in the past to be sent by facsimile, telex and mail. This situation is changing as the quality of information from overseas markets improves.

6.11 Instructions from investor

The investor will be given a deadline by which time they must convey any instructions to the global custodian, allowing the global custodian to pass them on to the appropriate bodies.

The investor must accept full responsibility for a missed event if instructions are sent after the custodian's pre-advised deadline.

6.12 Instructions to benefit distributor

Global custodians must ensure that clients' instructions are passed on to the appropriate bodies and also that the resulting entitlement is received in good time.

6.13 Registrars and Receiving Agents

A company's **Registrar** is responsible for identifying which investors are eligible to receive a benefit or who will be subject to a stock event. It does this by maintaining the register of stockholders on a given date, the record date. The Registrar is then responsible for distributing details of the event to eligible investors and distributing (or withdrawing) the stock results of an action.

Sometimes a **Receiving Agent** is appointed by a company to assist in the processing of documents and payments associated with a particular corporate action. This may result from the extra volume of work created by the issue (e.g. collection of payments after a rights issue or maintaining secrecy in a takeover situation).

In a rights issue the receiving agent distributes nil/partly paid rights and collects the call payments. In a takeover the receiving agent is appointed by the bidding company to maintain a record of those investors who accept the offer. In practice, a receiving agent is typically a department within the Registrar.

7 DIVIDENDS AND STOCK DISTRIBUTIONS

A dividend is a cash distribution paid to shareholders out of distributable reserves. For **preference shares**, the dividend is fixed. For **Ordinary shares**, the dividend is decided by the board. Most UK companies pay a dividend, if any, every six months. The **interim dividend** is paid during the year and the **final dividend** is paid after the financial year end. Dividends can only be paid out of retained profits, also known as distributable reserves.

7.1 Timings

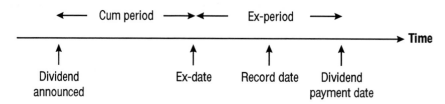

All UK equity dividends are announced on a Monday. The dividend is announced in the Stock Exchange Weekly Official Listing as well as on Bloomberg and Reuters. Firms can buy software which extracts relevant information from Bloomberg.

Whoever holds the stock on the stock register on record date will be entitled to receive the dividend.

The Exchange determines when the share price includes the dividend. If the share price is 'cum dividend' then the benefit is passed to the buyer. If the share price is 'ex-dividend' then the benefit remains with the seller. Cum and ex mean with or without the dividend. The ex-date marks the dividing line between the cum and ex-periods.

The dividend is actually paid on payment date to the holder on the record date.

7.2 Claims

Frequently the ex-date is between two and four days prior to the record date. If the share changes hands between the ex-date and the record date, then there will be a claim.

For example, suppose that on the third of the month, Customer A buys stock at the ex-div price from B. The record date is the fifth. On payment date, Customer A will receive the dividend. As Customer A bought the share ex-div, the dividend belongs to Customer B. Customer B will therefore need to make a claim to Customer A.

7.3 Stock claims

It is usual for the record date for stock distributions to be in advance of the announcement and ex-div date. This increases the likelihood of a claim.

7.4 Stock distributions

Stock distributions can be mandatory or optional. Mandatory stock events include bonus and scrip issues. Optional stock events include rights issues.

7.5 Rights issues

A rights issue is a popular method for raising new equity capital in the UK. Shares in rights issues are offered on a *pro rata* basis to existing shareholders. The main advantage for the shareholders is that they can maintain their relative percentage of the shareholding whilst for the company it is cheaper as less marketing is required.

An example of a rights issue would be a 'one in four', which means that for every four shares a shareholder owns they are allowed to buy one extra share thereby potentially increasing the number of shares by 25%. In order to encourage people to take up the rights, the rights are offered at a discount to the current market price.

Shareholders can either take up the rights and buy the new shares at the discounted price. Alternatively, the shareholder can sell the rights for cash. As mentioned earlier, the rights may be renounceable and, if the shareholder does nothing, the rights will lapse.

A rights issue is an offer by a company to sell a new offering of securities, normally common shares, to its shareholders, proportionate to their holdings. Usually an offer to sell newly issued shares or additional shares is at a lower price than the publicly offered shares.

The global custodian's first task is to provide all the clients who have a shareholding with full details of the issue including dates and payment amounts.

There are several options available to a shareholder.

- Nil-paid rights can be traded
- Nil-paid rights can be allowed to lapse, i.e. neither traded nor accepted
- Rights can be accepted and paid for by making a cash payment

It is, therefore, likely that the global custodian will have to give a series of different instructions to the company. All the clients' instructions must be received in time and accurately passed on to the company. Late or incorrect instructions will result in the global custodian, if at fault, making good the client's position. This may involve financial loss.

7.6 Bonus issues

As you will probably recall, a **scrip issue, bonus issue** or **capitalisation issue** (different terms for the same corporate action) creates new shares without raising capital. Shares are given without charge to existing shareholders in proportion to the shares already held. There are no direct advantages to the shareholder. For the company, the share price will reflect the increase in the number of shares, e.g. a 1 for 1 scrip issue will cause the share price to halve as it dilutes the share value (there being twice as many shares in existence following the action). The new share price might 'appear' more attractive to investors, it might camouflage poor historic results or the publicity surrounding the bonus issue might increase liquidity. The bonus issue will mean that the company converts its retained profit and loss reserves in the balance sheet into share capital consequently increasing the company's external credit rating and debt/equity ratio.

In this case, the client does not need to give any instructions. However, he should be informed of the issue by the global custodian as the number of shares currently held in the account will change.

The share price, however, will change as the overall market value of the old and the bonus shares remains the same.

Some bonus shares do not qualify for the next dividend payment.

7.7 Stock splits and consolidations

A **stock split** occurs where a company splits the nominal value of its shares. For example 1,000 £1 shares become 2,000 50p shares. This is unusual as the nominal value is usually meaningless.

A **consolidation** is the opposite of a stock split in that a number of shares with a low nominal value are converted into one share with a higher nominal value. It is easier to maintain the share register in this case but there are a few other advantages.

7.8 Conversions

A **conversion** takes place when debt securities are converted into equities. Convertible debt is often used as a marketing tool to encourage people to invest in debt in the early days of a company. The conversion also improves the debt/equity ratio.

Investors who are holders of convertible debt securities (bonds) may wish to convert the debt into equity. The full terms for the conversion are specified at the original issue date and generally allow the investor the right to convert at pre-determined rates and times set by the company.

The actual conversion is optional except that the last possible date for conversion is itself non-optional, i.e. the bond is either redeemed for cash or automatically converted into equity according to the issue terms.

7.9 Scrip dividends

Scrip dividends are a method companies use to distribute profits in the form of shares instead of cash. The shareholder is offered the benefit of receiving cash or given the option to receive shares.

The global custodian must also ensure that the client's instructions are obtained and passed on. Although the company will usually pay the cash dividend in the absence of any instructions to the contrary, it is important to check the terms of the issue in case the basic offer is for scrip.

7.10 Redemptions

A **redemption** or **repayment** is a stock situation where the company repays its debt holders in order to redeem part or all of its loan.

- A callable security is one which the issuer can repay at his choosing at any pre-determined time during the life of the loan.

- A putable security is one where the investor has this choice.

The redemption becomes non-optional at maturity – the final date of the loan.

7.11 Ranking *'pari passu'*

This is an area which can cause many problems for the global custodian and investor alike. A company might issue securities which are identical to existing securities already in circulation except that, for a pre-determined period of time, the new securities do not qualify for a particular dividend or are subject to some other type of restriction (active participation at shareholder meetings). Once this period is over, the two lines of securities are merged and become *pari passu:* they rank equal in all respects.

Until the two lines of securities become *pari passu*, they are given separate security identification codes and in addition will trade at different prices. Both global custodian and investor must be aware of these differences and reflect the holdings accurately in safe keeping records.

7.12 International dividends

International dividends are more complex than UK dividends. Firstly, it can be hard to identify the dividend announcement as it is disclosed through a variety of different information sources. Secondly, the stock prices tend to be quite volatile so that it can be harder to identify when the share price goes ex-dividend. Thirdly, the time scale between record date and payment can be quite lengthy. In Russian stocks it is often 12 months. The international markets are not as well organised as the European markets and there are different market conventions as to when a claim dividend is due, e.g. record date or ex-div date.

8 EUROCLEAR AND CORPORATE ACTIONS

8.1 Overview

CREST has had the functionality to deal with corporate actions since its inauguration in 1996. In January 2003 Euroclear extended its range of services to introduce electronic proxy voting for its customers. In July 2004, Euroclear added a further facility whereby issuers and their agents are able to transmit electronically both the payment of dividends and the associated tax voucher in a single message, thus streamlining the old paper-based process. In parallel with this, clients are able to transmit electronically to an issuer's Registrar their dividend election instructions, such as whether to take all or part of their dividend entitlement in cash, or to reinvest all or part of the proceeds in more shares.

Note that the use of CREST (or Euroclear as it is now known) for processing corporate actions is optional and a company whose securities are eligible for settlement through the Euroclear system is not obliged to process its benefit distribution or other events via the system. Almost all companies whose shares are eligible to settle through Euroclear choose to distribute dividends to members and sponsored members via Euroclear.

There are **six types of Euroclear transactions** for processing corporate actions:

- Registrar Adjustment (REG)
- Unmatched Stock Event (USE)
- Many to Many (MTM)
- Transfer to Escrow (TTE)
- Transfer from Escrow (TFE)
- Escrow Adjustment (ESA)

8.2 REG

When a firm has a capitalisation or bonus issue or a stock consolidation, a REG instruction is input to amend the share register details.

8.3 USE

When the firm announces a dividend, it gives the shareholders the option to receive the dividend through Euroclear. For Euroclear members who opt to receive the dividend, a USE will be created two days prior to payment date.

When a rights issue is announced, Euroclear creates a new stock with a new ISIN number via either a REG or USE instruction. If the rights lapse, this new stock is deleted. If the rights are sold, a normal DEL instruction is input. If the rights are taken up there is USE transaction to move the cash.

8.4 MTM

In a conversion when debt is converted into equity, a MTM instruction would be input. Similarly, a MTM would be used for the exercise of warrants.

8.5 TTE/TFE

During a takeover, the shareholders in the target company have between 21 and 60 days to respond. They can respond through Euroclear by submitting a TTE transaction to transfer the shares to the control of the bidding company. Once the shares are in escrow, only the bidder's receiving agent can move them out via a TFE.

Euroclear deals with claims through the CPU (Claims Processing Unit). The CPU automatically identifies claims and issues a CLA (Claim Notification).

8.6 ESA

This is a single input transaction that requires verification (acceptance) by a receiving (escrow) agent and is used to move stock between escrow balances within a stock account or else to move stock from an escrow balance to an available balance. In a takeover in which electronic acceptances are allowed, this transaction enables the accepting member to instruct the receiving agent for the bidding company that they wish to change their preferred option for the out-turn (change for example from a cash option to a stock option). Providing the receiving agent accepts the ESA, Euroclear will deal with the stock movement. The ESA transaction removes the need for any paper to move between the parties and this improves the processing efficiency.

9 OVERVIEW OF UK TAXATION

HM Revenue & Customs (HMRC, formerly the Inland Revenue) is responsible for the direct taxation of both individuals and corporations. Customs and Excise are responsible for indirect taxation. This section aims to give a brief and simple overview of the UK tax system. UK taxation has many detailed rules and exemptions which will be ignored for this purpose.

9.1 Personal tax

In the UK, individuals are subject to three types of direct taxation.

- Income tax
- Capital gains tax
- Inheritance tax

For income and capital gains, individuals are classified as both resident and ordinarily resident. Any individual who spends more than 162 days (counted at midnight) in the UK in a year is resident. Any individual who normally resides in the UK is termed ordinarily resident. Ordinarily resident individuals are taxed on their worldwide income, whereas residents are just taxed on their UK income. Hence, pop stars and celebrities might arrange worldwide tours to avoid being a UK resident for a year. There are worldwide tax treaties to avoid residents paying tax on the same income to two tax authorities. This is known as double taxation relief.

9.2 Income tax

Income tax is a tax on all income e.g. salaried earnings, rental income, dividends and interest. The whole of taxable income for the tax year (6 April) is totalled to create the statutory taxable income (STI).

All individuals have a tax free 'personal allowance'. The personal allowance is increased for those over 65. There are additional reliefs such as additional persons and widow bereavement.

The remaining income is then taxed according to the following taxable bands (2007/08).

	%
Starting rate	10
Basic rate	22
Higher rate	40

- PAYE ('pay as you earn') is personal income tax deducted at source by the employer and remitted to HMRC. Salaries are paid into the bank net of income tax. The remaining tax is calculated on the Self-assessment Tax Return.

- UK loan stock interest, bank deposit interest and building society interest are debited to an individual net of 20% tax. The first 20% is deducted at source and individuals just have to pay the remaining tax on the self-assessment form.

- Gilt interest and eurobond interest are usually paid gross. No tax is deducted at source.

- Dividends from UK companies are received net of a 'notional' 10% tax credit. Dividends are classed as the top slice of income. They will be taxed further at the highest tax rate.

9.3 Capital gains tax

Capital gains tax (CGT) arises when there is a chargeable disposal of a chargeable asset by a chargeable person.

- A chargeable disposal is a sale, a sale at under value, a gift or the liquidation of a company. Assets which were bought and sold for under a stipulated amount are exempt.

- A chargeable asset is any asset belonging to an individual except principal private residences, gilts and gilt futures, and qualifying corporate bonds. (A qualifying corporate bond is a non-convertible bond issued in sterling.)

- A chargeable person is any resident or ordinarily resident individual. The tax includes all assets located in both the UK and the rest of the world. Movements between spouses are tax free.

The gain is calculated by taking the consideration (sales price less stamp duty less broker's fees) less the purchase price less an indexation allowance. The indexation allowance is to take account of inflation and is based upon the retail price index.

The gains and losses for the fiscal year are aggregated and then the annual exemption is deducted. The remaining gain is then taxed at the current income tax rates.

'Bed and breakfasting' used to be a loophole to reduce CGT whereby assets were sold to crystallise the gain or the loss and then bought back the following day. This loophole has now been closed but it is possible to transfer assets to a spouse (known as 'bed and spousing') or transferring to an ISA (known as 'bed and ISA').

9.4 Inheritance tax

Inheritance tax is based on assets owned at death and also in the seven years prior to death. There is a stipulated amount that is tax-free, but then the remaining estate is taxed at 40%.

9.5 Partnerships

Partnerships are taxed as a collection of individuals.

9.6 National Insurance Contributions

National Insurance Contributions are paid by both employees and employers. The employee's contribution is deducted at source.

9.7 Corporation tax

Corporation tax is based on profits less any disallowable expenditure. Disallowable expenditure includes client entertaining and provisions. Staff entertaining is typically a considerable balance for securities firms.

Under quarterly accounting, companies must make a payment to HMRC every quarter on their CT61 form. Small companies pay tax at the lower rate and companies between the size bands get marginal tax relief.

Companies with common ownership are known as 'associated companies' and are treated as one group for corporation tax. It is possible for these companies to transfer losses between each company. This is known as **loss surrender**.

Transfer pricing is an issue for many securities firms with operations around the world. HMRC is concerned that companies are transferring profits to countries with lower tax rates. Thus HMRC needs to see documented explanations as to why international charges are reasonable and on an arm's length basis.

9.8 Indirect taxes

Stamp duty is the oldest form of UK taxation. **Stamp Duty Land Tax** is payable on land transfers, leases and conveyances.

In respect of securities, **stamp duty** is 0.5% of the consideration on transfer which requires a change in registered title, e.g. share transfer, rounded up to the nearest £5. Gilts, UK debentures, and foreign registered and bearer shares are exempt.

Within Euroclear there is electronic entitlement to shares. **Stamp duty reserve tax (SDRT)** then applies and functions similarly to stamp duty except that the duty is 0.5% rounded up to the nearest 1p. It is applied to the purchase side of bargains.

Irish stamp duty is charged at 1% on stocks registered in **Ireland**.

There is ongoing debate as to whether stamp duty on securities transactions should be abolished. Those in favour of its abolition say that it discourages investors and threatens the efficacy of London as a leading financial centre as there is no stamp duty equivalent in Europe. Many argue that stamp duty is very effective at raising revenue and has not caused any detrimental effect to date.

VAT (Value Added Tax) was introduced in the UK in 1973. The standard rate for UK value added tax is 17.5% on purchases although most security transactions are exempt. VAT registered companies can set off VAT on purchases against VAT on sales. Therefore firms need to monitor input/output tax carefully.

10 WITHHOLDING TAXES AND EXCHANGE OF INFORMATION

10.1 Overview

Withholding taxes (WHT) are taxes deducted from payments to non-residents, usually by a standard rate of tax applied to dividends and other payments such as interest.

The problem this causes for non-resident investors is that the net income is additionally subject to further taxation in their own country. Most governments allow most or all of the WHT to be reclaimed entering into a **Double Taxation Treaty** or **Agreement**. Countries do this in order to prevent income being taxed twice and to assist each other in combating tax evasion.

Income arising from a securities portfolio is generally subject to deduction of withholding taxes in the issuers' countries. Depending on the owner's tax status, the type of security and other factors, relief from some of the withholding tax may be due. The basis for tax relief lies in exemptions and lower tax rates in the local laws of some issuers' jurisdictions and in the double taxation treaties which the government of the owner's country may have concluded with a range of issuers' countries.

Global custodians must maintain complete, accurate, up-to-date information and declarations from their clients as proof of eligibility for tax relief. Above all, there must be absolute clarity as to the tax status of the owner and, to the greatest extent possible, in the treatment of portfolios held by commingled funds.

The tax authorities of the country in which the company is based determine the rate of WHT.

10.2 Double taxation treaties

Governments enter into DTTs with other countries in order to:

- Prevent income being taxed twice, and
- Render reciprocal assistance to prevent tax evasion

WHT reclamation may be allowable if:

- Certain classes of income are made taxable only in one of the countries who are party to a DTT, e.g. in the country of the tax payer's residence

- Income is taxable in both countries but, in the case of UK residents, the overseas tax is allowable as a credit against UK tax

If there is no DTT in operation, it is possible to gain unilateral relief, i.e. a UK resident may offset any overseas tax that he has paid against the UK tax liability on the same income.

10.3 Issues with withholding taxes

With the increase in cross-border investment activity, investors are subject to different tax regimes. Tax reclaims must be made in the issuer's country of origin by the global custodian on behalf of the client who will submit them.

There is no standard global approach to tax reclamation in terms of the timing of claims and repayment.

Calculating quite how much tax is kept back is far from a simple exercise, either for custodian banks or those who have entrusted their investments to them. The tax element on dividends and interest is paid direct to the tax authorities, with the onus on investors to reclaim.

Tax rates vary from country to country, as do the amounts withheld. Amounts can also vary depending on whether the money is invested in bonds or equities, and the exact nature of the double taxation treaty in force between withholding nations and the investor's country of residence.

The larger custodians may each make up to 30,000 individual reclaims a week. The figures explain why tax reclamation is such a complicated business. Tax recovery is becoming an important competitive factor for fund managers in determining performance figures.

The subject of withholding tax reclamation is often swept under the carpet because investors, their fund managers and custodian banks have no reliable data sources which indicate the true scale of losses being incurred. In this atmosphere, leading custodians have recognised the market opening represented by effective tax reclaiming services, both for their fund manager clients and as an interbank services opportunity.

Of pertinence to global risk management transactions, most governments impose a withholding tax ranging from 15% to 30% on some interest payments and nearly all dividends paid on securities owned by foreign investors. Reciprocal withholding tax treaties usually reduce the withholding tax among the major industrial countries to 15%.

Custodians particularly have a major problem with tax reclaims. It is a complex business covering institutions and countries all over the world. Tax recovery is an important issue for custodians and their clients.

10.4 UK Government

The UK Government introduced, with effect from April 2001, new measures to help promote the UK as a competitive environment for business. The withholding tax on international bond interest was abolished and replaced by simpler and less burdensome requirements to provide information to HMRC. At the same time the UK Government announced changes to allow HMRC to improve the effectiveness of exchange of information arrangements under double taxation agreements with other countries and allow the UK to enter into new exchange of information agreements helping to prevent individuals and companies evading or avoiding tax.

The tax rules for paying and collecting agents of quoted Eurobonds and foreign dividends apply to about 600 financial institutions. Previously, they were required to deduct and account for tax on payments to UK residents, and to obtain and keep for inspection various types of declaration from non-UK residents and others entitled to receive payments without deduction of tax.

HMRC is able to exchange taxpayer information with other countries with which the UK has a double taxation agreement. Information exchanged under these agreements is on a reciprocal basis. However, the UK does not receive information from other countries unless it is able to provide similar information in return.

The UK Government has emphasised the need for greater international co-operation in particular exchange of information to tackle financial crime, harmful tax competition, tax evasion and avoidance. A G7 initiative seeking to improve the supply of information from tax havens by the negotiation of effective information exchange agreements was launched by the Chancellor during the UK Presidency in 1998.

Withholding taxes vary from country to country, but some examples are given below.

10.5 Australia

Dividend Withholding Tax. Where dividends are paid or credited to non-residents, a franked dividend (one for which taxes have already been paid by a corporation) does not attract any withholding tax. Unfranked dividends however will be taxed at 30% unless paid to residents in a treaty country where a reduced rate applies (generally 15%). The payment of a dividend that consists of bonus shares from a capital reserve issued to a non-resident shareholder is subject to withholding tax. Where a franked dividend is paid to a non-resident, however, there is no refund of unutilised franking credits. An exemption from dividend withholding tax may be available where the following conditions are satisfied.

- The Australian company receives qualifying foreign-sourced dividend income (e.g. dividends exempt under the Controlled Foreign Corporations rules).

- The qualifying dividend income is credited to a Foreign Dividend Account (FDA), and

- The company makes an FDA declaration and pays the dividend from this account.

A deduction is allowed for the on-payment of unfranked non-portfolio dividend by an Australian resident company to its foreign parent.

No withholding tax applies to dividends distributed to Australian shareholders.

Interest Withholding Tax. A 10% withholding tax is levied on all interest remittances to foreign companies. The definition of interest has been modified to include: (1) amounts that can reasonably be regarded as equivalent to; or (2) in substitution for; or (3) obtained in exchange for a right to receive interest. Borrowers that do not deduct interest withholding tax from interest payments to non-residents are denied a deduction for the interest costs. The tax is waived, however, for interest remitted abroad on certain foreign borrowings. Interest withholding tax is not payable on interest paid by a company in respect of a debenture if the following conditions are satisfied.

- The company was a resident of Australia when it issued the debenture
- The company is a resident of Australia when the interest is paid, and
- The issue of the debenture satisfied the prescribed 'public offer tests'

Australian entities are normally subject to a 10% withholding tax for interest paid to overseas lenders. This is a final tax.

10.6 Germany

Dividend Withholding Tax. Under the German Tax Reform Act 2000, the standard rate of withholding tax (Kapitalertragsteuer) was reduced to 20% for local and foreign shareholders. Foreign parent companies often pay a lower withholding tax under tax treaties.

Interest Withholding Tax. Under domestic law and several tax treaties, interest on loans secured by German real estate remains subject to income or corporation tax for non-residents subject to limited taxation. The same is true for participating loans and profit-sharing bonds (instead of fixed interest, the creditor is entitled to a profit portion).

A 30% withholding tax applies to interest paid by domestic banks, provided the recipient has a German domicile or its seat or place of management is in Germany. This also applies to interest on special bonds and on income from investment funds. In the case of an over-the-counter trade (i.e. payment on presentation of interest coupons), a 35% withholding tax is imposed that may be refunded upon application to treaty-protected non-residents. A solidarity surcharge of 5.5% increases the interest withholding tax rates to 31.65% and 36.925%, respectively, effective 1 January 1998.

10.7 Japan

Dividend Withholding Tax. Dividends from a Japanese corporation are subject to a 20% withholding tax at source. The rate may be reduced under existing tax treaties for non-residents that do not have a permanent establishment in Japan. For domestic corporations, the income tax withheld is considered a prepayment against corporate income tax liability and withheld tax in excess of the liability is refundable.

Dividends. Paid by foreign corporations to Japanese shareholders are also taxable, but any foreign income taxes imposed on the dividends may be used as foreign tax credits.

Interest Withholding Tax. The normal withholding tax on interest payable to non-residents is 15% – except for interest on loans, which is 20% – but this may be reduced by tax treaties. The lower treaty rates apply, however, only to income that is not attributable to a permanent establishment.

10.8 United States

In the USA, Non-Resident Alien 1441 Regulation came into force in January 2001. This had major implications for institutional investors.

Previous withholding tax practices relied upon the address of the recipient. With the introduction of the new regulation, the US Internal Revenue Service (IRS) clamped down on beneficial owners, the ultimate owner of the dividend paid, to ensure 30% US withholding tax was paid on US source income. To qualify for a reduced rate of tax or exemption, additional documentation of the beneficial owner's tax status needs to be provided. For example, the W-8BEN form and others must be presented.

CHAPTER ROUNDUP

- Securities may be held either in certificated (paper) or dematerialised (electronic) format.

- A bearer document does not show the owner's name. With registered documents, ownership is recorded in a central registry.

- A depository is operated by a clearing house or settlement agency and is a place in where securities are 'immobilised'. With Euroclear, there are no physical securities as they are 'dematerialised'.

- Under the pooling (or omnibus) system, investors' holdings are registered in a single nominee's name.

- Custodians provide specialist asset safe-keeping services.

- The establishment of a Central Securities Depository aims to create efficiency gains and risk reduction.

- The ICSDs Euroclear and Clearstream provide clearance and custody for Euromarkets, and have also become involved in settlement and custody of international equities.

- Global custody is about processing cross-border securities trades, keeping financial assets safe and servicing associated portfolios.

- Cash management techniques seek to predict cash funding requirements and handle the movement of cash.

- Custodians seek to differentiate themselves from competitors through value-added services such as securities lending, fund administration, collateral management and risk management.

- Risks associated with global custody include credit risk, delivery risk, foreign exchange risk, operational risk, political risk and settlement risk.

- A corporate action is an action by which a company distributes cash, stock or a combination of them to stock holders, usually in proportion to their existing holdings (a benefit or entitlement distribution) or which changes the nature or description of a company's stock (a stock event).

- Corporate actions include dividends, rights issues, redemptions, consolidations and placings.

- Corporate actions can be processed as Euroclear transactions.

- The UK taxation system is operated by Her Majesty's Revenue & Customs (HMRC).

- Withholding tax is a tax deducted from payments made to non-residents, such as payments of dividends and interest.

- Double taxation treaties between various countries can prevent income or gains of non-resident investors being taxed twice and withholding tax may be claimed as a credit.

TEST YOUR KNOWLEDGE

Check your knowledge of the Chapter here, without referring back to the text.

1   Securities can be held in either paper (or ....) or electronic (or ....) form. *[Fill in the blanks.]*

2   Different types of institution may hold securities. A .... is a financial institution which provide a 'safe keeping service' for customers. A .... is a clearing house or settlement agency whose primary role is to facilitate settlement. *[Fill in the blanks.]*

3   The principal I........... C........... S............ D............s are .... and .... *[Fill in the blanks.]*

4   List five of the typical core service requirements of client investors and asset managers in respect of custody services.

5   Give another name for 'Herstatt risk'.

6   Give two examples of situations in which stock lending services may be required by an investor.

7   What is meant by 'systemic risk' in the context of global custody risks?

8   What are the full names for the six types of Euroclear transactions for processing corporate actions: REG, USE, MTM, TTE, TFE, ESA?

TEST YOUR KNOWLEDGE: ANSWERS

1   Securities can be held in either paper (or *certificated*) or electronic (or *dematerialised*) form. (See 1.)

2   A *custodian* is a financial institution which provide a 'safe keeping service' for customers. A *depository* is a clearing house or settlement agency whose primary role is to facilitate settlement. (See 2.7.)

3   The principal International Central Securities Depositories are Euroclear and Clearstream. (See 4.)

4   You could have mentioned five from the following list. (See 5.4.2.)

- Settlement
- Safe keeping
- Corporate actions
- Proxy voting
- Foreign exchange
- Cash management
- Reporting

5   Overnight delivery risk. (See 5.7.)

6   You could have mentioned examples from the following list. (See 5.12.1.)

- To cover settlement failures where participants do not have sufficient securities to settle a delivery
- To cover short positions where participants sell securities that they do not hold
- To support a derivatives activity where exercising options may require the delivery of the security

7   Systemic risk is the risk that the disruption (at a company, in a market segment, at a central clearing entity or central securities depository) causes widespread difficulties for other companies, in other market segments or in the financial system as a whole. (See 5.20.5.)

8   In full, the terms are as follows. (See 8.1.)

- Registrar Adjustment (REG)
- Unmatched Stock Event (USE)
- Many to Many (MTM)
- Transfer to Escrow (TTE)
- Transfer from Escrow (TFE)
- Escrow Adjustment (ESA)

Offshore funds, 112
One-off financial promotion, 372
Open Ended Investment Companies (OEICs), 96, 109
Open outcry, 186
Open outcry (LME), 206
Open-ended funds, 97
Operational risk, 3, 398
Operational system failure, 401
Operations management, 2
Optimisation, 100
Options, 154
Options on futures, 161
Order allocation policy, 383
Order-driven markets, 186
Ordinary income shares, 122
Organisational structure, 404
Outgoing ECA provider, 331
Overnight delivery risks, 246, 441
Overseas government bonds, 23
Overseas persons, 310
Over-the-Counter (OTC) market, 146

Packaged products, 374
Packaged units (investment trusts), 124
Paperless office (CREST), 258
Par value, 34
Part IV permission, 312
Participants (CREST), 260
Participating preference shares, 14
Passive fund management, 99
Passporting, 327
Per se eligible counterparties, 368
Per se professional clients, 367
Performance-based fees, 102, 108
Perimeter Guidance Manual, 300
Periodic statements, 386
Permanent Interest Bearing Shares (PIBS), 41, 47
Perpetual bonds, 35, 44
Perpetual subordinated bonds, 47
Personal account dealing, 384
Placement (money laundering), 343
Placings, 20
PLUS Markets, 182, 209, 295
Politically exposed persons (PEPs), 351
Pooling system, 427
Power of attorney, 425
Powerhouse firms, 4
Pre-emption rights, 19
Preference shares, 14

Premium
    Forward rates, 140
    Options, 155
    To NAV, 120
    Warrants, 16
    Put convertibles, 51
Prescribed markets, 340
Preventive controls, 411
Price indices, 99
Price stabilisation, 337
Primary dealers, 65
Principal risk, 396
Principles for Businesses, 285
Principles-based regulation, 287
Private company, 10
Private limited company, 183
Private person, 304
Private Warning, 302
Procedures manual, 412
Proceeds of Crime Act 2002, 345
Product-based organisations, 5
Professional clients, 367
Project BOAT, 210, 211
Project Turquoise, 187, 210
Promissory note, 134
Prospectus Directive, 333
Protected disclosure, 289
Protection (levels), 366
Proxy voting, 444
Public censure, 302
Public Interest Disclosure Act 1998, 289
Public limited companies, 10, 182, 183
Public Sector Net Cash Requirement, 70, 71
Purchase fund (bonds), 49
Purchase of own shares, 21
Put option, 155
Putable bonds, 35

Qualified investor schemes, 101, 108
Qualifying corporate bonds, 41, 47
Quanto swap, 172
Queues (CREST), 257
Quote-driven markets, 186

Range (of products advised on), 374
Ratio percentage test (401k Plans), 128
Real-time settlement, 436
Recognised Clearing Houses (RCHs), 296, 300
Recognised Investment Exchanges (RIEs), 295, 300